Quebec

" ... et pour les prendre dans ses brumes et dans ses vagues, les emmener sur ses caps et dans ses anses, les étonner par ses oiseaux et ses poissons, les brasser dans la tempête et les apaiser quand il calmit, les gâter par ses aurores et les endormir avec ses crépuscules."

Jean O'Neil, *Le Fleuve*

" ... and it will take them into its mists and waves, lead them over its capes and coves, surprise them with its birds and fish, wrap them in its storms and soothe them with its calm, delight them with its dawns, and at dusk, lull them to sleep."

Jean O'Neil, *Le Fleuve*

Travel Publications

Michelin North America
One Parkway South, Greenville SC 29615, U.S.A.
Tel. 1-800-423-0485
www.michelin-travel.com
TheGreenGuide-us@us.michelin.com

Manufacture française des pneumatiques Michelin

Société en commandite par actions au capital de 2 000 000 000 de francs
Place des Carmes-Déchaux – 63000 Clermont-Ferrand (France)
R.C.S. Clermont-Fd B 855 200 507

Typesetting: NORD COMPO, Villeneuve-d'Ascq
Printing: Canale
Cover design: Carré Noir, Paris 17ᵉ arr.

THE GREEN GUIDE:
The Spirit of Discovery

*The exhilaration of new horizons,
the fun of seeing the world,
the excitement of discovery: this is
what we seek to share with you.
To help you make the most of your
travel experience, we offer first-hand
knowledge and turn a discerning eye
on places to visit.
This wealth of information gives
you the expertise to plan your own
enriching adventure. With THE
GREEN GUIDE showing you the way,
you can explore new destinations
with confidence or rediscover old
ones.
Leisure time spent with THE GREEN
GUIDE is also a time for refreshing
your spirit, enjoying yourself, and
taking advantage of our selection
of fine restaurants, hotels and other
places for relaxing.
So turn the page and open a window
on the world. Join THE GREEN
GUIDE in the spirit of discovery.*

Contents

Carré Saint-Louis, Montreal

Guard at the Citadel, Quebec City

4

Practical Information 326

Index 346

Café on Rue Saint-Denis, Montreal

Canadian and Quebec Flags

5

Maps and Plans

COMPANION PUBLICATIONS

Map 491 Northeastern USA/Eastern Canada

Large-format map providing detailed road systems; includes driving distances, interstate rest stops, border crossings and interchanges.
– Comprehensive city and town index
– Scale 1:2,400,000 (1 inch = approx. 38 miles

LIST OF MAPS AND PLANS

Regional Maps

A View of the Taking of QUEBEC September 13. 1759   *Vue de la Prise de QUEBEC le 13 Septembre 1759.*

Battle of the Plains of Abraham

Montreal

Quebec City

Using this guide

● The guide is organized alphabetically according to the entry's French name. Each **Entry Heading** is followed by a map reference; its tourist region and population figure (where applicable).

● Following the names of sights mentioned in this guide you will find useful information in *italics*: (sight location) addresses, recommended visiting times, opening hours, admission charges, telephone numbers and web addresses. Symbols used in sight, hotel and restaurant descriptions include ♿ handicapped access, ✗ on-site eating facilities, ⊓ on-site parking.

● Sections with a blue background offer practical information, such as available transportation, how to contact visitors bureaus and recreation opportunities, for a city or region. Blue sections edged in a marbleized band also provide hotel and restaurant recommendations.

● We welcome corrections and suggestions that may assist us in preparing the next edition. Please send your comments to Michelin Travel Publications, Editorial Department, P. O. Box 19001, Greenville, SC 29602-9001 or to our web site: www.michelin-travel.com.

© Heiko Wittenborn

Legend

★★★ **Worth the trip**
★★ **Worth a detour**
★ **Interesting**

Sight Symbols

Recommended itineraries with departure point

Church, chapel – Synagogue | Building described
Town described | Other building
AZ B Map co-ordinates locating sights | Small building, statue
Other points of interest | Fountain – Ruins
Mine – Cave | Visitor information
Windmill – Lighthouse | Ship – Shipwreck
Fort – Mission | Panorama – View

Other Symbols

Interstate highway (USA) | US highway | Other route
Trans-Canada highway | Canadian highway | Mexican federal highway

Highway, bridge | Major city thoroughfare
Toll highway, interchange | City street with median
Divided highway | One-way street
Major, minor route |
15 (21) Distance in miles (kilometers) | Pedestrian Street
2149/655 Pass, elevation *(feet/meters)* | Tunnel
△6288(1917) Mtn. peak, elevation *(feet/meters)* | Steps – Gate
Airport – Airfield | Drawbridge - Water tower
Ferry: Cars and passengers | Parking – Main post office
Ferry: Passengers only | University – Hospital
Waterfall – Lock – Dam | Train station – Bus station
International boundary | Subway station
State boundary, provincial boundary | Digressions – Observatory
Winery | Cemetery – Swamp

Recreation

Gondola, chairlift | Stadium – Golf course
Tourist or steam railway | Park, garden – Wooded area
Harbor, lake cruise – Marina | Wildlife reserve
Surfing – Windsurfing | Wildlife/Safari park, zoo
Diving – Kayaking | Walking path, trail
Ski area – Cross-country skiing | Hiking trail

Sight of special interest for children

Abbreviations and special symbols

National Park | Subway station (Montréal)
Interpretation centre | Calvary, sanctuary
Hydroelectric plant | Ghost town
National historic site | Covered bridge

Amerindian reservation

All maps are oriented north, unless otherwise indicated by a directional arrow.

9

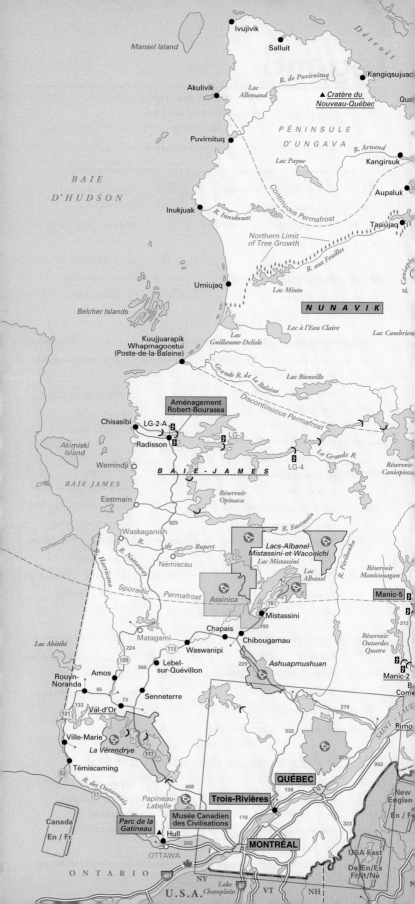

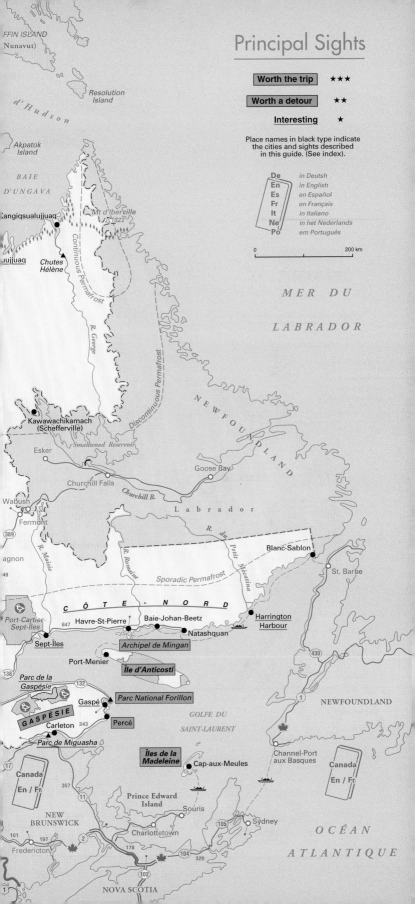

Principal Sights

Worth the trip	★★★
Worth a detour	★★
Interesting	★

Place names in black type indicate
the cities and sights described
in this guide. (See index).

De	in Deutsch
En	in English
Es	en Español
Fr	en Français
It	in Italiano
Ne	in het Nederlands
Po	em Portugués

0   200 km

FFIN ISLAND
Nunavut)

d'Hudson

Resolution
Island

BAIE
D'UNGAVA

Akpatok
Island

Kangiqsualujjuaq

Mt d'Iberville
△ 1622

uujjuaq

Chutes
Hélène

Continuous Permafrost

R. George

MER DU

LABRADOR

Kawawachikamach
(Schefferville)

Esker

Smallwood Reservoir

Churchill Falls

Churchill R.

Goose Bay

NEWFOUNDLAND

Discontinuous Permafrost

Wabush

Fermont

389

agnon

49

R. Moisie

Labrador

R. du Petit Mécatina

Blanc-Sablon

St. Barbe

Sporadic Permafrost

R. Romaine

CÔTE - NORD

Port-Cartier-
Sept-Îles

647   Havre-St-Pierre

Baie-Johan-Beetz

Natashquan

Harrington
Harbour

430

Sept-Îles

138

Archipel de Mingan

Port-Menier

Île d'Anticosti

Parc de la
Gaspésie

132

Parc National Forillon

Gaspé

GOLFE DU
SAINT-LAURENT

NEWFOUNDLAND

1

GASPÉSIE

Carleton

343

Percé

Parc de Miguasha △

Îles de la
Madeleine

Cap-aux-Meules

Channel-Port
aux Basques

Canada
En / Fr

17

Canada
En / Fr

357

11

Prince Edward
Island

Souris

105

Sydney

OCÉAN

NEW
BRUNSWICK

2

Charlottetown

104

329

ATLANTIQUE

101

197

178

Fredericton

102

1   0

NOVA SCOTIA

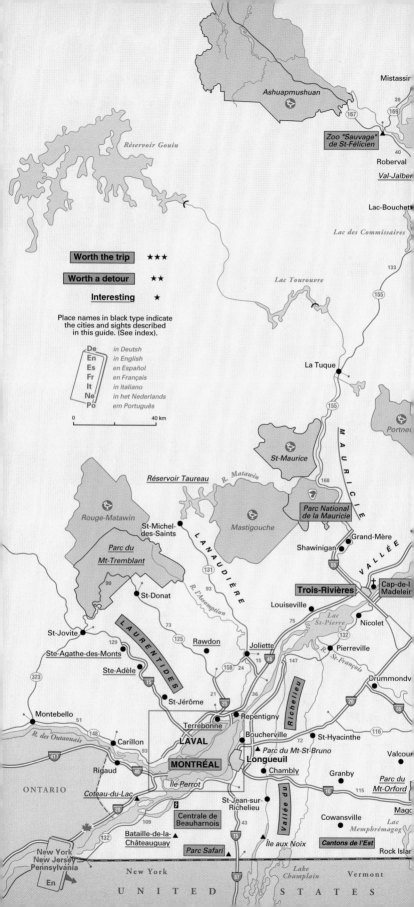

Mistassir

Ashuapmushuan

39
(169)

(167)

40

Zoo "Sauvage"
de St-Félicien

Roberval

Val-Jalber

Réservoir Gouin

Lac-Bouchett

Lac des Commissaires

133

Lac Tourouvre

(155)

Worth the trip	★ ★ ★
Worth a detour	★ ★
Interesting	★

Place names in black type indicate
the cities and sights described
in this guide. (See index).

De	*in Deutsch*
En	*in English*
Es	*en Español*
Fr	*en Français*
It	*in Italiano*
Ne	*in het Nederlands*
Po	*em Português*

La Tuque

(155)

M
A
U
R
I
C
I
E

Portneu

0 ————————— 40 km

St-Maurice

Réservoir Taureau

R. Matawin

168

Parc National
de la Mauricie

Rouge-Matawin

St-Michel-
des-Saints

Grand-Mère

VALLÉE

Parc du
Mt-Tremblant

Mastigouche

Shawinigan

55

*Cap-de-l
Madelei*

Trois-Rivières

St-Jovite

St-Donat

73

Louiseville

*Lac
St-Pierre*

75

Nicolet

(132)

L
A
U
R
E
N
T
I
D
E
S

99

L
A
N
A
U
D
I
È
R
E

(131)

R. l'Assomption

93

(125)

Rawdon

Joliette

15

40

147

Pierreville

St-François

Drummondv

Ste-Agathe-des-Monts

129

Ste-Adèle

(158)

24

21

36

R
i
c
h
e
l
i
e
u

20

55

(323)

15

St-Jérôme

25

Montebello

51

Repentigny

(148)

Terrebonne

Boucherville

72

St-Hyacinthe

(116)

R. des Outaouais

Carillon

93

LAVAL

▲ Parc du Mt-St-Bruno

411

MONTRÉAL

Longueuil

Granby

Valcour

Rigaud

40

Île Perrot

● Chambly

Parc du
Mt-Orford

ONTARIO

Coteau-du-Lac

St-Jean-sur-
Richelieu

10

115

Mago

20

Centrale de
Beauharnois

43

Cowansville

*Lac
Memphrémagog*

109

**New York
New Jersey
Pennsylvania**

Bataille-de-la-
Châteauguay

Parc Safari ▲

V
a
l
l
é
e

d
u

Île aux Noix ▲

Cantons de l'Est

Rock Islan

En

(132)

New York

*Lake
Champlain*

Vermont

U N I T E D

87

S T A T E S

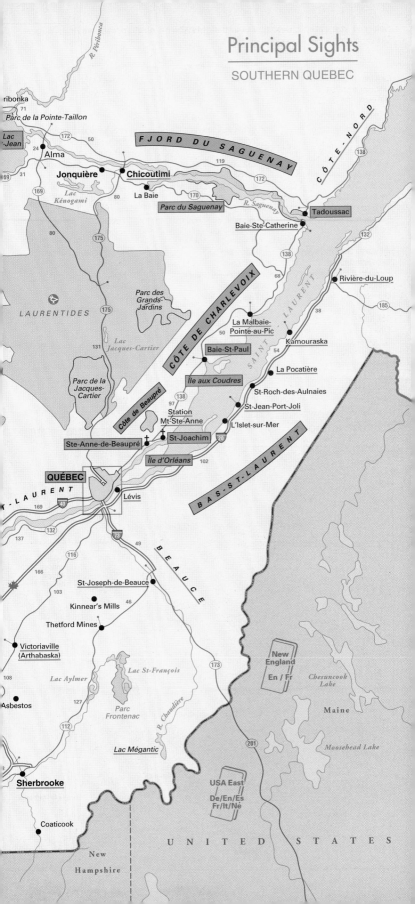

Principal Sights

SOUTHERN QUEBEC

Selected star-rated cities, towns and sights shown on maps on previous pages.
Consult the index for sight descriptions.

★★★

Canadian
  Museum of Civilization
Charlevoix, Côte de

Gaspésie
Montreal
Percé

Quebec City
Saguenay,
  Fjord du

★★

Anticosti, Île d'
Baie-Saint-Paul
Bas-St-Laurent
Beauharnois,
  Centrale de (Power Plant)
Beaupré, Côte de
Cap-de-la-Madeleine,
  Sanctuaire du
Coudres, Île aux
Est, Cantons de l'

Forillon, Parc national
Gatineau, Parc de la
Laurentides
Madeleine, Îles de la
Manic-5
Mauricie, Parc national de la
Mingan, Archipel de
Nunavik
Orléans, Île d'
Richelieu, Vallée du

Robert-Bourassa, Aménagement
Safari, Parc
Saguenay, Parc du
Saint-Félicien, Jardin zoologique de
Saint-Jean, Lac
Saint-Joachim, Église de
Sainte-Anne-de-Beaupré,
  Sanctuaire de
Tadoussac
Trois-Rivières

★

Arthabaska (see Victoriaville)
Baie-Sainte-Catherine
Bataille-de-la-Châteauguay
Beauce
Chambly
Chicoutimi
Côte-Nord
Coteau-du-Lac
Gaspé
Gaspesie, Parc de la
Harrington Harbour
Hull
James, Baie
Joliette

Kamouraska
Kuujjuaq
La Malbaie-Pointe-au-Pic
La Pocatière
Lévis
Magog
Manic-2
Mauricie
Mégantic, Lac
Miguasha, Parc de
Mont-Orford, Parc du
Mont-Sainte-Anne,
  Station
Mont-Tremblant, Parc du

Nouveau-Québec, Cratère du
Rawdon
Rimouski
Rivière-du-Loup
Saint-Jean-Port-Joli
Saint-Joseph-de-Beauce
Sainte-Adèle
Sainte-Agathe-des-Monts
Sept-Îles
Sherbrooke
Taureau, Réservoir
Terrebonne
Val-d'Or
Val-Jalbert

TOURIST REGIONS
as defined by Ministère du Tourisme (Québec)

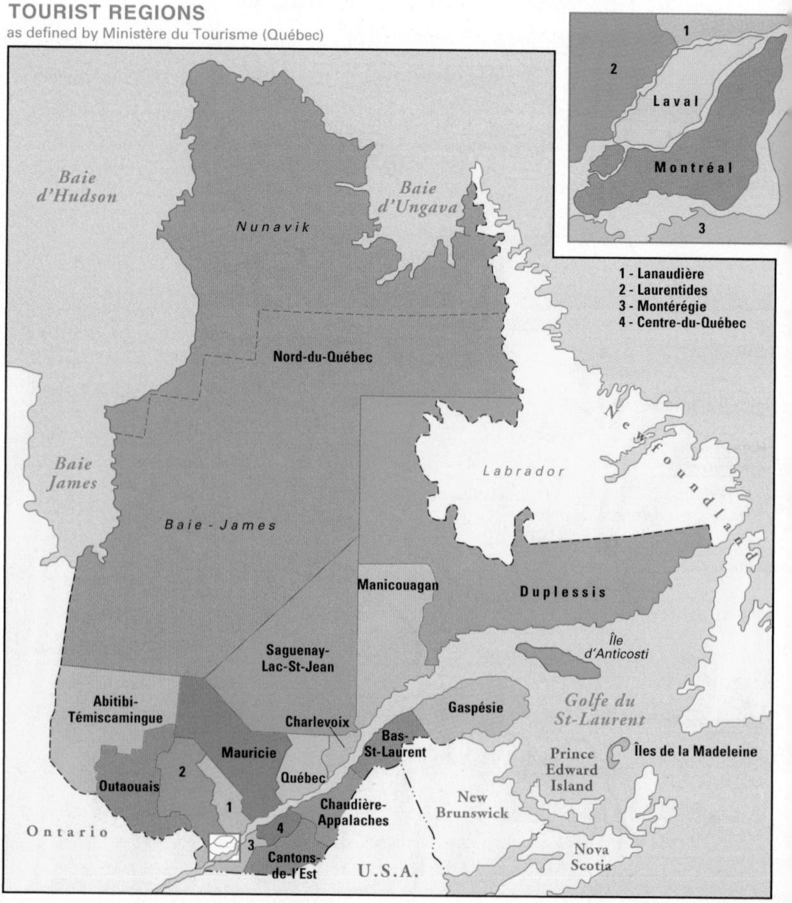

1 - Lanaudière
2 - Laurentides
3 - Montérégie
4 - Centre-du-Québec

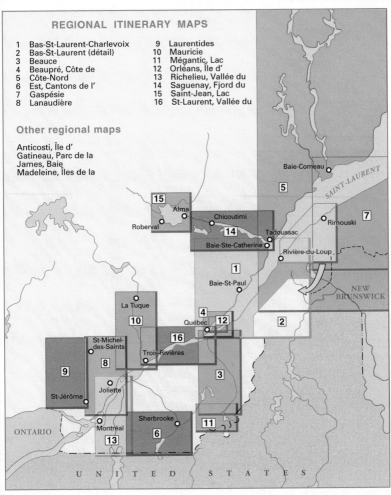

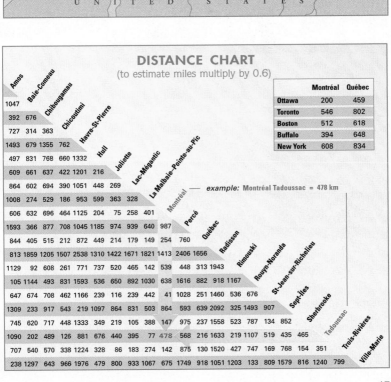

Rivière Jacques-Cartier

© Malak, Ottawa

Introduction
to Quebec

Quebec's Natural Environment

Quebec ranks as Canada's largest province, occupying roughly 15 percent of the country's landmass. With a total area of 1,540,680sq km/594,860sq mi, Quebec is slightly larger than Alaska and nearly three times the size of France. At its largest dimensions, Quebec's territory spans nearly 1,500km/930mi from east to west and 2,000km/1,240mi from north to south.

Regional Landscapes

This immense province boasts a striking range of landscapes and climates, from the often-steep shores of the mighty St. Lawrence River to the cultivated terraces of the Appalachian valleys to the wide-open spaces of the northern tundra.

The Canadian Shield – The granitic and gneissic rocks of this immense craton, which covers over 80 percent of Quebec's territory, are the roots of ancestral mountain ranges that were repeatedly uplifted and eroded over billions of years. During the Paleozoic era, much of the ancient Shield surface was covered by shallow seas and buried under thick marine sediments. Today this expanse is generally flat and monotonous, rising no higher than 600m/1,968ft above sea level. The landforms of the Shield consist of extensive plateaus interrupted by a few mountain massifs. Only near the rim of the Shield is the land deeply incised by rivers flowing towards the surrounding lowlands. Within the Canadian Shield, the following sub-regions are commonly identified.

The Northern Plateaus – Known for its many lakes, this was the only area in Quebec still glaciated during the final stages of the last ice age, approximately 6,000 years ago. The Otish Mountain massif and its summits of over 1,000m/3,280ft dominate the plateau's southern half. Located to the southeast of the Otish Mountains, the Manicouagan Reservoir now fills the impact crater of a meteor. Westerly winds from Hudson Bay deposit over 100cm/39in of precipitation per year, nearly half of it as snow – a remarkable total for this high latitude. Separating Ungava Bay from the Labrador Sea, the imposing Torngat Mountains rise to Mt. Iberville (1,622m/5,320ft), the highest summit in Quebec.

Abitibi-Témiscamingue – This area of the Shield lies along the border with Ontario between the Ottawa River and the Eastmain Plain, south of James Bay. To the south, the recurving upper Ottawa River frames the region of Témiscamingue, noted for its dairy farms nestled among spruce-covered hills.

The Laurentians – When viewed from a sufficiently high vantage point, the sea of well-rounded crests is remarkably even in elevation (600m/1,968ft-800m/2,624ft).

Canadian Shield Landscape

Sainte-Rose-du-Nord, Fjord du Saguenay

On the other side of the Saguenay Fjord lies the sparsely inhabited expanse of Côte-Nord, the north shore of the Gulf of St. Lawrence. Stretching over 1,000km/620mi of wind-buffeted coast, a spruce-covered coastal plain lies in front of the Laurentian scarp into which tumultuous rivers have cut narrow, rock-strewn valleys.

Saguenay–Lac-Saint-Jean – The Saguenay–Lac-Saint-Jean region owes much of its economic dynamism to an oasis-like situation within the Shield. The basin has an extensive cover of fertile soils, a notably warm, if brief summer as compared to the coastal areas farther south, and almost ubiquitous industrial power potential stored in the region's numerous rivers. From depths of 275m/902ft, the sheer rock faces of Cape Éternité and Cape Trinité form canyon-like walls, soaring many feet above the water surface.

The St. Lawrence Lowlands – Shaped like a triangle with its apex near Quebec City, the lowlands are lodged between the Canadian Shield to the north, and the Appalachian Mountains to the southeast. The lowlands rise gradually to the northeast so that the area around Quebec City has a higher elevation (100m/328ft above sea level) than the Montreal plain, which rarely surpasses the 70m/230ft mark.

Between Montreal and the first Appalachian ridges to the east, a string of isolated, massive outcrops known as the **Monteregian Hills** looms above an otherwise uniformly flat landscape.

Graced with fertile soils and a moderate climate, the lowlands have traditionally supported a variety of agricultural activities.

The Appalachian Mountains – Separated from the St. Lawrence lowlands by **Logan's Line**, the Appalachian Mountains cross into Quebec from Vermont and New Hampshire and run to the northeast along the boundary with the US and the province of New Brunswick. Broadleaf forests cover the higher elevations and ridges, while mixed agriculture occupies the larger valleys. Towards the northeast and the Gaspé Peninsula, agricultural land use becomes increasingly marginal and forests of coniferous trees predominate.

Eastern Townships and Beauce – These two regions are the most populated areas in Appalachian Quebec. The Eastern Townships occupy the southwestern portion of the Appalachian region between the US border and the Chaudière River basin. The Beauce region is centred on the upper Chaudière River. While fruit orchards and even vineyards can be found among the pastures and dairy farms along the western margin of this region, forests of sugar maple predominate in the Beauce area.

The similarity in landscape between the Eastern Townships and northern New England is unmistakable. Vermont's Green Mountains continue north of the border as the Sutton Mountains which, in turn, are followed by a ridge of low hills in the upper Bécancour basin near Thetford Mines.

The Lower St. Lawrence and the Gaspé Peninsula – To the northeast of the Chaudière River, the Green Mountains-Sutton Mountains belt is known as the Notre-Dame Mountains, whose northern slopes descend to a narrow coastal plain along the lower St. Lawrence River. Shielded by the Chic-Chocs from Arctic north winds, this area, once called "Quebec's Mediterranean," is known for its favourable microclimate.

To the south and east of the Gaspé Peninsula, the Appalachian zone includes mostly flat-lying red sandstone and schist strata that underlie the Magdalen Islands and Prince Edward Island in the Gulf of St. Lawrence.

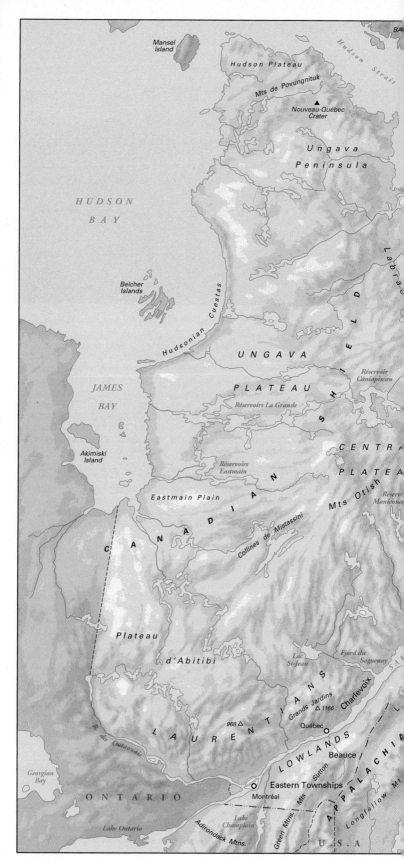

Mansel Island

Hudson Plateau

Hudson Strait

BA

Mts de Povungnituk

▲ Nouveau-Québec Crater

Ungava Peninsula

HUDSON BAY

Belcher Islands

Hudsonian Cuestas

UNGAVA PLATEAU

Réservoir Caniapiscau

L a b r a d

S H I E L D

Réservoirs La Grande

JAMES BAY

Akimiski Island

Réservoirs Eastmain

Eastmain Plain

CENTRA

PLATEA

Mts Otish

Réserv Manicoua

Collines de Mistassini

C A N A D I A N

C A

Plateau d'Abitibi

Luc St-Jean

Fjord du Saguenay

SA

Georgian Bay

R. des Outaouais

L A U R E N T I A N S

Grands Jardins △ 1166

Charlevoix

968 △

Québec ○

L

LOWLANDS

Beauce

A C H I A

ONTARIO

Eastern Townships

○ Montréal

Green Mtns.

Sutton Mts.

A P P A L A C H I

Longfellow Mt

Lake Ontario

Adirondack Mtns.

Lake Champlain

U. S. A

20

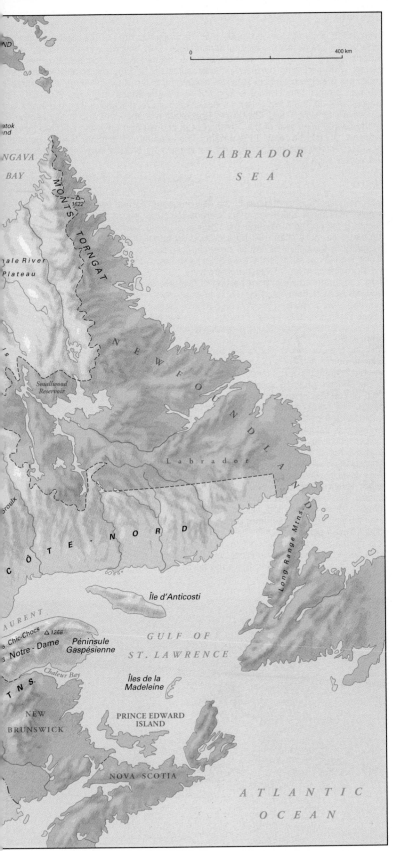

Climate

Owing to its high latitude and location at the eastern margin of the continent, Quebec undergoes extreme fluctuations in temperature. Cold winters and surprisingly warm periods during the summer months are the hallmarks of a continental climate. Of course, with increasing northern latitude, summers become cooler and winters turn frigid, but the sizeable gap in seasonal temperatures remains. For example, Montreal's average summer temperature is 22°C/72°F, and the winter averages -9°C/16°F. For Kuujjuarapik, an Inuit settlement on the eastern shore of Hudson Bay, the equivalent figures are 11°C/52°F and -23°C/-9°F. Precipitation is abundant and locally reinforced by the nearby open seas of the Atlantic Ocean and Hudson Bay. Annual totals average between 35cm/13in and 110cm/43in. The amount of annual rainfall generally decreases inland and northward and is fairly evenly divided between summer rains and winter snows.

Flora

Latitude is an important factor in the distribution of natural vegetation cover since it largely determines the length and average temperatures of the growing season. In Quebec's far northern reaches, the nominal growing season is less than 40 days as compared to more than 180 days around Montreal. Elevation above sea level and proximity to the ocean as well as local microclimates that develop in response to particular landforms, such as the Lake Saint-Jean basin, are additional factors modifying the latitudinal pattern of vegetational cover.

Most common in the southern portion of Quebec, the mainly broadleaf hardwood or **deciduous forest** is dominated by maple species mixed with beech, hickory, basswood, ash, and oak. Stretching from the southern Laurentians to the coastal areas of the Gaspé Peninsula, this forest persists in mostly hilly and mountainous areas. With increasing latitude and altitude it gradually mixes with balsam fir and yellow or white birch.

Covering the Côte-Nord, Abitibi and Saguenay–Lac-Saint-Jean regions, the dense **boreal forest** is dominated by straight-trunked, coniferous (cone-bearing) trees. Extending broadly in homogeneous stands, these needle-leaf softwood forests are better adapted to the shorter growing season. Common associations include fir stands with white birch or black spruce, lichen-spruce woodlands as well as Jack pine and birch-aspen stands. The boreal forest constitutes the largest reserve of wood fibre in Quebec. The ambitious reforestation program launched by the government of Quebec in 1984 to protect this valuable resource calls for the planting of 36 million saplings annually.

Farther north at the fringes of the high-latitude boreal forest begins the **taiga**. An extensive forest of softwood species, it is controlled by the subarctic climate and grows increasingly sparse as one travels northward. Well-spaced clusters of trees – mainly black spruce, white birch, or tamarack – already stunted in their growth, decrease in height to shrublike forms and give way to ground cover such as lichens and arctic mosses. The tree line marks the northern limit of the taiga. Two factors – low average summer temperatures and lack of available water – limit the growth and reproduction of trees. The brief summer period melts only a shallow layer of soil on top of the solidly frozen permafrost.

The northernmost vegetational zone, the **tundra**, has been called a cold desert. Interspersed by bedrock outcrops and fields of shattered rocks, a thin carpet of grasses, mosses, lichens, and flowering herbs clings tenuously to the ground. Widely

Caribou Herd

scattered low shrubs of willow and birch manage to survive only in sheltered pockets. In the tundra, year-round moisture is scarce and summers are too short and cold to support the growth of trees. The ground is perennially frozen and impermeable. Inadequate drainage at the surface creates the tundra's characteristic landscape of bogs, or "muskeg". During the few long summer days, the grassy tundra hastily completes its spectacular annual flowering cycle in both colour and intensity.

Fauna

Considering the immensity of Quebec's landmass, the variety of animal life is relatively poor. Slightly more than 50 species of mammals, such as beaver, deer and bear (brown and polar); 350 bird species, of which only 5 to 7 percent winter in the area; and 120 species of fish have been identified.

From south to north, animal diversity decreases in Quebec: from 50 mammal species in the Ottawa Valley to some 20 on and around the Ungava Peninsula. In the southern portion of Quebec, herds of white-tailed deer and moose (Laurentians and Chic-Chocs) predominate, contributing to Quebec's reputation as a hunter's paradise. Indeed Quebec offers 24 wildlife reserves abounding in popular game animals, such as moose, caribou, white-tailed deer and black bear. Birds of prey include the red-tailed hawk, merlin, kestrel and great horned owl. Quebec is on the flyway of migrating Canada and snow geese, and several areas on the St. Lawrence shores are renowned for bird-watching in spring and fall.

Further north, the taiga provides habitat to herds of **caribou**, such as the George River herd, which roams the area south of Ungava Bay and numbers 300,000 heads. Seven smaller herds are found along the transitional zone between taiga and tundra. The area is punctuated by myriad lakes and waterways teeming with salmon, smelt, pike and trout. Among animal species indigenous to the rugged tundra are the arctic hare, fox and polar bear as well as the gyrfalcon and snowy owl.

Many species of **marine mammals** travel up the St. Lawrence River on their migratory routes. They include the common seal as well as the beluga, humpback, fin and minke **whales**. Whale watching is a popular attraction, especially in the Saguenay Fjord and Côte-Nord regions.

We welcome corrections and suggestions that may assist us in preparing the next edition. Please send us your comments:

Michelin Travel Publications
Editorial Department
P. O. Box 19001
Greenville, SC 29602-9001
TheGreenGuide-us@us.michelin.com

Population and Language

According to the 1996 census, Quebec's population totalled 7,138,795 inhabitants, making up 25 percent of the entire Canadian population. Quebec ranks as the second most populous province behind Ontario (population 10,753,573). Almost four out of every five Quebecers (a total of 5,543,060) reside in urban areas.

Earliest Inhabitants – In 1996, 71,415 Quebecers (approximately one percent) claimed native ancestry. This includes **Amerindians**, Inuit and Metis. The largest of the three groups, the Amerindians (population estimated at over 47,600) are divided into Nine Nations, namely (in descending order of population) the Mohawk, Cree, Montagnais, Algonquin, Attikamek, Micmac, Huron, Naskapi and Abenaki.

Currently, the largest spoken language families in Quebec are the Iroquoian (Mohawk and Huron dialects) and Algonquian (Cree, Montagnais/Naskapi, Micmac and Abenaki dialects). Today the majority of Quebec's Amerindian population lives in Pointe-du-Buisson, Mashteuiatsh, Odanak, Lorette and Kahnawake. A large Cree-speaking population (around 10,720) is concentrated in the villages of the James Bay region. The **Inuit**, the inhabitants of Canada's arctic regions, number approximately 8,300. The province's Inuit population lives primarily in the coastal villages of Nunavik, the vast region occupying Quebec's northernmost territory. Their language is Inuktitut.

Non-indigenous Population – In the 1996 census, 2,881,395 Quebecers (approximately 80 percent) declared themselves of French origin. Quebecers of British descent accounted for 9 percent of the population, while 3 percent claimed Italian origin. Eastern Europeans represented 2 percent of the province's ethnic mosaic.

Approximately 47 percent of Quebec's population resides in Montreal's metropolitan area, although the city proper is home to only 14 percent of Quebecers. Since World War II, and especially between 1965 and 1980, the anglophone population that settled in Quebec City, Montreal and the Eastern Townships during the post-1815 wave of immigration has seen its numbers decline. Montreal's cosmopolitan flavour developed at the turn of the century with the arrival of Italian and Eastern European immigrants. After 1945, immigration intensified, originating mainly from Mediterranean countries. International events have since modified this trend and, in the 1970s, Southeast Asians, mostly French-speaking Vietnamese, emigrated to Quebec in unprecedented numbers, as did Latin Americans (particularly Chileans) in the following decade. Asians are the largest immigrant group today; 61,800 entered Quebec between 1991 and 1996.

The Language Debate – According to the 1996 census, 3,931,745 of Quebecers consider French their mother tongue. Three factors gave rise to the language controversy that culminated in the 1960s: a vivid awareness of the fragility of French culture in North America, which first led Quebecers to perceive and refer to themselves as "Quebecois" rather than "French Canadians"; the first signs of a decrease in fertility (the birth rate declined by 50 percent between 1951 and 1986); and lastly, an acute awareness of the consequences of heavy postwar international immigration (immigrants overwhelmingly integrated into the English minority rather than the French majority).

In Quebec, the language problem became focused on the issue of education. Conscious of the role of schools in the development of cultural identity, the Government of Quebec passed laws (Bill 63 in 1969, Bill 22 in 1974) establishing restrictions on the admission of immigrants into English schools. The pro-sovereignty francophone party, the parti Québécois, elected in 1976, passed the landmark **Bill 101** in the following year. Bill 101 is a veritable charter defining the status of the French language and regulating its use. In the field of education, current legislation allows children of parents who completed an English elementary school curriculum anywhere in Canada to attend English public elementary and secondary schools. In 1988 the government passed **Bill 178**, amending Bill 101's stipulation that commercial signs appear only in French. The new law required businesses to post French signs outdoors, while allowing the use of bilingual signs indoors, provided that the French language appear more prominently than the other language. The law was further amended in 1993 with the passage of Bill 86 permitting bilingual exterior signage, again under the condition that the French language clearly predominate.

Political System

Quebec's political system derives from the Constitution of 1867, which defines the jurisdiction of the provincial and federal governments.

Government – Legislative power rests with the unicameral **National Assembly**, created in 1968 to replace the Legislative Assembly. The 125 members of the National Assembly are elected by universal suffrage for a maximum of five years. The members belong to a wide range of parties reflecting the various political tendencies among the electorate. The **Lieutenant-Governor**, the official representative of the British Crown, joins with the National Assembly to form the **Parliament**.

The government is headed by the party that obtains the most seats in the National Assembly. The leader of this majority party – who is designated the **Premier** – appoints his **Executive Council** from among the National Assembly members. This council, which constitutes the government's **executive branch**, is responsible for introducing bills to the Assembly. Much of the Assembly's work is carried out by parliamentary committees, which review and investigate various matters brought before the legislative body.

National Assembly (1997)

Quebec's **judicial branch** is composed of two levels: the lower courts and the Court of Appeal. The first level is made up of the municipal courts, the Quebec Court and the Superior Court. The Quebec Court (1988), comprising the Provincial Court, the Courts of Sessions of the Peace and the Juvenile Court, is responsible for certain civil, criminal and penal issues. Judges serving on the Quebec Court are appointed by the provincial government. Appointed by the federal government, the Superior Court rules on all cases outside the jurisdiction of the other courts and acts as a court of appeal for offences concerning penal law. The federally appointed Court of Appeal is the general appellate court for the entire province.

The Supreme Court of Canada, with nine judges appointed by the federal government, is the highest court in the land and as such can hear appeals on decisions reached by Quebec's Court of Appeal.

The Electoral System – The principle of universal suffrage applies to all citizens 18 years of age and over. The plurality single-member electoral system is based on the concept of territorial representation. Each of the 125 Quebec members of Parliament represents the population of one constituency or "riding." Since 1963, Quebec electoral law stipulates that all parties must file financial statements and sets a limit on expenses, while at the same time providing state contributions for the financing of standard administrative and electoral expenses of parties that obtain a minimum level of electoral success. For the purposes of public administration, Quebec is divided into seventeen administrative regions.

Federal Government – Quebecers also elect members to the Canadian House of Commons, and are represented in the Canadian Senate by legislators appointed by the federal government. Representation in Ottawa is usually proportional to a province's population. In 1998, Quebec was represented by 75 of the 301 federal members of Parliament and 24 of the 104 senators.

International Relations – Under the Canadian Constitution, international relations fall within federal jurisdiction. However, since 1960, Quebec has instituted its own foreign delegations and offices and created a Ministry of International Affairs, using the principle of international extension of internal powers, in an effort to fully assume its responsibilities in matters of immigration, foreign loans, the environment and, above all, culture. With an increasingly prominent role in the French-speaking world, Quebec has achieved a unique status within the context of Canadian representation at international French-language events. Quebec City hosted the *Second Sommet de la Francophonie* (1987) and since 1988, Quebec and Canada have both participated in TV5, the international French language television network.

Economy

Historically, Quebec's abundant natural resources have constituted its primary economic base. Although Quebec's vast forests, farmlands and waterways continue to be widely exploited, the province's 20C economy has relied heavily on services and manufacturing. In 1996, over 65 percent of the gross domestic product derived from the service industries, compared to 34 percent from the goods industries (of which 22 percent of the total GDP was manufacturing).

The Fur Industry – A driving force in the settlement of northern Quebec and a traditional activity of the Amerindian and Inuit populations, trapping has become a somewhat marginal activity at the national level. Nonetheless, Canada and the former Soviet Union are the world's largest fur producers and in North America, Montreal is the centre of the fur industry. Amerindian and Inuit trappers and breeders are now grouped into cooperatives. Quebec trappers hunt mostly muskrat, beaver and marten. Over 240 thousand wildlife pelts are sold each year in Quebec.

Agriculture – Until the turn of the 20C, agriculture was the cornerstone of the Quebec economy. Commercial agriculture began in the 1880s with the marketing of milk and dairy products. Today agriculture accounts for less than 2 percent of the gross domestic product.

The principal farming areas developed in the fertile regions bordering the St. Lawrence River (e.g., Bas-Saint-Laurent, Beauce, Gaspé Peninsula). Quebec's agricultural industry is primarily based on animal products (milk, pork, poultry and cattle), large-scale cultivation of cereal products (corn, barley, oats and wheat), as well as vegetable and fruit farming. The main seasonal fruits are apples, strawberries, raspberries and blueberries.

The Forest – The exploitation of Quebec's extensive forested lands has generated considerable revenue since the colonial period. In many regions, farmers turned to forestry to supplement their livelihood during the long winter months. Early in Quebec's history, shipbuilding, construction and heating created a great demand for wood on the domestic market as well as in England, where much of Quebec's timber production was exported. At the onset of the 20C, new technologies and an increasing demand for newsprint fueled a phenomenal market for **pulp and paper**. Commercial forest land is essential to the regional economy and is located mainly in Abitibi-Témiscamingue, Côte-Nord and Saguenay-Lac-Saint-Jean. Sawmills and workshops generate half the jobs and products in the lumber industry. One third of Canada's pulp and paper production originates from Quebec, particularly from the Mauricie Region. One out of every seven tons of newsprint produced worldwide comes from Quebec. The province exports half of its total yield to the United States.

© Sheila Naiman/REFLEXION

Commercial Fishing, Gaspé Peninsula

Fisheries – Virtually all major fishing centres are located on the Gaspé Peninsula, the Magdalen Islands and Côte-Nord. In recent years, annual catches brought in by Quebec's fishermen have contributed relatively little to the gross domestic product (approximately $134 million in 1996). Once treated, these catches generate products reaching a value of $305 million.

Ocean catches generally include cod, Greenland halibut, rockfish, mackerel, herring, salmon, and shellfish (crab, shrimp and lobster).

Inland, most commercial fishing is concentrated to the west of Cape Tourmente and particularly in the region of Lake Saint-Pierre (Yamaska, Maskinongé, Nicolet and Sorel). The main catches are sturgeon, perch and eel.

Mines – The history of Quebec's mining industry is closely linked to three distinct eras and three regions. Asbestos mining started in the last quarter of the 19C in the Eastern Townships. In the 1920s, gold and copper were discovered in the Abitibi region. Finally, after 1945, iron ore was mined in Côte-Nord (Fermont, Duplessis) and in northern Quebec (Schefferville).

Today Quebec's mineral production accounts for 7 percent of the national total. Half of this production involves metallic minerals (gold, silver, iron, copper, lead, zinc), one quarter is non-metallic (asbestos) and another quarter is composed of various mineral substances. The Côte-Nord and Northern Quebec region produce nearly half of Quebec's mineral resources. One quarter of the province's minerals and virtually all its gold production emanate from the mines of Abitibi-Témiscamingue. Quebec is the world's largest exporter of asbestos. Although mining remains the principal activity in several regions, total production accounts for less than 2 percent of the gross domestic product.

Hydroelectric power – Quebec imports oil and natural gas but produces its own hydroelectric power. The province's industrialization is closely linked to its hydroelectric resources which, as early as 1900, provided low-cost energy for the lumber, petrochemical and electro-metallurgic industries, particularly aluminium plants (Alcan, Reynolds, Pechiney).

Traffic on the St. Lawrence Seaway between Montreal and Lake Ontario (1997)

Vessel Transit		Commodity	%	tonnes
Cargo vessels	2,083	Grains	36.5	13,482,327
Non-cargo/ballast vessels	726	Mining products	39.8	14,676,645
		Processed products	23.6	8,689,054
Pleasure craft	13,029	Other products	0.1	53,197
Traffic revenue	**$34,374,650**	**Total cargo**	**100.0**	**36,901,223**

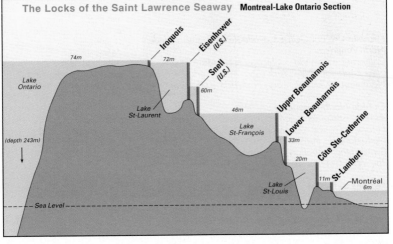

The Locks of the Saint Lawrence Seaway — Montreal-Lake Ontario Section

Proponents of economic nationalism soon demanded the nationalization of the province's hydroelectric industry, a step already taken by Ontario at the beginning of the century. From the days of the Shawinigan Water and Power Company (1902) to the creation of **Hydro-Québec** (first nationalization in 1944 to be followed by large-scale nationalizations in 1962-1963 on the initiative of René Lévesque, as minister under the government of Jean Lesage), hydroelectricity became a key element of Quebec's economic policy. The first hydroelectric dams on the Manicouagan River reflected the will of Quebecers to take charge of their economy and develop an engineering expertise that is now in demand worldwide.

Quebec electricity is mainly produced by its hydroelectric plants, three quarters of which are owned by Hydro-Quebec. There are also a few thermal plants and one nuclear power plant (Gentilly-2). Quebec exports 10 percent of its production to other Canadian provinces and to the United States. In recent years, the ambitious James Bay project has sparked great controversy over the environmental and cultural consequences on the northern regions of the province.

New Directions – The Quiet Revolution *(Révolution tranquille)* was characterized by increased government intervention in education, social affairs and the economy. Viewed in the North American context, Quebec's political economy has distinct characteristics reflected in its nationalization programs (asbestos and hydroelectricity), corporate aid and investment institutions, large-scale infrastructure projects (Expo '67, Montreal subway, Montreal's 1976 Olympic Games) and linguistic policies that promote the role of francophones in the commercial, industrial and financial sectors. Montreal, already the headquarters of several Canadian banks and insurance companies and of the Montreal stock exchange, benefited from these linguistic policies, which enabled more and more francophones to take part in the city's economy. Even though Montreal's role as a financial centre was eclipsed by Toronto in the 1970s, the Greater Montreal area dominates the provincial economy. The Montreal metropolitan area contains approximately one-half of Quebec's manufacturing companies and jobs.

Although in recent years, traditional sectors of the Quebec economy have suffered owing to increased competition, mainly from Asian nations, the province has found new markets for its high-tech expertise in aeronautics, telecommunications and engineering. The **service industry** has been the stronghold of the economy since the 1950s; by 1996 it had expanded to over 65 percent of the gross domestic product.

Since the establishment of a north-south railway network in 1850 and the opening of the **St. Lawrence Seaway** (1959), which enabled ships to sail into the very heart of the United States by way of the Great Lakes, the economies of Quebec and the United States have become more closely integrated. Through their investments and the opening of branch offices in Quebec, the United States has remained the province's main economic partner. Some 80 percent of Quebec's foreign exports are bound for the United States while 45 percent of its foreign imports originate from Quebec's southern neighbour.

Time Line

Pre-Colonial Period

BC	
c. 20000-15000	Earliest human migration into North America from Asia during the last ice age.
c. 5000-1000	Nomadic hunters of the Archaic culture occupy most of the continent.
c. 1000	Development of the Woodland culture: appearance of pottery and agriculture.
AD	
c. 1000	Norse sailors reach the shores of present-day Newfoundland.
c. 1100	The Thule people, ancestors of the Inuit, migrate into the Ungava Peninsula.
1492	Christopher Columbus lands on the island of San Salvador.

New France

1534	**Jacques Cartier** claims Canada in the name of François I, King of France.
1534-1608	The Huron and the Algonquin force the Iroquois out of the St. Lawrence Valley.
1535	On his second voyage, Cartier travels upstream on the St. Lawrence to Hochelaga, the site of present-day Montreal.
1608	**Samuel de Champlain** founds **Quebec City**.
1609-1633	French and Huron form an alliance against the Iroquois.
1610	British navigator **Henry Hudson** discovers the strait and bay that today bear his name, in his quest for the Northwest Passage.
1627	The Company of One Hundred Associates is founded.
1642	**Maisonneuve** founds Ville-Marie, later renamed **Montreal**. **Iroquois Wars** begin.
1648-1649	Iroquois destroy Huronia and regain control of the St. Lawrence Valley.
1670	The **Hudson's Bay Company** is founded.
1673	Father Marquette and Louis Jolliet explore the Mississippi.
1701	Montreal Peace marks the end of the Iroquois Wars.
1730s-1750s	La Verendrye family explores the Canadian West.
1744	Pierre-François-Xavier de Charlevoix publishes *History and General Description of New France*.
1755	Acadian deportation.
1756	Beginning of the Seven Years' War, in which Austria, Russia, France and Spain oppose Great Britain and Prussia.
1759	British defeat the French at the **Battle of the Plains of Abraham** (Quebec City) on September 13. On September 18, Quebec City surrenders to the British.
1760	Montreal surrenders to the British.
1763	The **Treaty of Paris** marks the end of the Seven Years' War. New France is ceded to Great Britain.

British Regime

1774	**Quebec Act** recognizes the French social system and civil laws and grants the freedom to practice the Roman Catholic religion.
1775-1776	American invasion and occupation of Montreal; American defeat in Quebec City.
1783	American Independence recognized by Great Britain. Americans loyal to the British Crown begin emigrating to Canada and Quebec.
1789	French Revolution and spreading of new ideas. Counter-revolutionary current after the death of Louis XVI.
1791	Constitutional Act divides the country into Lower (Quebec) and Upper (Ontario) Canada; each province is granted a legislative assembly.
1806	*Le Canadien*, first francophone newspaper, is founded in Montreal.
1812-1814	War of 1812; second American invasion; Quebec victory at the Battle of the Chateauguay, under the command of Salaberry.
1837-1838	**Patriots' Rebellion** in the Montreal region. Suspension of the Constitution of 1791.
1841	**Act of Union** creates the United Canadas.
1845-1848	François-Xavier Garneau publishes *History of Canada*. Major wave of Irish immigration.

1852	Laval University, first francophone university in North America, founded in Quebec City.
1854	Seigneurial regime is abolished.

Canadian Confederation

1867	British North America Act (renamed **Constitution Act, 1867** in 1982) creates the Canadian Confederation.
1870	Rupert's Land is sold to the Canadian Confederation.
1892	Construction of the **Chateau Frontenac** begins in Quebec City.
1900	Creation of the first cooperative savings and loan company *(caisse populaire)* by Alphonse Desjardins.
1910	Montreal newspaper, *Le Devoir*, is founded by Henri Bourassa.
1912	The Canadian government gives Quebec province a portion of Rupert's Land, thereafter known as Nouveau-Québec.
1918	Quebec women obtain the right to vote in federal elections; right to vote in provincial affairs is granted in 1940.
1927	Labrador Boundary Dispute: after years of dispute, the territorial limit between Quebec and Labrador is established; Quebec does not officially recognize the border.
1939-1945	World War II; large wave of immigration from southern Europe.

Contemporary Quebec

1948	Quebec adopts its provincial flag.
1959	Opening of the **St. Lawrence Seaway** enabling ships to navigate from the Atlantic to the Great Lakes in the United States.
1960	Government of Prime Minister Jean Lesage heralds the beginning of the **Quiet Revolution** *(Révolution tranquille)*.
1967	Universal Exposition in Montreal; publication of the Rapport of the Royal Commission on Bilingualism and Biculturalism in Canada.
1968	The Parti Québécois is founded.
1969	Passage of Bill 63, first law promoting the use of the French language in Quebec.
1970	A hostage-taking by the Quebec Liberation Front (Front de libération du Québec) leads to the October Crisis and the enactment of the War Measures Act.
1973	Construction of phase 1 of the James Bay project begins.
1976	**Summer Olympic Games** in Montreal; election of the Parti Québécois, under the leadership of **René Lévesque**, first nationalist-sovereign party to become elected.
1977	**Bill 101**, the charter on the French language, is passed.
1980	Referendum on sovereignty is rejected by 60 percent of the voters.
1982	The Canadian Constitution of 1867 is repatriated from London. The **Constitution Act, 1982** calls for a new constitution. Quebec is the only Canadian province that refuses to sign the new constitution.
1985	Historic Quebec City becomes the first urban centre in North America to be inscribed on UNESCO's World Heritage List.
1987-1990	**Meech Lake Accord:** Quebec sets five conditions upon which it will adhere to the Constitution of 1982.
1988	The socio-cultural region of Nunavik is recognized by the provincial government as homeland of Quebec's Inuit.
1990	Two provinces (Newfoundland and Manitoba) refuse to sign the Meech Lake Accord by the June 23 deadline. Quebec refuses to sign the 1982 Constitution. Amerindian crisis at Oka.
1992	Montreal celebrates the 350th anniversary of its foundation.
1993	The Bloc Québécois becomes the official Opposition in the Canadian House of Commons.
1994	The Parti Québécois is elected in Quebec, headed by Jacques Parizeau. Lucien Bouchard is elected to replace Parizeau in January 1996.
1995	A second referendum on Quebec sovereignty is rejected by 50.6 percent of the voters.
1996	Severe floods devastate the Saguenay region.
1998	The worst ice storm in the region's history slams into southwestern Quebec, damaging the hydroelectric system and leaving millions without electrical power.
2000	Montreal becomes the home of the first Nasdaq stock exchange satellite market in Canada.

Historical Notes

Early Settlement

According to recent archaeological excavations and interpretations, the earliest migration of humans into the North American continent occurred some 15,000 or more years ago. The first settlers are believed to have journeyed from Asia, crossing over the land bridge that joined Siberia and Alaska during the glacial period. After a few thousand years, the ice sheet retreated from the central part of present-day Canada, clearing the way for human occupation.

Two principal cultural periods mark the many centuries separating the initial settlement of central Canada and the arrival of the Europeans in the 11C. The first, known as the "Archaic" culture (5000 to 1000 BC) were nomadic peoples, who relied on hunting and gathering for sustenance. During the subsequent cultural period known as "Woodland" (1000 BC to AD 1500), native peoples adopted a sedentary lifestyle characterized by the production of pottery and the development of agriculture (particularly corn) to complement their diet of fish and game. It is thought that at least three million people inhabited the North American continent immediately prior to European contact.

For centuries after the shortlived Viking settlements on the coast of present-day Newfoundland in AD 1000, Europe appeared to have forgotten about the existence of the North American continent. It wasn't until the 16C that Quebec's indigenous peoples first came into contact with Europeans – primarily the cod fishermen who had ventured up the St. Lawrence beyond the famous breeding grounds of Newfoundland's Great Banks.

The arrival of European missionaries and fur traders had a profound effect on indigenous cultures, bringing about changes in their lifestyle and political alliances. However, native peoples largely resisted the Church's attempts to convert them to the Catholic faith, as described in *Relations*, the Jesuits' historic account of their missionary work in New France. In fact, the native cultures already possessed their own elaborate systems of beliefs and customs. Nonetheless, the modification of intertribal political relations, traditional trade routes, devastating wars, zealous colonization and endemic diseases brought to the New World by Europeans eventually brought about the permanent disruption of native lifestyles.

New France

In the 15C, European explorers set sail in hopes of finding the route to India. Among these was Christopher Columbus who, in 1492, claimed the island of San Salvador for the Spanish Crown. Although French explorer **Jacques Cartier** (1491-1557) sailed to the New World between 1534 and 1542, France did not establish a firm presence on the North American continent until 1608, when **Samuel de Champlain** (c.1570-1636) founded Quebec City. Shortly after, Europeans began exploring the continent in search of beaver and mink, the mainstay of the lucrative **fur trade** that played a decisive role in Quebec's history.

In the early 17C, the administration and development of the colony was entrusted to private companies such as the Company of One Hundred Associates (Compagnie des Cent-Associés, 1627), composed of merchants and aristocrats intent on colonizing New France for commercial gain. However, settlement progressed slowly; by 1663, there were approximately 3,000 inhabitants, fewer than half of whom were born in the New World. The Jesuits' attempts at evangelization had little success, and the fur trade led to alliances and to the **Iroquois Wars**. Between 1627 and 1701, the Iroquois nations repeatedly raided Algonquian-speaking Amerindians, notably

Jacques Cartier by Théophile Hamel

the Huron, Montagnais and Algonquin, who had allied themselves with the French settlers. Beginning in 1642, the French retaliated by building a series of forts and providing their allies with firearms. However, the attacks continued until 1701, when the Iroquois signed the Montreal Peace Treaty and established their neutrality.

A Royal Colony (1663-1763) – Under the reign of Louis XIV (1643-1715), the administration of New France mirrored that of other French colonies. A governor conducted the colony's military and external affairs; another appointed official ruled over judicial and financial matters and landlords, or *seigneurs*, performed various administrative functions. The seigneurs also enforced the law, erected mills, collected dues (tithes, annuities and grain taxes) and could, at will, subject their tenants to forced labour. Seigneurs, military personnel and religious communities allocated land plots to tenant farmers under a mode of land distribution and occupation known as the **seigneurial system**. These land plots, known as *rangs*, formed long, narrow rectangles perpendicular to a body of water or a road. Farmers comprised 80 percent of the population, which stood at 20,000 at the beginning of the 18C and at approximately 70,000 in 1760.

In a truly epic adventure, explorers pushed back the geographical boundaries of New France. Between the 1730s and 1740s, the La Vérendryes engaged in an extensive exploration of North American waterways, travelling as far as Manitoba, Saskatchewan, Wyoming, Montana and Dakota. They built forts and opened a fur trade route that was used by their successors.

Arrival of Champlain (1608) by George Agnew Reid

The British Conquest – The traditional rivalry between France and England, exacerbated primarily by conflicting interests in the fur trade, led to recurring wars between New France and the surrounding British colonies, ultimately resulting in the capture of Quebec City in 1629. In 1632 the city returned to the French following the signing of the Treaty of Saint-Germain. The Treaty of Utrecht (1713) brought about a temporary peace that lasted until the Seven Years' War (1756-1763), in which France, Austria, Spain and Russia opposed Great Britain and Prussia. On September 13, 1759, British General Wolfe defeated French General Montcalm on the Plains of Abraham, heralding the end of the French colony. Montreal surrendered to the British on September 8, 1760, and the colony was ceded to England in 1763, by the Treaty of Paris.

The British Regime

The Era of Constitutions (1760-1791) – The military conquest opposed French Catholics, subjects of an absolute monarchy, and English Protestants, governed by a constitutional monarchy. The constitution of 1774 (known as the Quebec Act) gave the great majority of francophones the right to maintain the seigneurial system and French civil laws, and the freedom to practice the Roman Catholic religion.

The late 18C is known as the "era of constitutions". The inhabitants of the thirteen American colonies won their independence from England in 1776, trying in vain to convince Canadians to join them during an invasion that was finally crushed at Quebec City. Loyalists – American citizens faithful to the British Crown – made their way north; many of them settled in the area known as the Eastern Townships.

Quebec remained sympathetic to the French Revolution of 1789 until the regicide of Louis XVI in 1793. British colonial authorities looked unfavourably upon the abolition of monarchy and the execution of its royal representative, and the Catholic Church, witnessing the overthrow of royal and ecclesiastical authority, fostered a counter-revolutionary current through its sermons and editorials. Despite attempts to maintain the status quo, a liberal-minded middle class was gradually taking shape. In 1791, the British parliament gave its North American colonies a new constitution, granting a separate legislative assembly to Quebec (Lower Canada) and Ontario (Upper Canada). This was Quebec's first experience in parliamentary democracy.

From Constitutional Debates to Popular Uprisings (1791-1840) – French Canadians grew accustomed to British institutions, and by the turn of the century, they constituted a majority in the elected assembly, hoping to draw attention to their grievances. Led by **Louis-Joseph Papineau** (1786-1871), the Patriot Party (Parti patriote), also known as the Parti canadien until 1826, was hindered by a British governor and legislative council that frequently defeated bills submitted by the peoples' representatives. The constitutional impasse and British colonial policies eventually led to several uprisings, known as the **Patriots' Rebellion**, particularly in the region of Montreal (Saint-Denis-sur-Richelieu, Saint-Charles-sur-Richelieu, Saint-Eustache). Various beliefs and convictions were reflected in this rebellion of 1837-1838: a democratic ideology that valued the supremacy of the House of Assembly, an anti-British and anti-colonial sentiment based on a belief in the right to self-government, and a movement away from the power held by the seigneurs and the clergy. After the failure of the rebellions, Governor-General Lord Durham was sent to assess the state of the colony; in 1839, he submitted a report recommending the union of the two Canadas.

The Act of Union (1840-1867) – Passed in 1841, the Act of Union joined Lower and Upper Canada into one province. At the time, Lower Canada's population stood at 750,000 (510,000 French Canadians) and Upper Canada numbered 480,000 inhabitants. Although Upper Canada's debt was far greater, the two public debts were consolidated, and the Legislative Assembly adopted English as the language of the Province of Canada.

By the mid-19C, the extremely high birthrate of the seigneurial era had led to over-population in Lower Canada, and large numbers of people moved to new settlements in the Mauricie, Saguenay–Lac-Saint-Jean and Bas-Saint-Laurent regions or to the industrial towns of New England. Although vast new regions were opened to colonization in Quebec, nearly one million French-Canadians immigrated to the United States between 1850 and 1930.

Weakened by its lack of clergy and official recognition, the Catholic Church proved staunchly loyal to the British government from 1763 to 1840, even during the Patriots' Rebellion; it was rewarded for its good faith after 1840, when it received a special legal status that allowed it to retain its assets. As it became more involved in the political scene and forged close ties to the party led by **Louis-Hippolyte Lafontaine** (1807-1864), the Church gained control over public education. Working with Upper Canada Reformists, Lafontaine (1807-1864) secured the right to a "responsible government" formed by the parliamentary majority.

Although the Union began in a period of renewed political liberalism, it ended with the emergence of an ideological and political conservatism. Frequent political crises finally led to a new political system of government known as Confederation, which French-Canadian Liberals opposed in vain.

Canadian Confederation

Ratified by the British Parliament in 1867, the **British North America Act** (today known as the Constitution Act, 1867) established the Canadian Confederation – a new political entity that included Quebec among its four founding provinces (along with Ontario, Nova Scotia and New Brunswick). The Confederation's **Constitution of 1867** called for a parliamentary system of government and a separation of federal and provincial powers. Education was among the areas of jurisdiction granted to the provinces. To guarantee the rights of the Protestant minority in Quebec and the Catholic minority elsewhere in Canada, the controversial **Article 93** created a school system divided along religious rather than linguistic lines.

The Constitution used the term French Canada to refer to francophones living in Quebec, New Brunswick, Ontario and Manitoba. It was during this time, when British imperialism reached its apogee, that **Wilfrid Laurier** (1841-1919) became the first French Premier of Canada (1896-1911). Among the other important events of the early 1900s was Quebec's opposition to the draft imposed by the federal government. Between 1870 and 1917, francophone Catholic minorities outside Quebec gradually lost a number of educational and linguistic rights.

A Nationalist Revival – This progressive loss of rights as well as the issue of autonomy, and the threat to the French language stemming from business, publicity and industrialization, gave rise to two nationalist trends. The first, embodied by **Henri Bourassa** (1868-1952), founder of Montreal's francophone daily Le Devoir (1910), advocated greater autonomy for Canada within the British empire, and greater autonomy for each province within the Confederation. Historian **Lionel Groulx** (1878-

1967), promoted a nationalist ideology based on the threefold identity of French Canadians: Catholic, francophone, and rural. Groulx's campaign began just as Quebec's rural culture was disappearing and ended as the role of Catholicism in Quebec society was fading.

In Quebec, the economic crisis of 1929, coupled with turmoil wrought by World War II, lasted into the 1940s; both these events led to economic and social interventions primarily backed by the federal government. So began an era of federal centralization vividly opposed by **Maurice Duplessis**, premier of Quebec from 1944 to 1959.

New Identity

The Quiet Revolution – With the onset of the 1960s there appeared a climate of social and economic change that contrasted sharply with the staunch conservatism of Duplessis's successive governments. Among the events that led to the so-called Quiet Revolution of 1960 *(Révolution tranquille)* were the economic prosperity engendered by the mining industry of the Côte-Nord region, Quebecers' introduction to consumerism through the automobile and television (1952) and the strengthening of the labour movement during the miners strike (1949) in Asbestos.

The Quebec government launched a series of economic and social programs. In 1962, it nationalized its hydroelectric industry, creating Hydro-Québec; in 1965 it created the *Caisse de dépôt et placement* to manage the assets of a new pension plan, and it helped promote francophone business in Quebec. The government also intervened in social and cultural matters by taking over the management of health and social services from the Church, administering public education and creating the Ministry of Cultural Affairs (1961). By taking charge of the educational and cultural sectors, the provincial government was in fact, after a century-long interval, realizing an objective first set by Liberals in the 19C.

A Sovereign State? – The increasing role of the provincial government paralleled the rise of a nationalist ideology in most of the province's political parties. The issue of Quebec sovereignty became a hotly debated topic between supporters of a federalism – personified by **Pierre Elliot Trudeau**, prime minister of Canada from 1968 to 1979 and 1980 to 1984 – and partisans of Quebec sovereignty – embodied by **René Lévesque**, leader of the Parti Québécois and premier of Quebec from 1976 to 1985. Lévesque (1922-1987) transformed what was primarily a cultural nationalism into a political nationalist ideology. Nonetheless, on May 20, 1980, Lévesque's Parti Québécois lost a referendum on Quebec sovereignty when 60 percent of Quebecers voted against separation.

The tension between the provincial and federal governments reached new heights when Quebec declined to sign the new **Canadian Constitution of 1982**, and the Charter of Rights and Freedoms, mainly because the agreement provided for no transfer of legislative powers between federal and provincial governments. Pierre Elliot Trudeau left politics in 1984 as the Progressive-Conservative party of Quebec-born Brian Mulroney took power in Ottawa.

René Lévesque retired from the political scene in 1985. Six months later, the Parti Québécois was defeated by the Quebec Liberal Party, headed by Robert Bourassa. The Liberal government announced it would sign the 1982 Constitution provided five conditions were met. At a meeting held at Meech Lake, near Ottawa, the Canadian prime minister and the ten provincial premiers tentatively agreed to these conditions. The **Meech Lake Accord** (April 30, 1987) which provided a special status for Quebec as a "distinct society," had to be ratified by the federal government and all ten provinces before June 23, 1990. However, a consensus was not reached and the failure of the Meech Lake Accord once again renewed doubts about Quebec's adherence to the Canadian constitution.

No generally acceptable solution to this thorny issue has yet been reached. The narrow failure of a second referendum on Quebec sovereignty, held in October 1995 (50.6 percent of Quebecers voted "no") indicates that the questions of sovereignty and Quebec's relationship with other Canadian provinces will likely continue to dominate the political scene in the years to come.

Michelin GREEN GUIDES available in English for North America include:
California
Canada
Chicago
Florida
Mexico
New England
New York City
New York, New Jersey, Pennsylvania
Pacific Northwest
Quebec
San Francisco
USA East
USA West
Washington DC

Architecture

Marked by both French, British and American influences, Quebec's rich and varied architecture constitutes a unique cultural heritage within the North American landscape.

17C – Owing to the ephemeral nature of Amerindian constructions, very little remains from the period preceding the arrival of Europeans. The earliest structures found in Quebec date from the late 17C. Erected by craftsmen and architects imported from France, these simple constructions bear the influence of various regional styles, in particular those of Brittany and Normandy. With a view to defending and protecting the strategic location of both Quebec City and Montreal, the colonial administration encouraged the building of fortifications around the early settlements. The villages that grew inside fortified walls provided a model for the urban centres that subsequently developed. Among fortification vestiges, only the old powder magazine and redoubt of the Quebec Citadel remain as examples of French regime military design. The dearth of trained craftsmen and tools gave rise to domestic architecture characterized by simplicity of design and lack of ornamentation. Illustrating the austerity of these early constructions, the Jacquet House (1699), in Quebec City, was built of rough fieldstone, and topped by a steep roof. Toward the end of the century, the principal urban areas were embellished by impressive administrative and religious edifices, erected by the French-born architects **Claude Baillif** and **François de la Joüe**. The Château Saint-Louis and the Quebec Basilica-Cathedral figured among those imposing monuments; unfortunately, neither of the original structures has survived intact. The arrival of religious orders (Ursuline, Augustine and Jesuit) gave rise to an institutional style that reflected the influence of French classicism. Noteworthy buildings from this period are Quebec City's Ursuline monastery, whose interior courtyard is reminiscent of 16C French chateaux, and the Old Sulpician Seminary of Montreal. These buildings, as well as several opulent residences, were erected with stone vaulting.

Early to mid-18C – Following several devastating fires, such as the one in Quebec City's Lower Town, local administrators established new ordinances that "canadianized" the architecture. Constructions were adapted to the North American context, giving rise to a vernacular style that later evolved into the *maison québécoise*. Strict regulations required the use of slate roofs and stone vaults, while prohibiting decorative elements liable to help spread fire. Erected in 1798, the Calvet House in Montreal exemplifies this common building type by its simple fieldstone walls, firebreaks (the part of the wall extending beyond the roof as a shield against flying sparks), corner consoles, wide chimney stacks, and gabled roof.

18C House, Quebec City

© Robert Holmes

The Baillairgé Family – The 18C saw the emergence of this dynasty of prolific architects, painters and sculptors. **Jean Baillairgé** (1726-1805) left France to work on new Canadian projects under the renowned military engineer **Chaussegros de Léry** (1682-1756). Shortly after landing in Quebec, he was selected to draw up plans for several buildings, including the Quebec cathedral. After studying in France at the Académie Royale de peinture et sculpture, his son, **François** (1759-1830), returned to Quebec and elaborated designs for the cathedral's interior. **Thomas** Baillairgé (1791-1859), Quebec's preeminent 18C architect, studied sculpture with his father, François, and with the Montreal woodcarver and sculptor Louis-Amable Quévillon (1749-1823), known especially for his interior decoration of the church at Sault-au-Récollet. Thomas contributed to the Quebec cathedral and later supervised the construction of churches throughout the province. Drawing on British architectural trends, Thomas developed an original style, which combined neoclassical influences and

Quebec's mixed architectural heritage. Thomas and his father collaborated on the elaborate interior of the Saint-Joachim church between 1815 and 1825. Thomas' nephew, **Charles** (1826-1906), was trained as an architect and engineer. He became Quebec City's engineer in 1866, beautifying the city with monumental edifices, such as the main pavilion of Laval University, new public spaces and imposing staircases.

Late 18C – Following the British Conquest, the province's urban areas lay in ruins. Though post-French Regime architecture still dominated until 1800, British influence drastically altered the architectural landscape in the early 19C. The neoclassical style, in particular Palladianism *(below)* bore a determining influence on constructions. Transformed into single-family homes, domestic structures of this period, based on the British model, occupied a relatively small area of land, but were built with two or three storeys. Massive chimneys rising from a four-sided gently sloped roof replaced the characteristic steeply pitched roof of the French Regime constructions.

The development of commerce and a relatively prosperous economy fostered the growth of new urban areas around industries, such as Sherbrooke and Saint-Hyacinthe. Cities also sprung up around military fortifications (Chambly, Sorel and Vaudreuil). Beginning in the 1780s, resort areas along the banks of the St. Lawrence attracted a wealthy bourgeoisie, who developed a taste for the "picturesque style" imported from Great Britain

19C – **Palladianism** continued to dominate the early part of the century. This popular style, inspired by the works of the 16C Italian architect Andrea Palladio, is characterized by austerity and symmetry of design and employs elements from classical antiquity, including pediments, pilasters, Doric and Ionic columns, cornices and quoins. In addition, the structures designed in this style were often faced with a smooth layer of cut stone. The Holy Trinity Anglican Cathedral in Quebec City represents a colonial version of Palladianism. A more resolutely classical style appears about 1830, as exemplified by the elegant Bonsecours Market in Montreal.

The **maison québécoise**, the Quebec equivalent of the rustic English cottage, came into vogue in the 1830s and 1840s. Offering a harmonious synthesis between the French heritage and British influence, this type of building is embellished by picturesque ornaments and incorporates amenities such as large windows, balconies, reception rooms, and heating systems.

The mid- and late 19C reflects an eclectic mix of more exuberant revival styles, inspired by architectural trends of the past and made possible by new materials and building techniques developed in the century. Numerous churches in Quebec City were erected in the **Gothic Revival style** popularized by the French architect and restorer Viollet-le-Duc, who is credited with resurrecting the prevailing style of the Middle Ages. Catholic churches were generally based on French Gothic architecture, while Protestant places of worship adopted the British model. Victor Bourgeau's Notre Dame Basilica in Montreal and the Chalmers-Wesley Church, by John Wells, in Quebec City, exemplify two variants of this style.

Modelled on Italian palaces and villas, the **Renaissance Revival style** was associated with the wealthy elite and therefore used mainly for commercial buildings. The Ritz-Carlton, in Montreal, exemplifies this style, characterized by wide cornices, exuberant ornamentation and rustication.

The **Second Empire style**, in fashion during Napoleon III's reign, gained prominence in the 1870s, under the Quebec architect **Eugène-Étienne Taché** (1836-1912). In search of a unified architecture for governmental buildings of the new province, Taché drew on this style for his plans of the Parliament Building in Quebec City. Recognizable by its distinctive double-sloped mansard roof pierced by dormer windows, the style also introduced arched lintel windows, a profusion of columns and wrought-iron roof cresting, as seen in the Shaughnessy House in Montreal.

After creating several works in Gothic Revival, the architect **Victor Bourgeau** (1809-1888) became a proponent of the **Baroque Revival style**. His masterpiece, Mary Queen of the World Basilica-Cathedral, a small-scale replica of St. Peter's Basilica in Rome, illustrates the tenets of this style by its massive proportions, enormous dome and elaborate interior embellished by an imposing baldachin.

While striving to adapt the Second Empire style to the Canadian environment, Eugène-Étienne Taché proposed structures that would reflect the era of New France's discoverers, Cartier and Champlain. Inspired by the French chateaux of the Loire valley, Taché designed monumental edifices replete with towers and turrets, conical roofs and machicolation. The most famous example of the **Chateau style** remains the Château Frontenac, erected by **Bruce Price** (1843-1903) in 1892.

In the late 19C, another interpretation of medieval architecture, the **Romanesque Revival**, was mainly used for religious buildings. This style was appropriated by H.H. Richardson, the prominent American architect who later modified it into the Richardsonian Romanesque, characterized by rounded arches and buttresses, squat columns, arcades and deep-set windows. Montreal's Windsor Station is an excellent example of this distinctly North American style.

20C – The turn of the century saw a wave of architects turning to the École des Beaux-Arts in Paris for inspiration. The exuberant **Beaux-Arts style**, which employs a classical vocabulary in monumental compositions, became the preferred institutional style and

A selection of architectural terms used in this guide

Apse	The rounded or polygonal termination of a church, in which the altar is housed.
Baldachin	An ornamental canopy over an altar supported by columns.
Barrel vaulting	Continuous arched vault of semicircular cross-section.
Bas-relief	Low relief. A form of sculpture in which figures or shapes project slightly from the background plane.
Bastion	In military architecture, a masonry structure projecting from the outer wall of a fortification.
Battlement	The uppermost portion of a fortified wall with alternate solid elements and openings (embrasures or crenels).
Blockhouse	In 18C and 19C military architecture, a fortified structure, commonly of wood, with a square floor plan and an overhanging upper floor.
Buttress	A masonry structure built against a wall to add support or strength.
Capital	Crowning feature of a column or pilaster.
Choir	That part of a church at the end of the nave reserved for singers and the clergy.
Cornice	A molded projection crowning the top of a building or wall.
Curtain wall	In modern architecture, a non-bearing exterior wall suspended on the face of a building like a curtain.
Dormer window	A small window projecting from a sloped roof.
Embrasures	A series of crenels or intervals cut into the top portion of a battlement.
Fanlight	A semicircular window over a door or window.
Gable	The vertical triangular section of wall closing the end of a double-sloped roof.
Mansard roof	A roof with two slopes on all four sides, the lower slope being the steeper of the two (named after the 17C French architect, François Mansart).
Nave	The central main body of a church designed to accommodate the congregation.
Pediment	Any triangular or semicircular crowning element used over doors, windows or niches.
Pilaster	An engaged pier or pillar projecting slightly from a wall surface, generally with base and capital.
Portal	A monumental entrance or gate.
Porte-cochere	A large covered entrance porch.
Portico	A porch or covered walk consisting of a roof supported by columns.
Pulpit	An elevated platform in a church occupied by a member of the clergy during religious services.
Quoin	A cornerstone often distinguished from the adjoining masonry by a special surface treatment.
Redoubt	A small free-standing fortification.
Reredos	A decorative screen or wall behind an altar sometimes forming part of the retable.
Retable	A decorative screen placed above and behind an altar and generally containing a work of art.
Rose window	A large circular stained-glass window dissected by stone members or mullions arranged like the spokes of a wheel.
Turret	A small tower generally placed at the corner of a building.

Place de la Cathédrale, Montreal

proliferated under the government of Louis-Alexandre Taschereau. Montreal's Museum of Fine Arts, replete with a imposing staircase and portico colonnade illustrates this style, which relies on monumentality and symmetry. Introduced to the province at a time of economic prosperity, the Beaux-Arts also symbolized wealth and power. The Château Dufresne with its elegant coupled columns, balustrades and elaborate ornaments reflects the tastes of the opulent bourgeoisie of the day.

The invention of steel-frame constructions heralded the beginning of the first skyscrapers, or buildings with more than 10 storeys. Influenced by the Chicago school, these structures reveal a complete break with past architectural trends. New techniques and building materials, such as reinforced concrete, provided architects with innumerable possibilities.

Introduced at the Paris Exposition in 1925, the **Art Deco style** made its appearance in Quebec's large corporation buildings. Hallmarks of the style include vertical lines and geometric ornaments carved on marble, bronze and other expensive building materials. The Price Building in Quebec City presents a stunning Art Deco ensemble.

After a period of artistic stagnation, the 1950s marked the beginning of urban renewal and the growth of modern architecture. Modern architecture embodied practical and functional thinking, developed in the works of Le Corbusier and Gropius. Simple, geometric lines, devoid of ornamentation, typified a style that did not rely on any past tenets of architecture. The influential architect, Mies van der Rohe, proponent of the **International style**, made use of glass curtain walls, black metal and reinforced concrete, seen in the Westmount Square. Montreal's Place Ville-Marie, erected by I.M. Pei, and Habitat, designed by **Moshe Safdie**, also illustrate these modern trends.

Ecclesiastical architecture experienced a renaissance under **Dom Paul Bellot** (1876-1944), a Benedictine monk, who drew inspiration on Viollet-le-Duc's works and introduced modern church architecture into Quebec. Known as "modern Gothic," his style is best illustrated by the Abbey of Saint-Benoît-du-Lac and St. Joseph's Oratory, in Montreal.

In recent years, **Postmodern** currents have presented an eloquent reply to the monotony and anonymity of the architecture of the 1960s. The style often incorporates existing structures and uses elements from previous styles, such as pointed arches, fanlights and other embellishments, to produce a harmonious ensemble, that blends with its environment. Montreal's La Place de la Cathédrale, Maison Alcan and the Canadian Centre for Architecture, by **Peter Rose** and **Phyllis Lambert**, all exemplify this trend.

Consult the practical information section at the end of the guide for travel tips, useful addresses and phone numbers, and a wealth of details on shopping, recreation , entertainment and annual events.

The Arts

Amerindian Art

Through the centuries, Quebec's Amerindian peoples have developed diverse modes of artistic expression that bear witness to their distinctive lifestyles and beliefs.

Traditional Art – Most Algonquian-speaking Amerindians (notably Abenaki, Algonquin, Cree, Micmac, Montagnais and Naskapi) are descended from nomadic peoples who excelled in the art of beadwork (shell, bone, rock or seed) and embroideries (porcupine quills and moose or caribou hair). Caribou-hide vests and moccasins, and various birchbark objects were often decorated with geometric incisions and drawings. Red, the symbol of continuity and renewal, was the predominant colour. Elaborate belts of **wampum** (beads made from shells) feature motifs illustrating the main events in Amerindian history. Wampum was exchanged at peace ceremonies and during the signing of treaties. The smaller, quasi-sedentary, Iroquoian-speaking groups included Hurons, Mohawks, Onondagas and Senecas. As agricultural societies, they formed semi permanent villages and constructed multi-family dwellings known as longhouses; out of their sedentary lifestyle evolved an artistic repertoire free from the constraints of nomadism. Among their most beautiful works are exquisite moosehair embroideries that gradually began incorporating floral motifs under European influence. Huron women were the most adept at this delicate art; the complex techniques they applied with remarkable skill have never been replicated. Also of interest are the wooden masks known as "False Faces" that represented mythological figures associated with traditional healing practices.

Chair Back Panel, Micmac (19C)

McCord Museum

The Contemporary Scene – Amerindian art has undergone a profound transformation in the past ten years. Whereas artists traditionally relied on the use of natural materials such as hide and bark, today they are exploring new media such as canvas, acrylics and charcoal; consequently, new techniques have emerged although inspiration is still drawn from social and cultural traditions. The result is a new, contemporary vision of aboriginal art that keeps alive the memory of the past.

Inuit Art

Art forms developed over centuries have brought no small renown to the inhabitants of North America's arctic regions.

Origins – The earliest known artifacts produced by the Inuit are small stone projectile points attributed to the Pre-Dorset and Dorset cultures, which developed in the first millenium BC. Petroglyphs or rock carvings attributed to these cultures have been found in the steatite hills of Kangiqsujuaq. The Thule people, generally considered to be the ancestors of the present-

FCNQ/drawing by R. Corbel

Soapstone Engraving

day Inuit, crafted more refined objects including combs and figurines. Generally small in size, these early artifacts were closely associated with religious beliefs and practices. Beginning in the 19C, many miniature sculptures made of stone, ivory (walrus tusks) and whalebone were traded for staples such as salt and firearms, provided by Europeans. With the decline of traditional lifestyles resulting from increased contact with the non-indigenous peoples, sculpture and other forms of arts and crafts gradually lost their magic or religious significance and provided a new source of income to the Inuit population.

Inuit Art in the 20C – Today the term "Inuit art" evokes images of steatite carvings. Abundant in the northern regions, **steatite** (known as soapstone) is a soft rock ranging from greyish green to brown. Other harder rocks commonly used include green serpentine, argillite, dolomite and quartz. Modern Inuit sculptures, which can reach im-

FCNQ/drawing by R. Corbel

Soapstone Sculpture

pressive dimensions, represent local fauna, life in the great northern regions and other arctic themes popular with the public. Other art forms include printmaking, sculpted caribou antlers, rock engravings and tapestries. In recent decades, the art trade has become an extremely lucrative economic activity for the Inuit population.

In order to prevent the exploitation of Inuit artists by retailers from the south, local **cooperatives** were created in the 1960s. Since 1967, they have been regrouped under the Fédération des Coopératives du Nouveau-Québec, which controls the marketing of artworks. The most renowned centres for Inuit sculpture are the villages of Povungnituk and Inukjuak, located on the shores of Hudson Bay. Salluit and Ivujivik are also well-known artistic communities. Three artists had a profound effect on the development of Inuit sculpture: Joe Talirunili (1893-1976), Davidialuk (1910-1976) and Charlie Sivuarapik (1911-1968). Among the foremost sculptors of the current generation are Joanassie and Peter Ittukalak, from Povungnituk, and Eli Elijassiapik, Lukassie Echaluk and Abraham Pov of Inukjuak.

Painting and Sculpture

17C-18C – The arrival of French and British colonists in the early 17C introduced European aesthetics and forms to Quebec's artistic landscape.

Religious Art – Religion was the very fabric of life in New France. Each village had its own church and great pains were taken to decorate its interior. As most canvases were imported from France, very few local votive paintings were executed in this early period. A notable exception to this are the works of Brother Luc (1614-1685), a member of the Récollet order.

In early colonial times, altars, retables, baldachins and statues were all imported from France. The transportation of such large objects proved problematic, however, and craftsmen were eventually trained locally. Sculptures, always made of wood, were carved in relief and gilded. The Baroque style, very much in fashion in France at that time, remained the preferred style until the mid-19C among Quebec sculptors.

The art of church decoration was handed down through generations; certain families became famous for their artistic accomplishments. In the 1650s, brothers Jean and Pierre **Levasseur** became the first of a dynasty of sculptors that continued into the 18C with Noël and Pierre-Noël Levasseur. Although they were best known for their religious artwork, they also sculpted ships' figureheads and other naval ornaments.

In the years following the British Conquest (1759), religious art came to a virtual standstill. But in the late 18C, church building resumed at a rapid pace. In Quebec City, the **Baillairgé** family was gaining wide recognition for its wood sculptures; three generations, represented by Jean (1726-1805), François (1759-1830) and Thomas (1791-1859), would perpetuate the tradition.

At the same time, **Philippe Liébert** (1733-1804) was winning acclaim in Montreal, particularly for his decoration of the church at Sault-au-Récollet, which contains sculptures by his student, **Louis-Amable Quévillon** (1749-1823). This renowned sculptor and designer developed a distinctive style inspired by Louis XV decoration, replete with foliage, arabesque and finely adorned vaults. Throughout the early 19C, the so-called Quévillon school embellished the interiors of numerous ecclesiastical edifices throughout Quebec. Later in the century, a new form of religious statuary made with plaster casts appeared, and eventually led to the decline of traditional wood sculpting. While most artists were turning to new art forms, sculptor **Louis Jobin** (1845-1928) was an exception. In 1881, he created the monumental statue (wood and metal) known as **Notre-Dame-du-Saguenay**, which overlooks the Saguenay from high atop a cliff. His equestrian sculpture of **Saint-Georges** (1912), in the Church of Saint-Georges-de-Beauce, was the last work created by a traditional wood sculptor. The craft of wood carving has nonetheless survived in certain areas of Quebec, such as Saint-Jean-Port-Joli, but it is above all a popular folk art, with no connection to the religious art that adorns many Quebec churches.

Military Topographic Art – In the period following the Conquest, British army officers were sent to Quebec to paint topographic views of the colony for military purposes. Some, inspired by the romantic ideals of late 18C England, are best exemplified by the carefully executed watercolours of officer Thomas Davies (1737-1812). Equally remarkable are the works of George Heriot (1766-1844) and James Cockburn (1778-1847).

19C – Quebec art entered its Golden Age in the late 18C, at a time of economic prosperity. The primarily European-trained artists began producing works focusing on such popular subjects as **landscapes** and, above all, **portraits**, commissioned by an emerging and wealthy bourgeoisie. The work of self-taught painters like Louis Dulongpré (1754-1843), François Beaucourt (1740-1794) and **Jean-Baptiste Roy-Audy** (1778-1848) may seem somewhat naive by European standards. The next generation of portraitists were trained in France where they acquired a more classical style. The best known among these is **Antoine Plamondon** (1802-1895), who also painted religious themes. Théophile Hamel (1817-1870) gained recognition as a leading portraitist of his day. Breaking with the tradition of portraiture, **Joseph Légaré** (1795-1855) created paintings that depicted contemporary events against dramatic backgrounds, such as *L'incendie du quartier Saint-Roch.*

Throughout the 19C, the arrival of European artists had a decisive impact on Quebec painting. Paul Kane (1810-1871), born in Ireland, came to Canada as a child. He travelled extensively and perfected his skills as a painter in Europe. His splendid portraits of native peoples are now of great historical interest. Among the painters who developed a marked interest in regional themes is **Cornelius Krieghoff** (1815-1872). This Dutch-born painter reproduced superb landscapes as well as scenes of daily life in the Montreal region in unprecedented detail.

By the mid-19C, Montreal had evolved into a sophisticated city, prosperous enough to lend financial assistance to an association whose goals were to promote the arts, organize exhibitions and mount a permanent collection. The oldest art gallery in Quebec, the **Art Association of Montreal**, was founded in 1860. It is the former name of the present-day Montreal Museum of Fine Arts.

The late 19C is marked by the emergence of photography. Acclaimed for his portraits and his renditions of the increasingly urban landscape of Montreal, **William Notman** (1826-1891) figures among Canada's most prominent photographers.

The Montreal Museum of Fine Arts

Still Life with Daisies by Marc-Aurèle de Foy Suzor-Côté

20C – At the onset of the 20C, the influence of the so-called Paris school was already visible in Quebec art, particularly in the works of Wyatt Eaton (1849-1896) and Montreal art professor William Brymner (1855-1925). Their followers include Impressionist-style painters **Marc-Aurèle de Foy Suzor-Côté** (1869-1937), Maurice Cullen (1866-1934), Clarence Gagnon (1881-1942) and Modernist-Fauvist **James Wilson Morrice** (1865-1924).

Although a contemporary of these artists, **Ozias Leduc** (1864-1955), a native of Mont-Saint-Hilaire, stood apart from the rest with his deeply mystical, luminous paintings. His still-lifes and landscapes reveal a spiritual symbolism that goes far beyond their subject, reflecting the long-lived union of art and religion in Quebec. In addition to the frescoes adorning the church of Mont-Saint-Hilaire, Leduc's works can be viewed in the Notre Dame Basilica in Montreal, and in several public collections.

Sculpture – Through the turn of the century, Quebec sculpture lost its exclusively religious character. This was the era of great commemorative monuments. Among the most notable sculptors were artist-architect Napoléon Bourassa (1827-1916) and the celebrated **Louis-Philippe Hébert** (1850-1917). Applying the techniques of French Realism to his art, Hébert created, among others, the famous Maisonneuve monument, and the statues of Jeanne Mance and Msgr. Ignace Bourget, all located in Montreal. **Alfred Laliberté** (1878-1953) fashioned sculptures along the fluid lines of Art Nouveau while maintaining an academic approach. One of his best-known works is a monument dedicated to Dollard des Ormeaux. Suzor-Côté, a close friend of Laliberté, used the same Art Nouveau techniques to create a series of bronzeworks. His *Femmes de Caughnawaga* (Montreal Museum of Fine Arts) showing a group of women fighting against the wind is so brilliantly executed that it seems the wind itself has sculpted the silhouettes.

The Contemporary Arts Society – In the 1930s, Montreal artists began to rebel against the "wild landscape nationalism" of the so-called "Group of Seven," artists from Toronto, who claimed sole authorship of a typically Canadian style of painting. A staunch critic of the Group, **John Lyman** (1886-1967) attempted to redirect Canadian art according to the precepts of the Paris school of thought. In 1939, he created the Contemporary Arts Society and organized a group known as the Modernists. Its members included André Biéler, **Marc-Aurèle Fortin** (1888-1970), Goodridge Roberts (1904-1974), Stanley Cosgrove and **Paul-Émile Borduas** (1905-1960).

The Automatist and Plasticist Movements – World War II marked a turning point in the evolution of Quebec art. In 1940, Alfred Pellan (1906-1988) returned to Quebec after an extended stay in France, to exhibit paintings strongly influenced by Picasso and other proponents of Cubism. Paul-Émile Borduas and several fellow artists, including **Jean-Paul Riopelle** (b.1923), Pierre Gauvreau, Fernand Leduc and Jean-Paul Mousseau, founded the **Automatist** group, whose paintings reflected the goal of Surrealism to transfer onto canvas the creative impulses of the psyche. In 1948, they published the **Refus Global,** a manifesto whose virulent attacks on the established order of Quebec society had a far-reaching impact that went well beyond the artistic milieu.

As a response to the lyricism and spontaneity of the Automatists, Guido Molinari and Claude Tousignant founded the **Plasticist** group (1955), freeing painting from the surrealist idiom through the use of an abstract geometric vocabulary. Form and colour were the key elements of their work. However, no single school of thought prevailed over the inspirational and creative effervescence of contemporary art, although several Montreal painters such as Charles Gagnon, Yves Gaucher, Ulysse Comtois and sculptors Armand Vaillancourt, Charles Daudelin and Robert Roussil developed their own highly personal styles.

The Current Art Scene in Quebec – Since the 1970s, Quebec has experienced a renewed interest in public art. Under a provincial law passed in 1978, building constructors must allocate one percent of construction costs for all new public buildings erected in the province to artwork. Sculptors often collaborate with architects to integrate their art into the building design. The most remarkable example of this can be seen in Montreal's subway system. Each station is designed by different architects and incorporates pictorial art and sculptures. The work of Marcelle Ferron, at the Champ-de-Mars station and Jordi Bonet (1932-1976), at the Pie-IX station are among the most interesting.

In recent years, Quebec art has evolved alongside major international currents; it has distanced itself from traditional painting while emphasizing more diversified forms and techniques, including "installation," a primarily sculptural idiom that also includes other art forms such as painting and photography. Among its proponents are Betty Goodwin, Barbara Steinman, Geneviève Cadieux, Jocelyne Alloucherie and Dominique Blain. Michel Goulet and Roland Poulin have made important contributions to the field of sculpture. Melvin Charney, an architect and urban planner, has also produced remarkable works; his most important creation is the garden of Montreal's Canadian Centre for Architecture.

Literature

Throughout the era of exploration and colonization, the literature of New France was limited to travel memoirs (Cartier, Champlain), stories, descriptive writings (Sagard, Charlevoix) and the famous historical missives known as the **Relations,** written by Jesuit missionaries recording their life and work in the New World.

The Emergence of Quebec Literature – Two newspapers, *Le Canadien*, founded in 1806 in Quebec City, and *La Minerve*, founded in 1826 in Montreal, were instrumental in the development of French-Canadian literature.

In 1837, the young Philippe Aubert de Gaspé published the first French-Canadian novel, entitled *L'influence d'un livre*, inspired by legends. The first fiction novels were influenced mainly by rural traditions, as evidenced in *The Canadians of Old (Les anciens canadiens)*, written in 1863 by **Philippe Aubert de Gaspé** senior. Nationalist and conservative ideologies were also a source of inspiration as in Pierre Joseph Olivier Chauveau's novel *Charles Guérin* (1846-1853). Indeed, Quebec literature was long influenced by a wave of conservative ideology that arose in the 1860s, promoting the moral values and precepts of the Catholic Church.

Historical novels, inspired by **François-Xavier Garneau**'s *History of Canada (Histoire du Canada)*, published in the 1840s, became very popular in the mid-1800s, as did the romantic poetry of Octave Crémazie (1827-1879). Louis-Honoré Fréchette (1839-1908) published his *Légende d'un peuple* in 1887.

20C – The early 20C was dominated by the nationalist works of writer and historian, **Lionel Groulx** (1878-1967), leader of the "Action française", and by the poet, Émile Nelligan (1879-1941), who produced his entire work between the ages of 17 and 20, before being confined to a mental asylum. In 1916, French-born **Louis Hémon**'s novel *Maria Chapdelaine*, depicting life in rural Quebec, was published posthumously, and is now translated into eight languages. In 1933, **Claude-Henri Grignon** wrote his celebrated novel *The Woman and the Miser (Un homme et son péché)*.

Urbanization and the trauma of the World War II resulted in greater introspection among Quebec writers as they questioned the established order. Novelist Robert Charbonneau abandoned his tales of rural life for psychological novels. Quebec poetry was redefined through the works of Alain Grandbois (1900-1975) and Hector de Saint-Denys Garneau (1912-1943). **Roger Lemelin**'s *The Town Below (Au Pied de la Pente Douce*, 1944) was the first novel to explore the lifestyle of the urban proletariat. The theme of city life also permeated the works of **Gabrielle Roy**, such as *The Tin Flute (Bonheur d'occasion)*, published in 1945.

The Quiet Revolution *(Révolution tranquille)* of the 1960s reflected Quebecers' growing awareness of their distinct cultural identity and their reappraisal of traditional values and institutions. The literature of the day faithfully reflected this period of upheaval as writers explored a rich variety of subjects and styles. It is the poets, however, who instilled the most strength and energy into Quebec literature at that time: **Gaston Miron** (1928-1996), Gatien Lapointe, Jacques Brault and Fernand Ouellette. Also during the 1960s new novelists rose to prominence, and already well-known writers became associated with the finest of Quebec letters, among them Hubert Aquin *(Hamlet's Twin/Neige noire)*, Marie-Claire Blais *(A Season in the Life of Emmanuel/Une Saison dans la vie d'Emmanuel)*, Roch Carrier *(La guerre, yes sir!)*, Réjean Ducharme *(The Swallower Swallowed/L'avalée des avalés)*, Jacques Ferron *(The Juneberry Tree/L'amélanchier)*, Jacques Godbout *(Knife on the Table/Le couteau sur la table)*, **Anne Hébert** *(Kamouraska* and *In the Shadow of the Wind/Les fous de Bassan)* and Yves Thériault *(Agaguk)*. Also during the 1960s, playwright Michel Tremblay *(below)* made a resounding entrance onto the literary scene with *Les Belles-Sœurs*. Two of the best-known anglophone Quebec novelists are Hugh MacLennan and Mordecai Richler,

LOUIS HÉMON

MARIA CHAPDELAINE

Récit du Canada français

Précédé de deux préfaces: par M. Émile Boutroux, de l'Académie française, et par M. Louvigny de Montigny, de la Société royale du Canada.

Illustrations originales de Suzor-Côté

Ouvrage honoré d'une souscription du Secrétaire d'État du Canada et du Secrétaire de la province de Québec

MONTRÉAL
J.-A- LeFebvre, éditeur,
LA COMPAGNIE D'IMPRIMERIE GODIN-MÉNARD LIMITÉE
41, RUE BONSECOURS, 41
1916

Thierry Marcoux/Bibliothèque nationale du Québec

who has won numerous literary prizes including the prestigious Prix du Gouverneur Général. Following the trend of the 1960s, the early 1970s were characterized by a broad diversity of styles, most notably the "psychological" novel. Prominent authors from this extremely prolific period of Quebec literature include Louis Hamelin *(La rage)*, Suzanne Jacob *(Laura Laur)*, Claude Jasmin *(Mario/La sablière)*, Sergio Kokis *(Le pavillon des miroirs)*, Marie Laberge *(Julliet)*, Robert Lalond *(Le petit aigle à tête blanche)* and Monique Larue *(True Copies/Copies conformes)*.

Theatre

The theatrical arts were introduced somewhat late in Quebec: the first permanent French theatre companies appeared in the 1880s. But it was only in the late 1940s to early 1950s that the foundations of what has become an enduring theatrical tradition were laid. At that time, an original repertoire and several theatrical institutions gradually took shape, as a generation of actors, trained for the most part with Father Legault's Les Compagnons de Saint-Laurent, paved the way for their successors. Professional theatre companies were created: the Théâtre du Rideau Vert (1949), the Théâtre du Nouveau Monde (1951), the Quat'Sous (1954) and the avant-garde Apprentis-Sorciers and Égregore.

© Jean F. Leblanc/AGENCE STOCK

Le Cirque du Soleil

Gratien Gélinas created Tit-Coq (1948), a play based on a popular character whose deceptively naive demeanour hid a mind capable of astute social criticism. In 1959, Gélinas wrote *Bousille et les justes* while heading the Comédie-Canadienne, a name that reflected the will to create a truly French-Canadian theatrical repertoire. A friend of Jean Anouilh and Arthur Miller, Marcel Dubé staged *Un simple soldat* at the Comédie-Canadienne in 1958; his ability to explore universal themes won him wide recognition. The Compagnie Jean Duceppe was founded by the comedian **Jean Duceppe** (1923-1990) in 1973, and garnered an excellent reputation for its contemporary repertoire.

Michel Tremblay, whose plays have had more international exposure than those of any other Quebec playwright, pursued his predecessors' exploration of city life. From *Les Belles-Sœurs* (1968), which is considered a milestone in the development of Quebec theatre, to *The Real World?* (*Le vrai monde?*, 1987), Tremblay has created a veritable human comedy, with a cast of characters who speak the street slang heard in the working class neighbourhoods of Quebec City and Montreal.

The strength and originality of Quebec's modern theatre lie in the **experimental works** of authors like Jean-Pierre Ronfard *(Vie et mort du roi boiteux*, 1981*)* at the Théâtre Expérimental de Montréal, and Gilles Maheu at Carbone 14. Playwright Normand Chaurette came on the scene in the 1980s with such pieces as *Provincetown Playhouse* and *Fragments of a Farewell Letter Read by Geologists* (*Fragments d'une lettre d'adieu lus par des géologues*, 1986); in 1996, his *Le passage de l'Indiana* gained wide acclaim at the Avignon Festival, and garnered the prestigious Prix du Gouverneur Général. Other renowned names of Quebec theatre include Michel Marc Bouchard *(The Orphan Muses/Les muses orphelines*, 1989), René-Daniel Dubois (*Don't Blame the Bedouins/Ne blâmez jamais les Bédouins*, 1985) and Marie Laberge (*Night/L'homme gris*, 1986). In Quebec's internationally renowned Ligue nationale d'improvisation, actors improvise dialogue in the context of a hockey game, Quebec's best-loved sport. The widely acclaimed **Cirque du Soleil** (Circus of the Sun) has delighted audiences around the world with its innovative and enchanting blend of traditional circus entertainment, music, theatre and dance.

Music

The Montreal Symphony Orchestra, conducted by Charles Dutoit, has represented Quebec throughout the world, with its widely acclaimed tours and recordings. Since 1963, the Montreal International Music Competition (Concours international de Montréal) has welcomed young musicians from all over the world. Both the Mount Orford and Lanaudière music camps are vibrant training centres. The Festival de Lanaudière, a summer music festival in Joliette, has gained international recognition.

Composers, Conductors and Musicians – The authors of Canada's national anthem, *Ô Canada*, are two French-Canadians; Adolphe-Basile Routhier (1839-1920) wrote the lyrics and Calixa Lavallée (1842-1891) composed the music.

Conductor Wilfrid Pelletier (1896-1982) launched Montreal's dynamic music scene while Claude Champagne (1891-1965), composer of the *Symphonie gaspésienne*, opened the way for numerous other composers. Among the foremost are Alexander Brott (founder of the McGill Chamber Orchestra), Jean Papineau-Couture and Jean Vallerand. The Contemporary Music Society of Quebec (Société de musique contemporaine du Québec), founded in 1966, includes composers such as Serge Garant, Pierre Mercure, Gilles Tremblay and André Prévost.

Pianists Henri Brassard, André Laplante and Louis Lortie have all triumphed in international music competitions, while violinist Angèle Dubeau and pianist Marc-André Hamelin have carved brilliant careers at home as well as abroad. Kenneth Gilbert is known for his research and remarkable renditions of 17C and 18C harpsichord music. Raymond Daveluy, Mireille and Bernard Lagacé are famous for their mastery of the pipe organ. Founded in 1879, the Casavant Frères company of Saint-Hyacinthe has maintained its reputation as one of the world's foremost organ manufacturers.

Opera – Since the days of Emma Lajeunesse (1885-1958), better known as **Albani**, several Quebec voices have been heard in Milan, New York, Paris and London: soprano Pierrette Alarie, contralto **Maureen Forrester** (1930), tenors Raoul Jobin and Leopold Simoneau, bass Joseph Rouleau and baritones Louis and Gino Quilico.

The Montreal Opera has staged several productions each year since its creation in 1980.

Traditional and Popular Music

Music is the heart and soul of Quebec's oral tradition. From the songs of the "voyageurs" to *Un Canadien errant* (1842), popularized by Nana Mouskouri, Quebec's folk repertoire, inspired by traditional French songs, was part of everyday life.

Félix Leclerc (1914-1988) was Quebec's preeminent folk musician. A raconteur and poet, he introduced Quebec culture to France after World War II, leading the way for many other Quebec folk singers or *chansonniers*.

In the late 1950s, several chansonniers and musicians formed a group known as "les Bozos," named after one of Leclerc's songs. They included Raymond Lévesque, Clémence Desrochers, André Gagnon, Claude Léveillé *(Frédéric)* – who worked with Edith Piaf – and Jean-Pierre Ferland *(Je reviens chez nous)*. Joining this talented new generation of singers and songwriters was **Gilles Vigneault**, the poet of Natashquan. His song *Gens de mon pays* accompanied the rise to power of the Québécois Party. Pauline Julien and Renée Claude are known today for their renditions of works by Quebec's great folksingers.

The rock music of **Robert Charlebois** reflected a more critical social outlook typical of the 1960s. At that time, large-scale shows and a recording industry heavily influenced by American culture were adding a whole new dimension to Quebec music. The California counterculture was echoed in the music of groups such as Harmonium and Beau Dommage.

Diane Dufresne created a highly personal and dramatic style that has won her numerous awards at home and abroad. She often sings compositions by **Luc Plamondon**, one of the most famous Quebec songwriters. Plamondon founded the Quebec Society of Professional Authors and Composers (Société professionnelle des auteurs et compositeurs du Québec) and worked on the rock opera *Starmania* in 1976. Sylvain Lelièvre, whose musical career took shape in the early 1970s, is today considered among Quebec's finest singer-songwriters. Richard and Marie-Claire Séguin, the rock group Offenbach, and Claude Dubois also rose to prominence in the 1970s, and Ginette Reno is considered one of Quebec's most acclaimed pop singers.

Such singers and composers as Richard Desjardins, Luc de Larochelière and Paul Piché appeared on Quebec's musical scene during the 1980s. The 1990s witnessed the phenomenal rise of songstress **Céline Dion**, whose acclaim today extends worldwide. Other musical stars of note include Laurence Jalbert, Luce Dufault, Isabelle Boulay, Bruno Pelletier and Garou.

Céline Dion in Concert

Cinema

Since 1895, most of the films shown in Quebec were imported from the US. The first feature films were produced in the province between 1944 and the introduction of television in 1952. But the birth of the Quebec film industry really dates back to the 1960s.

Several executive directors and directors of photography were trained at the National Film Board of Canada, a federal institution (1939) based in Montreal since 1956. The NFB has acquired an international reputation for its animation films (Norman McLaren and Frederick Back, two-time Oscar winner for *Crac!*, 1982 and *The Man Who Planted Trees*, 1988) and its documentary tradition, which evolved into a new genre known as "cinéma-vérité," a widely recognized trend in the Quebec film industry, best reflected in the works of **Pierre Perrault** (*The Moontrap*, 1963; *Wake up, mes bons amis!*, 1970) and Michel Brault (*Les Ordres*, 1974).

Claude Jutra won international fame for *Mon Oncle Antoine* (1971) and *Kamouraska* (1973), based on a novel by Anne Hébert. Jean Beaudin's film *J.A. Martin, photographe* (1976) won an award at the Cannes Film Festival.

Denys Arcand reached the European and American publics with his films *The Decline of the American Empire* (1986) and *Jesus of Montreal* (1989); the latter was nominated at Cannes and Hollywood. Jean-Claude Lauzon's *Night Zoo* won 13 of the 17 Genies awarded during the Canadian film industry's annual gala awards celebration in 1987. Robert Lepage's 1995 film *The Confessional (Le confessionnal)* won the prestigious Prix Claude-Jutra; other 1995 films of note include Charles Binamé's *Eldorado*, and *Thirty-two Short Films about Glenn Gould*, by François Girard.

SELECTED FILMS

Titles listed below represent Quebec filmmaking highlights from 1961 to the present.

Very Nice, Very Nice (1961)	Arthur Lipsetty
The Act of the Heart (1970)	Paul Almond
The Apprenticeship of Duddy Kravitz (1974)	Ted Kotcheff
Lies My Father Told Me (1975)	Jan Kadar
The Street (1976)	Caroline Leaf
Joshua Then & Now (1985)	Ted Kotcheff
The Decline of the American Empire (1986)	Denys Arcand
The Man Who Planted Trees (1987)	Frédéric Back
Night Zoo (1987, English subtitles)	Jean-Claude Lauzon
Train of Dreams (1987)	John N. Smith
Jésus de Montréal (1989, English subtitles)	Denys Arcand
Bethune, the Making of a Hero (1990)	Phillip Borsos
The Company of Strangers (1990)	Cynthia Scott
An Imaginary Tale (1990, English subtitles)	André Fournier
Léolo (1992)	Jean-Claude Lauzon
Love and Human Remains (1993)	Denys Arcand
The Confessional (1995)	Robert Lepage
Thirty-two short films about Glenn Gould (1995)	François Girard
The Boys (1997)	Louis Saia

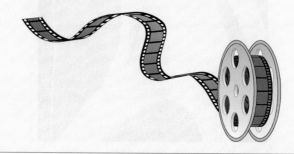

Customs and Traditions

Quebec's customs and traditions reflect the values of a rural people whose everyday life was greatly influenced by the Catholic Church and the rigours imposed by the natural environment. The oral and material heritage of Quebec is permeated with reminders of harsh winters, the era of the *coureurs des bois*, the settlement of forest regions and the predominance of the Church.

The Catholic Church long remained the focus of Quebecers' social and cultural life. Although the role of this institution has gradually diminished since the mid-1900s, reminders of its once powerful presence are everywhere, in countless churches and silver-coloured steeples, tiny processional chapels and wayside crosses.

Industrialization and urbanization have of course radically transformed the traditional Quebec lifestyle. In the city and countryside, many old customs have given way to the 20C while others endure.

Legends – The numerous stories, childhood tales, legends and proverbs of Quebec are of French inspiration. Long winter nights were ideal for the telling of fantastic tales. A favourite is the legend of the *chasse galerie* or "wild chase." As winter approached, young men often joined logging camps to supplement their income. Life was harsh in these camps, and the men's dreams sometimes drifted to a wife or girl-friend back home. On New Year's Eve, the devil appeared with a tempting offer: he would take the lovelorn men to their sweethearts in a special canoe capable of travelling through the air at great speed. In exchange, the men would promise to refrain from using swear words during the entire trip lest they be eternally damned. The men stood by their word on the way home, but on the return trip, they would sometimes forget their promise and speak the forbidden words. The flying canoe would come crashing to earth and the souls of the unfortunate passengers plummeted into hell. Another popular tale is the story of Rose Latulippe, the girl who danced with the devil. One night, during a dance, the door opened and a handsome stranger strolled in. Subjugated by his charm, Rose left her usual partner to dance with the newcomer. After several hours of dancing, the exhausted young girl tried to stop but discovered she could not. Her partner continued to whirl and twirl her 'round the dance floor until she thought this hour must surely be her last. Just as she despaired, the village

The Seasons – The traditions and festivities that have developed over the centuries in the southern part of the province are intimately linked to the four seasons.

Spring – In late March, the maple sap starts running, heralding the return of spring and the celebrations associated with the making of maple syrup. This sweet "water" was traditionally collected in pails hung on spouts inserted into the trunks of maple trees. The water was then boiled down to the proper consistency, producing maple syrup. This tradition known as sugaring-off is still very much a part of Quebec culture, but the pails have for the most part disappeared; today, maple water is collected in plastic tubing that brings the sap directly to a central evaporator. For the traditional sugaring-off parties, families and friends congregate in large wooden cabins known as sugar shacks, built at the edge of maple groves. Inside, long picnic tables are laden with a variety of hearty dishes and desserts cooked or covered in maple syrup. Hot syrup is also poured over snow to form a taffy-like substance known as tire, which is deftly rolled onto a stick.

Summer – The 24th of June is dedicated to St. John the Baptist, but it is also Quebec's national holiday. As a religious and national holiday, the "Saint-Jean-Baptiste" as it is commonly called, is a major annual event, celebrated throughout the province as a sign of Quebec's cultural and linguistic distinctiveness. Floats, flag parades, bonfires and live shows by some of Quebec's major entertainers are typically part of the celebrations.

Autumn – The hot, humid summer is followed by Quebec's most beautiful season, fall. As the nights grow cooler, maple trees display their autumn finery: vivid reds, rusty orange and golden yellow. This is the best time to visit the Laurentians and the Eastern Townships. It is also harvest time in apple-growing country. Many orchards are open to the public and resound with the sounds of families and friends who turn apple-picking into a pleasant outing.

Winter – The snow usually starts falling in late November or early December and melts in April. Although the days are cold and short, the winter months are generally very sunny and bright because of the sparkling snow. Quebecers celebrate winter with carnivals, the most famous of which is the **Quebec Carnival**, with its parades and ice sculpting contests. Another traditional winter activity is ice fishing on lakes and rivers.

priest appeared. Recognizing the work of the devil, he chased him off with prayers and a few drops of holy water. Poor Rose was exorcised and vowed never again to dance with any other than her appointed beau

...and Folk Heroes – Logger **Louis Cyr** (1863-1912) became a legend in his own time. Weighing more than 165kg/364lbs, he acquired a reputation as the strongest man in the world by lifting a platform on which 18 people stood, weighing altogether 1,967kg/4,336lbs. Of course, his record still stands.
Born in the Lake Saint-Jean region, **Alexis Lapointe** owed his nickname "trotteur" or trotter to his amazing speed. He could run 240km/149mi in a single day and often raced horses and even trains. It is said that the autopsy performed on him revealed double joints, bones and muscles akin to those of horses.

Vernacular Objects – Quebecers' appreciation of beauty and form is reflected in the design and decoration of buildings, furniture and everyday objects. Even the most functional items were decorated with symbols and motifs that are still visible in the countryside: wooden maple-sugar molds in the shape of hearts and leaves, weather vanes with animal motifs, barn doors and shutters with floral motifs.
From the earliest days of the colony, clothing was designed to protect Quebecers from the bitterly cold winters. Tuques, mittens, woolen scarves and boots are still essential from December to mid-March and sometimes even longer. A hooded coat known as a "canadienne" and fur coats made of fox, racoon and mink are popular winter gear.

Culinary Tradition – Quebec's varied regions offer a wide variety of dining experiences, from fancy restaurants to quaint neighbourhood bistros. Certain parts of Montreal, including Old Montreal, the Mount Royal Plateau, Boulevard Saint-Laurent and the downtown areas, are famous for their restaurants. Quebec also boasts a wide assortment of fine restaurants, mostly along Rue Sainte-Anne, Rue Saint-Jean, Rue Saint-Louis and the Grande Allée in the Upper Town, and in the Rue du Petit-Champlain area and along Rue Saint-Paul in the Lower Town.
No trip to Quebec would be complete without savouring some of the famed **regional specialties**. The Beauce region is famous for its delicious maple products: syrup, taffy, maple sugar, pie, yogurt, ice cream and liqueur. In the region of Saguenay-Lac-Saint-Jean, people claim as seriously as can be: "One blueberry, one pie!" Blueberries are also used to make an aperitif. The Saguenay–Lac-Saint-Jean also serves up other culinary delights such as *cipaille*, a six-layer meat pie with short crust, and *soupe à la gourganne*, a soup made with a type of very large bean. Other traditional dishes include pork and beans, a thick stew known as *ragoût* and a meat pie called *tourtière*. Fish and all kinds of seafood abound in several regions: fresh or smoked salmon from the Côte-Nord, lobster from the Magdalen Islands, cod from the Gaspé Peninsula, shrimp from Matane and winkles from Bas-Saint-Laurent.
For dessert, sugar pie and maple syrup are traditional favourites.

Courtesy La Cabane à Sucre Millette

48

SUGGESTED READING

20C Literature

Two Solitudes by Hugh MacClennan *(McClelland & Stewart, 1945)*
Home Truths, Selected Canadian Stories by Mavis Gallant *(Stoddart, 1956)*
The Watch that Ends the Night by Hugh MacClennan *(General Paperbacks, 1958)*
The Apprenticeship of Duddy Kravitz by Mordecai Richler *(McClelland & Stewart, 1959)*
The Favorite Game by Leonard Cohen *(McClelland & Stewart, 1963)*
Beautiful Losers by Leonard Cohen *(McClelland & Stewart, 1966)*
St. Urbain's Horseman by Mordecai Richler *(McClelland & Stewart, 1966)*
A North American Education by Clark Blaise *(General Paperbacks, 1973)*
Joshua Then and Now by Mordecai Richler *(McClelland & Stewart, 1980)*
Voices in Time by Hugh MacLennan *(Stoddart, 1980)*
Montréal mon amour, Short stories from Montreal ed. Michael Benazon *(Penguin, 1989)*
Solomon Gursky was Here by Mordecai Richler *(Penguin, 1989)*
Across the Bridge by Mavis Gallant *(McClelland & Stewart, 1993)*
Evil Eye by Ann Diamond *(Véhicule Press, 1994)*
The Jaguar Temple and Other Stories by Julie Keith *(Nuage Editions, 1994)*
The Tragedy Queen by Linda Leith *(Nuage Editions, 1995)*
Sonia and Jack by David Homel *(Harper Collins, 1995)*
7 Waves: Quebec Women Writers by Clare Braux *(Morgaine House, 1999)*

Quebec Authors in Translation

Maria Chapdelaine by Louis Hémon *(1916)*
The Town Below by Roger Lemelin *(McClelland & Stewart, 1944)*
The Tin Flute by Roger Lemelin *(McClelland & Stewart, 1945)*
The Outlander by Germaine Guèvremont *(McClelland & Stewart, 1945)*
The Madman, the Kite and the Island by Félix Leclerc *(Oberon Press, 1958)*
A Season in the Life of Emmanuel by Marie-Claire Blais *(McClelland & Stewart, 1965)*
Kamouraska by Anne Hébert *(General Paperbacks, 1970)*
The Alley Cat by Yves Beauchemin *(McClelland & Stewart, 1981)*

History and Architecture

A Short History of Quebec, 2nd ed. by John A. Dickinson and Brian Young *(Copp Clark Pitman Ltd., 1993)*
Children of Aataentsic by Bruce Trigger *(McGill-Queen's University Press, 1976)*
Inuit Stories by Nungak and Arima *(University of Toronto Press, 1988)*
The Living Past of Montreal by R.O. Wilson and Eric McLean *(McGill-Queen's University Press, 1993)*
Montreal Architecture, A Guide to Styles and Buildings by Francois Rémillard and Brian Merrett *(Méridian Press, 1990)*
Loing du Soleil: Architectural Practice in Quebec City during the French Regime by Marc Grignon *(Peter Lang, 1995)*

Photographic Essays

Wide Landscapes of Quebec *(Libre Expression, 1991)*
Montréal: a Scent of the Islands by François Poche *(Stanké, 1994)*

Soirée Québécoise

Tourtières (deep-dish meat pie), pea soup and sugar pie are just a few of the delicious specialties that will tempt your palate during your voyage. Below are some renditions that will bring back mouth-watering memories that you can share with your family and friends.

Soupe aux pois (Pea Soup)

Serves 6
Preparation: 20min (plus overnight soaking time)
Cooking Time: 2hrs 15min

1 lb dried peas
8 cups water
1/2 lb piece of salt pork
1 large onion, chopped
1/2 cup celery, chopped
1/4 cup carrots, grated
1/4 cup fresh parsley, chopped
1 small bay leaf
1 tsp dried savory
pepper to taste

1. Wash and sort peas. Soak overnight in cold water.
2. The next morning drain peas and place in a large pot.
3. Add water, parsley, salt pork, onion, celery, carrots, parsley, bay leaf, savory and 1 tsp salt. Bring to a boil.
4. Reduce heat and simmer until peas are very tender, about 2hrs adding water as needed.
5. Remove salt pork; chop and return to soup.
6. Discard bay leaf.
7. Season to taste with salt and pepper and serve.

Tarte au Sucre (Sugar pie)

Serves 6
Preparation: 20min
Cooking Time: 40min

1/2 cup maple sugar
1/2 cup brown sugar
2 tsp flour
1/3 cup whipping cream
Pastry for single-crust pie (see below)
Brown sugar can be substituted for maple sugar.

1. Combine maple sugar, brown sugar and flour.
2. Sprinkle evenly in bottom of unbaked pie shell.
3. Pour cream over sugar mixture and bake at 350°F until pastry is golden brown (35 to 40 min). Serve warm.

From *Food – à la canadienne*

Tourtière (Deep-dish meat pie)

Serves 6
Preparation: 30min
Cooking Time: 1hr 30min

1 lb lean ground pork
1 tsp salt
1/8 tsp pepper
1/2 tsp celery salt
1 large garlic clove, peeled
1/4 tsp ground cloves
1/4 tsp cinnamon
1 tbsp cornstarch
1 cup water
Double crust pie pastry (see below)

1. In a skillet, cook ground pork over low flame until warmed through.

2. Dilute cornstarch in water and add spices to the liquid.

3. Pour over pork stirring constantly. Cover and let simmer for 30 min.

4. Uncover and continue simmering another 10 min. Remove garlic clove and allow mixture to cool.

5. Spoon off most of fat leaving just enough for flavor.

6. Line a deep pie plate with pie crust.

7. Spoon meat mixture into crust. Top meat mixture with pastry for top crust. Trim top crust 1/2 inch beyond edge of pie plate. Fold extra pastry under bottom crust. Seal crusts together by fluting edge using thumb and fore-finger.

8. Bake at 425°F for 10min then lower heat to 350°F and bake 30 to 40min. Serve warm.

Most popular eateries and roadside *casse-croûtes* (snack stands) offer the very popular **poutine**. This filling dish of french fries topped off with brown gravy and cheese curd comes in different varieties ranging from Italian where spaghetti sauce is substituted for the brown gravy to galvaude—fries topped with chopped chicken, peas and coleslaw.

Basic Pastry Dough:
Single crust

1 1/2 cups flour
1/2 tsp salt
8 tbsp butter, chilled
1/4 cup ice water

1. Combine four, salt and sugar together in a bowl. Add butter and cut into dry ingredients with a pastry blender or 2 knives until mixure resembles coarse meal.

2. Sprinkle on and blend in enough of the ice water to make a workable dough, mixing in water with a fork.

3. Turn dough out onto work surface; using the heel of hand press dough away from the body. Make a ball out of the dough, wrap, and refrigerate for at least 2hrs.

4. Unwrap dough, place on floured work surface, and knead a few times with rolling pin to soften. Roll out to desired thickness.

L'Anse Saint-Jean

© Malak, Ottawa

Sights

AMOS

Abitibi-Témiscamingue
Population 13,955

Originally called Harricana after the river that flows through its centre, the town was later renamed Amos in honour of Alice Amos, wife of Lomer Gouin, premier of Quebec in the early 1900s. Amos is truly the cradle of the Abitibi region, as well as its first capital. It was here, in 1912, that the first settlers stepped off the train from Quebec City after a seemingly endless detour through the province of Ontario. Since 1913, the town has been linked to Quebec City by the transcontinental railway.

The "agriculturalist" movement promoted by French Canadian religious and political leaders, who painted a return to the land as a panacea for the great economic crisis of the 1930s, brought a rush of settlers to the area. The Catholic Church played a major role in the development of the region; in addition to providing moral and at times even political support, priests often acted as social mediators. Agriculture, mining and forestry remain the region's principal industries.

Access – *Amos is located 604km/375mi from Montreal by Rtes. 117 and 111; 56km/35mi from Val-d'Or by Rte. 111. Daily flights from Montreal to Val-d'Or by Air Alliance* ☎ *514-393-3333.*

SIGHT

Cathédrale Sainte-Thérèse d'Avila (Cathedral of St. Teresa of Avila) – *11 Blvd. Dudemaine. Open year-round daily 9am–5pm.* ♿ 🅿 ☎ *819-732-2110.* Located in the heart of town, this cathedral (1923) was designed by Montreal architect Beaugrand-Champagne, and by Msgr. J.O.V. Dudemaine, Amos' first parish priest. An example of the Romano-Byzantine style, the structure features a circular floor plan crowned by a spectacular dome. Noteworthy decorative elements include a 2.75m/9ft painted dove adorning the dome's interior, pink Italian marble, and stained-glass windows imported from France.

EXCURSIONS

Pikogan Village – *4km/2.5mi north of Amos. Turn left on Rue Principale, left again on 1ère Ave. Ouest and then right on 6ᵉ Rue Ouest, which becomes Rte. 109. Continue another 2km/1.2mi to the village, located on the left side of the road.* The residents of this Algonquin village, which is also home to several Crees, are all originally from the Lake Abitibi region. Founded in 1954, the village is now administered solely by indigenous people, reflecting their desire to reclaim their culture. All the services of a vital community exist here, including several classes in the Algonquin language at the local school. The **chapel★** *(open May-Sept Mon-Fri 9am-5pm; rest of the year & holidays by appointment only;* ♿ 🅿 ☎ *819-727-1242)* of the St. Catherine's Mission, built in 1968, is reminiscent of a wigwam, a characteristic Amerindian architectural form. The chapel's interior is decorated in the local Amerindian style.

Centre des Marais (Pageau Refuge) – *8km/5mi east of Amos. Take Rte. 111 East toward Val d'Or, and turn left on Rang Dix, at Figuery, toward Saint-Maurice (Rang Croteau). Open Jun 24–Aug Tue–Fri 1pm–5pm, weekends & holidays 1pm–8pm. $10.* ♿ 🅿 ☎ *819-732-8999.* Formerly a trapper, owner Michel Pageau has been an animal lover for thirty years. Forest rangers and hunters alike direct him to

Tending the Animals at Refuge de Pageau

hurt, mistreated or abandoned animals which he then takes in and cares for. Once nursed back to health, the animals are set free; those unable to survive in the wild remain here permanently. A **zoo** has thus sprung up in an undergrowth strewn with cages tagged with the Algonquin, French and English names of each animal. Whether a bear, deer or long-tailed buzzard, each animal's story provides new insight into wildlife and the dangers that threaten its survival.

Preissac – *35km/22mi southwest of Amos by Rte. 395.* Lost in time, the lovely village of Preissac is nestled along the road in a rural setting on the edge of the Kinojévis River. Next to the bridge over the rapids is a lovely spot for a picnic. A "dépanneur" (small grocery store) and a gas station can be found at the Preissac Exit on Route 395.

Just before reaching the Lake Preissac outfitter *(approximately 15km/9mi from Rte. 117)*, a lookout point on Route 395 affords a splendid **view**★ overlooking the lake. Fishing and tourism services, a marina and a campground are located on the shores of the lake, facing the outfitter.

Le Dispensaire de la Garde – *In La Corne, 26km/16mi southeast of Amos on Rte. 111. Open Jun–Sept daily 9:30am–5pm. $5. www.cabit.qc.ca/dispensaire ☎ 819-799-2181.* Experience the history of colonization, the beginning of rural clinics, the social role and personal life of nurses as well as the evolution of Quebec's health system in this house used by Nurse Gertrude Duchemin to treat the people of Abitibi-Témiscamingue. Guides dressed as nurses lead visitors through the multimedia presentation that brings rural medicine to life.

Île d'ANTICOSTI★★
Duplessis
Map pp 56-57

A true ecotourism destination, this island paradise stretches more than 222km/138mi in length and 56km/35mi at its widest point. Pastoral Anticosti Island lies in the estuary of the St. Lawrence River, south of the Mingan Archipelago (Côte-Nord) and northeast of Forillon National Park (Gaspé Peninsula). Mantled with lush coniferous forests and crisscrossed by more than a hundred rivers teeming with Atlantic salmon and trout, Anticosti is a favorite of deer hunters for its abundance of game. French industrialist Henri Menier, who purchased the island in 1895, created a private hunters' paradise upon it. Today the 125,000 white-tailed deer are everywhere-on the streets and even on people's front lawns.

Most of Anticosti Island forms part of a 4,575sq km/1,766sq mi provincial reserve. The island is not only a pleasant vacation spot for nature lovers, who can admire a rich variety of birds and wildflowers in a pastoral setting, but a great place for the adventure of a coastal tour by sea kayak. Limestone formations laden with fossils provide for fascinating rock collecting. Some fossils dating from the early Paleozoic era (420 to 500 million years ago) are considered by geologists to be unique.

Practical Information

Access – There are two means of getting to Anticosti Island. **By air:** from Montreal, Quebec City or Sept-Îles to Port-Menier, contact SÉPAQ ☎ 418-535-0156; chartered flights with Aviation Québec Labrador ☎ 418-962-7901. **By boat:** Relais Nordik Inc., departures from Rimouski ☎ 418-723-8787, Sept-Îles ☎ 418-968-4707, Havre-Saint-Pierre ☎ 418-538-3533.

Car rental – Sauvageau, Port-Menier ☎ 418-535-0157. Only one road traverses the island. It is paved between Port-Menier and the airport (7km/4mi), but elsewhere has a gravel surface. Dirt roads link Port-Menier to hunting and fishing lodges and camps on the Jupiter River. To visit the island, a four-wheel drive vehicle or van is indispensable.

Accommodation – The Anticosti Reserve is operated by SÉPAQ ☎ 418-890-0863 or 418-535-0156 (Port-Menier), which organises vacation packages that include airfare from Mont-Joli (on the Gaspé Peninsula), room, board, and rental of a four-wheel drive vehicle. Vacation packages with accommodation in Anticosti Reserve cottages vary in length from 7 to 14 days.

In addition to vacations organised by SÉPAQ or other outfitters – Pourvoirie du lac Geneviève ☎ 418-535-0294 – accommodation is available at the Auberge de Port-Menier ☎ 418-535-0122. The Carleton Pavilion, managed by SÉPAQ, takes reservations without vacation packages, provided space is available.

Historical Notes

Archaeological excavations on the island trace the presence of humans here back 3,500 years. The name Anticosti may be a modification of the Indian word *notiskuan*, meaning "the place where bear are hunted," or it could have originated with Basque or Spanish fishermen who called it *anti* costa, or "before the coast."

Jacques Cartier mentioned the island after his first voyage to New France in 1534, but settlement occurred there only after 1680 when Anticosti was granted to Louis Jolliet in recognition of his discovery of Illinois and his expedition to Hudson Bay. The initial settlement was destroyed by Admiral Phips' fleet in 1690. Anticosti was passed down to Jolliet's three children, and in 1763, following the Conquest, it was annexed to Newfoundland, which had become a colony of the British Crown according to the terms of the Treaty of Utrecht (1713).

During the next century, the island changed owners several times. In 1873, an English enterprise known as the Anticosti Island Company (or Forsyth Company) made an unsuccessful attempt at colonizing the island as did its successor, the Stockwell Company, and others.

The Menier Era: 1895-1926 – French industrialist and heir to a fortune from the chocolate industry, **Henri Menier** set out in the late 19C to find a piece of land which would serve both as a sound investment property and as a hunting and fishing retreat for himself and his friends. On December 16, 1895, Menier

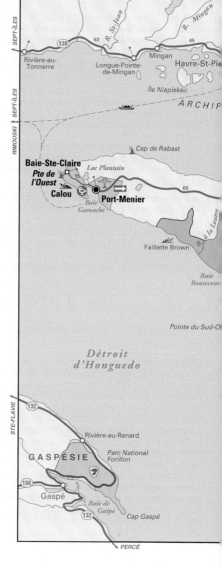

purchased Anticosti Island for the sum of $125,000.

Georges Martin-Zédé, as administrator of the island, was responsible for enforcing the strict regulations established by his friend Menier as well as for developing the village of Baie-Sainte-Claire and the lumber and fishing industries. To facilitate transport of the island's resources, a deep-water port was established on Ellis Bay, and the village of Port-Menier developed on the site.

No expense was spared in transforming the island into Menier's private paradise. To improve hunting opportunities, the natural abundance of indigenous wildlife such as otter, fox and bear was augmented by the introduction of beaver, moose, caribou, hare and some 220 white-tailed deer. A breeding farm was created to raise red and silver fox. Of the animals brought in by Menier, the most prolific by far were the white-tailed deer whose numbers were estimated at approximately 120,000 in 1989. Some biologists now claim that overpopulation has already begun to damage the vegetation.

In order to ensure his comfort on visits to Anticosti and to entertain his guests, Menier constructed a hunting lodge overlooking the bay between Port-Menier and Baie-Sainte-Claire. The sumptuous mansion, known as the "chateau" by local residents, was of Norwegian and Norman inspiration. The western wing of the structure was illuminated by an enormous stained-glass window in the shape of a fleur-de-lis. The lavish interior of the mansion reflected Menier's taste for luxury and elegance, boasting Norwegian antiques, priceless oriental rugs, fine porcelain and crystal, sculpted wooden doors, valuable paintings, and even a hand-carved "throne" for the Chocolate King. The house included an immense reception hall,

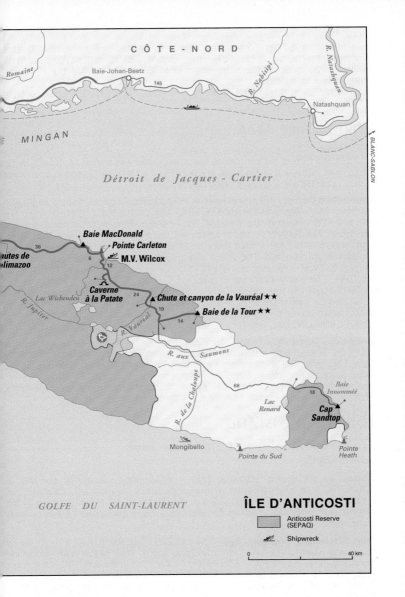

ÎLE D'ANTICOSTI

Anticosti Reserve (SEPAQ)

Shipwreck

0   40 km

an extensive library and twelve bedrooms with adjoining marble bathrooms. The chateau was fully equipped with running water and electricity, a real luxury on Anticosti Island.

Upon Henri Menier's death in 1913, Anticosti was inherited by his brother Gaston Menier who, although appreciative of the island's beauty, was somewhat intolerant of his brother's extravagances.

In 1917, due to economic difficulties in France that weakened the powerful chocolate industry, the Menier family closed down their lumber operation on the island and, in 1926, Anticosti was sold for $6.5 million to the Anticosti Corporation, a consolidated venture of three Canadian pulp and paper companies.

Over the years, the furnishings of the mansion were sold or transported to company holdings on the mainland. Chateau Menier fell into such disrepair that the structure was considered a hazard, particularly to local children who would wander on the site. In the autumn of 1953, orders were issued to burn it down.

New Developments – The Anticosti Corporation engaged in forestry activities and brought prosperity to the island for a brief period after the Menier era. An influx of forestry workers increased the local population from about 300 to almost 4,000. However, in the early 1930s, the islanders experienced hard times when exploitation of the forests was once again suspended, mainly due to the Great Depression. Unable to find employment, many residents were forced to leave the island.

For years the secrets of the island's rivers, forests and abundant wildlife, had been reserved for a privileged few, but at last, an increased interest in developing the tourism potential of Anticosti was recognised by the corporation, which changed its name in 1967 to Consolidated Bathurst Limited. In 1974, the Quebec Government acquired Anticosti for the sum of $23.78 million. Citizens were allowed to purchase land and residences in 1983, and in 1984 a municipal government was established.

Most of the island is now part of the Anticosti Reserve, a natural reserve covering 4,575sq km/1,766sq mi.

PORT-MENIER AREA

Port-Menier – The only remaining village on the island, Port-Menier was established at the turn of the century as the island's deep-water port. A general store, bank, post office and laundromat are housed in a complex located in the village centre, and there is a grocery store nearby.

Baie-Sainte-Claire – *15km/9mi west of Port-Menier.* Originally known as English Harbour, the village was renamed by Henri Menier in honour of his mother. The site was first settled in the mid-19C by fishermen from Newfoundland and the Maritimes. The Forsyth Company attempted unsuccessfully to develop the village, and when Martin-Zédé arrived there on behalf of Menier in 1895, he found only 11 families in residence. The village was transformed into a viable planned community, but was eventually abandoned in favour of the new village of Port-Menier. By 1931, Baie-Sainte-Claire lay in ruins.

In 1985 a lime kiln was rebuilt to the west of the village site. The original kiln had been used for nine years under Menier, producing slake lime for mortar and whitewash. Laws prohibiting hunting at Baie-Sainte-Claire make it an ideal spot to observe **white-tailed deer**, which can sometimes be seen in herds of up to 100.

Pointe de l'Ouest (West Point) – *1km/.6mi south of Baie-Sainte-Claire.* Despite the many lighthouses along the Anticosti shore, shipwrecks were numerous. Since the early 18C, over 200 ships have sunk in the vicinity of the island. Remains of the **Calou**, which shipwrecked in 1982, can be seen from this point.

The first lighthouse built on this site (1858) was one of the most powerful on the St. Lawrence; its light could be seen for 50km/31mi in clear weather.

TOUR OF THE ISLAND

From Port-Menier to Baie de la Tour
169km/105mi.

Chutes de Kalimazoo (Kalimazoo Falls) – *65km/40mi. Access to the falls is 1.7km/1mi from the main road. Follow signs to the campground. Take the trail on the right of the campground down to the stream, cross it, then turn left to get a good view of the falls.* The falls cascade into a small, clear pond flanked by limestone cliffs.

Baie MacDonald (MacDonald Bay) – *36km/22mi.* This scenic bay with its sandy beach was named for a fisherman from Nova Scotia, Peter MacDonald – popularly known as Peter the Hermit – who settled on Anticosti in the late 19C. After some time, his wife returned to Nova Scotia, but the fisherman stayed on, living as a hermit. According to legend, Martin-Zédé coaxed MacDonald into coming to Baie-Sainte-Claire when he became ill, but after his recuperation the feisty old fellow (age 87) made the trip home, travelling some 120km/74mi through the forests on snowshoes.

Pointe Carleton (Point Carleton) – *6km/4mi from Baie MacDonald.* The road passes along sandy beaches offering good views of the sea. The picturesque lighthouse on the point was built in 1918. *Lodging is available here at the Carleton Pavilion. For information, contact SÉPAQ.*

Wilcox Shipwreck – Near Point Carleton, at the mouth of La Patate River, the beached hull of the *M.V. Wilcox*, lies exposed to the pounding surf. This former mine sweeper wrecked here in June 1954.

Caverne à la Patate (La Patate Cavern) – *12km/7mi. Turn off the main road approximately 3km/2mi beyond the two bridges that cross La Patate River and one of its tributaries. With a four-wheel drive vehicle, it is possible to continue on the forest road for about 2km/1.2mi. Then, on foot, follow the path indicated by coloured ribbons for approximately 1hr to reach the entrance to the cavern. It is advisable to bring along a safety helmet when visiting the cavern.* Discovered in 1981, the cavern was explored and mapped by a team of geographers the following year. The entrance to the cavern measures 10m/33ft high and about 7m/23ft wide. The total length of the passages is 625m/2,050ft.

★★**Chute et canyon de la Vauréal (Vauréal Falls and Canyon)** – *The trail to the waterfall begins 24km/15mi east of La Patate Cavern. To reach the canyon, return to the main road and turn back toward Point Carleton. The turn-off is at 1.5km/1mi.*

© Yves Marcoux/PUBLIPHOTO

Baie de la Tour

The Vauréal River was originally called Morsal in honour of a descendant of the Huguenots who arrived on Anticosti in 1847 and spent 45 years near the river. Menier renamed it Vauréal after one of his properties in the Oise region of France. The one-hour hike along the riverbed to the base of the waterfall offers spectacular scenery. The greyish limestone walls, sometimes patterned with red and green schists, are carved into an undulating pattern by the forces of nature. Along the way, the steep walls are dotted with crevasses and caves. The waterfall plunges 70m/230ft into the canyon.

★★**Baie de la Tour (Tour Bay)** – *Turn off the main road 10km/6mi beyond Vauréal Falls. Continue on the secondary road for 14km/9mi.* Limestone cliffs dramatically plummeting into the sea create a breathtaking view from the sandy beach of the bay.

Return to the main road.

Detour to Cap Sandtop (Cape Sandtop) – *172km/107mi round-trip.* The road ends at Cape Sandtop. A dirt road stretches over this part of the island; in poor weather, deep ruts can sometimes make driving difficult. The Natiscotec River marks the boundary of the Anticosti Reserve. Low, sparse vegetation characterizes the marshlands found on this part of the island.

The Renard River leads back into the Anticosti Reserve. Renard Bay was once the site of an early settlement, where the Menier family eventually established a lobster-packing plant. A bird sanctuary is nestled in the small inlet between La Chute River and Innommée Bay.

Return to Port-Menier by the same road.

BAIE-SAINT-PAUL★★

Charlevoix
Population 7,379
Map p 80

This community occupies a beautiful **site**★ at the confluence of the Gouffre and St. Lawrence Rivers. The first settler was Noël Simard, who moved here from the Beaupré Coast in 1678 and cleared an area of fertile land in the Gouffre valley. The community he founded long remained the only settlement between Saint-Joachim and Tadoussac.

Surrounded by rolling green hills, Baie-Saint-Paul has inspired many artists and today boasts more than a dozen art galleries, an exposition hall and an art centre, and charming auberges set in traditional *Québécois* houses. During the 1970s, the town was frequented by the acrobats, clowns, jugglers and contortionists who later founded the Cirque du Soleil, an internationally acclaimed circus troupe.

August brings the annual **Canada Young Painters Symposium** to the Baie-Saint-Paul Arena; during the event, young artists from around the nation produce large scale works of art while the public looks on.

Access – *Baie-Saint-Paul lies some 95km/59mi northeast of Quebec City by Rte. 138.*

SIGHTS

Arriving in Baie-Saint-Paul from the south on Route 138, the visitor can admire a **view★★** of the fertile valley, dotted here and there with the buildings of the region's numerous religious communities.

Take time to stroll the village's narrow streets and enjoy the charming old houses that line the picturesque Rue Saint-Jean-Baptiste. Note in particular nos. 143-145. Wander down Saint Joseph street to window shop at its many art and antique boutiques then head over to the wharf to take a cruise or go sea kayaking. Next to the wharf lies a beach and small pine forest with walking trails.

Centre d'art de Baie-Saint-Paul (Baie-Saint-Paul Art Centre) – *4 Rue Ambroise-Fafard. Open Jun 24–early Sept daily 9am–7pm. Rest of the year daily 9am–5pm.* ▣ ☎ *418-435-3681.* This art gallery (1967, Jacques Deblois), built as a commemorative monument to the Canadian Confederation, displays the works of Charlevoix artists. In the weaving and tapestry studios, local craftsmen create works using both traditional and modern techniques.

Centre d'Exposition de Baie-Saint-Paul (Baie-Saint-Paul Exposition Center) – *23 Rue Amboise Fafard. Open late June–late Aug daily 9am–7pm. Rest of the year daily 9am–5pm.* ☎ *418-435-3681.* Designed by architect Pierre Thibault, the Center's primary purpose is playing host to traveling exhibits from around the world.

Seen from the wharf on Rue Sainte-Anne, the Île aux Coudres seems to block the entrance to the bay.

EXCURSIONS

Leaving the city by Route 362 Est, pause at the rest stop where an overlook provides another **view★★** of Baie-Saint-Paul, the St. Lawrence and the south shore. Nearby, on the right, the Chemin Vieux Quai descends to the shore, bordered by railroad tracks, and affords a closer view of the Île aux Coudres.

★★★Charlevoix Coast – *See Côte de Charlevoix.*

★★Île aux Coudres – *See Entry Heading.*

BAIE-SAINTE-CATHERINE★
Charlevoix
Population 295 – Map p 81

The community is set on a low plateau bordering a bay at the mouth of the Saguenay River, on the north shore of the St. Lawrence. In 1609, Samuel de Champlain met the Montagnais chief, Sagamo, at the southern point of the bay. Their meeting led to the alliance against the Iroquois, which was to have grave consequences for New France. The first settlers arrived in Baie-Sainte-Catherine in 1820 and for many years, they logged trees to produce timber destined for the European market. Today, whale watching is the major attraction in Baie-Sainte-Catherine as well as in Tadoussac, across the fjord.

Access – *Baie-Sainte-Catherine is approximately 210km/130mi northeast of Quebec City by Rtes. 40 and 138.*

SIGHTS

★★Whale-watching cruises (Croisière d'Observation des Baleines) – *Depart from the municipal wharf May–Oct daily at 10:15am & 1:30pm (late Jun–Labour Day additional cruises at 2:30pm & 4:30pm). Round-trip 3hrs. Commentary. Reservations required. $32.* ✗ ⅏ ▣ *Croisières AML.* ☎ *418-692-2634.* Several cruises offer visitors the chance to view whales up close, and to discover the marine environment of the St. Lawrence.

Centre d'interprétation et d'observation de Pointe-Noire (Pointe-Noire Observation and Interpretation Centre) – *On Rte. 138, just before the descent to the Saguenay. Open mid-Jun–Labour Day daily 9am–6pm. Early Sept–mid-Oct Fri–Sun 9am–5pm.* ⅏ ▣ ☎ *418-237-4383.* Situated on a cape overlooking the mouth of the Saguenay River, the Pointe-Noire promontory affords a superb panoramic view of the St. Lawrence estuary and the cliffs embracing the Saguenay Fjord. The interpretation centre (part of the Saguenay-St. Lawrence Marine Park) offers various activities to introduce visitors to this unique natural environment.

EXCURSIONS

Ferry to Tadoussac – *Depart from Quai de l'Anse-au-Portage year-round daily every 20min, 40min or 60min. One-way 10min.* ♿ *Société des Traversiers du Québec www.traversiers.gouv.qc.ca* ☎ *418-235-4395.* This year-round ferry service is the only means of crossing the deep waters of the Saguenay when travelling on Route 138. It is an impressive trip with the deep fjord on the left and the broad and majestic St. Lawrence on the right. Whales and other sea mammals are sometimes sighted from the ferry.

★★**Fjord du Saguenay** – *See Entry Heading.*

★**Côte-Nord** – *See Entry Heading.*

BAS-SAINT-LAURENT★★

Chaudière-Appalaches–Bas-Saint-Laurent
Map pp 80-81

Situated on the south shore of the St. Lawrence River, between Quebec City and the Gaspé Peninsula, the regions of Chaudière-Appalaches and Bas-Saint-Laurent are characterized by fertile plains and plateaus; to the north loom the foothills of the Appalachian Mountains. The peaceful rural landscapes along the shore are divided into long, narrow strips of farmland, laid out perpendicular to the river in the manner of the old seigneurial *rang* system. To the north, the Laurentian Mountains plunge into the St. Lawrence, creating picturesque scenery.

① FROM LEVIS TO RIVIÈRE-DU-LOUP *187km/116mi.*

★**Lévis** – *See Entry Heading.* Outside Lévis, Route 132 runs alongside the St. Lawrence, affording views of Quebec city, and of the Montmorency Falls on the north shore.
After 13km/8mi, turn left to Beaumont.

Beaumont Built between 1726 and 1733, the **church** of Beaumont is one of the oldest in Quebec (after St. Peter's Church on Île d'Orléans and the votive chapel at Cap-de-la-Madeleine). It was here that the commander of the British troops, General Wolfe, posted a proclamation of British supremacy in 1759. When the villagers removed the proclamation, Wolfe's soldiers attempted to destroy the church by burning it, but the structure survived intact.
The church was enlarged by extending the facade and adding a chapel on the north side, as well as a sacristy. Its simple nave ends in a circular apse. The church interior boasts a magnificent carved wood **decor** fashioned by Étienne Bercier, a craftsman from the Montreal studio of Louis-Amable Quévillon. Executed between 1809 and 1811, the choir is graced with Louis XV-style panelling and a coffered vault. The finely sculpted tabernacle of the main altar dates from the 18C. Above it hangs a painting by Antoine Plamondon, *The Death of St. Étienne.*
Continue through the village to rejoin Rte. 132.

Moulin de Beaumont (Beaumont Mill) – *7km/4mi beyond the village of Beaumont, turn left. Open Jun 24–Aug Tue–Sun 10am–4:30pm. May–Jun 23 & early Sept–Oct weekends 10am–4:30pm. $6.* ✗ ♿ 🅿 ☎ *418-833-1867.* This four-storey mill overlooking the Maillou Falls was built in 1821 to card wool for the seigneury. In 1850, it became a grain mill and, later, a saw mill. The mill, restored to operating condition, was reopened in 1967, and local residents furnished the third floor and attic with early French-Canadian pieces. On the premises, visitors can purchase bread made with freshly ground flour.
Behind the mill, a panoramic stairway leads to the base of the cliff, on the shores of the St. Lawrence, where the foundations of the Péan Mill can be seen. This late 18C mill operated for 144 years until 1888. Archaeological excavations have been underway on this site since 1984.
Return to Rte. 132, continue for 4km/2.5mi and turn left.

Saint-Michel – Located in the centre of the village, the **church** dates from 1858. The **presbytery** (1739), built in the typical Quebec style, is adorned with shutters carved with a fleur-de-lis on the top and a maple leaf on the bottom. In the late 18C, it was bombarded by the British and subsequently renovated.
Return to Rte. 132.

This agricultural region is dotted with several homes with brightly coloured trim. The road follows the water's edge, offering good views of the St. Lawrence and the islands that make up the Île aux Grues Archipelago.

Montmagny – *31km/19mi from Saint-Michel. After passing the bridge, turn left at the manor.* This charming city features several noteworthy sights. At the **Musée de l'Accordéon** (Accordion Museum) housed in the historic Manoir Couillard-Dupuis (1789),

Saint-André, Bas-Saint-Laurent

visitors may observe accordions being made, and learn the history of the famed, bellowed instrument *(301 Blvd. Taché Est; open June 24–Labour Day Mon–Fri 9am–5pm, weekends 10am–4pm; rest of the year Mon–Fri 9am–5pm; $4;* ♿ 🅿 *www.globetrotter.qc.ca/accordeon* ☎ *418-248-7927)*. At the **Centre éducatif des Migrations** *(53 Rue du Bassin Nord; open May-Oct daily 9am-5pm; $3.50;* ♿ 🅿 ☎ *418-248-4565)*, interactive exhibits on white geese and a multimedia presentation on the Grosse Île quarantine complex are displayed. At the Snow Goose Festival held every October, you can sample the variety of ways the locals serve up their feathered friends.

Archipel de l'Île-aux-Grues (Île-aux-Grues Archipelago) – *Guided excursion to the Archipelago departs from Berthier-sur-Mer late Jun–Labour Day Mon, Wed & Fri at 6:30pm. Rest of the year, call in advance for hours. Round-trip 2hrs 15min. Commentary. Reservations required. $23.* ♿ 🅿 *Croisières Lachance www.croisieres-lachance.qc.ca* ☎ *418-259-2140*. Of the twenty-one islands comprising the archipelago, Grosse Île, Île aux Grues and Île aux Oies are the most important. **Île aux Grues**, the only permanently inhabited island, is 10km/6mi long, and is accessible by air *(depart from Montmagny late Apr–Nov daily; reservations required; one-way $18.75;* ♿ 🅿 *Air Montmagny* ☎ *418-248-3545)* or ferry *(depart from Montmagny Apr–Dec daily; one-way 25min; reservations suggested;* ♿ 🅿 *Navigation Lavoie Inc.* ☎ *418-248-6869)*.

European settlement of Île aux Grues dates from 1679. In the following century, the forces of British General Wolfe devastated the island. Today this tranquil haven draws lovers of nature, peace and quiet to its many inns and bed-and-breakfasts. Snow geese flock here during the spring and fall. On the southeast tip of the island, outside the village of Saint-Antoine, stands an elegant manor house overlooking the St. Lawrence.

Former Hospital, Grosse-Île

© Paul G. Adam/PUBLIPHOTO

★ **Le Lieu Historique National de la Grosse-Île-et-le-Mémorial-des-Irlandais (Grosse-Île and the Irish Memorial National Historic Site of Canada)** – *Open May–Oct daily 9am–6pm. www.parkscanada.gc.ca/grosseile ☎ 418-563-4009. Several companies offer ferries to Grosse Île departing from Berthier-sur-Mer & Montmagny May–Oct. One-way 30min. Commentary. Reservations required. Visit & ferry $29–$55. ✗ ▣ Further information: Office du tourisme de la Côte-du-Sud ☎ 418-248-9196.* The ever-increasing number of European immigrants to Canada prompted the government to establish, in 1832, a quarantine station on Grosse Île in order to protect the country from the infectious and epidemic diseases (especially cholera) that were then ravaging Europe. In the first year of operation some 50,000 immigrants, weary from the long and uncomfortable ocean voyage, first set foot on Canadian soil here. In another wave of immigration in 1847, thousands of Irish fleeing famine, political repression and typhus arrived. As many as 5,000 perished on Grosse Île before ever reaching Quebec.

The island was divided into three zones. The western part of the island was known as the Hotel Sector. Healthy immigrants were lodged in hotels according to the class of passage they took on the ship coming from Europe. The first-class hotel was built in 1914 on a promontory overlooking the St. Lawrence and each room had running water and electricity – an amenity that would not arrive on the mainland until some twenty years later. The Village Sector in the middle part of the island housed the employees of the quarantine station and their families. To the east, the Hospital Sector included 21 structures, of which one is still standing.

The quarantine station on Grosse Île closed in 1937, after operating for more than a century. The facility was taken over by Canadian and US military authorities as a research station for biological and chemical warfare. It then became a research centre for animal diseases and animal quarantine station. In 1990, it became a national historic site.

A veritable Ellis Island *(consult THE GREEN GUIDE New York City)* of Canada, Grosse Île offers the visitor a touching rendez-vous with the past. On the island, a guided walk in the Hotel Sector includes a visit to the third-class hotel, the cemetery, the Bay of Cholera, and the monument erected in 1909 in memory of the thousands of Irish immigrants buried on the island. Visitors continue aboard a tourist trolley to the Village Sector, to view the chapels for employees and their families. The tour ends at the Hospital Sector.

L'Islet-sur-Mer – *23km/14mi. See Entry Heading.*

★ **Saint-Jean-Port-Joli** – *13km/8mi. See Entry Heading.*

Saint-Roch-des-Aulnaies – *14km/9mi. 2hrs.* Located on the south shore of the St. Lawrence, this peaceful community takes its name from the alder trees *(aulnes)* lining the Férée River. Granted to Nicholas Juchereau de Saint-Denis in 1656, the Aulnaies seigneury is among the oldest in the region. However, the land remained unsettled until the late 17C, owing to Iroquois hostilities. In 1837, the seigneury was sold to Amable Dionne (1781-1852), a wealthy merchant and mayor of Kamouraska for over 30 years, who erected the magnificent manor house for his son, Pascal-Aimable.

Completed in 1849, the Gothic Revival **Église Saint-Roch** *(3km/2mi east of the village entrance on Rte. 132; open mid-Jul–mid-Aug daily 10am–5pm; ₺ ▣ ☎ 418-354-2552)* contains several paintings by Joseph Légaré (1795-1855). The carved choir and altar were designed by François Baillairgé. Situated 400m/1,312ft beyond the church, the small fieldstone **processional chapel**, was erected in 1792 *(open Jun 24–Labour Day daily 10am–5pm)*.

Set on a promontory overlooking the junction of two rivers, the **Aulnaies Seigneurie** *(3km/2mi east of the church on Rte. 132; turn right, go up the hill to the parking area and information booth; open mid-Jun–Labour Day daily 9am–6pm. Mid-May–early Jun & mid-Sept–mid-Oct weekends 10am–4pm. $5.* ✗ 🅿 ☎ *418-354-2800)*, a Victorian-era wooden house flanked by two octagonal towers, was completed in 1853, according to a design by the noted architect, Charles Baillairgé. Guides dressed in late 19C costumes conduct tours through the house and describe the life of the period. Outside, visitors can enjoy walks through the lovely manicured gardens and the wooded park as well as visit the adjacent 1842 **grist mill** (moulin banal).

★**La Pocatière** – *10km/6mi. See Entry Heading.*

Rivière-Ouelle – *10km/6mi.* Originally known as Rivière-Houel in commemoration of one of Samuel de Champlain's officers, the territory was conceded by the Intendant Jean Talon to Jean-Baptiste Deschamps, also known as Boishébert de la Bouteillerie, in 1672.

Saint-Denis – *11km/7mi.* Located in the centre of the village, the **Maison Chapais** dates back to 1834 *(visit by 45min guided tour only, Jun 24–mid-Oct daily 9am–5pm; $3;* 🅿 ☎ *418-498-2353)*. Built by Jean-Charles Chapais, one of the signers of the Confederation, the house remained in the Chapais family until 1968. In 1866, the porch and spiral staircases were added, and the present interior furnishings were bought. The living room furniture dates from the early 19C, while the dining room and bedroom are appointed in the Second Empire style.

The road passes across a very wide flood plain affording expansive views of the Laurentian Mountains across the St. Lawrence. Perpendicular to the shoreline, eel traps extend into the river.

★**Kamouraska** – *10km/6mi. See Entry Heading.*

★**Rivière-du-Loup** – *41km/25mi. See Entry Heading.*

② FROM RIVIÈRE-DU-LOUP TO SAINTE-LUCE
130km/80mi by Rte. 132.

Cacouna – *10km/6mi from Rivière-du-Loup.* The seigneury was conceded to Daulier Duparc in 1673, but the first colonists began settlement only around 1750. Amerindians living in the region named it Kakouna, meaning "land of the porcupine." In the mid-19C, Cacouna became a popular seaside resort, and large hotels and luxurious vacation homes were constructed. Today, only the sumptuous Victorian houses along the water's edge recall the town's heyday.

Église Saint-Georges (St. George's Church) – *Turn right off Rte. 132 onto Rue de l'Église and continue for 2 blocks. Open year-round daily 8am–6pm.* ♿ 🅿 ☎ *418-862-4338.* The fieldstone church (1848) was partially reconstructed in 1896. The interior by F.-X. Berlinguet (1852) is richly decorated with carved and gilded detailing, crystal chandeliers and Italian paintings from the late 19C. The organ dating from 1888 is one of the few remaining works of Eusèbe Brodeur, a predecessor of the Casavant Brothers of Saint-Hyacinthe. Nearby, the neoclassical **presbytery** was built between 1835 and 1841.

Trois-Pistoles – *36km/22mi.* The town derives its name from an old monetary unit used throughout Europe until the late 19C. According to local legend, a small vessel shipwrecked on the coast of Île aux Basques in the early 17C. One of the sailors holding a silver mug lost it in the river and exclaimed: *"Voilà trois pistoles de perdues!"* (There go three pistoles.) The seigneury was granted to Denis de Vitré in 1687, but the region was frequented much earlier by Basque fishermen whose presence is confirmed by the remains of ovens on the **Île aux Basques**, located 4km/2.5mi offshore.

Église Notre-Dame-des-Neiges (Church of Our Lady of the Snow) – *From the centre of town, turn right on Rue Jean-Rioux. Open May–mid-Oct Mon–Sat 9am–4pm, Sun 11am–4pm (except during services).* 🅿 ☎ *418-851-1391.* This monumental edifice was constructed in the 1880s according to plans drawn up by David Ouellet. The church's exterior is distinguished by its bell towers and by the angular lines of its four facades. The ornate interior is the work of Canon Georges Bouillon, a proponent of the Romano-Byzantine style. Note the abundance of gilding, and the wooden Corinthian columns painted to resemble marble.

After 29km/18mi turn right towards Saint-Fabien and continue for 2km/1.2mi.

Saint-Fabien – Built in 1888, the octagonal **Adolphe Gagnon barn** *(not open to the public)*, located at the centre of the village, is the only one of its kind in the Bas-Saint-Laurent region. Blending into the landscape, the almost-round construction conceived by American theorist Orson Squire Fowler was designed to offer greater wind resistance, eliminate wasted space and facilitate storage of fodder. According to popular belief, the octagonal form made it impossible for demons to take refuge in the corners of the structure.

★**Parc du Bic (Bic Park)** – *Principal entrance at Cap-à-l'orignal, 6km/4mi from centre of Saint-Fabien. Open daily year-round.* ✕ & ▯ *www.sepaq.com* ☎ *418-736-5035.* This 33sq km/13sq mi provincial conservation park was created in 1984 to preserve the plants and wildlife along the southern shoreline of the St. Lawrence River. The jagged, rocky cliffs, consisting primarily of slate and limestone conglomerates, extend in a northeastern direction. These formations, as well as tiny islands, reefs and marshes, punctuate the magnificent views of the majestic St. Lawrence. The park boasts a variety of flora including both deciduous and boreal forests. An abundance of birds including eiders, cormorants, seagulls and herons can be observed. Grey and harbour seals, using the rocky coast in Orignal Bay as a resting ground, are occasionally spotted by fortunate visitors.

Activities – *Hiking, cycling (bicycle rentals available), sea kayaking, picnicking and camping (☎ 418-736-4711). Various nature programs are organised during the summer months at the Interpretation Centre (open Jun–mid-Oct daily 9am–5pm; ☎ 418-869-3502).*

Southern Shoreline of the St. Lawrence River from the Parc du Bic

Michel Gagné/REFLEXION

Bic – *15km/9mi from Saint-Fabien.* This small town is renowned for its spectacular **setting**★★ on the shores of the St. Lawrence. According to local legend, when the world was created, the angel responsible for distributing mountains happened to have a surplus at the end of the day while passing over Bic. To lighten his load, he emptied the remaining mountains on this spot.

★**Rimouski** – *16km/10mi. See Entry Heading.*
After 14km/9mi, at the junction with Rte. 298, turn left towards Sainte-Luce and continue for 4km/2.5mi.

Sainte-Luce – Cottages line the shore in this pleasant summer resort town, which occupies a picturesque site on the St. Lawrence.

BEAUCE★

Chaudière-Appalaches–Cantons de l'Est
Map p 66

The name Beauce refers to the area drained by the Chaudière River as it flows from Lake Mégantic, just north of the American border, into the St. Lawrence River. Like its French namesake, a region to the southwest of Paris that is sometimes referred to as the "granary of France," the Beauce is a vast, flat area of fertile farmlands. The region becomes more mountainous farther south.

Throughout this region, visitors will see the greatest concentration of maple groves in Quebec. A popular tradition rich in folklore and special events has developed around the theme of the maple tree and is reflected in regional folk art. During the sugaring-off season in spring, people gather in sugar shacks to sample maple taffy *(tire d'érable)* and take part in the festivities known as sugaring-off parties *(parties de sucre).*

BEAUCE

Cascading over numerous falls interspersed with more tranquil areas, the Chaudière River is navigable in only a few places, and its frequent floods often make newspaper headlines. Despite the construction of a dam at Saint-Georges-de-Beauce, the Chaudière still inundates the villages along its banks.

The region's inhabitants *(Beaucerons)* are known for their sense of tradition and entrepreneurial spirit.

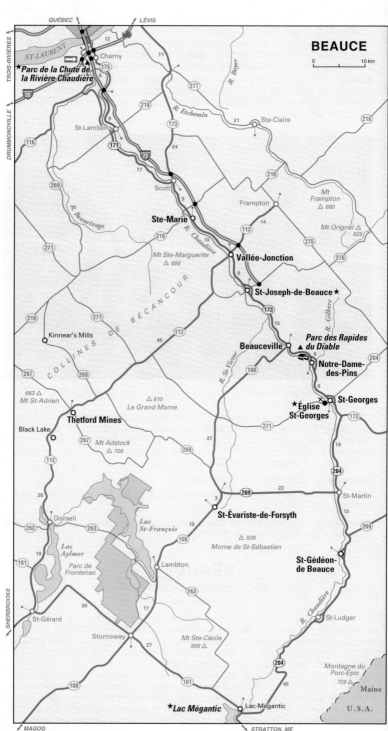

Historical Notes

President Kennedy Road (Route du Président Kennedy) – In 1775, twelve years after New France was ceded to England in the Treaty of Paris, an American expeditionary force of 1,100 men led by Colonel Benedict Arnold travelled along the Kennebec River to the state of Maine, and from there marched northward along the Chaudière River in an attempt to capture Quebec City. The thirteen American colonies engaged in the fight against British rule hoped to persuade the Canadians to join their cause. A great many soldiers died during the arduous northern trek; the survivors were defeated by troops under the command of Guy Carleton.

Every year, some 600,000 Americans en route to Quebec follow this road (Route 173), now named the President Kennedy Road.

The Gold Rush of 1846 – In the 19C, the Beauce region was the El Dorado of Canada. In 1846, a gold nugget the size of a pigeon's egg was discovered on a tributary of the Chaudière, and prospectors poured in to sift the sands of the stream between Notre-Dame-des-Pins and Saint-Simon-les-Mines. By the beginning of the 20C, $1 million worth of gold ore had been extracted. Vestiges of the mining heyday are still visible today.

© Malak, Ottawa

Children sampling Maple Syrup

FROM QUEBEC CITY TO LAC-MÉGANTIC *221km/137mi.*

Leave Quebec City by Rte. 73 Sud and cross the Pierre-Laporte Bridge continuing south; 1km/.6mi after the bridge, turn off at Exit 130. Follow the signs to Parc de la Chute de la Rivière Chaudière.

★**Chaudière River Falls Park** (Parc de la chute de la rivière Chaudière) – *In Charny. Open daily year-round.* 🅿 *Chaudière-Appalaches regional tourist association www.chau-dapp.qc.ca* ☎ *418-831-4411.* Just before it joins the St. Lawrence, the Chaudière River drops over a cliff in spectacular falls, 35m/115ft high and 121m/397ft wide. The Abenaki Indians named these falls *asticou,* meaning "boiler," because of the kettle-shaped basin at the foot of the cascades. The name *chaudière,* the French word for "boiler," was subsequently given to the entire river.

Steps descend to a suspension bridge hung across the river. From here, visitors can enjoy exceptional views of the falls, magnificent during the spring run-off.

Return to Rte. 73 and at Exit 123 take Rte. 175 Sud. At Saint-Lambert, cross the Chaudière River and take Rte. 171 Sud. At Scott (34km/21mi), the road crosses the river again and becomes Rte. 173 Sud.

Sainte-Marie – *9km/6mi from Scott.* One of the oldest communities in the region, Sainte-Marie was part of the seigneury given to **Thomas-Jacques Taschereau** in 1736. Taschereau was a member of an influential family which included Elzéar-Alexandre

Taschereau (1820-1898), the first Canadian to be made a cardinal in the Roman Catholic Church, and Louis-Alexandre Taschereau (1867-1952), premier of Quebec from 1920 to 1936. Sainte-Marie was also the birthplace of **Marius Barbeau** (1883-1969), writer, ethnomusicologist and founder of the Quebec folklore archives at Laval University, in Quebec City.

Today, Sainte-Marie's economy thrives on the baked goods industry. In 1923, Arcade Vachon and his wife, Rose-Anne Giroux, purchased a bakery in Sainte-Marie and began making snack cakes that are now sold throughout the province.

St. Mary's Church (Église Sainte-Marie) – *Open year-round Mon–Sat 8am–7:30pm, Sun 8am–noon.* & ▯ ☏ *418-387-5467.* The church (1856, Charles Baillairgé) is one of the first Gothic Revival structures built for the Catholic Church in Quebec. The exterior is English in inspiration while the interior is modelled after the work of Viollet-le-Duc. Of a rare harmony in its overall effect, the interior can be compared to the interior of Montreal's Notre Dame Basilica, designed by Victor Bourgeau.

After 10km/6mi, the road passes through **Vallée-Jonction**. Located at a railway junction, this small community overlooks the Chaudière River. Route 112 to Thetford Mines crosses the river at this point.

Turn off Rte. 173 and enter Saint-Joseph-de-Beauce.

★ **Saint-Joseph-de-Beauce** – *9km/6mi from Vallée-Jonction.* Set in the valley of the Chaudière River, this former seigneury was conceded to Joseph Fleury de la Gorgendière, a wealthy Quebec merchant, in 1737. The town was named in his honour. Saint-Joseph was also the home of Robert Cliche (1921-1978), a judge, politician and writer.

Downtown – *Intersection of Rue Sainte-Christine and Ave. du Palais.* Designed by F.X. Berlinguet, **St. Joseph's Church** (Église Saint-Joseph) features a narrow facade surmounted by a tall steeple. Its interior was completed in 1876 by J. F. Peachy. Facing the church, a large brick **presbytery** (1892, G.-É. Tanguay) evokes the design of small 16C French chateaux. The former **convent** (1889, J. F. Peachy) and **orphanage** (1908) are in the Second Empire style. Behind the church stands the **Lambert School** (1911, Lorenzo Auger), a functional edifice enlarged in 1947 and again in 1995. The institutional ensemble is completed by the **courthouse-prison**, a neoclassical structure erected between 1857 and 1862. To the rear, a Postmodern addition blends harmoniously with the original structure.

Continue on Ave. du Palais which rejoins Rte. 173 south of the town centre.

Beauceville – *15km/9mi.* Built on the steep slopes of the Chaudière River valley, this community was the birthplace of the poet **William Chapman** (1850-1917), emulator and rival of Louis Fréchette.

Across the river, stands the **Church of St. Francis of Assisi** (Église Saint-François d'Assise; *open during services only;* ☏ *418-525-8158*). Of note in its interior are the main altar and angel statues.

Devil's Rapids Park (Parc des Rapides du Diable) – *3km/2mi south of town.* The park is strewn with paths leading to the Chaudière River and the "devil's rapids" that tumble over the rocky riverbed. The foundations of a mill used to extract gold from quartz rock during the gold rush are still visible.

Turn off Rte. 173 and head toward Notre-Dame-des-Pins.

Notre-Dame-des-Pins – *8km/5mi from Beauceville.* In the mid-19C, gold prospectors gathered here before embarking on their journey along the Gilbert River to Saint-Simon-les-Mines.

Covered bridge – *Turn right on 1re Ave., just before the modern bridge (illustration below).* The 154.5m/507ft covered bridge across the Chaudière River is the longest in the province. First built in 1927, it was carried away by ice during the winter of 1928. Rebuilt in 1929 with three central piers, the bridge remained in use until 1969 when it was closed to vehicular traffic *(picnic area near bridge).*

Continue south; turn off Rte. 173 at Saint-Georges exit.

Saint-Georges – *9km/6mi.* The industrial capital of the Beauce region was originally named Sartigan, meaning "changing river," by the indigenous Abenaki villagers. In 1807, a German settler by the name of **Pozer** bought the land and gave the town its present name. Saint-Georges experienced some growth after the American invasion of 1775, but its greatest economic expansion followed the opening of the Kennebec Route to New England in 1830. In 1967, the Sartigan dam was erected to control the capricious flow of the Chaudière River.

★ **St. George's Church** (Église Saint-Georges) – *On 1re Ave. in Saint-Georges-Ouest, across the river. Open year-round Mon–Sat 8:30am–11:30am & 1pm–4pm. Closed major holidays.* & ▯ ☏ *418-228-2558.* This beautiful church (1902, David Ouellet), with its monumental cut stone facade, dominates the west bank of the Chaudière. Three spires, one 75m/246ft tall, rise above the edifice. The present church replaces a previous stone building (1862) and an earlier wood structure (1831). Before the entrance stands a copy of Louis Jobin's masterpiece, *St. George*

Covered Bridge, Notre-Dame-des-Pins

Slaying the Dragon. The original (1912), an enormous wooden sculpture, sheathed in bronze and gilded, is displayed nearby at the Centre Culturel Marie-Fitzbach on the third floor.

The ornate **interior** of this three-storey church features tiered balconies embellished with painted and gilded woodwork. The altar is surmounted by a broad canopy with St. George at its summit. The organ (1910) came from the renowned house of Casavant, in Saint-Hyacinthe.

Saint-Évariste-de-Forsyth – *44km/27mi by Rtes. 173, 204, 269 and 108.* Perched on a hill, this community affords lovely views of the surrounding countryside.

★**Museum of the Upper Beauce** (Musée de la Haute-Beauce) – *Museum & church open Jun 24–Labour Day daily 8:30am–6pm. Rest of the year Mon–Fri 10am–5pm. $5.* ♿ 🅿 ☎ *418-459-3195.* Next to the church, in Saint-Évariste-de-Forsyth, stands an old presbytery that now houses this Saint-Évariste regional centre and museum. Housed within is the Napoléon Bolduc collection of traditional objects and artifacts; changing exhibits on local themes are also mounted here.

The museum serves as the starting point for the visit of six interpretative sites located throughout the area *(site map available at the presbytery)*. The centres provide the visitor with additional insight into the traditional lifestyle of the Upper Beauce. Among these, the House of Granite, located in an abandoned quarry, offers detailed information on granite quarrying. Wool is carded on site at the Groleau mill, whose original bucket wheel still functions. The museum also sponsors activities throughout thirteen neighbouring villages, with a view to promoting local participation.

Return to Rte. 204.

Saint-Gédéon-de-Beauce – *38km/24mi.* The countryside opens onto Lake Mégantic – source of the Chaudière River – and the surrounding mountains.

★**Lac Mégantic** – *45km/28mi. See Entry Heading.*

BEAUHARNOIS
Montérégie
Population 6,435

This industrial community, founded in 1819, was named for the **Marquis de Beauharnois** (1671-1749), 15th governor of New France, who was granted a seigneury in this area. Today, the town is the site of a major power plant and a canal that diverts ships on the St. Lawrence Seaway around the rapids connecting Lakes Saint-François and Saint-Louis. Construction of the power plant by the Beauharnois Light, Heat and Power Company began in 1929, but was not completed until 1948. In 1953 and 1961, the canal was widened and the power station enlarged, making the Beauharnois power plant the largest hydroelectric plant in Canada at the time.

The present **Beauharnois Canal** was completed in 1932. Water is diverted from the original channel of the St. Lawrence into the canal by a system of dams and control works near Coteau-du-Lac. It is nearly 25km/16mi long by 1km/.6mi wide and 9m/29ft deep, and has two locks.

Access – *Beauharnois is situated some 40km/25mi from Montreal by the Mercier Bridge and Rte. 132.*

69

SIGHTS

★★ Centrale de Beauharnois (Beauharnois Power Plant) — This enormous power plant is among the most productive in Quebec, with a generating capacity of 1,645,810 kilowatts. With a total length of 864m/2,834ft, it is also one of the longest in the world. Its run-of-the-river dam uses neither reservoir nor falls to control or speed the water flow. Instead, the station harnesses the powerful flow of the St. Lawrence River, notably the 24m/79ft drop between Lakes Saint-François and Saint-Louis. Water passes through the canal at a rate of 3km/2mi per hour or 8 million litres/2.1 million gallons per second. During the long winter, Quebec consumes all the power generated; for the remainder of the year, excess capacity is transmitted to Ontario and the US by 735,000-volt power lines.

Visit — *Visit by guided tour (1hr 30min) only, Fête de Dollard–Jun 24 Mon–Fri 9:30am–5pm. Late Jun–Labour Day Wed–Sun 9:30am–5pm.* & 🅿 ☏ *450-289-2211 (ext 3080).* In the interpretation centre, a permanent exhibit offers an excellent introduction to the guided tour of the power plant. On the tour, visitors will see the enormous **alternator hall** (864m/2,833ft long), where electric vehicles or tricycles are used by staff to check the turbines. Each of the 36 turbines weighs over 100 tons, is 4m/13ft high and 6m/20ft in diameter; their installed capacity, or optimal output, is 1,645,810 kilowatts. The tour also includes a visit to the **control room**, where computers monitor operations and regulate output. The rooftop of the plant affords a spectacular view of the intricate network of power lines extending in all directions. Montreal and the St. Lawrence are visible in the distance.

Beauharnois Locks — *2km/1.2mi west of the power plant by Rte. 132 Ouest. Parking area next to the lock.* From this vantage point near the power plant, visitors can view the lower of the two Beauharnois locks. It enables vessels to bypass the power plant by raising them 12.5m/41ft. The upper lock, located 3.2km/2mi upstream, provides an additional 12.5m/41ft lift to the level of the Beauharnois Canal. The lock system is best viewed from the parking area.

★ Parc archéologique de la Pointe-du-Buisson (Pointe-du-Buisson Archaeological Park) — *Melocheville. 5km/3mi west of lock by Rte. 132. Open mid-May–Labour Day Mon–Fri 10am–5pm, weekends 10am–6pm. Labour Day–mid-Oct weekends noon–5pm. $4.* & 🅿 ☏ *450-429-7857.* This pleasant, wooded peninsula protruding into the St. Lawrence is popular with fishing enthusiasts in search of sturgeon, brill and eels in the rapids. Remains of human life dating back to 5000 BC have been found here, making this peninsula an important archaeological site.

The park offers various educational activities, as well as guided tours. In the summer season, visitors can watch archaeologists from the University of Montreal in action as an accompanying film *(15min)* explains their work. Two **interpretation centres** display the recovered artifacts and recreate the different phases of human activity at Pointe-du-Buisson.

Several paths lead through the park, providing good views of the rapids. Note the **Potsdam sandstone**, the oldest sedimentary rock in the Montreal area, exposed here by river erosion.

EXCURSION

★ Lieu historique national de la Bataille-de-la-Châteauguay (Battle of the Châteauguay National Historic Site) — *On Rte. 138 between Howick and Ormstown, 24km/15mi southwest of Beauharnois.* The valley of the Châteauguay River, situated southwest of Montreal, is a peaceful land of farms and small rural communities. However, for a short time during the War of 1812, it became the setting of an important battle that marked the turning point in the American invasion of Canada. On October 26, 1813, a Canadian force of about 300 men under the command of Lieutenant-Colonel **Charles-Michel de Salaberry** (1778-1829), met an American army of 2,000 soldiers led by Major-General Wade Hampton. Salaberry managed to outwit the larger force by playing on the Americans' lack of familiarity with the territory, and succeeded in repelling the attack.

Visit — *Open mid-May–Oct 2 Wed–Sun 10am–5pm. $3* & 🅿 ☏ *450-829-2003.* An interpretation centre stands beside the Châteauguay River, adjacent to the battle site. A film *(30min)* outlines the conflict of 1812 and dramatizes the event from Salaberry's point of view. In the belvedere overlooking the site of the battlefield, a model shows the positions of the American and Canadian forces as they manœuvred along the river. Exhibits illustrate the hardships of army life in the early 19C.

Sights described in this guide are rated:

★★★	Worth the trip
★★	Worth a detour
★	Interesting

Côte de BEAUPRÉ★★

Région de Québec

Map p 71

The Beaupré Coast is a narrow stretch of land nestled between the Canadian Shield and the St. Lawrence River, east of Quebec City. It extends from the Montmorency Falls to the massif of Cape Tourmente (660m/2,165ft). The name of the region is attributed to an exclamation made by Jacques Cartier who, noting the meadowland alongside the river, said *"Quel beau pré!"* (What a fine meadow!). The Beaupré Coast, dotted with numerous villages established during the French Regime, is renowned for the popular shrine at Sainte-Anne-de-Beaupré and the resort area of Mt. Sainte-Anne.

Historical Notes

The seigneury of Beaupré was among the largest in New France, stretching from the Montmorency River to Baie-Saint-Paul. Champlain established his first farm here in 1626; it was destroyed by the notorious adventurers, the Kirke Brothers, in 1629. Settlers began working this fertile land in the 1630s and founded the first rural parishes in New France. Beaupré's seigneur from 1668 to 1680 was François de Laval, the first Bishop of Quebec City. Msgr. de Laval was responsible for planning the King's Highway (Chemin du Roy), which ran from Quebec City to Saint-Joachim and is known today as the Avenue Royale. After Msgr. de Laval's death, the seigneury remained in the hands of the Quebec Seminary until the end of the seigneurial regime in 1854.

Access – *The Beaupré Coast is accessible from Quebec City by Rte. 440, which becomes Rte. 40 and then Rte. 138. If time allows, visitors are advised to take the much more interesting Rte. 360 (Ave. Royale) from Beauport.*

FROM QUEBEC CITY TO CAP-TOURMENTE

48km/30mi.

From Quebec City, take Rte. 440 east to Exit 24, then Ave. d'Estimauville to Rte. 360 (also called Ave. Royale as far as Beaupré); turn right and continue 3km/2mi.

Beauport – This community, the oldest settlement on the Beaupré Coast, is now a suburb of Quebec City. The first settlers arrived in 1634 and named the village after a medieval abbey on the north coast of Brittany.

★**Bourg du Fargy** – In the heart of Beauport stands an impressive group of buildings known as the Bourg du Fargy. The **Maison Bellanger-Girardin** *(600 Ave. Royale)* is typical of the residential architecture found throughout the Beaupré Coast. Its elongated form is the result of two distinct construction stages (1722 and 1735); its steep roof is characteristic of the heavy beam framework popular in the late 17C. Restored in 1983, the house is now used to display the work of local artists. Also situated in this neighbourhood are a number of attractive Victorian houses.

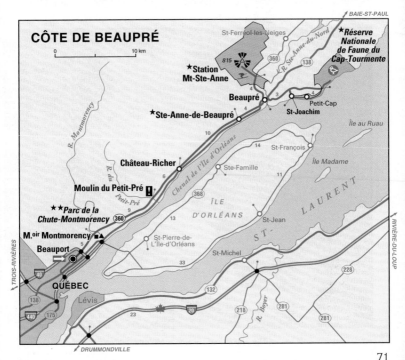

Note the **Beauport Convent** (1866, F.-X. Berlinguet) with its mansard roof topped by a large statue of the Virgin Mary. The **Église Notre-Dame-de-la-Nativité** (Church of Our Lady of the Nativity), originally designed by Charles Baillairgé, was built in 1849. Twice destroyed by fire, the church was subsequently rebuilt within the same walls. Only its two towering spires were not replaced after the fire of 1916. The stone **presbytery** (1903) stands nearby.

The road continues along an escarpment overlooking the Île d'Orleans.

★★ Parc de la Chute-Montmorency (Montmorency Falls Park) – 5km/3mi. Open year-round daily 8:15am–9pm. &. 🅿 ($7/car) www.chutemontmorency.qc.ca ☎ 418-663-3330.

Before emptying into the St. Lawrence, the Montmorency River cascades over a cliff in spectacular falls 83m/272ft high (30m/98ft higher than Niagara Falls). Named by Samuel de Champlain for Charles, Duc de Montmorency, who was Viceroy of New France from 1620 to 1625, the falls have long been a major attraction. In the winter months, the spray creates a great cone of ice known as a sugarloaf, which sometimes exceeds 30m/98ft in height. Before the last ice age, the Montmorency Falls emptied directly into the St. Lawrence River. They are now about 450m/1,476ft away from the river and mark the edge of the Canadian Shield.

With its enormous energy potential and its excellent site near the St. Lawrence, the site proved the ideal location for a powerful commercial empire that grew up here during the 19C. In 1811, a sawmill was established at the foot of the falls, an enterprise that by mid-century had become the most important of its kind in British North America. Under the direction of Peter Patterson and subsequently his son-in-law George Benson Hall, the company grew and diversified, but did not survive an economic crisis that eventually crippled the demand for lumber. In 1884, a power plant was established here, the first in the world to transmit hydroelectric power over long distances (11.7km/7mi). A second power plant began service in 1895, and in 1905, a cotton mill was built at the foot of the cliff. Only a few traces remain today of these nearly two centuries of intense industrial activity.

Manoir de Montmorency (Montmorency Manor) – This elegant house with terraces overlooking the Montmorency Falls has changed hands several times and undergone numerous modifications over the years. It was built in 1780 as a vacation home for Frederick Haldimand, Governor-General of British North America. From 1791 to 1794, it was inhabited by Edward, Duke of Kent, and his morganatic wife. Peter Patterson and his descendants made their home here. At the turn of the century it was renovated as a popular luxury hotel known as "Kent House." Destroyed by fire in May 1993, the structure was rebuilt along its original architectural lines. Today Montmorency Manor houses a restaurant and reception rooms in addition to a **visitor centre★** (open May–Oct daily 9am-11pm; rest of the year Thu–Sat 9am–11pm, Sun–Wed 9am–4pm; ✗ &. 🅿 ☎ 418-663-3330) presenting the area's historic, economic and human heritage.

Upper Lookout – From the Montmorency Manor, a footpath traces the flank of the cliff leading to the bridge above the falls. From here, a spectacular **view★★** embraces the furious waters tumbling over the cliff. The silhouette of the Île d'Orléans is

The "Sugarloaf" at Chute Montmorency

visible in the distance. The footpath continues on the other side to a smaller bridge over a side crevice; from here, you can see the sites of the power plant and the former cotton mill, with the towers of Quebec City and the Château Frontenac looming in the distance. Farther along, note the traces of a redoubt built here in 1759 by the British General Wolfe during his siege of Quebec. Helped by their Amerindian allies, the French militia overtook this redoubt using combat techniques developed by the indigenous population.

Lower Lookout – A panoramic stairway dotted with numerous lookout points leads to the bottom of the falls, allowing superb, closeup **views** of the powerful waters *(rain gear is advised to protect from the spray)*. Over time, the falls have carved out a large cauldron at their base, creating an immense, powerful whirlpool. The force of these turbulent waters (an average 35,000 litres/9,248gal per second) was harnessed in 1885 to activate sawmills and provide electricity for Quebec City. An **aerial tram** returns visitors to the upper level *(late Apr–mid-Jun daily 8:30am–7pm; mid-Jun–early Aug daily 8:30am–11pm; early Aug–early Sept daily 8:30am–9pm; early Sept–late Oct 8:30am–7pm; rest of the year hours vary; round-trip $7)*.

Return to Rte. 360.

Observe the high-tension power lines strung on large pylons, which carry electricity from the Manic-5 power station to Montreal, across the St. Lawrence. Past this point, the road takes on a more rural character.

Moulin du Petit-Pré (Petit-Pré Mill) – *9km/6mi from Montmorency Manor.* This large three-storey stone mill located just beyond the Petit-Pré River was built in 1695 by the Quebec Seminary to supplement its income and to supply the needs of Quebec City merchants; it was therefore the first "industrial" mill in New France. The mill was destroyed during the Conquest and rebuilt in 1764. It remained in operation until 1955. The **Beaupré Coast Interpretation Centre** *(open Jun–Oct daily 10am–6pm; Nov & Mar–May Mon–Fri 9am–4pm; $2;* ⚕ ▣ ☏ *418-824-3677)*, housed in the mill loft, provides information on the geology, history and socio-economic development of the region. Displays include photographs, documents, sketches, games and videos.

Château-Richer – *6km/4mi.* First settled in 1640, this community was named after a priory in France. The Église La-Visitation-de-Notre-Dame (Church of the Visitation of Our Lady, 1866) dominates the village from high on the cliff above the river. From the church, **views** of the coast reach as far as Cap-Tourmente. A quarry carved out of the cliff is visible to the north of the town. In the 18C and 19C, limestone from Château-Richer was often used in the construction of buildings in Quebec City. Regular in form and light grey in colour, the stone from this quarry replaced the darker limestone of Beauport by the early 19C.

On Avenue Royale, large bread ovens stand next to some of the older homes; they were often built separately from the houses because of the danger of fire. One is still in use, and visitors can purchase freshly baked bread.

Route 360 gradually descends to river level as it approaches Sainte-Anne.

★**Sainte-Anne-de-Beaupré** – *10km/6mi. See Entry Heading.*

Beaupré – *4km/2.5mi.* Located on the Sainte-Anne-du-Nord River, just before it joins the St. Lawrence, Beaupré was part of the town of Sainte-Anne-de-Beaupré until 1927. Now it is a separate community, dominated by its pulp mill.

★**Station Mont-Sainte-Anne** – *4km/2.5mi. See Entry Heading.*

Return to Beaupré (4km/2.5mi) and take Ave. Royale to Saint-Joachim. Turn right onto Rue de l'Église.

Saint-Joachim – *3km/2mi from Beaupré. See Entry Heading.*

★**Réserve nationale de faune du Cap-Tourmente (Cape Tourmente National Wildlife Reserve)** – *4km/2.5mi. Open mid-Apr–mid-Nov daily 8:30am–5pm. Late-Dec–mid-Mar daily 8:30am–4pm. $5.* ✗ ⚕ ▣ ☏ *418-827-4591.* Cape Tourmente (roughly translated as "windswept") was named for the winds that sweep through the valley at this point. The wildlife reserve was created here in 1969 as a haven for more than 290 species of birds. In April, May and October of every year, thousands of snow geese invade this massif overlooking the St. Lawrence during their spring and winter migrations, and each year, thousands of visitors gather here to witness their flight. The huge birds are a magnificent sight as they rise from the river or descend on the neighbouring mudflats in a white flurry of beating wings and raucous cries. The bulrushes that proliferate on the marshy edges of the St. Lawrence provide the sustenance required for the thousands of kilometres the geese must travel between their winter home on the coast of Virginia and their summer nesting grounds north of the arctic circle, on Baffin Island.

The snow geese are a protected species that can only be hunted by special permit. Displays and films can be seen in the **Interpretation Centre** situated 1.5km/1mi from the entrance *(open late Apr–late Oct daily 9am–4:45pm)*.

At the entrance to the reserve stands **La Petite-Ferme** *(little farm)*, built on the spot where Samuel de Champlain established, in 1626, the first farm of New France.

BOUCHERVILLE

Montérégie

Population 34,989 – Map p 175

Situated on the shores of the St. Lawrence opposite Montreal, Boucherville is one of Quebec's oldest communities. In 1667, the seigneury was granted to **Pierre Boucher**, governor of Trois-Rivières. The first settlers arrived the following year, and for almost three centuries, Boucherville developed as an agricultural community. In 1843, a fire originating from the chimney of a steamboat ravaged Boucherville, destroying many of its original buildings. The construction of the Louis-Hippolyte Lafontaine Tunnel under the St. Lawrence in 1965 transformed the city into an industrial and residential suburb of Montreal.

Boucherville is the birthplace of Louis-Hippolyte Lafontaine (1807-1864), prime minister of the United Canadas from 1842 to 1843 and from 1848 to 1851.

Access – *Boucherville lies approximately 20km/12mi from Montreal by Rte. 20 Est and Rte. 132.*

SIGHTS

Boulevard Marie-Victorin, the city's main thoroughfare, is lined with beautiful 19C houses, several of which belonged to descendants of the city's founder. Note the mid-18C manor house at no. 470, built for François-Pierre Boucher de Boucherville, and the 19C brick structure at no. 486, built for Charles-Eugène Boucher de Boucherville, premier of Quebec from 1874 to 1878 and from 1891 to 1892.

Maison Louis-Hippolyte-Lafontaine (Louis-Hippolyte Lafontaine House) – *314 Blvd. Marie-Victorin, near tunnel. Open year-round Thu–Fri 7pm–9pm, weekends 1pm–5pm.* ▯ ☎ *450-449-8347.* Located in a park near the St. Lawrence, this dwelling belonged to the father-in-law of Louis-Hippolyte Lafontaine. Constructed in 1766 and rebuilt after the fire of 1843, the house was moved from Boucherville's historic centre to its present site in 1964. It is now an art gallery featuring temporary exhibits.

Lafontaine lived here from 1813 to 1822, before undertaking his law studies in Montreal. A small display presents the highlights of his career. Lafontaine is generally considered to be the main proponent of "responsible government," a term used to designate a government empowered by a locally elected assembly rather than the British Crown.

In the park, visitors can see a statue of Lafontaine sculpted by Henri Hébert and view the remains of La Broquerie, formerly the Château Sabrevois, built in 1735 and destroyed by fire in 1970.

★ Église de la Sainte-Famille (Church of Sainte Famille) – *560 Blvd. Marie-Victorin. Open year-round Mon–Sat 9am–5pm, Sun 8am–noon.* ⚐ ▯ *www.total.net/~saintefa* ☎ *450-655-9024.* This church (1801) rises above a small square also occupied by a cultural centre and a nursing home. It was designed by the parish priest, Father Pierre Conefroy, who also supervised the construction. His efficient and cost-effective management of the project became codified as the "Conefroy plan specifications" *(plan-devis Conefroy),* which were thereafter adopted as a blueprint for the construction of churches throughout the province. Father Conefroy adopted the Latin cross floor plan to provide much-needed space for rural parish churches, which had experienced a veritable population explosion in the late 18C. In recognition of his successful endeavour, Father Conefroy was named vicar-general of the diocese and supervised all church construction in Quebec.

Interior – The original interior decor, commissioned from the studio of Louis-Amable Quévillon, was destroyed in the fire of 1843. Renovated by Louis-Thomas Berlinguet, the architectural treatment is typical of the style of Thomas Baillairgé. The Louis XV panelling exemplifies Berlinguet's attention to detail and ornamentation. The main altar and side altars, designed by Quévillon, survived the fire of 1843. The massive Baroque **tabernacle**, a major work dating from the French Regime, is attributed to Gilles Boivin and is believed to date from the year 1745. Across the street, a monument to Pierre Boucher commands a view of the Boucherville islands and East Montreal. The neighbouring streets, especially Rue de la Perrière and Rue Saint-Charles, are lined with 19C houses.

Parc des Îles-de-Boucherville (Îles-de-Boucherville Park) – *Hwy 25 (exit 1). Open year-round daily 8am–dusk. Golf, bicycle & boat rentals.* ⚑ ⚐ ▯ *www.sepaq.com* ☎ *450-928-5088.* Located on the St. Lawrence, close to Boucherville, this archipelago, formerly called Îles Percées, meaning "pierced islands," was part of Pierre Boucher's seigneury. The islands seem little changed today, although one of them, Île Grosbois, was the site of an amusement park at the turn of the century. Today, five of them form a provincial park created by the Quebec government in 1984. From the park information office on Île Sainte-Marguerite, a passenger ferry and footbridges provide access to the other islands. Bike paths *(20km/12mi),* hiking trails *(20km/12mi)* and canoe circuits lace the islands, affording pleasant **views** of Montreal across the river.

CAP-DE-LA-MADELEINE

Mauricie
Population 33,438 – Map p 288

Cap-de-la-Madeleine is situated on the north shore of the St. Lawrence at the mouth of the St. Maurice River, opposite the city of Trois-Rivières. Founded in 1635 by the Jesuit Father, Jacques Buteux, who was later murdered by the Iroquois, Cap-de-la-Madeleine is today a renowned pilgrimage site.

Historical Notes

The Miracles – In the mid-17C, a wooden chapel to Mary Magdalen was erected on this site by European settlers. A stone church did not appear until 1717, when a community was established here. **Father Luc Désilets**, who arrived in the mid-19C, renewed the ministry and by 1878, a larger church was required to accommodate the growing congregation. Father Désilets planned to bring stones for the new church across the St. Lawrence over an ice bridge. But unusually mild weather left the river free of ice, prompting Father Désilets to vow to preserve the existing 18C church in exchange for a miracle that would allow the stone to be transported across the river. On March 16, 1879, the temperature dropped and ice appeared on the river, remaining just long enough for the parishioners to bring the stones across. After the last load had arrived, the now-famous "Bridge of Rosaries" (pont des Chapelets) promptly broke up.

Regarding the ice bridge as a miracle from Our Lady of the Rosary, Father Désilets kept his vow and preserved the old church, adorning the interior with a statue of the Virgin donated by a parishioner. On the night of the consecration in June of 1888, the priest, along with Father Frédéric Jansoone and Pierre LaCroix, an afflicted pilgrim, witnessed a second miracle when the eyes of the statue of the Virgin appeared to open in their presence.

Pilgrimage Centre – Although organised public pilgrimages to the church had begun as early as 1883, news of the second miracle brought worshippers flocking to Cap-de-la-Madeleine. Specially constructed steamship quays and railroad lines facilitated access to the shrine, and in the 1950s, a new basilica was built to receive growing numbers of pilgrims. Today, thousands of people make the pilgrimage annually. The Oblate Fathers have administered the shrine since 1902.

Access – *Cap-de-la-Madeleine is located 150km/93mi northeast of Montreal by Rtes. 40 and 755 (Exit 10).*

Sanctuaire Notre-Dame-du-Cap

Detail of Window 1, Sanctuaire Notre-Dame-du-Rosaire

★★SANCTUAIRE NOTRE-DAME-DU-CAP

On Rue Notre-Dame, east of town; follow signs.

Basilique Notre-Dame-du-Rosaire (Our Lady of the Rosary Basilica) – *Open May–mid Oct daily 8am–9pm (mid-Aug 10pm). Rest of the year 8am–5pm.* ♿ 🅿 📧 *819-374-2441.* This lovely octagonal basilica was designed by Adrien Dufresne, a student of Dom Paul Bellot (1876-1944), a Benedictine monk. Construction began in 1955, and the basilica was inaugurated in 1964. The conical central tower surmounting the structure is 78m/256ft tall, and a 7m/23ft stone statue of the Madonna adorns the facade. The weighty exterior hides an interior appointed in blue and gold, the colours of the Virgin. The basilica can accommodate 1,800 people, all of whom can enjoy an unobstructed view of the main altar. The magnificent Casavant organ, built in Saint-Hyacinthe in 1963-1965, has 75 stops and more than 5,500 pipes. The altar is of Italian marble.

Stained-Glass Windows – *Begin to the left of the main entrance.* The basilica's interior is renowned for its remarkable stained-glass windows. **Jan Tillemans** (1915-1980), a Dutch Oblate father, fashioned the windows in the medieval tradition between 1956 and 1964. Each bay contains five lancets and a rose window nearly 8m/26ft in diameter. The first rose window, to the left of the main entrance, depicts the shields of the Canadian provinces, while the lancets represent the patron saints of Canada. The second window, in delicate hues of white and green, portrays Christ triumphant on the cross in the centre and scenes from his life in the lancet panels. The third window, depicting the Mysteries of the Rosary, is coloured primarily in blues and reds. The window to the right of the altar presents the prophets and evangelists in bright greens and blues, and the fifth window provides a multi-coloured glance at some of Canada's pioneers. The sixth and loveliest window tells the story of Our Lady of the Cape.

The Small Shrine and Park – *Same hours as Basilica.* Beside the basilica stands the original stone church (1715-1720), now a votive chapel. Along with the church of St. Peter's (Île d'Orléans), this chapel shares the distinction of being among the oldest shrines in Quebec. The miraculous statue stands above the altar of painted and gilt wood. In 1973, a modern annex was added to the church, incorporating some of the stones transported across the ice bridge in 1879. The small shrine is set in a park overlooking the river. The Stations of the Cross wind their way through the southern half of the park, ending before replicas of the Crucifixion and the tomb of Jesus in Jerusalem. In another section, the Mysteries of the Rosary are embodied in fifteen bronze sculptures produced in France (1906-1910). A small lake and the Bridge of Rosaries *(pont des Chapelets)* commemorate the ice bridge of 1879.

CARILLON

Laurentides
Population 258

Located on the Ottawa River close to the treacherous Long-Sault rapids, this community was named after Philippe Carrion de Fresnay, a French officer who ventured here to trade furs in 1671. In 1682, Carillon was incorporated into the Argenteuil seigneury granted to Charles-Joseph d'Ailleboust, and it remained a trading post throughout the turbulent days of the fur trade.

In the 19C, Carillon became a military settlement designed to protect the canal system built to circumvent the rapids. More recently, Hydro-Québec built a power plant to harness the rapids.

Dollard des Ormeaux – The town's renown is linked to a legendary act of bravery that took place at Carillon in 1660. From the time it was founded in 1642, Montreal lived under constant threat of attack by the Iroquois. In May 1660, Adam Dollard des Ormeaux (1635-1660) intervened to save the very existence of the tiny settlement located east of Carillon. With the help of forty Hurons, he and seventeen other French-Canadian men held three hundred Iroquois warriors at bay for a full week. Dollard and his companions sacrificed their lives, but their heroism so impressed the Iroquois that they gave up their attack on Montreal. The following month, the first furs reached Montreal safely, marking the beginning of a thriving trade. Ever since, Dollard des Ormeaux has been celebrated as the saviour of the young colony.

Access – *Carillon is located on Rte. 344, approximately 70km/43mi west of Montreal by Rte. 40 (Exit 2). It can also be reached by the Pointe-Fortune ferry, on the Ontario border.*

SIGHTS

Musée régional d'Argenteuil (Argenteuil Regional Museum) – *On Rte. 344, just to the right of the ferry ramp. Open Jun–Labour Day Tue–Sun 10:30am–4:30pm. Mid-Sept–mid-Oct weekends 11am–5pm. $2.50.* 🅿 ☎ *450-537-3861.* This lovely stone structure was built as a military barracks between 1834 and 1837 and was used to protect the canal. During the Patriots' Rebellion (1837-1838), it accommodated 100 British soldiers and officers. It was later converted into a hotel. Since 1938, it has housed a museum dedicated to local history. Exhibits are devoted to Dollard des Ormeaux and Sir John Abbott (1821-1893), the member of parliament for Argenteuil County and prime minister of Canada from 1892 to 1893. Many 18C and 19C musical instruments, clocks and French and Canadian furniture on display were contributed by members of the community.

Centrale hydro-électrique de Carillon (Carillon Power Station) – *Entrance on Rte. 344 in Carillon. Visit by guided tour (1hr 15min) only, May 15–Jun 23 Mon–Fri 9am–3pm. Jun 24–Labour Day Wed–Sun 9:30am–3:30pm.* ♿ 🅿 *http://www.hydro-quebec.com/visit/laurentides/carillon.html* ☎ *450-537-8624.* Built between 1959 and

1964 at the foot of the Long-Sault rapids, this power station is a run-of-the-river plant with an installed capacity of 654,500kw, making it the fifteenth largest power station in Hydro-Quebec. Its 14 turbines harness the flow of the Ottawa River, which is estimated at 2,000cu m/7,842cu ft per second. The plant and its spillway span the entire river. The guided tour of the power plant includes a short film *(15min)* and a visit to the turbine chamber, the control room and the roof, from which the reservoir and power lines can be seen.

Lieu historique national du Canal-de-Carillon (Carillon Canal National Historic Site) – *Open mid-May–mid-Jun & early-Sept–early Oct Mon–Thur 12:30pm–3pm. Mid-Jun–mid-Aug daily 8:30am–8pm. Mid-Aug–early-Sept Mon–Thur 9:30am–6pm. $1.50. www.parcscanada.gc.ca/parks/quebec/canalcarillon/* ☏ *450-537-3534.* This 60m/197ft-long navigation **lock** was constructed to replace seven older ones. It provides the greatest single lift (nearly 20m/66ft) of any conventional lock in Canada. Navigation to Ottawa upstream from this lock is unimpeded. The stone building of the **Maison du collecteur** (Toll House) was built in 1843 for the toll collector, who levied the tolls on barges and other vessels using the canal system. Beside it, parts of the former 19C canal and lock system still remain.

Parc Carillon (Carillon Park) – *Entrance just upstream from the power plant. Information* ☏ *450-537-8400.* Extending about 3km/2mi along the shores of the reservoir, this park offers waterside picnic spots. Near the dam stands a **monument** to Dollard des Ormeaux and his comrades, erected in 1960. Jacques Folch-Ribas fashioned the 18 granite monoliths (8m/26ft high) to commemorate the battle fought by the gallant defenders.

CHAMBLY★

Montérégie
Population 19,716 – Map p 263

A residential suburb of Montreal, the city of Chambly occupies a beautiful **site** on the western shore of the Chambly Basin. Formed by the widening of the Richelieu River just below significant rapids, the basin is often dotted with sailboats. The rounded shape of Mt. Saint-Hilaire looms to the northeast.

In 1665, Captain **Jacques de Chambly** was ordered to build a fort here to defend the route to Montreal against raids by the Iroquois. For services rendered to the colony, he was granted the seigneury in 1672. Today, the town still bears his name.

The river rapids were harnessed early in the 19C to activate seven mills including carding, sawing, fulling and grist mills. In 1843, the Chambly Canal was completed, facilitating navigation and trade between Canada and the US. Strings of barges pulled alongside the shore by horses were traditionally used to transport wood and other raw materials south to the New England states. During this period, Chambly enjoyed great commercial prosperity. Today, the city still attracts some light industry.

Artists and Heroes – Chambly's beautiful setting has long attracted artists. The Impressionist painter **Maurice Cullen** (1866-1934) lived here, as did his stepson **Robert Pilot** (1898-1967). Chambly is also the birthplace of Emma Lajeunesse (1847-1930). Better known by her stage name **Albani**, Lajeunesse was an internationally acclaimed opera singer and one of the greatest sopranos of her generation. The city's most illustrious native son is **Charles-Michel de Salaberry** (1778-1829), hero of the Battle of the Châteauguay.

Access – *Chambly is about 30km/19mi from Montreal by Rte. 10 (Exit 22).*

SIGHTS

Start at City Hall at the corner of Rue Bourgogne and Rue de Salaberry.

The Charles-Michel de Salaberry **memorial**, erected in 1881 in front of Chambly's city hall, is one of the first historical bronzes created by the great sculptor, Louis-Philippe Hébert. Just north on Rue Martel, in front of St. Joseph's Church (1784), stands the sculptor's last known work: a statue of Father Pierre-Marie Mignault, parish priest of St. Joseph's for 40 years.

Follow Rue Bourgogne east to reach the Chambly Canal.

Chambly Canal – *Near the marina. Parking available across the bridge on Rue Bourgogne. Open mid-Jun–mid-Aug daily 8:30am–7pm. Hours vary mid-May–mid June & mid-Aug–mid-Oct.* ✗ ♿ ▣ *www.parcscanada.gc.ca/chambly* ☏ *450-447-4888.* Completed in 1843, this historic canal runs about 19km/12mi, from Saint-Jean-sur-Richelieu to the Chambly Basin, skirting numerous rapids in the Richelieu River. Its nine locks (of which eight are operated manually) raise passing vessels over 24m/79ft. At the turn of the century, the canal was a busy commercial waterway used by more than 4,000 crafts annually. Today, although the canal has lost its economic importance, it is still used for boating and other recreational activities.

Parks Canada owns the canal and manages with the Friends of the Canal an information office that displays photo exhibits. Some of the locks' original mechanisms still exist, and visitors can observe locksmen operating the cranks that open and close the sluices and gates.

A bicycle path follows the banks of the canal to Saint-Jean-sur-Richelieu. **Scenic cruises★** *(depart from Quai Fédéral early May–mid-Oct by appointment; commentary; reservations required; $8.50; Croisières Chambly ☎ 514-592-8478)* offer a pleasant trip on the calm waters of the Chambly Basin and the canal. From the deck, visitors can admire Fort Chambly, the rapids and Mt. Saint-Hilaire in the distance.

Continue along Rue Bourgogne to Rue du Fort.

★★**Lieu historique national du Fort-Chambly (Fort Chambly National Historic Site)** – *On 2 Rue de Richelieu beside the river. Open Mar–mid-May & mid-Oct–Nov Wed–Sun 10am–5pm. Mid-May–Jun daily 9am–5pm. Mid-Jun–early Sept daily 10am–6pm. Early-Sept–mid-Oct daily 10am–5pm. $4. & ▣ www.parcscanada.gc.ca ☎ 450-658-1585.* Located in a magnificent park where the river widens to form the Chambly Basin, this fort has been restored to its 18C appearance. Vestiges of the original stone structure, conceived by military engineer Josué Boisberthelot de Beaucours, can still be seen. Fort Chambly is the only remaining fortified complex in Quebec dating back to the French Regime. Erected between 1709 and 1711 during the Anglo-French wars, the stone fort replaced an earlier wooden structure erected by Jacques de Chambly in 1665, to defend the Richelieu rapids on the crucial trade route between Montreal and Albany, New York. The new fort was laid out in a square with bastions at each corner. The main entrance is located on the western flank. Several buildings with dormer windows overlook the inner courtyard. A chapel topped by a mansard roof and small steeple faces the main entrance. Located inside the fort, an **interpretation centre** features displays on the history of Fort Chambly and its occupants under the French Regime, and a description of the restoration project. Slide shows and dioramas recreate life at the fort and in the surrounding region.

Corps de Garde (Guard House) – *On Rue Richelieu near fort. Also accessible through the park.* After the Conquest, British officials established extensive military installations in Chambly. During the War of 1812, the fort was garrisoned with as many as 6,000 men and enlarged to accommodate the infantry, cavalry and artillery. Several expeditions launched against the Patriots in 1837-1838 originated from Chambly. The fort and military camp were abandoned when the garrison departed in 1851.

The facade of the stone guard house (1814) features an imposing pediment supported by columns, exemplifying the Palladian style adopted by the military throughout the British colonies. The house contains displays on the period of occupation by the British garrison (1760-1851), and on the development of the city.

Église Saint-Stephen (St. Stephen's Church) – *2004 Rue Bourgogne.* This fieldstone edifice built in 1820 to serve as the garrison church was modelled after the Catholic churches of the period. The liturgical furnishings and the sobre decor, however,

Bird's-Eye View of Fort-Chambly

distinguish the interior as a Protestant place of worship. The cemetery contains several interesting funeral monuments, among them one belonging to the Yule family, former seigneurs of Chambly.

Continue along Rue Richelieu to the junction with Rte. 112.

★**Rue Richelieu** – Several attractive houses line this street, a former portage route established along the rapids in 1665.

Near the guard house at no. 12 stands the **Maison Beattie**, a brick structure (1875) that now serves as the Chambly Tourist Office and the Historical Society of the Chambly Seigneury (Société d'histoire de la Seigneurie de Chambly).

The first section of Rue Richelieu, from the guard house to Rue des Voltigeurs, passes through the former military domain. Buildings erected by the British army were transformed into residences at the end of the 19C when Chambly became a popular vacation centre. Near the guard house, at no. 10, stands a former barracks (1814). The stone house at no. 14 was once the commandant's residence. From Rue des Voltigeurs to Rue Saint-Jacques, the second section of Rue Richelieu crosses the former seigneurial domain where several military officers settled in comfortable residences.

The **Manoir de Salaberry**, at no. 18, was constructed in 1814 for Charles-Michel de Salaberry, who lived here until his death in 1829. With its pediment and two-storey portico, the residence is one of the finest examples of Palladian-inspired architecture in Quebec.

At no. 27 stands a monumental stone house built in 1816 for the merchant John Yule, brother of seigneur William Yule. The house at no. 26, built in 1920, was once the studio of the noted painter Maurice Cullen.

Rue Richelieu stretches alongside the **Parc des Rapides** (Rapids Park), providing **views** of the tumultuous Chambly rapids and the Chambly dam. On this site stood the Willett wool factories and mills; powered by the river current, they were the source of Chambly's prosperity throughout the 19C. Modest wooden homes, remnants of the former industrial community, can still be seen on this street.

EXCURSION

★★**Vallée du Richelieu** – *See Entry Heading.*

Côte de CHARLEVOIX★★★
Charlevoix
Map pp 80-81

The Charlevoix Coast is one of Quebec's loveliest and most varied regions, its rugged landscape marked by mountains sweeping down into the mighty St. Lawrence River. In this area, the river becomes a veritable arm of the sea, and its wide banks are referred to as "the coast," suggesting that this is no longer a river in the true sense of the word. The pristine coast affords magnificent views of the river, and the opposite shore is visible on clear days. Designated a UNESCO World Biosphere Reserve in 1989, the region also is a mecca for art and nature lovers attracted by its natural beauty, maritime past, and old-time resort tradition.

The first settlers moved into the Charlevoix region toward the end of the 17C. They were predominantly lumberjacks and navigators, since the coast did not lend itself to agriculture. Some remote communities remained inaccessible by road until the mid-20C. Charlevoix is named for Pierre-François-Xavier de Charlevoix (1682-1761), a Jesuit historian who wrote the famous *History and General Description of New France (Histoire et description générale de la Nouvelle France).*

Historical Notes

The Charlevoix Schooners – Until the late 1960s, small schooners, called *goélettes*, sailed the St. Lawrence transporting provisions and wood destined for the Charlevoix Coast, the Côte-Nord, Bas-Saint-Laurent, and the Gaspésie. More than 300 of these vessels, known locally as *voitures d'eau* (literally "water cars"), were built in Charlevoix. The small vessels were originally equipped with sails, and later with motors. Today, their hulls lie abandoned along the shore.

Visitors stopping along the clifftop roads of this region can often hear the rumbling of powerful motors from freighters passing in the distance on the St. Lawrence River. These freighters gradually replaced the traditional schooners.

A Choice Resort – As early as the 1760s, visitors flocked to Charlevoix, attracted by the beauty of its landscapes. After the Conquest, two Scottish officers, Captain John Nairn and Lieutenant Malcolm Fraser, received the former seigneury of La Malbaie-Pointe-Au-Pic from military governor General James Murray (1721-1794), and named it Murray Bay.

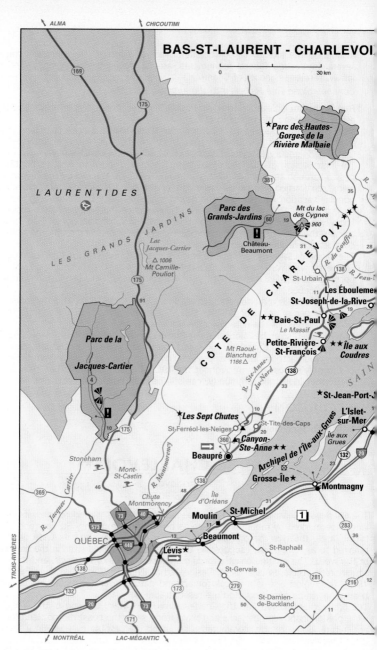

★ *Parc des Hautes-Gorges de la Rivière Malbaie*

LAURENTIDES

LES GRANDS JARDINS

Parc des Grands-Jardins

Mt du lac des Cygnes ★★★
△ 960

Château-Beaumont

Lac Jacques-Cartier
△ 1006
Mt Camille-Pouliot

St-Urbain

Les Éboulemen
St-Joseph-de-la-Rive

★★ *Baie-St-Paul*
Le Massif
Petite-Rivière-St-François ★★ *Île aux Coudres*

Parc de la Jacques-Cartier

CÔTE DE CHARLEVOIX

Mt Raoul-Blanchard
1166 △

R. Ste-Anne-du-Nord

★ St-Jean-Port-J

L'Islet-sur-Mer

★ *Les Sept Chutes*
St-Ferréol-les-Neiges

St-Tite-des-Caps

▲ *Canyon-Ste-Anne* ★★
Beaupré

Archipel de l'Île-aux-Grues

Île aux Grues

Grosse-Île ★

Montmagny

Stoneham

Mont-St-Castin

R. Montmorency

Chute Montmorency

Île d'Orléans

Moulin
St-Michel

Beaumont

QUÉBEC

Lévis ★

St-Raphaël

St-Gervais

St-Damien-de-Buckland

TROIS-RIVIÈRES

MONTRÉAL   LAC-MÉGANTIC

In the mid-19C, Charlevoix became a popular resort area. City dwellers began refurbishing traditional residences and later constructed elegant summer homes. Canada Steamship Lines brought many wealthy tourists to the region aboard their luxurious cruise ships and built the enormous Manoir Richelieu Hotel in 1899. Reconstructed in 1929 after a fire, the hotel is the sole survivor among the grand hostelries of the period. The great white boats *(bateaux blancs)* discontinued their visits in the 1960s, when the opening of the Côte-Nord road marked the end of an era. Today, numerous inns welcome tourists.

Artists' Haunt – Charlevoix has long attracted and inspired painters, poets and writers. Its villages and panoramas are immortalized in the works of such well-known Canadian artists as Clarence Gagnon, Marc-Aurèle Fortin, René Richard, Jean-Paul Lemieux and A.Y. Jackson. Baie-Saint-Paul, especially, is known as an artists' haunt, as are Port-au-Persil and Les Éboulements. Among the writers and poets who have lived here are Laure Conan and Gabrielle Roy.

Access – Charlevoix is accessible by Rtes. 40 and 138, northeast of Quebec City. Rte. 138 traverses the region which starts at the border of Cape Tourmente, about 40km/25mi from Quebec City. Rte. 362 also connects Baie-Saint-Paul to La Malbaie–Pointe-au-Pic.

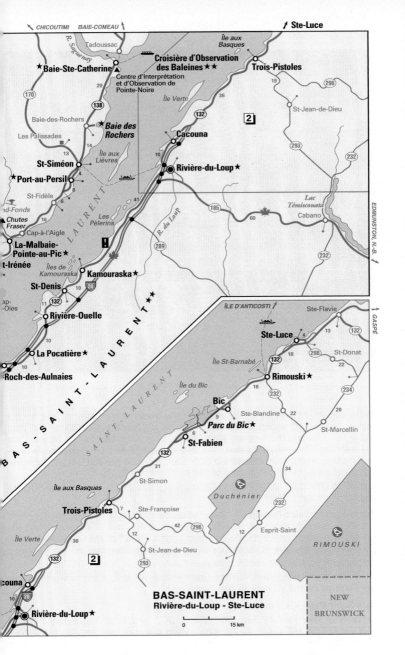

FROM BEAUPRÉ TO BAIE-SAINTE-CATHERINE 220km/136mi.

Leave Beaupré on Rte. 138. After 4km/2.5mi, turn left, following signs.

★★ **Canyon Sainte-Anne** – *Open Jun 24–Labour Day daily 8:30am–6pm. May–Jun 23 & early Sept–Oct daily 9am–5:30pm. $. ✗ ♿ 🅿 www.canyonste-anne.qc.ca ☎ 418-827-4057.* At this point, the Sainte-Anne-du-Nord River drops in a steep and narrow waterfall, plunging 74m/243ft into a mass of foam and whirlpools. Interpretative panels dot the paths leading through the woods to the river and falls; three footbridges span the river, allowing excellent views. A third footpath leads to the bottom of the canyon.

Rejoin Rte. 138; after 15km/9mi turn left on Rte. 360 for Saint-Ferréol-les-Neiges. Continue for 10km/6mi, following signs.

★ **Les Sept Chutes** (Seven Falls) – *Open Jun 24–Labour Day daily 9am–7pm. Late May–Jun 23 & early Sept–mid-Oct daily 10am–5pm. $6.50. ✗ ♿ 🅿 www.septchutes.qc.ca ☎ 418-826-3139.* Between 1912 and 1916, a dam and generating station were built here, where the Sainte-Anne-du-Nord River cascades over seven separate falls. The generators remained in operation until 1984.

81

Charlevoix Landscape

Today a pleasant park, the site affords lovely views of the falls, as well as the chance to discover a part of Quebec's natural and industrial heritage. The dam above the falls and the wooden aqueduct that carried water to the turbines are still standing. The **generating station**, one of the oldest of its type in Quebec, is open to the public *(visitors must descend 325 steps to reach the station)*. An interpretation centre recounts the history of the hydroelectric facility.

Return to Rte. 138. After 30km/19mi turn right to Petite-Rivière-Saint-François and continue for 10km/6mi.

Petite-Rivière-Saint-François – The road descends steeply through the forest to a small community located on the St. Lawrence, at the base of a great cliff. *In the village, turn left after the church.* The pier affords a **view★** of the Charlevoix mountains plunging into the St. Lawrence along the rock-strewn shores.

Return to Rte. 138 and continue to Baie-Saint-Paul.

There are wonderful **views★★** of the Gouffre valley, the St. Lawrence and the Île aux Coudres on the descent to Baie-Saint-Paul.

★★ **Baie-Saint-Paul** – *13km/8mi. See Entry Heading.*

Leave Baie-Saint-Paul by Rte. 362. Route 362, and later Route 138 from La Malbaie–Pointe-au-Pic, provide numerous views of the St. Lawrence and its shores. As the road leaves Baie-Saint-Paul, a rest stop overlooks the Gouffre valley and the Île aux Coudres.

Les Éboulements – *19km/12mi.* This community, perched on the mountain's edge 300m/948ft above the St. Lawrence, takes its name from the series of landslides *(éboulements)* that followed a violent earthquake in 1663, propelling half the mountainside into the river. In 1710, the seigneury was granted to Pierre Tremblay who settled here and built a mill.

Moulin banal (Mill) – *Just before the junction with the road to Saint-Joseph-de-la-Rive. The access road is located to the right, before the Du Moulin River. Open late Jun–early Sept daily 9am–5pm. Rest of the year by appointment. $2.* ▯ ☎ *418-635-2239*. This stone mill was built in 1790 by Jean-François Tremblay at the top of a small waterfall. The mill still functions with its original equipment, and visitors can watch the grain being ground into flour. The former seigneurial manor of the Sales-Laterrière family stands nearby. Along with the mill and other outbuildings, the manor illustrates life under the seigneurial regime, which was abolished in 1854.

Saint-Joseph-de-la-Rive – *3km/2mi. Turn off Rte. 362 to the right towards Saint-Joseph-de-la-Rive and follow a very steep descent to the St. Lawrence.* The community sandwiched between the St. Lawrence and the mountains, offers lovely views of Île aux Coudres and the river. It was one of the main shipbuilding centres for the traditional Charlevoix schooners, many of which lie scattered along the village shore. The ferry to Île aux Coudres leaves from this town.

Take time to tour the schooners at the **Exposition Maritime** *(305 Place de l'Église,* ☎ *418-635-1131)* for a taste of Charlevoix's maritime past. At the **Papeterie Saint-Gilles** *(304, Rue Félix-Antoine-Savard,* ☎ *418-635-2430)*, a traditional paper workshop founded by priest and writer Félix-Antoine Savard), guides explain the process of 17C paper production.

★★Île aux Coudres – *Ferry service: depart from Saint-Joseph-de-la-Rive Apr–Oct daily 7:30am–11:30pm every hour. Rest of the year daily 7:30am–7:30pm (Jan–Feb 8:30pm) every 2hrs. 15min.* ♿ *Société des traversiers du Québec* ☎ *418-438-2743. Visit: See Entry Heading.*

Return to Saint-Joseph-de-la-Rive and Rte. 362 to Les Éboulements and continue towards Saint-Irénée.

Along this stretch, the St. Lawrence can often be spotted. Take the unpaved Cap-aux-Oies road for 1km/.6mi and stop at the bottom of the steep hill for a panoramic **view** of the cape and the south shore of the St. Lawrence. As it sweeps down to river level, Route 362 again reveals spectacular **views**.

Old Boat on Île aux Coudres

Saint-Irénée – *15km/9mi from Les Éboulements.* Saint-Irénée lies at the confluence of the Jean-Noël and St. Lawrence Rivers. It was the birthplace of the lawyer and poet, **Adolphe-Basile Routhier** (1839-1920), who wrote the French lyrics to the Canadian national anthem, *Ô Canada*.

Rodolphe Forget (1861-1919), who built the railway that follows the north shore of the St. Lawrence, had a summer home here. Known as the **Domaine Forget**, this former estate is set in a lovely area overlooking the river. Today, it is a cultural centre devoted to the performing arts. Concerts are given throughout the summer.

The road passes through La Malbaie–Pointe-au-Pic, and Cap-à-l'Aigle.

★La Malbaie–Pointe-au-Pic – *14km/9mi. See Entry Heading.*

Rejoin Rte. 138.

The road leads up the mountainside to Saint-Fidèle-de-Mont-Murray, providing a view of the Îles de Kamouraska, and then descends to river level.

6km/4mi after Saint-Fidèle-de-Mont-Murray, turn right for Port-au-Persil.

★Port-au-Persil – *30km/19mi from La Malbaie–Pointe-au-Pic.* This cove on the St. Lawrence has long been a favourite with artists. Beside the old quay, a tiny Anglican church and a small waterfall add a picturesque note to the site.

Saint-Siméon – *4km/2.5mi.* This former logging community on the St. Lawrence is now the terminus for the ferry *(1hr)* that crosses the river to Rivière-du-Loup. At this point, the St. Lawrence reaches a width of about 20km/12mi.

Located near this community, at the foot of a 120m/394ft cliff, is a forest education centre known as Les Palissades *(about 13km/8mi by Rte. 170)*. The interpretation centre serves as the departure point for three footpaths that allow the visitor to explore the area's diverse flora.

★Baie des Rochers – *17km/10.5mi.* An unpaved road *(about 3km/2mi)* leads to this lovely deserted bay, dominated by an old wharf. The small island at its entrance is accessible at low tide.

Return to Rte. 138.

The St. Lawrence comes into view again near Baie-Sainte-Catherine.

★Baie-Sainte-Catherine – *23km/14mi. See Entry Heading.*

CHIBOUGAMAU

Saguenay–Lac-Saint-Jean–Nord-du-Québec

Population 8,664

This community is located in the Chibougamau region, a vast expanse of lakes and forests, bordered by Lakes Mistassini, Chibougamau and Aux Dorés. The name Chibougamau is derived from the Cree word *shabogamaw*, meaning "lake traversed by a river." The indigenous population in this region consisted of nomadic hunters and gatherers who separated into small multifamily groups for the long winter and reassembled into large bands at various strategic meeting places during the summer. Today, half the town's inhabitants are francophones of European descent and half are Cree, who live mostly around lakes and rivers, drawing their livelihood primarily from the immense boreal forest that is divided into familial hunting territories.

Historical Notes

Lake Chibougamau was situated along the northern route travelled by the first European explorers. Among these were Des Groseillers (1618-1696) and Radisson (1636-1710), followed closely by Father Charles Albanel (1616-1696). Trading posts gave way to the mining town of Chibougamau, built in the midst of the boreal forest on a sandy plain near Gilman Lake, 15km/9mi north of Lake Chibougamau.

Traces of ore were first discovered in the 1840s. Several companies in the mining industry recognised the area's great mineral wealth, and prospectors, mining engineers, promoters and geologists flooded into the area. Expansion came to an abrupt halt after the stock market crash of 1929, but by 1934, the speculators and promoters had returned. World War II again put an end to mining activities in the area and it was not until 1950, with the completion of a 240km/149mi winter road between Saint-Félicien and Chibougamau, that mining companies established themselves here permanently.

The first copper, zinc and gold mine opened in 1951 on the site of Chapais, 44km/27mi from Chibougamau. Here, mineralisation is not related to a geological fault such as the one encountered in VAL D'OR, but to the Chibougamau-Matagami belt, which comprises "zones" of ore that are in fact vertical veins about 1m/3ft thick and between 610m/2,000ft and 1,220m/4,001ft deep. Tunnels, or "drifts," 1.8m/6ft wide by 2.5m/8ft high, are dug along the veins to expose the ore.

Today, Chibougamau harbours mainly miners and forest workers. Several sawmills remain, along with several working mines. Prospecting continues mainly within the Lake Aux Dorés complex. At one time, only copper was mined in this area, but since the recession of the 1970s, gold has taken precedence. Once the extracted rock has passed through the local concentrators, it is shipped by train to Chapais and then on to the Noranda smelter in Rouyn-Noranda.

Access – *Chibougamau is located 700km/434mi from Montreal by Rtes. 40, 155 and 167 (starting at Lake Saint-Jean). One daily flight departs from Montreal on Air Creebec (depart from Montreal Mon–Fri at 8:50am, arrive Chibougamau at 10am; depart from Chibougamau Mon–Fri at 4pm, arrive Montreal at 5:15; call for fares ☎ 819-825-8355).*

Activities – *Canoes, pedal boats and sailboards can be rented at the beach in the centre of town, on the shore of Lake Gilman. Canoe races and ball games are the main sporting events. A campground is located at the town entrance, behind the tourist information booth. Mt. Chalko, on Rte. 167, offers skiing in winter and hiking trails in summer. Flights by floatplane offered May–Oct daily 8am–5pm; rest of the year daily 9am–4pm; reservations required; Propair Inc. ☎ 418-748-2659.*

SIGHT

Église Saint-Marcel (St. Marcel's Church) – This striking building was constructed during the 1960s. The roof, with its openwork centre, is composed of two concrete shells thrust upward in opposing curves; the resulting design evokes the form of a fish, an ancient Christian symbol.

EXCURSION

Réserve faunique des Lacs-Albanel-Mistassini-et-Waconichi (Albanel-Mistassini-and-Waconichi Lakes Wildlife Reserve) – *Reserve open Jun–Labour Day daily 7am–7pm. The entrance to the reserve is located 3km (1.9mi) from Chibougamau on Rte. 167. Chalco checkpoint open Jun–Labour Day daily 7am–7pm. Administrative offices open Mon–Fri 8:30am–5pm; closed major holidays; ☎ 418-748-7748.* This immense expanse of wilderness, stretching over 16,400sqkm/6,332sqmi, is covered with forests of black spruce and fir. A multitude of lakes, including Lake Mistassini – the largest lake in the province (2,019sqkm/780sqmi) – make this a haven for fishing enthusiasts.

Activities – *Hiking and fishing are the main activities. Wilderness camping (reservations ☎ 418-890-6527) is limited to 14 consecutive days. All waste must be packed out. Self-guided overnight canoe trips are possible; at least one-month advance notice is required. Rowboats may be rented on a daily basis, by reservation only; limit three persons per boat; no guide services available.*

Waconichi Reserve – Named after the hills to the west of Lake Waconichi that protect Amerindian encampments from the frosty northwest winds, the reserve includes a tourist complex with fishing facilities. Newly built log cabins *(27km/16.8mi from Chalco checkpoint, reservations required ☎ 418-890-6527)* are located on a lovely **site**★.

Mistassini – *From the Chalco checkpoint, drive 67km/41.6mi on Rte. 167 and turn left toward Mistassini (Baie-du-Poste); continue for 16km/10mi.* Mistassini is located on the old fur trading route leading to Fort Rupert (Waskaganish), on Hudson Bay. A Cree community, known as the Mistassini, already inhabited the area in 1640. The Hudson's Bay Company maintained a trading post at Fort Rupert for one hundred years, but competition from the Northwest Company eventually forced the HBC to move inland.

In order to intercept the furs before they arrived at Fort Rupert, the French established their own trading post in Mistassini in 1674, after Father Charles Albanel's visit to the area. The first trading post at Neoskweskau, on the Eastmain River, was moved to the north of Lake Mistassini in 1800 and to the south of the lake, where Mistassini is now located, in 1835.

FROM CHIBOUGAMAU TO VAL-D'OR

About 413km/250mi on Rtes. 167, 113 and 177.

Chapais – *44km/27mi from Chibougamau by Rtes. 167 and 113.* The town was named in honour of the politician and historian, Sir Thomas Chapais. The first major ore deposit in the Chibougamau-Chapais region was discovered on this site in 1929, by Leo Springner. In 1989, the Chapais sawmill was awarded a prize as the largest lumber producer in Eastern Canada. A new thermal mill converts wood residue into electric energy.

Waswanipi – *93km/58mi.* Like Mistassini, Waswanipi has been designated an Indian and wildlife reserve. Many Cree who live in this area are employed in the mines at Desmaraisville and Miquelon, south of Waswanipi; others work on reforestation projects in the region.

Lebel-sur-Quévillon – *120km/74mi from Waswanipi, 213km/132mi from Chapais.* In 1965, the shores of Lake Quévillon, fed by the Bell River, were still pristine wilderness. Since then, a small, vibrant community has developed, sustained by the Domtar **pulp mill** *(4km/2.5mi from town on the Chemin du Moulin; visit by guided tour (1hour 30min) only, year-round daily 2:30pm–4pm; reservations required;* △ ⋇ ⅍ ☐ ☎ 819-755-2153)*.* Located at the edge of town on Blvd. Quévillon is a municipal campground and beach with water sport equipment rental and charted walking trails.

Senneterre – *84km/52mi.* This dynamic little forestry town has changed considerably in just a few short years. Located at the town's three entry points, three sculptures, representing the forestry and railway industries and the Canadian armed forces, serve as reminders of a difficult but glorious past, while instilling hope for the future.

Lac Faillon – *45km/28mi east of Senneterre, on access road N-806.* Lake Faillon offers visitors a lovely setting enhanced by the unspoiled beauty of the Mégiscane River. Recreational activities on the lake include swimming, boating, canoeing and fishing.

★**Val-d'Or** – *67km/41mi by Rtes. 113 and 117. See Entry Heading.*

CHICOUTIMI★

Saguenay–Lac-Saint-Jean
Population 63,240 – Map p 272

Located at the confluence of the Saguenay, Chicoutimi and Du Moulin Rivers, the city is the economic, cultural and administrative centre of the Saguenay region as well as its episcopal seat. The University of Quebec maintains a campus here.

Chicoutimi was the site of a major fur trading post as early as 1676, but it was not founded as a community until 1842, when Métis trader Peter McLeod built a sawmill at the foot of waterfalls on the Du Moulin River. This marked the beginning of the area's important forestry industry. Chicoutimi draws its name from the Montagnais word *eshko-timiou,* meaning "to the edge of deep waters."

From the city, the visitor can behold a magnificent **view**★ of the rounded cliffs flanking the Saguenay River on its descent towards the St. Lawrence. The Saguenay can be crossed by car on the Dubuc Bridge *(pont Dubuc),* or on foot or bicycle by the Sainte-Anne footbridge.

In February, Chicoutimi celebrates its **Carnaval-Souvenir**, during which the inhabitants dress in period costume and recreate winter activities of a bygone era. *In July 1996, severe floods swept parts of the Saguenay–Lac-Saint-Jean region. Several sights were destroyed; others may be closed temporarily.*

Access – *Chicoutimi is located 200km/124mi north of Quebec City by Rte. 175.*

SIGHTS

★★**Scenic Cruises** – *Depart from dock at bottom of Rue Salaberry Jun–Sept daily at 8:30am & 12:30pm. Commentary. Reservations required. Return to Chicoutimi by bus. $34.75.* ✗ ▯ *Croisières Marjolaine Inc.* ☎ *418-543-7630.* Cruises on the majestic Saguenay fjord are among the most spectacular and popular excursions in Quebec. The boats descend the river to the lovely village of Sainte-Rose-du-Nord; stop below the rocky promontory known as the Tableau (150m/492ft high); pass by Saint-Basile-du-Tableau, one of the smallest villages in Quebec; and enter Eternity Bay (Baie Éternité), dominated by the towering peaks of Cape Éternité and Cape Trinité. The highlight of the cruise is the dramatic arrival at the foot of **Cap Trinité**. Set in this wild and rocky setting is a gigantic statue of the Virgin. The three ledges for which the cape was named are clearly visible from the boat; sometimes, rock climbers can be seen here.

On the return trip, the views of Ha! Ha! Bay and of Chicoutimi itself are equally magnificent.

★**Croix de Sainte-Anne** (St. Anne's Cross) – *On north side of the Saguenay, 3km/2mi from the Dubuc Bridge. Turn left on Rue Saint-Albert, right on Rue Roussel, and left on Rue de la Croix.* Located high above the Saguenay, the terrace offers a wonderful **view** of Chicoutimi and the area. The present 18m/59ft-high cross (1922) is the third to stand on this site. Msgr. Baillargeon constructed the first one in 1863 to guide the ferries sailing up the river and prevent accidents. The second cross (1872) was erected in gratitude for the protection accorded the city during the Great Fire of 1870, which devastated much of the land around the Lake Saint-Jean and the Saguenay River. Below this viewpoint one can see the lovely facade of Église Sainte-Anne (St. Anne's Church, 1901).

The Jacques Cartier lookout *(intersection of Rue Jacques Cartier Est and Blvd. Talbot)* and the Beauregard lookout *(east of the Jacques Cartier lookout, near the statue of Our Lady of the Saguenay)* also afford excellent views of the Saguenay.

★**La pulperie de Chicoutimi, Centre d'Interprétation** (Chicoutimi Pulp Mill Interpretation Center) – *300 Rue Dubuc. Open late-Jun 24–early-Sept daily 9am–5pm. Rest of the year by reservation for groups over 15. $8.25.* ♿ ▯ *www.pulperie.com* ☎ *418-698-3100. Note: The mill wil be closed until summer 2001.* This former pulp and paper mill, standing on a picturesque **site**★★ at the mouth of the Chicoutimi River, was one of the most important industrial complexes in Quebec. The mill was founded in 1896 by the Chicoutimi Pulp and Paper Company, which had become Canada's largest producer of pulp by 1910 thanks to its director Alfred Dubuc. At its height in 1920 the company employed over 2,000 people in its four mills and mechanical workshop. After the stock market crash of 1929, the mill was closed down. Today its ruins serve as the setting for cultural and artistic events.

Near the entrance at the top of the gorge stands Building 1921. This enormous former workshop of pink granite today serves primarily as an **interpretation centre** with an audio-visual presentation on the mill and the lumber industry in general.

Further down, along the river, stand the remains of two paper mills, dating from 1898 and 1912. Part of the enormous conduit that brought water down to power the mills still exists. A flight of steps leads up the river to a hillock overlooking the entire installation of the mill. The water tower is still functioning. Architect René-P. LeMay (1870-1915) designed several of these buildings using local stone instead of the brick traditionally used in industrial constructions. The choice of stone as a building material contributes to the charm of the site.

La pulperie de Chicoutimi

André Ellefsen

Maison Arthur-Villeneuve (Arthur Villeneuve Home) – *In Building 1921.* Beginning in 1994, local efforts to highlight the region's heritage resulted in the relocation to this sight of the home of painter Arthur Villeneuve, formerly located at 669, rue Taché Ouest. Villeneuve (1905-1990) worked for many years as a barber while painting in his spare time. A deeply religious man, he gave up his shop in 1957 and dedicated the rest of his life to painting after hearing a sermon on the use of one's talents. Today, the fame of this local folk painter has spread far beyond his simple home. Villeneuve decorated his house with colourful (and sometimes terrifying) murals.

★**Musée du Saguenay–Lac-Saint-Jean** (Saguenay–Lac-Saint-Jean Museum) – *In Building 1921. Scheduled opening summer 2001.* Building 1921 is slated to house the collections of this fine museum, formerly located in the chapel of the Chicoutimi Seminary. Visitors to the museum will gain insight into various aspects of regional history, such as the lifestyle of the Montagnais, the arrival of the first Europeans, the lives of the inhabitants in the 19C, and the development of the metallurgical (mainly aluminium), hydroelectric and forestry industries. Biographies of some of the region's key figures, including Peter McLeod, Alfred Dubuc, Sir William Price III and Arthur Vining Davis, will also be on view.

Cathédrale Saint-François-Xavier (Cathedral of St. Francis Xavier) – *Rue Racine at Rue Bégin. Open year-round daily 8am–11:30am & 1:30pm–4pm.* ☎ *418-549-3212.* The twin square towers flanking the stone facade of the cathedral (1915) overlook the city of Chicoutimi. The cathedral was rebuilt after a fire in 1919. Inside, note the sculpture of Christ by Médard Bourgault, the pulpit and Bishop's throne by Lauréat Vallières and the organ manufactured by the Casavant Brothers of Saint-Hyacinthe.

Village de la sécurité (Safety Village) – *200 Rue Pinel. On north side of Saguenay River, 4km/2.5mi from bridge. Turn right on Rue Pasteur, right on Rue Saint-Gérard, and left on Rue Pinel. Open late Jun–Aug daily 10am–6pm. Mid-May–mid-Jun & Sept by appointment only. $7.50.* ✗ ♿ 🅿 ☎ *418-545-6925.* Developed primarily to increase young persons' awareness of safety and security issues, this scale-model village offers a plethora of activities and attractions, including train rides and miniature motorised cars. Other attractions simulate an auto crash and a house fire, while a 30m/98ft high weather tower offers a splendid **view** of the region.

CÔTE-NORD★
Manicouagan–Duplessis
Map pp 88-89

The Côte-Nord, or North Shore, extends from the mouth of the Saguenay River north to the Labrador border. The Upper North Shore, the southernmost region, stretches from Tadoussac to Sept-Îles, and the Middle North Shore from Sept-Îles to Havre-Saint-Pierre. The Lower North Shore, so named because it is the closest to the ocean, encompasses the area between Havre-Saint-Pierre and Blanc-Sablon; in this vast expanse of taiga, towns and villages can only be reached by plane or boat.

The Inuit and Montagnais have inhabited the area for thousands of years, and the Montagnais, living in seven reserves scattered along the coast, still form a major part of the population. In the second half of the 15C, Basque fishermen came to this region to hunt whales. Fishing remained the primary industry until the 1920s, when pulp mill companies began exploiting the forest resources, thus creating an important forestry industry. In the 1950s, the discovery of rich mineral deposits, primarily iron ore, prompted another surge of economic growth as did the harnessing of the Manicouagan and Outardes Rivers for hydroelectricity in the early 1960s.

Access – *Rte. 138 traverses the Côte-Nord from Tadoussac to Havre-Saint-Pierre. The Lower North Shore is accessible by boat or plane.*

① FROM TADOUSSAC TO SEPT-ÎLES
450km/279mi by Rte. 138.

★★**Tadoussac** – *See Entry Heading.*

Grandes-Bergeronnes – *26km/16mi from Tadoussac; drive through Petites-Bergeronnes.* Named Bergeronnettes (wagtails) by Samuel de Champlain in 1603, after he spotted a flock of these yellow, long-tailed birds, the region had already been frequented by Basque fishermen and Montagnais long before. The first European settlers arrived in 1844 and erected a flour mill in Petites-Bergeronnes and a sawmill in Grandes-Bergeronnes.

Today **whale watching** is the main attraction. Favourable ecological conditions in the area produce an abundance of plankton, which in turn attracts belugas and blue whales to these waters. It is possible to observe them at sea or from the shore at Cap-de-Bon-Désir.

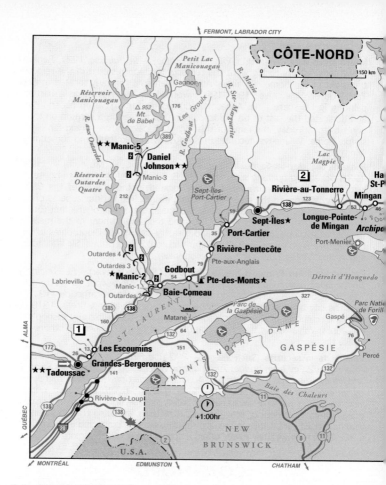

Map labels: FERMONT, LABRADOR CITY · CÔTE-NORD · 150 km · Petit Lac Manicouagan · Gagnon · Réservoir Manicouagan · R. Moisie · Les Groulx · △ 952 Mt de Babel · 176 · R. Godbout · R. Ste-Marguerite · Lac Magpie · 389 · ★★Manic-5 · Daniel Johnson★★ · Manic-3 · 212 · Réservoir Outardes Quatre · Sept-Îles-Port-Cartier · 2 · Rivière-au-Tonnerre · 123 · Ha St-P · Mingan · R. aux Outardes · 59 · 138 · 53 · Sept-Îles★ · Longue-Pointe-de Mingan · Archipe · Port-Cartier · 35 · Port-Menier · Outardes 4 · Rivière-Pentecôte · Outardes 3 · 79 · Pte-aux-Anglais · Détroit d'Honguedo · Godbout · ★Manic-2 · 54 · Pte-des-Monts★ · Labrieville · Manic-1 · Baie-Comeau · Outardes 1 · Parc de la Gaspésie · 327 · Parc Natio de Forill · 385 · 138 · ST-LAURENT · 160 · Matane · 132 · 64 · NOTRE DAME · Gaspé · ALMA · 1 · 172 · 26 · 13 · Les Escoumins · 151 · GASPÉSIE · 76 · Grandes-Bergeronnes · MONTS · Percé · ★★Tadoussac · 141 · 132 · 267 · 132 · Rivière-du-Loup · 132 · Baie des Chaleurs · 11 · QUÉBEC · 138 · +1:00hr · NEW · 20 · BRUNSWICK · 8 · U.S.A. · MONTRÉAL · EDMUNSTON · CHATHAM

Archeo-Topo Interpretation Centre – *498 Rue de la Mer. Open mid-May–mid-Oct daily 9am–6pm. $4.75. ☎ 418-232-6286.* Archaeological exhibits here focus on the excavations carried out in the Grandes-Bergeronnes region, which have uncovered traces of human occupation dating back 5,500 years.

Cap-de-Bon-Désir Nature Interpretation and Observation Centre – *6km/4mi east of Grandes-Bergeronnes. Open Jun–early-Sept daily 8am–8pm. Early-Sept–October daily 9am–6pm. $5. ☎ 418-232-6751.* Part of the Parc marin du Saguenay–Saint-Laurent (Saguenay–Saint-Laurent Marine Park), the centre provides various activities and information to introduce visitors to regional history and the underwater environment of the estuary. Whales and other marine mammals are often visible from the observation tower *(binoculars available for rent).*

Les Escoumins – *13km/8mi.* Basque fishermen established this small community in the late 15C, naming it Esquemin. Now known as Les Escoumins, the charming town offers ideal spots for whale watching and is noteworthy for its fishing and scuba diving. When crossing over the Escoumins River, visitors can see an unusual construction to the left: it is a **salmon ladder** designed to help the salmon as they swim upstream to spawn in the waters where they were born.

Baie-Comeau – *160km/99mi.* Named for Napoléon-Alexandre Comeau, a trapper, geologist and naturalist from the Côte-Nord, the city of 25,554 inhabitants traces its industrial beginnings to Colonel Robert McCormick (1880-1955) and his establishment of the Quebec North Shore Paper Company in 1936. Today the company, known as the Quebec and Ontario Paper Company, is one of the region's foremost employers.

Constructed of multi-colored granite stones and reminiscent of the works of the 20C French modernist, Auguste Perret, **Cathédrale Saint-Jean-Eudes** *(open Jun 24–Labour Day daily 8am–8pm; rest of the year during services only; ⅙ ⃞ ☎ 418-589-2370)* overlooks the mouth of the Manicouagan River. Situated in the Marquette sector to the east, **Amélie Quarter** boasts fine homes built in the 1930s. On Rue Cabot stands **Le Manoir Hotel**, rebuilt in the French Colonial style. **Église Sainte-Amélie** *(37 Ave. Marquette; open Apr–Dec daily 9am–6pm; ⅙ ⃞ ☎ 418-296-5528)* is dedicated to the memory of Amélie McCormick, wife of the town's founder and benefactor. The **frescoes★** adorning the interior are the work of Italian artist Guido Nincheri and were restored in 1996.

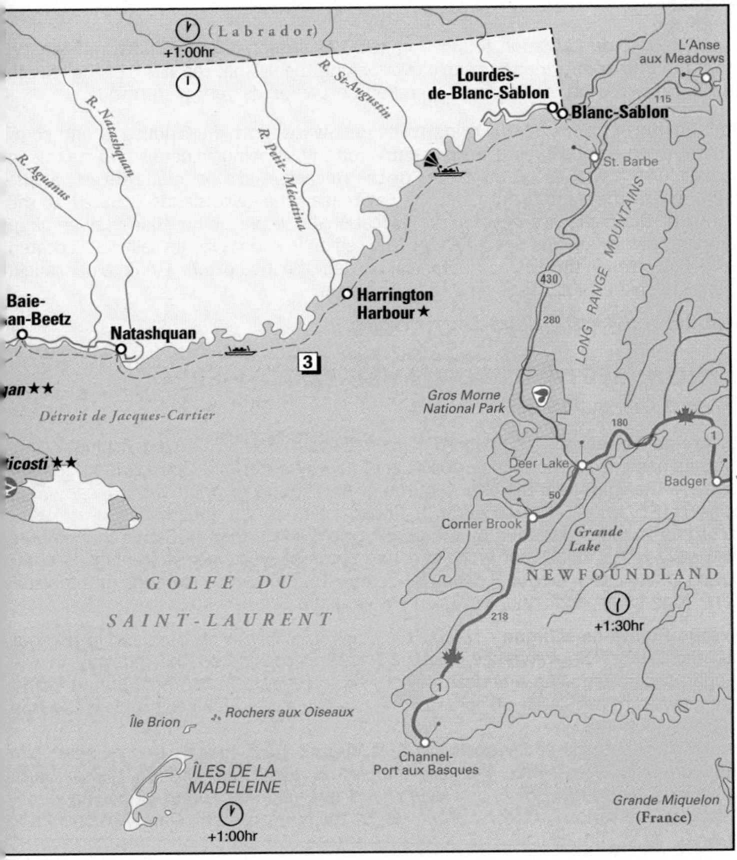

Excursion to the Manic-Outardes Complex – *430km/267mi round-trip from Baie-Comeau. See Entry Heading.*

Godbout – *54km/33mi from Baie-Comeau.* The village occupies a beautiful **site★** in the bay between Pointe-des-Monts Cape and the mouth of the Godbout River. The village and the river were named after the pilot and navigator, Nicolas Godbout, who settled on Île d'Orleans in 1670. A ferry connects the village to Matane, on the south shore.

Musée Amérindien et Inuit de Godbout (Amerindian and Inuit Museum) – *Facing the port, 2km/1.2mi south of Rte. 138. Open Jun–mid-Oct daily 9am–10pm. $3.* ⚠ ✗ ♿ 🅿 *www.vitrine.net/godbout ☎ 418-568-7306.* Directors Cécile and Claude Grenier have created a warm and intimate museum exhibiting a fine collection of Amerindian arts and Inuit sculptures, mostly from the Northwest Territories. Splendid photographs of arctic animals by Fred Bruemmer are hung throughout the museum. An authentic Algonquin bark canoe is suspended in the pottery workshop.

Continue on Rte. 138 for 29km/18mi, turn right and continue for 12km/7mi.

★ **Phare de Pointe-des-Monts (Pointe-des-Monts Lighthouse)** – *Open Jun 24–Aug daily 9am–7pm. Jun 7–Jun 23 & Sept daily 9am–5pm. $2.50.* ⚠ ✗ 🅿 *☎ 418-939-2332.* Built in 1830, the 28m/92ft lighthouse stands at the point where the St. Lawrence River widens into a gulf. For 150 years, the lighthouse served as a home for the lightkeepers and their families. Today, the interior houses a small museum that recreates the lives and duties of the various keepers; also on display are items salvaged from area shipwrecks. Activities organised here include trout and salmon fishing, deep sea fishing, scuba diving, whale- and seal-watching, and excursions to observe and photograph local fauna, including black bears, ospreys and gannets. A small inn and several vacation cottages are located on the site.

Return to Rte. 138.

Between Pointe-aux-Anglais and Rivière-Pentecôte, the road passes beside beautiful sandy beaches.

Rivière-Pentecôte – *79km/49mi from Godbout.* The village and nearby river were named in the 16C by Jacques Cartier, when he stayed here on Whitsunday *(Pentecôte)*. Rivière-Pentecôte was the birthplace of the North Shore's first newspaper, *L'Écho du Labrador*, founded in 1903 by Joseph Laizé, a Eudist missionary. From the tourist information centre overlooking the village, the **view**★ of the church and the tiny oratory of St. Anne, perched on a cape, is very picturesque.

Port-Cartier – *35km/21mi.* Owing to its deepwater port, this industrial and commercial town has become a major centre for transhipping minerals and cereals in Canada. The town lies on the banks of the Rochers and Dominique Rivers, at the point where they empty into the St. Lawrence. The two islands situated at the mouth of the rivers are devoted to recreational use, including hiking, swimming, camping, picnicking and sport fishing (the region is known for its salmon). Located on Île Patterson is the Taiga, a botanical garden of native plants. On Île McCormick, a café-theatre exhibits the work of local artists.

★**Sept-Îles** – *59km/37mi. See Entry Heading.*

② FROM SEPT-ÎLES TO HAVRE-SAINT-PIERRE
222km/137mi by Rte. 138.

Rivière-au-Tonnerre – *123km/76mi from Sept-Îles.* This pleasant fishing village takes its name from the thunderous rush of nearby waterfalls. Dominating the town centre is the **Église Saint-Hippolyte** (Church of St. Hippolyte; *open Jun 24–early Sept daily 8am–5pm;* ☏ *418-465-2842*). Construction of the church began in 1905, according to plans designed by the parish priest. More than 300 church members each gave three months of work and two cords of wood per winter for its completion (one cord = about 3.5cum/13.7cuft). The numerous carvings on the vault were done by a parishioner using only a penknife.

Longue-Pointe-de-Mingan – *53km/33mi.* Set on a narrow strip of land jutting out into the Gulf of St. Lawrence, Longue-Pointe is considered the gateway to the Mingan Archipelago. An American military base was established here during World War II. Visitors can catch glimpses of the islands of the archipelago from the Rue du Bord-de-la-Mer.
The **centre de recherche et d'interprétation de la Minganie** (*625 Rue du Centre; open late Jun–Aug daily 9am–9pm; mid-Jun–late Jun & early Sept–mid-Sept 9am–6pm;* ♿ ☐ ☏ *418-949-2126*) is a research and interpetation center providing information on the various activities organised by the Mingan Archipelago National Park Reserve, including educational programs and tourist excursions. Also presented here are the natural history of the region and marine mammals of the Gulf of St. Lawrence. Visitors can also make arrangements for **whale-watching cruises** (*depart from Longue-Pointe-de-Mingan mid-Jun–mid-Oct daily at 7:30am; round-trip 8hrs; commentary; reservations required; $65;* ♿ ☐ *Station de recherche des Îles Mingan* ☏ *514-465-9176*).

Mingan – *10km/6mi.* Of Basque origin, the name of this Montagnais reserve, created in 1963, means "strip of land." A trading post and fishing village during the French Regime, Mingan boasts one of the most productive fishing ports along the coast. The Montagnais operate a fish packing plant and marketing company known as Les Crustacés de Mingan. At the village entrance, on Route 138, the **Centre culturel montagnais** (Montagnais Cultural Centre; *open late Jun–mid-Aug daily 9am–6pm;* ☐ ☏ *418-949-2234*) exhibits tools, household items and photos illustrating the heritage of the Montagnais.

★**Montagnais Church** – *Rte. de l'Usine. Open year-round daily 8am–7pm.* ☏ *418-949-2272.* Located near the Cultural Centre, the church was built in 1918 by Jack Maloney, the legendary Jack Monoloy of Gilles Vigneault's song, *Les bouleaux de la rivière Mingan* (The Silver Birches of the Mingan River). In 1972, the church was remodelled in the Montagnais style: the pulpit is decorated with caribou antlers, the Stations of the Cross are painted on skins stretched across frames of birch branches, the baptismal font is hollowed out of a maple trunk, and the tabernacle is in the form of a wigwam.

Havre-Saint-Pierre – *36km/22mi.* This industrial town was first settled in 1857 by Acadian fishermen from the Magdalen Islands. The town's economy was based on marine resources until 1948, when the mining company, QIT-Fer et Titane (Quebec Iron and Titanium), began exploiting the world's largest known ilmenite deposits (naturally occurring iron and titanium oxides), discovered around Lakes Tio and Allard, 43km/27mi north of town.

Centre d'accueil et d'interprétation de la réserve de parc national de l'Archipel-de-Mingan (Welcome and Interpretation Centre of the Mingan Archipelago National Park Reserve) – *975 Rue de l'Escale. Open mid-Jun–late Aug daily 9am–6pm* ♿ ☐ ☏ *418-538-3285 or 418-538-3331 (off season).* The centre displays photographs of flora and fauna found in the Mingan Archipelago and provides information on organised activities on the islands.
Continue to Rue de la Berge and turn right.

Centre culturel et d'interprétation de Havre-Saint-Pierre (Havre-Saint-Pierre Cultural and Interpretation Centre) – *Open mid-Jun–mid-Sept daily 9am–10pm. $2.* ♿ ☎ *418-538-2450.* The tourist information service occupies the former Clarke Trading Company store (1926-1963). The interior has been refurbished to appear as it would have in the 1940s, and displays recall the cultural heritage of the village and its economic evolution. The centre also presents films and lectures on regional themes.

Excursions from Havre-Saint-Pierre

★★Archipel de Mingan – *See Entry Heading.*

★★Île d'Anticosti – *See Entry Heading.*

Havre-Saint-Pierre marks the end of Rte. 138. The Lower North Shore is not linked to the rest of Quebec by road network, although construction is underway on a continuation of Rte. 138 to Baie-Johan-Beetz.

③ FROM HAVRE-SAINT-PIERRE TO BLANC SABLON

The Basse-Côte-Nord (Lower North Shore) marks the eastern extremity of Quebec. The area is bordered by Labrador to the north; the island of Newfoundland lies to the southeast. Many villages along the Lower North Shore are former trading and fishing posts that date back to the French Regime. Yet of the 16 communities established within the 358km/222mi expanse between Kegasha and Blanc-Sablon, 12 are predominantly English-speaking (inhabited by descendants of fishermen from Newfoundland and the English Channel Island of Jersey), three are French and one is Montagnais.

Relais Nordik, Inc. operates a weekly **boat trip★** between Havre-Saint-Pierre and Blanc-Sablon aboard the *Nordik Express.* It is possible to purchase a ticket for passage only, but the plan including cabin and meals is recommended. The boat stops in most of the coastal villages *(depart from Havre-Saint-Pierre Apr–mid-Jan Wed at 10:45pm, arrive at Blanc-Sablon Fri at 7:45pm; one-way including cabin & meals $224.66; round-trip $438.23; reservations required for passage & vehicle transport 30 days in advance;* ▯ *Relais Nordik Inc.* ☎ *418-723-8787; return by plane possible: depart from Blanc-Sablon Mon–Fri at 4:30pm, Sun at 10:30am; one-way 1hr 20min; call for fares; Regionnair* ☎ *418-787-2328).*

Baie-Johan-Beetz – *31/4hrs from Havre-Saint-Pierre.* This small village bears the name of Johan Beetz, a Belgian aristocrat who immigrated to Canada in 1897. He first established a trade in luxury furs. Later on, he became a successful breeder of fur-bearing animals and attained international recognition for his breeding methods and scientific publications. His **house** (1899) is set on a rocky promontory overlooking the bay *(open May–Sept 9am–8pm; reservations required; $2;* ▯ ☎ *418-539-0137).* An accomplished artist, Beetz decorated several doors and walls of his home with his paintings of flowers and animals.

Natashquan – *3 3/4 hours from Baie-Johan-Beetz.* An atmosphere of calm and tranquillity permeates this fishing village, birthplace of the noted poet and singer, Gilles Vigneault. Natashquan was colonized by Acadians from the Magdalen Islands in 1855. On a sandy point jutting out into the St. Lawrence, weathered fishing sheds *(galets)* are remnants of a bygone era. The name Natashquan signifies in Montagnais "the place where they hunt bear." Since 1952, the nearby village of Pointe-Parent has been a Montagnais community.

★Harrington Harbour – *103/4hrs from Natashquan.* Brightly painted, pastel-coloured houses nestled at the foot of a hill welcome the *Nordik Express* as it approaches Harrington Harbor. The charming fishing village is situated on a small island; its port makes it one of the most accessible villages on the journey to Blanc-Sablon. Wide wooden sidewalks and bridges connect the rocky terraces dotted with colourful houses and shops. The large grey building dominating the village was the first hospital of the region and is now a home for the elderly. Nearby, the **craft shop** offers a fine selection of handmade sweaters, parkas and hooked rugs, as well as Montagnais moccasins and mittens.

In the afternoon of the second day, passengers can enjoy spectacular **views★** as the ship meanders by rocky islands speckled with lichens and moss, and skirts towering cliffs on which conifers form patterns of deep green.

Blanc-Sablon – *121/2hrs from Harrington Harbour.* Blanc-Sablon is situated 1.5km/.9mi from the Quebec-Labrador border. Since 1983, the area around the Blanc-Sablon River has been the site of important archaeological excavations, one of which revealed an Amerindian settlement dating back 7,200 years.

Lourdes-de-Blanc-Sablon – *5km/3mi by road.* Situated just west of Blanc-Sablon, this village is the largest of the region and boasts two very important facilities: an airport and a hospital. The town church houses the **Musée Scheffer Museum** (Scheffer

Harrington Harbour

Museum; *open year-round daily 9am–8pm;* 点 🅿 ☎ *418-461-2000*) dedicated to Msgr. Scheffer (1903-1966), first Bishop of Labrador (1946-1966). The mining town of Schefferville was also named after him.

Ferry to Sainte-Barbe, Newfoundland – *Depart May–early Jan (subject to change due to weather and ice conditions). No crossings Dec 25–26. One-way 1hr 30min. Reservations suggested mid-Jun–Oct. $9/person; $18.50/car. Northern Cruiser Ltd.* ☎ *418-461-2056 or 709-931-2309.* Ferry crossings connect Blanc-Sablon with Sainte-Barbe, Newfoundland, located 139km/86mi south of l'Anse-aux-Meadows *(consult THE GREEN GUIDE Canada)*, the site of the oldest known European settlement in North America. Artifacts, including iron work, excavated from the site, are Norse in origin and were dated back to approximately AD 1000 by carbon 14 testing.

Lieu historique national de COTEAU-DU-LAC★

Montérégie

Coteau-du-Lac is located on the northern bank of the St. Lawrence River at the point where it leaves Lake Saint-François. The history of this community is closely linked to the presence of turbulent rapids nearby. Over the years, various canal systems were constructed to avoid the rapids and facilitate navigation. The problem was finally resolved by the construction of the St. Lawrence Seaway.

Access – *Coteau-du-Lac is located approximately 60km/37mi southwest of Montreal by Rte. 20 (Exit 17) and Rte. 338.*

VISIT

Open mid-May–early Sept daily 10am–5pm. Early Sept–early Oct. Wed–Sun 10am–5pm. Rest of the year Mon–Fri 9am–5pm. Closed major holidays except Jul 1. $3. 点 🅿 *www.parcscanada.gc.ca* ☎ *450-763-5631.*

The vestiges of one of the first canal lock systems in North America are located on a pleasant **site**, at the confluence of the St. Lawrence and Delisle Rivers. A brief orientation stop at the Reception Centre, followed by a stroll along numerous walkways and among the ruins will give visitors an idea of how the local inhabitants lived and solved the difficulties of trade and transportation on the St. Lawrence River.

Until the early 20C, the rapids were most treacherous between Montreal and Kingston. The construction of the **Beauharnois canal** and hydroelectric plant in the 1920s necessitated a system of dams and waterworks to divert water into the hydroelectric station. As a result of this diversion, the river level dropped 2.5m/8ft lower than it was at the beginning of the century, and the rapids lost much of their force.

Conquering the rapids – When travelling downriver, the indigenous people who first settled the area portaged their canoes around the most dangerous parts of the rapids. The advent of the fur trade, however, brought crowds of trappers with heavier canoes and more goods to transport. In 1750, the French at Coteau-du-Lac solved the problem by building a *rigolet* canal, actually a stone dike, to facilitate passage to the Great Lakes. The remains of this dike are still visible from the park's walkways. After the American Revolution, British troops established outposts along the St. Lawrence River and the Great Lakes. The *rigolet* canal proved too small for their large boats so the British built a new **canal** in 1779. Approximately 300m/984ft long and 2.5m/8ft deep, the canal incorporated three locks which raised boats 2.7m/9ft. It remained in service until 1845, when the first Beauharnois canal opened. A boardwalk runs through the old, now-dry canal.

The fortification – The strategic importance of the site at Coteau-du-Lac led the British to establish a fortification here, to guard access to the river and protect the provisions intended for soldiers stationed in the Great Lakes area. Archaeological excavations have uncovered various parts of the warehouses and military barracks built during the American Revolution and the War of 1812.

Octagonal Blockhaus – Built during the War of 1812, this unusual eight-sided blockhouse was burned down in 1837 to prevent its falling into the hands of the Patriots. The log exterior and stone foundations were rebuilt by Parks Canada in 1967. It includes a ground floor and an overhanging upper floor. The walls are pierced by gun embrasures. Inside, informative displays describe the transport of goods on the canal.

Île aux COUDRES★★

Charlevoix
Population 1,066 – Map p 80

This enchanting island off the coast of Charlevoix occupies an exceptional **site** overlooking Baie-Saint-Paul. The small island, 11 km/7mi long by 5km/3mi across at its widest point, retains its rural peace and charm to delight the tourists who visit in the summer months. Île aux Coudres was named by Jacques Cartier, in 1535, for the hazel trees *(coudriers)* that once grew there in abundance. The first European settlers arrived in 1728. In addition to farming, they hunted the beluga whale, which they named *marsouin* (white porpoise), for oil. For a long time, the island was part of a seigneury owned by the Quebec Seminary.

Until the 1950s, the island housed several shipbuilding centres that manufactured the sail and motor schooners used for coastal navigation and for hunting the beluga. The centres also constructed heavy canoes allowing the inhabitants to reach the mainland shores even in winter, when the waterways were frozen. It was here that Pierre Perrault, from the National Film Board of Canada, filmed his renowned documentaries on the beluga whale hunt and the Charlevoix *voitures d'eau*, in the 1960s. Through his films, Quebecers discovered the beauty of the Charlevoix region and the Île aux Coudres. Today, these films are recognised internationally as classics in the field of social documentaries.

Crossing the River in Winter – Today, Île aux Coudres is linked to the mainland year-round by ferry. Before this link was established, however, crossing the icy St. Lawrence in the winter months required special skills acquired over many years of practice. The crossing was achieved by a combination of canoeing through the unfrozen waters and getting out of the canoe to pull it over the changing ice floes. This ability to navigate the icy waters is demonstrated each year, in February, at the **Quebec Winter Carnival** *(see Calendar of Events)*.

Access – *Île aux Coudres is about 120km/74mi northeast of Quebec City by Rtes. 138 and 362. The ferry from Saint-Joseph-de-la-Rive docks at the town of Île-aux-Coudres. Depart Apr–Oct daily 7am–11pm every hour. Rest of the year daily 7am–11pm every 2hrs.* ♿ *Société des traversiers du Québec www.traversiers.gouv.qc.ca* ☎ *418-438-2743.*

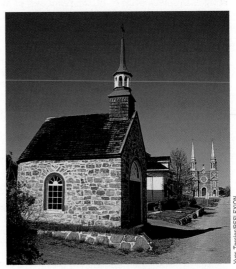

Yves Tessier/REFLEXION

Processional Chapel

93

VISIT

Visitors can make a **tour** of the island by car or on bicycle *(approximately 21km/13mi)*. Beached schooners, remnants of a past age, can be seen in several places. The site of Pointe du Bout d'en Bas, at the northern edge of the island, provides a picturesque **view★** of the lush green landscape of the village of Les Éboulements.

★ **Musée Les Voitures d'Eau (Schooner Museum)** – *In Île-aux-Coudres. Open mid-Jun–early-Sept daily 10am–5pm. Mid-May–mid-Jun & mid-Sept–mid-Oct weekends 10am–5pm. $4.* ⓺ ▯ ☎ *418-438-2208.* Devoted to the schooners known as *voitures d'eau,* literally "water cars," this maritime museum presents displays and photographs of a mode of transportation which, until the 1960s and the development of a road system, was a way of life for the islanders. The schooner *Mont-Saint-Louis,* built in 1939 and in service for 35 years, can be boarded.

Église Saint-Louis (Church of St. Louis) – *In Île-aux-Coudres. Open year-round daily 8am–6pm.* ⓺ ▯ ☎ *418-438-2442.* Built in 1885, this church boasts a charming interior decor and an altar sculpted by Louis Jobin. The statues of St. Louis and St. Flavien were carved by François Baillairgé between 1804 and 1810. The care with which the clothing and the anatomy of the statues were executed reflects the great talent of this eminent artist. Note the two **processional chapels** *(about 200m/656ft before and after the church),* built by volunteers in 1837.

★ **Les moulins de l'Isle-aux-Coudres (Isle-aux-Coudres Mills)** – *In Île-aux-Coudres. Open Jun 24–early Sept daily 9am–7pm. Late May–Jun 23 & early Sept–mid-Oct daily 10am–5pm. $2.75.* ▯ *www.charlevoix.qc.ca/moulins* ☎ *418-438-2184.* A stone windmill (1836) stands next to a watermill (1825) on this site beside the Rouge River. The two mills, respectively built by Thomas and Alexis Tremblay, operated until 1948. Restored by the Quebec government, they provide a rare opportunity to compare the two different mechanisms. An **interpretation centre** in the former miller's house explains their history. Visitors can also buy wheat flour ground by millstones. Farm equipment dating from the turn of the century is on display outside the mills.

DRUMMONDVILLE
Centre-du-Québec
Population 44,882

Drummondville was founded by British authorities after the War of 1812 as a military outpost on the Saint-François River. Frederick George Heriot, a Scottish officer, established a settlement here in 1815, naming it after the British governor, Sir Gordon Drummond. At Heriot's death in 1843, the community was well established, operating several riverside mills, factories and stores. The nearby falls were later harnessed for hydroelectricity.

Today, Drummondville is an important industrial centre, producing textiles and other manufactured goods. Every July, the **Mondial des cultures de Drummondville** is celebrated throughout the city.

Access – *Drummondville is 110km/68mi east of Montreal by Rte. 20 (Exit 177).*

SIGHT

★ **Village québécois d'antan (Quebecois Village of Olden Times)** – *Rue Montplaisir, Rte. 20 (Exit 181). Open Jun–Sept daily 10am–6pm. $15.* ✗ ▯ *www.villagequebecois.qc.ca* ☎ *819-478-1441.* As the village represents the history of Quebec, knowledge of French is essential for understanding the guides, signs and brochures. English-speaking visitors are advised to tour the village with someone who can act as an interpreter. Tours in English (large groups only) can be arranged in advance. The French-language multimedia extravaganza Légendes Fantastiques ($30) begins at sundown Wed–Sat.

This village recreates life in the region between 1810 and 1910. About 70 authentic period buildings have been brought from their original sites to this wooded terrain near the Saint-François River. Each dwelling, shop and barn is "inhabited" by a guide in period costume who welcomes visitors and explains the lifestyle of the former occupants. The structures exemplify a broad variety of architectural styles, from the log cabins of the first settlers through the *maison québécoise* with its cantilevered roof, to the mansard-roofed dwellings introduced by the Loyalists after the American Revolution.

Note in particular the village **church**, a reconstruction of Drummondville's Church of St. Frederick (1822); the stained-glass windows (1950) by Guido Nincheri were created for the Chapel of Mont-Saint-Antoine in Montreal, and brought to the village in 1984. The neighbouring presbytery (1833) is an excellent example of the *maison québécoise.* The Townships school (1892) is divided into two rooms, one for boys and one for girls. Visitors can tour the homes of the apothecary, the shoemaker and the notary, as well as the forge, the carding and saw mills, and the farm (1895) with its stables for horses and oxen. A covered bridge (1868) from Stanbridge spans a small stream. In the operator's home (1910), early telephones and an 1876 switchboard are exhibited. Visitors can buy bread made as it was in the 1870s, eat meals typical of the period, and have their photographs taken in period costumes.

EXCURSIONS

Domaine Trent (Trent Manor) – *In Parc des Voltigeurs, Rte. 20 (Exit 181). Open year-round daily.* ✗ 🅿 ☏ *819-472-3662.* Former officer of the British Navy, George Norris Trent decided to retire in Canada, and commissioned this handsome stone manor

© Malak, Ottawa

Life in the Village

house (1837) beside the Saint-François River. The house was expanded in 1848, and his descendants lived here until 1963. Today the building houses a museum featuring the rich culinary traditions of Quebec.

Moulin à laine d'Ulverton (Ulverton Woolen Mills) – *About 30km/19mi south by Rte. 143, turn right at Ulverton. Also accessible from Rte. 55. Visit by guided tour (1hr) only, Jun–Oct daily 10am–5pm. $5.* ✗ 🅿 *www.moulin.qc.ca* ☏ *819-826-3157.* The large shingled structure of this former carding mill rises above the Ulverton River, a tributary of the Saint-François River. Built by William Dunkerley in 1849, it changed hands several times. The mill fell into decay after 1949 but was renovated in the early 1980s. The operation of early 20C carding and spinning machines is demonstrated inside the mill.

Asbestos – *Asbestos is situated 60km/37mi southeast of Drummondville by Rtes. 143, 116 and 255; 170km/106mi from Montreal by Rtes. 20, 55 and 116; 60km/37mi north of Sherbrooke by Rtes. 143 and 249.* The community of Asbestos grew and prospered around a gigantic, crater-like open-pit asbestos mine, the second largest in the world. It is currently 335m/1,099ft deep, approximately 2km/1.2mi across, and yields 650 tonnes of fibre annually. The deposits extend to a depth of more than 1,450m/4,756ft. The complex process of separating the fibre from the rock is carried out in the 12-storey mill. Over 100 different types of asbestos, graded according to their temperature resistance, are produced here. Visitors can observe the functioning of the mine from a lookout.

Musée minéralogique et d'histoire minière d'Asbestos – *104 Rue Letendre, off Rte. 255. Follow signs. Open Jun 24–Labour Day Wed–Sun 10am–5pm. Apr–Jun & Sept–Nov by appointment only.* ☏ *819-879-6444, off-season* ☏ *819-879-5308.* At the Mineralogical and Mining History Museum, numerous samples of asbestos and ore-bearing rocks are displayed, alongside information on the history of the Jeffrey Mine and the entire asbestos region. A film *(20min)* explains the blasting, drilling and crushing methods used to extract asbestos fibre from the rock.

Cantons de l'EST★★

Cantons de l'Est
Map pp 98-99

Contrary to their name, the Eastern Townships (*Estrie* in French) occupy the south-west part of Quebec along the United States border. The area was thus named in the 18C because of its location east of Montreal. The Western Townships were located in what is now Ontario, but that designation is no longer used.

The Townships, as they are generally called, are situated in a mountainous region of the Appalachian chain, which extends from Alabama in the southern United States to the province of Newfoundland. In the Townships, tree-covered hills rising to nearly 1,000m/3,280ft are interspersed with deep valleys and lovely lakes. The region has become a popular retreat for Montrealers attracted by the recreational activities, including nautical sports in the summertime and skiing during the winter.

Historical Notes

After the American Revolution (1775-1783), the uninhabited land along the border to the southeast and southwest of Montreal was surveyed by the British authorities and plots were granted to Loyalists who had left the United States after the war. These first settlers were mainly from New England, and the towns and villages they established reflect this heritage. After 1850, however, increasing numbers of French-speaking people moved into the region; today its population is for the majority francophone.

Access – *Cowansville is about 80km/50mi from Montreal by Rtes. 10 and 139. Sherbrooke is 150km/93mi from Montreal by Rtes. 10 and 112.*

1 ROUND TRIP FROM COWANSVILLE *159km/99mi.*

Cowansville – Located on the south arm of the South Yamaska River, Cowansville is today a small industrial centre. This predominantly francophone community was founded by Loyalists in 1802, and named for its first postmaster, Peter Cowan. Numerous Victorian houses line Rue Principale and Rue Sud in the residential area. The Bromont ski centre is located nearby.

Follow Rue Sud (becomes Rte. 202 after crossing the Rte. 104 bypass), to Dunham.

Dunham – *10km/6mi.* One of the first Loyalist settlements, Dunham was established in 1796 on land granted to Thomas Dunn, a British administrator. The village is known for its vineyards. Its charm is enhanced by three steepled churches (Roman Catholic, Anglican and United) and several stone houses.

Continue west on Rte. 202 to Stanbridge East (10km/6mi).

The road between Dunham and Stanbridge East is often called the **Wine Route** (Route des vins) because it crosses the only region in Quebec where the climate is favourable to the cultivation of grapes. Elsewhere, the climate is too harsh and wine is made from imported, unprocessed grape juice.

★**Musée de Missisquoi (Missisquoi Museum)** – *In Stanbridge East. Open late May–mid-Oct daily 10am–5pm. Mid-Oct–late May Mon–Fri 9am–4:30pm. $3.50.* ▣ ☎ *450-248-3153.* Three buildings make up the rural museum created by the Missisquoi Historical Society. The main edifice is a three-storey brick **mill** built by Zébulon Cornell, a Vermont native, in 1832 to replace an earlier stone structure on the picturesque Brochets River (Pike River). When the mill closed in 1963, it was converted into a museum. Rooms on the main floor recreate life in the 19C, and the displays on the upper floor illustrate various activities and handicrafts of the era. From the basement, visitors can see the original water wheel, which still turns in the river current.

Farm, Eastern Townships

To the east *(20 River St.)*, **Hodge's General Store** is stocked with goods and provisions from the period, thus preserving its 19C charm. **Bill's Barn** *(River St., near the Rte. 202 intersection)* displays traditional farm machinery.

Take Rte. 237 southeast to Frelighsburg.

Frelighsburg – *10km/6mi.* A grist mill was established in 1794 on this enchanting site in the Brochets River valley, near Mt. Pinacle. A small community soon developed and was later named for Abram Freligh, a physician who moved here from New York in 1800. Today, Frelighsburg is best known for its apple orchards.

Turn left on Rue Principale (Rte. 213). After 2km/1.2mi turn right on Rue Selby, continue for 4km/2.5mi and turn right on Rue Dymond (proceed cautiously on gravel roads), which becomes Rue Jordan after 3km/2mi. Continue for 10km/6mi; turn left on Rte. 139 to Sutton and continue 2km/1.2mi.

The road passes to the north of **Le Pinacle** (675m/2,214ft), providing superb **views**★ of the Sutton valley.

★**Sutton** – *21km/13mi.* Mt. Sutton (972m/3,188ft) towers over this lovely winter resort, especially popular with skiing enthusiasts. The first settlers arrived in 1795 and constructed a foundry in the valley. In 1871, a new railway opened the area to vacationers. Today, numerous arts and crafts studios and shops enhance the town's charm.

Drive south on Rte. 139 for 2km/1.2mi, turn left on Rue Brookfall and immediately right on Chemin Scenic. After 11km/7mi, turn left on Rte. 105A and left again on Rte. 243 to Mansonville (24km/15mi).

The road offers several entrancing **views**★ of the Sutton area, then follows the valley of the Missisquoi River. The Jay Mountains in Vermont are visible to the south.

Mansonville – *37km/23mi.* This community in the Missisquoi River valley is named for its first settler, Robert Manson, who moved from Vermont in 1803 and built a grist mill and a saw mill. The town has a New England-style village green and also claims one of the few remaining round barns in Quebec *(visible from Main St. across from the Church of St. Cajétan)*. The circular structure was conceived by the Shakers, a religious sect of the Quakers. The purpose of the round barn was to keep the devil from haunting any corner.

Mt. Owl's Head – *12km/7mi, through Vale Perkins.* This mountain (751m/2,463ft) was named after Chief Owl, an Abenaki Indian. According to legend, his profile could be seen on the mountain after his death. Today, Owl's Head is a popular ski resort. The path leading to the top *(climb of about 1hr)* affords spectacular **views**★★ of Lake Memphrémagog.

Return to Mansonville. Take Rte. 243 to South Bolton (13km/8mi).

★**Detour to Saint-Benoît-du-Lac** – *26km/16mi round-trip from South Bolton. Take Rte. 245 to Bolton-Centre (5km/ 3mi), and turn right towards Austin. Turn right again on Fisher Rd., following signs. See Entry Heading.*

Return to South Bolton.

★**Lac-Brome (Knowlton)** – *14km/7mi from South Bolton.* Part of the municipality of Lac-Brome, the community of Knowlton enjoys a pleasant setting on Lake Brome. Founded by New England settlers in the early 19C, the town was named for Paul Knowlton, who built the community grist mill and a general store in 1834. Many of the brick and stone buildings have been converted into boutiques, art galleries and antique shops. Just to the south lies the community of Brome, home of the **Brome Agricultural Fair** *(see Calendar of Events)*, the largest annual agricultural event of the area.

★**Musée historique du comté de Brome** (Brome County Historical Museum) – *130 Rue Lakeside (Rte. 243). Open mid-May–mid-Sept Mon–Sat 10am–4:30pm, Sun 11am–4:30pm. $3.50.* ▣ ☎ 450-243-6782. This museum comprises several period buildings. The old Knowlton "Academy" (1854) offers the chance to see a schoolroom of yesteryear.

The Martin Annex houses military exhibits including a **Fokker DVII**, a German World War I fighter plane acquired for the museum by Senator G. G. Foster, a Knowlton resident. In the Courthouse (1854), a renovated reception room evokes the solemn atmosphere of a turn-of-the-century court. A recreated general store occupies the Fire Hall (1904).

Return to Cowansville (20km/12mi) by Rte. 104.

② ROUND TRIP FROM SHERBROOKE *153km/95mi.*

Leave Sherbrooke and take Rte. 143 to Lennoxville.

Lennoxville – *5km/3mi.* British Loyalists founded Lennoxville in 1794, naming the town for Charles Lennox, Duke of Richmond, who became Governor-in-Chief of British North America in 1818. The town is located at the junction of the Massawippi and Saint-François Rivers, a site formerly occupied by the Abenaki and later by French missionaries. Lennoxville is home to an agricultural research centre.

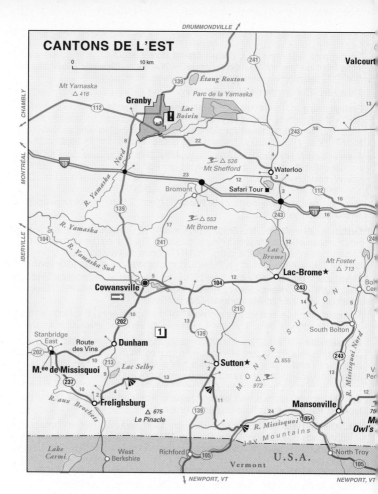

CANTONS DE L'EST

Bishop's University – Educational and cultural centre for the Estrie's anglophone community, this institution of higher education (1843), features medieval-style buildings surrounding a picturesque quadrangle laced with walking paths. Stroll over to **Saint Mark Chapel**, a Gothic Revival edifice adorned with luminous stained-glass windows and richly carved woodwork. In the manner of traditional collegiate chapels, the benches on each side face each other across the centre aisle.

Continue south on Rte. 143 for 3km/2mi, then turn left on Rte. 147 to Compton.

Compton – *17km/10mi.* This quiet village was the birthplace of **Louis-Stephen Saint-Laurent** (1882-1973), twelfth prime minister of Canada. The eldest of seven children, born to a French Canadian storekeeper and an Irish schoolteacher, Saint-Laurent studied law at Laval University. He went into private practice and soon gained recognition for his eloquence in both English and French. At the age of sixty, after a long and successful career as a lawyer, Saint-Laurent decided to enter politics. He was asked by Prime Minister Mackenzie King to serve as his Quebec lieutenant during World War II, and succeeded Mr. King as head of the Liberal Party in 1948. An ardent Canadian nationalist, "Uncle Louis," as he was fondly called, fought to establish a distinct Canadian identity during his years as prime minister (1948-1957).

★ **Louis S. St-Laurent National Historic Site** – *On Rue Principale (Rte. 147) in Compton. Open mid-May–early-Sept daily 10am–5pm. Early-Sept–mid-Oct daily 10am–noon & 1pm–5pm. $3.* & *www.parcscanada.gc.ca* ☎ *819-835-5448.* The authentically recreated general store of J.B.M. Saint-Laurent, the prime minister's father, is stocked with replicas of the goods sold here at the turn of the century. During its heyday, the general store served as a place for locals to visit and exchange ideas; politics were a frequent topic of discussion. Visitors can use headphones to eavesdrop on simulated conversations around the potbellied stove. A **multimedia biography** *(20min)* presents the highlights of Saint-Laurent's life and career. Also open to visitors is the simple clapboard house full of mementos of the Saint-Laurent family, who lived in it until 1969.

Coaticook – *14km/9mi.* This little community on the Coaticook River takes its name from the Abenaki word *koatikeku,* meaning "river of the land of pines." The first settler, Richard Baldwin, recognised the economic potential of harnessing the falls. Today, Coaticook is a small industrial town and the centre of a thriving dairy industry.

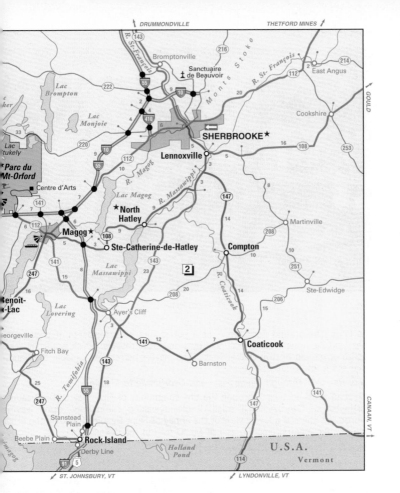

★ **Parc de la Gorge de Coaticook** – *Access from Rte. 147 at northern edge of town. Open Jun–Aug daily 9am–8pm. May & Sept–Oct daily 10am–5pm. Nov–Apr 9am–5pm. $7.* ✗ 🅿 ☎ *819-849-2331.* For nearly a kilometre, the Coaticook River is enclosed in a narrow, rocky gorge whose sides rise to 50m/165ft, then turns at a sharp angle and tumbles over several sets of falls. Whether skiing or hiking, you can make beautiful discoveries along the several kilometres of scenic pathway. A suspended footbridge (169m/554ft) affords a nice **view** of the gorge.

Musée Beaulne – *96 Rue de l'Union. From Rte. 141 (Rue Main), turn left on Rue Lovell at railway tracks, left again on Rue Norton, then right on Rue Union. Open mid-May–mid-Sept daily 11am–5pm. Rest of the year Wed–Sun 1pm–4pm. Closed Dec 25–Jan 1. $3.50.* 🅰 🅿 *www.museebeaulne.qc.ca* ☎ *819-849-6560.* Take a turn through time at this museum located in the refurbished **Château Norton★**, a magnificent mansion (1912) owned by **Arthur Osmond Norton** (1845-1919), proprietor of the most important manufacturer of railway jacks in the world at the turn of the century. Rooms, particularly the Victorian living room (adorned in fine oak panelling) and dining room, have been restored and decorated with period furniture.

From the town centre, take Rte. 141 towards Magog for 19km/12mi and turn left on Rte. 143. Continue 18km/11mi, crossing over Rte. 55 to Rock Island.

Rock Island – *37km/23mi.* Located on a rocky island in the Tomifobia River, this town overlooks the picturesque river valley.

The Tomifobia River marks the Canadian-American border. Vehicles crossing the bridge must proceed through US Customs (on the right) before continuing into Vermont or returning to Canada.

L'opéra et la bibliothèque Haskell (Haskell Free Library and Opera House) – *Just before reaching the US border on Rte. 143, turn left and cross the wooden bridge, then turn right on Rue Church. The Opera House is on the left, with the entrance in Vermont. Open year-round Tue–Sat 10am–5pm (Thu 8pm). Closed major holidays. $2.* 🅰 *www.haskellopera.org* ☎ *819-876-2471.* Martha Stewart Haskell funded the construction of this handsome building between 1901 and 1904. The half-stone, half-brick turreted building, erected in memory of Haskell's husband, sits squarely on the Canadian-American border; the line of demarcation is indicated on

North Hatley

the floor. The ground floor serves as a public library for residents of both countries, and the upper floor is occupied by a delightful theatre, which is a small-scale replica of the old Boston Opera House. The players perform in Canada; their audience sits in the United States.

Take Rte. 247 through Beebe Plain and Georgeville to Magog.

The road veers eastward through the tiny community of Fitch Bay before heading northwest to Georgeville, a small, English-speaking community. Upon leaving Georgeville, there is a lovely view of the abbey of Saint-Benoît-du-Lac on the other side of Lake Memphrémagog and of Mt. Orford in the distance.

★**Magog** – *41km/25mi. See Entry Heading.*

Leave Magog on Rte. 108.

Sainte-Catherine-de-Hatley – *8km/5mi.* Situated atop a hill in the centre of town, the Sanctuaire Saint-Christophe (Sanctuary of St. Christopher) affords expansive **views** of Lake Magog and Mt. Orford.

★**North Hatley** – *9km/6mi.* North Hatley (named for an English village near Cambridge) occupies a lovely **site** on the northern bank of Lake Massawippi where the river of the same name leaves the lake. A drive along the lakeshore provides glimpses of attractive homes and inns.

Return to Sherbrooke (11km/7mi) by Rte. 143.

Parc national FORILLON★★

Gaspésie

Map p 105

Created in 1970, **Forillon National Park** is located on the eastern tip of the Gaspé Peninsula, where the Gulf of St. Lawrence meets the Bay of Gaspé. The majestic, remarkably diverse landscape (245sq km/95sq mi), created largely by erosive forces, includes limestone cliffs towering over the sea; mountains of spruce, fir, poplar and cedar; wildflower meadows; and pebbly beaches tucked away in coves. Visitors can observe black bears, beavers, fox, moose, and porcupines; seagulls, cormorants, kittiwakes, and guillemots; seals and occasionally whales. In addition, the park provides a great variety of recreational activities.

Access – *The park is located 899km/557mi northeast of Quebec City on Rte. 132.*

Activities – *More than 40km/25mi of trails are maintained for hiking, and visitors can enjoy swimming, scuba diving, fishing, biking, and horseback riding. Campgrounds are located in the park at Des-Rosiers, Cap Bon Ami and Petit-Gaspé, and there are numerous picnic areas.*

VISIT

Open daily year-round. $3.75. ⚠ ✗ ♿ 🅿 www.parkscanada.gc.ca/forillon ☎ 418-368-5505.

Interpretation Centre – *Near Cap-des-Rosiers in the northern sector (Secteur nord) of the park. Open Jun–Aug daily 9am–6pm. Sept–mid-Oct daily 10am–5pm.* ♿ ☏ *418-892-5572.* An informative exhibit describes the history of fishing in the region and the interrelation between land and sea. Aquariums house many examples of marine life. Visitors can also see films about the flora, fauna and geology of the park. Pleasure cruises depart from the dock near the centre.

Cap Bon Ami – *3km/2mi south of the Interpretation Centre by a secondary road.* From the picnic lookout and along the walkway leading to the beach, **views★★** of the sea and the limestone cliffs of Cap Bon Ami are magnificent.

Return to Rte. 132, and follow signs leading to the southern sector of the park. At the junction with the secondary road, turn left.

★**Grande-Grave** – *16.5km/10mi from the Interpretation Centre.* A thriving fishing community from the 19C to the mid-20C, this small village was inhabited by settlers from the Channel Islands of Jersey and Guernsey. Today, several buildings have been restored to reflect the style of the 1920s. The first floor of the **Hyman Store** is stocked with goods that would have been found in a general store at that time. On the second floor, an exhibit describes the activities of fishermen and their families throughout the year.

Nearby, in **Anse-Blanchette**, stands the brightly painted house that belonged to Xavier Blanchette in the late 19C. The interior and outbuildings, including the *chafauds*, or racks for drying fish, recreate the life of a self-sufficient fisherman.

Continue on secondary road to Anse-Saint-Georges and Anse-aux-Sauvages.

★**Cap Gaspé** – *8km/5mi round-trip (at least 3hrs) on foot from l'Anse-aux-Sauvages.* This pleasant walk through newly forested lands that were cleared at the turn of the century to build homes for fishermen offers **views★** of the Bay of Gaspé and the Île Bonaventure.

Return to Rte. 132.

On the way back to Route 132, the road skirts the southern sector of the park, site of a Protestant church, an amphitheatre, a campground and a recreational and touristic centre.

Fort-Péninsule – *8km/5mi.* The blockhaus built here during World War II served as a complement to the naval base at Sandy Beach, on the south shore of the Bay of Gaspé. It was built by the Canadian government to prevent German submarines from entering the St. Lawrence.

Penouille – *1km/.6mi.* The sandy shores and taiga of this peninsula provide a sharp contrast to the immense limestone capes and boreal forests found in the rest of the park. Penouille, an old basque word meaning "peninsula," is the site of many organised activities in summer. The **beach** is the most popular one in the park.

Cap Bon Ami

GASPÉ★

Gaspésie
Population 16,517
Map p 105

On July 24, 1534, the Breton explorer Jacques Cartier set foot on this site and took possession of the land in the name of François I, King of France. Located on a hillside where the York River empties into the Bay of Gaspé, the city is now the administrative and commercial centre of the peninsula. The name Gaspé is derived from the Micmac word *gespec*, meaning "limits of the land."

Access – *Gaspé is located 738km/458mi northeast of Lévis (Quebec City) by Rte. 132.*

SIGHTS

★**Musée de la Gaspésie (Museum of the Gaspé Peninsula)** – *80 Blvd. Gaspé (Rte. 132). Open Jun 24–Labour Day daily 8:30am–8:30pm. Rest of the year Tue–Fri 9am–5pm, weekends 1pm–5pm. $4.* & 🅿 ☎ *418-368-1534.* This regional museum is dedicated to the preservation of Gaspésian culture and ethnological heritage. Its permanent exhibit highlights historical events, notably Jacques Cartier's discovery of the peninsula; the native Micmac population; and regional geography. In addition, the exhibit presents the lifestyles and traditions of the peninsula's Gaspesian inhabitants. Near the entrance to the museum is a handsome **quilt** bearing the symbols of 58 Gaspésian villages; it is the result of a collective effort by regional women's groups. Three other rooms house temporary displays of local art and regional heritage. Set on Jacques-Cartier Point, the museum offers good **views**★ of the Bay of Gaspé and the Forillon peninsula.

Jacques-Cartier Monument – In the park next to the museum, six cast-iron steles form a monument (1984) commemorating the discovery of Canada and the first encounter between Cartier and the native population. The dolmen-shaped steles, adorned with bas-reliefs illustrating Cartier's arrival in the New World on one side and excerpts of texts written by Cartier and Father LeClercq on the other, are the work of Jean-Julien and Gil Bourgault-Legros of Saint-Jean-Port-Joli.

From the museum, turn left onto Blvd. Gaspé in the direction of the town centre. At the traffic light, turn right onto Rue Adams, continue for two blocks and turn left onto Rue Jacques-Cartier; the cathedral is on the left.

★**Cathédrale du Christ-Roi (Christ the King Cathedral)** – *Open year-round daily 8am–7pm.* & 🅿 ☎ *418-368-5541.* The foundations of this cathedral were laid in 1934 to mark the 400th anniversary of Cartier's discovery of Canada, but financial constraints postponed its completion until 1969. Designed by Gérard Notebaert, the cathedral is distinguished by its unusual lines and a cedar exterior that blends into the environment.

In the strikingly simple interior, sunlight filters past massive beams creating a warm glow on the wooden sheathing. Claude Théberge designed the stained-glass window made of antique glass set in lead and the bronze representation of the triumphant Christ (Christ-Roi). The fresco, donated by France in 1934, illustrates Cartier's arrival in the New World.

Beside the cathedral stands the **Croix de Gaspé** (Gaspé Cross), also known as the Jacques-Cartier Cross. The 9.6m/31.5ft cross was carved in a single block of granite from a quarry near Quebec City. It was unveiled during the 1934 celebrations.

GASPÉSIE★★★

Gaspésie
Map pp 104-105

The Gaspé peninsula, commonly known as the "Gaspésie" in French, is bounded by New Brunswick and the Baie des Chaleurs to the south, the Gulf of St. Lawrence to the east, and the St. Lawrence River to the north. Tiny fishing villages nestled in coves dot the wild, rocky and sea-battered northern coast of the peninsula, culminating in the breathtaking beauty of Forillon and Percé. In the Chaleur Bay area, to the south, agriculture and forestry form the backbone of economic activity, but the scenic wonders of both coasts have made tourism the region's principal source of revenue. The spectacular scenery is complemented by the charm of the peninsula's simple lifestyle; its people are close to nature and respectful of the values and traditions of another age. The interior of the peninsula, with the exception of the mining village of Murdochville, is a dense wilderness of mountains and forests.

① FROM SAINTE-FLAVIE TO PARC DE LA GASPÉSIE

167km/104mi on Rte. 132.

Sainte-Flavie – This agricultural village and resort town is the gateway to the Gaspé Peninsula.

Le grand rassemblement by Marcel Gagnon

Centre d'art Marcel Gagnon (Marcel Gagnon Art Centre) – *564 Rte. de la Mer. Open mid-April–mid-Oct daily 8am–9pm.* ✗ ♿ 🅿 ☎ *418-775-2829.* The main attraction in this small arts centre is *The Great Gathering (Le grand rassemblement),* contemporary artist Marcel Gagnon's composite sculpture of more than 80 figures emerging from the St. Lawrence River. A permanent exhibit of the artist's paintings and smaller sculptures occupies the interior, and visitors can witness Gagnon himself at work in his studio.

★ **CISA, Centre d'interprétation du saumon atlantique** (Atlantic Salmon Interpretation Centre) – *900 Rte. de la Mer. Open late Jun–mid-Oct daily 9am–5pm. $7.* ✗ ♿ 🅿 ☎ *418-775-2969.* The informative exhibit highlights the life cycle of the Atlantic salmon. Photographs, models and a film document the importance of this fish to Quebec's economy and illustrate conservation measures intended to ensure its protection and reproduction. Aquariums enable the visitor to view salmon in various stages of development. A guided tour *(45min)* by minibus leads to the foot of the Mitis River hydroelectric dam, where visitors can observe salmon being lifted over the dam so that they can continue their upstream journey to the spawning grounds.

ADDRESS BOOK

For a legend of price listings for hotels and restaurants, see p 170. Other accommodations and restaurants listed under Percé and Parc de la Gaspésie.

Staying in Gaspésie

Centre d'art Marcel Gagnon – *564 Route de la Mer, Sainte-Flavie.* ✗ 🅿 ☎ *418-775-2829. 10 rooms.* **$$** *Description see above.* Simple and clean characterize the comfortable rooms located on the upper floor of the art centre. Breakfast is served in the restaurant on the ground floor where *Le grand rassemblement (The Great Gathering)* is ever-present.

Gîte l'Écume de mer – *21 Rue des Écoliers, La Martre.* ☎ *418-288-5274. 4 rooms.* **$** For a warm welcome and one of the hands-down most beautiful and delectable breakfasts in North America (ask for the crêpes), stop for a night or two at this cozy B&B run by the charming owner, Andréa Neu. While the two bathrooms are shared, her impeccably kept rooms will make you feel more than at home.

Dining in Gaspésie

Chez Pierre – *96 Boul. Perron Ouest, Tourrelle.* ☎ *418-763-7446.* **$$ Seafood**. For a proper introduction to the bounty of the St. Lawrence, take time for a meal at Chez Pierre. Order from the menu or try the *Dégustation Poissons* (fish sampler), a survey of delights such as profiteroles of crab and *filet de morue matanaise* (filet of Matane cod). Reasonable prices, efficient service, and a nice view of the water compliment the gastronomic experience.

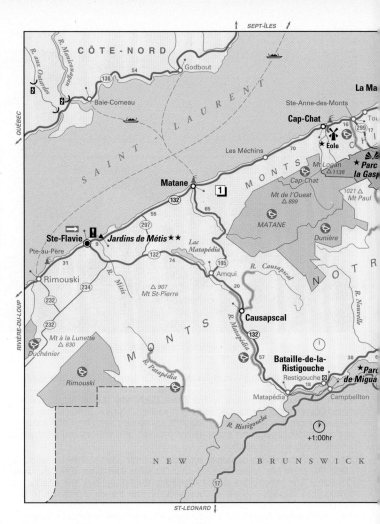

★★Jardins de Métis (Reford Gardens) – *9km/6mi. See Entry Heading.*

Matane – *55km/34mi.* The community of Matane is renowned for its salmon fishing and shrimp production. In the town centre, behind the city hall, a 44m/144ft **fish ladder★** *(passe migratoire)* built on the Mathieu-d'Amours dam enables salmon to travel upstream from mid-June to October *(visitors can view the salmon passing by through porthole windows).* Beside the dam, Parc des Îles (Islands Park) offers various recreational activities, including a playground, beach, picnic area and theatre. A lighthouse built in 1906 now serves as the town's tourist information office.

Cap-Chat – *70km/43mi. To see the wind turbine, turn right 3km/2mi west of Cap-Chat bridge.* Towering above the landscape at 110m/361ft, the vertical-axis **wind turbine★**, named Éole, is the largest of its kind in the world *(visit by 35min guided tour only, Jun 24–Oct daily 8:30am–5:30pm; reservations suggested; $7;* ♿ 🅿 ☎ *418-786-5719).* A rotor with two curved blades and a maximum speed of 13.25rpm is attached to a central column harnessing wind power into mechanical energy, which is then converted into electricity by means of a generator. Éole, a joint project of the National Research Council and Hydro-Québec, has been in full automatic operation since 1988. This feat of engineering was realized by LavalinTech of Montreal. On the tour of the facility, guides describe the turbine mechanism and discuss alternative energy sources for the future.

Cap-Chat Rock – *From Rte. 132, turn left 2km/1.2mi west of village. Follow gravel road for .5km/.3mi.* The village drew its name from this rock thought to resemble a sitting cat *(chat).* Nearby, a lighthouse dating from 1871 serves as the starting point for several nature trails.

★Parc de la Gaspésie (Gaspésie Park) – *33km/20mi. After 16km/10mi, take Rte. 299 from Sainte-Anne-des-Monts. See Entry Heading.*

② FROM PARC DE LA GASPÉSIE TO GASPÉ *259km/160mi.*

Return to Sainte-Anne-des-Monts and continue on Rte. 132 to La Martre.

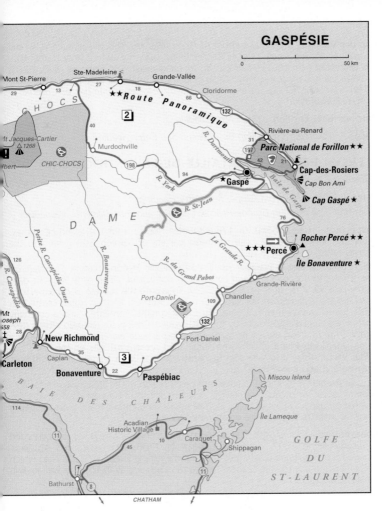

GASPÉSIE

0   50 km

La Martre – *26km/16mi.* From this little village perched atop a promontory, the **view** encompasses the surrounding capes and the ocean. The red octagonal **lighthouse** (phare) and adjoining building house temporary exhibits *(open Jun 24–Aug daily 9am–5pm; $2; ⚒ ৬ 🅿 ☎ 418-288-5605).*

★★Scenic Route from La Martre to Rivière-au-Renard – *153km/95mi.* Route 132 follows the contours of the coastline, up and over rocky cliffs, affording splendid views of hills, valleys, picturesque fishing villages and the ocean. In the region of **Mont-Saint-Pierre**, shale cliffs rim the bay, and at **Sainte-Madeleine-de-la-Rivière-Madeleine**, the lighthouse and surrounding buildings grace the lush, green hills. From the hilltop before arriving at **Grande-Vallée**, the view of the village and its bay is superb. In the town centre stands a covered bridge dating from 1923. Past the bustling fishing village of **Rivière-au-Renard**, located at the northern tip of Forillon National Park, expansive views sweep across fields to the Gulf of St. Lawrence.

Lighthouse at Cap-des-Rosiers

105

Cap-des-Rosiers – *21km/13mi from Rivière-au-Renard.* This village, named for the abundance of wild roses Jacques Cartier found when he arrived here in the 16C, has witnessed numerous shipwrecks off its rocky coast. The **lighthouse** *(37m/121ft)* is the tallest in Canada *(visit by 30min guided tour only, mid-Jun–Labour Day daily 10am–7pm; $2.50; for information: Cap-des-Rosiers Chamber of Commerce ☎ 418-892-5263).*

★★ **Parc national Forillon** – *See Entry Heading.*

★ **Gaspé** – *42km/26mi from Cap-des-Rosiers. See Entry Heading.*

③ FROM PERCÉ TO BATAILLE-DE-LA-RISTIGOUCHE
262km/162mi.

★★★ **Percé** – *76km/47mi from Gaspé. See Entry Heading.*

Take Rte. 132 through Grande-Rivière, Chandler and Port-Daniel to Paspébiac.

Paspébiac – *109km/68mi.* In 1767, Charles Robin, from the Island of Jersey, chose this location to establish the headquarters of his cod fishing empire, the Charles Robin Company (CRC).

Site historique du Banc-de-Paspébiac (Banc-de-Paspébiac Historic Site) – *Turn left off Rte. 132 onto Rte. du Banc and continue to waterfront. Open early Jun–Oct daily 9am–6pm. $5. ✗ ᰔ ▯ ☎ 418-752-6229.* To ensure the success of his exports of dried, salted cod (known as "Gaspé Cure") to Europe, Charles Robin created an entire town, complete with a naval yard, blacksmiths, carpenters and a company store. Eleven buildings erected by the CRC around 1783 were restored after a devastating fire in 1964. Seven of them (including a huge warehouse, a forge and a boatbuilder's shed) are open to the public, and present exhibits on the dried cod trade. Visitors may also view live demonstrations of such traditional activities as net-mending and barge-building.

West of Paspébiac extends the pleasant coastal region of the **Chaleur Bay**. This scenic body of water, which also washes the northern shores of New Brunswick, was discovered by Jacques Cartier in 1534. The area's moderate climate (*chaleur* means warmth) attracts visitors who enjoy water sports.

Bonaventure – *22km/14mi.* The seigneury of the Bonaventure River was conceded by Frontenac in 1697. Settlement began in 1760, when deported Acadians founded the village and established farms and a fishing industry. The village, which takes its name from a ship that sailed into the Chaleur Bay in 1591, is well known for its salmon river.

Musée acadien du Québec à Bonaventure (Quebec Acadian Museum) – *Located in the town centre, east of the church on Rte. 132. Open Jun 24–Labour Day daily 9am–8pm. Rest of the year Mon–Fri 9am–5pm, weekends 1pm–5pm. $3.50. ✗ ᰔ ▯ ☎ 418-534-4000.* Once used as the parish hall, this renovated building now houses a museum of history and ethnology. The permanent exhibit includes a collection of antiques and old photographs, and an audio-visual presentation recalling the influence of the Acadians on Quebec's culture.

New Richmond – *35km/22mi.* A Loyalist stronghold, the town boasts several charming residential areas that still maintain a turn-of-the-century Anglo-Saxon flavour.

Centre de l'héritage britannique de la Gaspésie (Gaspesian British Heritage Centre) – *351 Blvd. Perron Ouest. Open Jun–early-Oct daily 9am–6pm. $5. ✗ ᰔ ▯ ☎ 418-392-4487.* The centre located on Duthie's Point opened in 1989 to promote and preserve the British cultural heritage of the Gaspé Peninsula. The 20 buildings making up this reconstructed village came from the communities surrounding Chaleur Bay. The visit begins at **J.A. Gendron's General Store**, which serves as an interpretation centre. Next door, the **Harvey House** exemplifies the Colonial Revival style popular in the United States at the end of the 19C. Other dwellings dating from the late 17C through the early 20C reveal architectural styles typical of their respective periods. The visit ends at the lighthouse overlooking Cascapédia Bay.

Carleton – *28km/17mi.* Founded by Acadians between 1756 and 1760, the village was originally called Tracadièche, derived from the Amerindian word *tracadigash* meaning "the place where there are many heron." In the late 18C, Loyalists who immigrated to Canada after the signing of the Declaration of Independence renamed the settlement in honour of Governor General Guy Carleton, later known as Lord Dorchester. Nestled between the mountains and the sea, the town boasts a scenic location that has contributed to its success as a summer resort since the turn of the century.

Footpaths along Éperlan Creek (Sentiers de l'Éperlan) – A network of trails follows Éperlan Creek past several waterfalls, revealing splendid mountain scenery, and leads to the back of Mt. Saint-Joseph.

Mt. Saint-Joseph – *By car from the town centre, take Rue de la Montagne 6km/4mi to the summit.* From the top of Mt. Saint-Joseph at an altitude of 558m/1,830ft, the panoramic **view**★★ spans the Chaleur Bay, from Bonaventure to the Miguasha Peninsula, and extends south to New Brunswick. Inside the stone **Oratory of Our Lady** (Oratoire Notre-Dame, 1924), note the mosaic above the altar and the stained-glass windows; *open early Jun–mid-Oct daily 8am–8pm;* ✗ ⅙ ▣ ☎ *418-364-3723).*

After 18km/11mi, turn left and continue 6km/4mi.

★**Parc de Miguasha** – *See Entry Heading.*

Rejoin Rte. 132 and continue 38km/24mi.

Lieu historique national de la Bataille-de-la-Ristigouche (Battle of the Restigouche National Historic Site) – *In Pointe-à-la-Croix. Open Jun–Thanksgiving Day daily 9am–5pm. Mar–May & mid-Oct–Nov by appointment only. $5.* ⅙ ▣ *www.parcscanada.gc.ca/ristigouche* ☎ *418-788-5676.* France's last attempt to save its North American colony from British control was thwarted in the estuary of the Ristigouche River, in Chaleur Bay, in the summer of 1760. Two merchant ships

Pull on your boots, grab your tackle and take to the province's pristine waters for a fly-fishing experience! Fly-fishing requires proper equipment and casting technique, but with some practice can become an enjoyable activity and even some people's passion. Fishing with artificial flies dates as far back as AD 1 when they were used to simulate insects too delicate to use as natural bait.

Select your flies, rod, reel and fly line based on the type of fishing and the fishing conditions. Make sure your reel has a reliable drag and carries enough backing if your destination includes one of Quebec's many renowned salmon rivers. Accessories that may be helpful include boots or waders, a vest, hat, insect repellent, warm clothing, raingear and Polaroid glasses. Serious anglers study characteristics of rivers and streams, understand effects of weather and tides, and know how these variables relate to fly-fishing and fish behaviour in the different seasons. Local sporting goods stores can help outfit you with the appropriate gear and information about fishing permits. For additional information contact the Ministère de l'environnement et de la faune du Québec www.fapaq.gouv.qc.ca ☎ 418-643-3127.

R. Corbel

accompanied by the frigate *Le Machault*, under the command of François Chenard de la Giraudais, hoped to deliver troops, ammunition and supplies to New France. Upon reaching the Gulf of St. Lawrence, the French reinforcements learned that their British counterparts had arrived ahead of them. To avoid a confrontation, Giraudais moved his fleet toward the Ristigouche River hoping that the British ships would be unable to pursue them in shallower waters. Acadians and Micmac helped the French set up batteries to block the river channel. The British, however, penetrated the shallow waters, forcing the French to abandon ship. By nightfall the British had destroyed virtually the entire French flotilla.

Interpretation centre – In the reception area, the giant anchor and part of the hull recovered from *Le Machault* are on display. An animated film *(15min)* recounts the historic battle. In the exhibition halls, scenes depict life on board using many objects recovered from the wreckage, including personal items such as belt buckles, pipes, tobacco boxes, candle snuffers and clothing, as well as tools used to repair wood on board and tighten masts. The contents of the holds include fabric, shoes and clothing for troops and trade goods ranging from nails to combs. Earthenware, Chinese porcelain and other luxury merchandise are also on display.

Detour to New Brunswick – *An interprovincial bridge links Restigouche with Campbellton, New Brunswick. Rte. 11 leads to the Acadian Historic Village (Village historique acadien) located 10km/6mi west of Caraquet, and to the Marine Centre at Shippagan. For descriptions, consult THE GREEN GUIDE Canada.*

Continue on Route 132 through the Valley of the Matapédia where the landscape is composed of a mosaic of quaint villages, rolling forest, covered hills, and the ever-present Matapédia River, famous for its salmon fishing.

Causapscal – *75km/45mi.* Set at the confluence of the Causapscal and Matapédia Rivers, this town of 2,810 is a great departure point for salmon fishing expeditions. At the **Site Historique Matamajaw** *(53 Rue St-Jacques; open June–Sept 9:30am–8:30pm daily* ☎ *418-756-599)* relive the lifestyle of High Society fishing enthusiasts at the Matamajaw Salmon Club. In its specially designed channel, observe Atlantic salmon in their natural habitat.

Parc de la GASPÉSIE★

Gaspésie
Map pp 104-105

In the heart of the Gaspé Peninsula between the St. Lawrence River and Chaleur Bay lies an 800sqkm/309sqmi area devoted to the conservation of plant and animal life native to the province of Quebec. Created in 1937, the park is the only place in Quebec where woodland caribou, moose and white-tailed deer are known to coexist. A veritable "sea of mountains," the park encompasses two massifs, the Chic-Chocs and the McGerrigles, both part of the Appalachian range.

Three sectors of the park are devoted to recreational activities. In the **Mt. Albert Sector**, a hike to the mountaintop (1,151m/3,775ft) reveals a 13sqkm/8sqmi plateau strewn with vegetation characteristic of the northern tundra. In the **Lake Cascapédia Sector**, the ridges of the Chic-Choc massif offer spectacular **views★★** of the Appalachians and the St. Lawrence Valley to the north, and the Sainte-Anne River valley to the east. Mt. Jacques-Cartier (1,268m/4,159ft) is found in the **Galène Sector**. Its windy dome, home to caribou and arctic-alpine flora, affords an expansive **view★★** of the McGerrigle Mountains.

Access – *The park is located about 516km/310mi northeast of Quebec City by Rte. 132. From Sainte-Anne-des-Monts, take Rte. 229 south for 17km/10.5mi to the entrance of the park. The interpretation centre is 21km/13mi inside the park limits. From New Richmond, take Rte. 229 north for 99km/61mi to the interpretation centre. Accommodation is available at the Gîte du Mont-Albert (located next to the interpretation centre), and at various chalets and campsites throughout the park.*

Activities – *Hiking and nature programs are especially popular activities in the park. Visitors can also enjoy salmon fishing, trout fishing, canoeing, mountain biking and picnicking. For cross-country ski enthusiasts, day and overnight ski trips are organised from mid-December until mid-April in various sectors of the park (there are some 15 mountain shelters within park boundaries).*

ADDRESS BOOK

For a legend of price listings for hotels and restaurants, see p 170.

Staying at Parc de la Gaspésie

Gîte du Mont-Albert – *Route du Parc, Sainte-Anne-des-Monts.* ⚐ ♿ ▯ ☎ *418-763-2288, 1-888-270-4483. www.sepaq.com. 48 rooms. 19 chalets.* **$$** Located within the Parc de la Gaspésie, this charming inn provides a comfortable base for enjoying the park's seasonal activities. The clean and cozy rooms and efficient service make this a good bet for a romantic weekend getaway or the annual family vacation.

VISIT *Open daily year-round.* △ ✗ ♿ ▣ *www.sepaq.com* ☎ *418-763-3301.*

Centre d'interprétation de la nature (Nature Interpretation Centre) – *Open early Jun–early Sept daily 8am–8pm. Early Sept–mid-Oct Mon–Thu 8am–4:30pm, Fri–Sun 8am–7:30pm. Hiking & camping equipment rental & sales.* △ ✗ ♿ ▣ ☎ *418-763-7811.* A permanent exhibit provides an introduction to the fascinating landscapes found in the park and to the plants (arctic-alpine) and animals, especially caribou, that thrive on its mountaintops. During the summer months, naturalists answer questions at the summit of Mt. Jacques-Cartier and Mt. Albert. In the evening, lectures, slide shows, plays and films on themes related to the park are presented at the centre.

Parc de la GATINEAU★★
Outaouais
Map p 110

Covering 356sq km/137sq mi of lovely rolling hills interspersed with lakes, Gatineau Park lies nestled between the valleys of the Ottawa and Gatineau Rivers. This enchanting place is named after the French fur trader from Trois-Rivières, **Nicolas Gatineau**, who disappeared in 1683 during a trip up the river that now bears his name. Gatineau is also the namesake of the community, located at the junction of both rivers, and of the surrounding range of hills, part of which is included in the park. William Lyon Mackenzie King, tenth prime minister of Canada, helped create Gatineau Park in 1938. Formerly part of an Algonquin and Iroquois territory, the park is now administered by the National Capital Commission. Within its boundaries lie several Federal Government buildings, notably the prime minister's summer residence on Lac Mousseau (Harrington Lake); and the Willson House, the official meeting centre on Meech Lake, where negotiations on the controversial Meech Lake Accord took place in 1987.

Access – *There are three points of access to the park: Hull, Old Chelsea and Wakefield. The National Capital Commission operates an information centre in Old Chelsea.*

Activities – *The scenic drive that runs throughout the park is particularly beautiful in October, when the trees sport autumn's splendid colours. In summer, visitors can enjoy a wide variety of activities including cycling, hiking, swimming, boating, fishing and camping. In the winter months, the park becomes a skier's paradise, offering 190km/114mi of trails for cross-country skiing and downhill ski centres at Camp Fortune and Vorlage.*

VISIT

Park open daily year-round. Parkways closed from first snowfall until early May. Visitor Centre open mid-May–Labour Day daily 9am–6pm; rest of the year Mon–Fri 9:30am–5pm. $7/car. △ ✗ ♿ ▣ *www.capcan.ca* ☎ *819-827-2020.*

Scenic Parkway – *51km/31mi round-trip from Hull on Rte. 148; start on the Gatineau Parkway.* This beautiful drive skirts high walls of pink granite rock, then winds its way through the dense hardwood forests of the Gatineau Hills. Rounded by glaciers, these hills end in an abrupt slope, the Eardley escarpment, which demarcates the Canadian Shield. Several viewpoints afford superb views of the Ottawa River valley with its productive farms and sparkling lakes.

★★**Belvédère Champlain** (Champlain Lookout) – *6km/4mi round-trip from the intersection of the Champlain Parkway and the Lac Fortune Parkway.* The edge of the Eardley escarpment, at an altitude of 335m/1,098ft, offers a magnificent panoramic **view** of the Ottawa valley, where the Canadian Shield meets the St. Lawrence Lowlands. Below the lookout, a nature trail is dotted with eight observation stations, where various hardwood trees and other vegetation in the park are identified for visitors.

★**Domaine Mackenzie-King** (Mackenzie King Estate) – *3km/2mi round-trip from the Gatineau Parkway; take Kingsmere Rd. Open mid-May–mid-Oct Mon–Fri 11am–5pm, weekends 10am–6pm.* ✗ ♿ ▣ ☎ *819-827-2020.* At the heart of Gatineau Park lies the estate of the man who held power in Canada for a total of 22 years. **William Lyon Mackenzie King** was Canada's prime minister from 1921 to 1930 and 1935 to 1948. During these years, he retreated to the park to escape the pressures of power. When he died in 1950, he left his personal estate of 231ha/571 acres to the Canadian people. The estate comprises several houses and is crisscrossed by walks landscaped by Mr. King himself.

Kingswood – This rustic cottage was the first summer home built by Mr. King in 1903. He enlarged the house in 1924 and continued to live here until 1928. A pleasant walk to the lake offers a view of the boathouse **(1)**.

Moorside – This attractive clapboard house was purchased by Mackenzie King in 1924, and he lived here from 1928 to 1943. The upper floor rooms have remained intact; the ground floor now houses a delightful tea and lunch room. In the former garage **(4)**, an audio-visual presentation *(15min)* explains the life and career of former Prime Minister King.

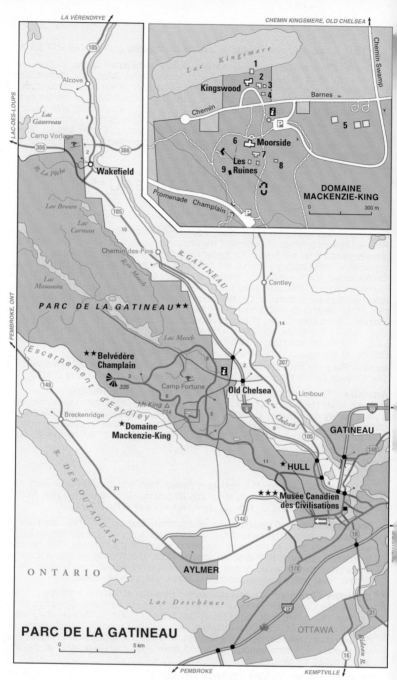

DOMAINE MACKENZIE-KING

1 – Boathouse	4 – Garage	7 – Garage
2 – Guest cottage	5 – The Farm	8 – Forge
3 – Ice house	6 – Garden	9 – Arc de Triomphe

The Ruins – Mr. King salvaged pillars, stones and other architectural features from buildings slated for demolition and had them installed on his estate as a means of landscaping his property. A few sections of the former Parliament Building, destroyed by fire in 1916, can be found, as well as some stones from the British Parliament bombed in 1941.

A third house, The Farm **(5)**, where King lived from 1943 until his death, is now the official residence of the Speaker of the House of Commons *(not open to public)*.

■ Old Chelsea Charmers

Neighboring Gatineau Park, Old Chelsea serves as a supply base for the recreational needs and creature comforts of park users as well as Old Chelseans. **Greg Christie's** *(148 Chemin Old Chelsea. ☎ 819-827-5340)* has been renting bikes, skis and other outdoor equipment to area visitors for years, while **Gerry and Isobel's Restaurant/Boutique** *(14 Chemin Scott ☎ 819-827-4341)* serves delicious homemade fare to hungry hikers, bikers, leaflookers and such, amid a wonderful assortment of local books, artwork and other wares. Next door is the **Old Chelsea Gallery** *(☎ 819-827-4945)*, a co-op that displays and sells the works of many local artists. Restaurants include **Péché Mignon** (in English "a little sin," or "weakness"), which is also a chocolatérie featuring everything chocolate for dessert *(205 Chemin Old Chelsea ☎ 819-827-4649)*, and the illustrious **Les Fougères** *(783 Rte. 105, Tenaga-Chelsea ☎ 819-927-8942)* where the hands-on chef-proprietors at this dining spot favored by capital residents offer locally smoked fish (from **Le Boucanerie Chelsea Smokehouse** ☎ 819-827-1925, just south of the restaurant) and other specialties. Try the fish of the day or the confit de canard (roast, salted duck), a Quebec favourite.

EXCURSIONS

Old Chelsea – *From Hull, take Rte. 5 for 8km/5mi to Exit 12 (Old Chelsea/Gatineau Park); turn west (left) onto Chemin Old Chelsea.* By the early 19C this tranquil village was a stopping place for lumbermen travelling into backcountry forests. Settlers recognized that picturesque Chelsea Creek could provide power for saw- and gristmills, and the hamlet grew, eventually becoming a service centre. By the 1870s four hotels-all owned by Irishmen-prospered, well-frequented watering holes that they were. Still a popular stopover for visitors and daytrippers, the community is home to Gatineau Park's **information centre** as well as shops, art galleries, cozy restaurants, and rental stores catering to outdoor enthusiasts. New England pioneers, attracted to area timber and agriculture, are buried in the **Old Protestant Burying Ground**. Genealogists, especially, will enjoy St. Stephen's Church and cemetery, where headstones date from the 1700s.

Wakefield – *From Old Chelsea, take Rte. 5 for 10km/6mi, then continue on Rte. 105 to Wakefield for another 10km/6mi. From Hull, take Rte. 5 and Rte. 105 for 32km/20mi.* This community occupies a beautiful **site**★ on the banks of the wide Gatineau River. In the early 19C, the first settlers arrived from Britain and named the village after a town in Yorkshire. Although a few mining operations have developed nearby, Wakefield remains a farming and forestry centre served by the railway that follows the Gatineau River.

Wakefield Steam Train

© Malak, Ottawa

GRANBY

Cantons-de-l'Est
Population 43,316
Map p 98

Settled by Loyalists in the early 19C, Granby was named for John Manners, Marquis of Granby, commander of British forces in North America in 1766. The rubber and tobacco factories that developed here on the banks of the Yamaska Nord River soon transformed the town into an industrial centre. The wealth generated from this development is evidenced by the large and gracious Victorian houses along Rues Elgin, Dufferin and Mountain. Palmer Cox (1840-1924), whose famous elf stories for children were inspired by Scottish folklore, is a native of Granby. Today, the nearby Yamaska Park, as well as the ski centres at Bromont and Mt. Shefford, draw outdoor enthusiasts to the community.

Access – *Granby is located 80km/50mi southeast of Montreal by Rtes. 10 (Exit 68), 139 and 112.*

SIGHTS

★**Jardin zoologique de Granby (Granby Zoo)** – *Entrance and parking on Blvd. Bouchard (Rte. 139), at the corner of Rue Saint-Hubert. Open Jun 2–Aug daily 10am–dusk. May, Sept–Thanksgiving Day times vary. $19.95.* ✗ ♿ 🅿 www.lets zooit.com ☎ 450-375-3861. This popular zoo features more than 1000 animals from all over the world. More than a third of the 225 species housed here are endangered. In addition to indigenous species and African mammals, the zoo boasts a nocturnal animals' cave, Bear Mountain, Cats Pavillion and farm animals. Of particular interest is the Reptile House, featuring turtles, iguanas, rattlesnakes and anacondas.

Centre d'interprétation de la nature du lac Boivin (Lake Boivin Nature Interpretation Centre) – *700 Rue Drummond. Turn left on Rue Drummond from Rue Principale. Open year-round Mon–Fri 8:30am–4:30pm. Weekends 8:30am–5pm.* ♿ 🅿 ☎ 450-375-3861. Set on the shores of Lac Boivin, formed by the widening of the Yamaska River, this nature centre offers visitors a choice of four short trails through the marshland surrounding the lake. This site harbours many species of fauna and flora. From the observation tower, visitors can admire **views** of Mt. Brome and Mt. Shefford.

EXCURSION

Waterloo – *19km/12mi west on Rte. 112.* This city, founded by Loyalists in 1796, was named Waterloo to commemorate the Duke of Wellington's victory over Napoleon in 1815. Best known for the mushrooms grown in the area, Waterloo is a pleasant community located on the lake of the same name. Visitors with a taste for adventure should not miss the **Safari Aventure Loowak** *(5km/3mi south of town by Rte. 241, at 475 Chemin Horizon),* with its exciting treasure hunts and daring "missions" *(open year-round daily 10am–5pm; $10;* ♿ 🅿 www.safari loowak.qc.ca ☎ 450-539-0501). Insects, plants and minerals are on view in the Loowak Museum.

Parc des GRANDS-JARDINS

Charlevoix
Map p 80

Just over an hour's drive from Quebec City, visitors can sample a taste of the province's northern regions in Grands-Jardins (literally "great gardens") Park. Clear blue lakes surrounded by forests of black spruce and a ground cover of lichen *(cladonie),* on which caribou feed in winter, are typical of the taiga found in subarctic climates. The park was created in 1981 to preserve the caribou's habitat. As many as 400 caribou roamed the land at the beginning of the century, but by the 1920s they were already extinct as a result of over-hunting. Between 1969 and 1972 some 80 caribou were reintroduced to the area; today the population has increased to between 100 and 125 caribou.

Access – *Parc des Grands-Jardins is located 133km/83mi northeast of Quebec City. Take Rte. 138 to Baie-Saint-Paul (91km/56mi) and then continue on Rte. 138 for another 11km/7mi to the junction with Rte. 381 Nord. Take Rte. 381 past Saint-Urbain (4.5km/3mi) and continue an additional 18km/11mi to the Reception Centre of the park at Thomas-Fortin. Overnight accommodations available in the park include camping (wilderness or with facilities), cottages and huts. The park offers canoe and bicycle rentals. For more information, call Château-Beaumont interpretation centre* ☎ 418-846-2057.

Activities – *The Château-Beaumont interpretation centre organises hikes (depart at 10am and 1:30pm) led by naturalists. Several hiking trails wind their way across the taiga zone; for information contact the Thomas-Fortin Reception Centre ☎ 418-457-3945. For the very adventurous canoeing or kayaking enthusiast, the centre also organises trips of several days on the Malbaie River, which features a series of rapids ranging from class 1 to class 6. For more information, contact Château-Beaumont.*

VISIT

Open late May–Jun & Sept–Oct daily 9am–5pm. Jul & Aug 9am–8pm. $3.50 ☖ ▣ ☎ 418-439-3945 or 418-439-1227 (off-season).

Sector of Lac des Cygnes Mountain (Secteur du Mont du lac des Cygnes) – *1.5km/1mi from the Thomas-Fortin reception centre.* A 2.7km/1.7mi hiking trail *(11/2hrs)* leads to viewpoint where visitors can admire a **panorama★★** of the St. Lawrence River and the Charlevoix valley with its scattered lakes and villages. On the climb to the summit (980m/3,214ft), hikers encounter three distinct types of vegetation. Mountain vegetation is characterized by forests of silver birch, poplar and pine. In the subalpine environment taiga dominates, while tundra prevails in the alpine region.

Continue on Rte. 381 for approximately 19km/12mi. A reception centre marks the main entrance to the park.

Château-Beaumont Interpretation Centre – *19km/12mi. Open mid-Jun–late Aug daily 8am–8pm. Mid-May–mid-Jun & late Aug–Oct daily 9am–5pm. ▣ ☎ 418-846-2057.* Expositions here present the park and its unique natural environment. The centre also serves as the point of departure for various nature activities and excursions.

HULL★

Outaouais
Population 62,339
Map p 110

Facing Ottawa across the wide waters of the Ottawa River, Hull has become an annex of the federal capital in the province of Quebec. Renowned since 1989 as the home of the Canadian Museum of Civilization, the city also boasts numerous government buildings and a variety of cultural and recreational activities.

Historical Notes

The city was founded by Loyalist settler **Philemon Wright** in 1800, some 26 years prior to the establishment of Bytown (Ottawa) across the river. Wright built a mill beside the Chaudière Falls and named his community after the Yorkshire town from which his parents had emigrated. Logging activities developed quickly at the small farming settlement, owing to the region's abundance of red and white pine trees, which were excellently suited for shipbuilding. Wright and his fellow settlers rafted the long, straight trunks down the river to Montreal and from there to Quebec City, where they sold them to the British Navy, thus beginning an industry that continued throughout the 19C.

In 1851 another American, **Ezra Butler Eddy**, arrived in Hull. He started a clothespin business and a match factory that acquired national fame; "Eddy lites" are still sold all over the continent. Eddy's pulp mill dominates part of the Hull waterfront.

In recent years, the centre of Hull has witnessed a great deal of change, including the construction of two large federal government complexes (Place du Portage and Les Terrasses de la Chaudière), and the creation of a new University of Quebec campus. In addition, the city has laid out bike paths along the river. Not far from here, gamblers head for the enormous (23,400sq m/251,878sq ft) avant-garde structure on the banks of Lake Leamy that houses the **Casino de Hull** (Hull Casino). The Jacques Cartier Park *(off Rue Laurier)* affords particularly good **views★** of Ottawa on the opposite bank of the Ottawa River, including Parliament Hill, the Château Laurier and the National Museum of Fine Arts *(see THE GREEN GUIDE Canada).*

Access – *Five bridges cross the Ottawa River, linking Hull and Ottawa. From east to west they are: the Macdonald-Cartier, Alexandria, Du Portage, Chaudière and Champlain bridges. Boulevard Maisonneuve, the main thoroughfare, accesses the Gatineau Highway (A-5).*

★★★CANADIAN MUSEUM OF CIVILIZATION

100 Rue Laurier, between Alexandria Bridge and Rue Victoria.

Directly across the Ottawa River from Parliament Hill stands the Canadian Museum of Civilization, moved here from its former location in Ottawa and inaugurated in June 1989. The museum is dedicated to the history of Canada since the arrival of the Vikings, and to the art and traditions of indigenous peoples and various ethnic groups who have established themselves in Canada throughout the centuries.

Through its impressive collection of 5 million artifacts and the use of innovative and interactive displays, dioramas and high-tech projection systems, the museum seeks to promote intercultural understanding among the 275 different peoples who call Canada home and to preserve their cultural heritage. The museum concentrates primarily, although not exclusively, on Canadian culture.

Architecture – The two museum buildings represent architect Douglas Cardinal's breathtaking vision of the Canadian landscape. Using computer-assisted design techniques, Cardinal was able to create the sweeping curves that evoke the emergence of the North American continent and its subsequent molding by the wind, water and glaciers. Fossil impressions are visible in the Tyndall limestone sheathing the exterior walls. The building to the left of the main entrance, the **Canadian Shield Wing**, houses storage spaces, administrative offices and laboratories for conservation and restoration. On the right, the vast **Glacier Wing** (16,500sq m/177,600sq ft) contains the museum's exhibition halls. Some 3,300sq m/35,500sq ft of space is reserved for temporary exhibits organised by the museum or other institutions; the rest houses permanent exhibits.

Visit

Open Jul–Labour Day daily 9am–6pm (Thu–Fri 9pm). May–Jun & early Sept–mid-Oct daily 9am–6pm (Thu 9pm). Rest of the year Tue–Sun 9am–5pm (Thu 9pm). $8 (half-price Sun; free Thur 4pm–9pm). ✗ ⟨ 🅿 *($8) www.civilization.ca* ☎ *819-776-7000. The museum's restaurant, Les Muses, serves Canadian-French cuisine inside and, in summer, on the patio* ☎ *819-776-7009.*

IMAX/OMNIMAX – *Main level. Features change periodically; films are shown alternately in English and French. Tickets available at main entrance booth. Reservations recommended. $8. Films and screening times information* ☎ *819-776-7010.* A six-storey IMAX screen (10 times the size of a conventional movie screen) and an enormous OMNIMAX dome, which moves into place above the audience, provide unparalleled viewing opportunities for a maximum of 295 spectators *(latecomers not admitted).* The seats in the steeply inclined auditorium tilt backwards for greater viewing ease and comfort.

Canadian Museum of Civilization (Ottawa in the Background)

Canadian Children's Museum – *Main level.* This delightful place for "hands on" learning encourages children to discover the world by participating in activities they enjoy, either individually or aided by supervisors. Near the museum entrance, the **Kaleidoscope** features temporary exhibits specially created for children. In the **Crossroads** area, children can climb aboard a Pakistani bus for an imaginary trip to eight different countries, and the **Grand Adventure** offers a superlative opportunity to get to know other countries and cultures by way of the International Village, a veritable microcosm of the planet Earth. Here, kids can embark on several exciting adventures, including a trip across the desert with a mysterious pyramid looming in the background. A costume room, puppet theatre, toys and games section and an art studio complete the indoor activities. Weather permitting, **Adventure World**, an enclosed outdoor exhibition park, invites visitors to climb on a real tugboat, play a life-size game of chess or get into the cockpit of a Cessna 150.

Canadian Postal Museum – *Main level.* The postal history of Canada and other countries is delightfully presented via a multimedia theatre, an art gallery and thematic exhibits. The astonishingly varied collection of some 25,000 objects, 200,000 stamps and 5,000 works of art includes clay tablets (2043BC) from Mesopotamia; cancellation markings; Valentine's Day cards; and a broad assortment of mail boxes.

Grand Hall – *Lower level.* This immense elliptical space houses the museum's stunning, masterpiece exposition presenting the rich cultural and artistic heritage of the Amerindian peoples of Canada's west coast. Looking down across the wide expanse of the hall, visitors will see the facades of six chieftains' houses, symbolizing a traditional Amerindian village erected between the coastal rainforests (represented here by an enormous mural photograph) and the Pacific Ocean (evoked by a smoothly polished grey granite floor). Built on-site by native artisans using their ancestral techniques, each facade reveals the influences and particularities of a distinct culture: Coast Salish, Nuu-chah-Nulth (Nootka), Kwakwaka'wakw (Kwakiutl), Nuxalk, Haida and Tshimshian. Most of the artifacts incorporated into the facades date from the second half of the 19C. Majestic totem poles (some original, others of more recent provenance) illustrate the incredible artistic talent of the Pacific Coast peoples. Worth noting is the openwork Wakas pole (1893); this 12m/39ft masterpiece stood in Vancouver's Stanley Park for 60 years. Floor-to-ceiling windows on the left open onto the Ottawa River and Parliament Hill, flooding the hall with natural light.

First Nations Hall – *Lower level. Scheduled opening June 2001.* Dedicated mainly to the arts and culture of Canada's indigenous populations as well as their long history and their role in present-day society, this hall presents the richness and diversity of the First Nations through a wide variety of permanent and temporary exhibits. Comprising some 10,000 paintings, carvings, sculptures, photographs and diverse craft objects, the permanent collection of contemporary indigenous art – shown on a rotating basis – features works by established artists (Norval Morrisseau, Bill Reid, Alex Janvier, Kenojuak Ashevak, Pudlo Pudlat, Jessie Oonark) as well as rising talents (Edward Poitras, Shelley Niro, Arthur Renwick, David Ruben Piqtoukun, Toonoo Sharky, James Ungalaq).

Drawing by R. Corbel

Inuit Ublumi (1974) Sculpture by Pierre Karlik

Canada Hall – *Upper level.* A 17m vaulted ceiling surmounts this enormous exposition hall, in which reconstructed buildings and artifacts illustrate one thousand years of Canadian history and heritage. Some of the objects on display are authentic, while others are re-creations. Along a meandering passage through time, visitors witness the arrival of the Vikings in Newfoundland around the year 1000, and discover the life of the early European adventurers who fished the waters of the North Atlantic long before the great voyages of exploration. Early Acadian settlements and 18C farms and villages of the St. Lawrence Valley evoke the history of New France. Another scene explains how fur and timber trading encouraged westward movement, symbolized by a tent and a Conestoga wagon. An Ontario street scene depicts the development of commerce and communication during the second half of the 19C. The small turn-of-the-century Prairies railway station and a full-size grain elevator evoke the settlement of western Canada and the development of the rail system between 1870 and 1914. The journey through time ends with the era of industrialisation (a working-class neighbourhood in Winnipeg; a west coast fish cannery; and the Northwest Territory's Wildcat Café) and effects of modernisation on daily life and traditional values during the 20C.

ADDITIONAL SIGHT

Maison du Citoyen (Citizen's House) – *25 Rue Laurier between Rue Victoria and Rue Hôtel-de-Ville. Open Jun 24–Labour Day Mon–Fri 8:30am–4:30pm. Rest of the year 9am–4:30pm.*   *($10)* ☎ *819-595-7175.* This combined administrative, cultural and sports centre opened in 1980. The brick and glass structure houses Hull's city hall, an art gallery, library, theatre and conference rooms, all of which are set around a large glassed-in atrium called the **Agora**.
Outside the building is a pleasant park used as a skating rink in winter. The Citizen's House is connected to a conference centre (Palais des Congrès), hotel and shopping centre by enclosed passageways.

■ **A Restaurant Sampler**

Enjoy Outaouais regional French cuisine, presented as a three-course table d'hôte that changes daily, in the casual setting at **La Grimod** *(53 Rue Kent* ☎ *819-771-7386)*, or dine with diplomats and celebrities on linen-clad tables at tony **Café Henry Burger**, an Ottawa-Hull institution since 1922 *(69 Rue Laurier* ☎ *819-777-5646)*. You should know that this well-known restaurant provides meals for the Wakefield Steam Train's popular Sunset Dinner ride. Belgian dishes are served table d'hôte at **Restaurant Le Sans-Pareil** *(71 Blvd. Saint-Raymond* ☎ *819-771-1471)*. Try the mussels, prepared with a variety of sauces, and french fries covered in mayonnaise. Trendy, inexpensive bistro fare, such as Croque Monsieur and burgers (order the cream cheese and bacon), is the attraction at **Le Twist Café Resto Bar**. Operating within a funky, old, converted house, Le Twist makes a good spot for lunch, a snack or coffee *(88 Rue Montcalm* ☎ *819-777-8886)*.

EXCURSIONS

★★ **Parc de la Gatineau** – *See Entry Heading.*

Gatineau – *4km/2.5mi northeast by Rte. 148 (Lady Aberdeen Bridge).* This town located at the confluence of the Ottawa and Gatineau Rivers formerly served as the assembly point for the huge lumber rafts built for Philemon Wright, founder of Hull, in the 19C.

Aylmer – *12km/7mi west by Rte. 148.* In the mid-19C, Aylmer was designated the capital of the township of Hull. Charles Symmes, nephew of Philemon Wright, was one of the first settlers in this community, situated on Lake Deschênes, a widening of the Ottawa River. Known as Symmes Landing, it was later renamed for the fifth Baron Aylmer, who was Governor-in-Chief of British North America from 1831 to 1835.

Auberge Symmes (1832), the inn dominating the lake, has been restored to its original state. This monumental stone structure inspired the painter Cornelius Krieghoff. Today, the town's main street *(Rue Principale, from town centre to Hull)* is bordered by golf courses and sumptuous mansions.

Parc de la JACQUES-CARTIER

Région de Québec
Map p 80

Located in the highlands of the Laurentian Mountains, **Jacques-Cartier Park** covers an area of 670sqkm/259sqmi. The coniferous boreal forest extending from Quebec across to Alaska reaches its southernmost point here, on the rolling mountaintops of the massif, which ends in an abrupt 600m/1,968ft drop to the Jacques-Cartier River. Here, the coniferous forest gives way to deciduous vegetation.

Extensive logging of the plateau disrupted the fragile environmental equilibrium, causing the disappearance of caribou and salmon, two species well adapted to the harsh climate of the region. The park was created in 1981 in an effort to better monitor logging operations and preserve the area's magnificent natural heritage.

Access – *The park is located 50km/31mi north of Quebec City on Rte. 175.*

Activities – *In summer, visitors can enjoy canoeing, kayaking and whitewater rafting on the turbulent Jacques-Cartier River (19km/12mi). Atlantic salmon are being reintroduced between Donnacona and Pont-Rouge for the benefit of fishing enthusiasts. More than 60km/37mi of hiking trails, laid out along eight nature walks, meander through the forest and along the river. Six mountain bike trails cover more than 80km/50mi of the park over former logging and gravel roads. There are nine campsites in the park, and group camping facilities. Mountain bikes, rubber rafts and canoes can be rented at the interpretation centre. Fishing permits can be purchased here as well. In winter, the park is open to cross-country skiers.*

VISIT

Open late May–early Sept Mon–Fri 8am–5:30pm, weekends 7am–5:30pm. Early Sept–mid-Oct Mon–Fri 9am–5pm, weekends 8am–5:30pm. △ ▣ *www.sepaq.com* ☎ *418-848-3169.*

Centre d'accueil et d'interprétation (Reception and Interpretation Centre) – Turn left off Rte. 175 from Quebec City at the la Vallée secteur entrance. Continue 10km/6mi into the park. Open same hours as the park. Maps of the park and activity information are available at the welcome centre. A permanent exhibit on the Laurentian

Canoeing on the Jacques-Cartier River

Massif and an audio-visual presentation on the geographical formations found in the area provide explanations of the geological forces that shaped the park's spectacular landscapes.

The road into the park begins to the left of the interpretation centre and follows the Jacques-Cartier River behind the centre. After crossing the river, the road surface changes from asphalt to gravel.

The trail known as **Sentier des Loups** *(8km/5km round-trip, about 2 1/4hrs round-trip)* offers splendid **views**★★ of the entire Jacques-Cartier River valley.

Baie JAMES★
Nord-du-Québec
Map p 118

Covering an area of 350,000sq km/135,135sq mi between the 49th and 55th parallels, the James Bay territory makes up 20 percent of Quebec's total land area. A wilderness of innumerable lakes, mighty rivers and coniferous forests of spindly black spruce and grey pine, the region is home to some 40 species of animals including caribou, moose, black bear, beaver, lynx, beluga whales and seals, and a multitude of waterfowl and fish.

Historical Notes

The Cree Population – The Crees of Quebec are part of the large Algonquian linguistic family. Their spoken language is Cree. In 1997, the sedentary population numbered approximately 12,000 people, living in nine villages: Whapmagoostui (Kuujjuarapik–Poste-de-la-Baleine), Chisasibi, Wemindji, Eastmain and Waskaganish, on the east coast of James Bay and Hudson Bay; and Nemaska, Mistassini, Oujé-Bougoumou and Waswanipi, further inland. Native to the northern forests, the Crees have hunted (moose, caribou, beaver and geese) and fished in the region for thousands of years. Once organised in small nomadic groups, they practiced the barter system well before the arrival of Europeans.

Between 1672 and 1713, French trappers – called *coureurs des bois* – and merchants of the Hudson's Bay Company (HBC) engaged in fierce competition to acquire furs on Cree hunting grounds. From the onset of the fur trade, HBC employees depended upon the Cree for survival, quickly establishing a mutually dependent relationship.

The first Anglican missionaries arrived in the mid-19C to establish health and educational services, but the lifestyle of the Crees changed little until the 20C. In 1950, the Federal government became more involved in the region, establishing a compulsory English-language educational system.

Since the mid-1970s, the Crees have exercised a strong degree of autonomy, governing their own school system, health and social services as well as housing and economic development programs. Each community is administered by a local band council. The Crees have established numerous organizations and companies, such as Air Creebec.

James Bay and Northern Quebec Agreement (Convention de la baie James et du Nord québécois) – By the 1960s, the government of Quebec had determined that the province's economic expansion and its energy needs were closely tied to the devel-

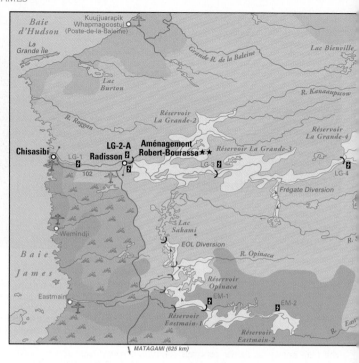

MATAGAMI (625 km)

opment of hydroelectric resources in the northern regions. As a result, it called on Hydro-Québec to undertake a long-term project aimed at harnessing the great northern rivers.

In 1971, the provincial government passed a law to develop Quebec's northern territory and created the Société de développement de la baie James (James Bay Development Corporation), or SDBJ, in order to ensure the proper exploitation of the region's natural resources. In the same year, the Société d'énergie de la baie James (James Bay Energy Corporation), or SEBJ, was established to oversee the technical and financial orchestration of the Hydro-Québec project.

The energy project immediately raised legal questions regarding native rights not taken into account by the provincial government. The Inuit and Cree nations obtained an injunction and eventually entered into negotiations with the Federal and provincial governments and three corporations, in order to resolve the issue of territorial claims. On November 11, 1975, all parties, including the Grand Council of the Crees of Quebec and the Northern Quebec Inuit Association, signed the James Bay and Northern Quebec Agreement. It was the first modern-day settlement of native claims in Canada. Under the agreement, the Inuit and Cree yielded certain claims and rights.

In return, they were awarded exclusive hunting, fishing, and trapping rights in designated areas; ownership of certain lands (16 percent of the claimed territory); the creation of aboriginal councils to oversee community and regional affairs and to participate in decisions concerning the various phases of the James Bay project; and financial compensation. In addition, programs for health care, education and economic development were implemented.

The James Bay Energy Project – Envisioned to exploit the vast hydroelectric potential of Quebec's remote northern reaches, this ambitious long-term project originally called for the construction of 19 power plants grouped in three distinct complexes: La Grande, Grande-Baleine (Great Whale) and Nottaway-Broadback-Rupert. To this day, only the **La Grande complex** is nearing completion. The first phase of the project extended over a 12-year period from May 1973 to December 1985, at a cost of almost $14 billion, and led to the construction of 2,000km/1,200mi of roads linking the area with the south, five airports and five working camps. At the peak of construction, in the summer of 1978, 18,000 workers were on site. The Robert Bourassa underground power plant was inaugurated on October 27, 1979, followed by La Grande-3 in 1982 and La Grande-4 in 1984. The project involved diverting the Eastmain and Opinaca Rivers from the south, and the Caniapiscau (Koksoak) River from the east, into the La Grande River, in order to create five reservoirs.

This colossal undertaking required the construction of 215 earth-and-rockfill dams and dikes, displacing 262,400,000cu m/1,028,870,400cu ft of gravel, rock and sand – enough to construct the Great Pyramid of Cheops 80 times over.

THE JAMES BAY PROJECT

|---|---|
| 0 | 75 km |

🔋 Existing/future power plant

〰	Natural drainage and direction of water flow		Tundra
〰	Reservoir and dam		Taiga
〰	Division dam and new direction of water flow		Swamps
			Boreal forest

The three power plants house a total of 37 generator sets and have a combined capacity of 10,282 megawatts (1 megawatt=100,000 watts). During the second phase of the project, between 1988 and 1996, construction of La Grande-1, La Grande-2-A, La Forge-1, La Forge-2 and Brisay were completed, bringing the total capacity of the La Grande complex to 15,244,000 kilowatts-more than half the electricity produced in Quebec. Construction on the final power plant, the Eastmain plant, has yet to begin; when that plant is finished, the La Grande complex will at last be complete.

Access – *Radisson (La Grande) is located 1,448km/898mi northwest of Montreal and 625km/387mi north of Matagami by the James Bay Rd. At the information booth located 6km/4mi north of Matagami, visitors can make reservations for guided tours of the power plants. At 381km/236mi, there is a 24-hour gas station with a mechanic on duty during regular working hours, and a snack cafeteria. Flights are available between Montreal, Quebec City, Val-d'Or and Radisson on Inter-Canadian, Air Wemindji and Air Creebec. Accommodation (camping, hotel rooms, studio apartments) is available in Radisson.*

LA GRANDE

Radisson – Of the five temporary villages established during the construction of the La Grande complex, Radisson is the only one that remains as a permanent settlement. It is located on the south shore of the La Grande River, just west of the Matagami Road and 5km/3mi west of the Robert Bourassa power plant. The hub of the village is the Pierre Radisson community centre; it houses shops, a post office and recreational facilities including a gymnasium and a swimming pool. Living quarters for employees of Hydro-Québec, and a hotel, are connected to the centre by enclosed passageways.

★★Aménagement Robert-Bourassa (Robert Bourassa Generating Facility) – *Visit by guided tour (4hrs) only, mid-Jun–early Sept daily at 1pm (French) and 2pm (English). Rest of the year by appointment only. Reservations required 48 hrs in advance.* △ ✗ ⓖ 🅿 ☎ *819-638-8486.* The guided tour includes a documentary on the construction and operation of the complex, explanations on the production of electricity and a visit to the power plant. The most powerful hydroelectric facility in Quebec, third in the world, the Robert Bourassa power plant has an installed capacity of 5,328,000 kilowatts. The reservoir covers an area of 2,835sq km/1,094sq mi and is contained by one dam and 31 dikes.

Spillway, Robert Bourassa Generating Facility

Hydro-Québec

119

Spillway – Used to release excess water accumulated in the reservoir during exceptionally strong floods, the spillway is extended in a **"giant's staircase"**★ made up of 10 steps, each 10m/33ft high and 122m/400ft wide. Carved out of rock, it is a visible testimony to the feats of engineering achieved at the La Grande complex.

Robert Bourassa Power Plant – The LG2 power plant is located 137m/450ft underground in an immense granite cavern, .5km/.3mi in length, equipped with 16 generator sets. A special surge chamber reduces the strong pressure changes that occur when switching equipment on or off.

The **La Grande-2-A** power plant, situated less than a kilometer west of the Robert Bourassa plant, began operating in late 1992. Designed to supplement production during peak periods through the use of six additional generator sets, it increases the installed capacity to 7,326,000 kilowatts.

EXCURSIONS FROM RADISSON

Driving tour of the Robert-Bourassa Generating Facility (Circuit de visite de l'Aménagement Robert-Bourassa) – *Depart from the Hydro-Québec information center in Radisson, which provides maps and information about the tour.* This pleasant drive, dotted with informative panels, winds for some 30km/18mi around the dikes of the Robert Bourassa reservoir and offers scenic views of the surrounding area.

Chisasibi – *From Radisson, head south on the Matagami Rd. for 20km/12mi. Turn right and continue on the asphalt road for 82km/51mi.* The hydroelectric development of the territory caused a sharp increase in the flow of the La Grande River as it empties into James Bay. In 1981, the Crees residing in the community of Fort George on an island at the river's mouth, demanded (by way of referendum) that their village be relocated to a site 8km/5mi upstream. The new village was called Chisasibi, meaning "Great River".

Activities – *The Agence Mandow* ☎ *819-855-3373 offers a variety of activities, including guided tours of the village. James Bay is located 15km/9mi from the centre of Chisasibi. To reach the shores of James Bay, leave the centre, turn right and continue straight toward the La Grande River for 2km/1.2mi. Turn left and follow the road for another 2km/1.2mi. At the fork, turn left and continue for 11km/7mi.*

JOLIETTE★
Lanaudière
Population 17,541
Map p 133

Set on the banks of the Assomption River, the industrial and commercial centre of Joliette is the capital of the Lanaudière region. An important artistic and cultural centre, it is also the seat of a Roman Catholic bishopric and home to several Catholic orders.

Historical Notes

In 1828, the notary, **Barthélemy Joliette**, a descendant of the famed explorer, Louis Jolliet, who discovered the Mississippi River with Jacques Marquette in 1673, built a mill on the banks of the Assomption River. First known as L'Industrie, the town was given its present name at its incorporation in 1863. Joliette and his wife, Marie-Charlotte de Lanaudière, were the town's first benefactors, providing land for the church and a college.

The town gained a reputation as a cultural centre through the efforts of various religious orders, especially the Viatorian Clerics. A member of this order, **Father Wilfrid Corbeil** (1893-1979), played a key role in developing the arts. One of his greatest achievements was the creation of the Joliette Art Gallery *(below)*. The town's prestigious music festival was the brainchild of Father Fernand Lindsay.

Festival international de Lanaudière (The Lanaudière International Festival) – From the end of June to early August, musicians from all over the world perform classical and popular music concerts during this celebrated international festival *(see Calendar of Events)*. Performances are held at various churches throughout the city and in neighbouring villages, as well as at a modern open-air amphitheatre set in a charming, wooded site. Blessed with excellent acoustics, the amphitheatre can accommodate more than 10,000 concertgoers in its seats and on the surrounding grassy slopes.

Access – *Joliette is about 75km/46mi north of Montreal by Rtes. 40 and 31.*

SIGHTS

★**Musée d'art de Joliette** (Joliette Art Museum) – *145, Rue Wilfrid-Corbeil. Open Jun–Aug Tue–Sun 11am–5pm. Rest of the year Wed–Sun noon–5pm. Closed Jan 1 & Dec 25. $4.* & ▣ *www.bw.qc.ca/musee.joliette* ☎ *450-756-0311.* Inaugurated in 1976, this regional art museum – considered one of the finest in Quebec – maintains a collection of more than 8,000 works. It is housed in a stark structure designed in the International style. In addition to permanent exhibits, the museum mounts temporary exhibits of contemporary art.

Lower Level – A diverse selection of works (Marc-Aurèle Fortin, Paul-Émile Borduas, and others) relates the evolution of the museum's collections from 1885 to the present.

Ground Floor – The gallery devoted to religious art contains beautiful Quebec and European religious works from the Middle Ages to the 1960s, including a finely decorated wooden pulpit from Saint-Arsène-de-Rivière-du-Loup (c.1840) and several altars, notably one from the village of Champlain (in the Mauricie region) attributed to François Normand. Also on view here are several 15C wooden sculptures.

Les oignons rouges by Ozias Leduc

Musée d'Art de Joliette

First Floor – The development of a distinctive Canadian art in this century is traced from the works of the Group of Seven to the Automatists and Plasticists. The collection features works by Ozias Leduc, Suzor-Côté, Emily Carr, Alfred Pellan, Jean-Paul Riopelle and Guido Molinari. Works by international artists such as Henry Moore, Arman and Karel Appel are exhibited occasionally.

The **"Pit" spring** is situated near from the museum, in Renaud Park, on the corner of Rue De Lanaudière and Rue Saint-Charles-Borromée. Residents and visitors alike can taste and bottle the sulphurous waters of this spring discovered in 1881 by Pierre Laforest, better known by his nickname "Pit." A statue of Barthélemy Joliette stands nearby.

Cathédrale de Joliette (Joliette Cathedral) – *2 Rue Saint-Charles-Borromée Nord. Open year-round daily noon–4:30pm.* ♿ 🅿 ☎ *450-753-7596.* Built between 1888 and 1892, this spacious church is dedicated to the 16C Italian

prelate, Charles Borromeo, who played a major role in the clergy reforms enacted at the Council of Trent (1545-1563). The church became a cathedral in 1904. Its architects adopted the Romano-Byzantine architectural style. The tall central spire can be seen from various points throughout the city. The stained-glass windows designed in 1912 by Henri Perdriau depict episodes from the Old Testament. Also worth noting are the Stations of the Cross, by Georges Delfosse (1869-1939) and the painting of St. Charles Borromeo by Antoine Plamondon, which hangs above the altar. Adorning the vault spanning the structure, twenty three works by Ozias Leduc tell the story of the life of Jesus and the mysteries of the Rosary.

In winter, behind the cathedral, a 4.5km/3mi section of the Assomption River is cleared to form Quebec's longest **skating rink** on a river. It is a lively and popular local attraction *(access by three parking areas in Joliette, Notre-Dame-des-Prairies and Saint-Charles-Borromée).*

Résidence Saint-Viateur (Viatorian Clerics House) – Beside the cathedral stands the old Joliette novitiate, a remarkable group of buildings dominated by a massive tower. This modern take on the Norman abbey of Saint-Georges de Boscherville (13C) was built between 1939 and 1941 under the supervision of Father Wilfrid Corbeil. The complex includes the residence and the infirmary for the Clerics of Saint Viator, a religious order founded in Lyon, France by Father Louis-Marie Querbes, in 1831.

★**Chapel** – *Visit by guided tour (30min) only, year-round daily. Reservations required ☏ 450-756-4568.* The harmonious interior was decorated between 1940 and 1945 by Marius Plamondon of Quebec City. He designed the **stained-glass windows** and also carved the Stations of the Cross and the Old Testament figures at the ends of the pews. The sculpture on the altar depicts Isaac's sacrifice. The chapel has retained all its original furnishings.

Maison Antoine-Lacombe (Antoine Lacombe House) – *Located in Saint-Charles-Borromée, 2km/1.2mi north of the centre of Joliette; take Rue Saint-Charles-Borromée (which becomes Rue de la Visitation) to the corner of Rue Davignon. Open year-round Tue–Fri 1pm–6pm, weekends 1pm–5pm. ☏ 450-755-1113.* This charming stone residence was built in 1847 and renovated in 1968. It now belongs to the municipality and serves as a cultural centre, hosting art exhibits, conferences and concerts.

JONQUIÈRE

Saguenay–Lac-Saint-Jean
Population 56,503
Map p 272

This major industrial centre located on the right bank of the Saguenay River was formed in 1975 by the merger of three municipalities: the small town of Jonquière, Arvida (named for its founder Arthur Vining Davis), and Kénogami. The original town of Jonquière was founded in 1847 by Marguerite Belley and her sons, who moved here from the Charlevoix region. They named the new community after the Marquis of Jonquière, Governor of New France from 1749 to 1752. Two major industrial concerns were established in the early 20C: the Price Paper Company at Kénogami in 1912, and the **Alcan aluminium smelter** at Arvida in 1926; Arvida is now the largest producer of aluminium in the western world. In 1941, a dam was erected on the Saguenay for the **Shipshaw power plant** *(visit by 1hr guided tour only, Jun–Aug Mon–Fri 1:30pm–4:30pm; closed Jun 24; reservations required; ♿ P ☏ 418-699-1547).*

Access – *Jonquière is 200km/124mi north of Quebec City by Rtes. 175 and 170.*

SIGHTS

★**Église Notre-Dame-de-Fatima (Church of Our Lady of Fatima)** – *3635 Rue Notre-Dame. Access from Blvd. du Royaume at the corner of Rue de Montfort. Open year-round daily 9am–5pm. ♿ P ☏ 418-542-5678.* Known as the "teepee," this modern church (1963) rises more than 25m/82ft above the surrounding area. It is shaped like a white concrete pyramid, split vertically. Two stained-glass windows by Guy Barbeau lend a striking luminosity to the interior; the windows rise the full height of the building, joining the two halves of the pyramid.

Mt. Jacob – *Access from Rue Saint-Dominique by Rue du Vieux-Pont.* Mt. Jacob dominates the western part of Jonquière and affords a superb **view** of the region. At its summit, the **National Exhibition Centre** *(open Jul–Aug daily 10am–8pm; rest of the year daily 10am–5pm; ♿ P ☏ 418-546-2177)* serves as the setting for cultural activities and events celebrating the city's history, art and architecture.

★**Mt. Fortin** – *Access from Blvd. du Saguenay by Rue Desjardins. The summit is accessible by car when the gate is open.* The view from this mountain, the site of a ski centre in winter, encompasses a splendid **panorama** of the entire area. The aluminium bridge and Shipshaw dam can be seen in one direction, while Kénogami and Jonquière, indicated by the spire of the Church of Our Lady of Fatima, are visible in the other.

Fish for speckled trout, rent a boat, or simply relax at the Parc et Promenade de la Rivière-aux-Sables *(2230 Rue de la Rivière-aux-Sables).* Located in the oldest part of the city, the park and promenade offers a playground, market place and public square-plenty of ways to enjoy the outdoors.

★**Pont d'aluminium (Aluminium Bridge)** – *Access from Blvd. du Saguenay by Rte. du Pont.* This 150m/492ft bridge weighs less than 164 tonnes, a third of what a comparable steel structure would weigh. Spanning the rocky gorge of the Saguenay, it was built by Alcan in 1948 to demonstrate the properties of aluminium. It needs no maintenance and has never been repaired.

EXCURSIONS

★★★**Fjord du Saguenay** – *See Entry Heading.*

★★**Lac Saint-Jean** – *See Entry Heading.*

★**Chicoutimi** – *See Entry Heading.*

KAHNAWAKE

Montérégie
Population 6,300
Map p 175

This Mohawk reservation is situated on the south shore of the St. Lawrence River, near Montreal. Kahnawake means "above the rapids" in the Mohawk language.

Historical Notes

In 1668, Jesuit missionaries founded the Saint-François-Xavier mission in La Prairie with the intent to convert the local native population to the Catholic faith. In 1717, the mission was moved to its current site in Kahnawake. Known for their amazing lack of sensitivity to vertigo, the Mohawks of Kahnawake have gained renown throughout North America for their expertise in tall construction projects, including skyscrapers. They often work on sites in the major cities of Canada and the US.

■ Kateri Tekakwitha

Born in 1656 in Auriesville (in present-day New York State) of an Iroquois father and an Algonquin mother, Kateri Tekakwitha was orphaned at the age of four by a smallpox epidemic that killed her parents and left her nearly blind. She was adopted by her uncle and named Tekakwitha, meaning "one who moves with hesitation." In 1676, she was baptised by the Jesuits and named for St. Catherine of Siena (Kateri). Ill treated in New York, she fled to the Mission of Saint-François-Xavier in 1677 and died three years later, at the age of 24. At the tricentennial of her death in 1980, she became the first person of Amerindian origin to be beatified by the Roman Catholic Church.

Access – *The Kahnawake reservation is located 12km/7mi south of Montreal by the Honoré-Mercier Bridge (Rte. 138). Take the first exit after crossing the bridge.*

VISIT

Church – *Open year-round Mon–Fri 10am–noon & 1pm–5pm, weekends 10am–5pm. Contribution requested.* ⬥ 🅿 ☎ *450-632-6030.* The church (1845) built by the Jesuit priest, Félix Martin, replaced the earlier chapel of 1717. It contains the tomb and relics of Kateri Tekakwitha. Inside, the small **museum** features displays on the young woman and the Mohawk way of life.

KAMOURASKA★

Bas-Saint-Laurent
Population 707
Map p 81

The seigneury of Kamouraska (which means "where rushes grow by the water's edge" in Algonquin) was granted to Olivier Morel de la Durantaye in 1674 by Louis de Buade, Comte de Frontenac, governor of New France. The first settlers arrived the following year and by the 18C, Kamouraska was one of the largest communities in the Bas-Saint-Laurent (Lower St. Lawrence) region. Since the 19C, grain, potato and dairy farming have constituted the town's principal economic activity.

The term **"Kamouraska roof"** refers to the curved overhanging eaves, a local architectural feature found gracing many of the houses throughout the region. The design, which first appeared on several public buildings (including the church at Saint-Jean-Port-Joli), seems to add height to the ground floor, which otherwise appears crushed by the heavy roof.

Access – *Kamouraska is located 163km/101mi from Quebec City by Rte. 73 (Pierre-Laporte Bridge) and Rte. 20 (Exit 465).*

SIGHTS

Musée de Kamouraska (Kamouraska Museum) – *69 Ave. Morel. Behind the church in the town centre. Open Apr–mid-Jun Mon–Fri 9am–5pm by appointment only. Mid-Jun–mid-Oct daily 9am–5pm. Oct–Dec Tue–Fri 9am–5pm, weekends 1pm–4:30pm. $4.* 🍴 ⬥ 🅿 ☎ *418-492-9783.* The edifice containing the museum was built as a convent in 1851. Devoted to the cultural history of the Kamouraska region, the museum displays household items and furniture typical of the homes and lifestyles of the early European settlers. Farm implements and craftsmen's tools

Kamouraska Roof

evoke the working conditions of the community's forefathers. A large collection of fishing tackle and models demonstrating eel fishing techniques emphasize the crucial role the St. Lawrence played in the lives of local residents. The museum also houses an altar carved in 1737 by François-Noël Levasseur for Kamouraska's second church (1727).

Berceau de Kamouraska (Old Kamouraska) – *3km/2mi east of town centre on Rte. 132*. The former heart of the village, now known as the "Kamouraska Cradle," was the location of the first two churches of the community (1709 and 1727) and the cemetery where 1,300 pioneers are buried. A simple, open-air chapel commemorates the spot.

■ How do you feel?

At the Site d'Interprétation de l'Anguille de Kamouraska *(205 Ave. Morel. ☎ 418-492-3935)*, take a guided tour and discover the secrets of traditional eel fishing. End the experience by sampling a smoked version of the snakelike fish.

Halte écologique des battures de Saint-André-de-Kamouraska (Kamouraska Salt and Marsh Ecological Centre) – *9km/6mi east of Old Kamouraska, 3km/2mi west of Saint-André; located near the rest area on Rte. 132. Open late Jun–early Sept daily 8am–9pm. Early May–late Jun & early Sept–late Oct Mon–Fri daily 8am–6pm. $2.* ⚠ ♿ 🅿 ☎ *418-493-2604.* The interpretation centre is designed to stimulate interest in and respect for the marsh and river ecosystems. Experienced guides lead organised activities related to ecological themes, including plant and animal life in the marsh, beluga whales, peregrine falcons and other birds. A trail *(6km)* leads to the salt marsh *(batture in French),* and on to a rocky promontory equipped with scenic belvederes and birdwatching stations.

LA BAIE

Saguenay–Lac-Saint-Jean
Population 21,807
Map p 272

This industrial centre occupies a magnificent **site★** on an inlet of the Saguenay Fjord popularly known as Ha! Ha! Bay. According to local legend, the bay was originally named after Ha! Ha! street, a one-way street in 17C Paris. Another story has it that early explorers of the area, mistaking the bay for a river, sailed up it as though it would lead them inland, and named it for the cries of laughter that erupted once they had discovered their folly. Arriving in 1838, the first settlers were members of a group called the **Society of Twenty-One** (Société des Vingt-et-Un), whose aim was to settle the Saguenay–Lac-Saint-Jean region. They created three villages at the site of present-day La Baie: Bagotville, Port-Alfred and Grande-Baie. La Baie was formed by the merger of these communities in 1976.

La Baie quickly grew into a forestry centre and today boasts a large pulp mill. The city's greatest asset, however, is its extensive port, which serves the large bulk carriers transporting bauxite from the Caribbean and South America to supply the aluminium smelters in La Baie and Jonquière.

In the summer months, the region's history is brought to life through the pageantry of **La fabuleuse histoire d'un royaume** (The Fabulous Story of a Kingdom). You can also catch a glimpse of salmon swimming upstream at the *passe migratoire* (fish ladder) on the Rivière-à-Mars located in the middle of the city.

Access – *La Baie is 212km/131mi north of Quebec City by Rtes. 175 and 170. It is 20km/12mi southeast of Chicoutimi by Rte. 372.*

SIGHTS

Scenic drive – Just before Route 372 begins its descent to the Mars River in Ha! Ha! Bay, a lookout provides an excellent **view**★★ of the bay. On clear days, the panorama can extend some 48km/30mi. Further on, Route 372 joins Route 170, which skirts the bay and offers several lovely vistas along a 12km/7mi stretch.

Parc Mars (Mars Park) – *At the junction of Rte. 170 (Rue Bagot) and Rte. 372 (Blvd. Saint-Jean-Baptiste), continue on Rue Bagot and turn left on Rue Mars.* This waterfront park offers superb **views**★ of the bay and its surrounding hills, as well as of the impressive shipping facilities. About 200,000 tonnes of newsprint and lumber and more than 3 million tonnes of bauxite pass through the port annually.

Musée du Fjord (Fjord Museum) – *3346 Blvd. de la Grande-Baie Sud (Rte. 170). Open Jun 24–Labour Day Mon–Fri 8:30am–6pm, weekends & holidays 10am–5pm. Rest of the year Mon–Fri 8:30am–noon & 1:30pm–5pm, weekends & holidays 1pm–5pm. $4.* ♿ 🅿 ☎ *418-697-5077.* This museum offers science, history and art exhibitions relating to the Saguenay region, the province of Quebec, and Canada.

> Don't miss **La Pyramide des Ha! Ha!** at the Parc des Ha! Ha! *(Rue Monseigneur-Dufour* ☎ *418-697-5050).* Conceived by the artist Jean-Jules Soucy, this 21m (69ft) high aluminum pyramid with a 24m (79ft) base is covered with 3,000 red and white triangular traffic yield signs and serves as a stage and an observation point.

EXCURSION

Saint-Félix-d'Otis – *43km/26mi from La Baie.* This village and its surroundings has attracted filmmakers interested in capturing "history on film." Once a film site, the **Site de la Nouvelle-France** *(Vieux Chemin www.nouvelle-france/royaume.com* ☎ *418-544-8027)* invites visitors to relive history in the reconstructed buildings of the French Regime. A small Huron village, a Montagnais camp, and an Old French country house and its *dépendances* (small farm) allow you to experience the customs and habits of the Amerindians and the first settlers.

LA MALBAIE–POINTE-AU-PIC★

Charlevoix
Population 4,918
Map p 81

Officially incorporated with the community of Pointe-au-Pic in 1995, La Malbaie enjoys a beautiful **site**★ on the north shore of the St. Lawrence at the mouth of the Malbaie River. Samuel Champlain dubbed this place *malle baye* (bad bay) in 1608, when he anchored his ships here only to discover, the following day, that they had run aground. After the Conquest, the land surrounding the bay was granted to two Scots, Malcolm Fraser and John Nairn. They called it **Murray Bay** in honour of General James Murray, chief administrator of the colony, and welcomed many visitors to the area. The most famous of the hotels that gradually replaced the hospitality of the local seigneurs is the **Richelieu Manor** *(Manoir Richelieu; access by Rte. 362 and Chemin des Falaises)*, a vast, picturesque, château-style edifice overlooking the St. Lawrence. Near the hotel, which was was rebuilt in 1929 after a fire, stands a second building (1930) housing the **Charlevoix Casino**.

Three communities hug the shores of the bay: La Malbaie–Pointe-au-Pic, Cap-à-l'Aigle and Rivière-Malbaie. A golf course is laid out along an escarpment at the south entrance to La Malbaie–Pointe-au-Pic. Winter activities include skiing at the Mont-Grand-Fonds centre nearby.

Access – *La Malbaie–Pointe-au-Pic is about 140km/87mi northeast of Quebec City by Rte. 138. The latter forms Blvd. de Comporté, which becomes Rue Principale in Pointe-au-Pic.*

Parc provincial des hautes-gorges de la rivière Malbaie

SIGHTS

Vacation Villas – Most of the villas and summer residences on the two hillsides surrounding La Malbaie were built between 1880 and 1945. The influence of the "shingle" style of architecture popular along the Atlantic Coast of the United States can be seen in the cedar-shingled dwellings. Vacationers visiting the region for hunting and fishing came to appreciate the rustic character of the sober interiors and simple furnishings that local architect Jean-Charles Warren (1868-1929) designed. Warren erected about 60 of these grand villas, initiating a "Laurentian" style that integrated buildings into their surroundings by using local materials and positioning the structure to take the fullest advantage of the magnificent scenery.

Musée de Charlevoix (Charlevoix Museum) – *1 Chemin du Havre. Open late Jun–Labour Day daily 10am–6pm. Rest of the year Tue–Fri 10am–5pm, weekends 1pm–5pm. $4.* ♿ 🅿 ☎ *418-665-4411.* Paintings, sculptures and textiles in the permanent collection provide an understanding of local Charlevoix art, heritage and history. The museum also presents changing exhibitions on various themes. The rotunda affords an impressive view of the surroundings.

EXCURSIONS

Chutes Fraser (Fraser Falls) – *In Rivière-Malbaie, about 3km/2mi. After the bridge over the Malbaie River, turn left and take Chemin de la Vallée for 1.5km/1mi, then turn right following signs for the campground. Open mid-May–Nov daily 8am–10pm. $2.25.* ⛺ ✗ 🅿 ☎ *418-665-2151.* These falls on the Comporté River are set in a pleasant area. The river drops about 30m/98ft forming a lace-like pattern across the rocky ledges.

La Ferme à Rosanna – *Notre-Dame-des-Monts, 16km/10mi by Rte. 138 Sud and by a small road (signed). Open mid-Jun–mid-Oct daily 10am–6pm. $6.* 🅿 ☎ *418-457-3595 or 418-457-3764.* This Radio Canada television series, which topped popularity charts in the mid-eighties, was set in the Charlevoix region. Scenes were shot in Les Éboulements, in the churches of Sainte-Agnès and Saint-Irénée and in **Notre-Dame-des-Monts**. The farm of Rosanna, one of the main characters, has been recreated in a wonderful mountain site near this village.

★**Parc provincial des hautes-gorges de la rivière Malbaie (Provincial Park of the High Gorges of the Malbaie River)** – *Take Rte. 138 and turn left toward Saint-Aimé-des-Lacs. Continue over 35km/22mi on a dirt road. Open early Jun–mid-Oct daily 9am–5pm. $3.50.* △ ✕ ᵬ ☐ *($5/car)* ☎ *418-439-4402.* Mountains rise more than 1,000m/3,280ft in this spectacular park, dominating the high gorges of the Malbaie River and the valley of the Martres River. A **cruise** leads to the steep-sided gorges of the Malbaie River *(depart from the wharf at the end of the dirt road mid-Jun–mid-Oct 11am, 1:15pm & 3:30pm; round-trip 1hr 45min; commentary; reservations required; $20;* ᵬ ☐ *www.sepaq.com* ☎ *418-439-1227).*

LA POCATIÈRE★

Bas-Saint-Laurent
Population 4,887
Map p 81

Birthplace of agricultural education in Canada, La Pocatière is situated on a terrace above the coastal plain. Various types of research are pursued here, particularly in agro-alimentary studies, continuing the city's vocation as an educational centre. The industrial sector is dominated by the Bombardier factory, renowned for its world-famous snowmobiles and rail transportation equipment.

Access – *La Pocatière is 131km/81mi from Quebec City by Rte. 73 (Pierre-Laporte Bridge) and Rte. 20 (Exit 439).*

SIGHT

★**Musée François-Pilote (François Pilote Museum)** – *10km/6mi east of Saint-Roch-des-Aulnaies, turn right off Rte. 132. At the top of the hill, turn right and immediately turn right again into the parking lot of the Collège de Sainte-Anne. The museum is situated behind the school. Entrance on the second floor. Open May–Sept Mon–Sat 9am–noon & 1pm–5pm, Sun 1pm–5pm. Rest of the year Mon–Fri 9am–noon & 1pm–5pm, Sun 1pm–5pm. $4.* ☐ ☎ *418-856-3145.* This museum of Quebec ethnology centers on rural life in the province at the turn of the century. The museum is named after François Pilote, who founded the first school of agriculture in Canada in 1859.

Yesteryear – *First floor.* The exhibit covers the history of maple sugar making, with a reconstructed sap house; a vast collection of vehicles, including sleighs, horse-drawn buggies and motorcars; trade implements used by lumberjacks, carpenters, blacksmiths, shoemakers and weavers; and numerous farm tools. A second exhibit on coastal navigation from the mid-18C to the mid-19C contains model ships and nautical instruments. At that time, goods were transported by small schooners called *goélettes*.

Natural Sciences – *Second floor.* Experience the history of the evolution of agriculture from the time of Champlain (1632) to the year 2000 with a glimpse of the future. In the adjoining rooms, Canadian mammals, seashells, firearms and religious objects are on display.

Family Life – *Third floor.* Three rooms (living room, dining room and bedroom) recreate the comforts of an upper class family in the 1920s, while a variety of household items in seven rooms reflect the lifestyle of a farming family in Quebec around 1900. A rural schoolroom, a general and a jewelry store, and professional offices of a country doctor, a dentist and a notary complete the exhibit.

Education – *Fourth floor.* This floor features a presentation on the history of agricultural education in Quebec and education in general. It includes exhibits on breeding, aviculture, biology, and zoology as well as chemistry, physics, astronomy and fisheries. Also on view is a soil laboratory and the magnificent Tanguay collection of 400 mounted birds including some 200 different species, nearly all native to Quebec.

The ☐ symbol indicates that on-site parking is available.

LA PRAIRIE

Montérégie
Population 17,128
Map p 175

Located on the southern shore of the St. Lawrence, this community is today a residential suburb of Montreal. In 1647, the seigneury of "La Prairie de la Magdelaine" was granted to Jesuit missionaries eager to convert the local Amerindians. However, the Iroquois wars delayed colonization for over 20 years. The first settlers protected themselves by erecting a wooden palisade around their settlement. In 1691, they were attacked by British forces from New England led by John Schuyler, a commander from Albany. The settlers won the battle, which left over one hundred soldiers dead on both sides. Iroquois hostilities ended with the Montreal Peace treaty in 1701, and the area enjoyed a period of rapid development during the first half of the 18C. After the Conquest, English merchants developed transportation and travel routes. In 1836, rivers and roads were supplemented by Canada's first railway, built by the Champlain and St. Lawrence Railroad Company, which ran from La Prairie to Saint-Jean-sur-Richelieu. The railroad company's major shareholder was the famous financier and brewer, John Molson. Several brickyards, still ranking among the largest in Canada, were established in the 1890s.

Access – *La Prairie is about 20km/12mi southeast of Montreal by the Champlain Bridge and Rte. 15 Sud (Exit 46). To reach the old section, take Rue de Salaberry to Blvd. Taschereau (Rte. 134), turn left (north) as far as Chemin Saint-Jean (Rte. 104) and turn left again.*

VIEUX-LA PRAIRIE (OLD TOWN)

The devastating fires of 1846 and 1901 destroyed most of the old buildings in the historic district known as Vieux-La Prairie. A few interesting buildings remain, most built of sandstone and reminiscent of the beginnings of English Classicism *(no. 120 Chemin de Saint-Jean and no. 166 Rue Saint-Georges)*. At least two buildings *(no. 115 and 150 Chemin de Saint-Jean)* illustrate the urban architectural style developed in New France. Most of the remaining buildings in the historic district are wood structures, typically found in the suburbs of Montreal at the beginning of the 19C *(no. 234, 238 and 240 Rue Saint-Ignace)*.

Église de la Nativité (Church of the Birth of the Virgin Mary) – *Chemin Saint-Jean. Open year-round daily 9am–5pm. Reservations required.* & 🅿 ☎ *450-659-1133.* The church (1841) dominates the old village, locally called Vieux-Fort (old fort). The monumental Neoclassical facade, topped by a slender spire, has over the years become the symbol of La Prairie. Two sets of colonnades and a domed bell tower recall Montreal's old Catholic cathedral. The interior, inspired by the Church of Saint Martin-in-the-Fields, displays Neoclassical symmetry.

Musée du Vieux-Marché (Old Market Museum) – *249 Rue Sainte-Marie. Open Jun–early-Aug Mon–Fri 9am–5pm, Sun noon–4pm. Rest of the year Tue–Thur 9am–5pm. Closed major holidays & Dec 24–early Jan. Contribution requested.* & 🅿 ☎ *450-659-1393.* Originally a market, this brick structure (1863) also served as a police and fire station. At present, the building houses the Historical Society of La Prairie de la Magdelaine, devoted to historic preservation, and the city's archives. Exhibits trace the history of the old town, and researchers may explore the genealogies, research holdings and reference books in the society's documentation room.

Réserve faunique LA VÉRENDRYE

Outaouais–Abitibi

Named for the famed explorer of the Rocky Mountains, Pierre Gaultier de Varennes, Sieur de la Vérendrye, this reserve (13,615sqkm/5,257sqmi) was created in 1939 and is a favourite with nature lovers in search of adventure or tranquility. The many lakes and watercourses that feed the Outaouais and Gatineau Rivers provide a habitat for over one hundred species of birds and fish such as pike, walleye, bass, lake trout and speckled trout. A variety of mammals, notably moose, bear, deer, beaver and fox roam the vast coniferous forests covering the territory.

Access – *The reserve is about 300km/186mi northwest of Montreal by Rte. 15 and Rte. 117. Its northern entrance is 54km/34mi from Val-d'Or. There are campsites, cabins and a lodge for visitors inside park limits.*

Activities – *Approximately 800km/ 496mi of canoe circuits are available, complete with wilderness camp sites and portage routes. The most popular place to begin is Lake Jean-Péré, which offers some relatively easy excursions for beginners. Canoes and small fishing boats are available for rent.*

Pine Grosbeak

© Wayne Lankinen /VALAN PHOTOS

VISIT

Open late May–Oct daily 8am–4pm. △ ⚔ ⚙ 🅿 *www.sepaq.com* ☎ *819-438-2017.*

Route 117 – The main road traversing the reserve *(180km/112mi)* affords pleasant views of the many rivers and lakes found throughout the park. **Lake Jean-Péré** is one of the park's main attractions and the starting point for various canoe excursions. The route passes by the Cabonga Reservoir and the Dozois Reservoir, controlling the flow of the Gatineau and Outaouais Rivers respectively, before crossing the dam that straddles the latter river.

LAC-BOUCHETTE

Saguenay–Lac-Saint-Jean
Population 1,445
Map p 280

This small community nestled between Lakes Ouiatchouan and Bouchette was founded in 1890. It is named in honour of Joseph Bouchette, an engineer and land surveyor who mapped this area in 1820.

Pilgrimage Centre – Lac-Bouchette is most famous for its shrine founded in 1907 by the abbot **Elzéar Delamarre** (1854-1925), Superior of the Chicoutimi Seminary. Father Delamarre spent his summers in the region, eventually building a summer retreat and a chapel near Lake Bouchette. In 1916, he discovered a natural grotto resembling the Massabielle grotto at Lourdes, France. Before his death, many pilgrims had made the trek to the grotto. Today, this former summer retreat is owned by the Capuchin Brothers, and is visited by more than 200,000 faithful every year.

Access – *Lac-Bouchette is 218km/135mi from Quebec City, and 25km/15mi south of Chambord on Lake Saint-Jean by Rte. 155.*

SIGHT

★**Ermitage Saint-Antoine** (**St. Anthony's Hermitage**) – *2km/1.2mi west of Rte. 155 across Lakes Ouiatchouan and Bouchette. Open year-round daily 7:30am–11pm.* △ ⚔ ⚙ 🅿 *www.destination.ca/ermitage* ☎ *418-348-6344.* The red brick monastery of the Capuchin Brothers, built in 1924, dominates the site.

First chapel – The first chapel built by Father Delamarre in 1907 was dedicated to St. Anthony of Padua. After discovering a grotto similar to the one in Lourdes, Delamarre expanded the chapel and dedicated it to Our Lady of Lourdes. This later chapel has a Gothic Revival interior, embellished with arches and fan vaulting. The earlier chapel, now a side aisle, contains the tomb of Father Delamarre. The walls of the modest chapel are decorated with a group of 23 **paintings★** representing the life and miracles of St. Anthony, executed between 1908 and 1920 by Charles Huot (1855-1930).

Marian chapel – Built in 1950, this modern chapel resembles a grotto. The stained glass windows (1971) were designed by Guy Bruneau. The large one at the back represents Bernadette Soubirous kneeling before Our Lady of Lourdes.

Chapel grounds – Steps lead from the Marian Chapel to the grotto discovered by Father Delamarre in 1916. Nearby stand an open-air chapel overlooking the lake and a copy of the Holy Steps of Rome; a path leads up the hillside to the 14 Stations of the Cross, sculpted in stone.

LACHINE

Région de Montréal
Population 35,171
Map p 175

Today a peaceful community on the banks of the St. Lawrence, Lachine has a rich history that is closely linked to the development of the French colony and to the commercial and industrial evolution of the province. In 1667, Robert Cavelier de La Salle was granted a seigneury by the Sulpicians at the point where the St. Lawrence emptied into Lake Saint-Louis. As he was forever in search of the elusive "passage" to the East, La Salle's seigneury was facetiously nicknamed La Chine (French for China).

Lachine soon became an outpost for the city of Ville-Marie, the original name of Montreal. On August 4, 1689, the community was the site of a brutal massacre. About 1,500 Iroquois attacked and burned the village to the ground, killing over two hundred people. Another hundred were taken prisoner. The massacre is thought to have been an act of revenge for the execution of several Iroquois chiefs that had been ordered by the governor of the colony two years earlier.

Access – *Lachine is about 19km/12mi from downtown Montreal by Rue Wellington and Blvd. LaSalle. The city can also be reached by Rte. 20 Ouest. Visitors can take a bicycle on the metro from Montreal (Saturday and Sunday only) and disembark at* ◑ *Lionel Groulx.*

SIGHTS

★Lachine Rapids and Canal – Beyond Lake Saint-Louis, the level of the St. Lawrence drops 2m/7ft over a distance of 2km/1.2mi. In 1603, from the top of Mt. Royal, Champlain had noted the existence of "the most impetuous rapids one is likely to see." These impressive rapids presented a considerable obstacle to the various explorers wishing to travel upriver.

As early as 1680, Dollier de Casson, Superior of the Saint-Sulpice seminary, proposed the construction of a canal to bypass the rapids. The project, however, was not undertaken until 1821. Completed in 1824, the 13.6km/8.5mi channel linked

Braving the Rapids: Jet Boat Excursion on Rapides de Lachine

Lake Saint-Louis and the Port of Montreal; seven locks raised ships a total of 14m/49ft. The canal was enlarged twice, from 1843 to 1849 and from 1873 to 1884. It remained the only passage around the rapids until the opening of the St. Lawrence Seaway in 1959.

No longer used for travel, the canal today forms a recreational corridor about 15km/9mi long. A pleasant bike path borders the old docks of Montreal and Verdun and connects the Old Port to Lachine. In winter it becomes a trail for cross-country skiers.

The rapids are visible from the Boulevard LaSalle in the city of LaSalle. Jet boats departing from the Old Port in Montreal offer heart-pounding **excursions★★** down this tumultuous stretch of the river. *The canal is currently under construction. Expected reopening date 2002.*

Musée de la ville de Lachine (Lachine Museum) – *On Blvd. LaSalle, turn left before crossing the canal.* ◐ *Angringon; bus 110 or 114. Open Apr–late Dec Wed–Sun 11:30am–4:30pm.* ☜ *514-634-3471 (ext. 346).* This museum is set around an old stone house built during 1669-1685 by Charles Le Moyne and Jacques Le Ber, two of the first merchants to settle in Lachine. The house is now known as the Maison Le Ber-Le Moyne. Displays of period furniture and tools complement the exhibits on historical themes and handicrafts. An adjacent modern structure, called pavillon Benoît-Verdickt, houses furniture dating from the 1850s to the present, as well as travelling contemporary art exhibits.

Outside the museum, the church in Kahnawake can be seen across the lake.

Parc René-Lévesque (René Lévesque Park) – *From Blvd. LaSalle, turn left onto Chemin du Canal.* Formerly called Grande-Jetée, this park is situated on a peninsula jutting out into Lake Saint-Louis. The peninsula was built up on land reclaimed from the river between 1873 and 1884 to shelter the third entrance to the Lachine Canal. The park was renamed after René Lévesque (1922-1987), premier of Quebec from 1976 to 1985. Foot and bike paths lead to the tip of the peninsula past 12 pieces of contemporary sculpture created for various symposia held every two years in the city's parks. Note in particular Georges Dyens' work *Les forces vives du Québec* (Quebec's Vital Forces), unveiled in 1988 to honour Lévesque. The park affords views of the St. Lawrence as it leaves Lake Saint-Louis, of the City of Lachine and, downstream, of the bridges spanning the river. A ferry operates between the tip of the peninsula and Saint Louis Park in summer.

Centre d'interprétation du canal de Lachine (Lachine Canal Interpretation Centre) – *711 Blvd. Saint-Joseph, on Monk Island, at end of 7ᵗʰ Ave. in Lachine.* ◐ *Angringon, then bus 195. Open mid-May–Labour Day Mon 1pm–6pm, Tue–Sun 10am–noon & 1pm–6pm.* ☐ ☜ *514-283-6054.* The Pavillon Monk (1974), a small stone building serving as an interpretation centre, exhibits photographs on the construction and history of the canal. In the canal's heyday, 15,000 ships a year passed through the locks, carrying wheat and wood. In the second half of the 19C, entrepreneurs eager to exploit the region's hydraulic power created the largest concentration of industry in Canada along its banks: nail factories, flour mills, saw mills, etc.

★**Fur Trade in Lachine National Historic Site** – *On Blvd. Saint-Joseph, across from 12ᵗʰ Ave. and from the Sainte-Anne College.* ◐ *Angrignon, then Bus 195. Open Apr–mid-Oct Mon 1pm–6pm, Tue–Sun 10am–6pm. Mid-Oct–Nov Wed–Sun 9:30am–5pm. $2.50.* ☐ ☜ *514-637-7433.* This stone warehouse, used to store furs and trade goods from 1803 to 1859, contains an interesting and evocative display on Montreal's fur trade. Strolling among bundles of fur and boxes of merchandise, visitors can identify the different stages of the industry's history. On display are maps of the fur country showing the trading posts of both the North West Company and the Hudson's Bay Company. Before the North West Company merged with the Hudson's Bay in 1821, nearly 80 percent of the furs exported to Europe passed through Lachine.

Promenade Père-Marquette (Father Marquette Walk) – *Main access on Blvd. Saint-Joseph, across from 18ᵉ Ave.* The walk along Lake Saint-Louis was named for Father Jacques Marquette (1637-1675), who discovered the Mississippi River with Louis Joliet in 1673. It affords views of the Couvent des Sœurs de Sainte-Anne (Sisters of St. Anne Convent), who run the St. Anne College (1861), across from the warehouse, and of the Église des Saints-Anges-Gardiens (Church of the Guardian Angels), erected in 1919.

The ✗ symbol indicates that eating facilities can be found on the premises of the sight.

LANAUDIÈRE

Lanaudière
Map opposite

Located on the southern edge of the Canadian Shield, the Lanaudière region forms a corridor of fertile plains extending from the St. Lawrence in the south to Lake Taureau in the north, and from the Laurentians in the west to the Mauricie region in the east. One of the earliest areas to be colonized by the French, the region takes its name from Marie-Charlotte de Lanaudière, daughter of the seigneur de Lavaltrie and wife of Barthélemy Joliette, who erected several mills in the area and financed the construction of the first railway in the mid-19C.

The Lanaudière region provides a wealth of outdoor activities, from boating and hiking in summer to skiing and snowmobiling in winter. The international music festival of Lanaudière *(see Calendar of Events)*, in Joliette, and the regional agricultural exhibition in Berthierville attract visitors from all over.

CIRCUIT FROM TERREBONNE *314km/195mi.*

★**Terrebonne** – *See Entry Heading.*

Take Rte. 125 to Rte. 25 and exit onto Rte. 640. At Exit 22 East take Rte. 138 east.

Repentigny – *23km/14mi. 1hr.* Set on the banks of the St. Lawrence River at the confluence of the Prairies and Assomption Rivers, this community of 53,824 inhabitants is named after Pierre Le Gardeur de Repentigny, who was granted the seigneury in 1647.

The strikingly modern **Église Notre-Dame-des-Champs**★ *(187 Blvd. Iberville; turn left from Rue Notre-Dame; open year-round Mon–Thu 8:30am–9:30am, Fri 3pm–4:30pm, Sat 4pm–5pm, Sun 9am–noon; ☎ 450-654-5732)* was conceived in 1963 by Roger d'Astous, a former student of Frank Lloyd Wright. The building's curved walls resemble a tent, enclosing a harmonious interior space lit from a row of windows that punctuate the upper portions of the walls. A modern clock tower stands beside the covered walkway leading to the church. **Église de la Purification** *(Rue Notre-Dame between Rue Hôtel-de-Ville and Rue Brien; open year-round Mon–Fri 9:30am–5pm. ⅋ ☎ 450-581-2484)* with its twin towers was built in 1723 during the French Regime.

Take Rte. 138 (Chemin du Roy) towards the northeast and continue 1km/.6mi after the junction with Rte. 158.

The road hugs the St. Lawrence shore affording numerous views of the wide and majestic river.

Chapelle des Cuthbert (Cuthbert Chapel) – *46km/28.5mi. Open Jun–Labour Day daily 10am–6pm. ⅋ 🅿 ☎ 450-836-8158.* In 1765 James Cuthbert, aide-de-camp to General Wolfe, purchased the seigneury of Berthier. Cuthbert's wife Catherine is buried in this chapel, which he constructed in 1786 to perpetuate her memory. Dedicated to St. Andrew, the chapel served as the first Presbyterian place of worship for the area, and remained in use until 1856.

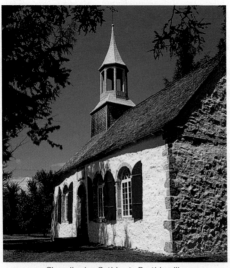

Chapelle des Cuthbert, Berthierville

© Sheila Naiman /REFLEXION

Return to the junction and continue on Rte. 158 towards Joliette.

★ **Joliette** – *27km/17mi. See Entry Heading.*

From Saint-Charles-Borromée, continue north along Rue de la Visitation (Rte. 343) and turn right on Rte. 348 which follows the Assomption River (through Sainte-Mélanie) until the junction with Rte. 131 (28km/17mi). Continue on Rte. 131 towards Sainte-Émélie-de-l'Énergie (29km/18mi).

As the countryside becomes more mountainous, Route 131 enters into the narrow **Noire River valley**★. The road crisscrosses the dark and shallow river punctuated with splendid cascades.

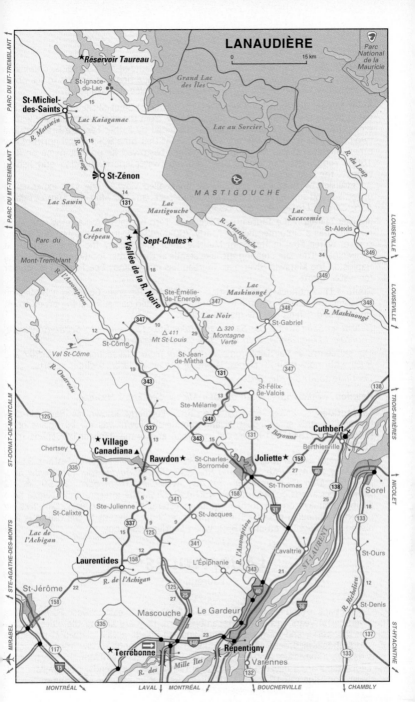

★Sept-Chutes de Saint-Zénon (Seven Falls of Saint-Zénon) – *20km/12mi from Sainte-Émélie-de-l'Énergie. Open mid-May–Oct daily 9am–5pm. $3.25.* 🅿 ☎ *450-884-0484.*
Only one of the cascades, the "Bridal Veil" (Voile de la mariée), is accessible. Though spectacular during the spring thaw, the 60m/197ft-high cascade dries up in summer. Sturdy wooden steps lead to the top of the falls and continue to Lake Guy. From there, the trail meanders through birch trees and moss-covered rocks to hidden cascades and, a little further, vast and peaceful Lake Rémi *(15min from Lake Guy)*. Across the lake, an impressive cliff rises abruptly out of the water.

Those eager to embark on a longer hike should return to Lake Guy and follow the Mont Brassard circuit *(3hrs)*, which leads the visitor to a lookout, at an altitude of 150m/492ft, offering a wonderful **view★** of the U-shaped valley of the Noire River to the south. The trail continues through a lush forest of birch and pine trees. Before reaching the steep descent to the cascades, the Mont-Brassard belvedere offers an expansive **view** of Lake Rémi and the Laurentians to the west.

Continue on Rte. 131 Nord.

Saint-Zénon – *14km/9mi.* This community, surrounded by mountains, dominates the valley of the Sauvage River. Beside the church, a fine **view** extends to the north of the valley known as the Nymph's Corridor (Coulée des nymphes).

Saint-Michel-des-Saints – *15km/9mi.* The village of Saint-Michel-des-Saints is situated beside the Matawin River, just upstream from the spot where its wild waters empty into the calm Taureau Reservoir. Founded by Father Léandre Brassard and two colleagues in 1862, the tiny village was at that time 80km/50mi north of any other inhabited place. Msgr. Ignace Bourget bestowed its present name on it in 1883. Today, the lumber industry, tourism, water sports, hunting and fishing support the local economy.

An **excursion** by floatplane provides an unequalled view of the vast expanses of unsettled land surrounding Lake Taureau *(depart Jan–Mar Mon–Fri; May–Oct daily; $35; Cargair Ltd. ☎ 450-833-6836).*

★ **Réservoir Taureau** (Lake Taureau) – Called Lac Toro by native Atikamekw, this large reservoir has a circumference of nearly 700km/434mi. It was created in 1931 to control water flow in the Saint-Maurice River and supply the power station at Shawinigan. The dam creating the lake stands at the former location of the Taureau Rapids on the Matawin River. Lac Taureau has many sandy beaches and is popular for water sports.

Route 131 continues to the Mastigouche Wildlife Reserve. Covering 1,574sqkm/608sqmi, the reserve is home to a variety of fish and game, including brook trout. Hunting and fishing are the main activities.

Return to Saint-Michel-des-Saints and take Rte. 131 south to Sainte-Émélie-de-l'Énergie (47km/29mi), then Rte. 347 towards Saint-Côme.

The ski centre at Val Saint-Côme *(12km/7mi from intersection of Rtes. 347 and 343)* with more than 20 slopes, is one of the area's largest winter resorts.

Continue south on Rte. 343.

★ **Rawdon** – *89km/55mi south of Saint-Michel. See Entry Heading.*

Laurentides – *25km/15mi by Rte. 337.* Formerly known as Saint-Lin-des-Laurentides, this small industrial and commercial town was the birthplace of **Sir Wilfrid Laurier** (1841-1919), lawyer, politician and prime minister of Canada from 1896 to 1911.

Lieu historique national de Sir-Wilfrid-Laurier (Sir Wilfrid Laurier National Historic Site) – *Corner of 12ᵉ Ave. (Rte. 158) and Rte. 337. Visit by guided tour (1hr) only; mid-May–Jun Mon–Fri 9am–5pm. Jul–Aug Wed–Sun 10am–6pm. $2.50.* ☁ ▣ *www.parkscanada.gc.ca/laurier ☎ 450-439-3702.* The interpretation centre here exhibits displays on the former prime minister's life and the important role he played in Canadian politics. The simple brick house adjacent to the centre is furnished to reflect life around 1850, when Laurier was a boy.

LAURENTIDES★★

Laurentides
Map opposite

The Laurentians extend across the province of Quebec from east to west. Formed more than one billion years ago in the Precambrian era, they are among the oldest mountains in the world, and form part of the Canadian Shield, a vast plateau in the shape of a horseshoe which nearly encircles Hudson Bay. The range of low, rounded mountains rises to a maximum altitude of 968m/3,175ft at Mt. Tremblant. To Montrealers, the Laurentians are a haven for recreational retreats; on weekends, city dwellers rush northward on Highway 15 to enjoy this vast summer and winter playground.

Historical Notes

Few people inhabited this area before the arrival of the legendary **Father Antoine Labelle** (1833-1891). Deputy-minister of agriculture and colonization, Father Labelle devoted his entire life to persuading his fellow French Canadians to settle the wilderness. He travelled by canoe and on foot to select sites for new settlements and was responsible for the establishment of more than twenty parishes in the Laurentians. Today, many of these communities still bear the names of their parish saints, particularly in the area just north of Montreal. Thus, the name **Valley of the Saints** has been given to the area beside the Nord River where Saint-Jérôme, Saint-Sauveur, Sainte-Adèle and Sainte-Agathe are located.

Despite Father Labelle's efforts to establish agriculture, farming proved to be unprofitable in the Laurentians. However, a new source of wealth developed during the 20C, when the ever-increasing population of Montreal began to retreat to the Laurentians in search of recreational activities.

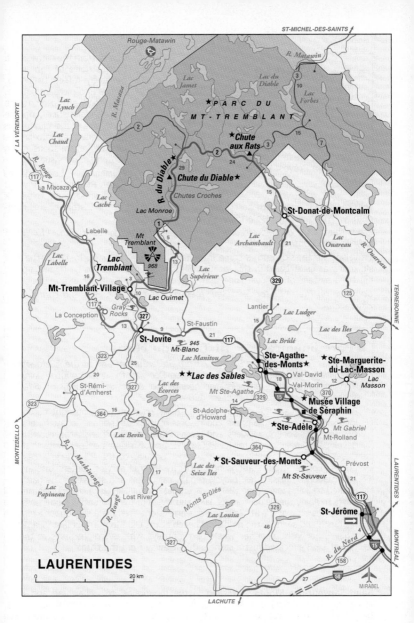

Today, boaters, swimmers and fishermen enjoy the many lakes of the region. The surrounding hills are the domain of the hikers, horseback riders and, golfers. In summer, several renowned theatres open their doors to visitors. During the fall season, the mountains display a dazzling array of fire red, orange, and gold foliage. In winter, the area attracts downhill and cross-country skiers and offers a wide range of *après-ski* activities. The Laurentians have the highest concentration of alpine ski centres in North America. Small chalets and luxurious homes are nestled in the mountains and along lakesides. The region's principal resorts cater to an international clientele.

FROM SAINT-JÉRÔME TO SAINT-DONAT *177km/109m.*

Saint-Jérôme – *51km/32mi from Montreal by Rte. 15 (Exit 43, Rue de Martigny Est).* Founded in 1830, this city grew rapidly, primarily through the efforts of Father Labelle. Known as the "Gateway to the Laurentians," it is an important administrative centre located on a pleasant site beside Nord River.

Cathedral – *Rue Saint-Georges. Open year-round daily 7:30am–4:30pm. Contribution requested.* ☎ *450-432-9741.* The long spires of this imposing stone church (1900) tower above the community of Saint-Jérôme. In 1951, the church was elevated to the rank of cathedral. The rounded forms of its portico and pinnacles, and the monumental treatment of the decor are hallmarks of the Romano-Byzantine style. Inside, note the stained glass by D. A. Beaulieu of Montreal.

■ The Jackrabbit

The community of Prévost was for many years the home of **Hermann Johannsen**, better known by his sobriquet, "Jackrabbit." This intrepid sportsman almost single-handedly introduced cross-country skiing to the Laurentians, laying out many trails, including the famous Maple Leaf Trail that ran from Prévost to Mt. Tremblant.

Across from the cathedral, a bronze **statue** of Father Labelle, by Alfred Laliberté, stands in a pleasant square. The former courthouse *(palais de justice)*, on the north side of the square, has been converted into an exhibition centre focusing on contemporary visual arts.

Promenade – Located between Rue de Martigny and Rue Saint-Joseph, this walk *(610m/.4mi)* is lined with descriptive panels that recount the history of this community. The walkway also affords views of the Nord River.

From the centre of Saint-Jérôme, take Rue de Martigny Est to Rte. 117 (Blvd. Labelle) and continue north.

Travelling north, ski centres come into view from the highway. In 1932, the first ski tow was established in this vicinity. Skiers paid five cents to be hauled up the hill by a system of pulleys, rope and tackle, powered by an automobile engine.

Continue on Rte. 117 for 5km/3mi, then turn left on Rte. 364 and continue for 2km/1.2mi.

■ Parc linéaire le P'Tit Train du Nord

Access – Rte. 15 and/or Rte. 117 from St-Jérôme or any of the 23 towns and villages that lie along the park. Open Dec–Apr for cross-country skiing and snowmobiling, May–Oct for hiking and bicycling. $5/daily or $10/season. www.laurentides.com ☎ 450-436-8532.

For over 70 years the railway line the P'Tit Train du Nord brought nature lovers to the many fine parks and resorts of the Laurentians. Today, hikers, cyclists, cross-country skiers and even snowmobilers cherish the recently developed "linear park" for its 200km/124mi of maintained pathways. Val-David and Mont-Tremblant are the most popular of the 23 village access points. Former train stations now operate as trail service centers offering information booths, cafés, bicycle repair, restrooms and showers. The hard-packed trail and low grade (2% on average) allow all levels of outdoor enthusiasts to enjoy the fields, forests, lake and rivers of the Laurentian wilderness. Day-trippers favor the St.-Faustin-Lac Carré-Mont-Tremblant section for a picnic lunch and swim at the municipal beach at the Old Mont-Tremblant Village, while other visitors prefer week-long journeys with overnight stays at the quaint B&B's located just a stone's throw away from the path.

★**Saint-Sauveur-des-Monts** – Nestled in the mountains, this charming and lively village boasts a variety of restaurants, fashion stores and handicraft shops, cafés, bars and discos, most of which are located along the busy main street *(Rue Principale)*, near the church of Saint-Sauveur (1903).

Saint-Sauveur is the oldest Laurentian resort, having welcomed visitors since 1930. The **Mont-Saint-Sauveur** ski centre is one of the largest in the Laurentians, boasting more than 25 ski lifts within 3km/2mi of the community.

Pavillon 70 – *From Rue Principale, turn left on Ave. Saint-Denis and continue 1km/.6mi to Mt. Saint-Sauveur. At the foot of slope no. 70.* This ski lodge, a veritable wooden palace designed by Peter Rose of Montreal, was completed in 1977. A monumental facade topped by two massive chimneys characterizes the internationally acclaimed building, credited with introducing the Postmodern style to Quebec.

Return to Rte. 117.

Route 117 continues its course through the mountains. The Rouge River offers sports enthusiasts exciting whitewater rafting opportunities as it flows past several communities.

★**Sainte-Adèle** – *9km/6mi.* Nestled in the Laurentian Mountains, this community occupies a lovely **site★** surrounding the small Lake Sainte-Adèle. In 1834, Augustin-Norbert Morin (1803-1865), lawyer and politician, founded this village named for his wife, Adèle. Today, the community is dominated by the vast and luxurious resort hotel, **Hôtel Chantecler** *(☎ 450-229-3555 www.lechantecler.com)*. Sainte-Adèle boasts two downhill ski centres, Côtes 40-80 and Chantecler, where the Canadian ski team trains regularly. Popular with artists and writers, the village features numerous restaurants and charming country inns.

Sainte-Adèle

★ **Sainte-Marguerite-du-Lac-Masson** – *From centre of Sainte-Adèle, take Rte. 370 to the right. About 24km/15mi round-trip.* After 4km/2.5mi, the road crosses the Nord River and passes the Alpine Inn, an imposing log structure built in 1934, in the rustic style. Several lakes can be glimpsed before the road reaches Sainte-Marguerite-du-Lac-Masson, a quiet village on **Lake Masson**. A narrow panoramic road circles the lake.

Many more ski centres can be seen, their ski trails cutting swathes of green down the mountain sides in summer. Route 117 passes through Val-Morin and Val-David, known for their summer theatre and resort hotels.

★ **Sainte-Agathe-des-Monts** – *18km/11mi. See Entry Heading.*

Over the next 21km/13mi, the road crisscrosses the former route of the famed "P'tit train du nord" (little train of the north), immortalized in a song by Félix Leclerc. This popular shuttle made the trip (in the years prior to the establishment of ski areas) between Montreal and the Laurentians throughout the winter, serving the region's agricultural communities. The service was eventually superseded by the automobile, and the tracks have been removed.

To the south of Saint-Faustin, the **Mont-Blanc** (945m/3,100ft) ski centre is visible.

Saint-Jovite – *30km/18mi.* This small tourist centre of recent vintage is located in the valley of the Diable River. Visitors will find many restaurants, antique and handicraft shops.

From Rue Ouimet turn right on Rue Limoges (Rte. 327).

The lovely **Lac Ouimet** *(6km/4mi)* has a graceful setting encircled by hills. It is dominated by the Gray Rocks resort hotel with its ski slopes, golf course and sailing facilities. The long ridge of Mt. Tremblant can be seen to the north.

Continue northward on Rte. 327.

Mont-Tremblant Village – *4km/2.5mi. Lake Mercier marks the entrance to the village. The road continues towards Lake Tremblant (3km/2mi) and the Mont-Tremblant ski centre.* Located on the shores of Lake Tremblant, the resort of Mont-Tremblant will delight visitors in all seasons with its beauty and wide range of activities. The village is renowned for its fine restaurants.

■ Claude-Henri Grignon

A native of Sainte-Adèle, the writer and journalist Claude-Henri Grignon (1894-1976) published his famous novel, *Un homme et son péché* (published as *The Woman and the Miser* in English), in 1933. Set in Sainte-Adèle and centered on the miserly **Séraphin Poudrier**, the novel takes the reader back to the days when the so-called *Pays d'en haut* (the highlands) were being settled. It won the Prix Anathase David in 1935 and was subsequently adapted for radio, television and film. Grignon's masterpiece, written in the realist-naturalist style, remains a classic in Quebec literature.

ADDRESS BOOK

For a legend of price listings for hotels and restaurants, see p 170.

Staying in Mont-Tremblant

Château Mont Tremblant – *3045 Chemin Principal, Mont-Tremblant.* ✗ ☐ ☐ ☎ *819-681-7000, 1-800-441-1414. www.cphotels.ca. 316 rooms.* $$$ Reigning above Mont-Tremblant Village, this Canadian Pacific resort hotel remains in character with the re-created 18C atmosphere of its surroundings. Its chateau-like exterior and rustic pine and stone interior recall the early days of New France. Costumed employees show you the way to rooms decorated with pine furnishings and plaid drapes and bedspreads. Besides offering immediate access to the slopes and other outdoor activities, the hotel boasts several restaurants, boutiques and a spa.

Dining in the Laurentides

Cabane à sucre Millette – *1357 Rue Saint-Faustin, Saint-Faustin–Lac Carré.* ☐ ☐ ☎ *819-688-2101. www.millette.ca.* $ **Quebecois**. For a truly authentic Quebecois experience, don't miss a meal *(see photo p 48)* at the Millette family's "sugar shack." Maple-syrup making implements like *outils à marquer le bois* (tree-marking tools) and even a *nid de guêpe* (wasps nest) decorate the rustic, wood-panelled interior. After touring the syrup making facilities, enjoy *musique folklorique* (folklore music) while you savor the copious servings of traditional favorites such as *soupe aux pois des Laurentides* (Laurentian pea soup), *l'omelette de grand-mère Millette* (Granny Millette's omelette), *jambon fumé au sirop d'érable* (maple syrup smoked ham) and *saucisses dans le sirop d'érable* (sausages in maple syrup). Finish it all off with *crêpes au sucre à la crème chaude* (crêpes in a maple-syrup crème sauce).

Restaurant aux Tourterelles – *1141 Chemin Chantecler, Sainte-Adèle.* ☐ ☎ *450-229-8160. www.bar-resto.com/tourt/.* $$ **French**. Nestled across from the lake, this cozy restaurant emanates romance with its stone fireplace, greenery and walls tinted in verdant hues trimmed in plum and sunset orange. The table d'hôte (fixed price) menu includes three courses that might include delicacies such as a *potage de carotte et gingembre* (carrot and ginger soup) accompanied by a *velouté de champignons* (cream of mushroom soup), *médaillons de cerf* (medallions of deer) and *miroir aux framboises* (raspberry coulis over pastry cream and lady fingers). Selections by sommelier François Chartier make a fine accompaniment to any dish.

Restaurant La Forge – *Place Saint-Bernard, Mont-Tremblant Resort* ☎ *819-681-4900.* $$$$ **Thai/French**. Encircled by evergreens bedecked in tiny white lights, this inviting octagonal, two-level restaurant, with a bistro on the main floor, is located right at the base of the ski lifts. White linen tablecloths, leather chairs and decorative iron tools help create its warm, yet sophisticated, ambience. Situated in the middle of the room, the circular bar stocks some 250 wines and a number of scotches. The open kitchen prepares regional dishes like Boileau deer tournedos with morello cherries and peppercorns or rack of Quebec piglet served with Oka cider and golden Sainte-Julie honey.

Lac Tremblant (Lake Tremblant) – A pleasant **cruise** sails over the long (10km/6mi) and narrow (1km/.6mi) expanse of Lake Tremblant *(depart from Quai Fédéral Jul–mid-Oct daily 10am–4:30pm (Tue–Thu 6pm & 7:30pm); limited number of cruises Jun & early Sept–mid-Oct; round-trip 1hr 10min; commentary; $12;* ☐ ☐ *Croisières Mont-Tremblant* ☎ *819-425-1045).* Near the boat dock, a tributary of the Diable River, known simply as Décharge-du-Lac, leaves the lake in a display of falls and whirlpools. Luxurious homes line the lake shores; the tall silhouette of the Sleeping Giant rises at the northern end of the lake while the imposing Mt. Tremblant looms to the east. At the beginning of the century, this was a logging area with no roads. The northern end of the lake is still inaccessible by car; residents reach their homes by boat in summer and snowmobile in the winter months. The lake is famous for its fish (landlocked salmon, trout, muskie) and its clean waters. It offers several beaches and water sports. At the Mont-Tremblant ski station, the great ridge of the mountain dominates the resort community at its base. The tiny Roman Catholic church with a prominent red roof is a replica of the church built in Saint-Laurent, on the Île d'Orléans, in the early 18C.

In summer, the peak of Mt. Tremblant (968m/3,175ft) can be reached by **chairlift**. On clear days, the peak offers a magnificent **view**★ of the lake and surrounding mountains.

★**Parc du Mont-Tremblant** – *From Lake Tremblant, follow the Chemin Duplessis (follow sign indicating Lac Supérieur) for 13km/8mi to the junction with the road from Saint-Faustin. The entrance to the park is 5km/3mi north of the junction. 1 day. See Parc du MONT-TREMBLANT.*

Skiing in Mont-Tremblant

In the summer season when all roads in the park are open, exit at the Saint-Donat entrance and continue to Saint-Donat. Out of season, visitors must return to the Lac Supérieur (Saint-Faustin) entrance.

The picturesque road follows the **Diable River★** from the Mont-Tremblant ski centre to the Croches Falls.

Saint-Donat – *10km/6mi from park entrance.* The resort community of Saint-Donat lies in the Lanaudière region at an elevation of 472m/1,548ft and is surrounded by mountains rising to 900m/2,952ft. It is set on the shores of Lake Archambault but stretches as far as Lake Ouareau to the east.

Continue on Rte. 329 Sud to Sainte-Agathe-des-Monts.

This is a lovely drive through mountains and past several lakes. Just outside Saint-Donat, the road affords beautiful views of Lake Archambault.

LAVAL
Région de Montréal
Population 330,393
Map pp 174-175

In the 17C, the Jesuits gave the name **Île Jésus** to this large island just to the north of Montreal. The first parish, Saint-François-de-Sales, was created in 1702 and the fertile land was quickly settled.

A master sculptor and principal designer of church interiors in Quebec in the early 19C, **Louis-Amable Quévillon** (1749-1823) was born and lived in the small parish of Saint-Vincent-de-Paul. With the help of apprentices, friends and associates, he created what historians labeled the "Quévillon school."

In the 20C, the advent of the automobile, together with the building of bridges and highways, rapidly changed Île Jésus, transforming it into the main industrial and residential suburb of Montreal. In 1965, the 14 municipalities on the island merged and selected their new name in honour of Msgr. Laval, former seigneur of Île Jésus. Today, Laval is the most populous city in Quebec after Montreal.

Access – *Laval is located 12km/7mi to the northwest of Montreal, on the north shore of the Prairies River.*

SIGHTS

★★**Cosmodôme** – *2150 Autoroute des Laurentides (Chomedey). From Montreal, take Rte. 15 (Exit 9) and follow signs.* The Cosmodôme opened in 1994 with a mission to "promote the study and practice of space science and technology." A 3/4 scale replica of an Ariane rocket stands in front of the ultramodern complex, making it easy to spot from afar.

Space Science Centre – *Open Jun 25–Aug daily 10am–6pm. Rest of the year Tue–Sun 10am–6pm. Closed Jan 1 & Dec 25. $9.75.* ✗ ⅋ ◻ *www.cosmodome.org* ☎ *450-978-3600.* Interactive consoles, mural panels, scale models, large-scale replicas, simulators and videos make for a fascinating, hands-on visit to Canada's only museum devoted to the history and exploration of space. A path through the exhibits traverses six different thematic sections, initiating visitors to the wonders of the universe. In the first section, a multimedia show *(20min)* traces the history of human space exploration. In the second section, various scientific instruments of yesteryear bring home the incredible technological strides achieved in human knowledge of the universe. The third section focuses on telecommunications, from prehistory to the present. Earth is next-the importance of water, continental drift, undersea mountains, and other aspects of our planet are examined. Don't miss the magnificent mural representation of the continents as viewed from space. The fifth section boasts two themes: teledetection and its various roles, ranging from meteorology to espionage; and human exploration of the moon. On view here is a space rock donated by NASA. The last section offers the chance to explore the solar system; note in particular a holographic image of the Hubble space telescope surrounded by meteor fragments. The visit ends with an exhibit entitled "Are We Alone?", on historic efforts to communicate across the universe.

Space Camp Canada – *Reservations required; for information* ☎ *450-978-3600.* Modeled after similar programs in the US, the camp offers an array of space-oriented educational activities for kids and adults. Programs of varying length, some necessitating overnight stays and all run by specially trained counselors, initiate campers to the life and work of real astronauts through workshops, exercises, training programs and mission simulations.

Maison André-Benjamin Papineau (André-Benjamin Papineau House) – *5475 Blvd. Saint-Martin Ouest (Chomedey). Leave Hwy 13 at Exit 15 and follow the signs to Maison Papineau. Open year-round daily 9am–5pm (Jun 24–early Sept Fri 7pm–10:30pm).* ⚐ 🅿 ☎ *450-688-6558.* This stone house, with its steep roof and high chimneys, was built between 1818 and 1832 by André Papineau. Its most famous resident was his son, André-Benjamin, cousin of Louis-Joseph, fellow Patriot, politician and mayor of Saint-Martin (one of Laval's municipalities). Moved to this spot when Highway 13 was constructed, the house now functions as a cultural centre and art gallery presenting works by professional artists.

Économusée de la Fleur (Flower Museum) – *In Sainte-Dorothée. 1270 Rue Principale. Guided tours available for groups of 8 persons or more ($3/person); reservations required. Open year-round Mon–Wed 9am–6pm, Thu–Fri 9am–9pm, Sat 9am–5pm, Sun 10am–5pm. $3.45 Closed Dec 25–26 & Dec 31–Jan 6.* ☎ *450-689-8414.* Located on the outskirts of the village of Sainte-Dorothée, this combination boutique/museum allows visitors a peek at the process of flower preservation. At the entrance, visitors are welcomed by a shop full of dried bouquets and flower arrangements, while an upper-level room displays examples of show flowers; a variety of objects with floral motifs; and a reading corner. To view the process of flower-drying, visit the studios and drying rooms situated at the rear of the building. A number of display panels outline the techniques of this traditional craft, and personnel are on hand to answer questions.

LÉVIS★

Chaudière-Appalaches
Population 40,407
Map p 259

The city of Lévis is located on the southern shore of the St. Lawrence, opposite Quebec City. In 1759, British General Wolfe built a redoubt on these rocky cliffs, from which he planned to bombard the French capital. Initially called Aubigny, the community was renamed in 1861 for François-Gaston, Duc de Lévis, who defeated the British at Sainte-Foy in 1760.

During the 19C, Lévis became a centre for timber exports to England. In 1828, the Davie Shipbuilding Company, from the neighbouring city of Lauzon, established the first shipbuilding centre in Canada here. With the arrival of the railway in 1861, Lévis became a major business centre. Today, the city is noted for its port, wood-related industries, and as the birthplace and headquarters of the Desjardins cooperative savings and loan company *(Caisse populaire Desjardins)*. Lévis and Lauzon were incorporated in 1990.

Alphonse Desjardins – On December 6, 1900, Alphonse Desjardins (1854-1920), a journalist and stenographer in the House of Commons, founded the first cooperative savings and loan company *(Caisse populaire)* in North America. This people's bank, based on a European concept and adapted to local conditions, sought to bring economic independence to French Canadians, thus slowing their exodus to the United States. With his wife Dorimène, Desjardins ran the first "caisse pop" from his home in Lévis and went on to open 184 branches throughout the province. Towards the end of his life, requests for federation with the *Caisse populaire Desjardins* were coming in from other Canadian provinces. Although Desjardins laid the basic groundwork, the

Caisse populaire centrale was not united until 1932, twelve years after his death. Today, the **Desjardins Cooperative Movement** (Mouvement Desjardins), with headquarters in Lévis, includes more than 1,300 *caisses populaires* and over 5 million members.

Access – *Lévis is located 250km/155mi east of Montreal by Rte. 20 (Exit 325). A ferry (below) connects Lévis to Quebec City, located just across the river.*

SIGHTS

Terrasse de Lévis (Lévis Terrace) – *From Rte. 132, take Rue Côte-du-Passage, bear left on Rue Desjardins, and turn left on Rue William-Tremblay.* Built during the Depression, this terrace was inaugurated in 1939 by George VI and Queen Elizabeth. Located high above the river, it offers an excellent

Alphonse Desjardins

Société historique A. Desjardins

view★★ of the older areas of Lévis and Quebec City, with the Citadel, Château Frontenac and port. The view extends to Mt. Sainte-Anne in the east, and as far as the Quebec City Bridge in the west.

Carré Déziel – In the heart of old Lévis, Déziel Square is surrounded by several interesting buildings, including the imposing Église Notre-Dame-de-la-Victoire (Church of Our Lady of Victory) erected in 1851. At the centre of the square stands a **monument** to Joseph-David Déziel sculpted by Louis-Philippe Hébert. Déziel (1806-1882) was the first parish priest and the superior of the Lévis College, which he founded in 1851. Today, he is considered to be the founder of Lévis.

★**Maison Alphonse-Desjardins** (Alphonse-Desjardins House) – *8 Ave. Mont-Marie at corner of Rue Guenette. Open year-round Mon–Fri 10am–noon & 1pm–4:30pm, weekends noon–5pm. Closed Jan 1 & Dec 25.* ♿ 🅿 ☎ *418-835-2090.* Built between 1882 and 1884 in the Gothic Revival style, this small, white clapboard house was the home of Alphonse and Dorimène Desjardins for more than 40 years. The house was restored in 1982 by the Mouvement Desjardins *(above)* as a tribute to its founder. Displays of artifacts describe Desjardins' life and the beginning of the cooperative movement. Desjardins' office and other rooms have been refurbished to reflect the period (1906) when the *Caisse Populaire De Lévis* had its head office in the house.

★**Lieu historique national Fort-Numéro-Un-de-la-Pointe-de-Lévy** (Fort No. 1 at Point Lévy National Historic Site) – *2km/1.2mi by Rte 132 Est and Chemin du Gouvernement. Open early-May–late Aug. daily 10am–5pm. Late Aug.–early-Oct Thur–Sun 1pm–4pm. $3.* ♿ 🅿 *www.parkscanada.gc.ca/levy* ☎ *418-835-5182.* The fort (1865-1872) stands opposite Quebec City, atop Point Lévy, the highest point on the south shore. It is the sole vestige of three such forts built to protect the city from possible American attack during the American Civil War, and from the **Fenian Raids**. The Fenians were members of a secret, New York-based Irish society fighting to liberate Ireland from British domination and occupy British North America, or the Dominion of Canada. The fort was never completely garrisoned, and was nearly abandoned after the Treaty of Washington in 1871.

Shaped like an irregular pentagon, the fort is composed of a series of massive earthen ramparts with a tall embankment protecting the casemates, ditches and vaulted tunnels leading to the caponiers (stone and brick structures armed with small cannons). Its design marks the transition between two styles of fortification: the classical system, which involved enclosing protected areas with contiguous walls; and the mid-19C system of erecting a series of detached forts. Overlooking the river, the fort affords splendid **views**★ of the Montmorency Falls Park and Île d'Orleans.

EXCURSIONS

★**Ferry for Quebec City** – *Depart from dock in Lévis (accessible on foot or by car) year-round daily at 6am & 7am, 7:30am–11am & noon–6pm every half hour, 7pm–2am every hour. $1.50/person, $3/car.* ♿ *Société des traversiers du Québec* ☎ *418-837-2408 or 418-644-3704.* This ferry, in operation since 1812, offers fine **views** of the old capital, its port installations and harbour, and is by far the most scenic way to arrive in Quebec City.

★★**Bas-Saint-Laurent** – *See Entry Heading.*

★**Beauce** – *See Entry Heading.*

L'ISLET-SUR-MER

Chaudière-Appalaches
Population 1,786
Map p 80

Built along the banks of the St. Lawrence, L'Islet-sur-Mer originally consisted of two seigneuries conceded to the Couillard and Bélanger families by Frontenac in 1677. Since the 18C, the community's economy has thrived on maritime activity. Through the years, the village's native sons have taken to the sea as captains, pilots, sailors or fishermen.

Access – L'Islet-sur-Mer is 92km/57mi from Quebec City by Rte. 73 (Pierre-Laporte Bridge) and Rte. 20 (Exit 400, Rte. 285).

SIGHTS

*★***Église Notre-Dame de Bonsecours (Church of Our Lady of Perpetual Help)** – Open Jun 24–Labour Day daily 10am–5pm. & 🅿 ☎ 418-247-5103. The fieldstone church was built in 1768 and enlarged in 1884, when the facade was refurbished and twin steeples added. The statues in the niches of the facade, representing St. John the Baptist on the left and St. Francis of Assisi on the right, are the work of Amable Charron, who also designed the cornices of the interior. The main altar was fashioned by François Baillairgé and the tabernacle by Noël Levasseur. Six paintings by Antoine Plamondon grace the walls. The Stations of the Cross were carved in 1945 by Médard Bourgault, a native of Saint-Jean-Port-Joli.

Musée Maritime du Québec (Maritime Museum of Quebec) – *200m/656ft beyond church. Open mid-Jun–early-Sept daily 9am–5pm. Mid-May–mid-Jun & early-Sept–late-Oct daily 10am–5pm. Rest of the year Tue–Fri 10am–noon & 1pm–4pm. $5 (museum & ice-breaker) or $9 (museum, ice-breaker and hydrofoil).* 🅿 www.mma.qc.ca ☎ 418-247-5001. Dedicated to the memory of Captain Joseph-Elzéar Bernier (1852-1934), a native of L'Islet-sur-Mer who was a navigator and a pioneer of Arctic exploration, the museum focuses on the maritime history of the St. Lawrence River.

The collection includes elaborate models of different ships, in addition to numerous objects recovered from the 1914 wreck of the *Empress of Ireland*. Behind the museum, visitors can board the *Ernest Lapointe*, an icebreaker built in 1940 for the fleet of the Canadian Coast Guard. The other vessel, the *Bras d'Or 400 (Golden Arm)*, is a hydrofoil used by the Canadian Navy between 1968 and 1972.

LONGUEUIL

Montérégie
Population 127,977
Map p 175

Located on the south shore of the St. Lawrence, Longueuil was part of the seigneury granted to **Charles Le Moyne** in 1657. Between 1685 and 1690, Le Moyne built a massive stone fort that would serve as an outer defence to protect Montreal against the Iroquois and named it Longueuil after his birthplace in Normandy, France.
The fort was demolished in 1810. Le Moyne fathered twelve sons, several of whom were famous in their own right. He left his seigneury to his eldest son, Charles, who was granted a patent of nobility by Louis XIV. Among his other sons were the explorer **Pierre Le Moyne d'Iberville**, who helped Pierre de Troyes defeat the English at James Bay in 1686 and became governor of the conquered trading posts. His son **Jean-Baptiste Le Moyne de Bienville** founded New Orleans in 1718.
Today, Longueuil has become an industrial suburb of Montreal and is home to manufacturing plants for aircraft parts, textiles, furniture and toys.

Access – *Longueuil is about 10km/6mi from Montreal by the Jacques-Cartier Bridge. It can also be reached by metro and by a water shuttle connecting Montreal to the Longueuil marina in the summer.*

SIGHTS

Cathédrale Saint-Antoine-de-Padoue (St. Anthony of Padua Cathedral) – *On the corner of Rue Saint-Charles and Chemin de Chambly. Open year-round daily 7:30am–5pm. Contribution requested.* & ☎ *450-674-1549.* This imposing stone church (1885-1887) with its single steeple and dome is actually a "co-cathedral" for the diocese of Saint-Jean—Longueuil along with the cathedral in Saint-Jean-Sur-Richelieu. It stands on the former site of Le Moyne's fort. The ornate interior has three naves, and features paintings by the noted artist, Jean-Baptiste Roy Audy.
From the end of the Chemin de Chambly, the tower of Montreal's Olympic Stadium is visible.

Maison Rollin-Brais (Rollin-Brais House) – *205 Chemin de Chambly*. Built between 1794 and 1801, this stone house with its shingle roof and high chimneys originally served as a forge, but was later transformed into an inn.

Rue Saint-Charles Est – A number of historic houses, most of them made of stone, line this picturesque section of Rue Saint-Charles. The **Couvent de Longueuil** *(no. 70)* was originally built in 1769, and a convent wing was added in 1844. The **Maison Daniel-Poirier** *(no. 100)* dates from 1749.
The **Maison André-Lamarre** *(no. 255)*, built in 1740, is Longueuil's oldest home. The original pitched gable was replaced by a mansard roof in 1895. Today, the house is the headquarters of the Longueuil historical society.

Behind the Maison André-Lamarre, four foot bridges cross Route 132, and lead to a network of bike paths along the St. Lawrence. At the eastern end of this network, a ferry crosses to Charron Island and the Boucherville Islands Park *(depart from the yacht harbor mid-Jun–Aug Mon, Thu–Sun 10am–5pm every hour; mid-May–mid-Jun & Sept–mid-Oct weekends 10am–5pm; 5min; $2 round-trip;* & **P** *Société Sogerive* ☎ *450-442-9575)*.

LOUISEVILLE
Mauricie–Centre-du-Québec
Map p 153

In 1665, Charles de Jay, Sieur de Mannereuil, built a wooden fort on this site. At the end of the 19C, the village was named after Princess Louise, daughter of Queen Victoria and wife of the Marquis of Lorne, governor-general of Canada from 1878 to 1883. Today, Louiseville is a pleasant agricultural community.

Access – *Louiseville is 100km/62mi northeast of Montreal by Rte. 40 (Exit 166) and Rte. 138, which forms the main street.*

SIGHTS

Église Saint-Antoine-de-Padoue (Church of St. Anthony of Padua) – *On Rte. 138 in centre of town. Open year-round daily 8am–8pm.* & **P** ☎ *819-228-2739*. This imposing church with its twin steeples was built in 1926. The interior is decorated with frescoes and mosaics. Blocks of coloured marble create a lovely contrast between the warm beige walls and columns and the cool incandescence of the rose and blue marble sheathing the apse. The frescoes on each side of the choir (*The Nativity* on the left and *The Annunciation* on the right) are by Father Antonio Cianci and Olga Storaci Caron, respectively.

■ La Seigneurie Volant

3000 Chemin du Seigneur, Saint Paulin, QC. www.baluchon.com ☎ *819-268-2555.* Visit the manor, forge, mill, chapel and sugar shack constructed for the filming of the popular *télé-série Marguerite Volant*, an historical drama that recalled the experiences of the Seigneurie Volant in 18C New France. Take a guided tour, ride horseback, or try your hand at cross-country skiing. An obligatory tasting of the beers produced following recipes of the era are a nice end to any sojourn. Accommodation available at the nearby Auberge Le Baluchon *(info above)*.

★**Parc des Chutes Sainte-Ursule** (Sainte-Ursule Falls Park) – *11km/7mi by Rte. 348 and a small well-marked road. Open Jun–mid-Oct daily 9am–6pm. Rest of the year daily 9am–4:30pm. $5.* ✗ **P** ☎ *819-228-3555*. The Maskinongé River drops 70m/230ft at this point where the Canadian Shield abruptly meets the St. Lawrence Lowlands. In 1663, an earthquake changed the course of the river to cut through this rocky gorge of gneiss and pink granite. Trails follow the river as it tumbles through the gorge, leading to the site of a 19C paper mill; only its foundations remain. An observation tower offers views of the entire series of seven falls.

Admission prices and hours published in this guide are accurate at press time.

Îles de la MADELEINE★★

Îles de la Madeleine
Population 13,802
Map opposite

This isolated and windswept outpost of Quebec lies in the middle of the Gulf of St. Lawrence, closer to Cape Breton and Prince Edward Island than to the Gaspé Peninsula. Of the eight islands and numerous islets that make up the archipelago, six are linked by a series of sandy isthmuses, forming a hook-shaped mass about 72km/45mi long, stretching southwest to northeast. The islands offer a wealth of outdoor activities to the visitor, ranging from sightseeing to swimming and hiking.

Historical Notes

Discovery – During the 15C, the Magdalen Islands were a frequent stopping point for Basque and Breton fishermen in search of fish, seals, walruses and whales. The archipelago was officially discovered in 1534 by Jacques Cartier during the first of his three expeditions in the Gulf of St. Lawrence. Cartier landed first at Rocher aux Oiseaux (Bird Rock), then at Île Brion, due north of the islands, which he described in the ship's log as "the best land we have yet seen. A single acre of this soil is worth more than all of Newfoundland. We found it full of beautiful trees, prairies, fields of wild wheat, and flowering pea plants as varied and as lovely as anything I have seen in Brittany, and appearing to have been planted with much labour."
In the decades following Cartier's discovery, the islands were inhabited sporadically by Micmac Indians and by French explorers and fur traders. The archipelago is thought to have been named for Madeleine Fontaine, wife of **François Doublet**, the nobleman who colonized the territory in the name of the French Crown in 1663.

The Acadian Deportation – The archipelago was not permanently inhabited until after 1755, when it became a refuge for French colonists who had settled Acadia (now the west coast of Nova Scotia). An area of territorial dispute between Britain and France from 1604 to 1710, Acadia was ceded to Britain in 1713 under the Treaty of Utrecht, which ended the Spanish Succession War in Europe.

Practical Information

Time – The Magdalen Islands are on Atlantic time, which is one hour ahead of Eastern time (rest of Quebec).

Access – **By air:** Service between Montreal and Havre aux Maisons Island on Regionaire ☎ 888-373-4466 and Air Nova ☎ 888-247-2262. **By car/boat:** From Montreal, take Rte. 20 to Rivière-du-Loup, then Rte. 185 to Edmunston (New Brunswick), and Rte. 2 to Moncton (N.B.). From there, take Rte. 15, then Rte. 16 to Cape Tourmentine (N.B.), and cross the new toll bridge *(10min)* linking New Brunswick to Prince Edward Island. From Borden, take Rte. 1 to Charlottetown (P.E.I.), then Rte. 2 to Souris (P.E.I.) for the ferry to Cap-aux-Meules. *Ferry from Souris–Cap-aux-Meules (5hrs): daily service (except Mon) Apr 1–Jun & Sept–Oct from Cap-aux-Meules (8am) and from Souris (2pm). Daily service (except Tue) Jul–Aug from Cap-aux-Meules (8am) and from Souris (2pm). Limited service Nov–Jan. One-way $34.50/person, additional $65.75/car. Reservations required.* ✗ ᕋ ◨ *CTMA Traversier Ltd. Cap-aux-Meules ☎ 418-986-3278 or Souris ☎ 902-687-2181. Additional information ☎ 418-986-6600.*
A cargo ship accommodating 15 passengers departs year-round weekly from Montreal to Cap-aux-Meules *(2 days)*. Two months advance reservation required. Contact CTMA in Cap-aux-Meules ☎ 418-986-6600 or in Montreal ☎ 514-937-7656.

Accommodations – Inns, hotels, motels and B&Bs are concentrated on the islands of Cap aux Meules, Havre aux Maisons and Havre Aubert. In addition, many residents offer rooms, cottages and houses for rent. It is advisable to reserve lodging well in advance for a stay during the peak tourism months of July and August. Contact the Tourism Association *(below)*.

Visiting the Islands – The Tourism Association (Association Touristique des Îles-de-la-Madeleine) information office *(128 Chemin du Débarcadère, at the corner of Chemin Principale, Cap-aux-Meules ☎ 418-986-2245)* provides literature and information about guided tours of the islands, scenic cruises, outdoor activities, restaurants and accommodation.
Several private operators offer tours of the island (by van or boat) varying in length from several hours to a full day. To watch seals and view the cliff formations, scenic cruises are highly recommended. For close-up views of the cliffs and wildlife, hike along one of the many trails around the islands *(for information, contact the "Club vacances Les Îles" centre on Grande Entrée Island ☎ 418-985-2833)*.

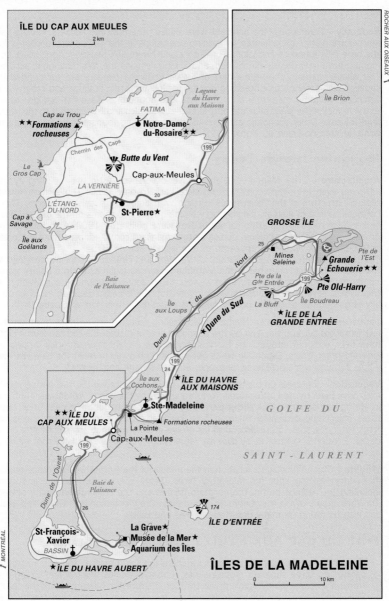

ÎLE DU CAP AUX MEULES

ROCHER AUX OISEAUX

ÎLES DE LA MADELEINE

When the Acadian settlers refused to swear an oath of unconditional allegiance to Great Britain, the governor of Nova Scotia, Charles Lawrence, issued a **Deportation Order** (August 1755), which forcibly expelled the Acadians to the American colonies. Several hundred escaped, fleeing to the Magdalen Islands and France's other remaining colonies, the islands of Saint-Pierre and Miquelon, off the southern coast of Newfoundland *(consult Michelin Green Guide to Canada)*.

In accordance with the terms of the Treaty of Paris (1763), the Magdalen Islands were ceded to Britain, while France retained control of Saint-Pierre and Miquelon. In the wake of the French Revolution, the Acadian refugees on these two islands joined their compatriots on the Magdalen Islands, preferring the British monarchy to the new French republic. These former Acadians are the ancestors of many of the islands' present population, known as *Madelinots*.

After the Conquest, the British government annexed the Magdalen Islands to Newfoundland but they soon became a seigneury of the Province of Quebec under the Quebec Act of 1774. King George III granted seigneurial title to Admiral Isaac Coffin in 1798 as a reward for his services to the British Empire, and the Coffins retained control of the islands for the next century. The hardships they exercised on their Acadian tenants forced many of the settlers into exile, this time to the north shore of the St. Lawrence. It was not until 1895 that the Acadians settlers obtained the rights to the land that they had painstakingly cleared and developed.

Economy – Traditionally the Acadians were skilled fishermen and farmers. Fishing and agriculture were supplemented by logging operations in the 19C, which accounts for the bare hills found on the islands of Entrée and Havre aux Maisons. Agriculture and logging have now greatly diminished, and fishing remains the chief economic activity. The islands, actually the visible part of a vast undersea plateau, are surrounded by shoals which are a natural breeding ground for lobster, crab, scallops and other shellfish. Cod, flounder, mackerel and perch are also abundant. These fish are processed at the Madelipêche plant near the port at Cap-aux-Meules and transported to the mainland for sale. Other economic activities include a growing tourism industry and a salt mine, located on Dune du Nord.

Magdalen Islands Today

Architecture – The Magdalen Islands have developed distinctive building types, although even the oldest constructions date back to only 1850. The earliest known type of structure is the fisherman's cottage with adjoining subsistence farm. These cottages consist of a small, single-storey building with two rooms on the ground floor and a small room in the attic. Larger houses were built after 1900, with four rooms on each floor. Many traditional homes feature mansard roofs, adopted from the presbyteries and convents that appeared on the islands about 1875.

The large wooden churches at Bassin, La Vernière and Grande-Entrée are designed in the style of Catholic churches in the Maritime Provinces (such as Church Point), while numerous Protestant churches bear witness to an active anglophone community. In the 1960s, several new parishes were created on the islands, resulting in an unusually large number of contemporary religious churches in this part of Quebec.

Landscape – The Magdalen Islands' most striking features are without question the **rock formations** cut into the land by the pounding sea. In places, the red sandstone cliffs have been sculpted into arches, tunnels, caves, and defiant promontories topped by emerald-green grass. Expansive white beaches stretch away to meet the blue sea, the whole forming a multicoloured seascape, at once savage and serene.

Vegetation – Tall trees on the island are rare: those that escaped the 19C lumbermen's axes have been twisted into unique, tortured shapes by the winds. Wildflowers abound in spring and summer. The **pitcher plant**, a carnivorous plant found in peat bogs, captures insects by drowning them in fluid secreted in its pitcher-shaped leaves. In freshwater marshes, the **multicoloured iris** grows in colonies that are sometimes quite dense. Erosion is controlled by **dune hay** *(ammophile)*, with its expansive root system, and moss, covering the dunes.

Wildlife – The archipelago's location in the middle of the Gulf of St. Lawrence makes it an ideal resting spot for migratory birds. Many species nest here year-round, including the Atlantic puffin, the northern gannet and the endangered piping plover. The rare snowy owl is indigenous to the islands. Grey, common and Greenland seals can also be found on many deserted beaches and islets.

★★ÎLE DU CAP AUX MEULES (CAP AUX MEULES ISLAND)

The largest of the islands, this is the archipelago's commercial and administrative centre. Its three separate municipalities (Cap-aux-Meules, Fatima and Étang-du-Nord) are connected by scenic drives through the forested hills and along the coast. The island was named for the millstones, or *meules*, found on the cape overlooking the port.

The quaint **port** at Cap-aux-Meules is the archipelago's lively gateway. Evenings are a good time for a stroll, to observe a variety of boats and trawlers, some dry-docked for repairs, others being readied for the next day's fishing.

Take Rte. 199 (Chemin Principal) west to La Vernière.

★**Église Saint-Pierre de La Vernière (Church of St. Peter of La Vernière)** – *Rte. 199 at the intersection of Chemin de l'Église in La Vernière. Open year-round Mon–Fri 8:30am–7pm.* ♿ 🅿 ☎ *418-986-2410.* This vast, wooden edifice dominates Plaisance Bay, and its white silhouette is visible from the islands of Havre Aubert and Havre aux Maisons. The original church, erected in 1876, has been incorporated into the transept of the present structure; the nave and choir were added at the turn of the century. The polygonal tower, surmounted by an elegant spire, recalls the architecture of churches in the Maritime Provinces, evidence of an affiliation between the island parishes and the diocese of Charlottetown, Prince Edward Island, that ended in 1947.

Butte du Vent (Vent Hillock) – The Chemin de l'Église leads up into the hills toward the butte du Vent, *(turn left on Chemin Cormier and immediately right on Chemin des Arsène. Caution is advised on the unpaved roads; 4-wheel drive vehicle strongly recommended).* This is the highest point on the island, affording extensive **views**★★ of the entire archipelago and Plaisance Bay.

Return to Chemin de l'Église, turn left on Chemin des Huet, then right on Chemin des Caps to the municipality of Fatima.

★★ **Église Notre-Dame-du-Rosaire (Church of Our Lady of the Rosary)** – *Chemin des Caps in Fatima. Open year-round daily 8am–5pm.* ☎ *418-986-2685.* A lovely example of contemporary religious architecture, the church celebrates the archipelago's maritime way of life. From the outside the building resembles a scallop shell; the interior abounds in nautical symbolism, including porthole windows, an altar and pulpit evoking a breakwater, and recessed Stations of the Cross scattered across the wall in a wave pattern. The church's design, by Jean-Claude Leclerc, is reminiscent of the Ronchamps chapel in eastern France by the renowned 20C architect, Le Corbusier.

Return south on Chemin des Caps. Turn right on Chemin de la Belle-Anse and drive to the coast.

★★ **Formations rocheuses (Rock formations)** – Visitors can walk northward along the coast from Chemin de la Belle-Anse to **Cap au Trou** (Cape Trou) to see some of the most dramatic formations on the archipelago. Here the sea has bitten savagely into the red sandstone, leaving deep fissures and jutting promontories. In places, where the arches have collapsed, only solitary columns of stone withstand the force of the sea. *(Note: the cliffs are unstable; avoid the edges and use extreme caution when walking in this area).*

Cliffs on Île du Cap aux Meules

Continue south on Chemin de la Belle-Anse; turn right on Chemin des Caps, then right on Chemin de l'Étang-du-Nord.

Other impressive rock formations can be found along the coast near Étang-du-Nord, where a small, lively port provides a haven for numerous fishing trawlers. A stroll along rugged **Cap à Savage** (Cape Savage) is highlighted by good views of Cap aux Meules' western coast and of tiny **Île aux Goélands** (Goélands Island), named for the gulls *(goéland in French)* that flock there.

Return to Cap-aux-Meules.

★ÎLE DU HAVRE AUBERT (HAVRE AUBERT ISLAND)

The gently rolling hills of the southernmost island in the archipelago are the setting for some of the prettiest examples of local domestic architecture. The community of Havre-Aubert is the centre of the islands' cultural life.

★ **La Grave** – *Northeast of Havre-Aubert.* This historic site takes its name from the word *"a grave"* in reference to the meeting place where merchants came to buy the fishermen's salted and dried products. Here, some 15 grey-shingled buildings line the road that skirts a small bay and leads out to Cape Grindley. This historic site includes stores, an ironworks, two **chafauds** (sheds where cod was dried and prepared) and several warehouses. Abandoned by the fishing industry, the buildings now house artisans' boutiques, where craftsmen create and sell objects made from local materials such as sand, alabaster and sealskin.

Aquarium des Îles (Island Aquarium) – *Open mid-Jun–mid-Aug daily 10am–6pm. Mid-Aug–mid-Oct 10am–5pm. $4.* ♿ ▯ ☎ *418-937-2277.* Tanks of fish native to the archipelago surround a large, open pool where visitors can handle the fish. On the upper floors, a gallery features displays which explain and demonstrate the methods of fish preservation and processing (drying, smoking, and canning) that enable Madelinot fishermen to export their products.

★**Musée de la Mer** (Maritime Museum) – *Point Shea, adjacent to La Grave. Open Jun 24–late Aug Mon–Fri 9am–6pm, weekends 10am–6pm. Rest of the year Mon–Fri 9am–noon & 1pm–5pm, weekends 1pm–5pm. $4.* ♿ ▯ *www.ilesdela-madeleine.com/musee/index.htm* ☎ *418-937-5711.* Here, displays of boats, navigational instruments and diverse artifacts acquaint visitors with the maritime history and culture of the Magdalen Islands. The exhibit also covers fishing methods and presents the story of the "ponchon," a mail barrel that was the only means of communication during February of 1910, when a severed telegraph cable resulted in the archipelago's complete isolation from the mainland.

From La Grave, return to the centre of the island via Rte. 199, bearing left at Chemin du Bassin.

The scenic drive through the community of Bassin and along Anse-à-la-Cabane winds past colourful houses typical of the islands. Many structures feature mansard-style roofs; others have verandas and balconies, with finely crafted posts and railings and intricately carved corbels.

Église Saint-Francois-Xavier (St. Francis-Xavier Church) – *In Bassin. Open daily year round.* ♿ ▯ ☎ *418-937-5580.* This large wooden church was built in 1939, in the Romanesque Revival style. The presbytery (1876), topped by multiple mansard roofs, is the best example of Second Empire architecture on the islands.

★ÎLE DU HAVRE AUX MAISONS
(HAVRE AUX MAISONS ISLAND)

One of the loveliest islands of the archipelago, Havre aux Maisons has retained its rural charm, with its scattered houses, winding roads, farmland and **baraques** – small buildings with sliding roofs designed to shelter hay. Several scenic drives skirt the coastline, affording charming views.

Île du Havre aux Maisons

At Havre aux Maisons Island, turn left at Chemin du Cap-Rouge, and again at Chemin des Cyrs for views of Petite Bay, Cochons Island and La Pointe.

At **La Pointe**, small wharfs buzz with activity. Lobster is sold live or cooked, and visitors can watch clams being cleaned and prepared.

Return to Rte. 199 and continue to Chemin Central.

Église Sainte-Madeleine (St. Magdalen Church) – *On Chemin Central. Open year round daily 8am–8pm.* ♿ ☎ *418-969-2212.* Built in 1969, the structure features great upward curves that unite the church and the presbytery around a central entrance. The nave, lit by a windowed wall, is in the form of an amphitheatre. Its low ceiling confers a sense of intimacy to the vast space.

Return to Rte. 199 and turn left on Chemin de la Pointe-Basse.

The drive to the harbour at Pointe-Basse, along the Chemin du Quai *(on the right)* passes by a complex of abandoned *fumoirs*, large wooden smokehouses filled with rods on which the fish were hung during the smoking process.

Return to Chemin de la Pointe-Basse.

The road offers views of this island's **rock formations**, which are concentrated around Anse-à-Firmin and Cape Alright. At **Dune du Sud★**, visitors will find a superb, wide beach and relatively calm currents.

Continue on Chemin de la Pointe-Basse which runs along the coast and becomes Chemin des Échoueries before rejoining Rte. 199.

EASTERN ISLANDS

The easternmost islands of the archipelago are connected to the others by **Dune du Nord**, a narrow ridge. North of the dune is a government-operated **salt mine** (mines Seleines), which produces salt used to de-ice Quebec's roads in winter.

Grosse Île – The smallest of the contiguous islands is inhabited mainly by descendants of Scottish tenant farmers who arrived in the early 18C, having been forced off the lands they tended in their native Scotland, as a result of the development of sheep-raising. It is here that the traditional lifestyle based on fishing and agriculture has changed the least.

Pointe-de-l'Est National Wildlife Reserve – *Open Jun 24–Aug. Information on hiking trails located within the reserve: "Club vacances Les Îles"* ☎ *418-985-2833.* Bordered to the southeast by a vast beach, this 1,440ha/3,557 acre area offers an excellent introduction to the world of sand dunes: their wildlife (seals, migratory birds), their flora (dune hay), and their glorious topography (beaches, marshes).

★★**Plage de la Grande Échouerie** (Grand Échouerie Beach) – This seemingly endless expanse of sand that stretches out and around the easternmost point of the wildlife reserve is considered the archipelago's loveliest beach. The term *échouerie* refers to the rocky ledges where walruses basked in the sun.

★**Île de la Grande Entrée** – Lobster fishing formed the basis for settlement of this small stretch of land, which was colonized in 1870.

Pointe Old-Harry (Old Harry Point) – Grand Échouerie Beach leads to this point, now a small harbour protected by a typical Madelinot jetty made of *dolosses*, or anchor-shaped cement blocks. Walrus hunting, which began in the 17C, brought the first European settlers to the islands. The walruses were slaughtered and cut up at Old Harry.

Route 199 runs the length of the island, ending at the small fishing port of Grande Entrée, where docks and fishing boats are painted in bright colours.

Coastal hiking trails – These trails afford some of the archipelago's most impressive **views★★★** onto jagged cliffs and jutting promontories, tidal pools and vast beaches, twisted trees and colourful wildflowers. From the parking lot at the end of Chemin des Pealey, hikers in search of vast panoramas can explore La Bluff and Boudreau Island, for vistas extending as far as Pointe-de-l'Est.

ÎLE D'ENTRÉE (ENTRY ISLAND)

Ferry from Cap-aux-Meules. Contact Tourist Association office for schedule and reservations.

The only inhabited island that remains detached from the others, this outpost is home to approximately 200 English-speaking residents. Its smooth, treeless hills are laced with trails from which hikers can view fascinating rock formations and wildlife, especially the cormorant, a long-necked seabird.

From Big Hill, the highest peak in the islands (174m/571ft), the **view** embraces the entire archipelago.

MAGOG★

Cantons de l'Est
Population 14,050
Map p 99

This community on the shores of beautiful Lake Memphrémagog was originally named Décharge du Lac (the "outlet"), because of its location at the source of the Magog River. In 1888, the town adopted the name Magog, a shortened version of the Abenaki word Memphrémagog, meaning "large expanse of water." The first settler was Loyalist Ralph Merry who arrived in 1799. Today, Magog is a textile manufacturing centre and a popular resort owing to its lakeside location and the proximity of Mt. Orford Park.

Access – *Magog is 120km/74mi east of Montreal by Rte. 10 (Exits 115 or 118) and 25km/ 15mi from Sherbrooke by Rte. 112, which becomes Rue Principale.*

SIGHTS

★**Parc de la Pointe-Merry** (Pointe-Merry Park) – *Just south of Rue Principale (Rte. 112).* This pleasant green space affords splendid **views★** of the northern end of the lake, which stretches over 50km/31mi, crossing the border into Vermont. The wooded peaks of Mt. Orford and Owl's Head are visible from the lake.

★**Scenic Cruises** – *Depart from Quai Magog Jun 24–Labour Day daily 10am–6pm, mid-May–Jun 23 & early Sept–mid-Oct weekends noon–2pm. Round-trip 1hr 45min ($14, reservations suggested) or 7hrs ($52, reservations required), according to destination. Commentary.* ✗ ⅊ 🅿 *Croisiéres Memphrémagog Inc. www.croisiere-memphremagog.com* ☏ *819-843-8068.* The cruise leads passengers to some of the loveliest areas of Lake Memphremagog. A longer cruise *(7hrs)* makes the journey from Magog to Newport, Vermont.

Abbaye de Saint-Benoît-du-Lac

EXCURSIONS

★**Abbaye de Saint-Benoît-du-Lac (Saint-Benoît-du-Lac Abbey)** – *20km/12mi. Leave Magog on Rte. 112 Ouest; turn left after 5km/ 3mi. Open year-round daily 5am–noon & 1pm–8pm.* ⅊ 🅿 ☏ *819-843-4080.* The drive to Saint-Benoît-du-Lac, whose only inhabitants are the monks of the Benedictine abbey, offers lovely glimpses of Lake Memphrémagog. The abbey (1912) was founded by members of the Saint-Wandrille-de-Fontenelle abbey in Normandy, who were exiled to Belgium after being banned from France in the early 20C. The monks founded a novitiate on the site in 1924, and Saint-Benoît-du-Lac was elevated to the rank of abbey in 1952. The monastery complex, surmounted by an impressive bell tower, occupies a magnificent **site★★**, striking for its peace, serenity and sheer beauty. With the exception of the original buildings, most of the structures were designed in 1937 by French Benedictine monk, **Dom Paul Bellot** (1876-1944), who lies buried in the abbey cemetery. Montreal architect Dan S. Hanganu conceived the plans for the abbey church, consecrated on December 4, 1994.

Visitors can attend vespers in the oratory and listen to Gregorian chants at daily services. The monks produce two well-known cheeses, L'Ermite and Mont-Saint-Benoît, which are sold in a small shop on the premises.

★**Parc du Mont-Orford (Mt. Orford Park)** – *See Entry Heading.*

Complexe MANIC-OUTARDES

Manicouagan
Map p 88

Begun in 1959, the mammoth undertaking of harnessing the energy of the Manicouagan and Outardes Rivers took 20 years to complete. The project led to the development of new technologies that surpassed any previous engineering feats and established several world records. The completion of the seven power plants involved the mobilization of thousands of men and women and the transportation of tonnes of material into the vast forest wilderness of the Manicouagan region.

Beneath the site chosen for the construction of the main dam at Manic-3, permeable alluvial deposits threatened to allow water seepage into the projected structure. In order to prevent this, engineers sank a double concrete wall 131m/430ft into the earth's surface, thus creating the world's largest waterproof shield.

The electricity produced at the Manic-Outardes Complex is transmitted to major cities by 735,000-volt lines. Never before had such high voltage lines been used for commercial purposes.

Today, the combined capacity of Manic's seven power plants is 6,821 megawatts (1 megawatt = 1,000,000 watts). A network of 735,000-volt power lines (the first of this type used for commercial purposes) transport electricity from the plants to major cities. The three power plants comprising the **Outardes Complex** *(not open to the public)* are fed by a 652sq km/252sq mi reservoir established 93km/58mi upstream from the confluence of the Outardes and St. Lawrence Rivers. Most of the dams and dikes of the Outardes complex are earth-and-rockfill constructions made of material found near the sites.

Access – *Manic-5 is located 211km/130mi north of Baie-Comeau on Rte. 389, a paved but winding road known as "Chemin de la Manic." Manic-2 is 21km/14mi north of Baie-Comeau by the same route. Rte. 389 is partially paved beyond Manic-5 but it continues to Fermont (345km/214mi from Manic-5) and Wabush (390km/242mi). A campground with gas station and snack bar is located near Manic-2; a restaurant and gas station are located near Manic-3; a motel (reservations required) with restaurant and gas station is situated 3km/2mi from Manic-5. Accommodation is also available in Baie-Comeau.*

VISIT

★**Manic-2** – *Visit by guided tour (1hr 30min) only, Jun 24–Labour Day daily at 9am, 11am, 1:30pm & 3:30pm.*   ⭳   🅿   *www.hydro.qc.ca*   ☎   *418-294-3923.* Operating since the mid-1960s, Manic-2 was the first power plant of the Manic-Outardes Complex to produce electricity. The giant concrete wall is 94m/303ft high and 692m/2,270ft long and is one of the largest hollow joint gravity dams in the world. Because of its tremendous weight, a gravity dam can withstand the enormous pressure exerted by the water trapped in its reservoir; the hollow joints, extending from the foundation to the top of the dam, reduce the amount of concrete required to build the structure by 15 percent. The power plant, located at the base of the dam, has a head of 70m/230ft. The facility's eight turbine-alternators can generate up to 1,015,200kwh.

★★**Manic-5** – Measuring 214m/702ft in height and 1,314m/4,307ft in length, the spectacular **Daniel Johnson Dam**★★ is the largest arch-and-buttress dam in the world. The dam was completed in 1968 after seven years under construction, and is named for the former prime minister of Quebec, Daniel Johnson, who died on the site of the complex on the morning of its inauguration. The dam regulates the water supply to all the power stations of the Manic-Outardes complex.

With the construction of the dam, two semicircular lakes – the Manicouagan and the Mouchalagane – were united into an immense ring of water encircling an island. The diameter of the reservoir is 65km/40mi. A study of the reservoir led geo-

Daniel Johnson Dam at Manic-5

Hydro-Québec

physicists to theorize that the natural depression of the lakes may have been created by a meteorite that crashed to earth some 200 million years ago. The depression is comparable to a moon crater, and rock found at the site is similar to samples of moon rock brought to earth by astronauts.

The Manic-5 power plant is located approximately one kilometre downstream from the dam. Its head is 150m/492ft high, and its turbines are capable of producing 1,532,000kwh.

Visit – *Visit by guided tour (1hr 30min) only, Jun 24–Labour Day daily at 9am, 11am, 1:30pm & 3:30pm.* & ☐ ☎ *418-294-3923.* Guides describe the Manic-Outardes dams and explain how electricity is produced and transmitted to consumers. Scale models complement the talk. A bus then takes visitors to the base of the massive arches and across the top of the dam overlooking the countryside and the Manicouagan River.

Manic-5 PA – This underground power plant began production in 1989 with four generator sets. The initials "PA" stand for *puissance additionnelle* (additional power) because this new facility provides supplementary power to Manic-5 during peak periods. The total energy potential of the two Manic-5 power plants is 2,747 megawatts.

MAURICIE★

Mauricie–Centre-du-Québec
Map opposite

The Maurìcie region encompasses the valley of the Saint-Maurice River, which flows southward for 560km/347mi, from the Gouin Reservoir in the northern part of central Quebec to the St. Lawrence River. The Saint-Maurice River was named after Maurice Poulin de la Fontaine, who explored the waterway in 1668. Capital of the Mauricie, Trois-Rivières is the major industrial centre of the region.

Historical Notes

The valley of the Saint-Maurice River has been an important industrial region since the 18C. Rich veins of iron ore were first mined here in 1730, and forestry has dominated the regional economy since 1850. In the late 19C, hydroelectric plants were established in Grand-Mère, Shawinigan and La Gabelle. Their energy supply, together with the invention of floating booms (chains of logs enclosing free-floating logs), led entrepreneurs to establish pulp mills between 1890 and 1900. Chemical plants later opened in Grand-Mère and Shawinigan, and eventually, a major aluminium plant was built in Shawinigan. Because of the major aluminium smelter in Shawinigan, the valley ranks among the most industrialized regions in both the province and the nation.

Access – *The valley of the Saint-Maurice River extends from Trois-Rivières north to La Tuque, along Rtes. 55 and 155.*

FROM TROIS-RIVIÈRES TO LA TUQUE *170km/105mi.*
Leave Trois-Rivières by Boulevard des Forges.

★★**Lieu historique national des Forges-du-Saint-Maurice** (Les Forges-du-Saint-Maurice Saint-Maurice National Historic Site) – *13km/8mi. Open mid-May–mid Sept daily 9:30am–5:30pm. Early Sept–mid-Oct daily 9:30am–4:30pm. $4* & ☐ *www.parkscanada.gc.ca ☎ 819-378-5116.* The ironworks on the banks of the Saint-Maurice River operated 150 years (1729-1883) and engendered Canada's first industrial community. Today this National Historic Site commemorates the inception of Canada's massive iron and steel industry.

By special warrant of King Louis XV, François Poulin de Francheville established the first blast furnace in 1730 as part of an initiative to exploit the natural resources of New France. At its productive zenith, the furnace was capable of reducing 19 tonnes of raw ore per day to 4 tonnes of liquid cast iron. Iron was smelted here until 1883. The **Grande Maison** (1737), which housed managers' offices, a store and living quarters, today serves as the park's welcome centre. Displays on the ground floor explain the economic and social conditions in Canada during the early years of the forge's operation. Objects produced at the forge, which included guns and ammunition, cooking pots, wheel hubs, horseshoes and cast iron bedsteads, are on view in the basement. On the upper floor a "sound and light" narration uses a scale model of the forge village as it appeared around 1845.

From the Grande Maison, a path leads to the vestiges of the **blast furnace**. The shape of the structures comprising the ironworks have been recreated by a three-dimensional metal structure. At the blast furnace (haut fourneau), an excellent interpretation centre explains the smelting process in layman's terms; particularly interesting is reconstructed hydraulic machinery of the type used during the 18C. Other displays present the sources and types of ore, and a small, furnished cabin illustrates the life led by forge workers and their families during the late 18C.

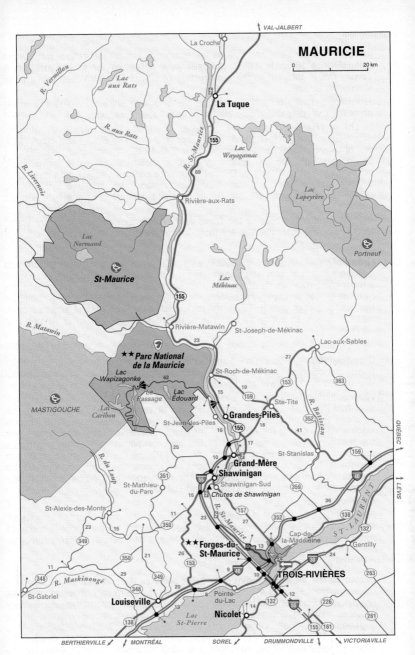

A pleasant path leads down to the Saint-Maurice River; along the way, other vestiges are visible, including the **upper forge** (haute forges), the finerystack of the **lower forge** (basse forges), and the **mill** (moulin). Beside the river, a spring known as the **Devil's Fountain** (Fontaine du Diable) is a source of natural gas.

Continue northward on Blvd. des Forges and take Rte. 55 (Exit 196).

Shawinigan – *23km/ 14mi (Exit 217 South).* This community was formerly referred to as "electric city" because it generated all the power needed to supply Montreal. The name Shawinigan comes from the Algonquian word *ashawenikan,* meaning "portage on the crest."

Hôtel Sacacomie

4000 Rang Sacacomie, St-Alexis-des-Monts. www.sacacomie.com ☎ 819-265-4444. $139-$169/night Located in pristine wilderness and bordering a majestic lake, the Hotel Sacacomie with its powerful log exterior and simple and rustic interior makes for great weekend and week-long getaways. Horseback riding, diving, seaplane tours, golf, snowmobiling and many other outdoor activities await.

In 1852, a water slide was built to transport logs around the various falls on the Saint-Maurice River. In 1899, the falls were harnessed for their hydroelectric power; this in turn led to the construction of pulp mills, chemical plants and an aluminium smelter.

From town, take Rte. 157 Sud across the bridge to Shawinigan-Sud and follow signs for the "parc des chutes de Shawinigan" and Shawinigan-Sud.

La Cité de l'énergie – *1000 Ave. Melville. Open late June–early Sept Mon–Fri 10am–8pm. June–late-June & early Sept–mid-Oct Tue–Sun 10am–5pm. $14. ঙ P www.citedelenergie.com ☎ 819-536-4992.* Constructed next to the Shawinigan Falls, the City of Energy enlightens visitors to the role hydroelectric power plays in the history of Quebec. A science center complete with interactive displays and multimedia presentation, observation tower and two hydroelectric power plants bring to life the innovations and inventions of the hydroelectric industry.

Although the rocky beds of the **Chutes de Shawinigan** (Shawinigan Falls) are scenic throughout the year, the falls are most impressive during the spring run-off.

Return to Rte. 55.

Grand-Mère – *10km/6mi (Exit 223).* In 1890, a hydroelectric power station was built here and pulp mills were constructed shortly afterwards. The town was named after a giant rock which protruded from the middle of the river, resembling the head of an old woman (Grand-Mère means "grandmother"). To make room for the Hydro-Québec dam in 1916, the rock (rocher de Grand-Mère) was relocated, piece by piece, to a tiny park in the centre of town *(corner of 5ᵉ Avenue and 1ʳᵉ Rue).*

Leave Grand-Mère by the bridge over the Saint-Maurice River and take Rte. 155.

Grandes-Piles – *17km/10mi.* Founded in 1885 as a transfer point for lumber boats, this community is perched on a cliff overlooking the river. The municipality was named for the pile-shaped rocks located in the waterfall south of the village.

★**Village du Bûcheron** (Lumbermen's Village) – *On Rte. 155 in Grandes-Piles. Open mid-May–mid-Oct daily 10am–5pm. $8. ✗ ঙ P ☎ 819-538-7895.* Twenty-five buildings and a collection of more than 5,000 objects recreate a typical Québécois logging village during the early 20C. The rough, axe-hewn timber structures evoke the rudimentary living conditions of the men for whom the cutting and transportation of wood were a way of life. In each of the buildings, objects and furnishings highlight the living conditions of loggers, fire watchmen and storage guards. Visitors can enjoy a snack in the restored cook's house and visit the sawmill, forge, lumbermen's quarters and stables.

Continue on Rte. 155.

Between Grandes-Piles and Saint-Roch-de-Mékinac, the drive affords lovely **views**★ of the powerful Saint-Maurice River and the rocky cliffs on the opposite shore. In spring, osprey *(balbuzard)*, large fish-eating hawks, nest here and visitors can often see them circling above the river.

Continue to Rivière-Matawin (38km/24mi).

Detour to the Réserve faunique du Saint-Maurice (Saint-Maurice Wildlife Reserve) – *Access by bridge across the Saint-Maurice River (toll: $12/car). A welcome center (2km/1.2mi from Rivière-Matawin) provides maps and information for various activities (lodging, camping, fishing, hunting, canoe-camping, nature study, dogsledding, hiking). Open mid-May–mid-Sept daily 7:30am–9:30pm. Mid-Sept–Nov Mon–Fri 8am–4:30pm, weekends 8am–9:30pm (certain roads may closed in the winter; call in advance). ✗ ঙ P ☎ 819-646-5680.* This vast wilderness of forests, lakes and streams is a haven for fishermen and canoeists. Numerous campgrounds are scattered around Lake Normand, famous for its clear waters and long, sandy beaches.

The 22km/13.5mi **Pionniers Circuit**, a canoeing and camping circuit, runs through the hills and woods of the reserve. Other sights include waterfalls (the Dunbar waterfall is most spectacular), rock formations (including the "boat-rock", shaped like a boat) and a nature trail through the boreal forest.

La Tuque – *69km/43mi.* A former fur trading post, La Tuque, like many other towns in this region, owes its existence to vast forested areas and a powerful waterfall. It boasts a pulp and paper mill and a hydroelectric plant (1909). Its name is derived from a hill shaped like the popular woollen hat known as a *tuque*.

La Tuque is the birthplace of singer-composer **Félix Leclerc** (1914-1988), who became the first Quebec songwriter to acquire international fame. His songs praise the beauty of the forests and rivers of Quebec, with special emphasis on the St. Lawrence River.

Unless otherwise indicated, distances given after each stop on an itinerary are calculated from the previous town or sight described.

Parc national de la MAURICIE★★

Mauricie–Centre-du-Québec

Map p 153

Established in 1970 with a view to preserving a representative slice of the Laurentian Mountains, the Mauricie National Park comprises 536sq km/205sq mi in a transition area between the deciduous woods of the south and the boreal forest. Maples and conifers thickly cover rounded hills rising some 350m/1,148ft and interspersed with numerous rivers and lakes. For 5,000 years, the region's rich natural resources have attracted indigenous peoples, trappers, loggers, raftsmen, fishermen and hunters. Before being designated a national park, it was one of the largest private hunting and fishing grounds in North America.

Access – *Mauricie National Park is located some 70km/42mi north of Trois-Rivières by Rte. 55. Its two principal entrances are the west entrance near Saint-Mathieu (exit 217) and the east entrance near Saint-Jean-des-Piles (Exit 226; follow the signs). West entrance open May–Oct. East entrance open May–Oct & Dec–Mar. Accommodation limited to camping, although the Wabénaki and Andrew lodges (open year-round) provide dormitory-style sleeping arrangements. Reservations required for the lodges ☎ 819-537-4555.*

Activities – *Canoeing and canoe-camping are among the best ways of exploring the park (canoes and security equipment can be rented on site). Several trails with rudimentary campsites run through the back country. Some circuits require difficult and extensive portaging over relatively rough terrain, and canoeing lessons are strongly recommended. Visitors can swim, hike, and fish for speckled and lake trout.*

VISIT

Park open year-round. Visitor centers at the Saint-Jean-des-Piles and Saint-Mathieu entrances offer information, entrance permits, canoe rentals and interpretative displays; open mid-May–Labour Day daily 7am–10pm; early Sept–early Oct daily 9am–4:30pm (Fri 10pm). $3.50. ⚠ ✂ ♿ 🅿 www.parkscanada.gc.ca/mauricie ☎ 819-538-3232.

Scenic Drive – *62km/38mi between the two park entrances.* This wonderful drive meanders through the pink metamorphic rocks of the Canadian Shield. The road follows the long, finger-shaped **Lac Wapizagonke** over 16km/10mi, providing several viewpoints of cliffs and sandy beaches. The observation deck at Le Passage *(30km/19mi)* affords a superb **view** of the area.

The road leads to **Lac Édouard**, a narrow stretch of water surrounded by a pleasant, natural beach, then winds, curves and descends to the eastern entrance of the park, offering pleasant views of the Saint-Maurice River.

Lac MÉGANTIC★

Cantons-de-l'Est

Map p 156

Situated in the southeast corner of Quebec, this lovely lake covers 26sq km/10sq mi and reaches depths of 75m/246ft. Located near the American border, its southern end is surrounded by the Blanches Mountains. From Lake Mégantic, the Chaudière River flows northward across the southern part of the province to join the St. Lawrence near Quebec City.

Discovered by Father Druillettes in 1646, the lake region was settled by the Abenaki in 1700. They called it *Namesokanjik*, meaning "place where fish abound." Formerly a logging centre, Lake Mégantic is now a haven for fishermen and vacationers.

Access – *Lake Mégantic is located 190km/118mi south of Quebec City by Rte. 73 and Rtes. 173 and 204. The community of Lac-Mégantic lies at the junction of Rtes. 204 and 161.*

VISIT

Lac-Mégantic – This community is located on the northern shores of Lake Mégantic, where it empties into the Chaudière River. It was founded in 1885 by Scottish settlers who left their architectural signature in the numerous red brick buildings along the main street. Today the town is a small industrial and commercial centre. A pleasant park beside the lake *(behind the courthouse)* provides good views of the mountains, notably the peak of Mt. Mégantic to the west.

The **Église Sainte-Agnès** (Church of St. Agnes) houses a lovely **stained-glass window**, depicting the Jesse Tree, created in 1849 for the Church of the Immaculate Conception, located in London's Mayfair district *(open Jun–Sept Mon 9am–4pm, Tue & Fri 9am–7:30pm, Wed–Thu & Sat–Sun 9am–5pm; rest of the year Mon 9am–4pm, Tue & Fri 9am–7:30pm, Wed & Sat 9am–5pm, Thu & Sun 9am–4pm; ♿ 🅿 ☎ 819-583-0370).*

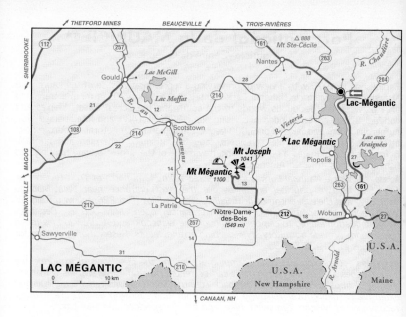

EXCURSION TO MT. MÉGANTIC *59km/36mi.*

Leave Lac-Mégantic by Rte. 161.

The road rises above the lake, overlooking the Blanches Mountains to the south. *At Woburn (27km/17mi), turn right on Rte. 212 and continue for 18km/11mi.* The road reaches **Notre-Dame-des-Bois**, the village with the highest altitude (549m/1,801ft) in the province.

In Notre-Dame-des-Bois, turn right following signs to the Mt. Megantic Conservation Park.

Mt. Mégantic – *13km/8mi.* Near the top of this peak (1,100m/3,608ft) is the **ASTROlab** *(open mid-May–mid-June weekends noon–5pm & 8pm–11pm; mid-Jun–Aug daily noon–midnight; Sept–mid-Oct weekends noon–5pm & 8pm–11pm; reservations required for evening tours; $10; http://astrolab.qc.ca ☎ 819-888-2941),* a small observatory operated jointly by the Universities of Montreal and Laval. The telescope here is one of the most powerful in eastern North America, measuring 1.6m/5.2ft in diameter and weighing approximately 26 tons.

Return 3km/2mi and turn left, following a rough road that climbs steeply for 1km/.6mi up Mt.Joseph.

Mt. Joseph – Father Corriveault of Notre-Dame-des-Bois constructed the small sanctuary here in 1883 after the village inhabitants were miraculously saved from devastating tornadoes after praying to St. Joseph. The summit affords a stunning **view★★** of the surrounding mountainous region.

Jardins de MÉTIS★★
(Reford Gardens)

Gaspésie
Map p 104

In 1886, Lord Mount Stephen (1829-1921), president and founder of the Canadian Pacific Railway Company, purchased this tract of land at the confluence of the Métis and Saint Lawrence rivers from the Seigneur of Grand-Métis, Archibald Ferguson. The land was to be Stephen's salmon fishing retreat, but he spent very little time at Grand-Métis, and in 1918 he gave the land to his niece, Elsie Stephen Reford. From 1926 to 1959, Mrs. Reford gradually transformed the estate into magnificent gardens. Over 3,000 varieties of flowers and ornamental plants, including many rare species, flourish in six distinct gardens that rank among the loveliest in the world.

Access – *The gardens (Jardins de Métis) are located in Grand-Métis, 350km/217mi east of Quebec City. They are accessible by Rtes. 73 (Pierre-Laporte Bridge in Quebec City) and 20 to Rivière-du-Loup (198km/123mi) and Rte. 132 to Grand-Métis (152km/94mi).*

VISIT

Open Jun daily 8:30am–6:30pm. Jul–Aug daily 8:30am–8pm. Sept–mid-Oct 8:30am–6:30pm. $8. ✗ ⅙ ▣ www.refordgardens.com ☎ 418-775-2221.

Entrance Garden – This floral massif displays the brilliant colours of annual flowers from July through August. Perennials such as peonies, lupins and daylilies bloom earlier in the season. Peeking among the spruce trees bordering this colourful array of flowers are forget-me-nots and horsetails. Tuberous begonias flower near the rock garden from mid-summer until fall.

Les Rocailles (Rock Garden) – On a slope beside a meandering stream lies a small alpine garden of saxifrage, spiraea, phlox and alpine pinks. In the centre bed is the rare **Bock willow**, a small shrub of Chinese origin introduced by Mrs. Reford. Nine types of ferns including the ostrich fern, the Canadian maidenhair fern and the interrupted fern can be found here.

Rhododendron Garden – The spectacular floral display of rhododendrons in early summer is followed by the blooming of roses, which continues until the first frost. A favourable microclimate and careful maintenance (soil enrichment, acidity testing, winter protection) account for the beauty of this garden, which also includes red Japanese maples and the pride of the gardens, the **blue poppy** *(meconopsis betonicifolia)*. The floral emblem of the gardens, the blue poppy is native to the alpine prairies of the Himalayas and was introduced by Mrs. Reford who painstakingly adapted it to her gardens. This rare and beautiful flower blooms from mid-June through mid-July.

Allée royale (The Long Walkway) – A tribute to the English garden, the Long Walk is lined with annuals, perennials and shrubs is designed so that at least one species is in flower throughout the season. From the end of July until mid-August, blooming delphiniums attract a multitude of ruby-throated hummingbirds.

Yves Tessier/RÉFLEXION

Villa Reford – To the left of the Long Walk, the sumptuous Victorian residence called Estevan Lodge by Mrs. Reford overlooks the gardens. Built by her uncle in 1887 as a fishing retreat, the house was enlarged as a summer home for the Refords in 1927. The first floor of the villa now houses a restaurant, snack bar and handicrafts boutique. A garden shop is located in the adjacent coach house. In the **museum**, located on the upper floors, visitors can see the Refords' sitting room overlooking the bay, their apartments, the darkroom and the attic. On the other side of the attic, furnished rooms re-create several aspects of daily life on the estate: the kitchen, the one-room schoolhouse, the church, the general store and the doctor's office.

At the end of the well-manicured lawn leading from the villa to Mitis Bay, a low wall constructed along the waterside promontory is bordered by poplars and conifers that protect the gardens from harsh winter winds.

Jardin des pommetiers (Crab Apple Garden) – A stroll along the woods leads to this garden's beautiful flower beds, arranged in patterns of sweeping curves accented by crabapple trees and patches of lawn and ground cover.

Jardin des primevères (Primula Glade) – The conifer with drooping branches at the entrance is a **False Sawara cypress** imported by Mrs. Reford from Japan. In spring, different varieties of primrose burst into bloom.

Sous-bois (Woodland Garden) – The remaining land of the estate is a wooded area containing shrubs and other plants native to Quebec.

Parc de MIGUASHA★

Gaspésie

Map p 104

On the north shore of the Ristigouche River, in Chaleur Bay, lies an escarpment containing fossils embedded in sedimentary rock since the Upper Devonian Period (370 million years ago). The site of Miguasha was once probably a tropical lagoon fed by several rivers and surrounded by lush plant life. The shifting of sands and deposit of sediments gradually buried aquatic and plant life layer by layer. Over millions of years, the sediments became rock, and the embedded life forms were preserved as fossils. Two geological formations are visible at Miguasha: the Fleurant conglomerate, consisting mainly of sandstone (at the base); and the greyish Escuminac formation (at the top). The latter consists mostly of silt, sandstone and argillaceous schist, and measures only 8km/5mi long by 1km/.6mi wide.

The storehouse of paleontological information contained in this cliff was first discovered in 1842, although scientific study here did not begin until 1880. Soon afterwards, the site gained popularity with European geologists, who collected and removed many of the fossils. In the 1970s, as part of a move to protect the fossil deposits from unauthorized removal, the provincial government purchased portions of the cliff. Since 1985 Miguasha has been a national conservation park, where visitors are introduced to the fascinating world of fossils through exhibits and on-site observation of the cliff in the company of researchers and park personnel. In 1999 the park was designated a UNESCO World Heritage Site.

Access – *Miguasha Park is located 242km/150mi from Rimouski by Rte. 132, or 294km/182mi from Gaspé.*

Fred Klus /M.L.C.P.

VISIT

Open Jun–Aug daily 9am–6pm. Sept–early-Oct daily 9am–5pm. ✗ ♿ 🅿
www.sepaq.com ☎ *418-794-2475.*

Interpretation Centre – Fossils on display represent ferns, invertebrates and twenty groups of fish from the Upper Devonian Period. Among the outstanding finds of the Miguashan fossils is *Eusthenopteron foordi*, which resembles the earliest known amphibian, *Ichthyostega*. Fossils found in Greenland indicate that this amphibian may have lived some 20 million years after the Miguashan fish.

Laboratory – Guides explain methods of disengaging fossils from the host rock. With the use of microscopes, visitors can examine fossil samples.

Cliff Walk – A short walk down to the cliff offers a firsthand look at the sedimentary strata. Guides help visitors locate fossils. A 1.9km/1mi hiking trail surrounds the site. *Note: it is forbidden to remove fossils from the park.*

Archipel de MINGAN★★

Duplessis

Map pp 88-89

The Mingan Archipelago is made up of approximately 40 islands lying in the Gulf of St. Lawrence, north of Anticosti Island. The string of islands measures 95km/59mi in length. The Mingan Archipelago National Park Reserve, created in 1984, extends from Longue-Pointe to Baie-Johan-Beetz, on the Côte-Nord.

The sedimentary rocks of the Mingan Archipelago were formed by the accumulation of limestone deposits at the edge of the Canadian Shield some 500 million years ago. The weight of glaciers, constant freezing and thawing, and the relentless pounding of the sea caused fissures to form. Over time, these fissures eroded, slowly creating the string of islands and their characteristic monoliths.

Geographical Notes

Monoliths – These spectacular rock formations were wrought by the elements over millenia. Because all the monoliths are approximately the same height (from 5m/16ft to 10m/33ft), it is believed they were once part of the same rock. The monoliths are nicknamed "flower pots" *(pots de fleurs)* in reference to the vegetation sprouting from their tops. Over the years, the residents of the area have come to recognize familiar shapes in the forms created by nature, and have given the monoliths whimsical names such as "Bonne Femme" (Matron) and "Tête d'Indien" (Indian Head).

Flora – The icy Labrador current, distinctive soil deposits, high humidity and a powerful sea all contribute to the islands' unique bioclimate. Approximately half of the land on the islands is covered with coniferous forest, but exceptional ecological conditions have fostered a diverse collection of plants, including ferns, orchids, mosses and lichens, some of which are normally found only in arctic or alpine climates. Some forty plants growing on the islands are extremely rare. The most notable is the **Mingan thistle** *(chardon)*, not known to be found anywhere else in eastern Canada; it was discovered in 1924 by Brother Marie Victorin, the founder of Montreal's Botanical Garden.

Fauna – Of the many seabirds living in the archipelago, probably the most endearing one to residents and visitors alike is the **Atlantic puffin** *(macareux)*, whose red, yellow and blue beak and bright orange feet have earned it the nickname "sea parrot" *(perroquet de mer)*. Other birds to look for are the common eider, the black guillemot, and the common and arctic tern. Three types of seals are found in the waters around the islands: the grey seal, the harp seal and the harbour seal. The fin whale can sometimes be spotted.

© Yves Marcoux /PUBLIPHOTO

Monoliths, Archipel de Mingan

Access – *Access from Havre-Saint-Pierre or Mingan by boat. Havre-Saint-Pierre is located 855km/530mi northeast of Quebec City and 214km/133mi northeast of Sept-Îles, at the end of Rte. 138. Motorized vehicles are forbidden on the archipelago.*

VISIT

Nature Information Centres – Parks Canada operates two information centres in the Mingan Archipelago National Park Reserve; one at Longue-Pointe-de-Mingan and the other at Havre-Saint-Pierre. During the summer months, the centres organise workshops on plants, wildlife, geology and geomorphology, as well as films, lectures and special exhibits on island-related themes. Visitors interested in organised interpretation programs, wilderness camping, scuba diving and kayaking in the reserve must register at one of the centres.

★ **Sea Cruises** – To fully appreciate the natural wonders of the Mingan archipelago, visitors should tour the islands by boat. Cruises departing from Havre-Saint-Pierre specialize in geological interpretation; visitors disembark on Niapiskau Island for a closer look at the monoliths *(depart from the Havre-Saint-Pierre marina mid-Jun–Labour Day daily 7:45am, noon & 3:45pm; round-trip 3hrs 30min; commentary; reservations suggested; $29.50; & ◙; La Relève du Poète Jomphe*

Inc. ☎ *418-538-2865).* Cruises leaving from Mingan offer views of the "flower pots", and also concentrate on sighting marine life and sea birds *(depart from the Parks Canada wharf early Jun–early Sept daily 8am, noon & 4pm; round-trip 3hrs 30min; commentary; reservations suggested; $29.50; ✗ ⴲ* ⴼ *Randonnée des Îles Ltée* ☎ *418-949-2307).* Naturalists accompany the trips. The Mingan Islands research centre in Longue-Pointe-de-Mingan schedules whale-watching cruises that leave from the dock.

Parc du MONT-ORFORD★

Cantons-de-l'Est

Map pp 99

Created in 1938, the park covers an area of 58sq km/23sq mi in the Appalachian Mountains of Quebec. Mt. Chauve (600m/1,968ft) towers to the northeast, while Mt. Orford (881m/2,890ft), a well-known ski centre, dominates the southwest horizon.

Access – *The western entrance of the park (116km/72mi east of Montreal) is reached by Rte. 10 (Exit 115) and Rte. 141. The latter passes through the southern section of the park and exits by the eastern entrance, connecting with Exit 118 of Rte. 10. The park is 7km/ 4mi from Magog.*

Activities – *The park includes lakes for sailing and swimming; hiking trails through forests of sugar maple, birch, fir and pine; downhill and cross-country skiing and ice-skating in winter; a golf course; an arts centre (below) and several beaches, picnic areas and campgrounds.*

VISIT

Park open daily year-round. Le Cerisier Interpretation Centre open year-round daily 8am–5pm. $5/car. △ *(mid-May–mid-Oct)* ✗ ⴲ ⴼ *www.sepaq.com* ☎ *819-843-9855.*

Mont Orford (Mt. Orford) – *On Rte. 141, 1km/.6mi from western park entrance. Access by chairlift or on foot.* From the top of the chairlift, splendid **views★** extend over Lake Memphrémagog and the surrounding mountains. The summit *(short walk around television tower)* offers a panoramic **view★★** north to the St. Lawrence Valley, west to the Monteregian hills, south to Lake Memphrémagog and east to the Appalachian Mountains.

Lac Stukely (Lake Stukely) – *Turn left off Rte. 141, 4km/2.5mi from western entrance, and follow secondary road for 6km/4mi.* This pretty lake is reached after a pleasant drive beside the Cerises River and the Cerises Pond. The lake is bordered by sandy beaches and has several rocky islets.

Centre d'arts Orford (Orford Arts Centre) – *On Rte. 141, 1km/.6mi from eastern entrance or 1km/.6mi from road leading to Lake Stukely. Open May–Nov daily 9am–9pm.* ✗ ⴲ *www.arts-orford.org* ☎ *819-843-3981.* The Orford Arts Centre, founded in 1951, enjoys a fine reputation for its courses in musical training. The great concert hall, in the shape of an amphitheatre, is located on a lovely, wooded site and served as the Man and Music pavilion of Montreal's Expo '67. A theatre, several residences and outdoor sculptures are scattered among maple and birch woods. The celebrated centre draws artists from around the world to its annual summer **Festival Orford** *(see Calendar of Events).*

Parc du MONT-SAINT-BRUNO
Montérégie
Map p 263

One of the best-known Monteregian hills, Mt. Saint-Bruno rises 218m/712ft above the surrounding plain. The public park, created in 1985, covers a 5.9sq km/ 2.3sq mi section of the mountain. The park is part of the former seigneury of Montarville, granted in 1710 to Pierre Boucher by the Sieur de Vaudreuil, Governor of New France. Mills were developed to harness the waterways of the mountain, and apple trees were planted in the sandy soil. In 1829, part of the seigneury was sold to François-Pierre Bruneau, a Montreal lawyer whose name (with modified spelling) was subsequently given to the mountain.

Access – *Mt. Saint-Bruno Park is about 20km/12mi east of Montreal by Rte. 20 (exit 102) or Rte. 30 (exit 121). It is situated near the community of Saint-Bruno-de-Montarville.*

Activities – *Mt. Saint-Bruno is popular with walkers, hikers and bikers during the summer; with skiers during the winter.*

VISIT

Open daily year-round 8am–dusk. $5/car. ⚅ ♿ 🅿 ☎ *450-653-7544.*

From the parking lot, a pleasant trail *(1hr round-trip)* leads past the former site of the Mont-Saint-Gabriel College through woods of red oak and maple, to two lakes: Lake Moulin and Lake Seigneurial. Beside the former stands an old stone **mill** dating from 1761, the only survivor of the numerous mills that once harnessed these waters. It nows serves as a nature interpretation centre. Beside it, and along the lake shore, apple trees recall the era of the Montarville seigneury.
Longer trails lead to the three other lakes of the park: Lake Bouleaux, Lake Tortue and Lake Atocas (an Amerindian word meaning "cranberry").

Station MONT-SAINTE-ANNE★
Région de Québec
Map p 71

Created in 1969 as a sports centre for the city of Quebec, this provincial park covers the broad slopes of Mt. Sainte-Anne as well as part of the Jean-Larose River valley. An internationally known ski centre that has hosted several World Cup races, the park boasts abundant snowfall, especially on the north side of the mountain.
Ski areas include more than 200km of cross-country trails and over 50 downhill runs (vertical drop: 625m/2,060ft). At night, the trails are lit over several kilometres, creating a magical effect.

Access – *Mt. Sainte-Anne is about 40km/25mi northeast of Quebec City by Rte. 440 and Rtes. 138 and 360.*

Activities – *Cross-country skiing, downhill skiing, snowboarding, dogsledding, hiking, mountain biking, canyoning, horseback riding, golf, paragliding and mountain climbing, depending on the season.*

VISIT

Park open daily year-round. Ski season mid-Nov–Apr. $40.85 (downhill ski package), $13.05 (cross-country ski package). ⚅ ♿ 🅿 *www.mont-sainte-anne.com* ☎ *418-827-4561.*

★★**Panorama** – *Access to the summit (15min) by gondola late Jun–Aug daily 10am–4:45pm. Sept–mid-Oct weekends 10am–4:45. Round-trip 30min. $12. Mountain biking May–Oct Mon–Fri 9am–5pm, weekends 8:30am–5pm. $6. Gondola/mountain bike package and rentals available* ⚅ ♿ 🅿 The summit of Mt. Sainte-Anne affords an outstanding view of the mighty St. Lawrence. To the south, the Beaupré Coast, punctuated by the twin spires of Sainte-Anne-de-Beaupré's Basilica, is visible, as well as Île d'Orleans and Quebec City. East of Île d'Orléans, the St. Lawrence reaches a width of 10km/6mi and separates two distinct landscapes: the Laurentian Shield (Beaupré Coast) and the Appalachians, on the south shore. The Laurentian mountains rise on the horizon to the north.

Chutes Jean-Larose (Jean-Larose Falls) – *From ski centre, walk eastward about 700m/2,296ft to a charted path.* Before joining the Sainte-Anne River, the Jean-Larose River drops about 68m/223ft in a steep, narrow canyon, creating a series of falls, one of which is 33m/108ft high. The rock has been carved away by the water, and the falls, hidden in the trees, are very picturesque. The path descends steeply *(397 steps)*, providing several good viewpoints.

Parc du MONT-TREMBLANT★

Laurentides

Map p 135

Designated a forest reserve in 1894, Mt. Tremblant is Quebec's oldest provincial park. The recreational wonderland, covering 1,500sq km/930sq mi, abounds in lakes and rivers, notably the Diable and Assomption Rivers, with their tumultuous rapids and waterfalls. Mountains rise to an altitude of over 931m/3,063ft. Kilometres of winding roads and trails beckon hikers, especially in the fall when the bright red foliage of the maple trees blends with the soft yellow hues of the birches. The park has a rich and diverse fauna (moose, black bear, and beaver), and a multitude of birds, including the great blue heron and the bald eagle.

"Trembling Mountain" – According to one legend, the Algonquin named the mountain *Manitonga Soutana* (Mountain of Spirits), because of the trembling caused by the streams tumbling down its sides. According to another Amerindian version, the name *Manitou Ewitschi Saga* (Mountain of the Fearsome Manitou) was chosen, in reference to the nature god who made the mountain tremble when man came and interfered with it.

Access – *Mt. Tremblant Park is located about 140km/87mi north of Montreal. There are three main entrances: from Saint-Donat (Rte. 15 and Rte. 329); from Saint-Faustin (Rte. 15 and Rte. 117); and from Saint-Côme (Rte. 25 and Rte. 343). Sections of these roads are unpaved. Campsites and shelters are available in the park.*

Activities – *Summer: canoe-camping, sailing, nature interpretation, fishing, swimming, hiking, horseback riding and mountain biking. Winter: snowshoeing and snowmobiling, cross-country skiing, camping and downhill skiing at Tremblant resort.*

VISIT

Park open daily mid-May–Sept 7am–9pm. Oct–April daily 9am–4pm. Sections of the parks roads are closed during winter. $4. △ ✗ ᕦ ᐱ www.sepaq.com ☎ 877-688-2289.

From the Lac Supérieur entrance, take park road no. 1.

This picturesque route follows the **Diable River★**, from the Mt. Tremblant ski area to the Croches Falls.

Lac Monroe (Lake Monroe) – *11km/7mi from entrance.* This large and attractive lake has many facilities for visitors, including a beach, canoe and bicycle rentals, hiking trails and campsites. The road follows the shoreline for several kilometres, offering good views. On the other side of the road, a nature trail *(2.7km/2mi–11/2hrs round-trip)* leads to Femmes Lake. Lake Lauzon is located a bit father.

Continue on park road no. 1.

★**Chute du Diable (Devil's Falls)** – *8km/5mi from Lake Monroe. Park and follow the trail on foot for 800m/2,624ft. Allow 20min round-trip.* The dark waters of Diable River drop steeply in a forceful fall and suddenly change course, leaving a mass of shattered rocks at the base of the falls.

■ Snowshoes, Saunas and Such

With hiking trails, bike paths, golf courses and plenty of organized events, Tremblant is a cornucopia of recreational choices in summer. Opportunities for exercise don't wane much in winter either. Diversions include **Aquaclub La Source** (☎ 819-681-5668), an indoor pool with waterfalls; snowshoe excursions (☎ 1-88-Tremblant); or dogsledding (☎ 800-425-8846) at a neighbouring forest trail. For muscle-bruised skiers, the nearby **Le Scandinave** (☎ 819-425-5524 www.scandinave.com) offers a different spa experience in a woodsy outdoor setting along Rivière du Diable. The idea is to slowly raise your body temperature in a repeating cycle of heat, cold and rest while nerving up to jump into the hole cut in the frozen river! The Finnish sauna, Jacuzzi or Norwegian steam baths are joined by outdoor heated sidewalks. Compared to the river-which less than a quarter of visitors brave-the bracing Nordic waterfall seems tame. Swedish massages are offered here too.

Diable River

10km/6mi after the waterfall, the road turns away from Diable River. Head east towards Saint-Donat and Chute aux Rats on park road no. 2 and continue over 24km/15mi.

★**Chute aux Rats (Muskrat Falls)** – *The Pimbina River plunges 18m/59ft over a layered cliff. The graceful fall is one of the prettiest in the Lanaudière region.* Picnic tables are located in the swimming area and a wooden stairway scales the side of the mountain, following the falls to the top.

Continue on park road no. 3 to exit (5km/3mi).

MONTEBELLO

Outaouais
Population 1,066

This community on the north shore of the Ottawa River, between Hull and Montreal, was the home of **Louis-Joseph Papineau** (1786-1871), member of Parliament, president of the Legislative Assembly, eloquent speaker and leader of the Patriots. Since 1930, it has also been the location of a famous hotel that hosts numerous international conferences.

Historical Notes

In 1674, Msgr. de Laval was granted the seigneury known as Petite Nation, then inhabited by Algonquins. The notary Joseph Papineau, father of Louis-Joseph, purchased the seigneury in 1801 and established the first settlement. In 1845, upon returning from eight years of exile after the failed Rebellion, Louis-Joseph built a manor on the land, naming it after a friend, the **Duke of Montebello**, son of one of Napoleon's generals. In 1878, the community that had developed around the manor also took this name. Montebello was also home to Papineau's son-in-law, artist and architect Napoléon Bourassa (1827-1916), and his illustrious grandson, Henri Bourassa (1868-1952), politician and founder of Quebec's first French-language newspaper, *Le devoir*.

Access – *Montebello is 130km/81mi west of Montreal and 70km/43mi east of Hull by Rte. 148.*

SIGHTS

★**Château Montebello** – *Entrance off Rte. 148.* This enormous octagonal log structure with its six radiating wings, stands beside the Ottawa River on the former Papineau estate. It was built in 1930, in 90 days, by the Montreal architect, Harold Lawson, for the exclusive Seigniory Club. Ten thousand red cedar logs were used in the construction.
Today an exclusive hotel, the Château Montebello has hosted many international events including the 1981 Economic Summit, the 1983 Bilderberg Meeting and the 1983 NATO Conference. The grounds are very pleasant in winter and summer.

163

Manoir-Papineau

★ Lieu historique national du Manoir-Papineau (Papineau Manor National Historic Site) – *The manor will be closed for restoration until 2001. The granary and funeral chapel will remain open. Call for hours.* ⟨ ⟩ ☎ *819-423-6455.* The manor was built between 1848 and 1850 for Louis-Joseph Papineau. It is an extraordinary structure with castle-like towers.

The estate was sold to the Seigniory Club in 1929. Many alterations have been made to the interior over the years, but some of the massive furnishings belonging to the Papineau family still remain, notably in the dining room and the grand salon. A fireproof library (a novelty at that time) built in a four-storey tower, once held Papineau's 6,000 volumes. From the manor, the tranquil Ottawa River is visible through the trees.

Addresses, telephone numbers, opening hours and prices published in this guide are accurate at press time. We apologize for any inconvenience resulting from outdated information, and we welcome corrections and suggestions that may assist us in preparing the next edition. Please send us your comments:

Michelin Travel Publications
Editorial Department
P. O. Box 19001
Greenville, SC 29602-9001
TheGreenGuide-us@us.michelin.com

MONTREAL★★★

Population 1,016,376

Maps p 174-175 and pp 176-177

Located on the largest island of the Hochelaga Archipelago in the waters of the mighty St. Lawrence River some 1,600km/1,000mi from the Atlantic Ocean, the cosmopolitan city of Montreal offers the visitor a wealth of attractions. Owing to its key position at the head of a vast inland waterway connecting the Great Lakes, the city is Canada's foremost port as well as a leading industrial, commercial and financial centre. The second-largest city in Canada after Toronto, Montreal is home to the world's largest francophone population after that of Paris, which accounts for its vibrant and distinctive French culture. The city's anglophone community, concentrated primarily on the West Island, is particularly prominent in the business world. Montreal thus has the distinction of being the only major Canadian urban centre where these two communities – traditionally opposed throughout their long history – have achieved a considerable degree of integration.

Old World cultures mesh in the modern setting of Montreal, creating a fascinating vitality with an international flair. The city's numerous and varied ethnic groups sometimes make it seem like a miniature mosaic of the world.

Geographical Notes

Lying at the confluence of the Ottawa and St. Lawrence Rivers, the island of Montreal measures 50km/31mi in length and 17km/10mi at its widest point. The island is connected to the mainland by a tunnel and fifteen road bridges, five of which span the St. Lawrence.

Twenty-nine municipalities on the island make up the Montreal Urban Community; the largest municipality is the City of Montreal itself which, having annexed numerous smaller villages in the 1880s, now occupies over a third of the island. The centre of Montreal Island is dominated by a 233m/764ft hill, known as **Mt. Royal**. Nicknamed "the Mountain," Mt. Royal is one of the Monteregian Hills, a series of eight peaks in the St. Lawrence valley.

Historical Notes

Montreal Island was inhabited by Mohawks of the Iroquois nation long before Europeans set foot in North America. In 1535, **Jacques Cartier** landed on the island while searching for gold and a route to the Orient, and encountered the Mohawk village of **Hochelaga** at the foot of the mountain. Legend has it that Cartier, having climbed the mountain, was so taken by the view before him that he exclaimed "It's a royal mountain!" *(C'est un mont réal)*. According to historian Gustave Lanctot, however, Montreal was named by Cartier in honour of Cardinal de Medici, bishop of the Sicilian town of Monreale.

When **Samuel de Champlain**, the "Father of New France," sailed up the river from his newly established settlement of Kebec (Quebec City) in 1611, Hochelaga had ceased to exist. Champlain considered founding a new community on the Île Sainte-Hélène, but his project never materialised.

The City of Mary – The 17C was a period of zealous evangelization on the island. The Roman Catholic Church, hoping to regain the ground lost during the Protestant Reformation, viewed colonisation as a means of spreading the faith. During this period, two French men decided to establish a mission on Montreal Island: **Jérôme Le Royer de la Dauversière** and **Jean-Jacques Olier**. The latter had founded the Sulpician Order in Paris in 1641. They raised money and chose **Paul de Chomedey, Sieur de Maisonneuve** to lead their mission, which they called **Ville-Marie** (City of Mary).

Maisonneuve and about 40 companions crossed the Atlantic in 1641. After wintering in Quebec City, they arrived on the island in May 1642. Despite their high-minded ideals, the Catholic missionaries ultimately came into conflict with the peoples they had hoped to convert. The hostilities continued until peace with the Iroquois was established by treaty in 1701.

18C – After the failure of evangelization initiatives, Ville-Marie (soon renamed Montreal) began to grow as a centre of the fur trade. Explorers set off across the Great Lakes and their attendant waterways, returning loaded with pelts. The furs were prized in Europe, where they were transformed into luxurious apparel. The fur trade became Montreal's principal commercial activity, one strong enough to spawn other businesses and farms all over the island. By the time of the **British Conquest**, the city of Montreal was firmly established. After the surrender of Quebec City in 1759, British troops commanded by General Jeffery Amherst marched on Montreal. In 1760, Chevalier de Lévis prepared a gallant defence of the city, but Montreal's governor, Marquis de Vaudreuil, ordered him to surrender without a fight.

Following the Conquest of Canada, most of the French nobility returned to France. The first English-speaking people to settle in the city were Scots, attracted by the fur trade. After the American Revolution, an influx of Loyalists from the United States swelled Montreal's anglophone population.

Montreal: view from Mount Royal

In 1775-1776, Montreal was again occupied. American troops under General Richard Montgomery invaded the city in an attempt to persuade Montrealers to join the thirteen colonies in revolt against the British Crown. During the seven-month occupation many leading Americans, including **Benjamin Franklin**, visited Montreal. Early in 1776, the occupying troops departed for Quebec City, where they were defeated by the British

19C – The fur trade in Montreal reached its heyday in the late 18C and early 19C Trading posts, where the local indigenous population brought furs to exchange for a wide range of goods, were established all over northern Canada. The furs were subsequently transported to Montreal by canoe. The **North West Company**, a partnership between some of the great figures in Montreal history, including Fraser, Frobisher Mackenzie, McGill, McGillivray, McTavish and Thompson, was created in 1783. These men and others founded the **Beaver Club**, an association of fur traders who had frequently wintered in the northwest.

In 1821, the merger of the North West Company with its rival, the **Hudson's Bay Company** **(HBC)**, marked the decline of Montreal's dominance in the fur trade. The HBC exported its furs to Europe via Hudson Bay, bypassing Montreal and reducing the city's importance. Fortunes had nonetheless been made in Montreal, and the profits were invested in other sectors of activity as the 19C progressed.

Even though Montreal did not participate in the American Revolution, the city and its region were the centre of a revolt against British rule in 1837. The colony was administered by a Crown-appointed governor and his council. The assembly elected by the

Montréal 1812 by Thomas Davies

© Malak, Ottawa

Canadian people lacked the power to enforce its decisions. Many leading French-Canadians, among them **Louis-Joseph Papineau** and **George-Étienne Cartier** raised their voices in protest. The motivations behind the so-called **Patriots' Rebellion** were not lost on the British, who subsequently granted full representative government to French Canada. After several years of exile, Papineau briefly returned to politics before retiring to Montebello; Cartier went on to become a great Quebec politician and one of the Fathers of Canadian Confederation.

An Expanding Economy – About 1820, Montreal's economy experienced a conversion to commerce and import-export activities. The anglophone business community established Rue Saint-Jacques as a financial centre, and founded the Bank of Montreal (1817) and the Board of Trade (1822), institutions whose investment activities promoted development in the city and throughout Quebec and Canada. Today, Rue Saint-Jacques is home to the Montreal Stock Exchange as well as the city's dominant financial and banking institutions.

After 1815 the anglophone community's economy was fueled by additional British immigrants, coming mainly from Ireland. In the 1860s, Montreal experienced an influx of rural French-Canadians, who restored its francophone character. About 1840, the enlargement of the **Lachine canal**, which had enabled vessels to circumvent the Lachine rapids since 1821, spurred further industrialization. A new system of canals, on the St. Lawrence River as far as the Great Lakes and on the Richelieu River as far as New York via Lake Champlain and the Hudson River, opened new commercial axes, which were quickly supplemented by railroad lines. The first short-line railroad (1836) linked La Prairie to Saint-Jean-sur-Richelieu.

Montreal rapidly became the headquarters of financing, construction, employment and maintenance for the rail system. The opening of the Victoria bridge in 1859 brought rail traffic across the river, establishing a continuous, north-south railroad link between Montreal and Vermont.

Montreal's **port** grew with the construction, in the 1880s, of the Canadian Pacific railway line linking the nation's Atlantic and Pacific coasts. Development of the Prairie provinces created new markets for Montreal: inland grain made its way by rail to the port's storage silos before being exported across the Atlantic, and products manufactured in the city were transported west in wagons.

20C – The period of growth that followed World War I came to an abrupt halt during the Great Depression. Lack of funds lead to widespread unemployment, and the skeletal outlines of unfinished projects marked the cityscape. The post-World War II years brought renewed prosperity and dynamism to the city. Under the leadership of Mayor Jean Drapeau, the downtown and eastern areas of Montreal underwent complete renovation. Since the 1960s, Montreal has emerged as an international city, hosting several important international events: the World Fair, **Expo'67**, which celebrated the centennial of Canada's Confederation; the 1976 summer **Olympic Games** and in 1980 and 2000, the renowned flower exhibition, the **International Floralies**.

During the 1970s, several companies relocated their headquarters to Toronto, relegating Montreal to the status of second-largest metropolis in Canada. The city also remains a major centre of francophone culture. Montreal celebrated the **350th anniversary** of its foundation with elaborate festivities in 1992.

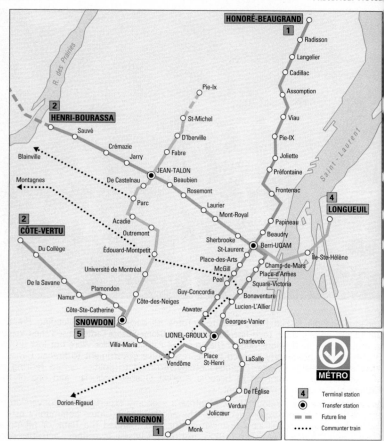

The Montreal Metro – *Map above*. Inaugurated in 1966 in time for Expo '67, the four lines of the metro now extend over 64km/40mi with 65 stations. It was designed according to the French "tire on rail" technology and is completely underground. The stations are connected by a double tunnel to prevent accidents; in places the tunnel is close to the surface, but sinks to a maximum of 55m/180ft as it passes under the St. Lawrence River to Longueuil. The decor of each metro station was conceived by a different architect, in relation to its surroundings, and enhanced by works of art. All of the metro stations were created as extensions of the street. Whereas in other cities the word "metro" has become synonymous with long, narrow tunnels leading to departure platforms, in Montreal the voyager exits the train to find himself in a bustling subterranean city centre. Some of the more noteworthy stations in the system include Berri-UQAM, Champ-de-Mars, McGill, Place-des-Arts, Papineau, and Pie-IX.

In Montreal, the Sun Rises in the South

■ Travellers accustomed to determining their geographical orientation by the position of the sun will have to make an adjustment in Montreal. The St. Lawrence River is considered to flow from west to east, a correct assumption for the most part. However, as it approaches the downtown area, the river makes an abrupt northward swing, and thus flows almost due north as it passes the city. Montreal streets at right angles to the St. Lawrence are thereby considered to be oriented north-south (when actually they extend east-west), and streets parallel to the river are designated east-west (though in reality they run north-south).

Ville Souterraine – *Map pp 192-193*. Temperatures in Montreal change dramatically from season to season, but pedestrians can move throughout most of the business district without exposure to climactic extremes via the "city beneath the city." Montreal's pedestrian city began in the 1960s with the construction of **Place Ville-Marie**. Particularly remarkable for the spaciousness of its corridors and for its aesthetically "landscaped" atmosphere, the system connects the

Getting There

By Air – **Dorval** International Airport: 22km/14mi *(approximately 30min)* from downtown by shuttle bus *($11)*, taxi *($28)* or STCUM network (train, bus, metro); free shuttle to Dorval hotels; airport departure tax $10; for information ☎ 694-7377. **Mirabel** International Airport, 55km/34mi *(approximately 45min)* from downtown by shuttle bus *($18)* or taxi *($69)*; charter and cargo flights only; information ☎ 694-7377.

By Train – Central Station (Gare centrale): 895 Rue de la Gauchetière Ouest (Ⓜ Bonaventure). Information & reservations ☎ 989-2626.

By Bus – Montreal Terminal (Orléans Express or Vermont Transit): 505 Blvd. de Maisonneuve Est (Ⓜ Berri-UQAM). Information ☎ 842-2281.

Getting Around

Metro & Bus – Local metro and bus service are provided by Société de Transport de la Communauté Urbaine de Montréal (STCUM) ☎ 288-6287. The system generally operates from 5:30am–1:30am *(lines 1, 2 & 4)* or 11pm *(line 5)*. Each metro line is designated by a number and a colour; the direction is indicated by the name of the station at the end of the line in that direction. Metro tickets (which may also be used on buses) are available at metro stations and may be purchased individually *($2)*, or in a book *(carnet)* of six *($8.25)*. Tourist passes *(cartes touristiques)* are also available *($5/day or $12/3 days)*. Lost and found ☎ 280-4637.

Car Rental – Major rental car companies are located at the airports and throughout the downtown area. Agencies include Avis ☎ 866-7906; Budget ☎ 866-7675; Discount ☎ 286-1554; Hertz ☎ 842-8537; Thrifty-Québec ☎ 845-5954; National-Tilden ☎ 481-1166.

Taxis – La Salle ☎ 277-2552; Diamond ☎ 273-6331; Champlain ☎ 273-2435.

General Information

Tourist Information – Infotouriste office: 1001 Rue du Square-Dorchester (Ⓜ Peel). Open Jun–Labour Day daily 8am–8pm, rest of the year daily 9am–6pm. Internet surfers can check out www.tourisme-montreal.org for tourist info as well as up-to-date images of the city on its LiveCam Network.

Accommodations – Reservation services: Hospitality Canada ☎ 393-9049; Montreal Reservations Centre ☎ 284-2277.

Local Press – English: *The Gazette*. French: *Le journal de Montréal, Le devoir, La presse* (daily).

Post Office – 1500 Rue Ottawa ☎ 846-5290 (Mon–Fri 8am–5:45pm). General information (Société canadienne des postes) ☎ 344-8822.

Currency Exchange Offices	☎
Dorval Airport – ICE Currency Services (offices at Arrivals & Departures, open daily)	828-0061
Calforex International Currency – 1250 Rue Peel	392-9100
Mint Master International – 390 Rue Saint-Jacques Ouest	844-2549

Useful Numbers

	☎
Police–Ambulance–Fire (emergency calls)	911
Directory Assistance	411
Tourisme Québec	873-2015
Office des Congrès et du Tourisme	844-5400
Canadian Automobile Association (CAA)	861-7575
Road conditions	284-2363
Weather (24hrs/day)	283-4006
Jean Coutu Drugstore (Mon–Fri 9am–11pm, Sat 10pm; Sun 10am–10pm)	527-8827

Entertainment – Montreal offers visitors a wide variety of activities year-round. For current entertainment schedules and addresses of principal theatres and concert halls, consult the free tourist publications *Mirror* or *Hour* (English), *Le guide Montréal* (bilingual), and *Voir* (French), or review the arts and entertainment supplements in local newspapers (weekend editions). Tickets for major enter-

© Michel Gagné/REFLEXION

Winter Festival, Île Notre-Dame

tainment or sports events may be purchased at the venue or through the following offices: **Admission** ☎ 790-1245; **Telspeck** ☎ 790-1111; **Voyages Astral Inc.** ☎ 866-1001. Most major credit cards accepted.

Sports – Montreal is home to several professional sports organizations. **Hockey:** Montreal Canadiens (National Hockey League), season from Oct–Mar at the Molson Centre (Ⓜ Lucien-L'Allier) ☎ 932-2582. **Baseball:** Montreal Expos (National Baseball League), season from Apr–Sept at Olympic Stadium (Ⓜ Viau) ☎ 846-3976. **Soccer:** Montreal Alouettes; season from mid-Jun–early Nov at McGill Stadium (Ⓜ McGill) ☎ 871-2255. **Horse races:** year-round; Blue Bonnets Hippodrome (Ⓜ Namur) ☎ 739-2741.

Recreational Activities – Bicycle rental (summer) or ice skating (winter): Vélo Aventure Montréal ☎ 847-0666. Year-round skating *($5.50)* and rentals at Atrium Le1000, 1000 Rue de la Gauchetière (Ⓜ Bonaventure) ☎ 395-0555. IMAX Cinemas (movies & laser shows) ☎ 496-4629. Casino de Montréal (Ⓜ Île Sainte-Hélène) ☎ 392-2746.

Shopping and Dining – A large number of boutiques, movie theatres and malls in the **Underground City** *(map pp 192-193)* are connected by the metro. Hours: Mon–Fri 9:30am–6pm (Thu & Fri until 9pm; in summer, Mon–Fri until 9pm), Sat 10am–5pm; some stores may also be open on Sunday:

Complexe Desjardins, 170 Rue Sainte-Catherine Ouest (Ⓜ Place-des-Arts or Place-d'Armes) ☎ 281-1870.

Eaton Centre, 705 Rue Sainte-Catherine Ouest (Ⓜ McGill) ☎ 288-3708.

Place Montréal Trust, 1500 McGill College Ave. (Ⓜ McGill or Peel) ☎ 843-8000.

Place Ville-Marie, 1 place Ville-Marie (Ⓜ Bonaventure or McGill) ☎ 861-9393.

Promenades de la Cathédrale, 625 Rue Sainte-Catherine Ouest (Ⓜ McGill) ☎ 849-9925.

A variety of boutiques, clothing stores, antique shops, art galleries and fashionable restaurants can be found along Sainte-Catherine, Sherbrooke, Peel, Crescent and de la Montagne streets. Galleries, gift shops offering aboriginal art, cafes and restaurants in Old Montreal. Elegant fashion boutiques, art studios, cafes and restaurants along Rue Saint-Denis. Ethnic groceries and restaurants, franchise stores, nightclubs and discotheques along Blvd. Saint-Laurent.

Address Book

Staying in Montreal

The accommodations listed below have been chosen for their location, character, or value for money. Rates are for a standard room, double occupancy in high season, not including taxes; some hotels offer lower weekend rates. Rates may vary widely according to season. The ⌇ symbol indicates a swimming pool on the premises.

$$$$	$200-$300	$$	$75-$125
$$$	$125-$200	$	under $75

Hôtel Place d'Armes – *701 Côte de la Place d'Armes.* ✗ ⌖ ▣ ☎ 514-842-1887, 1-888-450-1887. www.hotelplacedarmes.com. 48 rooms. **$$$$** This charming boutique hotel is strategically located on Place d'Armes in the center of the ecclesiastic and financial district of Old Montreal. Calming colors and rich mahogany furnishings characterize the elegant rooms; amenities include bathrobes, down comforters, whirlpool baths and FAX and internet access for business travellers. Large windows afford splendid views of Chinatown, downtown Montreal and the Notre-Dame basilica.

Hôtel Le Germain – *2050 Rue Mansfield.* ❌ ♿ ▱ ☎ *514-849-2050, 1-877-333-2050 www.hotelgermain.com. 101 rooms.* **$$$$** Rated one of the 21 coolest hotels in the world by *Condé Nast Traveler* magazine, this office-building-turned-boutique-hotel oozes refined luxury. Oriental minimalism prevails in the light-filled loft-like rooms, done in earth tones and ecru with dark wood furnishings handcrafted by local artisans. Sumptuous bedding and upscale amenities such as irons and ironing boards, CD players and daily newspapers make these some of the most sought-after rooms in the city.

Hôtel Le Reine Elizabeth – *900 Blvd. René-Lévesque West.* ❌ ♿ ▱ ⨊ ☎ *514-861-3511, 800-441-1414. www.cphotels.ca. 1,066 rooms.* **$$$** The cavernous Queen Elizabeth's convenient location above Montreal's underground city and the railway station makes it a favorite with touring celebrities: in 1967 John Lennon and Yoko Ono recorded *Give Peace a Chance* here during their summer "bed-in." Spacious rooms have recently been renewed with wallpaper and chintz bedspreads. Besides incorporating a large health club, a beauty salon and a shopping arcade, the hotel boasts the **Beaver Club**, known for its fine French cuisine.

Hostellerie Pierre du Calvet – *405 Rue Bonsecours.* ❌ ▱ ☎ *514-282-1725 www.pierreducalvet.ca. 10 rooms.* **$$$.** *(See entry heading.)* Step back in time at the oldest home open to public accommodation within the walled city of Montreal. Former home of French merchant Pierre du Calvet, the 18C structure has been restored as an elegant European house chockablock with family heirlooms, antiques and Oriental rugs. Romantic rooms exude Old World ambience with original stone walls, fireplaces and four-poster canopy beds. Enjoy breakfast in the airy, plant-filled Victorian greenhouse.

Hôtel de l'Institut – *3535 Rue St-Denis.* ❌ ♿ ▱ ☎ *514-282-5120, 1800-361-5151. www.ithq.qc.ca/. 42 rooms.* **$$$** Occupying the top floors of the modern bunker-like structure that houses the Institut de Tourisme et d'Hôtellerie du Québec, the hotel offers comfortable, modern rooms and the impeccable service you would expect from closely supervised students of the art of hospitality. A few steps away lie some of the trendiest places in Montreal-the Plateau Mont-Royal district and the Quartier Latin.

Auberge de la Fontaine – *1301 Rue Rachel East.* ♿ ▱ ☎ *514-597-0166, 1-800-597-0597. www.aubergedelafontaine.com. 21 rooms.* **$$$.** A 19C Victorian mansion, Auberge de la Fontaine sits in the heart of the Plateau Mont-Royal district facing beautiful La Fontaine Park. Colorful contemporary rooms, access to the kitchen for snacks and beverages, and a generous breakfast buffet served each morning in the sunny dining room make for a restful stay outside the frenzy of downtown.

Château Versailles – *1659 Rue Sherbrooke West.* ❌ ♿ ▱ ☎ *514-933-3611, 1-800-361-7199 (CAN), 1-800-361-3664 (USA). www.montrealnet.ca/versailles. 172 rooms.* **$$** Composed of four interconnected 19C Victorian town houses and a modern tower annex across the street, this former pension is prized for its price, personal service and convenient location in the museum district. The large rooms were completely renovated in 1997.

L'Auberge de jeunesse – *1030 Rue Mackay.* ☎ *514-843-3317, 1-800-663-3317. www.hostellingmontreal.com. 243 beds.* **$** Organized into rooms that accommodate between four and ten people, this youth hostel a few minutes from downtown offers a non-smoking environment, kitchen services, a television room and laundromat.

Dining in Montreal

The establishments below were selected for their character, location or value for money. Prices indicate the average cost of an appetizer, entrée (main course) and dessert for one person (not including tax and tip, beverages or alcoholic drinks). Call for hours of operation and reservation requirements.

$$$$ =over $50   **$$** =$20-$35
$$$ = $35-$50   **$** =under $20

Toqué! – *3842 Rue St-Denis.* ☎ *514-499-2084.* **$$$$ French.** Montrealers and international food critics alike consider this postmodern restaurant, located in the Plateau Mont-Royal district, one of the finest in the city. Chef Normand Laprise's contemporary French cuisine, artfully presented using the freshest – and often unusual (milkweed buds, fiddlehead ferns) – local produce is the reason why. Signature dishes served by the professional waitstaff include *gigot d'agneau de Rimouski et son jus fumé au thym* (leg of lamb in its own juices scented with thyme), and *poêlée de mousserons* (sautéed St. George's mushrooms).

Dining in Old Town

La Marée – *404 Place Jacques-Cartier.* ☎ *514-861-8126.* **$$$ Seafood.** Situated in one of the most-trafficked sections of the city lies Montreal's best bet for seafood. Enjoy favorites such as *escalope de saumon au ragoût de pineau des charentes* (grilled salmon in a sauce flavored with pineau des charentes liquour), *potiquet de poissons et crustacés au porto blanc et morilles* (fish and shellfish braised in white port wine with cream and morels), and *poêle de homard à la tomate et basilic* (sautéed lobster in tomato, butter and fresh basil).

Hélène de Champlain – *200 Tour de l'Île, Île Ste-Hélène.* ☎ *514-395-2424.* **$$$ Continental.** Five minutes from downtown and the Casino de Montréal, this Quebecois-style home provides a beautiful park setting on Île Ste-Hélène. Steaks, lamb and escargots are standard fare, but the romantic dining rooms with their fireplaces and views of the city and rose garden make for a delightful dining experience.

Moishes – *3961 Blvd. St-Laurent.* ♿ ☎ *514-363-3509.* **$$$ North American.** A Montreal institution for over 60 years, this steak house is justifiably renowned for its house-aged, charcoal-grilled steaks, which are even better when paired with a selection from Moishes' fine wine list. The courteous and efficient wait-staff serves up favorite accompaniments like pickled salmon and broiled peppers.

BYOW – Bring your own wine. Restaurants that don't have a liquor license can allow patrons to bring in their own favorite vintages. Most BYOW *(apportez votre vin)* eateries are located in the Plateau Mont-Royal district and the Quartier Latin.

Table d'hôte – These fixed-price meals typically include a three-course menu consisting of a starter, main dish and dessert.

Daou – *519 Rue Faillon East.* ☎ *514-747-7876.* **$$ Lebanese.** The lively ambience here, occasionally spiced with belly dancers in the evenings, compliments Middle Eastern specialties such as tabbouleh, kibbeh, shish kebab and hummus, making you feel like you've just stepped into a big, joyous Lebanese wedding party. The décor is ordinary, but expect good food for a good price.

Le Piton de la Fournaise – *3784 Rue Mentana.* ☎ *514-526-3936.* **$$ Réunion/Creole.** Upon entering this vibrant restaurant, you'll feel as if you've stepped off the boat at Île de la Réunion smack dab in the middle of the Indian Ocean. The cuisine blends Indian, African and French influences and the décor highlights arts and crafts from the island. Just listening to the staff speak Creole is a treat in itself. Bring your own wine.

Beauty's – *93 Ave. Mont-Royal West.* ☎ *514-849-8883.* **$ Diner.** If breakfast or brunch is your thing, come wait in line with *les gens branchés* (everyone who is anyone) at this 1950's-style diner. Bagels, smoked salmon, and blueberry pancakes are the main attractions at this crowded eatery in the Plateau Mont-Royal district.

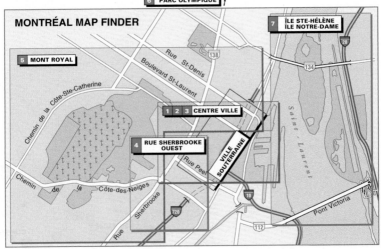

MONTRÉAL MAP FINDER

6 PARC OLYMPIQUE

7 ÎLE STE-HÉLÈNE
ÎLE NOTRE-DAME

5 MONT ROYAL

1 2 3 CENTRE VILLE

4 RUE SHERBROOKE
OUEST

VILLE SOUTERRAINE

principal downtown hotels and office buildings, major department stores (La Baie), hundreds of boutiques, several cinemas, numerous restaurants, two railway stations, the bus terminal, the city's major cultural centre, **Place des Arts**, and two major convention centres, **Place Bonaventure** and **Palais des Congrès**. (In Quebec, the French word *place* commonly designates large interior spaces and commercial centres).

★★★ 1 VIEUX-MONTRÉAL (OLD MONTREAL) *Map p 177.*

The term "Old Montreal" refers to the section of the city formerly surrounded by fortifications. The imposing stone walls (5.4m/18ft high and 1m/3ft thick) were built early in the 18C and removed a century later. They contained the area today bounded by Rue McGill to the west, Rue Berri to the east, Rue de la Commune beside the river to the south and a line between Rues Saint-Jacques and Saint-Antoine to the north. As the 18C progressed, several distinct neighbourhoods developed outside the walls: Faubourg de Québec to the east, Faubourg des Récollets to the west, and Faubourg Saint-Laurent to the north.

During the 19C, the city gradually expanded beyond the old walls. Montrealers built their houses further from the river, and businesses were established in what is presently the downtown area. Warehouses sprang up where homes and gardens had previously flourished and the area fell into a period of decline. By the 1960s, however, interest in Old Montreal revived. The surviving 18C homes were renovated and the warehouses were transformed into apartment and office buildings. Shops and restaurants opened, signaling the renewal of the area.

Today, all development in Old Montreal is controlled by the Viger Commission, which ensures that the historic, architectural and cultural nature of the area is respected. As a result, Old Montreal has become an attractive place to live and work, as well as a major tourist attraction.

Horse-drawn carriages (calèches) depart from Rue Notre-Dame, Place d'Armes, Rue de la Commune and Place Jacques-Cartier, enabling visitors to discover Old Montreal in the manner of bygone eras.

Walking Tour *2.2km/1.4mi. Map p 175.* ◐ *Square-Victoria*

★ **Rue Saint-Jacques** – Financial heart of Canada until the 1970s, Rue Saint-Jacques, lined with a homogeneous ensemble of 19C and early 20C buildings, still retains much of its former grandeur. Note in particular the **Canada Life Assurance Building** *(no. 275)*, Montreal's first steel-framework skyscraper (1895), and the **Banque de Commerce Impériale** (Canadian Imperial Bank of Commerce, *no.265; open year-round Mon–Fri 9:30am–4pm;* ♿ ☎ *514-876-2119)*, whose facade is adorned with fluted Corinthian columns. The bank features a monumental interior **banking hall**. The decline of Rue Saint-Jacques was accelerated during the mid-1970s when the major financial institutions moved their headquarters to the downtown area or to Toronto. Today, however, the street is experiencing a revival, with several significant new constructions and the conversion of older buildings. The street was named by Dollier de Casson in 1672 after Jean-Jacques Olier, the founder of the Sulpician Order.

Visible to the west is the black, 47-storey **Tour de la Bourse**★ (Stock Exchange Tower, *no. 800 Square Victoria)*, home of the Montreal Stock Exchange *(open year-round Mon–Fri 9:30am–4:30pm; closed major holidays;* ♿ ▣ ☎ *514-871-2424.*

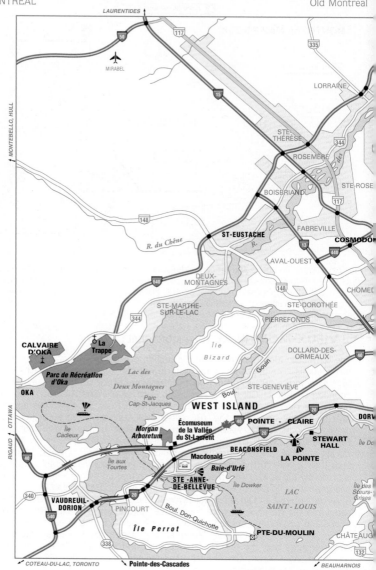

⭐ **Banque Royale du Canada** (Royal Bank of Canada) – *360 Rue Saint-Jacques. Open year-round Mon–Fri 10am–4pm. Closed major holidays.* ♿ ☎ *514-874-2959.* This building (1928) was the first erected in Montreal after the 1924 modification of zoning regulations authorizing the construction of buildings of more than 10 storeys on the condition that setbacks be incorporated into their design. Inspired by the "Setback Law" of New York, the new regulation left more latitude to architects, who were thereafter restricted more by the laws of engineering than by city regulations. The 20-storey bank was, at the time, the tallest building in the British Empire. The bottom tier – of Renaissance Revival design – is a severe, monumental composition influenced by the Teatro San Carlo in Naples. The entire tower, whose traditional roof has long dominated the skyline of Montreal's financial district, is best viewed from the opposite side of Rue Saint-Jacques. The bank's headquarters were located here until the 1962 completion of the Royal Bank of Canada Tower at Place Ville-Marie.

Interior – The bronze main entry doors open onto a vast vestibule adorned with a coffered, richly ornamented, vaulted ceiling. Blue, pink and gold enliven the ground floor, from which four arched doorways give access to the wings and elevators. A magnificent marble staircase leads to the immense **banking hall**, which is 45m/148ft long, 14m/46ft wide and 14m/46ft tall.

Walk eastward on Rue Saint-Jacques.

★**Place d'Armes** – As superior of the Sulpician Order in 1670, Dollier de Casson devised a city plan for Montreal, outlining new streets north of Rue Saint-Paul and a large open square in the centre, later to become the site of the Notre Dame Basilica. According to legend, Casson's central square occupied the site of the 1644 battle during which Maisonneuve killed the local Indian chief, causing two hundred of the chief's followers to flee the settlement. The Place d'Armes, as the square has been called since 1723, traditionally served as drill grounds where troops presented arms to the sovereign or his representative, in this case, the Messieurs de Saint-Sulpice, seigneurs of the island.

In 1775-1776, during the American occupation, vandals mutilated the bust of Georges III which stood at the centre of the square. Rediscovered in an old well on the site, the bust is now part of the collection of the McCord Museum. In 1832, the square was the site of an electoral riot against the Tories, led by the legendary Patriot **Jos Montferrand**, who is immortalized in the songs of Gilles Vigneault.

Today, Place d'Armes is home to some of the most prestigious buildings in the city, many of them erected by major companies and financial institutions.

★**Banque de Montréal (Bank of Montreal)** – *119 Rue Saint-Jacques.* Dominating the north side of the vast square, Montreal's main branch of Canada's oldest bank presents an imposing facade, evoking the Pantheon in Rome. Along with the Bonsecours market, the edifice (1847) is one of Montreal's finest examples of the

175

MONTRÉAL
CENTRE VILLE

0   400 m
0   1/4ml

🚢 Harbour cruise   🚌 Amphibus
⛵ Boat trip to the Lachine Rapids

Centre Canadien d'Architecture ╱

Neoclassical style. Step inside to see the elaborate interior redecorated in 1905. From the entrance hall under the dome, huge columns of green granite lead into the massive **banking hall** with its beautiful coffered ceiling.

The bank's small **museum** *(turn left at entrance and go through revolving doors; open year-round Mon–Fri 10am–4pm; closed major holidays; ☎ 514-877-6810)* features displays relating to the bank's history, bank notes of different denominations and a collection of whimsical money boxes.

★**Maisonneuve Monument (1)** – The monument in the centre of the square honours the founder of Montreal, Paul de Chomedey, **Sieur de Maisonneuve** (1612-1676). A masterpiece by Louis-Philippe Hébert, the sculpture was completed in 1895 to celebrate the city's 250th anniversary. Maisonneuve is depicted brandishing the standard of France, while grouped below him are some of the prominent figures of Montreal's history: Jeanne Mance, founder of Montreal's General Hospital; Lambert Closse, defender of the fort, and his dog Pilote, who first heard and gave warning of the enemy's approach; Charles Le Moyne, with a sickle and a gun to represent life in the colonies; and an Iroquois warrior.

The words Father Vimont proclaimed at the first mass in 1642 are engraved on the monument (in translation): "You are the grain of mustard seed which will germinate, grow and multiply all over this country."

New York Life Insurance Building – *511 Place d'Armes*. Sheathed in red sandstone, this 8-storey edifice (1888) was Montreal's first skyscraper. A synthesis of Romanesque and Renaissance Revival styles, the structure features corner towers, arched-lancet windows and rough-hewn stone. Although at the time, steel was beginning to be widely used as a means of interior support in architectural construction, this building's floor weight is borne by its walls.

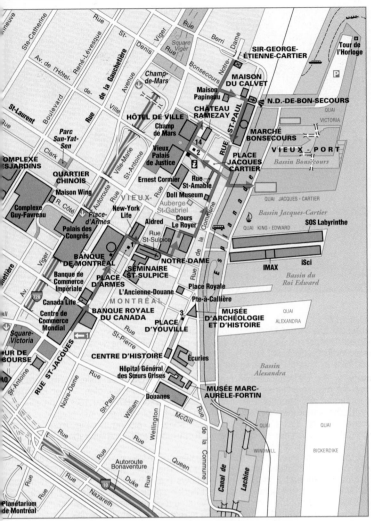

Aldred Building – *507 Place d'Armes*. The form and ornamentation of this Art Deco skyscraper (1930) were inspired by New York City's Rockefeller Center, then under construction.

★★★**Basilique Notre-Dame** (Notre Dame Basilica) – *Open Jun 24–Labour Day daily 8am–8pm. Rest of the year daily 8am–6pm. ($2)* ♿ ☎ *514-842-2925*. The twin towers of Montreal's most famous religious edifice rise over 69m/226ft on the southern edge of Place d'Armes. At the time of the basilica's construction, they dominated the entire city but have since been overshadowed by the taller structures housing Montreal's financial institutions.

Rulers of Montreal Island, the **Sulpician** seigneurs long opposed the division of their territory into small parishes administered by the bishop of Quebec. To impede such a division, and a lessening of their power, the Sulpicians decided to erect this church, large enough to accommodate the entire community at worship (seating capacity of 3,500). Despite the Sulpicians' efforts, the Diocese of Montreal was established in 1830 and the island subsequently divided into parishes.

The basilica, Quebec's first major building in the Gothic Revival style, was designed by James O'Donnell (1774-1829), an Irish architect from New York, who supervised its construction from 1824 to 1829. A Catholic convert, O'Donnell is buried in the basilica's basement crypt. John Ostell finished the towers in 1843 according to the original plans. Lack of funds halted progress on the interior until after 1870, when it was finally completed under the direction of Victor Bourgeau.

Notre Dame is Montreal's first large-scale limestone edifice. Its construction necessitated the opening of new quarries, and stonecutters had to be hired and trained to work the stone, thus leading to its widespread application as a sheathing material. The three Baccirini statues adorning the facade were purchased in Italy and

Basilique Notre-Dame

represent the Virgin Mary, St. Joseph and St. John the Baptist. The east tower, named Temperance, contains a ten-bell carillon while the west tower, known as Perseverance, houses "Jean-Baptiste," a magnificent, 10,900kg/24,030lb brass bell, cast in London and rung only on special occasions.

Interior – The church's central nave is flanked by two side aisles surmounted by deep-set double galleries. Without deviating from this basic plan, Victor Bourgeau reappointed and enriched the interior decor between 1872 and 1880, embellishing it with the sculptures, wainscoting and giltwork typical of provincial religious architecture. Notre Dame's Gothic Revival style is distinguishable from that of non-Catholic churches by the interior furnishings and ornamentation, inspired by the French Gothic style.

The magnificent interior is a veritable gallery of religious art in hand-carved white pine, painted and gilded with 22 carat gold. The nave, measuring 68m/223ft long, 21m/69ft wide and 25m/82ft high, follows the natural slope of the terrain from the entrance to the altar, and the interior space is illuminated by three rose windows piercing the polychromed vaulted ceiling. Designed by Bourgeau and carved by Henri Bouriché, the altar and **reredos** incorporate white oak statues, which stand out against the background's soft blue hues. The massive black walnut **pulpit★** is the work of Louis-Philippe Hébert; note especially the statues of Ezekiel and Jeremiah at its base. The **stained-glass windows** of the lower level were designed by Jean-Baptiste Lagacé and produced at the Chigot studio in Limoges, France. Commissioned at the basilica's 1929 centenary and installed in 1931, the windows depict scenes from the history of Montreal.

The massive **organ**, one of the world's largest, was produced in 1887 by Casavant Brothers of Saint-Hyacinthe, and has 6,800 pipes, 84 stops, four manual keyboards and a pedal-board. To the right of the entrance, note the baptistry, decorated by Ozias Leduc in 1927.

Because of its excellent acoustics, Notre Dame is frequently the setting for organ recitals and Montreal Symphony Orchestra concerts.

Sacred Heart Chapel (Chapelle du Sacré-Cœur) – *Entrance behind the choir.* Added to the church in 1891, the original chapel was intended mainly for intimate celebrations and weddings. It was completely destroyed by arson in 1978 and reconsecrated in 1982. Its ornamentation combines elements from the original chapel with contemporary additions. The vault is of steel sheathed in linden wood, and side skylights permit daylight to filter into the interior. Dominating the whole is an impressive **bronze reredos**, the work of Charles Daudelin. Measuring 17m/56ft high by 6m/20ft wide and weighing 20 tonnes, its 32 panels were cast in England and represent a man's difficult journey to heaven.

Museum (Musée Notre-Dame) – *Beside Sacred Heart Chapel. Renovation in progress. Scheduled reopening late 2001.* ☎ *514-842-2925.* Among the church plates and vestments on display are the silver crozier, throne and embroidered canopy of Henri-Marie de Pontbriand (1708-1760), the last bishop of Quebec under the French Regime, and an altar cloth embroidered of gold and silver threads of silk by the recluse, Jeanne LeBer (1662-1714).

★ **Vieux Séminaire de Saint-Sulpice (Old Sulpician Seminary)** – *130 Rue Notre-Dame Ouest*. Located next to the Notre Dame Basilica, the freestone building is the oldest structure in Montreal. It was built in 1685 as a residence and training centre by **Dollier de Casson** (1636-1701), Superior of the Messieurs de Saint-Sulpice and Montreal's first historian.

The Sulpician Order – Founded in Paris by Jean-Jacques Olier in 1641, the Sulpician Order was established in Montreal in 1657. In 1663, the Compagnie de Saint-Sulpice acquired the mission of Ville-Marie, including its land titles and seigneurial power, from the Société de Notre-Dame. As seigneurs of the island, the Sulpicians exercised great authority over the population and were responsible for the construction of Notre Dame Basilica. The seminary also served as the administrative centre of Ville-Marie. Today, the seminary building continues to serve as a residence for the Sulpicians.

A Classical Building – Like numerous other structures in Montreal, the architecture of the seminary bears traits of 17C French classicism. Its palatial, U-shaped plan was adopted by all of the island's religious orders.

The main building, topped by a mansard roof, was enlarged in 1704 and 1712, under the direction of the Sulpician Vachon de Belmont (1654-1732). Two lateral wings around a court of honour were constructed during this period, along with staircase turrets at the juncture of the main buildings. The seminary building conceals from view the main garden which, until the 19C, overlooked the St. Lawrence River.

The facade **clock**, created in Paris, was installed in 1701. Its face was engraved by Paul Labrosse and gilded by the Sisters of the Congregation. Believed to be the oldest public timepiece in North America, the clock's original movement was fabricated entirely of wood. It was replaced by an electric mechanism in 1966.

Walk down Rue Saint-Sulpice.

Cours Le Royer (Le Royer Courtyard) – *Bounded by Rues Saint-Dizier, de Brésoles, Le Royer, and Saint-Paul*. After 1861, a series of warehouses designed by Victor Bourgeau was constructed on the former site of the Montreal General Hospital. These buildings were renovated into housing units during the 1980s in a large-scale project that began the movement to transform Old Montreal into a residential area. The structures, designed in the protorationalist style, overlook a charming courtyard, dotted with flower-filled planters.

Follow Rue Saint-Dizier to Rue Saint-Paul and turn left.

★★ **Rue Saint-Paul** – Along with Rue Notre-Dame, this narrow street is one of the oldest in Montreal. Its curves and dips are explained by its origins as a footpath along the river banks between the fort and the hospital. In 1672, Dollier de Casson straightened the street somewhat in his formal plan of the city, and named it in honour of Paul de Chomedey, Sieur de Maisonneuve.

Lovely, well-proportioned 19C buildings presently line Rue Saint-Paul. The section between Boulevard Saint-Laurent and Place Jacques-Cartier incorporates former warehouses, now transformed into shops and artists' studios.

Located in the former International Centre of Design *(no. 85)*, Montreal's centre for arts and new technologies, the Cité des Arts et des Nouvelles Technologies de Montréal (**A**), now serves as a conference center. You can pause for a drink or a snack in the **Café Électronique** (Electronic Café), while trying out a new CD-ROM or surfing the Internet.

> **Music and ambience**
>
> **L'Air du Temps** *(191 Rue Saint-Paul Ouest;* ☎ *514-842-2003)* is a favourite of jazz-lovers for its high-quality live performances as well as its magnificent décor and relaxed ambience. For an entirely different kind of musical evening, stop by **Les Deux Pierrots** *(104 Rue Saint-Paul Est;* ☎ *514-861-1270)*. A veritable Montreal institution, this nightclub is the perfect place to expose your ears to traditional Quebec music in a most convivial setting.

Take a short detour to admire the Auberge Saint-Gabriel *(no. 426 Rue Saint-Gabriel)*, built in 1754 and today renovated as a restaurant.

★★ **Place Jacques-Cartier** – With its outdoor cafés, street performers, and flower vendors, this cobblestone square is lively all summer, especially in the evenings. The public square was created in 1847 by the city council and named for the famous explorer who, according to tradition, docked his ship at its foot in 1535. During the early 18C, the Marquis de Vaudreuil erected his chateau on the spot now covered with blooming parterres; the building was destroyed by fire in 1803. A bustling fruit, vegetable and flower market operated on the square for over forty years, until the construction of the Bonsecours Market.

Place Jacques-Cartier

The numerous early 19C buildings surrounding Place Jacques-Cartier today house mainly restaurants. Montreal's City Hall stands on the north side of the square, and the Old Port is accessible from its southern end.

A statue of **Horatio Nelson** (**2**) crowns a 15m/49ft column at the top of the square. Erected in 1809, this monument was the first to honour Nelson (1758-1805), who defeated French and Spanish forces at the battle of Trafalgar in 1805 (a similar, more renowned monument in London's Trafalgar Square dates from 1842).

The **Tourist Information Centre** located at the west corner of Place Jacques-Cartier and Rue Notre-Dame *(open late Mar–mid-Jun daily 9am–5pm; late Jun–early Oct daily 9am–7pm; rest of the year Thu–Sun 9am–5pm;* 🅿 ☎ *514-844-5400)* occupies the former site of the Silver Dollar Saloon. Named for the 300 American silver dollars embedded in the floor, the saloon attracted clients who "walked on top of a fortune."

A tiny side street off Place Jacques-Cartier, **Rue Saint-Amable**, is renowned for the artists who, during the summer, show and sell works depicting Montreal and the quarter. The street is named for the wife of Jacques Viger, first mayor of Montreal.

★**Hôtel de Ville (City Hall)** – *275 Rue Notre-Dame Est. Visit by guided tour (1hr) only, year-round Mon–Fri 8:30am–4:30pm. Closed major holidays.* ♿ ☎ *514-872-3355.* The first important building in Quebec to adopt the Second Empire style was originally built in the 1870s. After a fire in 1922, the building was reconstructed by Joseph-Omer Marchand, who preserved the original walls but added a storey.

General Charles de Gaulle delivered his famous "Vive le Québec libre" speech in 1967 from the balcony overlooking the main entrance. Just inside the main door stand two sculptures, recast from the original bronze works, *The Sower* and *Woman with Bucket*, by Alfred Laliberté. The elegant **main hall** (hall d'honneur) is 31m/102ft long by 12m/39ft wide and features a marbled floor and walls, and a huge bronze chandelier weighing over one tonne. The **Council Chamber** can be visited if there is no session in progress *(access from the door under the clock)*. Its stained-glass windows represent various aspects of city life during the 1920s.

Walk to the back of City Hall for a beautiful view of downtown Montreal. Excavation of the **Champ de Mars**, now a vast expanse of lawn, has revealed the base of a section of the old stone fortification wall.

★**Château Ramezay** – *280 Rue Notre-Dame Est. Open Jun–Sept daily 10am–6pm. Rest of the year daily 10am–4:30pm. Closed Jan 1–2 & Dec 25–26. $6.* ♿ *www.chateauramezay.qc.ca* ☎ *514-861-3708.* Across from the City Hall stands one of Montreal's loveliest examples of early-18C domestic architecture (1705). Constructed for Claude de Ramezay (1659-1724), eleventh governor of Montreal during the French Regime, the building underwent numerous transformations, always emerging relatively unchanged in appearance but for the tower, which was added in the early 20C. The building's walls are formed of stone fragments and topped with a lead-covered copper roof pierced by dormers. In 1745, Ramezay's heirs sold the house to the **West India Company**, and master builder Paul Tessier (also known as Lavigne) was hired to reconstruct it in 1756. The original structure was doubled in size, allowing for the addition of an "apartment," imposing vaults and firebreak walls.

The house became known as a "chateau" after the Conquest, when British governors resided in it from 1764 to 1849. For seven months in 1775-1776, during the American occupation, it served as the headquarters of Richard Montgomery's army. Benjamin Franklin lodged here during this period while on a diplomatic mission. In 1929, the chateau was one of the first three buildings to be classified as an historic monument of Quebec, along with Quebec City's Church of Our Lady of the Victories and Sillery's Jesuit House.

Musée du Château Ramezay (Château Ramezay Museum) – The chateau, restored and transformed into a museum in 1895, presents Montreal's economic, political and social history. Several rooms on the main level house long-term temporary exhibitions using objects drawn from the permanent collection, including furniture, paintings, newspapers, letters, costumes and manuscripts. Note especially the room embellished with hand-carved mahogany **panelling**. Produced in 1725 in Nantes, France, for the headquarters of the West India Company, this remarkable woodwork is attributed to the French architect, Germain Boffrand (1667-1754), a proponent of the Louis-XV style. Shipped to Montreal for display in the French pavilion during Expo '67, the panelling was ultimately presented to the Chateau Ramezay because of the latter's connection with the company.

The basement, with its huge vaults, houses the museum's permanent exhibits, a series of rooms designed to resemble a common room. Other displays here present traditional arts and crafts and furniture.

Continue east on Rue Notre-Dame to its intersection with Rue Berri.

★**Lieu historique national de Sir George-Étienne Cartier** – *458 Rue Notre-Dame Est. Open Jun–Aug daily 10am–6pm. Apr–May & Sept–late Dec Wed–Sun 10am–noon &1pm–5pm. $4.25.* ♿ *www.parkscanada.gc.ca/cartier* ☎ *514-283-2282.* This limestone, mansard-roofed building consists of two houses linked by a covered passage that today serves as a reception area. From 1848 to 1872, the structure was the sometime home and legal office of the renowned statesman, **George-Étienne Cartier** (1814-1873). An influential member of the Sir John A. Macdonald cabinet until his death, Cartier was a prominent figure in Canadian politics during the 19C.

The visit begins on the ground floor of the building's eastern section, where colourful signs, mannequins and panels introduce visitors to 19C Montreal society. The second level illustrates Cartier's life and work, highlighting his role as one of the proponents of Canada's railway development, and as a Father of Canadian Confederation.

The meticulously restored western half sends visitors backward in time to the Victorian era. Period furnishings and recorded voices evoke the rather pampered lifestyle of middle-class Montrealers during the late 19C.

Return to Rue Bonsecours and turn left.

Maison Papineau (Papineau House) – *440 Rue Bonsecours.* This large edifice was erected in 1785 by Jean-Baptist Cérat, also known as Coquillard. With its steeply pitched roof pierced by two rows of dormer windows and carriage door leading to a rear courtyard, the structure represents a typical French Regime house. During a reconstruction in 1831, the original stone walls were covered in wood, sculpted and painted to resemble limestone. This modification lent a Neoclassical appearance to the traditional-style structure. The house was owned by six generations of the Papineau family, including **Louis-Joseph Papineau** (1786-1871), leader of the Patriot party, who lived in it periodically between 1814 and 1837.

The charming **view** down Rue Bonsecours to the little church of Our Lady of Perpetual Help *(below)* is one of the most photographed perspectives in the city.

★**Maison du Calvet (Calvet House)** – *401 Rue Bonsecours at corner of Rue Saint-Paul Est.* Constructed in 1725 on a lot belonging to Pierre du Calvet, this structure is Montreal's finest existing example of a traditional urban residence. Typical elements include unadorned fieldstone walls, firebreaks (the part of the wall extending beyond the roof as a shield against flying sparks), corner consoles, tall chimneys incorporated into large gables, and a pitched roof unrelieved by dormers. The third level, with three small windows, evokes the mansard roofs introduced by the Loyalists. The interior, today renovated as a café, features beamed woodwork characteristic of the 18C.

Pierre du Calvet (1735-1786), a French Protestant merchant who came to Montreal in 1758, was the house's most famous resident. He offered his services to the British in 1760 and to the Americans in 1775. These shifts of allegiance endeared him to no one, and he was imprisoned for treason in 1780. After his release in 1784, he set sail for London to appeal this punishment. His ship was wrecked on the return voyage and he was drowned.

★**Chapelle Notre-Dame-de-Bon-Secours** **(Chapel of Our Lady of Perpetual Help)** – *400 Rue Saint-Paul Est. Open May–Oct Tue–Sun 10am–5pm. Mid-Mar–Apr & Nov–mid-Jan Tue–Sun 11am–3:30pm.* ♿ ☎ *514-282-8670.* This small edifice is distinguished by its copper steeple, and by a 9m/30ft statue of the Virgin with arms outstretched towards the river, created by Philippe Laperle. Commissioned by Marguerite Bourgeoys in 1657, and dedicated in 1678, the original stone chapel burned to the ground in 1754. The present structure dates from the mid-18C. The facade and interior decoration were added in the late 19C. The tower was constructed over the apse between 1892 and 1894 to house the statue of the Virgin. Also added at this time were an "aerial chapel" and an observatory accessible from the tower *(climb of 100 steps)*. From here, the **panoramic view★** extends over the St. Lawrence River, St. Helen's Island, the Jacques-Cartier Bridge, and the Old Port.

The chapel, nicknamed "the Sailors' Church," was hung with small carved ships offered to the Virgin by devout seamen. Some of these votive offerings can still be seen today in the chapel. The oak statue of the Virgin, located in the chapel to the left of the altar, is the focus of special devotion, having been repeatedly recovered intact after several fires and a theft. Beneath the nave of the chapel, the foundation walls of the original building have been uncovered, along with the traces of a wood fort and indications of the Amerindian presence here as early as 400 BC.

Musée Marguerite-Bourgeoys (Marguerite Bourgeoys Museum) – *Open May–Oct Tue–Sun 10am–5pm. Mid-Mar–Apr & Nov–mid-Jan Tue–Sun 11am–3:30pm. $5.* ♿ ☎ *514-282-8670.* A former school next to the chapel as well as the tower and crypt house a museum dedicated to the life and work of **Marguerite Bourgeoys** (1620-1700). This legendary woman arrived in Ville-Marie with Maisonneuve in 1653 and founded the first non-cloistered religious community in Canada, the **Congregation of Notre Dame**. For many years, Sister Bourgeoys sheltered the **Filles du Roy** (the "King's wards"), young women who came from France with dowries provided by Louis XIV to marry the first settlers. A special feature of the museum is its collection of charming figurines, dressed in regional and period costume and displayed in 58 scenes that relate the extraordinary life of this famed Montréal nun. Marguerite Bourgeoys was canonized in 1982.

Walk west on the Rue Saint-Paul Est.

★**Marché Bonsecours** **(Bonsecours Market)** – *350 Rue Saint-Paul Est.* Ⓜ *Champ-de-Mars. Open year-round Mon–Wed & weekends 10am–6pm. Thur & Fri 10am–9pm.* ✂ ♿ 🅿 *www.marchebonsecours.qc.ca* ☎ *514-872-7730.* Originally constructed to house Montreal's first interior market, this building (1845) occupies the former site of the Intendant's Palace, destroyed in 1796. With its 163m/535ft freestone facade and lofty dome, the elegantly ornamented structure is best viewed from the river side. The ground-floor merchant stalls were accessible from the outside through large bays. After fire destroyed the Parliament Buildings in 1849, the market became the seat of the Legislature of the United Canadas. From 1852 to 1878, it served as the City Hall, and today is leased for a variety of charming shops, craft boutiques, temporary exhibitions, and other purposes.

Excalibor
122 Rue Saint-Paul Est. ☎ *514-393-7260.* Take a trip back in time to the age of chivalry and knights on horseback at this unusual boutique, purveyor of objects to tempt aficionados of things medieval. Even non-history buffs will enjoy perusing the stock of medieval-inspired clothing, jewelry, swords, coats of mail and shields.

Continue west on Rue Saint-Paul Est to the foot of Place Jacques-Cartier. Turn left, cross Rue de la Commune and enter the Old Port area.

★Vieux-Port **(Old Port)** *Map p 177.* Ⓜ *Place-d'Armes or Champ-de-Mars.*

In Montreal's early years, barges and canoes were hauled by hand onto the muddy St. Lawrence banks. In the mid 18C, several wooden quays were built on the site of the present port. These were replaced in 1830 by stone piers, loading ramps and a breakwater, constructed by the newly created Harbour Commission. Concrete piers, steel sheds, docks, jetties and a huge grain elevator (demolished in 1978) were erected in 1898. During the 1920s, Montreal had become the largest grain port on the continent, with a traffic volume second only to the port of New York, even though at the time, ice forced an annual shutdown of several months.

Today, much of the maritime traffic bypasses Montreal on the St. Lawrence Seaway, and the port's principal activities centre around the handling of shipping containers. The older section of the port has been converted into a park featuring cultural and recreational activities during the summer months.

Michel Gagné/REFLEXION

Vieux-Port Esplanade

Esplanade – *Entrances at Rue Berri, Place Jacques-Cartier, Blvd. Saint-Laurent, and Rue McGill.* With its sunny, breeze-swept spaces and paths for walking, skating or biking, this immense waterfront park comes alive during fine weather, especially during the summer months. The esplanade boasts excellent **views★** of the city and river, boat trips, bike rentals, and **iSci** the Montreal Interactive Science Centre *(see below)*. **Tram tours** allow visitors to discover the entire esplanade and the history of the old Port *(depart from Jacques-Cartier pier year-round daily; $3; ☎ 514-496-7678)*.

★**iSci** – *King Edward pier at Blvd. St. Laurent and Rue de la Commune.* Three main exhibition areas, the LIFE lab, MATTER Works and INFORMATION Studio compose the **Interactive Science EXHIBITIONS** *(open daily mid-June–early Sept 10am–9pm; rest of the year 10am–6pm; $9.95 ✗ ♿ P www.isci.ca ☎ 514-496-4724)*. The **IMMERSION Interactive Cinema** *(open daily 10am–11pm; $5.50 ✗ ♿ P www.isci.ca ☎ 514-496-4724)* allows spectators to control the action of the adventure by voting on interactive screens, and the **IMAX** cinema *(open early May–Sept daily 10am–10pm; rest of the year Tue–Sun 10am–9pm; reservations suggested; $9.50; ✗ ♿ P www.isci.ca ☎ 514-496-4724)* continues to thrill viewers with its 3-D sensations.

Le Tour de Ville

Le Delta Centre-Ville, 777 Rue Université. ☎ 514-879-1370. For a great view of Montreal, ride the elevator to the 28th floor of the Radisson Hôtel des Gouverneurs to the city's only revolving dining room. The bar is a great place for an evening cocktail and the restaurant's buffet features international and seasonal themes.

At the eastern end of the quai de l'Horloge, note the **Tour de l'Horloge** (Clock Tower). Completed in 1922, the 45m/148ft tower honours the sailors who perished during World War I. You can climb the 192 steps to the top for a nice panorama of the city *(donation requested)*.

★★**Jet Boat Trips on the Lachine Rapids** (**Expéditions dans les rapides de Lachine**) – *Ⓜ Champ-de-Mars. Depart from Quai de l'Horloge May–Aug daily 10am–6pm. Sept–mid-Oct 10am–4pm. Round-trip 1hr. Commentary. Reservations suggested. $49. ♿ P ($7) Lachine Rapids Tours/Saute-Moutons www.jetboatingmontreal.com ☎ 514-284-9607).* On the wettest, most exciting ride in Montreal, passengers embark upriver to the ferocious Lachine Rapids in unique "jet boats." These specially designed vessels repeatedly mount and descend the tumultuous rapids. Despite the protective clothing provided, passengers can anticipate a thorough soaking.
The **views★★** of Montreal and the surrounding areas are spectacular, particularly if the excursion occurs around sunset.

★ Harbour Cruises (Croisières du port de Montréal) – *Depart from Quai de l'Horloge & Quai Jacques Cartier May–Oct daily noon, 2:30pm & 4:30pm; round-trip 2hrs; commentary; reservations required; starting at $25.31. Dancing & dinner cruises available; depart at 7pm; round-trip 4hrs; commentary; reservations required; starting at $30 (plus price of meal).* ✗ ⚐ ☎ ($9) Croisières AML ☎ 514-842-3871. Cruises of various lengths offer visitors a fine perspective of Montreal from the river. The port installations, bridges, islands, the St. Lawrence Seaway and the Olympic Stadium are among the highlights.

Amphibus – *Depart from the corner of Blvd. Saint-Laurent & Rue de la Commune May–Jun 23 daily 10am–10pm every 2hrs. Jun 24–Aug daily 10am–midnight every hour. Sept–Oct daily 10am–8pm every 2hrs. Round-trip 1hr. Commentary. Reservations required. $18.* ⚐ Amphibus Inc. ☎ 514-849-5181. The "Kamada," a specially designed amphibious bus, tours part of Old Montreal before descending into the St. Lawrence River for a cruise around the Cité du Havre.

★ Place d'Youville Area *Map p 177.* Ⓜ *Square-Victoria.*

Stash Café

200 Rue Saint-Paul Ouest. ☎ *514-845-6611.* Montrealers as well as tourists are drawn to this Polish restaurant for its welcoming ambience. Break here for a slice of cake with coffee, or sample savoury traditional dishes such as *pierogis* (dumplings stuffed with cheese, meat or cabbage), sausages and cabbage rolls.

The St. Pierre River ran along this square to join the St. Lawrence at Pointe-à-Callière, until it was channelled underground in the 19C. The square was named after **Marguerite d'Youville**, who founded the Grey Nuns in 1737.

In 1849, it was the site of the Colonial Legislature created after the Patriots' Rebellion of 1837 with representatives from Lower Canada (Quebec) and Upper Canada (Ontario). Tories burned the building to the ground to show their objection to a law compensating anyone whose land had been damaged during the Revolt (including rebels). The Legislature moved briefly to Bonsecours Market and then left for Kingston, Quebec, and finally Ottawa, never again to risk meeting in Montreal.

The buildings surrounding the pleasant square represent different epochs in the city's history, from the 17C Grey Nuns hospital, to the 19C warehouses, and the immense, Beaux-Arts style **Édifice des Douanes** (Customs House), erected between 1912 and 1936. Today, numerous residences are undergoing renovations, adding to the charm of this up-and-coming area.

L'Arrivage

350 Place Royale. ☎ *514-872-9128.* A pleasant spot to break for lunch, this restaurant located within the Montreal Museum of Archaeology and History serves forth delightful creations in an airy space blessed with a view of the Old Port. It's particularly nice in summer, when the terrace is open.

Pointe-à-Callière (Callière Point) – Montreal was born on this small triangle of land, where the St. Pierre River joined the St. Lawrence, in May 1642. The spot had already been cleared in 1611 by Samuel de Champlain, who deemed it an excellent location for a harbour. Thirty-one years later, Maisonneuve established the settlement of Ville-Marie on the site, surrounding it with a wooden stockade. A 10m/33ft **obelisk (3)**, *Les Pionniers,* commemorates the occasion of Maisonneuve's landing. Callière Point is named for Louis-Hector de Callière, Governor of Montreal from 1684 to 1698, whose home formerly occupied the site.

★★ Musée d'Archéologie et d'Histoire de Montréal (Montreal Museum of Archaeology and History) – *350 Place Royale. Open Jul–Aug Tue–Fri 10am–6pm, weekends 11am–6pm. Rest of the year Tue–Fri 10am–5pm, weekends 11am–5pm. $8.50.* ✗ ⚐ *www.musee-pointe-a-calliere.qc.ca* ☎ 514-872-9150. Opened in 1992, this museum complex brings alive the fascinating history of Montreal from its very beginnings here at Callière Point.

In the striking, contemporary Éperon Building, visitors can view a wonderfully absorbing multimedia presentation *(16min)* on the evolution of Montreal. Temporary exhibits are mounted on the second floor, and from the third floor belevedere, a lovely **view★** extends over the Old Port Esplanade.

An underground passage leads from the Éperon Building to the **archaeological crypt** located directly beneath Place Royale. Artifacts on display here bear witness to Montreal's many centuries of human occupation. In the crypt, visitors can see the actual vestiges of early Montreal, foundations and even walls of structures uncovered in the course of archaeological excavations. Scale models of the city illustrate its appearance during various periods, and interactive monitors allow visitors to interact with the images of some of Montreal's early inhabitants.

The underground passage terminates at the **Old Customs House** (1838, John Ostell). Above ground, the edifice's Neoclassical facade dominates the Place Royale. Today tranformed as an interpretation centre, the dignified building houses exhibits on the history of Montreal as a centre of trade and commerce.

Place Royale – In 1645, Maisonneuve erected his dwelling on this square, originally known as the Place d'Armes. By 1706, it had become the public market place, the popular setting for official announcements by the town crier, criminal punishments including whippings and hangings, and occasional duels. The square was officially named Place Royale in 1892.

★**Centre d'histoire de Montréal (Montreal History Centre)** – *335 Place d'Youville. Open May–Aug daily 10am–5pm. Sept–early Dec Tue–Sun 10am–5pm. $4.50. ⚹ ▯ ($7) www. ville.montreal. qc.ca/chm/ chm.htm ☎ 514-872-3207. The Centre d'histoire de Montreal is currently under renovation. Call for new opening times.* Restored in 1981, this red brick edifice (1903), a former fire station, features elements of Dutch baroque architecture: an elegantly gabled roof, an imposing dormer and sculpted ornamentation. The rear tower was used to hang the water hoses to dry and stone arches at the front provided access for firefighting vehicles. Today, the building houses a delightful

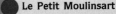

Le Petit Moulinsart

139 Rue Saint-Paul Ouest. ☎ *514-843-7432.* A warm welcome and attractive décor make visitors feel right at home in this charming Belgian restaurant. Images of Tintin (a Belgian comic character) on the walls and menu only increase its appeal. Relax and partake of succulent mussels or a fabulous crème brûlée.

interpretation centre dedicated to Montreal's history from 1642 to the present. The presentation employs hands-on displays, videos, audio tracks, tableaux, animated mannequins, and original and reconstructed objects to illustrate the economic, social and urban trends that influenced the city's colourful past and furnish insight into the lives of Montrealers. Temporary exhibitions also explore various aspects of Montreal's history.

Écuries d'Youville (Youville Stables) – *298-300 Place d'Youville.* Enclosing a pleasant, garden courtyard, these low stone structures (1828) were built as warehouses for the Grey Nuns, and later used to store grain. The complex never actually served as a shelter for animals; however, it is thought that its present name derives from 19C stables that were located nearby. Restored in 1967, the complex currently houses offices and a restaurant, and the surrounding buildings have been renovated as condominiums. Enter the courtyard through the central carriage door.

Hôpital général des Sœurs Grises (Grey Nuns Convent) – *Bounded by Rue Saint-Pierre, Rue d'Youville, Rue Normand and Place d'Youville.* In 1680, the Sulpicians ceded the marshland near the St. Pierre River to François Charron de la Barre and his brothers, who constructed a hospital on the site in 1694. In 1747, Marguerite d'Youville and the Grey Nuns assumed direction of the hospital, rebuilding it after it was largely destroyed by fire in 1765.
In 1871, due to frequent flooding of the site and increased activity in the adjacent port, the Grey Nuns left the area for a quieter location to the west of the centre. Their chapel on Rue Saint-Pierre was demolished, the street was extended to the river, and warehouses were erected.
In 1980, the convent building was renovated to house a novitiate and the general administration offices for the Grey Nuns. The oldest section of the convent can be seen from Rue Normand.

★**Musée Marc-Aurèle-Fortin (Marc-Aurèle Fortin Museum)** – *118 Rue Saint-Pierre. Open year-round Tue–Sun 11am–5pm. Closed late Dec–early Jan. $4.* ☎ *514-845-6108.* Located in one of the warehouses built by the Grey Nuns in the 1870s, this museum presents the works of the artist **Marc-Aurèle Fortin** (1888-1970). In his quest to create a school of Canadian landscape art entirely devoid of European influence, he produced colourful representations of his native Quebec, concentrating on regional flora and fauna, and views of the St. Lawrence. Among notable works (shown in rotation) are: *Bœufs aux Labours* (1947), *Bagotville au Saguenay* (1953) and *Arbre à Lafresnière* (1962). The museum also mounts changing exhibits of works by local artists.

★★②**FROM DORCHESTER SQUARE TO McGILL UNIVERSITY** *2.4km/1.5mi. Map p 176. Ⓜ Peel. Begin the walking tour at Dorchester Square.*

This walk through the commercial heart of present-day Montreal leads past some of the city's landmark skyscrapers. The highrises along Avenue McGill College illustrate the diverging tendencies that mark the Postmodern movement.

★ **Dorchester Square** – Surrounded by a group of remarkable buildings, this pleasant green square has long been considered the heart of the city, though more recent skyscrapers have stolen some of the limelight. Formerly known as Dominion Square, it was renamed in 1988 to commemorate Lord Dorchester, Governor of British North America from 1768 to 1778 and from 1786 to 1795. Situated outside city limits prior to 1855, the area originally served as a cemetery, especially for the many victims of the 1832 cholera epidemic. The cemetery was eventually moved to Mt. Royal, and the second bishop of Montreal, **Msgr. Ignace Bourget** (1799-1885), decided to erect a cathedral on the site, much to the chagrin of his parishioners, residents of the old town who objected to having to walk so far to church.

The square contains several notable memorials, including a statue of **Sir Wilfrid Laurier** (**4**) by Émile Brunet. Laurier (1841-1919) was the first French-Canadian prime minister of Canada; his famous words carved on the pedestal read (in translation): "The governing motive of my life has been to harmonize the different elements which compose our country." The monument to Laurier faces one of **Sir John A. Macdonald** (**5**) across the street in Place du Canada. The monument to **Lord Strathcona's Canadian Horse Regiment** (**6**), honouring the Canadians killed in the Boer War (1899-1901), is the work of George Hill, who also sculpted the nearby lion commemorating **Queen Victoria's Jubilee** (**7**). The statue of **Robert Burns** (**8**) was erected by devotees of the renowned Scottish poet (1759-1796).

★ **Dominion Square Building** – *On northern side of Dorchester Square between Rue Peel and Rue Metcalfe*. This imposing Renaissance Revival structure (1929) evokes the grandeur of 15C Florentine palaces. Reputed to be the "largest commercial building in Canada," the edifice displayed several features considered innovative for the time: an underground parking area and two-level shopping mall, and the first wooden escalators to appear in Montreal. Also considered novel was the fact that the building housed both offices and boutiques.

The **Infotouriste** Tourist Office is located on the ground floor, at the corner of Rue Peel and Rue Metcalfe *(open late Jun–Labour Day daily 8:30am–7:30pm; rest of the year daily 9am–6pm; closed Jan 1 & Dec 25;* ⎕ ☎ *514-873-2015)*. Visitors will find many services here, including an information desk, guided tours of the city, a bookstore, currency exchange, accommodation reservations and car rentals.

★ **The Windsor** – *1170 Rue Peel*. Today one of Montreal's most distinctive office buildings, the Windsor hotel was inaugurated in 1878 with a ball honouring the Marquis de Lorne (then governor-general) and his wife Louise, daughter of Queen Victoria. Seriously damaged by fire in 1906 and destroyed in 1957, the structure's main wing was replaced by the Bank of Commerce *(below)*. The hotel continued to operate in the remaining wing until 1981. The stone and brick facade is topped by a mansard roof pierced with dormers and œil-de-bœuf windows. The renovation of the hotel interior into office space preserved the Adamesque decor of the ground floor, exemplified in the sumptuous ballroom.

★★ **Sun Life Building** – *1155 Rue Metcalfe*. This magnificent Beaux-Arts edifice (1913), constructed of steel sheathed in white granite and adorned with colossal colonnades on its four facades, occupies the entire east side of Dorchester Square. Headquarters of the Sun Life Insurance Company, the building could accommodate 2,500 employees and was touted as the "tallest building in the British Empire." Its construction and subsequent expansions (1923-1933) contributed to Montreal's status as Canada's most important financial city during those years. During World War II, the British government stored its Treasury bonds and gold reserves in this building. Today it houses the Sun Life administrative headquarters and other prestigious insurance and brokerage firms.

Cross Blvd. René-Lévesque and continue down Rue Peel.

Place du Canada – Several high rises tower over this green plaza, facing Dorchester Square. The elongated **Banque de Commerce** (Bank of Commerce, 1962), presents an unusual contrast between the slate window frames and the glass and stainless steel facade. Across the street rises the Postmodern, copper and glass **La Laurentienne** (Laurentian Building, 1986). Popularly known as the "cheese-grater," the **Château-Champlain Hotel** stands on the south side of the square. The slender building (1967) marked by convex, half-moon windows, bears the influence of Frank Lloyd Wright, mentor of architect Roger d'Astous. The prevailing architectural tastes of the 1990s are reflected in the **1000 de la Gauchetière** office building dominating the southeast corner of the square; it is Montreal's tallest structure, at 205m/672ft.

★ **St. George's Anglican Church** (**Église anglicane Saint-Georges**) – *Entrance on Rue de la Gauchetière. Open Jun–Aug Tue–Sun 8:30am–5pm. Sept–May Tue–Sun 8:30am–4:30pm.* ⎕ *www.st-georges.org* ☎ *514-866-7113*. Erected in 1870, this charming Gothic Revival church is the oldest building on Place du Canada. The well-proportioned interior features a striking double hammer-beam vaulted **ceiling** of red pine and spruce. Of special interest are the oak reredos with its delicate open tracery, the choir stalls and the chancel screens. The side screens and sculptures, also of oak, were produced by the Casavant Company of Saint-Hyacinthe, who installed the organ in 1896.

Gare Windsor (Windsor Station) – *Corner of Rue Peel and Rue de la Gauchetière.* Designed by Bruce Price, famed architect of Quebec City's Château Frontenac, this distinctive railway station (1889) is one of Montreal's finest examples of the Richardsonian Romanesque style, characterized by the towers, crenellations, turrets and round arches. The station was created to house the administrative centre of Canadian Pacific Railways, and now serves as the terminus of the suburban transit network.

Return to Blvd. René-Lévesque and continue east.

★★**Basilique-Cathédrale Marie-Reine-du-Monde (Mary Queen of the World Basilica-Cathedral)** – *Main entrance on Blvd. René-Lévesque. Open year-round Mon–Fri 7am–7:30pm, Sat 7:30am–8:30pm, Sun 8:30am–7:30pm.* ♿ ☏ *514-866-1661.* Designed by Victor Bourgeau, this monumental edifice is distinguished by large Greek columns, ornate decoration and a row of statues lining the cornice. After a fire destroyed the St. James Cathedral (Cathédrale Saint-Jacques) located on the east side of Montreal, Msgr. Ignace Bourget decided to erect a new cathedral in the west quarter to reinforce the importance of the Catholic Church in this anglophone, Protestant district. A proponent of papal supremacy, the bishop of Montreal selected as a model St. Peter's in Rome, the mother church of Roman Catholicism. The scale of this Baroque Revival replica was reduced to one-third the size of the 16C Italian basilica.

Work on the structure did not begin until 1870, and was interrupted in 1878 due to lack of funds. Construction resumed in 1885, and the church was consecrated in 1894. Originally dedicated to St. James the Major, the structure was recognized as a minor basilica in 1919 and adopted its present name in 1955.

Alphonse Longpré (1881-1938) carved the cornice figures, representing patron saints from parishes comprising the Montreal diocese in 1890. The copper dome was added in 1886; its original iron cross was replaced by an aluminium version in 1958. The **statue (9)** of Msgr. Bourget, standing to the right of the cathedral, is the work of Louis-Philippe Hébert. The bishop also appears on the statue's pedestal in the company of the architect of the cathedral, Victor Bourgeau.

Interior – In the entrance vestibule hang the portraits of all the bishops of Montreal, among them the late Msgr. Paul Grégoire, appointed Cardinal in 1989. Cast in copper covered with gold leaf, the magnificent **baldachin** (1900) by Victor Vincent dominating the nave is a replica of the 16C masterpiece by the Italian sculptor, Bernini, created for St. Peter's Basilica. The interior is decorated with large paintings by Georges Delfosse representing episodes in the history of Canada, including the martyrdoms of the Jesuit priest Jean de Brébeuf and Gabriel Lalement; and the drowning of Nicolas Viel, the first Canadian martyr, and Ahuntsic, his Amerindian disciple. In the chapel behind the altar stands a delicate statue of the Virgin by Sylvia Daoust, the renowned 20C Canadian sculptress.

Located on the left side of the nave, a **mortuary chapel** (1933) contains the tombs of several archbishops and bishops. The Italian marble walls and floor are embellished with beautiful mosaics. In the centre, note Msgr. Bourget's mausoleum, executed in Rome. Above the altar in the back of chapel, a magnificent bronze bas-relief represents St. Peter's of Rome.

Cross Blvd. René-Lévesque and continue east.

Montreal's largest hotel, Le Reine Élizabeth (1957), occupies the block of Boulevard René-Lévesque between Rue Mansfield and Rue University. The Central train station, terminus for VIA and Amtrak trains, is located beneath the hotel.

★★**Place Ville-Marie** – Centrepiece of the underground city before its development around the McGill metro station, Place Ville-Marie initiated the rebirth of Montreal's downtown and has become the forerunner of many such developments across the country. Inspired by New York City's Rockefeller Center *(consult THE GREEN GUIDE New York City),* the project was planned in 1930 to fill the enormous pit caused by the pre-World War I passage of a railway tunnel under Mt. Royal. However, construction of Place Ville-Marie did not begin until 1959 due to a lack of funds during the Great Depression.

Restaurant Julien

1191 Rue Union.
☏ *514-871-1581.* Be careful not to overlook the side streets when seeking out fine dining opportunities in Montreal. Hidden away from the main boulevards, this elegant French restaurant well deserves its years-long reputation for unfailingly high standards in both dining room and kitchen. Prepare to enjoy fine cuisine in a polished setting, either inside or, in summer, out on the lovely terrace.

The **Banque Royale Tower**★ (1962; I.M. Pei, Affleck and Associates) dominates the complex. The cruciform structure, sheathed in aluminium, boasts 3,534sq m/ 38,000sq ft of office space on each of its 42 storeys.

The Banque Royale and the three other buildings making up the complex enclose a concrete esplanade that is especially lively in summertime. From this raised vantage point, an unparalleled **vista**★ extends to the north of the city, down Avenue McGill College to the McGill University campus, dominated by the bulk of Mt. Royal. Gerald Gladstone's bronze fountain, entitled *Female Landscape* (1972), stands in the foreground. From the shopping centre beneath the esplanade, large skylights afford intriguing views of the surrounding towers. *Access to underground city (open during business hours) via glass pavilions in front of the Banque Royale Tower.*

From Place Ville-Marie, proceed northward on Ave. McGill College.

Extending from Place Ville-Marie to the gates of McGill University, **Avenue McGill College** has become Montreal's busiest thoroughfare and a showplace for Postmodern architecture. Planned in 1857 as a prolongation of the main campus axis towards the downtown area, the avenue is now home to several important architectural projects initiated during the 1980s and 1990s.

★★**Place Montréal Trust** – *1500 Ave. McGill College. Open year-round Mon–Wed 10am–6pm, Thu–Fri 10am–9pm, Sat 10am–5pm, Sun noon–5pm.* ✗ & ▯ ☎ *514-843-8000.* This enormous edifice (1989) of rose marble blocks partitioned by sheets of pastel blue glass occupies the entire left side of the block between Rue Sainte-Catherine and Boulevard de Maisonneuve. Conceived by the architects **E. Zeidler**, **E. Argun** and **P. Rose**, the tower's bold design features a cylinder encased in a square base. The glass-walled **atrium** rises five floors from the metro level; a panoramic elevator permits visitors to admire the three-tiered central bronze fountain. With more than a hundred boutiques, a restaurant and numerous exotic food vendors, the atrium is a popular lunchtime spot for downtown Montrealers.

Walk east on Rue Sainte-Catherine.

Montreal's main commercial artery, **Rue Sainte-Catherine** is lined with such major department stores as **Ogilvy** and **La Baie**; huge commercial centres, including the Faubourg Sainte-Catherine; and numerous boutiques. After business hours, this thoroughfare is transformed into a lively nightspot, abounding in bars and clubs.

Magasin Eaton (Eaton Store) – *677 Rue Sainte-Catherine Ouest.* Formerly, one of the province's most important department stores, this well-known commercial outlet incorporated the original building (1925) – acquired by Timothy Eaton and enlarged to nine floors in 1930 – and a modern shopping complex, known as Centre Eaton (**B**).

★**Christ Church Cathedral** – *Entrance from Rue Sainte-Catherine between Rue University and Ave. Union. Open year-round daily 8am–5:30pm.* & *www. montreal.anglican. org/cathedral* ☎ *514-288-6421.* Distinguished by its triple portico and embellished with gables and gargoyles, this lovely structure (1859) reflects the Gothic Revival style. The limestone edifice, topped by a slender central spire, was erected as Montreal's second Anglican cathedral, after the first one burned down in 1856.

Place Montréal Trust

Before entering, note the **monument (10)** *(to the right of the church)* dedicated to Francis Fulford (1803-1868), the Anglican bishop at the time of the cathedral's construction.

A sinking building – From its inception, the church's foundations posed problems: they were so fragile that by 1927 the 39m/128ft stone spire was leaning 1.2m/3.9ft to the east and had to be removed. It was replaced in 1940 by the present spire of aluminium treated with acid to resemble stone. During the 1980s, the base of the church was discovered to be sinking. In response, the Anglican Church of Canada leased the land to a development company, which saved the church from destruction by shoring up the foundations and constructing an underground commercial complex (Les Promenades de la Cathédrale) beneath it. A gleaming office tower (La Place de la Cathédrale) completes this rather unique architectural ensemble.

Interior – A pointed arched nave and ogive windows decorated with trefoil and quatrefoil elements distinguish the calm, graceful interior. The capitals of the arcaded nave are embellished with leaves that appear in watercolour paintings of the McCord family gardens. On the vault, various decorative motifs evoke the Old Testament and symbols of the Christian faith. The chancel features a beautifully carved stone **reredos**. The William Morris studio of London produced many of the magnificent stained-glass windows. Note the organ, below the rose window at the south end: of North German inspiration, it was built in 1980 by Karl Wilhelm of Mont-Saint-Hilaire. *(Organ recitals are regularly held in the cathedral).*

Enter Les Promenades de la Cathédrale by the doors on either side of the cathedral's main entrance.

Les Promenades de la Cathédrale – *Open year-round Mon–Wed 10am–6pm, Thu–Fri 10am–9pm, Sat 9am–5pm, Sun noon–5pm. Closed major holidays.* ✗ ♿ ☎ *514-849-9925.* Linking the Eaton Centre and La Baie department store, this shopping centre (1988) is the result of one of Montreal's most spectacular feats of engineering. Excavation and construction occurred beneath the church over a period of several months, during which the structure's weight was borne only by slim pylons. Ogive ornamentation in the underground concourses is a reminder of the presence of the religious monument above.

Ascend to the street level "cloister," an attractive park located between the cathedral and La Place de la Cathédrale.

★**La Place de la Cathédrale** – *600 Blvd. de Maisonneuve Ouest.* Postmodern in design, this distinctive, 34-storey office tower (1988; Webb, Zerafa, Menkès and Houdsen) reveals the influence of the adjacent cathedral, as much by its pointed arched entrances, colonnades and deep embrasures as by its pitched roof and tall, arched windows. A prominent landmark among Montreal's downtown skyscrapers, the building is sheathed in copper-coloured reflecting glass. Step into the nave-like **foyer** for the sight of Christ Church Cathedral and its steeple through the 5-storey curvilinear glass wall. The building houses the cathedral and diocesan offices.

Exit to Blvd. de Maisonneuve and walk west to Ave. McGill College.

★**Tours de la Banque Nationale de Paris/Banque Laurentienne (National Bank of Paris (BNP)/Laurentian Bank Towers)** – *1981 Ave. McGill College.* Completed in 1981, the sprawling, twin-towered structure is designed in a play of angles and shapes. The metallic-blue glass exterior of the office complex camouflages the actual number of storeys within (16 and 20 storeys) and reflects the neighbouring buildings. Its jagged, abstract form surrounds a small forecourt highlighted by *La foule illuminée*, a fibreglass group sculpture by the French artist, Raymond Masson. The "blue building," as it is called by many Montrealers, symbolizes the economic growth experienced by the city during the early 1980s.

Tour l'Industrielle Vie (Industrial Life Tower) – *2000 Ave. McGill College.* This granite-clad tower (1986) features a rather conventional exterior enlivened by Postmodern ornamentation. The huge fanlight window at its entrance is repeated at the top of the building.

> **Hidden jewels**
> An unassuming location in the middle of a business district belies the culinary riches put forth at **Le Grand Comptoir** *(1225 Square Phillips;* ☎ *514-393-3295),* where classic bistro dishes like ris de veau (sweetbreads) and bavette a l'echalote (sirloin with shallots) are easy on both palate and wallet. Looking for a quick, tasty meal, especially in the wee hours? Try the famous smoked-meat sandwiches at **Ben's** *(990 Blvd. de Maisonneuve Ouest, at the corner of Rue Metcalfe;* ☎ *514-844-1000),* which has been serving up traditional deli fare for decades in its large, if spartan, dining room.

On the sidewalk, note the delightful bronze **sculpture**, *"Le banc du secret,"* by Léa Vivot of two children on a bench. The work bears numerous bilingual inscriptions, poems and sentiments, all anonymous but for one: "Montreal, a secret to share," signed Jean Doré, former mayor of Montreal.

Maison Ultramar (Ultramar Building) – *2200 Ave. McGill College.* This edifice (1990) successfully integrates the former University Club *(892 Rue Sherbrooke)* and the Molson House *(2047 Rue Mansfield)*. The building's recessed entranceway surmounted by a rounded glass facade displays the architect's skillful handling of a corner lot.

Place Mercantile – *Across from the Ultramar Building; entrance at 770 Rue Sherbrooke Ouest.* This aluminium and glass complex (1982) incorporates, on the Rue Sherbrooke side, the facades of a row of greystones dating from 1872. One of these, Strathcona Hall (1904), was sold by McGill University with the stipulation that the hall be preserved. It collapsed during construction of Place Mercantile, but was entirely rebuilt. Today the building houses the offices of Cacades Inc., Cascades Etcan Inc., and Etcan International Inc.

Turn right on Rue Sherbrooke.

★★**Musée McCord d'Histoire canadienne (McCord Museum of Canadian History)** – *69C Rue Sherbrooke Ouest. Open year-round Tue–Fri 10am–6pm, weekends 10am–5pm (Jul–Sept Mon 10am–5pm). $8.50.* ✗ ♿ *www.mccord-museum.qc.ca* ☎ *514-398-7100.* Founded in 1921, the McCord figures prominently among Canada's foremost historical museums, and is particularly renowned for the incredible breadth and variety of its collections.

Biddle's

2060 Rue Aylmer. ☎ *514-842-8656.* Jazz-lovers in the mood for excellent live music and a laid-back ambience should keep this famed local hangout in mind when planning an evening on the town. Stop in for a set or two and sample tasty barbecued chicken or ribs, either inside or on the outdoor terrace in fine weather.

With a view to founding a museum dedicated to Canada's social history, David Ross McCord (1844-1930) donated his extensive personal collections to McGill University in 1919. Today the museum's holdings include over 100,000 artifacts and more than 750,000 historic photos, offering insight into various facets of Canadian history from the settlement of the Amerindians to the present.

Building – In 1968, the museum moved its collections to this sober structure of grey limestone, originally a social centre for McGill University students. Erected in 1906 by Percy E. Nobbs, the edifice is highlighted by an elaborate portal flanked by Tuscan pilasters. An extension (1992) has been added to the south of the structure, permitting additional exhibit space, conservation laboratories, a library and various amenities. The new building's facade reflects the elegant style of the original structure. Galleries on two floors showcase the museum's permanent and temporary exhibits.

Collections – A magnificent Haida facade pole of Queen Charlotte Islands red cedar in the stairwell leads to the second floor. This level houses the permanent exhibit "Simply Montréal: Glimpses of a Unique City," which offers an enlightening look at life in Montreal from the 17C to the present. The unusual variety of objects draws from the museum's holdings of Amerindian art, decorative art (metalware and jewelry, furniture, basketry, glassware, ceramics), sporting equipment and toys. Also illustrating the Canadian lifestyle are examples from the museum's extensive costumes and textiles collection as well as selections from the **Notman Photographic Archives**. This outstanding collection of negatives and photographs, 400,000 of which were shot by master photographer William Notman (1826-1891), portrays historical figures, events and Canadian sites over a 78-year period and constitutes a comprehensive chronicle of Canadian life in the 19C and early 20C.

Cross Rue Sherbrooke to main entrance of the campus.

★**McGill University (Université McGill)** – *End of Ave. McGill College.* Graced with an attractive downtown campus on the slopes of Mt. Royal, Canada's oldest university originated when its benefactor, the Scottish fur trader, James McGill (1744-1813), bequeathed Burnside, his country estate, and £10,000 for the foundation of an English-speaking university. Granted a Royal Charter by George IV in 1821, McGill's first classes (in medicine) were held in 1829, following the incorporation of the Montreal Medical Institute. In the years since, the university has witnessed enormous growth and today claims an enrollment of over 30,000 students at the 32ha/79 acre downtown campus and at the Macdonald College campus located at Sainte-Anne-de-Bellevue, in the West Island.

Campus – Enter the campus by the Greek Revival **Portail Roddick** (Roddick Gate, 1924), erected in memory of Sir Thomas Roddick, dean of the Medical School; embedded in the gate is a clock, the gift of Lady Roddick in honour of her husband's extreme punctuality. The more than seventy buildings located on the university's downtown campus reflect a wide variety of architectural styles. Ornate facades, towers and turrets embellish early 19C limestone structures. Executed in an eclectic 19C style, they contrast with the unadorned concrete of more recent buildings. To the west of the main avenue, note the beautiful stone fountain (1930), attributed to Gertrude Vanderbilt-Whitney.

Pavillon des Arts (Arts Building) – *At the end of the main avenue.* The central and east sections of the campus' oldest structure were designed by John Ostell between 1839 and 1843. The west pavilion (Molson Hall) and the wings linking the three sections date from between 1861 and 1880. The Doric portico and interior were rebuilt in 1924, in the austere neoclassical style. From the steps of the portico there is a good **view** of downtown through the trees of the campus. The tomb of the university's founder, James McGill, stands in front of the building.

Avenue McGill and McGill University

★ **Musée d'histoire naturelle Redpath** (Redpath Museum of Natural History) – *To the west of Arts Building. Open Jun 24–Labour Day Mon–Thu 9am–5pm, Sun 1pm–5pm. Rest of the year Mon–Fri 9am–5pm, Sun 1pm–5pm. Closed Dec 25–Jan 1.* ♿ *($1) www.mcgill.ca/redpath* ☎ *514-398-4086.* This building (1882) was the first in Canada designed to hold a natural history museum. Its generous benefactor was Peter Redpath, a wealthy industrialist and founder of the nation's first sugar refinery. The building's eclectic Greek and Renaissance facade evokes an antique temple.

Inside, visitors can see an incredible array of treasures, including a set of samurai armor, a funerary canopy and the skeleton of an *Albertosaurus*. The first floor houses offices and classrooms, as well as a selection of objects drawn from the museum's zoology, paleontology and mineral collections. The upper floors re-create the charming, studious atmosphere of Victorian-era museums, and house an amazing number of invertebrate and vertebrate fossils, mollusks, minerals and other zoological artifacts. Also on view here are African art objects and Egyptian antiquities, including several human and animal mummies and fine examples of pottery.

Exit the campus by the Roddick Gate and turn right.

Located on the edge of campus bordering Rue Sherbrooke, just west of the Roddick Gate, a **plaque** (**11**) commemorates the Indian village of Hochelaga which (as was supposed in the 19C) stood on this spot at the time of Jacques Cartier's arrival in 1535.

Additional Sight

Planétarium de Montréal (Montreal Planetarium) – *1000 Rue Saint-Jacques.*
🚇 *Bonaventure. Open late Jun–Labour Day daily 12:45pm–5pm & 7pm–8:30pm.
Rest of the year Tue–Wed 9am–5pm, Thu–Fri 9am–5pm & 7:30pm–8:30pm,
weekends 10:30am–5pm & 7:30pm–8:30pm. Call for show times. $6.* 🦽 🅿
www.planetarium.montreal.qc.ca ☎ *514-872-4530.* Each year, visitors can take
in superb multimedia shows *(50min)* presented in the planetarium's 385-seat **Star
Theatre**, where a German-made Zeiss V projector utilizes 150 separate projectors
to create the image of the starry sky on the theatre's immense, hemispheric dome.
Temporary and permanent exhibits offer an introduction to the natural phenomena
of our universe, and provide updates on recent astronomical events.

★③ FROM PLACE DES ARTS TO CHINATOWN
Map below. 🚇 *4 Place des Arts.*

Long neglected by the city's leaders, this area experienced a renaissance during
and after the French counterculture movement of the 1960s. The decision to erect
the modern Place des Arts Complex in the eastern part of the city, made by the
municipal administration under mayor Jean Drapeau, reflected a growing interest
in francophone culture and marked the beginning of a series of investments in the
then somewhat abandoned French sector of Montreal.

The inception of Place des Arts engendered other major projects such as the
Desjardins Complex, the University of Quebec at Montreal, the Olympic stadium,
the Guy-Favreau Complex and the Convention Centre.

*Begin at Place des Arts. This walk takes the visitor through a section of the under-
ground city.*

★★**Place des Arts** – *North side of Rue Sainte-Catherine between Rue Jeanne-Mance
and Rue Saint-Urbain. Open daily year-round.* ✗ 🦽 🅿 *($9) www.pda.qc.ca* ☎ *514-
285-4200.* Montreal's premier cultural complex for the visual and performing arts
consists of three structures bordering a central square. The imposing concert hall
(1963) is flanked by a theatre building (1967) and the city's contemporary art
museum (1992). The buildings are situated around a vast esplanade where lively
crowds gather during fine weather. Several annual festivals and events take place
here, among them the International Jazz Festival, held in the area near the intersection of Rues Jeanne-Mance and Sainte-Catherine.

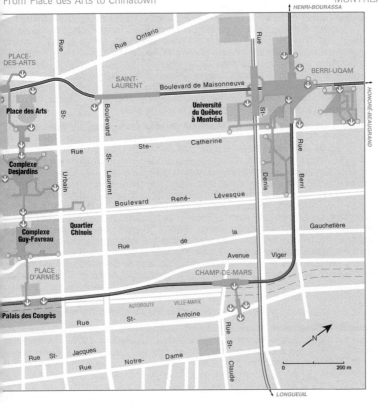

Salle Wilfrid-Pelletier (Wilfrid Pelletier Auditorium) – Highlighted by an elliptical facade of windows and slim concrete columns, the building is home to the Montreal Symphony Orchestra (Orchestre symphonique de Montréal), the Grands Ballets Canadiens and the Montreal Opera. The auditorium has a seating capacity of 2,982. The interior central hall, called the Piano Nobile, features works of art by renowned Canadian artists: flamboyant tapestries by Robert Lapalme and Micheline Beauchemin, an imposing sculpture by Anne Kahane, and Louis Archambault's brass-leaf *Anges radieux* (Radiant Angels), which dominates the hall's main staircase. On the lower level, note the aluminium mural by Julien Hébert, ceramic panels by Jordi Bonnet, a marble swan by Hans Schleech and a sculpture by the Inuit artist Innukpuk. Jean-Paul Riopelle's *La Bolduc* and a painting by Fernand Toupin also decorate the hall.

Place des Arts

Complexe Théâtral (Theatre Building) – The complex's three theatres are housed in this imposing building situated on the corner of Rues Sainte-Catherine and Saint-Urbain. The Jean-Duceppe theatre is designed exclusively for plays and musicals. Directly above it is the Maisonneuve Theatre, of Italian inspiration. These "stacked" performance spaces are separated by an ingenious system of springs which acts as a floating floor for the Maisonneuve, above, or as a suspended ceiling for the Jean-Duceppe, below. A complete soundproofing system permits separate productions to occur in the two theatres simultaneously. The Studio Théâtre, a smaller and more intimate space, is located on the metro level.

★★ **Musée d'art contemporain de Montréal** (Montreal Contemporary Art Museum) – *185 Rue Sainte-Catherine Ouest. Open year-round Tue–Sun 11am–6pm (Wed 9pm). $6.* ✕ ♿ ▯ *($6) www.macm.org* ☎ *514-847-6226.* Rising to the west of the Place des Arts, this imposing edifice houses Canada's only institution devoted exclusively to contemporary art. Spacious, well-lit galleries display works selected from the permanent collection of more than 5,000 paintings, sculptures, prints, drawings, photographs and large-scale installations. More than 60 percent of the pieces are by Quebec artists, enabling the museum to showcase major trends in Quebec contemporary art with the work of Paul-Émile Borduas, Jean-Paul Riopelle, Guido Molinari, Claude Tousignant, Alfred Pellan, Ulysses Comtois and Armand Vaillancourt. International contemporary artists are also represented in the collection. A **sculpture garden** is accessible from the second floor *(closed in winter)*; from here extends a view of the Place des Arts. Situated in the public space between by the Place des Arts complex and the Contemporary Art Museum is the **Fifth Gallery** (Cinquième Salle), a multipurpose theatre space that can be reconfigured according to the requirements of the piece being presented.

Take the underground passageway leading to the Desjardins Complex.

★ **Complexe Desjardins** (Desjardins Complex) – *South side of Rue Sainte-Catherine between Rues Jeanne-Mance and Saint-Urbain.* Opened in 1976, this complex appears heavy and austere from the outside. The vast interior plaza, better suited to the Montreal climate than an outdoor plaza, consists of four towers embracing an immense polygonal atrium lined with three levels of shops. This layout is reminiscent of an amphitheatre, in which passersby are both spectators and players. The atrium is the site of exhibits and popular cultural activities, in contrast to the Place des Arts, which during the 1970s acquired a reputation as a symbol of elitist culture.

The Wilfrid Pelletier Auditorium and the Guy-Favreau Complex are visible from the atrium through huge windows to the north and south.

Follow the passage under Blvd. René-Lévesque to the Guy-Favreau Complex.

A taste of the exotic

While Montreal's Chinatown is not large, it boasts a plethora of food shops and restaurants. To build your appetite, wander the shelves at **Kim Phat** *(1059 Blvd. Saint-Laurent)*, stocked with an extraordinary variety of exotic foodstuffs: bamboo shoots, jackfruit, dried seaweed, Oriental candies and fragrant spices. Step across the street to simply appointed **Cristal de Saïgon** *(1068 Blvd. Saint-Laurent;* ☎ *514-875-4275)* to sample the famed "soupe tonkinoise," a savoury blend of broth, noodles and meat. The restrained, yet attractive dining room at Le **Pavillon Nanpic** *(75A Rue de la Gauchetière Ouest;* ☎ *514-395-8106)* offers a variety of Cantonese and Szechuan dishes; try the excellent General Tao chicken.

Complexe Guy-Favreau (Guy-Favreau Complex) – *200 Blvd. René-Lévesque.* Completed in 1984, this complex was named for **Guy Favreau** (1917-1967), a lawyer, politician, public prosecutor and minister of justice in John Diefenbaker's administration (1957-1963). Consisting of six interconnected structures, it contains Montreal's federal administration offices and numerous apartments, as well as a mall. The red brick exterior complements the handsome stainless steel and brick interior atrium. Exhibits are regularly organised in the main hall and in the mall. Offering a respite from the downtown bustle, the tranquil exterior **garden** is dotted with fountains and sculptures.

Exit on Rue de la Gauchetière for Chinatown.

The massive concrete and glass construction (1983) that forms a bridge over the Ville-Marie Expressway is the **Palais des Congrès de Montréal** (Montreal Convention Centre). Erected in 1983, this mammoth building, capable of accommodating up to 10,000 people, hosts conventions, trade shows and exhibits throughout the year. The centre is linked to the Place d'Armes metro and the underground city.

★**Chinatown** (Quartier chinois) – *Along Rue de la Gauchetière between Rue Jeanne-Mance and Blvd. Saint-Laurent, and on cross streets.* Montreal's Chinatown developed during the 1860s, with the arrival of immigrants fleeing the working conditions on the railroads and in the gold mines of the American West. Originally grouped in ghettos as a means of self-defense against official ostracism, the Chinese population in the area declined in the 1950s. Persons of Asian descent now reside throughout the city; primarily retirees and newly arrived immigrants live in Chinatown. On Sundays, however, many families gather in the area, and all shops are open.

Restricted to and frequently jammed with pedestrians, these few blocks of Rue de la Gauchetière have become the social hub of Montreal's Far Eastern community, with numerous Chinese and Vietnamese restaurants and grocery stores. Two large Chinese-style arches (1963) span Rue de la Gauchetière, and a series of bronze medallions on the ground represent Chinese virtues. Murals along Rue Saint-Urbain depict Oriental legends such as that of the Monkey King. On Rue Clark, a small park is dedicated to **Sun-Yat-Sen** (1866-1925), "Father of the Republic and Founder of modern China."

Erected in 1826, the **Maison Wing** (Wing House, *1009 Rue Côté*), one of the oldest houses in the neighbourhood, is now a bakery supplying fortune cookies for restaurants throughout the city.

★★④ RUE SHERBROOKE OUEST *1.4mi/2.3km. Map below.* ☉ *Peel.*

Begin the tour at the corner of Rue Sherbrooke West and Rue Peel. All addresses are on Rue Sherbrooke West, unless otherwise indicated.

One of the city's busiest and most prestigious downtown arteries, Rue Sherbrooke combines a bustling retail sector with some of Montreal's choicest residences. Flamboyant Victorian, Gothic and Romanesque-style structures combine with less decorative 1950s office buildings to form the city's most architecturally heterogeneous district. Rue Sherbrooke marks the southern border of the historic **Mille Carré**

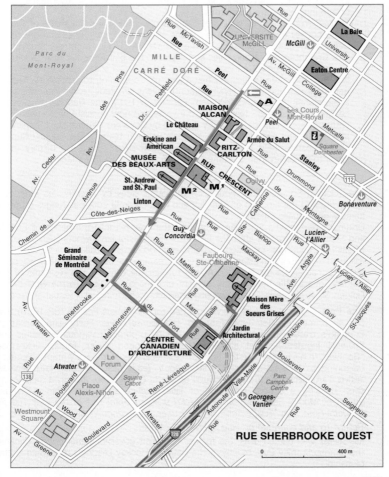

RUE SHERBROOKE OUEST

Rue Sherbrooke Ouest

■ Ice Hockey

A winter preoccupation for more than 100 years, hockey is truly Canada's national game. And the enthusiasm isn't limited to televised games of the major leagues either: more than 580,000 young Canadians in some 25,000 teams participate in organized minor hockey tournaments. Community rinks are ubiquitous.

Derived from the French *hoquet* ("shepard's crook") for the shape of the stick, hockey originated from variations of stick and ball games brought to Canada by English soldiers in the 1850s. In 1875, Montreal student J.G. Creighton formalized rules and replaced the ball for a flat disk (puck) to give better control on ice.

The fast and often rough play made the sport appealing to spectators. The game spread quickly as rivalry among college amateur teams intensified. Professional teams soon followed. Formed in 1917, the National Hockey League has added US teams over the years and now consists of 30 teams, with only six in Canada. A trophy donated by Governor General Lord Stanley in 1893 is still awarded to the league's winning team in the Stanley Cup championships held each June. The original silver cup is on display in Toronto's Hockey Hall of Fame *(see THE GREEN GUIDE Canada)*.

Doré (Golden Square Mile), bound on the other sides by Avenue des Pins, Rue University and the junction of Rue Guy and Chemin de la Côte-des-Neiges (approximately one square mile).

Originally part of the Sulpician seigneury, the area fell into the hands of English and Scottish fur traders after the Conquest. Successful landowners such as James McGill built country estates near the renowned orchards on the slopes of Mt. Royal, followed in 1885 by an affluent bourgeoisie reaping the benefits of the newly completed Canadian Pacific Railway. At the turn of the century, the residents of the Golden Square Mile held seventy percent of Canada's wealth. To the west of the Golden Square Mile lies the town of **Westmount**, a charming, residential enclave.

Rue Peel – This elegant street was named for Sir Robert Peel (1788-1850), the British prime minister who founded the Conservative Party and facilitated England's transition into the industrial era by promoting various economic and financial legislation. Peel also created the London police force, nicknamed "Bobbies" in his honour. To the north, Rue Peel is lined with lovely mansions, many belonging to McGill University. A stroll south leads past the **Guilde canadienne des métiers d'art Québec** (**A**) (Canadian Guild of Crafts Quebec, *no. 2025*), a gallery and shop housing a superb collection of **Inuit sculpture** and Amerindian art *(open Jun–Sept Mon & Sat 10am–5pm, Tue–Fri 9:30am–6pm; rest of the year Tue–Fri 9:30am–6pm, Sat 10am–5pm; www.dsuper.net/~cdnguild ☎ 514-849-6091).* *Return to and continue on Rue Sherbrooke West.*

Rue Stanley was named after the former Canadian governor-general who donated the famous Stanley Cup, trophy of the National Hockey League's renowned championship.

★Maison Alcan – *No. 1188; main entrance at 2200 Rue Stanley*. The headquarters of Alcan Limited, a major producer of aluminium, features an innovative amalgamation of old and new. Designers of the structure (1983) successfully followed preservation regulations by integrating into its facade the five 19C buildings on the south side of Rue Sherbrooke between Rues Stanley and Drummond.

At the far left, the **Atholstan House** *(no. 1172)* was commissioned by Lord Atholstan (1848-1938), famed philanthropist and founder of the now-defunct *Montreal Star*. Constructed in 1895 in the Beaux-Arts style then associated with the wealthy elite, the limestone building features an Adamesque interior and presently houses the offices of Alcan's president.

A superb glass-roofed **atrium** links the five structures to the Davis Building, a modern aluminium-sheathed edifice located at the rear. Worth noting here are several works of art, including colourful textile panels, Inuit steatite sculptures, and *Paolo et Francesca*, a 1985 sculpture by Esther Wertheimer.

Stroll down the pleasant pedestrian walkway linking Rues Stanley and Drummond behind the Maison Alcan building to see the massive, gray **Armée du Salut** (Salvation Army Citadel, *2050 Rue Stanley*), erected in 1884 in the style of an Ionic temple.

Return to Rue Sherbrooke West.

★The Ritz-Carlton Hotel – *No. 1228*. Montréal's last surviving grand old hotel, the Ritz-Carlton conjures up nostalgic thoughts of the Roaring Twenties. The elegant structure (1912) features a Renaissance Revival facade of limestone embellished with terra-cotta ornamentation, and a wrought-iron canopy illuminated by superb lamps. The western section of the building was added in 1956; note especially the decorative panels surmounting

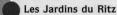

Les Jardins du Ritz

1228 Rue Sherbrooke West. ☎ *514-842-4212*. Located behind the luxurious Ritz-Carlton Hotel, this lovely terrace – with its peaceful duck pond – seems far from the bustle of downtown Montreal. Stop here for high tea, served in the traditional English fashion with scones, finger sandwiches and petits-fours accompanied by thick Devonshire cream and delicious assorted jams.

the windows. The richly decorated lobby and the hotel's reception rooms are replete with marble, bronze, leather and rich wood panelling.

Numerous members of royalty and chiefs of state – among them Charles de Gaulle – have stayed at the hotel. Elizabeth Taylor and Richard Burton were married here in 1964, and the hotel remains a favourite stopping point for celebrities today.

Cross Rue de la Montagne.

Across the street, the imposing **Château** apartment complex *(no. 1321)* topped by a sloped roof, is decorated with stone crenellations and turrets. The building (1925) was constructed of Tyndall fossilized limestone, which also adorns the interior of the Ottawa Parliament.

Erskine and American United Church – *No. 1339. Entrance at 3407 Ave. du Musée. Open year-round Tue & Thu–Fri 10am–4pm, Sun 11am–1pm.* ♿ ☎ *514-849-3286.* Along with Windsor Station, this splendid edifice is an excellent example of the Richardsonian Romanesque style, exemplified here by massive rounded arches, rusticated stone, narrow windows and pinnacled buttresses adorning the tower. Erected in 1894, the building has united two religious groups, the Erskine Church and the American Presbyterian Church, since 1934.

Considerably modified and enlarged in 1938, the interior is remarkable for its painted and ornamented dome, resting on a finely chiseled cornice, and for the 24 stunning Tiffany **stained-glass windows** illustrating Biblical themes. Other stained-glass windows depict floral motifs, as well as themes of the Protestant faith.

★Rue Crescent – The two blocks of this street between Rues Sherbrooke and Sainte-Catherine are lined with charming Victorian structures, today occupied by fashionable boutiques, art galleries, fine fabric shops and restaurants. During the summer months, many of these restaurants open balconies and terraces, adding to the area's lively ambience.

★Musée des Arts décoratifs de Montréal (Montreal Museum of Decorative Arts) (**M¹**) – *2200 Rue Crescent. Open year-round Tue–Sun 11am–6pm. $12.* 🍴 ♿ *www.mbam.qc.ca* ☎ *514-284-1252.* Formerly located at the Château Dufresne, the international design collections of this museum were moved in 1997 to a 8,073sq ft exhibition space adjacent to the new wing of the Montreal Museum of Fine Arts, which began administering the collection in 2000; a glassed-in passage allows access between the two museums. Conceived by the famed architect Frank Gehry (designer of the new Guggenheim Museum in Bilbao, Spain), the galleries house furnishings, ceramics, glass and metal sculptures, jewelry, textiles and graphic arts drawn from a splendid collection numbering more than 4,000 objects. Covering the 20C, with particular emphasis on the period from 1965 to the present, the holdings trace the major trends in decorative arts from Art Nouveau to Postmodernism.

Rue Crescent Revelry

What do meat on skewers and gyrating dancers have in common? Go to **le Milsa** *(2045 Rue Crescent ☎ 514-985-0777)* featuring traditional Brazilian barbeque for the answer. Servers come to your table and carve off slices of everything from beef to turkey to lamb letting you eat to your heart's desire. If you are in the mood for something a bit lighter, head across the street to **Restaurant Chang Thai** *(2100 Rue Crescent ☎ 514-286-9994).* Reasonable prices and an inviting décor make for an enjoyable evening of sampling an extensive variety of Thai specialties.

Formule 1 Emporium
2070B Rue Crescent.
☎ 514-284-3799. Fans of auto racing, especially Formula 1, will revel in the atmosphere of this small shop. Race team memorabilia and clothing shares space with a selection of small-scale, die-cast replicas of notable competition and passenger cars. Ferrari merchandise is a specialty.

★★Musée des Beaux-Arts de Montréal

(Montreal Museum of Fine Arts) – *No. 1380. Open year-round Tue–Sun 11am–6pm (Wed 9pm). Closed Jan 1 & Dec 25. $12 (free for permanent collection).* ✕ ᠘ *www.mbam.qc.ca* ☎ *514-285-1600.* Located in the centre of the Golden Square Mile, this 140-year old institution ranks among Canada's finest museums. The encyclopedic permanent collection comprises over 30,000 objects, ranging from Old Masters to contemporary Canadian art.

The strengths of the collection lie in the areas of Canadian and Inuit art, prints and drawings, decorative arts ranging from archaic Chinese bronzes to 20C glassware, and the world's largest collection of Japanese incense boxes (over 3,000 pieces).

The Buildings – First established in 1860 as the Art Association of Montreal, the museum moved into the current North Pavilion (also known as the Benaiah Gibb Pavilion) half a century later, with a collection of 467 works of art. Replete with a majestic staircase, a portico colonnade of white Vermont marble, and solid, massive doors, the 1912 edifice exemplifies the Beaux-Arts style commonly employed in museum constructions of the period. One floor of the magnificent structure is dedicated to Canadian art and the other to decorative arts and antiquity.

Enlarged twice, in 1939 and 1977, the museum underwent a third major expansion, onto the south side of Rue Sherbrooke in 1991 with the addition of the South Pavilion (also known as the Jean-Noël Desmarais Pavilion) **(M²)**. A series of underground galleries connects the two pavilions. The new annex, which provides much-needed additional space, is the work of the architect **Moshe Safdie**, renowned for such prestigious commissions as Habitat, Ottawa's National Gallery of Canada, and Quebec City's Museum of Civilization. Adorned with a monumental entry portal, the building incorporates the Renaissance Revival brick facade of the New Sherbrooke apartment complex (1905), the site's former occupant. The large windows and skylights afford expansive views of the city. Facing Rue Bishop, a set of five large vaulted galleries, devoted to temporary exhibits, opens onto a skylit interior.

Owing to the museum's extensive program of long-term temporary exhibitions, certain galleries may be closed and specific works of art may be exhibited in locations other than those indicated here. For information, inquire at the reception desk.

Benaiah Gibb Pavilion – *North side of Rue Sherbrooke.* This magnificent structure is largely devoted to the display of Canadian Art and Decorative Art. On the second floor, paintings, sculpture, furniture and decorative arts cover the sweep of **Canadian** art from the 18C to 1945. Works on view may include sculptures by Louis Archambault and Robert Roussil, and paintings by Antoine Plamondon and Cornélius Krieghoff. Visitors may also find paintings by Paul Kane (1810-1871) and Suzor-Côté (1869-1937), as well as canvases by the Group of Seven and works of Montreal artists James Wilson Morrice (1865-1924), Ozias Leduc (1864-1955) and Alfred Laliberté (1878-1953). The museum possesses stunning examples of 18C-20C Quebec **sacred silverware**, featuring pieces by François Ranvoyzé (1739-1819). Of particular interest on the first floor is the museum's collection of Amerindian and Inuit art.

Galleries of Ancient Cultures – The underground galleries linking the Benaiah Gibb Pavilion to the Jean-Noël Desmarais Pavilion house African and Oceanic art featuring sculpted masks and other striking ritual objects, while the Asiatic art section houses porcelains, funerary objects of Chinese antiquity and sculptures from India and Pakistan. The **Islamic art** section offers a large number of ceramics, from Persian pieces of the Sassanian period (3C-7C) to Hispano-Moresque wares.

Jean-Noël Desmarais Pavilion – *South side of Rue Sherbrooke.* The fourth floor is devoted exclusively to **European art** from the Middle Ages to the 19C. Polychromed wood sculptures, triptychs, frescoes and stained-glass windows beautifully illus-

The Montreal Museum of Fine Arts

Autumn Landscape by Cornelius Krieghoff

trate the artistic richness of the medieval era. Renaissance art includes the superb *Judith* and *Didon* by Andrea Mantegna, and Flemish artists are represented by Peter Brueghel the Younger's *Return from the Inn*, as well as *Portrait of a Young Man* by Hans Memling. European art of the 17C and 18C includes masterpieces by Rembrandt *(Portrait of a Young Woman around 1665)*, El Greco, Ruysdael, Canaletto and Gainsborough *(Portrait of Mrs. George Drummond)*. The 19C section features painters of the Barbizon school, Impressionists and Postimpressionists. Two additional galleries present the museum's impressive collection of prints and drawings, including several works by Albrecht Dürer. *For conservation purposes, prints and drawings are occasionally removed from view.*

Displayed in galleries on the third level and the second underground level, the museum's rich collection of **20C Art** and international and Canadian **contemporary art** (since 1960) features works by Picasso, Sam Francis, Christian Boltansky, Gerhard Richter, Rebecca Horn and other artists, as well as works by renowned Canadian contemporary artists Jean-Paul Riopelle, Paul-Émile Borduas, Betty Goodwin, and Geneviève Cadieux.

Church of St. Andrew and St. Paul
– *No. 1431. Visit by guided tour only, Jul–Aug Thu 10am–4pm (organ recital at noon). Rest of the year for mass & by appointment.* ♿ ☎ *514-842-3431.* Erected in 1932, this Gothic cathedral-like edifice is home to the Black Watch (Royal Highland) Regiment of Canada. Constructed of steel and reinforced concrete sheathed in Indiana limestone, the Presbyterian church features an immense stained-glass window above the main altar, commemorating the victims of World War I. The first two windows in the left nave were designed by **Edwin Burne-Jones** of the William Morris Studio, an early practitioner of the Arts and Crafts style.

At the northwest corner with Rue Simpson, stands the ornate, Beaux-Arts **Linton** apartment complex *(no. 1509)*, one of the largest buildings of its type at the time of its construction (1907). Its brick exterior is lavishly embellished with terra-cotta ornamentation.

Across the street, an attractive row of grey townhouses *(nos. 1400-1460)* contain some of Montreal's most prestigious art galleries.

Grand séminaire de Montréal (Sulpician Seminary)
– *No. 2065 at junction with Rue du Fort.* Two **towers** with "pepper-box" roofs mark the former site of a small fort constructed by the Sulpicians in 1676 to protect their mission and its Amerindian converts. In 1685, the fort was reconstructed in stone with four towers and a defending wall to protect the chapel, the priests' residence and a barn. The two north towers were destroyed in 1854 to make room for the construction of the seminary (1857). The remaining towers are, along with the Sulpician Seminary on Rue Notre-Dame, among the oldest structures on the island of Montreal. Now restored, the towers are supplemented by a small outdoor panel display illustrating the history of the fort and of the Sulpician congregation.

Inside the main building, the striking seminary **chapel★** was designed by Joseph-Omer Marchand in 1904 and completed in 1907 *(open year-round daily 9am–4pm;* ♿ 🅿 ☎ *514-935-1169).* The monumental interior features a large nave reminis-

cent of early Christian architecture, spanned by cedar beam vaulting. Note the mosaics adorning the floor, the exquisitely carved oak stalls facing each other in the manner of collegiate chapels, and, in the portico, *Descente de la croix*, an enormous painting by Napoléon Bourrassa. In 1991, the chapel acquired its superb Guilbault-Thérien organ, manufactured in the classical French tradition of the 18C.
Follow Rue du Fort to its intersection with Rue Baile.

★**Centre Canadien d'Architecture** (Canadian Centre for Architecture) – *1920 Rue Baile. Open Jun–Sept Tue–Sun 11am–6pm (Thu 9pm). Rest of the year Wed–Fri 11am–6pm (Thu 8pm) & weekends 11am–5pm. $6.* & ▣ *www.cca.qc.ca* ☎ *514-939-7026.* Inaugurated in 1989 with a view to fostering the study and appreciation of the built environment, this unique institution is an acclaimed research facility and Montreal's most original example of Postmodern architecture.

The Project – The Canadian Centre for Architecture (CCA) is the brainchild of **Phyllis Lambert**, architect, noted preservationist and heiress to the Seagrams fortune. Lambert initially conceived the centre as the repository of her vast collection of architectural documents. The site selected for the project was a dilapidated Second Empire mansion, the Shaughnessy House, located in a 19C residential quarter that had suffered decline. Lambert collaborated with the prominent Canadian architect Peter Rose to restore the Shaughnessy House and incorporate it into a new construction. The presence of the Centre has contributed enormously to the rehabilitation of the quarter.

Renowned as a comprehensive reference and research centre, the CCA contains over 180,000 books, 65,000 prints and drawings, 30,000 plans and more than 50,000 photographs. In addition, the museum features temporary exhibits on architectural themes, a conservation laboratory and a book store.

Visit – Forming the core of the CCA building, the **Shaughnessy House** (1874) is enclosed on three sides by the new structure, which was designed to be sympathetic to the mansion through its simple lines and symmetrical facade. The modern edifice's only embellishment is the curious aluminium cornice crowning the building that echoes the wrought-iron roof cresting on the Shaughnessy House.

Trenton limestone, black granite, maple panelling and flooring and aluminium fittings grace the interior of the main building. Located on the first floor, seven galleries display temporary exhibits on architectural themes. Also open to the public are the Shaughnessy House reception rooms and the delightful **conservatory** and **tea room**, restored to 19C splendour and furnished with works of contemporary design.

Jardin Architectural (Architectural garden) – Located across Boulevard René-Lévesque, this unusual outdoor space designed by architect Melvin Charney was conceived as a tribute to the buildings of the neighbourhood and to the architectural heritage of the Western world. Among the pieces on display in the esplanade overlooking a maze of highways are ten raised sculptures, or "allegorical columns," depicting various architectural elements.

Maison mère des Sœurs Grises (Grey Nuns Convent) – *North side of Blvd. René-Lévesque between Rue Guy and Rue Saint-Mathieu. Entrance for visitors at 1185 Rue Saint-Mathieu.* ▣. *The interior of the convent is not open to the public. The chapel and certain rooms can be visited during the guided tour of the Marguerite d'Youville Museum.* Designed in the neoclassical style, this elegant building (1869-1903) housed the Grey Nuns after their departure from Old Montreal in 1871. The plan is typical of 19C convent architecture. To highlight the chapel at the centre

Sleigh Ride in Parc du Mont-Royal

of the building, the architect Victor Bourgeau adopted the Romanesque style of medieval French abbeys. The slender steeple, one of the tallest in the city, was added in 1890.

In 1737, Marie-Marguerite Dufrost de Lajemmerais (1701-1771), widow of François d'Youville, founded a lay order to care for the old, poor and sick in Montreal. Officially recognized by Louis XIV as the Sisters of Charity in 1753, the members are now known as the Grey Nuns. Marguerite d'Youville's lifetime of service was recognized when she was beatified in 1959 and canonized a saint by Pope John Paul II in December 1990.

The **Musée Marguerite-d'Youville** (Marguerite d'Youville Museum) presents an exhibit on Mother d'Youville's life and on the origins and achievements of the order *(visit by guided tour only, year-round Wed–Sun 1:30pm–4pm; closed week of Easter, Jun 24, Jul 1 & late Dec–early Jan;* 🚻 🅿 ☎ *514-937-9501).* Visitors are shown the memorial chapel dedicated to her, and the crypt with her tomb and those of 200 of the first members of the Grey Nuns.

★★⑤ MONT-ROYAL AND SURROUNDINGS
Map pp 202-203.

Nicknamed "the Mountain," Mt. Royal rises some 233m/764ft over the centre of downtown Montreal. Residents and out-of-town visitors alike flock to Mt. Royal Park, a popular leisure spot located on the highest of the mountain's three peaks. Historically an anglophone district, the town of **Westmount** (founded 1874), situated on the western flank of Mt. Royal overlooking downtown and the St. Lawrence River, is one of Montreal's choicest residential areas. Westmount's steeply sloping streets are bordered with imposing 19C mansions of brick and stone interspersed with modern residences surrounded by manicured gardens. From the **Westmount Belvedere** *(between 18 and 36 Summit Circle),* the **view★** plunges over the rooftops of lovely residences to the three towers of **Westmount Square★** *(corner of Rue Sainte-Catherine and Ave. Green),* designed by Mies van der Rohe in 1966. The glass and black metal towers house elegant apartments, offices and shops. The Victoria Bridge is visible in the distance. The community of **Outremont**, founded in 1875 on the mountain's eastern flank, is the enclave of Montreal's francophone bourgeoisie and is Westmount's counterpart for beautiful homes, private mansions and green lawns and parks. Two cemeteries are located on Mt. Royal, in addition to several reservoirs for drinking water, and the Radio Canada transmission tower (1963).

★★Parc du Mont-Royal (Mt. Royal Park) – *Access on foot: 20min climb from downtown. Walk to top of Rue Peel at Ave. des Pins and take the path with small flights of steps to a steep flight of 204 steps.* **By car:** *drive up Voie Camillien-Houde or Chemin Remembrance to the parking areas.* **By metro:** Ⓜ *Mont-Royal. Open year-round daily 6am–midnight.* ✗ 🚻 🅿 ☎ *514-843-8240.* A jewel in Montreal's crown, the city's premier urban park opened to the public in 1876. Planned by the preeminent American landscape architect, **Frederick Law Olmsted** (1822-1903), creator of New York City's Central Park, Mt. Royal Park exemplifies the naturalistic manner of garden design popular in the late 19C.

At the time of the park's inception, a $1 million investment was required to appropriate the land. Today the property bears some 60,000 trees, 650 species of plants and flowers, and is home to a proliferation of wildlife including grey squirrels, chipmunks and birds.

The park also features a lake, two excellent lookout points, a chalet/welcome centre, an illuminated cross and numerous paths winding through the forest.

Belvédère du Chalet (Chalet Lookout) – *From the parking lot, take the footpath to the chalet (7min).* The splendid **view★★★** from the front of the small chalet here encompasses the bustling downtown. Below the lookout lies the campus of McGill University, notably the distinctive, cylindrical form of the McIntyre Medical Sciences Building. The downtown skyscrapers are prominent, especially the IBM Marathon Building, Bank of Commerce Tower, 1000 de la Gauchetière, the cruciform structure of Place Ville-Marie and Place de la Cathédrale, with its double-sloped roof and copper-coloured exterior. From this vantage point, the St. Lawrence River appears as a silver ribbon stretching away to the distance, and looming on the horizon are the shadowy Monteregian Hills, notably the imposing mass of Mt. Saint-Hilaire.

Croix (Cross) – *Accessible on foot from the chalet.* The 36.6m/120ft metal structure on the summit of Mt. Royal commemorates an episode in Montreal's early history. In December 1642, Paul de Maisonneuve, founder of Ville-Marie (Montreal), took an oath to carry a cross up the mountain if the settlement were saved from a flood, expected to occur on Christmas Day. The fortress was spared, and Maisonneuve kept his promise on January 6, 1643, erecting a wooden cross at the summit. Today's metal cross dates from 1924. Illuminated at night, it is visible from as far away as 100km/62mi.

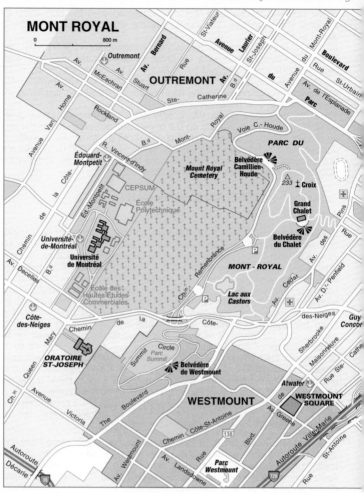

Belvédère Camillien-Houde (Camillien Houde Lookout) – *Accessible by car on the Voie Camillien-Houde*. From this popular vantage point, the **view★★** of eastern Montreal is dominated by the Olympic Stadium. To the south, several of the Monteregian Hills are visible. The foothills of the Laurentian Mountains rise to the north. Camillien Houde (1889-1958), the namesake of the viewpoint, served as Montreal's mayor for several nonconsecutive terms between 1928 and 1954.

Université de Montréal (University of Montreal) – *Entrance on Blvd. Édouard-Montpetit at its intersection with Ave. Louis-Colin.* ◐ *Université de Montréal.* Created in 1878 as a branch of Laval University in Quebec City, the university became an independent institution by papal decree in 1919. Originally located on Rue Saint-Denis in what is currently the UQAM area, the university moved to its present site in 1942.

Construction of the main pavilion began in 1928, but was interrupted by the Great Depression in 1930 and not resumed until 1941. Designed by Ernest Cormier, the building consists of a central section topped by a lofty tower, with perpendicular wings branching toward the front. Replete with stylized ornamentation, geometric surfaces and setbacks, this striking edifice exemplifies the Art Deco Style. The central hall and the large auditorium have retained their original Art Deco interiors. With an enrollment of nearly 60,000 students, the university is the largest francophone university in the world outside Paris. Its 13 departments are supplemented by the École Polytechnique *(northeast of main building)* and the École des Hautes Études Commerciales *(Ave. Decelles)*.

★★**Oratoire Saint-Joseph** (St. Joseph's Oratory) – *Entrance on chemin Queen Mary.* ◐ *Côte-des-Neiges. Open May–Sept daily 6:30am–9:30pm. Rest of the year daily 6:30am–9pm.* ✕ ♿ ☐ *www.saint-joseph.org* ☎ *514-733-8211.* Set on the northwest slope of Mt. Royal, this renowned Roman Catholic shrine is visited yearly by millions of pilgrims. Its enormous dome dominates northern Montreal.

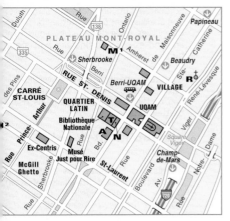

Brother André – Alfred Bessette (1845-1937) entered the Congregation of Holy Cross in 1870 and took the name Brother André. During forty years as a doorkeeper at Notre-Dame College *(across from the Oratory)*, he preached the healing power of devotion to St. Joseph. In 1904 he erected a small chapel on the path which led from the college to Mt. Royal. Many afflicted people who came to pray with him left the chapel cured, abandoning their crutches, canes and wheelchairs as testament to their recovery, and spreading the lay brother's reputation as a healer. By the early 20C, the crowds of pilgrims had grown to such proportions that the present basilica was planned to receive them.

★**The Basilica** – Towering 154m/505ft over the city, this colossal temple is surmounted by an octagonal, copper-clad dome. Built of reinforced concrete sheathed in granite, the basilica is 104m/341ft long, 64m/210ft wide and 112m/367ft high. Rising 44.5m/146ft above the roof of the basilica, the dome has a diameter of 38m/125ft. The cross crowning the structure is 8m/26ft high.

Construction of the huge building began in 1924, but was interrupted by lack of funds, the economic depression and technical difficulties. In 1936 the renowned Benedictine monk-architect, **Dom Paul Bellot**, was called upon to act as chief architect of the oratory. He selected concrete rather than granite for the construction of the dome, and revised the interior plans in a modern style. The monument was completed in 1967.

The visitor is struck by the immensity and austerity of the basilica's **interior**. Henri Charlier carved the stone main altar, the crucifix and the tall wooden carvings of the apostles *(in the transept)*; the stained-glass windows were designed by Marius Plamondon. Roger Prévost executed the bronze grilles and Roger de Villiers the life-size Stations of the Cross statues *(around the nave)*. The altar in the Chapel of the Blessed Sacrament *(behind the choir)* is the work of Jean-Charles Charuest, and the mosaic of the life of St. Joseph was produced at the Labouret Studio, in Paris. *During the summer, organ recitals are held here on Wednesday evenings at 8pm (☎ 514-337-4622).*

Within the main edifice are a **votive chapel** enshrining the remains of Brother André; a 56-bell **carillon**, originally cast in Paris for installation on the Eiffel Tower; the **crypt**, where daily masses are held; and the **Musée du Frère André** (Brother André Museum; *same hours as the Oratory*), displaying a collection of photographs and mementos tracing the friar's history. Brother André's **original chapel** (chapelle du Frère André)

Oratoire Saint-Joseph

● Le Duc de Lorraine

5002 Chemin de la Côte-des-Neiges. ☎ *514-731-4128.* Renowned for many years for the excellence of its breads, pastries, cheeses and meats, this charming, windowed tearoom is also a fine spot to sample croissants or a light meal.

Aux Deux Gauloises

5195 Chemin de la Côte-des-Neiges. ☎ *514-733-6867.* It's true that there are other dishes on the menu at this charming restaurant besides crêpes. But these crêpes are excellent, the selection is enormous, and the service is hard to beat for friendliness. You can hardly go wrong here, whatever you choose.

is located outside the main structure. The **Stations of the Cross★** statues built into the hillside were designed by Louis Parent and executed in Indiana buff stone by the Italian sculptor, Ercolo Barbieri, in 1960.

Outside the basilica, the wide terrace affords a superb **view** of northern Montreal and of the Laurentian Mountains rising on the horizon.

★Plateau Mont-Royal
🕒 *Sherbrooke.*

Musée des Hospitalières de l'Hôtel-Dieu de Montréal (Hospitallers Museum) (**M²**) – *201, Ave. des Pins Ouest, entrance at Rue Saint-Urbain and Ave. des Pins. Open mid-Jun–mid-Oct Tue–Fri 10am–5pm, weekends 1pm–5pm. Rest of the year Wed–Sun 1pm–5pm. Closed Good Friday, Easter Monday & Dec 25–Jan 1. $5.* ♿ ☎ *514-849-2919.* Housed in a former chaplain's residence (1925), this museum traces the history of the Hospitallers of St. Joseph (a religious order devoted to caring for the sick) and their role in the development of Montreal. In addition to temporary exhibitions, the museum displays a selection of some 400 objects (historic documents, medical instruments, sacred art) drawn from its permanent collection of more than 19,000 artifacts.

A massive oak staircase (17C) from the Hôtel-Dieu hospital in La Flèche, France, dominates the entrance hall of the museum's new addition (1992). The ground floor presents the history of Montreal and of the Hospitaller order, and boasts a a magnificent gold-leafed retable (1777) sculpted by Philippe Liébert. Exhibits here illustrate the cloistered life of the Hospitaller nuns from the 19C and the early 20C. Displays on the second floor focus on the Hospitallers' nursing vocation. A fine collection of historic medical instruments offers an excellent glimpse at the evolution of medical techniques. The visit ends with a video presentation *(15min)* about the Hospitaller order throughout the world.

Boulevard Saint-Laurent – This lively thoroughfare is the starting point for numbering of east-west streets. Traditionally, it represents the linguistic border between the anglophone west and the francophone east. Established in 1672 during the formal planning of the city, and extended to the Prairies River, near Sault-au-Récollet, the artery long formed Montreal's principal passageway, hence its nickname "the

Rue de Bullion (Plateau Mont-Royal)

Main." After a devastating fire in 1852, the road was extended to the city's new limit at Mile End; it became a boulevard in 1905. For more than a century, the Main has welcomed immigrants who have in various ways affected its development. Chinese immigrants settled in the southern section during the 19C, while Jewish merchants arriving around 1880 concentrated in the northern section as far as Rue Sainte-Catherine and established a textile industry (now largely defunct). Greek immigrants moved into the area during the early 20C, but left the Main after 1940 to relocate on Avenue du Parc. More recently, Slavs, Portuguese and Latin Americans have settled in the area.

Although its popularity diminished somewhat between 1960 and 1980 the boulevard now attracts a diverse crowd to its shops and restaurants (many of which are unchanged since the 1940s) and to the newer cafés and "in" boutiques. A wide range of specialty stores manifest the

> **Traditional...**
>
> **Schwartz's** *(3895 Blvd. Saint-Laurent; ☎ 514-842-4813)* is a veritable Montreal institution. Don't go for the service, or for the décor. Do go for the excellent smoked-meat sandwiches, which have won this old-time delicatessen a devoted following.
>
> **... or trendy**
>
> There's always a crowd at **Shed Café** *(3515 Blvd. Saint-Laurent; ☎ 514-842-0220)*, where a hip clientele devours pizzas, salads, panini, sandwiches and sinful desserts, all in a most original setting (don't miss the ceiling and the light fixtures).

area's ethnic diversity, and its sidewalk sales remain very popular.

Rue Prince-Arthur – *From Blvd. Saint-Laurent, east to Saint-Louis Square.* This small pedestrian street, named for Prince Arthur, third son of Queen Victoria and governor-general of Canada from 1911 to 1916, was a popular centre of the counterculture movement during the 1960s. Today the area is home to Italian and Greek restaurants, and is populated in fine weather by musicians, magicians, acrobats, portrait painters, and other street performers.

★**Carré Saint-Louis (Saint-Louis Square)** – *Rue Saint-Denis between Rue Sherbrooke and Ave. des Pins.* Named for Emmanuel and Jean-Baptiste Saint-Louis, two eminent local businessmen, this picturesque, tree-shaded square is surrounded by lovely Victorian structures distinguished by their whimsical roof lines and gables. The district became a select neighbourhood during the late 19C, when the francophone bourgeoisie began moving to the area, attracted by its tranquil atmosphere. Long popular with Quebec artists and poets (Louis Fréchette, Émile Nelligan and, more recently, Gaston Miron lived here), the square was the centre of the nationalist movement during the 1970s. Although the fleur-de-lis is still in evidence, today the square is more likely to resound with American folk songs than with separatist chants. It is still considered a francophone bastion for Quebec writers, musicians, filmmakers and actors.

★**Rue Saint-Denis** – This avenue is lined with attractive townhouses, today occupied by restaurants, art galleries and fashionable stores. Named after Denis-Benjamin Viger, an affluent landowner during the mid-19C, the street was frequented by wealthy francophones who erected charming Victorian homes. The area became known as Montreal's

La Rue Saint-Denis

The bakery-café **La Brioche Lyonnaise** *(1593 Rue Saint-Denis; ☎ 514-842-7017)* is absolutely charming, with its stone walls and lace curtains. Light meals, melt-in-your-mouth croissants and excellent pastries round out the bill of fare. **The Café Cherrier** *(3635 Rue Saint-Denis; ☎ 514-843-4308)* serves up tasty meals from breakfast to dinner; take a seat out on the terrace in fine weather and watch the crowds pass by. Stop by the elegant showroom of renowned florist **Marcel Proulx** *(3835 Rue Saint-Denis; ☎ 514-849-1344)* to admire glorious dried arrangements, rare flowers and beautiful pieces of decorative art. Enduringly chic, **L'Express** *(3927 Rue Saint-Denis; ☎ 514-845-5333)* is one of the most popular bistros in Montreal; its relentlessly high standards are apparent in the outstanding wine list, faultless service and excellent cuisine that never disappoints. Tucked away in a tiny shop swathed in rose-colored fabric, **Confiserie Louise Décarie** *(4424 Rue Saint-Denis; ☎ 514-499-3445)* sells delectable treats such as chocolates, English toffee and Italian nougat, all wrapped in beautiful packages that are as pleasing to the eye as their contents are to the palate.

Quartier Latin (Latin Quarter) when several institutions of higher education were established here during the early 20C. The polytechnical institute opened in 1905, followed by the École des Hautes Études Commerciales *(Viger Square)*, and the University of Montreal. The **Saint-Denis Theatre** (T) (Théâtre Saint-Denis) was erected during this period, followed in 1912 by the Saint-Sulpice Building *(no. 1700)*, now home to the **Bibliothèque nationale de Québec, BNQ** (National Library of Quebec). The houses were divided into smaller apartments to accommodate the many students attending these institutions.

The area's economic stability suffered when the University of Montreal moved to its present campus on the north slope of Mt. Royal, and the street only regained its original vibrancy during the 1960s. Cafés, intimate restaurants, small boutiques and bookshops proliferated, drawing a young crowd back to the area.

Today, the Rue Saint-Denis is a favourite with Montrealers and tourists alike. Known as the "restaurant strip," the section between Rue Sainte-Catherine and Rue Duluth is extremely popular during the summer months, when tables and chairs spill out onto the street.

Université du Québec à Montréal (University of Quebec at Montreal) – *Traversed by Rue Saint-Denis, the main section of campus extends between Blvd. René-Lévesque and Blvd. de Maisonneuve.* Founded in 1969, this university (known as UQAM) is housed in a series of contemporary brick buildings integrated with older structures. One of these occupies the former site of Église Saint-Jacques (St. James Church), designed in the Gothic Revival style by John Ostell in 1852. All that remain of the church today are the facade of the south transept facing Rue Sainte-Catherine and the bell tower on Rue Saint-Denis. This spire, which was added to the church about 1880, is the tallest in Montreal at 98m/321ft. With an ever-increasing enrollment of over 40,000 students, the institution is undergoing major expansion, and now occupies some of the buildings that formerly housed the polytechnical institute. A second campus between Place des Arts and Rue Sherbrooke houses an enormous complex for the study of the sciences.

★★★ 6 OLYMPIC PARK AREA *Map p 207.*

Situated in the heart of Montreal's growing East End, this vast, recreational area is dominated by the striking silhouette of the Olympic Stadium.

Historical Notes

In 1883, leading French Canadian businessmen established the community of Maisonneuve 10km/6mi outside of downtown Montreal in an attempt to rival the anglophone economic domination of the city. After 1896, Maisonneuve experienced a significant economic boom, becoming a major centre for the manufacture of

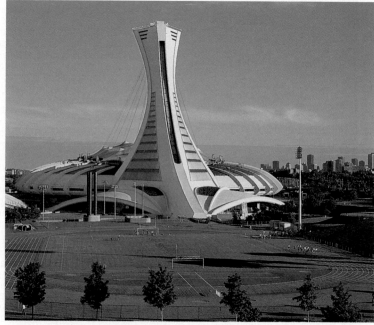

The Tower and Stadium, Parc Olympique

© Malak, Ottawa

shoes, textiles, baked goods and candy. A shipbuilding industry also took root. To emphasize its prosperity, the city launched a program of aesthetic and structural development based on the tenets of the American "City Beautiful" movement, building the immense **Maisonneuve Park**, grand boulevards and prestigious buildings, including Château Dufresne. However, the exorbitant cost of development, combined with the postwar recession, gradually drove Maisonneuve into bankruptcy; by 1918, the government of Quebec decreed that the city be annexed by Montreal. Covering 204ha/504 acres, the Maisonneuve Park today encompasses the **Botanical Garden**, an extensive bike trail, a picnic ground and a snack bar. Families flock here during the summer to enjoy walks and picnics in this pleasant, natural setting. During the winter, sports enthusiasts can partake of the five cross-country ski trails lacing the park, and skate on the floodlit ice rink. Situated across from the Botanical Garden on Rue Sherbrooke, the **Olympic Park** has contributed greatly to the economic boom experienced by Eastern Montreal in the past decade.

★★Parc olympique (Olympic Park)

⚛ *Viau, or by car (entrance to the parking lot from 3200 Rue Viau). Information desk and ticket office at base of tower. Free shuttle service between the park, the Montreal Botanical Garden and the Biodome.*

To accommodate the 1976 summer Olympic Games, a gigantic sports complex covering 55ha/136 acres was erected at the heart of Montreal's East End, in the former City of Maisonneuve. The city's most controversial public project, the Olympic complex is nonetheless a stunning architectural achievement. The various constructions present a harmonious synthesis of form and function, their lines evoking movement and activity in a concrete monument to the glory of sport. The park includes the stadium and tower complex; a sports centre with six pools for swimming, diving and recreation; a concrete esplanade stretching above the largest underground parking garages in Canada; the Pierre Charbonneau Centre and the Maurice Richard Arena, both built in 1954. Long idle, the former velodrome has been converted into the Biodome, a living museum of natural sciences.

History of the Project – Excavation work in the park was begun in 1973, but only the stadium, velodrome, aquatic complex and Olympic Village were completed in time for the 1976 Games. Tremendously expensive ($1.2 billion), the park

Jardin Leslie-Hancock † Arboretum

installations remained incomplete for many years. A series of technical difficulties delayed construction of the stadium tower until 1979. When it was discovered the tower would be too heavy if erected as planned, a moratorium was imposed for four years. Completion of the tower and the roof in 1987 was followed by a series of innovations and adaptations destined to turn the park into a profitable venture. Although the stadium still faces financial difficulties, it has made a valiant effort to remain lucrative.

Created in 1975, a government organization, the *Régie des installations olympiques* (RIO), has been in charge of completing, managing and transforming the complex as a recreational and tourist centre.The park has been home to the **Montreal Expos**, the city's professional baseball team, and regularly hosts sports and cultural events.

Stadium – *Visit by guided tour (30min) only, year-round daily. English tours 12:40pm & 3:40pm; French tours 11am & 2pm. Closed early Jan–early Feb. $5.25. ✗ & ▣ ($10) www.rio.gouv.qc.ca ☎ 514-252-8687. The visit of the park installations does not include ascent to the top of the tower.* Conceived by the French architect Roger Taillibert, the concrete structure consists of 34 enormous cantilevered ribs crowned by a structural ring containing lighting and ventilation systems. The stadium is dominated by the world's tallest inclined **tower**. From the top of the tower, 26 suspension cables descend to the retractable roof, made of Kevlar, an ultra-thin synthetic fibre with the strength of steel. At the time of its construction, it was the largest mobile roof in the world. When the cables were retracted by means of the 46 winches anchored at the tower's base, the entire roof was hoisted into a niche at the summit of the tower. The stadium could then be closed by redeploying the roof like a parachute over the opening. Despite its strong material, the roof has been subject to deterioration and tears owing to the city's harsh weather conditions.

With a seating capacity of 55,147, the gigantic interior space is large enough (18,950sq m/203,763sq ft) to accommodate Rome's Colosseum. Spectators seated in the terraces enjoy an unobstructed view of the playing surface. Intended as a complex for sporting events, the stadium also hosts rock concerts, operatic productions, conventions and religious meetings during summer. The stadium was the setting for the Mass delivered by Pope John Paul II during his 1984 visit to Montreal.

A good perspective of the stadium's exterior can be seen from the footbridge leading from the Pie-IX metro station to the esplanade; in the foreground is *La Joute*, a bronze sculpture-fountain by the Quebec artist, Jean-Paul Riopelle.

Tower – *Open mid-Jun–early Sept daily 10am–9pm. Early Sept–mid-Jun 10am–5pm. Closed early Jan–early Feb. $9. ✗ & ▣ ($10) www.rio.gouv.qc.ca ☎ 514-252-8687.* Completed in 1987, the 175m/574ft tower is composed of two parts: the lower concrete base bears the brunt of the weight, acting as the tower's centre of gravity. The steel upper section hovers over the stadium at a 45° angle. Today, the tower belongs to the prestigious World Federation of Great Towers. The spine of the stadium's tower can be mounted by a **funicular** elevator that travels 266m/872ft of rails in two minutes. Though the angle of the climb ranges from 23° to 63.7°, a gyroscope-controlled levelling system ensures that the cabin, which can hold up to 76 people, is always horizontal. The view during the ascent is spectacular: it encompasses the stadium and Montreal's East End. From the observation deck, the panoramic **view★★★** can extend as far as 80km/50mi, weather permitting. Three large skylights offer a breathtaking vertical view of the stadium. The windows lining the three sides of the triangular deck command expansive views of downtown Montreal, the Laurentian Mountains to the north and the Monteregian Hills to the south. The Botanical Garden is visible directly to the north.

Below the observation deck, a hands-on interpretation centre presents exhibits revolving around different themes: the park's conception and history, the technological innovations involved in its construction, and the materials used.

★**Biodome** – *Open late Jun–Labour Day daily 9am–7pm. Rest of the year daily 9am–5pm. $9.50. ✗ & ▣ ($7) www.ville.montreal.qc.ca/biodome ☎ 514-868-3000. Shuttle service (free) between the Biodome and the Botanical Garden.* Constructed as a velodrome for the Olympic cycling events, this imaginative **building★** resembles a cyclist's racing helmet. Its vast, scalloped roof spans 160m/526ft and is supported by four "feet." The ceiling's six ribs are composed of 144 jointed sections, each one weighing between 50 and 100 tons. These six arches are linked by transverse bands, forming a trellis to support the skylights, which admit natural light to the interior.

Lack of interest in indoor cycling led to the velodrome's conversion into the Biodome, an innovative museum of environmental and natural sciences. The museum, which opened its doors in 1992, re-creates the habitats of four "ecosystems." Equipped with sophisticated climatic regulators, the habitats support thousands of plants and animals indigenous to the ecosystem. Luxuriant vegetation and a variety of wildlife characterize the torrid **Tropical Forest**, inspired by the Amazonian jungle. Lynx, beaver, and otter frolic in the **Laurentian Forest**, domaine of maple trees, pines birches and spruce. Austere granite cliffs rise above the **St. Lawrence Marine Ecosystem**, where visitors can contemplate many types of fish and marine invertebrates. The frozen banks of the **Polar World** harbor penguins and other water birds, illustrating the rigors of life in the arctic and antarctic regions. In the discovery room, visitors can observe the mechanisms by which plants and animals adapt to cold, heat, drought, or darkness. An "environment place" offering films and video completes the installation.

Village olympique (Olympic Village) – *On north side of Rue Sherbrooke, east of Rue Viau.* Nicknamed "the Olympic Pyramids," these twin 19-storey buildings (1976) were constructed to house 11,000 athletes for the Olympic Games. Inspired by the complex at Baie-des-Anges in southern France, their exterior galleries and walkways are ill-suited to Montreal's cold winters. The buildings now contain a residential and commercial complex.

★★JARDIN BOTANIQUE DE MONTRÉAL
(MONTREAL BOTANICAL GARDEN)

4101 Rue Sherbrooke Est. ☉ *Pie-IX. Open mid-Jun–early Sept daily 9am–7pm. Early Sept–Oct 9am–9pm. Rest of the year daily 9am–5pm. $9.50.* ✗ ⚹ ▣ *($7) www.ville.montreal.qc.ca/jardin/* ☎ *514-872-1400. Shuttle service (free) between the Biodome, Olympic Park, and the Botanical Garden.*

Covering 75ha/185 acres, the Montreal Botanical Garden is located across from the Olympic Park and the Biodome. Ranked among the world's finest horticultural facilities, the garden was founded in 1931 by Brother Marie-Victorin (1885-1944). The garden contains more than 21,000 species from all over the world including 10,000 trees, 1,500 types of orchids and an extensive collection of bonsais. Since 1939, the Research Institute on Plant Biology has been housed in the Art Deco-style Administration Building. Not far from the building lies the **reception garden**, which displays vividly coloured annual flowers from April to October. Nearby, the new **Reception Centre** (1995) leads to the Molson introduction greenhouse, where visitors can get a first glimpse into the plant kingdom before exploring the ten greenhouses and some thirty thematic gardens that make up the Botanical Gardens.

★**Serres d'exposition (Conservatories)** – A stroll through the garden's ten magnificent exhibition greenhouses leads through reproduced botanical environments from around the world. From the Main Greenhouse, where temporary exhibits change seasonally, continue on to the Chinese Greenhouse, also known as the Jardin céleste. Here you'll find the superb **Wu Collection** of *penjings*, given to the Botanical Garden in 1984 by Wu Yee-Sun, a Hong Kong banker who mastered the art of *penjing* or "landscape in a pot." Following is a re-created Mexican hacienda, its courtyard and walls covered by cacti and succulent plants. Plants from arid regions occupy the next greenhouse, and the next features over 100 species of begonia and gesneriads. Tropical flora occupies two greenhouses, one devoted to rainforest vegetation, the other to **tropical economic plants** destined for exportation, such as cocoa, coffee, teak, mahogany, palm, mango and bamboo. Orchids and aroids flourish in the last conservatory.

★**Jardin de Chine (Chinese Garden)** – Opened in 1991, this enchanting landscape is a replica of a typical Ming dynasty (14-17C) garden from southern China, near the Yangtze River. The largest Chinese garden in the world outside China, it emphasizes natural appearance. Architect Le Wei Zhong skillfully combined two key elements of Chinese gardens, mountains and water, to encourage contemplation. The seven pavilions, with their steeply curving grey roofs, were prefabricated in Shanghai and assembled on site by Chinese workers. The ornate main pavilion – also called the "Friendship Pavilion" – hosts temporary exhibitions to provide the visitor an opportunity to explore the philosophy, art and customs of another world. The large terrace affords sweeping views over the lakes and gardens. Across the lake rises a jagged rock mountain (9m/29ft), replete with a stone stairway, cave and tumbling waterfall. Another structure houses a fabulous collection of *penjings*.

Jardin japonais (Japanese Garden) – Designed by the Japanese landscape architect, Ken Nakajima, this 2.5ha/6.2 acre garden (1988) presents a wonderful juxtaposition of water, boulders and plants – including a pond and a waterfall – in the traditional Oriental style, creating an atmosphere of peace and harmony that attracts visitors year-round. The unusual green rocks are peridotites from the EASTERN TOWNSHIPS. Exhibit spaces in the **Japanese pavilion** (1989), styled as a traditional Japanese family home, offer visitors a glimpse into Japanese artistic and cultural expression. The pavilion complex includes a Zen garden, composed of raked pebbles and stones considered conducive to meditation. The Japanese garden also features a garden of **bonsais** cultivated according to the Japanese tradition *(on view seasonally)*.

The Botanical Garden offers a wealth of other points of interest to delight and absorb plant lovers. The lovely, seasonal **Exhibition Garden** (arranged in traditional French patterns) features shrubs, plants of Quebec, toxic plants, medicinal plants, trial vegetables and hardy perennials. In the **Rose Garden**, visitors can admire over 10,000 specimens planted among the trees and shrubs. Ornamental plants indigenous to aquatic environments, such as lotuses, water lilies and water hyacinths, grow in the **Marsh and Bog Garden**'s 110 pools. In the **Shade Garden**, 1,000 species of primulas and begonias are shaded beneath lime, maple and ash trees; and the **Flowery Brook** features irises, peonies, asters and other flowers arranged in a traditional English garden. Not to be missed are the **Alpine Garden**, with plants from the world's major mountain ranges displayed in a rock garden setting; the **Leslie Hancock Garden** of azaleas and rhododendrons; and the **Arboretum**, which covers more than half of the total area with over 10,000 specimens of about 3,000 different species.

★**Insectarium de Montréal (Montreal Insectarium)** – *North side of Rue Sherbrooke in the Botanical Garden. www.ville.montreal.qc.ca/insectarium* Built in the shape of a giant bug, this museum (1990) displays a vast selection of insects from all over the world (approximately 150,000 specimens). Most of the insects on exhibit are preserved, although a few living specimens can be observed (including a beehive). The collections are presented as thematic exhibits that highlight the fascinating world of entomology and the role insects play in our environment. The insectarium also features a fine collection of monarch butterflies.

★Château Dufresne

South corner of Rue Sherbrooke and Blvd. Pie-IX; entrance on Blvd. Pie-IX. ◐ Pie-IX. Currently closed to the public.

The Château Dufresne was constructed between 1915 and 1918 for two eminent figures of the French Canadian bourgeoisie – the brothers Oscar (a shoe industrialist) and Marius (architect and civil engineer) Dufresne. The symmetrical facade, with eight monumental Ionic columns and a dentiled cornice surmounted by a balustraded terrace, illustrates the tenets of the Beaux-Arts style in vogue at the time of construction. One of the most luxurious homes in Maisonneuve, the reinforced concrete building reflected the grandiose aspirations that eventually led the city into bankruptcy and its subsequent annexation to Montreal.

Interior – Two identical wings, one for each brother, contained a total of 44 rooms decorated with mahogany panelling, ornamentation and furnishings evoking the lifestyle of Montreal's moneyed class in the 1920s and 1930s. An innovation of the period, many of the decorative elements were prefabricated, ordered from catalogues. The **rooms of Marius Dufresne** *(west side)*, are characterized by abundant use of oak and Neoclassical woodwork. Mahogany panelling, Italian marble and French wallcoverings characterize the **rooms of Oscar Dufresne** *(east side)*, which feature delicately tinted **mural panels★** by Guido Nincheri (1885-1973), in the parlor. Coffered ceilings, mahogany embellished with gilded foliage, Renaissance-style mural wallcoverings...each room here reveals perfection in its myriad details.

OTHER AREAS OF INTEREST *Map opposite.*

★**Île Sainte-Hélène (St. Helen's Island)** – **By car:** *take either Jacques-Cartier Bridge or Concorde Bridge.* **By metro:** ◐ *Île Sainte-Hélène.* In 1611, Samuel de Champlain named the small island in the St. Lawrence, east of the main island of Montreal, after his wife, **Hélène Boulé.** Prior to 1665, when it became part of the Longueil seigneury, the island served as a strategic defense point for the Amerindians in their battle against European invasion. After Canadian Confederation in 1867, the island became the property of the federal government until the city purchased it as a park early this century. In 1967, Île Sainte-Hélène was extended to cover 138ha/341 acres, in order to host the world fair, Expo '67, along with neighbouring Île Notre-Dame.

Today, most of the island is a public park, popular with Montrealers for cross-country skiing in winter, and swimming in the outdoor pools in summer. The road skirting the west side of the island provides excellent **views★** of the city and its port installations.

Vieux-Fort (Old Fort) – *Open mid-May–Aug daily 10am–6pm. Rest of the year Mon & Wed–Sun 10am–5pm. $6. ⚄ ▣ www.stewart-museum.org ☎ 514-861-6701.* St. Helen's Island was sold in 1818 to the British government, which subsequently erected a citadel. Today the fort houses the **Musée David M. Stewart★** (David M. Stewart Museum) devoted to the history of European settlement in Quebec. The museum presents displays on the early discoverers and first settlers, their explorations across the continent, the British Conquest, the effects of the American Revolution, the War of 1812 and the Patriots' Rebellion. Note also the wonderful collection of maps and globes, ship models, kitchen utensils, weapons and navigation instruments and many archival documents.

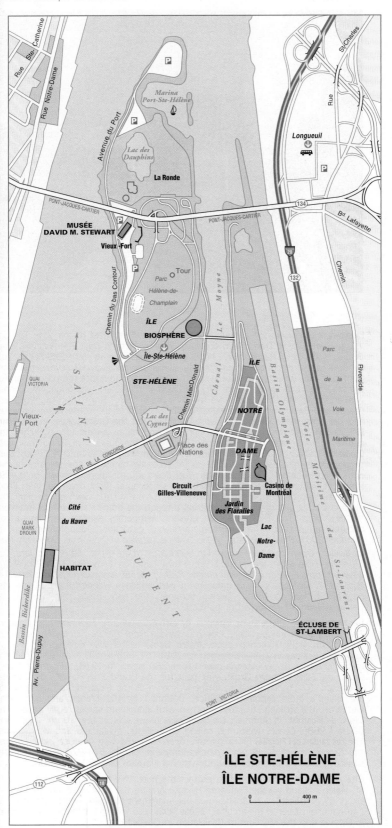

ÎLE STE-HÉLÈNE
ÎLE NOTRE-DAME

0   400 m

Biosphere, Île Sainte-Hélène

★ **Biosphere** – *Open Jun 24–Labour Day daily 10am–6pm. Rest of the year Tue–Sat 10am–4pm. Closed Dec 25–26 & Jan 1, Easter, Victoria Day, Thanksgiving Day $8.50.* ✗ ⚹ ▣ *($10/summer). http://biosphere.ec.gc.ca ☏ 514-283-5000.* This geodesic dome designed by Buckminster Fuller for the Expo'67 reveals the form the future was expected to take in the 1960s. Erected to house the US pavilion for the fair, the immense structure (76.2m/250ft in diameter) was originally covered with an acrylic sheath that was destroyed by fire in 1976. Since 1995 the Biosphere has housed Canada's first eco-watch centre devoted to the conservation of water and the ecosystems of the St. Lawrence River and the Great Lakes. In the **Water Delights Hall** *(1st floor)*, interactive consoles and hands-on exhibits highlight the nature of water and the crucial role it plays in the survival of living things. In **Connexions Hall** *(2nd floor)*, visitors can view a multimedia presentation *(25min)*, then participate in discussions designed to increase awareness of the fragility of our natural environment. The **Visions Hall** *(top floor)* affords glorious views of the St Lawrence via telescopes; monitors simulate a helicopter flight over the river. From this level, step out to the exterior belvedere, for a futuristic **view★** of Longeuil, the Victoria Bridge and downtown Montreal through the dome's skeleton of interconnecting tubes. The Biosphere also presents temporary exhibits and houses an documentation centre for environment-related publications and information. In Summer 2001, the new exhibit "Aqua" will be installed in the former Discovery Hall.

La Ronde – *Open mid-May–early Jun weekends 10am–9pm. Early Jun–late Jun Mon–Fri 10am–9pm, weekends 10am–11pm. Late Jun–early Sept Mon–Thu & Sun 11am–11pm, Fri–Sat 11am–midnight. $29.* ✗ ⚹ ▣ *www.laronde.com ☏ 514 872-4537.* Montreal's major amusement park enjoys a wonderful site at the east end of St. Helen's Island. During summer, the park hosts the International Benson&Hedges Fireworks Competition.

★ **Île Notre-Dame** (Notre Dame Island) – **By car:** *Bonaventure Highway and Concorde Bridge.* **By public transportation:** *free bus service from the Île Sainte-Hélène metro station.* An artificial construction, Notre Dame Island was created for the St Lawrence Seaway in 1959. Enlarged for Expo '67 with landfill excavated from the metro, the island now extends over 116ha/286 acres. In 1978, a Formula 1 race track, the **Gilles Villeneuve Circuit**, was built for the Grand Prix Player's du Canada. The Expo '67 French Pavilion, formerly known as the Palais de la Civilisation, is the island's most prominent edifice. Designed by the French architect, Jean Faugeron, the striking structure adorned with aluminium spikes today houses the **Casino de Montreal**. In summer, **Lac Notre-Dame** *(west side of the island)*, lined by a 600m/1,968ft beach, welcomes sailing enthusiasts, swimmers and windsurfers. The **Les Jardins des Floralies** (floral garden, *open daily mid-May–late Oct; closed during the Grand Prix;* ✗ ⚹ ▣ *www.parcjeandrapeau.com ☏ 514-872-4537*) features superb gardens created for the International Floralies of 1980 and 2000.

Cité du Havre – Constructed to protect the port, this peninsula links the city to St. Helen's Island via the Concorde Bridge. Among the structures remaining from Expo '67 is **Habitat★**, a futuristic, modular apartment complex, which launched the international career of the architect **Moshe Safdie**, also known for the National Gallery in Ottawa and the Museum of Civilization in Quebec City.

EXCURSIONS ON THE ISLAND

The West End *Map pp 174-175.*

This shoreline drive offers the visitor to Montreal a pleasant break from the bustle of the city. Beginning on the southwestern outskirts of the City of Montreal, a **panoramic road**★ leads to the western tip of the island. The meandering lakeshore drive hugs the St. Lawrence River and Lac Saint-Louis shores and borders affluent residential districts interspersed with numerous parks, equipped with picnic spots and playgrounds. First named Boulevard LaSalle, in LaSalle, the street becomes Boulevard Saint-Joseph, in Lachine, then Chemin du Bord-du-Lac (or Chemin Lakeshore) between Dorval and Sainte-Anne-de-Bellevue.

★**Maison Saint-Gabriel (Saint-Gabriel House)** – *2146 place Dublin, 4km/2.5mi from downtown Montréal by Rue Wellington. Turn left at parc Marguerite-Bourgeoys, and follow signs. Visit by guided tour (1hr 30min) only, mid-Feb–mid-Dec Tue–Sun 1:30pm, 2:30 & 3:30pm (Jun 24–Labour Day Tue–Sun 10am–5pm tours on the hour). $5.* ☐ *www.maisonsaint-gabriel.qc.ca* ☎ *514-935-8136.* In 1668, **Marguerite Bourgeoys** built a house here to care for the *filles du roy*, the King's wards. Destroyed by fire in 1693, the house was rebuilt five years later on the old foundations. Restored in 1965 and today considered one of the oldest structures on Montreal Island, the house today serves as a historical museum.

Located on the ground floor, the community and reception rooms contain much of the original 18C furniture, and present displays on Marguerite Bourgeoys and her order. Domestic equipment and utensils are on display in the kitchen. A dormitory and the bedroom of one of the *filles du roy* can be seen on the upper floors. Still joined by the original wooden pegs (1698), the rafters and beams of the attic attest to the house's solid construction.

Return to Rue Wellington and continue to Blvd. LaSalle.

LaSalle – *5km/3mi.* Named for Robert Cavelier de La Salle (1643-1687), this community was formerly part of Lachine, but became independent in 1912. At the end of 6th Avenue, take the path across the old hydro dam (1895) to enjoy superb **views**★ of the Lachine Rapids. Offshore lies Île aux Hérons, an island designated as a nature reserve to protect herons. The long-necked wading birds fish in the rapids and can often be spotted along both banks of the river.

Boulevard LaSalle passes under the double span of the **Honoré-Mercier Bridge** before entering Lachine. Opened in 1934, the bridge was named for Mercier, premier of Quebec from 1887 to 1891.

Lachine – *7.5km/5mi. See Entry Heading.*

West of Lachine, the communities on Montreal Island are collectively known as the **West Island**. Lined with opulent residences boasting their private boat docks, yacht clubs and lush parks, the "island's" communities are home to most of Montreal's English-speaking residents. The first suburb, **Dorval** *(4.5km/3mi)*, was named for Jean-Baptiste Bouchard, a native of Orval, France, who acquired land here in 1691. Today, Dorval is best known for its international airport.

★**Pointe-Claire** – *6km/4mi.* This wealthy, traditionally anglophone suburb on the shore of Lac Saint-Louis, was named for the fine and clear *(claire)* **views**★ available from the strip of land that extends into the lake *(below)*.

★**Stewart Hall** – *On left side of Chemin Bord-du-Lac–Lakeshore; follow signs. Cultural Centre open Jun–Aug Mon–Fri 8:30am–9pm. Rest of the year Mon–Fri 8:30am–9pm, Sat 9am–5pm, Sun 1pm–5pm. Hours vary for the art gallery and library.* ♿ ☐ ☎ *514-630-1220.* Built in 1915, this copper-roofed stone mansion is a half-scale model of a castle located on the Isle of Mull in Scotland. In 1963, Mr. and Mrs. Walter Stewart purchased the property and donated it to the City of Pointe-Claire as a cultural centre. Today, the building contains a library, an art gallery with changing displays, and a superb wood-panelled reception room, site of meetings, plays, concerts and other activities organised by the Cultural Centre. The lovely garden affords magnificent **views**★ of the lake.

★**La Pointe** – *Turn left off Chemin Lakeshore onto Rue Sainte-Anne and park beside church.* Located on the end of this peninsula jutting into Lac Saint-Louis, the convent (1867) belongs to the Congregation of Our Lady. Behind it, an old stone **windmill** dates from 1709 *(access on foot only)*. Once an outer fortification for Montreal, this structure served as a retreat in case of Amerindian attack.

Topped by a single steeple, the Église Saint-Joachim (Church of St. Joachim) was built in 1882. Adjacent to it stands the presbytery with its wraparound porch and distinctive roof line, enlivened by numerous pyramidal forms. The **views** from this site are superb.

After Pointe-Claire, the Chemin du Bord-du-Lac becomes Boulevard Beaconsfield. It traverses the affluent suburb of **Beaconsfield** *(5km/3mi)*, named for the British prime minister, Benjamin Disraeli (1804-1880), who was conferred the title of Lord Beaconsfield by Queen Victoria on his retirement.

The road returns to being called Chemin du Bord-du-Lac as it passes through **Baie-d'Urfé** *(6km/4mi)*, named for François-Saturnin Lascaris d'Urfé, who founded a mission here in 1686.

The garden beside the Baie-d'Urfé Town Hall *(20410 Chemin Lakeshore)*, commands superb **views** of the lake and Île Dowker offshore.

★**Sainte-Anne-de-Bellevue** – *3km/2mi*. Located at the western tip of Montreal Island, this community was part of the Bellevue seigneury granted in 1670. Dedicated to St. Anne in 1714, the parish took its present name in 1878.

The main street *(Rue Sainte-Anne)* runs beside the Ottawa River, whose rushing waters join those of the St. Lawrence in Lac Saint-Louis after passing through a lock. Above the lock, the twin spans of Highway 20 and a railway bridge cross to Île Perrot.

An attractive waterfront **boardwalk** lined with restaurants is a popular spot for watching small and large boats plying the river.

Macdonald Campus – *Located on Rue Sainte-Anne, at entrance of the community.* In 1907 Sir William Macdonald (1831-1917), Chancellor of McGill University and founder of the Macdonald Tobacco Company, donated 650ha/1,605 acres to the university. Distinctive red brick buildings were erected on the site, today home to McGill's Faculty of Agriculture and Environmental Sciences.

Especially popular with children, the campus' **experimental farm** *(open May–Jul 9am–5pm; ✕ ⅋ ◻ ☎ 514-398-7701)* features a dairy barn and an animal farm where sheep, goats, pigs, rabbits and other animals thrive. Covering 245ha/600 acres, the Morgan **arboretum** *(open year-round daily 9am–4pm; $5; ◻ ☎ 514-398-7811)* boasts the most complete collection of tree species indigenous to Canada.

★**Boat Trips** – *Depart from Ste-Anne-de-Bellevue Jun 24–Labour Day daily 1:30pm & 3:30pm. Mid-May–Jun 23 & Labour Day–late Sept by appointment. Round-trip 1hr 30min. Commentary. Reservations required. $15.* ✕ ⅋ ◻ *Croisières Bellevue Ltd.* ☎ 514-457-5245. Boat trips are offered on Lac Saint-Louis and Lac Deux Montagnes (Lake of Two Mountains). On the former, the boat sails along Île Perrot as far as Pointe-du-Moulin, affording splendid **views** of the lakeshore, downtown Montreal in the distance, and of the industrial area around Beauharnois.

To enter Lac Deux Montagnes, the boat passes through the Sainte-Anne lock, then under Highways 20 and 40. The deck offers expansive **views** of the magnificent homes lining the shores of Senneville and OKA, and the hills of Rigaud, rising on the horizon.

Return on Rue Sainte-Anne and turn left on Blvd. Saint-Pierre. Continue for 2km/ 1.2mi and take Rte. 40 east for 20km/12mi towards Montreal. Take Exit 62 on Chemin de la Côte-Vertu. To reach the museum, continue for 5km/3mi then turn right on Blvd. Sainte-Croix. The museum is 1km/.6mi further on the left.

Saint-Laurent – *28km/17mi from Sainte-Anne-de-Bellevue or about 10km/6mi north of downtown by Rue Sherbrooke Est (Rte. 138), Rte. 15 Nord, Rte. and Blvd. Décarie.* This industrial suburb of Montreal was founded about 1687, when the brothers Paul, Michel and Louis Descaries arrived to farm the land they called the Côte Saint-Laurent.

★**Musée d'art de Saint-Laurent** (Saint-Laurent Art Museum) – *On grounds of Cégep Saint-Laurent, on Ave. Sainte-Croix. From Blvd. Décarie, turn right on Rue du Collège. The college is straight ahead at the junction with Blvd. Sainte-Croix.* ◍ *Du Collège. Open year-round Wed–Sun 1pm–5pm (Wed 9pm). Closed Dec 25–26. $3.* ⅋ ◻ ☎ *514-747-7367.* This small museum is located in the Presbyterian Church of St. Andrew and St. Paul (1867), moved from Dorchester Boulevard to this site in 1931. The striking Gothic Revival structure served as a chapel until 1975 when it was converted into a museum. Inside, the intricately carved wooden vault and luminous stained-glass windows can still be seen.

The museum owns an impressive collection of French-Canadian artifacts. Displayed in exhibits concentrating on particular themes, the objects illustrate such trades as tin smithing, textile fabrication, ceramic making, furniture making, silver and gold smithing and wood sculpting. Of particular interest is the authentic reconstruction of a silversmith's shop. A large collection of religious sculpture and some fine pieces of furniture complement the exhibits. The museum also mounts temporary exhibits on the area's cultural and artistic heritage.

The Northeast *Map p 174.*

Sault-au-Récollet – *Located about 12km/7mi north of downtown Montreal by Rue Sherbrooke Est (Rte. 138), Rue Cartier, Rue Rachel and Ave. Papineau. Blvd. Gouin is a one-way street east.* Today part of the City of Montreal, Sault-au-Récollet is one of the oldest communities on Montreal Island. Set beside rapids on the Prairies River, it was visited by both Jacques Cartier, in 1535, and Samuel de Champlain, in 1615. It was named after a Récollet brother, Nicolas Viel, who drowned in the rapids in 1625 while returning from the Huron country with his Amerindian companion, Ahuntsic. The Sulpicians founded a mission here in 1696, and the parish came into existence in 1736. Sault-au-Récollet was a separate municipality until 1916 when it was annexed by Montreal. Since 1930, the rapids have been harnessed by Hydro-Québec for electricity.

★**Église de la Visitation-de-la-Bienheureuse-Vierge-Marie** (Church of the Visitation of the Blessed Virgin Mary) – *From Ave. Papineau turn left on Blvd. Henri-Bourassa and left on Rue des Jésuites.* ⊕ *Henri-Bourassa. Open year-round daily 9am–5pm. Closed Jan 1 & the afternoon of Dec 25.* & 🅿 ☎ *514-388-4050.* Erected between 1749 and 1752, this edifice is the oldest church on Montreal Island. Its large nave and absence of lateral chapels are in keeping with the style of Récollet churches in New France.

The stone **façade** (1850, John Ostell), flanked by two tall towers, was inspired by the church of Sainte-Geneviève de Pierrefonds (northwest of Montreal), designed a few years earlier by Thomas Baillairgé. Victor Bourgeau later used this same design throughout the region, notably for the Church of St. Rose, in Laval. The elaborate **interior**★★ illustrates the aesthetic principles of the Quévillon school. The turquoise and gold vault, adorned with diamond-shaped barrels, is of rare quality; like the sculpted decor in the chancel, it was installed by David Fleury David about 1820. Fashioned by Vincent Chartrand of the Quévillon studio, the magnificent **pulpit**★ (1837), with its finely decorated sound reflector, is one of the most beautiful pieces of liturgical furniture sculpted in Quebec. The tabernacle above the main altar is attributed to Philippe Liébert (1732-1804); the main altar and side altars were designed by Louis-Amable Quévillon (1749-1823). The portals (1820) leading to the sacristy are embellished with polychrome bas-reliefs inscribed into Louis XV-style panels.

Parc-nature de l'Île de la Visitation – *From Blvd. Gouin just east of the Papineau-Leblanc Bridge, turn left on Rue du Pont.* ⊕ *Henri-Bourassa. Open year-round daily dawn–dusk. Closed to cars. Reception centre open late Jan 1–October 29 & last 2 weeks of Dec daily 9:30am–4:30pm.* ✕ & 🅿 *($4) www.cum.qc.ca/parcs-nature* ☎ *514-280-7272.* L'île-de-la-Visitation is one of six nature parks operated by the Montreal Urban Community. Its 33ha/82 rolling acres are laced with paths for biking and skiing. Several mills have occupied the strip of land connecting the island to the banks of the Prairies River since the 18C. The last one operated until 1970. Before reaching the island, the attractive, early-19C **Maison du Pressoir** (Cider Press House) can be visited; the original mechanism is exposed, and displays illustrate the cider-making process *(open Jan 1–Oct 29 daily 11am–5pm;* ☎ *514-280-6783).* Nearby, the **Maison du Meunier** (Miller's House) now hosts local art exhibits *(open Jan 1–Oct daily 11am–5pm;* 🅿 ☎ *514-280-6709).*

EXCURSIONS FROM MONTREAL

★★**Vallée du Richelieu** – *See Entry Heading.*

★★**Laurentidesans** – *See Entry Heading.*

Lanaudière – *See Entry Heading.*

NICOLET
Centre-du-Québec
Population 4,352

Set on the banks of the Nicolet River, 3km/2mi from its junction with the St. Lawrence, this community is named for one of Samuel de Champlain's companions, **Jean Nicollet** (1598-1642). Settlement began in 1756, when Acadian refugees arrived and established their farms, transforming Nicolet into an agricultural centre. A diocese was inaugurated in 1877, and the city is now home to several religious orders. Nicolet is also the site of the Quebec Police Academy. In 1955, a landslide pushed much of the old city into the Nicolet River.

Access – *Nicolet is 170km/105mi from Montreal by Rte. 20, Rte. 55 (Laviolette Bridge), and Rte. 132. It is 25km/15mi southwest of Trois-Rivières.*

SIGHTS

★★**Cathédrale Saint-Jean-Baptiste** (Cathedral of St. John the Baptist) – *On Blvd. Louis-Fréchette at east end of town. Open year-round daily 9am–4pm.* ☎ *819-293-5492.* Distinguished by its detached campanile, this stunning cathedral (1962, Gérard Malouin) resembles a ship's sails. Built of reinforced concrete, it replaces the previous cathedral, which was destroyed in the 1955 landslide.

Interior – A magnificent **stained-glass window** (50m/164ft wide by 21m/69ft high), the work of Jean-Paul Charland, adorns the façade; surrounding a figure of St. John the Baptist (patron saint of Nicolet), the abstract design bursts into hundreds of colourful prisms as the morning sun shines through. The white oak and hickory nave seats 1,400 people. The Stations of the Cross are engraved on its slated walls beneath iconographic representations of Nicolet's former bishops. To the left o the black granite altar, a passage leads to a baptismal font embellished with mosaics. The stained-glass window in the apse, by Brother Éric de Thierry, is a stunning representation of the risen Christ.

Ancien collège-séminaire (Old College Seminary) – *350 Rue d'Youville*. Religious authorities established the college-seminary in 1805 to encourage young men from urban areas to join the priesthood. The building, designed by Father Jérôme Demers and Thomas Baillairgé, was constructed in 1828; a fire destroyed half o the structure in 1973. The building is now occupied by the Quebec Police Academy

Musée des Religions (Museum of Religions) – *900 Blvd. Louis-Fréchette, just off Rue Notre-Dame in the centre of town. Open Jun 24–Labour Day daily 10am–5pm Rest of the year Tue–Sun 10am–5pm (Nov–Apr Sat 1pm–5pm). Closed Jan 1 & Dec 25. $4.50.* & ▯ *www.museedesreligions.qc.ca* ☎ *819-293-6148*. Dedicated to the study and preservation of religious heritage, this museum reopened in 1991 in a new, contemporary structure topped by a glass pyramid. On the ground floor exhibits present various world religions (Buddhism, Christianity, Hinduism, Islam and Judaism) using objects from the permanent collection. Temporary thematic exhibits invite reflection on such topics as human spirituality. On the lower level the Nicolet Seminary Archives are available for research purposes.

Maison Rodolphe-Duguay (Rodolphe-Duguay House) – *195 Rang Saint-Alexis 1km/.6mi by Rte. 132 over the Pierre-Roy Bridge; turn left on Rang Saint-Alexis Open mid-May–mid-Oct Tue–Sun 10am–5pm. Rest of the year by appointment $3.50.* ▯ ☎ *819-293-4103*. The birthplace and home of artist Rodolphe Duguay (1891-1973) stands on a pleasant site overlooking the Nicolet River. The adjacent studio was added by the artist himself following his return from a long sojourn in Paris in 1927. In his lifetime, Duguay was best known for his wood engravings and was a follower of Suzor-Côté. Temporary exhibits present his life and works and allow a peek into the environment in which he worked.

EXCURSIONS

Baie-du-Febvre – *13km/8mi by Rte. 132*. Nestled along Lac Saint-Pierre lies this small village that serves as the welcome spot for the return of Quebec's Snow Geese each April. Surrounding fields flooded by the winter's melted snow become shallow lakes that serve as the perfect place for waterfowl who stop for a rest during their annual return home. To get more acquainted with the most important Snow Goose migration journey in Quebec, visit the **Centre d'Interprétation de Baie-du-Febvre** *(420 Route Marie-Victorin; open Mar–Nov daily 10am–5pm. $3 www.oies.com* ☎ *450-783-6996)*.

Odanak Indian Reservation – *25km/15mi by Rte. 132. Turn left in Pierreville fol lowing signs*. Located on the banks of the Saint-François River, this Abenaki reservation, known as Arsigontekw, was settled in 1700 by members of the Sokoki and Abenaki communities. The small **church**, the fifth on this site, was entirely decorated by the native population. Note the wooden frieze along the walls, and the statues, especially the one of Kateri Tekakwitha.

Musée des Abénakis (Abenaki Museum) – *In former convent beside church. Open May–Oct Mon–Fri 10am–5pm, weekends 1pm–5pm. Rest of the year Mon–Fri 10am–5pm. $4.* & ▯ ☎ *450-568-2600*. Temporary and permanent exhibits here offer glimpses of the traditional lifestyle of the Abenakis, Odanak history, and the foundation of the Catholic mission here. Works by native artists are displayed on a rotating basis.

Île aux NOIX
Montérégie
Map p 263

Situated near the US border, this 85ha/210 acre island in the Upper Richelieu was named Île aux Noix for the walnut trees (*noix* means "nut") that once flourished on it. As a reward for a brilliant career as a navy captain, Pierre Jacques Payan, Sieur de Noyan, was granted the island seigneury in 1733 by the Marquis de Beauharnois, Governor of New France. The first inhabitant of the island was a soldier named Pierre Jourdanet; his rent was fixed at one bag of nuts annually.

Historical Notes

Situated on a major north-south military and commercial route only a few kilometres from the outlet of Lake Champlain, Île aux Noix was first fortified by the French in 1759, during the Seven Years' War; it was captured by the British the following year. The island was occupied by Americans during the Revolution of 1775-1776. After their departure, the British once again fortified this strategic site. They built a ship-yard in order to establish a fleet that could foil the American warships on Lake Champlain. Shortly thereafter, the British constructed a second, larger military instal-lation named Fort Lennox.

With the American threat temporarily halted, the island was used as a juvenile reha-bilitation centre. It was briefly regarrisoned during the Civil War and during the Fenian Revolt, after which it became a holiday resort and then a World War II internment camp. Île aux Noix is now preserved as a national historic site.

Access – *The island is located 48km/30mi south of Montreal by Rtes. 10, 35 and 223, then by ferry service (same hours as Fort Lennox) from Saint-Paul-de-l'Île-aux-Noix. The island is also accessible by boat (4hrs) from Saint-Jean-sur-Richelieu.*

VISIT

★ **Lieu historique national du Fort-Lennox** (Fort Lennox National Historic Site) – Fort Lennox was erected between 1819 and 1829, at about the same time as the Citadel in Quebec City. It was named for Charles Lennox (1764-1819), Duke of Richmond, Governor-in-Chief of British North America, who ordered its construction.

The fort was completed just as an improved road system was established along the Richelieu River banks. The roads shifted the military threat from the water to the land, and the fort, no longer strategically positioned, was temporarily aban-doned by the military shortly after its construction. The Trent Affair and the Fenian uprising in the 1860s brought new threats to the British, who re-garrisoned Fort Lennox until 1870.

The bastion-type fortress is typical of 19C military architecture. The fort is sur-rounded by a wide moat, which forms a five-pointed star around a series of tall earthen ramparts. The corners are protected by bastions that open onto the inner yard. Visitors cross a footbridge and pass under a massive stone archway to enter the main courtyard, which is surrounded by a group of Neoclassical stone struc-tures. The guard house (1823) and officers' quarters (1825-1828) are arranged in a symmetrical pattern and are decorated with columns and arches. The soldiers' barracks are also ordered symmetrically around a pedimented pavilion. The fort complex includes two warehouses (1823), a powder magazine (1820) and 17 firing stations, or casemates, located under the ramparts.

Visit – *Open mid-May–Jun 23 Mon–Fri 10am–5pm, weekends 10am–6pm. Jun 24–Labour Day daily 10am–6pm. Sept 5–early-Oct weekends 10am–6pm. $5 (ferry & visit of fort).* ✗ ⟨⟩ *www.parkscanada.gc.ca/fortlennox/* ☎ *450-291-5700.* The fort occupies a pleasant **site**★ overlooking the Richelieu River. Visitors are led through the principal sections of the fort complex. The building interiors have been restored to recreate life on a British army base in the mid-19C. Among the numerous displays, visitors will see the guard room with its wood stove and jail; the prison; the soldiers' barracks with hard straw mattresses, uniforms and weapons; the officers' quarters, the brick-lined powder magazine, and the ware-houses with their cannon and gun carriages. The island itself features several relaxing picnic areas.

© Anne Gardon/REFLEXION

Soldiers' Barracks in Fort-Lennox

Île d'ORLÉANS★★

Région de Québec
Population 6,892
Map below

Wedged in the St. Lawrence, within view of Quebec City, this almond-shaped island covers an area of 192sq km/74sq mi. It boasts a varied landscape of maple groves in the north and on the central plateau, oak forests in the southwest, marshes in the centre and sand along the water's edge. Although joined to the mainland by bridge in 1935, the Île d'Orléans still retains the pastoral tranquillity that inspired the 19C artist Horatio Walker, and the *chansonnier* Félix Leclerc.

Historical Notes

Long before the arrival of Europeans, the indigenous population called the island Minigo, meaning "bewitched" in Algonquian, because they considered it to be a land of spirits. When Jacques Cartier came ashore in 1535, the abundance of vines growing on the island prompted him to dub the site the Isle of Bacchus. The following year the name was changed to Île d'Orléans in honour of the son of King François I, the Duke of Orléans. Under the French Regime, the seigneury was laid out in strips of land *(rangs)* perpendicular to the St. Lawrence, providing optimal access to the waterfront.

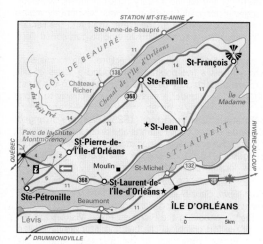

Today, vast expanses of farmland produce strawberries, raspberries, apples, asparagus and potatoes. The island is also known for its maple syrup. Many islanders trace their ancestry back to French colonists who arrived here more than three centuries ago, at a time when the island was more populous than the capital city. In fact, in 1667, the Île d'Orléans claimed a population of 529 while the residents of Quebec City numbered only 448.

Access – *Île d'Orléans is located 10km/6mi northeast of Quebec City by Rte. 138 or Rte. 40, exit 325.*

TOUR OF THE ISLAND 67km/41mi.

After crossing the bridge to Île d'Orléans (Pont de l'Île), turn right toward Saint-Pétronille. A tourist information centre (☎ 418-828-9411) is located at the intersection of the bridge road and Rte. 368.

Route 368 runs along the island's 67km/41mi circumference, passing through six communities. Driving along the road, the visitor will discover splendid scenery and magnificent **views★★** of the Beaupré Coast and the Bas-Saint-Laurent shoreline. The itinerary along the southern coast, from Sainte-Pétronille to Saint-François, is particularly picturesque. The return trip along the northern side of the island offers scenic views of the Montmorency Falls and Mt. Sainte-Anne.

Sainte-Pétronille – *5km/3mi from junction of bridge road.* Located on the site of the island's first settlement, this community was conceded in 1649. Hurons sought refuge here in the 1650s after warring with the Iroquois. The small chapel dating from that period has since disappeared. In 1855, a wharf was constructed to load island produce, and a steamship ferry service linked Sainte-Pétronille to Quebec City. This connection led to the development of tourism in the late 19C, and many affluent families erected Victorian-style villas here as summer homes. A three-hole golf course built in 1866 is one of the oldest in North America. The village was known as L'Anse-au-Fort, then as Bout de l'Île (tip of the island) and Village de Beaulieu before acquiring its present name in 1870.

Église de Sainte-Pétronille (Church of Sainte-Pétronille) – *Turn left on Chemin de l'Église, then right before the cul-de-sac facing the golf course. Open late Jun–Aug daily 10am–4:30pm. ☎ 418-828-2656.* The religious complex includes a convent (1875), a presbytery and a church (1871) designed by J. F. Peachy. The interior was decorated by David Ouellet.

Continue along Chemin de l'Église which runs into the Chemin du Bout-de-l'Île. A walkway borders the shoreline. Turn left, then right on Rue du Quai.

La Goéliche – *Rue du Quai.* Known as the Château Bel Air when it was constructed in 1880, and then as Manoir de l'Anse, this imposing Victorian hotel and restaurant stands majestically overlooking the St. Lawrence.

Return to Rte. 368 and continue to Saint-Laurent.

★ **Saint-Laurent-de-l'Île-d'Orléans** – *11km/7mi.* Traditionally the maritime centre of the Île d'Orléans, Saint-Laurent enjoyed a thriving shipbuilding industry in the mid-19C when some twenty family-owned shipyards produced flat-bottom boats, called *chaloupes*. Famous for their clean lines and sturdy construction, these boats remained the primary means of transportation for the islanders until a bridge joined the island to the mainland in 1935. The village still claims the island's only marina, which can accommodate up to 130 boats.

Situated 2km/1.2mi before the town limit of Saint-Laurent, the **Gendreau House** *(no. 2385 Chemin Royal)*, with its steep roof and unusual double row of dormer windows, was erected in 1720. For at least eight generations, it was inhabited by members of the Gendreau family. Next to the marina in the heart of the village, the **Église Saint-Laurent** (St. Lawrence Church, 1860), is topped by a tall, well-proportioned steeple. In the old section of the village, a small processional chapel stands beside the courthouse. Upon leaving town, note the early 18C flour mill, the **Moulin Gosselin** *(left side of road)*, which now houses a fine restaurant.

Saint-Jean, Île d'Orléans

★ **Saint-Jean** – *11km/7mi.* Founded in 1679 by Msgr. de Laval, this community was home to the island's pilots and navigators. Between 1850 and 1950, the village experienced a period of intense economic growth with the arrival of numerous Charlevoix pilots, who brought with them opportunities for maritime and industrial development. The maritime cemetery commemorates the lives of these seamen, many of whom perished in the course of difficult voyages on the tumultuous waters of the St. Lawrence. Today, the village's residents still pursue the maritime and agricultural activities of their ancestors. Their homes, decorated with nautical adornments, are clustered on the hillsides and along the St. Lawrence shoreline.

★ **Manoir Mauvide-Genest** (Mauvide-Genest Manor) – *Visit by guided tour (30 min) only, mid-Jun–early Sept daily 10am–5pm every half-hour. Early Sept–mid-Oct Tue–Sun 11am–5pm. $4.* ✗ ♿ 🅿 ☎ *418-829-2630.* The original house was constructed in 1734 for Jean Mauvide, surgeon to the King and a successful French merchant, and his wife, Marie-Anne Genest, of the Saint-Jean region. By the mid-18C, the wealth accumulated by Mr. Mauvide through his business ventures in the Antilles enabled him to enlarge the rural dwelling into a veritable manor. In 1752, Mr. Mauvide bought half of the Île d'Orléans seigneury. A few years later, when his business failed, he sold the seigneury to his son-in-law. In 1926, Judge J.-Camille Pouliot purchased the manor and undertook its restoration. It is now considered the finest extant example of rural architecture from the French Regime. The manor houses a restaurant and a museum exhibiting furnishings and objects collected by Judge Pouliot. Authentic Quebec pieces include a beggars' bench *(banc de quêteux)* and a church cabinet *(pigeonnier)*, as well as an elevated bed designed to provide protection from the cold floor.

Church – *Open mid-Jun–mid-Sept daily 10am–5pm. Contribution requested.* 🅿 ☎ *418-829-3182.* Topped by a red metal roof, the church (1736) dominates the seamen's cemetery beside the water's edge. Thomas Baillairgé designed the interior in 1831. The ornate pulpit and churchwarden's bench were carved about 1812 by Louis-Bazile David of the Montreal studio of Louis-Amable Quévillon. The paintings in the choir are the work of Antoine Plamondon. Note, in particular, his *St. Anne Saving the Shipwrecked* (1856).

Saint-François – *11km/7mi.* Formerly the seigneury of François Berthelot, the parish was founded in 1679. The community encompasses the eastern extremity of the island as well as the tiny Madame and Ruaux Islands. The St. Lawrence changes from fresh to salt water 20km beyond this point. Agriculture, mainly potato crops, is the primary means of revenue for the villagers.

Ravaged by fire in 1988, the **Église Saint-François** (Church of St. Francis, 1736) was reconstructed on its original foundations in 1992. On the southern side of the church, note the **presbytery** (1867), in the Quebec vernacular style, with a large balcony. A processional chapel marks the town limit. Just outside the village, a lookout tower affords **views**★★ of both banks of the St. Lawrence. The ski slopes of Mount Sainte-Anne and the Beaupré Coast lie to the west.

Sainte-Famille – *14km/9mi.* Msgr. de Laval founded this parish, the oldest on the island, in 1661, and had the first church erected here in 1669. Among the most interesting buildings in the village is the 17C fieldstone farmhouse of Norman inspiration, today occupied by a restaurant specializing in traditional French-Canadian cuisine. A horse and buggy picks up diners from the parking lot on the main road to the house.

★★ **Église de la Sainte-Famille** (Church of the Holy Family) – *Open late Jun–Labour Day daily 11am–5pm.* 🅰 🅿 ☎ *418-828-2656.* This tri-steepled edifice is considered the most important church dating from the French Regime. Built between 1743 and 1748, the church was modified in 1807 with the addition of two lateral bell towers. In the Neoclassical **interior** (1921, Thomas Baillargé), the nave slopes toward the altar and baldachin. The sculpted vault (1812) by Louis-Bazile David, a student of Quévillon, represents a starry sky. Dating from 1749, the tabernacle of the main altar is the work of the Levasseur family, while the tabernacles of the lateral altars are attributed to Pierre Florent, brother of François. Hanging to the right of the nave is a painting of the Holy Family attributed to Brother Luc, a Récollet painter who visited New France about 1670.

Saint-Pierre-de-l'Île-d'Orléans – *13km/8mi.* The parish of Saint-Pierre is distinguished by its two churches. When the parishioners decided to build a new church in 1955, the government acquired the old church, erected between 1715 and 1719, to protect it from demolition.

★ **Old Church** – *Open Jun 24–Aug daily 9am–6pm. May–Jun 23 & Sept–Oct daily 10am–noon & 1pm–5pm.* 🅰 🅿 ☎ *418-828-9824.* Damaged during the Conquest, the church was restored and then enlarged in 1775 when the parish priest became auxiliary bishop of Quebec City. The church was again remodelled in the 1830s by Thomas Baillargé. The interior contains three altars executed by Pierre Émond in 1795 and a sanctuary lamp carved in wood. Note also the box pews, introduced in Quebec by Protestant groups, and, at the front and back of the church, the woodstoves with sheetmetal pipes that heated the nave.

PERCÉ★★★

Gaspésie
Population 3,993
Map p 105

Named for the massive rock pierced *(percé)* by the sea, standing just offshore, this village occupies a magnificent **site** that inspires artists and poets and attracts visitors from all over the world to the Gaspé peninsula. One of Jacques Cartier's landing points in 1534, the area was also frequented by European fishermen in the 16C and 17C. A mission was founded here in 1673, but was destroyed by the British in 1690, to be re-established only after the Conquest. A tiny, isolated fishing village until the advent of tourism at the turn of the century, Percé now boasts some of the peninsula's finest restaurants and tourist facilities.

Access – *Percé is located 750km/465mi northeast of Lévis (Quebec City) and 76km/47mi from Gaspé by Rte. 132.*

SIGHTS

★★ **Rocher Percé (Percé Rock)** – Once attached to the mainland, this mammoth rock wall is 438m/1,437ft long and 88m/289ft high. The limestone block was formed at the bottom of the sea millions of years ago, and contains innumerable fossils. At one time, it may have had up to four holes forming as many archways. One such archway crumbled in 1845, leaving a detached slab called the Obelisk. Today, only a 30m/94ft arch remains. The sculptured limestone is best viewed from **Mont-Joli**★★. The rock is connected to Mont-Joli by a sandbar, exposed at low tide. *Check tide tables at the tourist office. The stairway to the beach and sandbar is accessible from the Mont-Joli parking lot.*

View of Rocher Percé from Mt. Sainte-Anne

★★The Coast – The coast along Route 132 offers spectacular **views★★**. Just before entering Percé, a belvedere provides a good view of Aurore Peak (Pic de l'Aurore). Further along the road, a path leads up to **Cape Barré**, which affords a commanding view of the cliffs known as **Trois Sœurs** (Three Sisters) to the west, and Percé Rock, Anse du Nord, Mont-Joli, Île Bonaventure and the village, to the east. Leaving Percé, the promontory at **Côte Surprise** offers yet another superb view of Percé Rock, the village and the island.

ADDRESS BOOK

For a legend of price listings for hotels and restaurants, see p 170.

Staying in Percé

Au Pirate, L'Auberge à Percé (The Pirate's House) – 169 Route 132 Oeust. ✕ ▯ ☎ 418-782-5055 (e-mail getty@quebectel.com). 5 rooms. **$$$** Wonderfully comfortable rooms, gregarious proprietors, and beautiful views of Percé rock can only mean you were lucky enough to get a reservation at the Pirate's House. Its award-winning **dining room ($$$)** attracts visitors from around the country with specialties such as *fondants de chair de crabe en mille-feuille* (fondant of crab in a puff pastry), *brandade de morue et sa compote de tomates fraîches* (brandade of cod in a fresh tomato compote), and *le trio du golfe beurre blanc au vinaigre de framboises–saumon, pétoncles, crevettes grillées* (salmon, scallops and grilled shrimp in a raspberry vinegar beurre blanc). Reservations required for lunch and dinner.

Hôtel la Normandie – *221 Route 132 Oeust.* ✕ ♿ ▯ ☎ *418-782-2337, 1-800-463-0820. www.normandieperce.com. 45 rooms.* **$$$** A waterfront hotel in the most traditional sense, the Normandie offers comfortable rooms with views of Percé rock or of the mountains. Be sure to reserve a table in its acclaimed **dining room ($$$)**. An impressive wine list accompanies the ample choices of the *table d'hôte* (fixed price) menu with favorites such as *blanc de morue croûté au saumon fumé, et pesto de tomates séchées* (baked cod with smoked salmon topping, tomato pesto sauce) and *feuilleté de homard, au Champagne* (lobster in puff pastry, Champagne sauce).

Dining in Percé *(see above)*

La Maison du Pêcheur – *155 Place du Quai.* ☎ *418-782-5331.* **$$** Located next to the public pier, the Fisherman's House serves up breakfast, lunch and dinner. Choose from the delectable Québécois seafood specialties like *les escalopes de homard aux parfums d'érable* (lobster flavoured with maple syrup) or the mouth watering wood-fired pizzas such as *La Spéciale du Pêcheur avec sauce tomate, crevettes, pétoncles et chair de homard* (tomato sauce, shrimp, scallops and lobster).

Mont Sainte-Anne (Mt. Sainte-Anne) – *From Rte. 132, take Ave. de l'Église. Behind the church, a gravel road leads to Mt. Sainte-Anne. A steep but easy trail leads to the summit. Allow 2hrs round-trip.* Rising 320m/1,050ft above Percé, the flat topped mountain features extraordinary red rock formations that drop off on three sides. Lookouts stationed along the way to the summit provide increasingly expansive **views★★★** of Percé Rock, the bay, the village and the surrounding area. A statue of St. Anne crowns the mountain summit.

La Grotte (Grotto) – *On the return trip from Mt. Sainte-Anne, turn left at Chemin de la Grotte, and continue for 1km/.6mi.* In this scenic grotto, a waterfall cascades into a small pool surrounded by moss and ferns.

★**La Grande Crevasse (Great Crevice)** – *From the village, take Rte. des Failles up to the Auberge Gargantua (3km/2mi). The trail (1hr 30min round-trip) starts behind the inn; caution is advised as there is no guardrail.* Passing alongside the west cliff of Mt. Sainte-Anne, the trail offers glimpses of the peaks of the Chic-Choc mountains to the west and the Bay of Gaspé to the north. The Great Crevice *(also visible from Rte. des Failles)* is a deep fissure in the red conglomerate rock which is a part of Mt. Blanc, located northwest of Mt. Sainte-Anne.

★**Parc de l'île-Bonaventure-et-du-Rocher-Percé** (Île Bonaventure and Percé Rock Park) – *Open early Jun–mid-Oct daily 9am–5pm.* ✗ ▯ *www.sepaq.com* ☏ *418-782-2240.* In summer the Île Bonaventure is home to some 70,000 **gannets** that nest in the ledges and crevices of the 90m/1,259ft cliffs on the east side of the island. This sanctuary is considered the largest colony of gannets in North America. Other seabirds found here are kittiwakes, murres, puffins, razorbills, guillemots, cormorants and gulls.

The **boat trip** to Île Bonaventure takes visitors past Percé Rock and then around the island *(depart from Percé wharf late-May–mid-Oct daily 8am–5pm; May–mid-June & mid-Sept–mid-Oct daily 9am–4pm; round trip 1hr 15min; commentary; reservations required; $20;* ☐ ▯ *Les Bateliers de Percé Inc.* ☏ *418-782-2974).* In summer, passengers can disembark on the island for a closer look at the birds and walk along the nature trails.

Île PERROT

Montérégie
Population 9,178
Map p 174

Located at the confluence of the Ottawa and St. Lawrence Rivers, this tranquil island is 11km/7mi long by 5km/3mi wide. In 1672, it was granted to **François-Marie Perrot**, the governor of Montreal and a captain in the Auvergne Regiment, who had married a niece of Intendant Jean Talon a few years earlier. Perrot used the island's strategic location as a base for illegal trade in liquor and furs with the Amerindians.

It was not until 1703, when Joseph Trottier, Sieur Desruisseaux, acquired the land, that clearing and tilling began. Trottier built a manor house and a windmill *(moulin)* on the estate, known thenceforth as the Domain of Pointe-du-Moulin.

Today the island is a pleasant stopover on the route from Montreal to Toronto or Ottawa.

Access – *Île Perrot is about 45km/28mi west of Montreal by Rte. 20 (Exit 38).*

VISIT

★**Église Sainte-Jeanne-de-Chantal (Church of St. Jeanne of Chantal)** – *Rue de l'Église. Visit by guided tour (30min) only, July & Aug. Mon–Fri by appointment, 10am–5pm, weekends 9am–5pm. Rest of the year by appointment.* ☐ ▯ *http://pages.infinit.net/eglisejc* ☏ *514-453-2125.* Erected during the latter half of the 18C, this little stone church stands on the southern half of the island, in the Village-sur-le-Lac secteur. The view of the church's exterior from the cemetery evokes an image of old and rural Quebec. The elegant interior was decorated between 1812 and 1830 by Joseph Turcaut and Louis-Xavier Leprohon, two sculptors of the Quévillon school. From the church, the **view** over Lake Saint-Louis is splendid.

★**Parc historique Pointe-du-Moulin (Pointe-du-Moulin Historic Park)** – *2500 Blvd. Don Quichotte. Open mid-May–Aug daily dawn–dusk. Sept–early Oct weekends dawn–dusk.* ☐ ▯ *www.pointedumoulin.com* ☏ *514-453-5936.* This park, at the eastern end of Île Perrot, covers about 12ha/30 acres and encompasses the location of Joseph Trottier's manor house (now destroyed). The lovely site juts out into the water, offering sweeping **views** of Lake Saint-Louis and of Montreal in the distance. On clear days, the Adirondacks are visible to the southwest. Picnic sites dot the grounds, amid winding paths.

An **interpretation centre** *(open same hours as the park)* near the park entrance features displays and films *(15min)* tracing the history of the estate, and describing the seigneurial system and traditional 18C farming methods. Activities such as crafts demonstrations, theatrical productions and concerts are offered on weekends in summer.

At the extreme tip of the park stands Trottier's stone **windmill** (about 1705), which has been rebuilt and is in full working order. The entire upper section of the mill can be revolved with a pole, enabling the broad sails to catch the wind from any direction. On windy summer Sundays, the mechanisms are put into operation, offering an extraordinary view of the ingenious 18C processes involved in harnessing the wind to mill grain. The stone walls are pierced with loopholes, as the mill also served as a fortification in the 18C.

The **miller's house** stands nearby. Built about 1785, it contains displays on traditional family life in New France (cooking and baking, dress, furniture and architecture).

QUEBEC CITY★★★

Population 167,264
Map pp 258-259

Built atop a rocky promontory jutting into the St. Lawrence River, Canada's oldest city has delighted visitors for centuries. Today dominated by the imposing mass of the Château Frontenac, Quebec City has retained its historic character and Old World charm, presenting a mélange of fortifications, narrow cobblestone alleys, and elegant residences, all reflecting the city's traditional role as a military and administrative centre. The slender spires of numerous churches dot the skyline, attesting to the French colony's religious origins. Quebec's distinctive French flavour is enhanced by fine restaurants, outdoor cafés and a lively nightlife. In 1985, the city became the first urban centre in North America to be inscribed on UNESCO's World Heritage List.

Historical Notes

Birthplace of New France – Perched on a promontory at the confluence of the St. Charles and St. Lawrence Rivers, Quebec City draws its name from the Algonquian word *Kebec*, meaning "where the river narrows." In fact, the St. Lawrence is only 1km/.6mi wide at this point. Amerindian hunters and fishermen inhabited the area in the village of Stadacona long before the arrival of Europeans. In 1535, Jacques Cartier landed on the pristine shores and named the promontory "Cap Diamant" (Cape Diamond) for the precious stones he hoped to find here. Discovering only worthless minerals, Cartier soon abandoned the site.

After an exploratory voyage in 1603, Samuel de Champlain returned to New France in 1608 to establish a fur-trading post at Kebec. Champlain constructed a rudimentary wooden fortress, on the site of the church named Notre-Dame-des-Victoires. The structure, known as the **Habitation**, consisted of two main buildings, and served as fort, trading post and living quarters, and a garden. A second, larger U-shaped fortress was built on the same site in 1624. Champlain also established a fortification on the Cape Diamond heights and named it Château Saint-Louis.

In the 17C, the first settlers arrived in Quebec. Primarily craftsmen and merchants attracted to the profitable fur trade, they erected houses in the Lower Town, which became the centre of commercial activity. Seeking protection offered by the fortifications, the colonial government and numerous religious institutions settled in the Upper Town. Reluctant to divide up land plots in the Upper Town, the institutions effectively halted development on Cape Diamond for over a century. The Lower Town remained the main residential and commercial centre until the mid-19C.

Strategic Location – Quebec City's location enhanced its development as the political, administrative and military centre of New France. Towering 98m/321ft above sea level, the Cape Diamond promontory provided the colony with a strategic military location, thereby earning the sobriquet "Gibraltar of America." From this naturally fortified area, the French repelled successive attacks by the Iroquois and by the British. In 1629, the settlement was captured by British conquerors, the **Kirke Brothers**, and retaken by the French in 1632. In 1690, it was besieged unsuccessfully by the British **Admiral Phips**. Hostility between the small French colony and Britain escalated during the 18C, culminating in the Battle of the Plains of Abraham that precipitated the Conquest of 1759. Following the Treaty of Paris in 1763, Quebec City, the former capital of the French colony, assumed a new role as capital of the British dominion.

Château Frontenac and Lower Town

Economic growth – Situated on the north shore of the St. Lawrence, the town quickly assumed a dominant position as port of entry and exit for ocean-bound vessels carrying goods, travellers and immigrants to North America. During the 18C and 19C, the Old Port became the transit point for trade of raw materials needed by Britain. The loading of fur, cereal and wood cargoes destined for foreign shores, the unloading of goods imported from France, the Antilles, England and Scotland, and a major shipbuilding industry all contributed to the feverish activity along the shores of the St. Lawrence.

Expansion of the lumber trade with Britain, after Napoleon's embargo in the early 19C, enabled Quebec City to maintain a competitive position with Montreal until the mid-19C. Then the trade in raw timber, super-

Quebec Winter Carnival

seded by lumber, declined, and Quebec City gradually lost its position as centre of production and trade in New France.

Competition from railroad companies located on the south shore of the St. Lawrence increased, and the impact of technological development in oceangoing vessels, enabling them to bypass the city and sail to Montreal, contributed to the city's decline. In addition, the section of the St. Lawrence between the two cities was dredged, allowing larger ships passage. A sudden decrease in demand for wooden ships hastened the demise of the large shipbuilding industry.

To remedy the situation, Quebec City tried to attract various railroad companies, and built the Quebec City bridge to establish a rail link between the northern and southern shores, all to no avail. After 1850, Montreal became the centre of trade, finance, and industry, engendering a westward shift of population and economy. Quebec City experienced a short period of expansion with the footwear industry in the 1920s. However, most jobs today are related to public administration, defence, and the service sector.

Population – Prior to the Conquest, the town's population was made up of French settlers. The influx of British and Irish immigrants in the early 19C led to an increase in the anglophone population, which numbered 41 percent in 1851, and reached 51 percent by 1861. Following Quebec City's economic decline, the population shift westward decreased the number of anglophones to 31.5 percent in 1871, and 10 percent in 1921. In 1996, anglophones accounted for 1.85 percent of Quebec City's residents, thereby affirming the city's distinct francophone character.

Quebec City Today – Throughout the centuries, Quebec City has retained its role as a capital city and as a bastion of French culture. The colonial French city is much more in evidence here than in Montreal. In the past twenty-five years, the growth of the provincial government has given the city a new boost, and a bustling metropolis has developed outside the old walls. In contrast to the modern cities of North America, Quebec City has retained a cachet reminiscent of Old World capitals.

PRACTICAL INFORMATION ....Area Code: 418

Getting There

By Air – **Jean-Lesage** International Airport: 16km/10mi *(approximately 20min)* from downtown by shuttle bus *($9)* or taxi *($25)*. Airport information ☏ 640-2600.

Gare du Palais, roof detail

By Train – Gare du Palais: 450 Rue de la Gare-du-Palais; Gare de Sainte-Foy: 3255 Chemin de la Gare; Gare de Lévis: 5595 Rue Saint-Laurent. Information ☏ 692-3940.

By Bus – Gare du Palais Terminal: 320 Rue Abraham-Martin; Sainte-Foy Terminal: 925 Ave. de Roche-Belle. Information ☏ 525-3000.

Getting Around

Public Transportation – Local bus service is provided by Société de transport de la communauté urbaine de Québec (STCUQ) ☏ 627-2511. Buses operate from 5:30am–1am. Tickets may be purchased in local tobacco shops & newsstands *($1.75)* or on board the bus *($2.25)*. Day passes are also available *($4.70/day)*.

Cars – Rental car companies: Avis ☏ 872-2861; Budget ☏ 872-9885; Hertz ☏ 694-1224; National-Tilden ☏ 683-9000; Thrifty-Québec ☏ 877-2870. Streets are narrow and congested in the Old Town, Upper and Lower; it is easiest and most pleasant to visit these areas on foot. Visitors may wish to park in one of the city's designated parking areas. To find parking locations (indicated by the ℙ symbol), refer to the maps on *pp 232-233* and *240-241*.

Taxis – Taxis Coop Québec ☏ 525-5191; Taxis Québec ☏ 522-2001; Taxis Coop Sainte-Foy Sillery ☏ 653-7777.

General Information

Tourist Information – **Tourisme Quebec:** 12 Rue Sainte-Anne; open mid-Jun–Labour Day daily 8:30am–7:30pm, rest of the year daily 9am–5pm ☏ 514-873-2015 or 800-363-7777 *(from Quebec & the US)*. **Greater Quebec Area Tourism & Convention Bureau:** 835 Ave. Wilfrid-Laurier; open Jun–Thanksgiving Day daily 8:30am–7:30pm, rest of the year 9am–5pm; ☏ 649-2608.

Accommodations – Information: Greater Quebec Area Tourism & Convention Bureau ☏ 649-2608.

Local Press – English: *The Chronicle-Telegraph*. French: *Le Journal de Québec*, *Le Soleil*.

Post Office – Open Mon–Fri 8am–5:45pm. Main Branch: 300 Rue Saint-Paul ☏ 694-6175; Upper Town: 3 Rue Buade ☏ 694-6102.

The city's main event is its famous winter **Carnival.** Held in February, this festival attracts thousands of visitors. For ten joyous days, Quebec City bustles with festivities that include a great parade, the construction of a magnificent ice palace, an ice sculpture contest, and canoe races over the partially frozen St. Lawrence. The activities are overseen by an enormous snowman, nicknamed Bonhomme Carnaval.

Currency Exchange Offices: ☎
Caisse populaire Desjardins (Old Quebec) – 19 Rue des Jardins   694-1774
Caisse populaire Laurier (Sainte-Foy) – 2600 Blvd. Laurier   658-4870
Montreal Currency Exchange – 12 Rue Sainte-Anne   694-1014
Montreal Currency Exchange – 46 Rue du Petit-Champlain   694-0011
Transchange Inc. – 43 Rue Buade and 8 Rue du Trésor   694-6906

Useful Numbers   ☎

Police–Ambulance–Fire (emergency calls)   911

Directory Assistance   411

Brunet Drugstore (daily 24hrs/day)   623-1571

Tourisme Québec   514-873-2015

Canadian Automobile Association (CAA)   624-0708

Road conditions   514-284-2363

Weather (24hrs/day)   648-7766

Entertainment – For current entertainment schedules, consult the free tourist publications *Québec Scope, Voilà Québec,* and *Voir* (French), or review the arts and entertainment section of the newspapers (weekend editions). Tickets for major entertainment or sports events may be purchased at the venue or through the following: **Billetech** ☎ 643-8131; **La Baie** department stores (two locations in Quebec City, one in Sainte-Foy). Most major credit cards accepted.

Sports – **Ice Hockey:** The Rafales de Québec (International Hockey League), season from Sept–Mar at the Québec Coliseum ☎ 691-7211. The Ramparts de Québec (Junior League), season from Sept–Mar at PEPS Laval University, Sainte-Foy ☎ 656-2131. **Harness Racing:** Québec Hippodrôme, Parc de l'Exposition ☎ 524-5283.

Shopping and Dining – The following streets lend themselves well to strolling, window-shopping, and to discovering a good restaurant: Saint-Jean, Saint-Louis, Saint-Paul and Sainte-Anne, Petit-Champlain quarter, Côte de la Fabrique and Grande Allée.

Address Book

Staying in Quebec City

The accommodations listed below have been chosen for their location, character, or value for money. Rates are for a standard room, double occupancy in high season, not including taxes; some hotels offer lower weekend rates. Rates may vary widely according to season. The ⚊ symbol indicates a swimming pool on the premises.

$$$$	$200-$300	$$	$75-$125
$$$	$125-$200	$	under $75

Le Château Frontenac – *1 Rue des Carrières.* ✕ ♿ ⚊ 🅿 ☎ *418-692-3861, 800-441-1414. www.cphotels.ca. 603 rooms.* **$$$$** *(See entry heading).* Built in 1892, the regal copper-roofed château towers above Old Québec as one of the most enduring symbols of the city. Over the years, this grande dame has hosted the likes of Queen Elizabeth and Winston Churchill. The bustling lobby lined with elaborate wood paneling reflects the opulence of those bygone days. Well-appointed rooms vary in size, shape and view, according to price. Amenities include a large gym, as well as baby-sitting and limousine service.

L'Hôtel Dominion 1912 – *126 Rue St-Pierre.* ♿ 🅿 ☎ *418-692-2224, 1-888-833-5253. www.hoteldominion.com 40 rooms.* **$$$$** Located in a nine-storey commercial building constructed in 1912 for Dominion Fish and Fruit, Ltd., this boutique hotel sits in the heart of the Old Port district. Stained glass and ironwork highlight the exquisitely decorated lobby and reading room. Natural light floods the spacious, high-ceilinged rooms through tall windows, and goose-down duvets and pillows wrap guests in comfort. Rate includes continental breakfast.

Auberge Saint-Antoine – *10 Rue St-Antoine.* ♿ 🅿 ☏ *418-692-2211, 1-888-692-2211. www.saint-antoine.com. 31 rooms.* **$$$$** A renovated 1822 warehouse and an adjoining 1720's English merchant's house now compose one of the city's finest small hotels. Rooms and suites-many with the original stone walls and hand-hewn beams-are individually decorated, ranging from the feminine floral prints and rosy hues of the Rosalind Room to the sleek contemporary furnishings of the James Bond 007 Suite. Rate includes a buffet breakfast.

Château Bonne Entente – *3400 Chemin Ste-Foy, Ste-Foy.* ✗ ♿ 🅿 ☏ *418-653-5221, 1-800-463-4390. www.chateaubonneentente.com. 150 rooms.* **$$$** Occupying a wooded site convenient to both Old Quebec and the airport, the Bonne Entente offers the charms of a country inn while supplying the amenities of a modern hotel. Pamper yourself with a full range of massages and other spa services at the Health & Fitness Centre, then settle into an overstuffed chair in front of the fireplace in the cozy Tea Room, where tea and petit-fours are served each afternoon. Guest rooms boast distinct décor; family suites feature bunk beds and toys for the kids.

L'Hôtel du Vieux Québec – *1190 Rue St-Jean.* ✗ ♿ 🅿 ☏ *418-692-1850, 1-800-361-7787. www.hvq.com. 41 rooms.* **$$$** A good bet for families and student groups, this carefully restored century-old brick hotel in the Latin Quarter boasts recently renovated rooms with sofas – and some with kitchenettes. Free guided walking tours of Old Quebec are offered in July and August.

Hôtel Particulier Belley – *249 Rue St-Paul.* ✗ ♿ 🅿 ☏ *418-692-1694. 8 rooms.* **$$** Old World charm in the form of brick walls and exposed beams, coupled with a great location in the Vieux Port, make for a comfortable and reasonably priced stay here. Simply decorated rooms rest above **The Tavern Belley**, one of the city's most popular local hangouts. Apartments located across the street are also available for rent.

Brrrrr – Quebec City plays host to the first **ice hotel** in North America (second in the world after Jukkasjarvi, Sweden). Scheduled opening January 2001. *For more information:* ☏ *418-692-4499 (30) www.icehotel-canada.com.*

Centre international de Séjour de Québec – *19 Rue Ste-Ursule.* ♿ ☏ *418-694-0755, 1-800-461-8585. www.tourismej.qc.ca.* **$** Located within the walls of the Old City, this youth hostel is a member of Hostelling International. Open year-round, it offers 240 beds with individual rooms accommodating two to eight people. A cafeteria and kitchen are available on site.

Dining in Quebec City

The establishments below were selected for their character, location or value for money. Prices indicate the average cost of an appetizer, entrée (main course) and dessert for one person (not including tax and tip, beverages or alcoholic drinks). Call for hours of operation and reservation requirements.

$$$$ =over $50   **$$$** = $35-$50   **$$** =$20-$35   **$** =under $20

Le Champlain – *1 Rue des Carrières.* ♿ 🅿 ☏ *418-692-3861.* **$$$$** French/Quebecois. Chef Jean Soular constantly strives to create new dishes that celebrate produce from the *terroir* (region). A waitstaff dressed in period costume lends conviviality to the princely décor. A fine wine list complements signature dishes that include *roulade de ris de veau* (veal sweetbreads), *filet de sanglier* (wild boar filet), and *foie gras en crépine* (goose liver wrapped in caul).

★★★ ① BASSE-VILLE (LOWER TOWN)

Historical Notes

The Lower Town began in the early 17C as a fur-trading post, established by Champlain on the area around his "Habitation." In 1636, the year following Champlain's death, the first city plans were drawn up. Between 1650 and 1662, more than 35 parcels of land were conceded to merchants who began constructing shops and residences around the Habitation and its adjoining square, then called the Market Place (place du marché). Limited space in the Lower Town inspired the residents to fill in parts of the shore northeast of the square and erect wharves along present-day Rue Saint-Pierre.

In August 1682 a fire devastated the Lower Town. As a result of this disaster, building standards, such as the use of stone rather than wood, were imposed on new constructions, giving rise to the simple stone box construction visible throughout the quarter today.

Café du Monde

Le Continental – *26 Rue St-Louis.* ♿ 🅿 ☎ *418-694-9995.* **$$$ Continental**. One of the oldest restaurants in the city, this local favorite near Château Frontenac serves up classic continental specialties such as rack of lamb and orange duckling as well as seafood and steak. Professional service prevails in the dining room, where dark blue walls and wood paneling impart a simple elegance.

Le Café du Monde – *57 Rue Dalhousie.* ♿ ☎ *418-692-4455.* **$$ French**. A menu featuring *steak frites* (steak and fries), *magret de canard* (breast of duck) and *moules* (mussels) can only mean you've landed in the popular Parisian-style bistro. Gregarious waiters in white aprons and a cozy atmosphere make for a pleasant-and tasty-dining experience.

47ᵉ Parallèle – *24 Rue Ste-Anne.* ☎ *418-692-1534.* **$$ International**. Surrounded by a kaleidoscope of contrasting colors at this vibrant restaurant, you can sample regional dishes from around the world. Selections on the changing menu may include grilled medallions of European fallow deer, Morroccan lamb curry on vegetable couscous or alligator from a Louisiana bayou. Here, the world truly is your oyster.

Portofino – *54 Rue Couillard.* 🅿 ☎ *418-692-8888.* **$$ Italian**. In this boisterous trattoria you can choose from more than 20 varieties of homemade pasta and 30 different wood-fired pizzas, complimented by a good list of Italian wines. Throw in the noise level of a good time and the flags of popular Italian soccer teams and even the most reticent in your party will soon be singing "Amore."

La Playa – *780 Rue St-Jean.* ☎ *418-522-3989.* **$$ Creole**. Latin, Cajun and Thai flavors pepper La Playa's shrimp, fish and poultry specialties. To cool off from the spicy sauces, sip on one of the 60 exotically named martinis. In summer ask for a table on the terrace.

Les Épices du Szechwan – *215 Rue St-Jean.* ♿ ☎ *418-648-6440.* **$$ Chinese**. Located in an old house in the St-Jean-Baptiste district of Old Quebec, Les Épices offers good Chinese fare, which – true to its name – emphasizes the fiery spices typical of the Szechwan region in south-central China.

As commerce, shipbuilding and port activities grew, so did the prosperity of the community. After the Conquest, the English merchants and shipbuilders continued the expansion of the town, constructing numerous wharves along the banks of the St. Charles and St. Lawrence Rivers. Subsequently, the marshland between the different quays was filled in, and new streets, such as the Rue Saint-Paul, were created. By the 19C the area occupied by the Lower Town had doubled in size. Port activity declined after 1860, severing the economic life line of the Lower Town and resulting in progressive deterioration of the buildings in the area over the next century. In 1967 the Quebec Government passed legislation to support restoration of Place Royale. The archaeological and restoration work began in 1970 and continues today. The Lower Town's commercial vocation still marks the area, as evidenced in the market squares, wharves, and warehouses.

Walking Tour *2.2km/1.4mi. Map p 232-233.*

Access – *From Dufferin Terrace, take the steep Frontenac stairway to the Lower Town. Follow Côte de la Montagne down the hill to the Casse-Cou stairway on the* *right descending to Rue du Petit-Champlain. A funicular (cable car) also connects Dufferin Terrace to the Lower Town (in service Jun–mid-Oct daily 8am–midnight; rest of the year daily 7:30am–11:30pm; $1.25; ☎ 418-692-1132).*

Begin the tour at Rue du Petit-Champlain.

Maison Louis-Jolliet (Louis-Jolliet House) – *16 Rue du Petit-Champlain.* Completed in 1683 according to plans by the French stonecutter and architect, Claude Baillif, this two-storey stone structure was owned by Louis Jolliet, who "discovered" the Mississippi River along with Father Jacques Marquette in 1673. Since 1879 the house has served as the lower station for the funicular linking the Upper and Lower Towns.

★**Verrerie la mailloche** (Economuseum of Glass) – *58 Rue Sous-le-Fort, at the intersection of Rue du Petit-Champlain. Visit by guided group tour ($3/person) Nov–mid-Jun; reservations required. Studio open Jun–Oct Wed–Sun 10am–4:30pm (demonstrations 10am–noon & 1pm–4:30pm); rest of the year Mon–Fri 10am–4:30pm (demonstrations 10am–noon & 1pm–4:30pm). Gift shop (enter by the Casse-Cou stairway) open Jun–Oct daily 9am–10pm; rest of the year daily 10am–5pm (Thu–Fri 9pm). Closed major holidays. www.lamailloche.qc.ca ☎ 418-694-0445.* This studio/museum introduces visitors to the fascinating art of glassblowing. Begin in the studio, where examples of beautiful, richly coloured glass are on view. Blowers can be seen at work here, carefully extracting molten glass from red-hot ovens and using a variety of tools to shape the formless lumps into vases, carafes, plates and cups. Panels describe the various stages of the process, and the blowers themselves willingly answer questions.

Second-floor galleries display a variety of glassware from different countries, including Italy, France and England; note also panels recounting the history of glassmaking from the third millenium B.C.

★**Rue du Petit-Champlain** – Extending along the foot of the cliff, this cobblestone pedestrian alley was developed in the 1680s. First known as Rue De Meulles, the street was renamed Rue du Petit-Champlain (Little Champlain Street) when the larger Boulevard Champlain, situated

> ### Petit-Champlain shopping
>
> This appealing area boasts all sorts of shops, many specialising in regional fine arts and crafts. Writing home? Try **L'Oiseau du Paradis** *(80 Rue du Petit-Champlain; ☎ 418-692-2679),* where the selection of fine, handmade papers includes cards, tablets and other writing materials as well as lamps and masks. Colourful silk scarves and ties are displayed in all their shimmering glory at **Soierie Huo** *(91 Rue du Petit-Champlain; ☎ 418-692-5920),* where you'll also find scarves of wool and chiffon. **La Dentellière** *(56 Blvd. Champlain; ☎ 418-692-2807)* stocks an impressive selection of imported laces as well as lovely handmade examples by Quebec craftswomen.

Shopping along Rue du Petit-Champlain

parallel to it along the river, was created during the 19C. The early wooden dwellings along the street were inhabited by craftsmen and labourers until the 19C, when Irish immigrants who found work associated with the port moved into the district. Much of the neighbourhood fell into decay in the early 20C as a result of the economic decline of the port. Recent restoration work carried out by a joint public and private effort has transformed the street into a festive district enlivened by restaurants, boutiques and art galleries.

At the end of Rue du Petit-Champlain, turn left onto Blvd. Champlain.

★**Maison Chevalier** (Chevalier House) – *Corner of Rue du Marché-Champlain and Blvd. Champlain. Open Jun 24–Oct daily 10am–5:30pm. Early May–Jun 23 Tue–Sun 10am–5:30pm. Nov–Apr weekends 10am–5pm.* ♿ 🅿 *($10) www.mcq.org* ☎ *418-643-2158.* This three-storey stone building occupies the site of the **Cul-de-Sac**, a natural port discovered by Champlain in 1603. The King's shipyards, originally established at the mouth of the St. Charles River, were moved here in 1745, but its presence was short-lived. The basin was filled in during the mid-18C in an effort to enlarge the area of the Lower Town.

The imposing structure is composed of three separate buildings. The west wing was built in 1752 for the wealthy merchant and shipowner Jean-Baptiste Chevalier. The construction was so solid that the walls and foundation withstood bombardment by the British in 1759. However, the house was destroyed by fire and rebuilt in 1762. Throughout the 19C, the mansion was known as the London Coffee House, a choice inn frequented by the city's money-eyed class.

Acquired by the Quebec Government in 1956 to serve as part of the Museum of Civilization, the Chevalier House underwent extensive interior renovations, and now features exhibits on traditional Quebec architecture and furniture.

Continue to the corner of Rue du Marché-Champlain and Boulevard Champlain to enjoy the superb **view**★ of the imposing Château Frontenac, looming over the Lower Town.

Return to the Chevalier House; turn right on Rue Notre-Dame and right on Rue Sous-le-Fort.

> ● **Le Cochon Dingue**
>
> *46 Blvd. Champlain.* ☎ *418-692-2013.* One of Old Quebec's most inviting eateries sports an attractive façade of stone pierced by large windows. Friendly service and a relaxed ambience enhance the savoury bistro food, especially steak-and-fries (the house specialty), mussels and tempting desserts. Breakfast is also served daily.

Batterie Royale (Royal Battery) – *At the end of Rue Sous-le-Fort and Rue Saint-Pierre. Open daily year-round.* ♿ ☎ *418-643-6631.* Constructed in 1691 at the request of Louis XIV, King of France, this thick, four-sided earthen rampart formed part of the fortifications designed to strengthen Quebec City's defences against the British. Situated at the edge of the river, the battery suffered from the elements and was frequently in need of repair. Destroyed during the Conquest, the defence was not rebuilt. Instead, the British erected two warehouses and a wharf on the site. The royal battery was gradually buried and forgotten until two centuries later, when archaeologists excavating the area unearthed it in 1972. Today this historic rampart has been reconstructed, and replicas of 18C cannons are positioned in ten of the eleven embrasures; the eleventh was left empty, because any gun set at such an angle, if ever it was fired, would have destroyed buildings along Rue Saint-Pierre. During the summer, interpretive programs here demostrate the operation of cannons during the French Regime.

Turn right on Rue Saint-Pierre, then left on Ruelle de la Place, which leads to Place Royale.

> ● **Boutique Métiers d'Art**
>
> *29 Rue Notre-Dame.* ☎ *418-694-0267.* Specialising in the work of Quebec artisans, this little boutique features a broad selection of art objects – many of them truly unique – incorporating an enormous variety of materials. At the rear of the gallery you'll find lovely glass sculptures, ceramics, delicate works in blown glass and leaded-glass windows in vibrant colours.

★★**Place Royale** – This charming cobblestone square occupies the former site of the garden of Champlain's "Habitation." As the town developed around the fortress, a market appeared on the site. The square was known as "place Royale" after the Intendant Champigny erected a bust of Louis XIV on the site in 1686. The area flourished and became the hub of the city's economic activity until the mid-19C, when the port fell into decline.

In 1928, the French Government offered a bronze bust of Louis XIV (**1**) (a copy of Bernini's original 1665 marble sculpture conserved at Versailles) to the City of Quebec as part of that city's program to reaffirm its French heritage. However, through fear of offending the anglophone population in the city, the monument was not erected until 1948.

★Église Notre-Dame-des-Victoires (Church of Our Lady of the Victories) – *Open May–mid-Oct Mon–Sat 9am–5pm, Sun 1pm–5pm. Rest of the year Mon–Sat 10am–4pm, Sun 1pm–4pm.* ☎ *418-692-1650.* Built between 1688 and 1723, this stone edifice topped by a single spire stands on the site of Champlain's "Habitation." Built as an auxiliary chapel of Quebec City's main cathedral, it served the congregation of the Lower Town. Like most of the buildings in this part of the city, it was destroyed during the Conquest and rebuilt soon after.

The church was named in thanksgiving for two successful occasions on which Quebec City resisted the sieges of the British. Frescoes adorning the choir recall these victories: one in 1690, during which Admiral Phips' fleet was defeated by the troops of the Count de Frontenac, and the other in 1711, when most of Admiral Walker's fleet was shipwrecked during a storm. The model ship suspended in the nave represents the *Brézé*, a 17C vessel that transported French troops to Quebec.

To the left of the reliquary in the left side chapel hangs a painting of St. Genevieve (1865) by Théophile Hamel. Located above the high altar, the magnificent **retable** (1878, David Ouellet) represents the fortified city.

Leave Place Royale by Rue Notre-Dame.

Parc La Cetière (La Cetière Park) – Archaeological excavations undertaken here in 1972 revealed the remains of foundations from structures dating back to 1685. Destroyed during the Conquest, the five stone houses of the block were rebuilt on the same foundations. However, a fire in 1948 and another in 1957 levelled the area. In the scant ruins exposed in the park, it is possible to distinguish an internal partition wall of one dwelling and a chimney base and vent opening of another.

Take Rue du Porche and turn right on Rue Thibaudeau.

Place de Paris – To supplement the needs of the Lower Town's growing population, several market places developed near the one on Place Royale *(above).* Occupying a strategic position near the St. Lawrence, the prosperous Finlay market (1817) stood on this square until the early 1950s. Today, a contemporary sculpture entitled *Dialogue with History* (**2**) marks the centre of the vast, open square. Quebecers have nicknamed it "the colossus of Quebec." A gift from the city of Paris, the sculpture, by the French artist Jean-Pierre Raynaud, was conceived to be viewed in conjunction with the bust of Louis XIV, positioned along the same axis on Place Royale; it represents the dialogue between the present-day population (symbolized by a mass) and the absolute monarch (the bust). The **Place Royale Interpretation Centre** *(27 Rue Notre-Dame; open Jun 24–Oct 22 daily 10am–5:30pm; rest of the year Tue–Sun 10am–5pm; $3. www.mcq.org* ☎ *418-646-3167)* is located in the former home (1682)f of the successful merchant François Hazeur. A map of New France in 1688 and objects recovered from archaeological digs beneath the square bear witness to 400 years of history of this area. Multimedia presentations, exhibitions, a discovery space and guided visits help you relive history.

Leave the square by turning left on Rue Dalhousie, then turn left on Côte de la Montagne and right on Rue Saint-Pierre.

★Rue Saint-Pierre – During the 19C, this busy thoroughfare developed as Quebec's principal financial district. Numerous banks and insurance companies established their headquarters near or along this street. Among the noteworthy commercial buildings that have been preserved are the **National Bank** *(no. 71),* built by J.-F. Peachy in 1862; the former **Molson Bank** *(no. 105),* now occupied by the local post office; and the **Imperial Bank of Canada** *(nos. 113-115),* which dates from 1913. Between Rues Saint-Antoine and Saint-Jacques, note the low porte cochère of the Estèbe House, part of the Museum of Civilization. The former **Hochelaga Bank** *(no. 132)* stands next to the **Dominion Building** *(no. 126),* Quebec City's first skyscraper. Dominating the corner of Rues Saint-Paul and Saint-Pierre, the **Canadian Bank of Commerce** *(139 Rue Saint-Pierre)* exemplifies the Beaux-Arts style in vogue at the turn of the century.

Turn left and continue along Rue Saint-Paul.

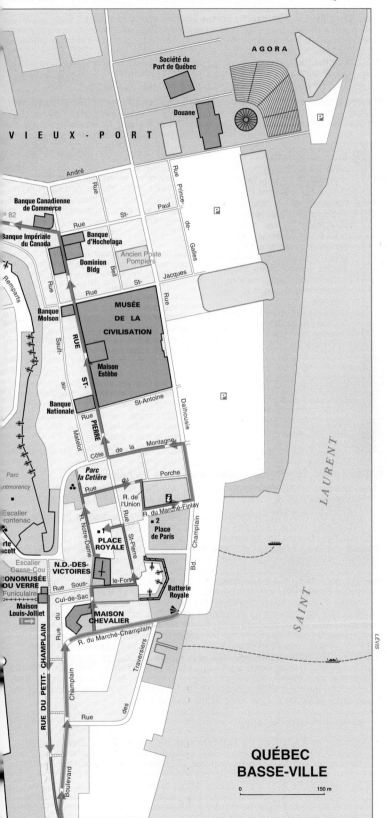

AGORA

Société du
Port de Québec

Douane

V I E U X - P O R T

André

Rue

Rue St-
Paul

Rue Prince-
de-
Galles

Banque Canadienne
de Commerce

° 82

Rue

Banque
d'Hochelaga

Banque Impériale
du Canada

Dominion
Bldg

Ancien Poste
Pompiers

Rue

Bell

St-

Remparts

Rue

RUE

Banque
Molson

Sault-

MUSÉE
DE LA
CIVILISATION

Rue

Jacques

St-

ST-

Maison
Estèbe

Banque
Nationale

Rue

PIERRE

au-

Matelot

Côte

St-Antoine

de la Montagne

Dalhousie

Parc
la Cetière

Rue

du

Porche

Montmorency

R. de
l'Union

R. du Marché-Finlay

Escalier
Frontenac

R. Notre-Dame

Rue

■ 1
PLACE
ROYALE

St-Pierre

■ 2
Place
de Paris

Champlain

Porte
Prescott

Escalier
Casse-Cou

N.D.-DES-
VICTOIRES

le-Fort

CONOMUSÉE
DU VERRE

Funiculaire

Rue

Sous-

Batterie
Royale

Maison
Louis-Jolliet

Cul-de-Sac

MAISON
CHEVALIER

du

RUE DU PETIT-
CHAMPLAIN

R. du Marché-Champlain

Traversiers

Champlain

Rue

des

Boulevard

S A I N T

L A U R E N T

LÉVIS

QUÉBEC
BASSE-VILLE

0   150 m

★**Rue Saint-Paul** – Built directly on the wharves of the St. Charles River in 1816, this portion of Rue Saint-Paul was widened in 1906. At that time, every building was demolished and replaced, with the exception of the old Renaud warehouse *(no. 82)*, which had been built in a slightly recessed spot in 1875. Most of the houses on the south side of the street date back to 1850 and have been converted into antique shops, art galleries and charming restaurants.

Turn right on Rue des Navigateurs and left on Rue Saint-André.

★**Centre d'interprétation du Vieux-Port-de-Québec (Old Port of Quebec Interpretation Centre)** – *100 Rue Saint-André on Louise Basin. Open early May–Sept 3 daily 10am–5pm. Sept 4–early Oct 1pm–5pm. Rest of the year by appointment. $3.*   *www.parkscanada.gc.ca/vieuxport*   *418-648-3300.* Housed in a former cement works near the bank of the St. Lawrence, this fascinating interpretation centre offers an excellent look at the importance of the timber and shipbuilding industries and the prominent place of Quebec as a port city during the 19C. On the ground floor, a diorama recreates the bustle of the wharves lining the banks of the St. Charles River during that period. Exhibits on the upper floors describe the processes involved in the logging and shipbuilding industries and explore the lives of the people of the time. Visitors can follow a log of wood as it is chopped in the forest, stored and prepared for export. Mannequins dressed in 19C costumes represent the workers who made the economic prosperity of the period possible. Several films on the port are shown in the activity room *(atelier d'animation)*. The glassed-in terrace on the top floor serves as an excellent **viewpoint** for observing modern port activities; the view onto Lower Town from here is superb. Across the basin, the cylindrical towers of the Reed Paper Mill (1927) dominate the waterfront.

Return to Rue Saint-Paul by Rue Rioux.

Build an appetite ...

After a long day of sightseeing, relax over a tasty meal in one of the Lower Town's inviting restaurants. **L'Ardoise** *(71 Rue Saint-Paul ; 418-694-0213)* bistro will win you over instantly with its cheerful combination of dark woods, wicker chairs and rustic stone. The service is friendly and the food is delicious – try one of the excellent fish dishes.
Or, stop in for breakfast. Located near the Museum of Civilization, **L'Échaudé** *(73 Rue Sault-au-Matelot; 418-692-1299)* serves a tempting variety of beautifully prepared and presented meat, fish and poultry dishes as well as salads. The service is always attentive, even when there's a crowd.

★★ Musée de la civilisation (Museum of Civilization)

Main entrance on 85 Rue Dalhousie. Open Jun 24–Labour Day daily 10am–7pm. Rest of the year Tue–Sun 10am–5pm. $7. ✗ & 🔲 *www.mcq.org 418-643-2158.*

Occupying the entire block between Rues Saint-Antoine and de la Barricade, the award-winning structure by the prominent architect, **Moshe Safdie** – acclaimed for his Habitat complex in Montreal and for the National Gallery of Canada in Ottawa – opened in the fall of 1988. Topped by a copper roof pierced by stylized dormers, the edifice consists of two sleek, angular masses of limestone accentuated by a glass campanile. Between the buildings, a monumental staircase leads to a terrace overlooking the **Estèbe House** (Maison Estèbe), a 1752 stone structure preserved and integrated into the museum as a reminder of the bond between past and present. Inside the spacious entrance hall note *La Débâcle*, a massive sculpture representing ice breaking up in spring, by the Montreal artist Astri Reusch.

The museum's stated purpose is to present life and culture in an open and objective manner in order to encourage the visitor to examine his or her own traditions and values with respect to those of other cultures and civilizations. The museum's collection comprises some 240,000 objects and documents in several divisions (costumes and textiles, arts, ethnology, etc.). In addition to permanent exhibits illustrating such themes as thought, language, natural resources, the human body and society, the museum organises eight to ten temporary exhibits throughout the year, some of which are mounted at the Chevalier House.

■ Rue Sous-le-Cap

Situated at the foot of the Cape Diamant rock, this narrow alley provided the only link between the Place Royale area and the smaller Faubourg Saint-Nicolas, located to the north, until the 19C. Before the development of Rue Saint-Paul, the houses that now face that artery were turned towards Rue Sous-le-Cap. Because the cramped design of the building made it impossible to build staircases inside the houses, outside sheds were constructed and connected to the main houses by footbridges spanning the street. These bridges are maintained by the owners.

Mémoires (Memories) – Second floor, hall 3A. Inspired by the impact of the past on Quebec's society today, this insightful presentation provides an opportunity for citizens to become reacquainted with their roots and for visitors from outside Quebec to understand the culture of the province. The objects presented evoke, with some nostalgia, the life of the French since their arrival here four centuries ago and their struggles to build a new life in an unknown land. Reminders of both happy and sad times span the emotions associated with the past. The journey ends with questions about the future.

Nous, les premières nations (Encounter with the First Nations) – *Second floor, hall 4A.* This emotion-based exhibit documents the history and culture of the eleven First Nations who inhabit Quebec. Inuit art, ceremonial costumes, canoes, Atikamekw and Algonquin crafted bark baskets, hunting and fishing implements and Huron and Micmac ornamental baskets help visitors explore themes such as personal and collective identity and historical and contemporary perspectives on territory, autonomy and traditional ways of life. The visit ends with interviews and legend-telling with members of the First Nations by film-maker Arthur Lamothe and internet stations for exploring Aboriginal sites.

★Vieux-Port (Old Port)

Access at the corner of Rues Dalhousie and Saint-André.

Covering an area of 33ha/81.5 acres, the port installations are located around the Pointe à Carcy where the St. Charles River joins the St. Lawrence. From the settlement of the colony until the mid-19C, the port played a major role in the development of Canada. Imported goods, exported furs and timber, and thousands of immigrants passed through this harbour. Activity declined in the second half of the 19C, and the port fell into disrepair.

In the mid-1980s, a revitalization project financed by the federal government changed the face of the old port with the creation of the **Agora**★ complex, which includes an open-air amphitheatre built between the St. Lawrence and the Customs House, and a wide boardwalk along the river. A marina for several hundred pleasure boats complements the former maritime hub.

Édifice de la Douane (Customs House) – *2 Rue Saint-André.* Overlooking the St. Lawrence, the majestic Neoclassical structure (1860) was designed by the English architect William Thomas. Cut stone masks and masonry dressing ornament the ground floor windows.

Fire ravaged the interior of the Customs House in 1864, and again in 1909, destroying the upper level and the dome. The door knocker on the main entrance originally hung on the first English Customs House established in Canada in 1793 in Quebec City. The building was completely restored between 1979 and 1981 and is still occupied by the administrative offices of the Customs Service.

Société du port de Québec (Port of Quebec Building) – *Rue Saint-André.* Designed by local architect Thomas R. Peacock, the building (1914) stands on the site where, in 1909, a fire destroyed a grain elevator and also damaged the Customs House.

★★★ 2 HAUTE-VILLE (UPPER TOWN)

Historical Notes

Originally described as an "inhospitable rock, permanently unfit for habitation," the massive Cape Diamond was the site of Champlain's strategic Fort Saint-Louis (1620), built in the centre of a staked enclosure. Enlarged in 1629 and renamed **Château Saint-Louis**, the modest wood structure was replaced by a single-storey building in 1692. At the request of the Count of Frontenac, it became the official residence of the governor of the colony. Rebuilt after sustaining severe damage during the Conquest, the edifice was razed by fire in 1834.

The Upper Town was not developed until a group of wealthy merchants, the Company of One Hundred Associates *(Compagnie des Cent-Associés)*, decided to increase settlement in the colony. The land belonging to a handful of seigneurs was redistributed, and the parcels owned by religious institutions were reduced. The first efforts to urbanize the Upper Town were initiated under Governor Montmagny's administration (1636-1648). Though constrained by the hilly topography of the site, as well as the presence of vast lands belonging to institutions, Montmagny planned to erect a large, fortified city. The first houses appeared towards the end of the 17C, near the Place d'Armes and along Rue Saint-Louis. However, the Ursuline, Augustine and Jesuit Orders long refused to divide up their land plots, and the military opposed the construction of buildings near fortifications, thus halting any rapid development of the town. By the late 18C, the buildings still reflected the administrative and religious presence in the district.

During the 19C, a new and very elegant residential neighbourhood evolved along Rues Saint-Louis, Sainte-Ursule and d'Auteuil, and Avenues Sainte-Geneviève and Saint-Denis, to be surpassed only in 1880, by the Grande Allée. Today, the Upper Town forms the heart of Old Quebec (Vieux-Québec), and still functions as the city's administrative centre.

Walking Tour *2km/1.3mi. Map pp 240-241.*
Begin the tour at Place d'Armes.

★★ Place d'Armes – Located outside the confines of the Fort Saint-Louis, the square (1620) originally served as grounds for drill exercises and parades. With the building of the citadel in the early 1900s, Place d'Armes lost its military function and became a public park. Today, this lovely green square is bordered by prestigious buildings. At its centre is the **Monument de la Foi (1)** (Monument of Faith), a Gothic Revival sculpture (1916, David Ouellet) standing atop a fountain; it commemorates the third centennial of the arrival of the Récollet missionaries in Quebec (1615). The bas-reliefs represent the arrival, in 1615, of Father Dolbeau, the city's first priest, as well as the missionary work of the Récollets and the first mass celebrated by that order.

★★ Château Frontenac – Quebec City's most prominent landmark, the Château Frontenac Hotel is inextricably linked with the image of the old city. Named after Louis de Buade, Count de Frontenac, governor of New France (1672-1682, 1689-1698), the hotel stands on the site of the Château Haldimand, also known as the "Vieux Château." Built in 1786 for Governor Frederick Haldimand, it faced the Château Saint-Louis, which housed the administrative services and reception rooms of the colonial government. In 1880, as part of the numerous beautification projects planned by Lord Dufferin, the idea of building a luxury hotel on the site finally took root.

R. Corbel

Château Frontenac and Terrasse Dufferin

Bruce Price (1843-1903), who was selected by the Canadian Pacific Railway to design the hotel, found inspiration in the chateau-style architecture that was very much in favour in the city. The American architect adapted an initial design by Eugène-Étienne Taché. He chose a horseshoe plan and selected copper roofing that contrasted with the brick walls adorned with cut stone. The French chateau style thus acquired a distinctly Canadian flavour which, up until the 1940s, became the trademark of railway companies and of Canada, a nation whose existence is closely linked to the development of railways from east to west.

Upon its opening in 1893 following completion of the Riverview wing, the hotel was an instant success. The Citadel wing (1899) and the Mont-Carmel wing (1908), bordering the Governors' Garden, were added according to Price's plans. The Rue Saint-Louis wing was annexed a few years later. Between 1920 and 1924, an imposing tower was constructed, reinforcing the hotel's monumental appearance. With the recent addition of the beautifully integrated Claude Pratt wing (1993), the hotel boasts 610 rooms, 24 suites and 20 meeting rooms.

The hotel's architects adorned the monument with coats of arms and emblems. The coat of arms of the Count de Frontenac (chicken claws) can be seen above the porte-cochere leading to Rue Saint-Louis. Above the arch overlooking the courtyard is a stone engraved with the Maltese Cross; it is dated 1647 and was taken from Governor Montmagny's Château Saint-Louis. The interior was rebuilt after a fire in 1926. The entrance and reception halls, the Salon Verchères and the Champlain dining room are eloquent examples of the careful attention brought to the design of this jewel of Canadian architecture.

The prominence of Château Frontenac in the city's landscape can best be appreciated from high atop the citadel, from the Marie-Guyart Building observatory or from the Lévis terrace.

Continue along Rue Saint-Louis.

★**Ancien Palais de Justice (Old Courthouse)** – *12 Rue Saint-Louis.* Now housing the Ministry of Finance, this Second Empire-style building (1887) was erected on the site of the former Récollet convent and church, both destroyed by fire during the late 18C. The facades were fashioned after 16C Loire Valley châteaux. On each side of the main entrance, note the coats of arms of Jacques Cartier and Samuel de Champlain. The capitals, adorned with fleurs de lis, add a distinctly French flair to the imposing edifice.

★**Maison Maillou (Maillou House)** (**A**) – *17 Rue Saint-Louis.* Located next to Château Frontenac, this large stone structure now houses the Quebec Chamber of Commerce. Built about 1736 by the architect Jean Maillou (1668-1753) as his personal residence, the single-storey dwelling was heightened in 1767 and enlarged on its western side in 1799. During the early 19C, the house was occupied by the British army. The metal exterior shutters on the windows date from this period. Carefully restored in 1964, the Maillou house constitutes a fine traditional urban ensemble typical of the 1800s.

At no. 25, the offices of the Consulate General of France occupy the former **Maison Kent** (Kent House) (**B**). Dating back to the 18C, this large white structure adorned with bright blue trim was rebuilt in the 1830s. The Duke of Kent, father of Queen Victoria, is said to have resided here from 1792 to 1794.

★**Maison Jacquet (Jacquet House)** (**C**) – *34 Rue Saint-Louis.* Reputedly the oldest house in Quebec City, this small, one-storey structure, topped by a steep red roof, was erected on land acquired by François Jacquet from the Ursuline Nuns in 1674. Architect François de la Joüe enlarged the original dwelling around 1690, adding a second story. The addition to the side was constructed in 1820. Philippe Aubert de Gaspé lived in the house from 1815 to 1824, giving the house its current name, Maison des Anciens Canadiens (home of the early Canadians), from the title of his 1863 novel. Today, a fine restaurant specializing in traditional Quebec cuisine occupies the premises.

View of Old Quebec by Fred H. Holloway

The Montreal Museum of Fine Arts

Aux Anciens Canadiens
34 Rue Saint-Louis. ☎ *418-692-1627.* Charmingly situated in a historic white house with red trim (1675), this venerable restaurant specialises in local cuisine, offering a delicious introduction to fine dining à la quebecoise. The menu lists both traditional favourites – thick pea soup, tourtière (meat pie) – and contemporary creations such as feuillete de saumon (salmon in puff pastry). For dessert, try maple-syrup pie, or sugar tarts drizzled with cream.

★ **Musée d'Art Inuit Brousseau (Brousseau Museum of Inuit Art)** (**M¹**) – *39 Rue Saint-Louis. Open year-round daily 9:30am–5:30pm.*& 🅿 ☎ *418-694-1828. $6.* Discover the magical world of the Inuit in this carefully arranged and well-organized museum. The permanent collection of 450 pieces ranges from the prehistoric to the contemporary. Maps and stone carvings recall the migration of these inhabitants of the Canadian Arctic and their first encounter with Europeans. Contemporary sculpture reveals the artists' sources for inspiration, creative techniques and materials. Their characteristic fantastical imagery is particularly evident in works by well-known artists such as Luke Airut, George Arluk, Lucy Tasseor and Judas Ullulaq. A video available in French and English *(23min)* concludes the visit.

Turn right onto Rue des Jardins and left onto Rue Donnacona.
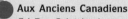

★★ **Monastère des Ursulines (Ursuline Monastery)** – Founded in 1639 by Madame de la Peltrie and Marie Guyart (mère Marie de l'Incarnation), the Ursuline monastery is the oldest educational institution for young women in America and is still in operation today. Begun in 1641, the complex was devastated by fire in 1650 and again in 1686. The Saint-Augustin and Sainte-Famille wings, as well as the kitchen area that links them, were built during a period of reconstruction lasting from 1685 to 1715, and provide the basic outline for the square inner courtyard. The Sainte-Famille wing's steeply pitched roof exemplifies the architectural style dominant under the French Regime. In 1836, the architect Thomas Baillairgé added the Sainte-Angèle wing. Despite several new constructions during the 20C, the imposing, grey complex has retained its vast garden and an orchard.

Chapel – *12 Rue Donnacona. Open May–Oct Tue–Sat 10am–11:30am & 1:30pm–4:30pm, Sun 1:30pm–4:30pm.* ☎ *418-694-0413.* Replacing an early-18C structure, the current chapel (1902) is designed in the eclectic style characteristic of religious architecture in Quebec at the turn of the century. The stair-turret visible at the back of the church is reminiscent of château-style architecture. It was added in 1889 and survived the demolition of the former chapel. The interior is composed of two sections: the "exterior chapel," where sat the lay faithful; and the "interior chapel" used by the cloistered nuns. The stunning interior **decoration★★** was taken from the 18C chapel and beautifully preserved, including the pulpit and sounding board surmounted by a trumpeting angel; the side retable dedicated to the Sacred Heart; and the main retable, a fine example of wood carving executed in the Louis XIV style, in the shape of a triumphal arch. These ornaments, as well as the high altar, were created between 1726 and 1736 under the supervision of the famed Quebec sculptor Pierre-Noël Levasseur. The sculptures are embellished with fine gilding applied by the Ursuline Nuns, who maintained a gilding workshop for over two centuries to supply the needs of their order. The sculpted decor found in this chapel is truly unique: figures of St. Augustine *(left niche)*, St. Ursula *(right niche)* and St. Joseph *(upper niche)* represent the epitome of the art of wood carving in Quebec. The vast nuns' choir,

Monastère des Ursulines

with its stalls and galleries, is surmounted by a wooden vault adorned with cupolas. Most of the paintings decorating the chapel were acquired in Paris around 1820 by Abbot Louis-Phillipe Desjardins (1753-1833), formerly the chaplain for the Ursulines. On the right side of the nave hangs *The Parable of the Ten Virgins* by Pietro Da Cortona. On the reverse side of the facade, note the painting by Philippe de Champaigne, *Jesus in the home of Simon the Pharisian*. The nun's choir features an anonymous work painted in France around 1670, entitled *France bringing Faith to the Hurons of New-France*. Located on the north side, a commemorative chapel houses the tomb of Marie de l'Incarnation (d. 1672), who was beatified in 1980.

★★Musée des Ursulines (Ursuline Museum) (M²) – *12 Rue Donnacona. Open May–Sept Tue–Sat 10am–noon & 1pm–5pm, Sun 1pm–5pm. Rest of the year Tue–Sun 1pm–4:30pm. $4. ☎ 418-694-0694.* Since 1979, this remarkable museum has occupied the former site of the small house belonging to the order's benefactor, Madame de la Peltrie. Representing the occupations and talents of the Ursuline Nuns, the collection includes works of art, archival documents, decorative arts, indigenous art and other materials tracing the heritage of the community from 1639 (the Ursulines' arrival in Quebec) to 1759 (the British Conquest).

The historical introduction offered in the first room on the museum's main floor immerses the visitor in that period's social and religious context. The second room, containing cabinets and various personal items, recreates the living quarters of Madame de la Peltrie. Handicrafts on view here illustrate the social and educational influences that the Ursuline sisters had on the young

Hunger pangs?

Restaurants along the Rue Saint-Jean have what it takes to satisfy every taste. The charming **Casse-Crêpe Breton** *(1136 Rue Saint-Jean; ☎ 418-692-0438)* puts forth delicious crepes, both savoury and sweet, served with a smile. Even the most formidable thirst doesn't stand a chance at **Pub Saint-Alexandre** *(1087 Rue Saint-Jean; ☎ 418-694-0015)*, where an amazing selection of 200 imported beers complements the menu of pasta, sausages and steak-and-fries, all served in an English pub setting. Steps away from the Rue Saint-Jean, **Petit Coin Latin** *(81/2 Rue Sainte-Ursule; ☎ 418-692-2022)* is the perfect spot to enjoy breakfast, a light meal or a peaceful cup of coffee; the staff keeps a selection of periodicals on hand for guests to peruse at their leisure.

French girls of the time, and the cultural exchanges that occurred between the nuns and the Amerindians (Marie de l'Incarnation completed the first Iroquois and Algonquian dictionaries).

On second floor, a room dedicated to the monastic life offers a glance at the organization and architecture of the first monastery – an Ursuline's cell, chapel, refectory – through such items as furniture, religious costumes and kitchen ustensils. On the same floor, a last room features gilding and glorious **embroideries**★, two art forms for which the Ursuline nuns were renowned. Religious art of the Ursulines included in the collection are altar frontals and ecclesiastic vestments from the 17C and 18C, delicately embroidered with gold and silver threads.

Return to Rue Saint Louis by Rue du Parloir and turn right.

Across from no. 58, on Rue du Corps-de-Garde, a cannonball is exposed in the roots of a tree. The wall of the Cavalier du Moulin park rises in the background. At no. 72, a plaque attests that General Montgomery's remains were brought here after the failed attack on Quebec City by Americans in 1775-1776.

Turn left on Rue Sainte-Ursule.

Chalmers-Wesley United Church/Église Unie Saint-Pierre – *78 Rue Sainte-Ursule. Open early Jul–late Aug Mon–Fri 10am–3pm. ☎ 418-692-0431.* Two protestant congregations, one francophone, the other anglophone, share this Gothic Revival structure (1853, J. Wells). Staggered buttresses flank the slender steeple. Inside, note the superb stained-glass windows dating from 1909, and the elaborate woodwork adorning the apse and the pews. The early 19C organ was restored in 1985.

Across the street stands the **Sanctuaire de Notre-Dame du Sacré-Cœur** *(no. 71)*, built by F.-X. Berlinguet in 1910. The sanctuary is a replica of the Gothic chapel dedicated to Our Lady of the Sacred Heart at Issoudun, in France.

Backtrack on Rue Sainte-Ursule past Rue Saint-Louis.

On the northwest corner of Rues Saint-Louis and Sainte-Ursule stood the first city hall of Quebec City, founded in 1833. When the present City Hall opened in 1896, combining under one roof the administrative and judicial offices for the city, row houses were erected by David Ouellet along Rue Sainte-Ursule *(no. 60-68)*, lending the street a picturesque appearance.

Continue to the intersection with Rue Dauphine, turn right and continue to Rue Saint-Stanislas.

Institut canadien (Canadian Institute) – *40-42 Rue Saint-Stanislas. Open year-round Tue & Thu noon–8pm, Wed & Fri noon–5pm, weekends 1pm–5pm. ⓓ ⓟ www.icqbdq.qc.ca ☎ 418-529-0924.* The first Gothic Revival religious building in Quebec, this former Methodist church (Wesleyan Church) was built in 1848. Since 1949 it has housed the headquarters of the Canadian Institute, a francophone cultural institution that oversees the city's network of municipal libraries. The nave has been converted into a performance hall *(closed for renovation)*, and the Old Quebec branch of the public library is located in the basement.

Turn right on Rue Cook.

Église presbytérienne Saint Andrew (St. Andrew's Presbyterian Church) – *5 rue Cook. Open Jul–Aug Mon–Fri 10am–4:30pm. ⓓ ☎ 418-694-1347.* Built in 1810 for presbyterian Scots in Quebec City, the church was enlarged in 1823. Its steeple recalls the one found on the Holy Trinity Anglican Cathedral *(below)*. Initially, the congregation consisted almost entirely of the Fraser Highlanders, a battalion in General Wolfe's army. Inside, the ornate main altar faces the former Governor's gallery.

Continue onto Rue Sainte-Anne.

★**Price Building** – *65 Rue Sainte-Anne.* Quebec City's first skyscraper rises conspicuously over the Upper Town. Designed by Montreal architects Ross and MacDonald, it was built in 1930 to house the head office of Price Brothers, famed for introducing the pulp and paper industry to the Saguenay region. The 16-storey building stands on a narrow piece of land some 24m/78ft wide. Its profile resembles a ziggurat, a pyramid with a series of upward steps. Like numerous other North American corporations at that time, Price Brothers selected the Art Deco style, integrating

QUÉBEC
HAUTE-VILLE
0   200 m

Marie-Guyart

Parc de l'Amérique-Française

BON-PASTEUR

Parc de Francophe

St-Cœur-de-Marie

La Laurentienne

Maison Stewart   Musée du ╱ Québec

embellishments that reflected its Canadian origin (pinecones, squirrels, aboriginals) and its business activities (lumber and paper). In order that the building blend in with the old city, the company opted for a pavilion roof with copper covering.
In the entrance hall, bas-reliefs and copper doors (entrance and elevator) combine to produce a fine Art Deco ensemble. The building has housed municipal offices since 1984.

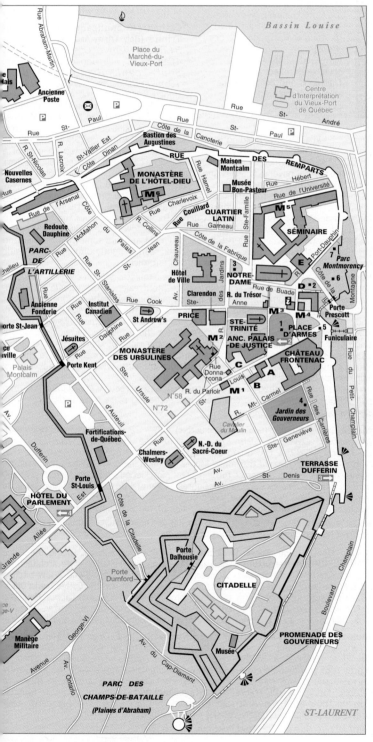

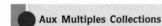

Aux Multiples Collections

69 Rue Sainte-Anne (☎ 418-692-1230) and 43 Rue Buade (☎ 418-692-4298). These galleries specialise in superb collections of authentic Inuit art from Nunavik, Keewatin and Baffin Island. Fashioned of stone (notably steatite or soapstone), caribou antlers, ivory and whalebone, the sculptures reflect the traditions and beliefs of the arctic regions' indigenous populations.

Hotel Clarendon – *57 Rue Sainte-Anne.* In 1858, Charles Baillairgé erected two houses for a printer named Desbarats, on this site. The property was converted into a hotel in 1875. The following year, an Art Deco entrance pavilion was annexed. In the entrance hall, two large bronze torchères provide rare examples of the Art Nouveau influence in Quebec.

★**Cathédrale anglicane de la Sainte-Trinité (Holy Trinity Anglican Cathedral)** – *31 Rue des Jardins. Open May–Jun daily 10am–6pm. July–Aug daily 9am–8pm. Sept–Thanksgiving Day daily 10am–4pm.* ᴕ ☎ *418-692-2193.* Designed in 1799 by the army engineers, Major Robe and Captain Hall, this edifice was the first Anglican (Episcopal) cathedral to be built outside the British Isles.

Completed in 1804, the building is modelled after the Church of St.-Martin-in-the-Fields, in London, designed by the architect, James Gibbs. Erected on part of a property formerly owned by the Récollet Order, the cathedral features a simple floor plan. The central nave, side aisles and lateral galleries dotted with a double row of windows contribute to the church's innovative design. The facade is turned away from Place d'Armes so that the chancel faces east, in the time-honoured Christian tradition. The church steeple, which contains an 8-bell peal, is actually several feet higher than that of the Our Lady of Quebec Basilica. The pitch of the roof had to be raised approximately 3m/10ft in 1816, since its low grade proved too weak to sustain massive snowfall. As a result, the pediment appears somewhat heavier and the great height of the massive church tower seems slightly diminished. A Celtic cross fashioned in 542 AD marks the church entrance.

Interior – The wooden vault spanning the nave simulates stucco coffers. The Ionic columns and pilasters were sculpted by the Montrealer, Louis-Amable Quévillon, who was nearly excommunicated for having participated in the interior decoration of a non-Catholic church. King George III provided the funding for the cathedral, and sent English oak from the Royal Forests of Windsor for the pews. On the left side of the tribune is a royal pew reserved for the British monarch, head of the Church of England, or his representative. To the right of the altar, the bishop's chair was carved out of wood from an elm tree that had flourished in the churchyard for some two hundred years. The cathedral treasure, which includes silverware donated by Georges III, is exhibited on special occasions.

To the right of the cathedral stand a large Neoclassical rectory (1841) and a church hall (1890). In summer, the courtyard is a gathering place for artists.

Return to Rue Sainte-Anne.

Musée Grévin Québec (Grévin Museum Quebec) (M³) – *22 Rue Sainte-Anne. Open mid-May–Labour Day daily 9am–11pm. Rest of the year daily 10am–5pm. $3;* ☎ *418-692-2289.* A 17C urban dwelling today houses this wax museum, the first North American branch of the famed Musée Grévin in Paris. With astonishing realism, scenes on the first floor depict turning points in Quebec's history. A stroll past the various tableaux reveals such famed figures as Samuel de Champlain, Madeleine de Verchères, Dollard des Ormeaux, Generals Montcalm and Wolfe, Émile Nelligan and Mackenzie King, among others. Personalities of the 20C inhabit the second floor.

In the quaint pedestrian street known as **Rue du Trésor**, artists exhibit sketches and engravings depicting typical scenes of the city.

Ancien Hôtel Union (Former Union Hotel) – *12 Rue Sainte-Anne.* Facing the Place d'Armes, the large structure (1805-1812) exemplifies Palladian-style architecture, characterized by a simple plan, a massive shape, sash windows and a low-pitched roof. Formerly occupied by the city's first hotel, it now houses the **Quebec Tourist Office**, which provides information for the entire province *(open late Jun–Labour Day daily 8:30am–7:30pm; rest of the year daily 9am–5pm; closed Jan 1, Easter, Dec 25;* ✕ ᴕ ▣*)* as well as a currency exchange, guided tours, car rentals and bookstore.

★**Musée du Fort (Fort Museum) (M⁴)** – *10 Rue Sainte-Anne. Open Feb–Mar Tue–Sun 11am–4pm. Apr–Jun & Sept–Oct daily 10am–5pm. Jul–Aug daily 10am–6pm. $6.75.* ☎ *418-692-2175.* Erected in 1840, this square white building topped by a grey roof was modified in 1898, giving it a whimsical appearance. An excellently narrated sound and light presentation *(30min)* cast upon a large scale model of Quebec during the 18C traces the city's military and civil history from its foundation in 1608 until the American invasion of 1775-1776. The maquette itself provides a unique perspective of the city's distinctive topography.

Turn left on Rue du Fort and continue to Rue Buade.

Ancien bureau de poste (Old Post Office) (**D**) – *Entrance on 5 Rue du Fort. Open year-round Mon–Fri 8am–5:45pm. Closed major holidays.* ♿ ☎ *418-694-6103.* Constructed as the city's main post office in 1873, this edifice presents an imposing facade adorned with Beaux-Arts embellishments. Faced with decorated cut stone, it was enlarged to more than twice its original size in 1914. Above the entrance, a carved bas-relief advertises the Chien d'or (The Golden Dog), an inn that occupied the site until 1837. The building was renamed the Louis S. St-Laurent Building in honour of the former Canadian prime minister and continues to operate as a working post office. Inside, the Canadian Parks Service presents exhibits on the development of historical and natural sites in Canada.

Monsignor de Laval Monument (**2**) – In front of the old post office stands a monument to Msgr. François de Montmorency-Laval (1623-1708), first bishop of Quebec. It was erected in 1908, as part of the celebrations marking the bicentennial of his death. Installation of the monument, designed by sculptor Louis-Philippe Hébert, necessitated the demolition of an entire block of eight houses, thus creating an imposing public square.

Rue Buade ends at the **Charles-Baillairgé Stairway** (1893), named in honour of the architect who, after an illustrious career designing buildings, devoted his talents to civil engineering. This cast-iron stairway is one of several Baillairgé designed for the city.

Descend the stairs and continue up Côte de la Montagne.

From the foot of the stairs, note the monumental false front of the old post office, dominating the Lower Town.

Palais archiépiscopal (Archbishop's Palace) (**E**) – *2 Rue Port-Dauphin.* This Neoclassical structure (1847) replaced the first archbishop's residence, erected in the late 17C in Montmorency Park. As part of Lord Dufferin's beautification projects in the late 19C, a false front was erected towards the Côte de la Montagne, thus making the building visible from the St. Lawrence River. The original facade of the large edifice dominates the main courtyard, leading to the old seminary.

Return to Rue Buade.

Facing the Beaux-Arts style presbytery *(16 Rue Buade at the corner of Rue du Fort)*, a plaque draws attention to the foundations of a funeral chapel thought to contain the tomb of Samuel de Champlain. There are in fact at least ten theories concerning the possible location of Champlain's tomb!

★ **Basilique-cathédrale Notre-Dame-de-Québec (Basilica-Cathedral of Our Lady of Quebec)** – *Open May–mid-Oct daily 9am–2:30pm. Rest of the year daily 9am–4:15pm.* ♿ *www.patrimoine-religieux.com* ☎ *418-694-0665.* Declared a historical monument in 1966, the basilica is the most European of Quebec churches. Its complex architectural history has yielded an impressive structure

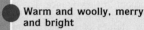

Warm and woolly, merry and bright

It's never too soon to prepare for winter, so head for the Upper Town to stock up on necessities for the frigid months. Stop in at **Lambert & Co.** *(42 Rue Garneau;* ☎ *418-694-2151)*, a diminutive boutique housed in a former stone residence, where in addition to stockings (ask the staff to share the history of the woollen essentials), you'll find hand-crafted soaps, maple products, and chocolates made by Trappist monks. No matter what the season,

La Boutique de Noël de Québec *(47 Rue Buade;* ☎ *418-692-2457)* entrances young and old with its brightly-lit trees and myriad decorations, including intriguing strands of lights and an enormous variety of Christmas-tree balls.

that bears witness to the contributions of three generations of Quebec's renowned family of architects.

Early construction – In 1674, following a papal order creating the Diocese of Quebec, the original structure here (1650) was consecrated as a cathedral. Under the direction of François de Laval, who had been appointed Bishop of New France, the building was enlarged and renovated. In 1743, Gaspard Chaussegros de Léry, the royal engineer, enlarged the apse, raised the nave and added to it a clerestory and side aisles by opening arches into the walls of the old nave, leaving thick pillars in place. A new facade was built overlooking the market square, now known as Place de l'Hôtel de Ville. Completed in 1749, the structure was destroyed during the Conquest of 1759.

A Baillairgé Masterpiece – Reconstruction of the church took place between 1768 and 1771 and was modelled on Chaussegros de Léry's work. Jean Baillairgé (1726-1805), the first in the renowned Baillairgé family of joiners, painters, sculptors and architects, rebuilt the south belfry with its two openwork drums surmounted by domes. In 1787, after studying at the Royal Academy of Painting and Sculpture in Paris, his son, François Baillairgé (1759-1830), undertook the task of decorating the interior. He designed the plans for the magnificent baldachin, executed by André Vermare.

François's son, Thomas Baillairgé (1791-1859), continued his father's work and, in 1843, designed the monumental Neoclassical facade whose construction was interrupted two years later when the base of the first of two projected towers showed signs of weakness. In 1857, Charles Baillairgé (1826-1906), cousin of Thomas, designed the plans for the brass-plated cast-iron gate that encloses the porch, which enabled him to declare that the building of the monument was indeed a family effort. The church was consecrated as a basilica in 1874 to emphasize its history and status as one of Canada's most important churches.

After the structure was destroyed by fire on December 22, 1922, the city's religious authorities decided to restore it to its original appearance in order to retain the familiar image of "Msgr. de Laval's church." The current monument was reconstructed between 1923 and 1925 from old plans and photographs.

Interior – Recreated after the devastating fire of 1922, the interior evokes the principal features of the 18C cathedral despite the use of concrete, steel and plaster. Immediately upon entering, the eye is drawn to the light and delicately sweeping baldachin executed by André Vermare. The luminous stained-glass windows of the upper level are French in origin and represent saints, evangelists and archangels. Those of the lower level are German and American and recall important events in the life of the Virgin Mary. The cathedral crypt *(guided tour only; inquire at the reception desk)* houses the sepulchres of Quebec's bishops and of some of the governors of New France. The lamp in the chapel on the right near the entrance to the crypt was a gift from Louis XIV. The Casavant organ of 5,239 pipes is flanked by statues of shepherds, one reading (symbolizing inspiration), and the other playing an instrument (symbolizing improvisation). In 1993, the remains of Msgr. de Laval were interred in a small commemorative chapel *(right side aisle)*; a small display to the right of the choir presents his life and works.

Well worth seeing is a multimedia "fresco" entitled *Feux Sacrés* ("Act of Faith"), which transports the viewer through time to tell the story of the basilica *(May–Thanksgiving Day Mon–Fri starting at 3:30pm, weekends starting at 6:30pm; $7.50; inquire at the reception desk)*.

Place de l'hôtel de ville – This large open square, designed in conjunction with the cathedral in 1650, became the principal marketplace of the Upper Town in the 18C. Its commercial vocation ended in the late 1880s with the construction of City Hall. Placed in its centre, the **Cardinal Taschereau monument** (**3**) (1923) by André Vermare, is dedicated to the first Canadian cardinal. The bas-reliefs represent the institution of the Forty Hour Prayer in the diocese *(facing the cathedral)*, the career of the Superior of the Quebec Seminary *(facing Rue des Jardins)* and the Cardinal aiding Irish victims of the typhoid epidemic at Grosse-Île, in 1848 *(facing Rue Buade)*.

Hôtel de ville de Québec (Quebec City Hall) – *2 Rue des Jardins.* The majestic structure stands on land formerly belonging to the Jesuit Order, who erected a college and church on this site, in the very centre of Old Quebec, in 1666. The College was demolished in 1877, to be replaced by the City Hall, built in 1896 according to plans by Georges-Émile Tanguay. Stylistically, Tanguay's building presents a curious blend of the Second Empire and French Château styles, embellished with Richardsonian Romanesque detailing.

Located north of the basilica, Quebec City's **Quartier Latin★** (Latin Quarter) is the oldest residential district in the Upper Town. Formerly belonging to the Quebec Seminary, the land was divided up during the late 17C, while the parcelling of other vast properties, belonging to the Ursulines, Jesuits and Augustinian Nuns, did not commence until a century later. The narrow streets crisscrossing the quarter are remnants of the passageways that once connected these large holdings. Between 1820 and 1830, the craftsmen who initially populated the district gave way to a French-speaking bourgeoisie, eager to reside in the vicinity of the Seminary and its clergy. After World War II, influences from the Parisian existentialist movement gave rise to a bohemian student life in Old Quebec at the same time as Laval University was expanding into the district, occupying dozens of old houses. Though still inhabited by a few longtime residents and families, the neighbourhood today caters mainly to students.

★★Séminaire de Québec (Quebec Seminary) – This influential institution was founded in 1663 by Msgr. de Laval to train and recruit priests destined to work in the newly created parishes of New France. In 1852, the seminary was formally granted a university (Laval University), Canada's first francophone higher education institution. In 1950, Laval University moved to a new campus in Sainte-Foy but the university's school of architecture remained here, and today occupies several of the structures in the complex.

© J.-F. Bergeron/ENVIRO FOTO

Quartier Latin

Vieux-Séminaire (Old Seminary) – *Entrance at 2 Côte de la Fabrique (Welcome Pavilion). Guided tours of the seminary available in summer. $3 (includes admission to the Museum of French America);* & ☐ *($11/day)* ☎ *418-692-2843.* The old seminary comprises three sections arranged around an inner court, as is typical of French monastic architecture in the 16C and 17C. The visitor enters by a porte-cochère framed by a portal designed by François Baillairgé and bearing the Seminary's coat of arms. Traditional building crafts were employed in the construction of the three wings, creating a stylistically homogeneous ensemble.

The **Procure Wing** was built between 1678 and 1681 to house the Grand Séminaire; its walls and vaults survived fires in 1701, 1705 and 1865. After the last fire, the building was raised by one stone storey. The sundial on the facade bears the inscription *Nos jours passent comme une ombre* ("Our days pass like a shadow"). Within this wing is the marvelous **Msgr. Olivier Briand Chapel★**, noteworthy for the fine wood panelling adorning its walls. Executed by the master sculptor Pierre Émond in 1785, the decor exemplifies two distinct styles – Louis XIII and Louis XV. Émond also designed the olive branches framing the engraving of the *Marriage of the Virgin* that dominates the altar piece.

To the right, the **Parloirs Wing** or former Petit Séminaire dates from 1823, as does the **Congregation Wing**, where the porte-cochère is located. The **Congregational Chapel** here, a low-ceilinged shrine devoted to the Virgin Mary, is divided into three naves, separated by two rows of Ionic columns. The main altar, flanked by two similar columns, is surmounted by a gilded **statue★** of the Virgin, one of the few known wood carvings crafted by the hand of the architect Thomas Baillairgé.

★ **Musée de l'Amérique Française** (Museum of French America) (**M⁵**) – *Entrance at 2 Côte de la Fabrique (Welcome Pavilion) or at 9 Rue de l'Université (Jérôme Demers Pavilion). Open Jun 24–Labour Day daily 10am–5:30pm. Rest of the year Tue–Sun 10am–5pm. Closed Dec 25. $4.* & ☐ *($9/day) www.mcq.org* ☎ *418-692-2843.* Operated since 1995 as part of the Museum of Civilization, the collections of the Museum of French America encompass objects and works of art reflecting France's rich historic, cultural and social heritage in North America. The museum's holdings include an extensive archive of historical documents; some 195,000 rare books and journals; European paintings from the 15C-19C and Canadian paintings from the 18C-20C; gold- and silverware for religious and domestic use; and extensive collections of textiles, furniture, scientific instruments, stamps and coins, birds and insects as well as botanical, zoological and geological specimens.

The collections are housed in three buildings, of which **Welcome Pavilion** serves as the museum's reception and information centre and temporary exhibition space. The second building occupies the seminary's former outer chapel. Erected between 1888 and 1900 according to plans by J.-F. Peachy, the chapel features an interior modelled after the 19C Trinity Church in Paris. The Quebec version, made of galvanized steel painted in trompe-l'oeil, provided better protection against fire. In addition to beautiful pieces of silverware by Francis Ranvoyzé, Guillaume Loir, Laurent

La Maison Serge Bruyère

1200 Rue Saint-Jean.
☎ *418-694-0618.* This famed dining establishment encompasses four separate restaurants. Old stone enhances the Bavarian atmosphere at Le Falstaff, which serves German specialties (including an excellent choucroute) and a wide variety of imported beers; the menu also includes dietetic creations. At Café Européen, diners can sample delicious sandwiches, salads, quiches and desserts on the terrace in fine weather. Chez Livernois bistro serves up creative concoctions in a relaxed, welcoming setting. The excellence of the cuisine and the quality of service at prestigious La Grande Table provide its guests with an altogether memorable dining experience.

L'Astral

1225 Place Montcalm, in Loews Le Concorde Hotel.
☎ *418-647-2222.* The 28th floor of Loews Le Concorde Hotel tops the list for dining rooms with a great view of the city. Quebec's only revolving restaurant affords views of the St-Lawrence, Old City, Île d'Orléans and the Charlevoix Coast. Watch the sun set to live piano music *(Tue–Sun evenings),* enjoy a nightcap or discover the popular Sunday brunch.

Amiot and others, the chapel contains one of the most important collections of **relics★** outside St. Peter's in Rome. The 16 gilded reliquary busts of the apostles were carved by Louis Jobin. The columns around the chapel are adorned with representations of the Seven Sacraments and each lamp symbolizes a gift of the Holy Spirit.

The third structure, the **Jérôme Demers Pavilion**, houses two permanent exhibits. The first, dedicated to the French experience in North America, presents the seven major francophone communities on the continent: Quebec, Acadia, Louisiana, French Ontario, Métis, and French-American communities in the West and in New England. The second exhibit incorporates the highlights of the Seminary's impressive collections to underscore the institution's religious, cultural and educational mission. Temporary thematic exhibitions here invite discovery of Quebec by its provincial arts, crafts, folklore and history.

Leave the museum by Rue de l'Université and turn right on Rue Sainte-Famille. Take Rue Couillard on the left.

Charming **Rue Couillard** received its name in the 18C, in honour of the sailor, Guillaume Couillard (1591-1663), son-in-law and heir of the lands of Louis Hébert. Its sinuous path leads past the former Hospice de la Miséricorde *(no. 14),* built between 1878 and 1880 for the Sisters of the Good Shepherd.

Musée Bon-Pasteur (Good Shepherd Museum) – *14 Rue Couillard, between Rue Ferland and Rue Saint-Flavien. Open year-round Tue–Sun 1pm–5pm. $2.* ♿ ☎ *418-694-0243.* This remarkable Gothic Revival structure, with its brick walls pierced by ogive windows, serves as the main building of the **Maison Béthanie★** (1878, David Ouellet). The structure formerly housed the Mercy Hospice, a caring institution founded and operated by the Sœurs du Bon-Pasteur (Sisters of the Good Shepherd) as a refuge and halfway house for young women. Today the structure has been renovated as a museum tracing the history of the Good Shepherd community, a lay order founded in 1850 by Marie Fitzbach (later known as Marie-du-Sacré-Cœur). Artifacts, sculptures, furnishings, musical instruments and articles of daily life illustrate the caring and teaching vocations of the sisters, life in the community, and the activities of the order today. Several rooms recreate the atmosphere of common rooms in present-day Good Shepherd convents. Note especially the fine religious art objects crafted by the sisters, including polychromed wood statues, rare books, and embroidered textiles. A video *(15min)* illustrates the mission of the community in the past and present.

Turn right on Rue Collins and continue to Rue Charlevoix.

★ **Monastère de l'Hôtel-Dieu de Québec (Augustine Monastery)** – *32 Rue Charlevoix.* The founding sisters of the Augustinian Hospitallers of Quebec, Marie Guenet de Saint-Ignace, Marie Forestier de Saint-Bonaventure and Anne Le Cointre de Saint-Bernard, took up residence in 1640 in a makeshift hospital located next to the Jesuit mission, in Sillery. In 1644, upon completion of the monastery, the nuns moved to this site in the old city. The first hospital erected by the nuns was made of wood. In 1695, François de la Joüe enlarged the structure by annexing a stone building; the two structures now form part of the convent and can be clearly seen from the garden. The hospital underwent several expansions during the 19C and 20C, reaching its current capacity in 1960.

★ **Musée des Augustines de l'Hôtel-Dieu de Québec (Augustine Museum) (M⁶)** – *Open year-round Tue–Sat 9:30am–noon & 1:30pm–5pm, Sun 1:30pm–5pm. Closed major holidays.* ♿ ☎ *418-692-2492.* Opened in 1958, the museum presents a collection of objects and artworks tracing the Augustinian nuns' history and heritage in New France. It includes one of the foremost collections of New France-era **paintings★** known in Quebec (including portraits of Louis XIV and the Intendant Jean Talon, as well as of the order's benefactors, the Duchesse d'Aiguillon and Cardinal Richelieu), various pieces of furniture including Louis XIII chairs from the Château Saint-Louis, and a fine collection of surgical implements. From the museum, it is possible to descend to the cellar, where the nuns took shelter during the Conquest (when more than 40,000 cannonballs fell upon Quebec).

The relics of the Blessed Catherine-de-Saint-Augustin, a nun who arrived in Quebec in 1648 and was beatified in 1989, are visible in the Catherine-de-Saint-Augustin Centre.

★**Church** — *Same hours as museum*. To counteract the proliferation of non-Catholic community chapels that appeared in Quebec City with the influx of Protestant Irish immigrants in the early 19C, the Church of Quebec encouraged the nuns to erect a large Catholic church. Designed by Pierre Émond in 1800, under the supervision of Father Jean-Louis Desjardins, the structure features polygonal chapels and an apse, connected to the convent.

The Neoclassical facade (1835) boasts a beautifully sculpted Ionic portal created by Thomas Baillairgé. The small belfry was placed over the facade in 1931.

The sculpted, gilded wood **interior decor** was crafted by Thomas Baillairgé, between 1829 and 1832. Highlights include the high-altar **tabernacle**, a veritable small scale model of St. Peter's in Rome; the retable, in the shape of a triumphal arch; and the basket-handle wooden vault. The painting above the altar, *The Descent from the Cross*, executed by Antoine Plamondon in 1840, was inspired by Rubens' famous masterpiece which now hangs in the Antwerp Cathedral in Belgium. The church features a collection of paintings confiscated from churches in Paris during the Revolution and sent to Quebec in 1817. One of these, *The Vision of Sainte-Thérèse d'Avila*, now hangs in the Notre-Dame-de-Toutes-Grâces chapel.

★★ ③ FORTIFICATIONS

In the 17C, Quebec City played a key role in the defense of northeastern French America. As a consequence of the city's strategic location, several fortification projects were undertaken over the years. However, the construction of batteries, redoubts and cavaliers in both the Lower and Upper Towns ceased following the signing of the Utrecht Treaty of 1713, which temporarily suspended hostilities between the European factions. During the peace that followed, peripheral forts were the most common means of defense.

The fortification of Quebec City resumed in 1745 in reaction to the capture of Louisbourg, on the island of Cape Breton in present-day Nova Scotia. French military engineer Gaspard Chaussegros de Léry initiated the new fortification project, which was completed by the British, after the Conquest of 1759. The British erected a temporary citadel in 1783, then added four circular Martello towers (1805-1812), and finally built a new, permanent citadel between 1820 and 1832. The fortifications were faced with red sandstone from a Cap-Rouge quarry.

Following the departure of the British garrison in 1871, local military authorities approved the demolition of certain city gates in order to facilitate passage between the Lower and Upper Town and the Saint-Jean and Saint-Louis faubourgs. Influenced by the historical romantic movement then popular in Europe, **Lord Dufferin**, governor-general of Canada from 1872 to 1878, insisted on the preservation of Quebec's fortifications. In 1875, he submitted a plan for the beautification of Quebec City, which included refurbishing the fortified enceinte, rebuilding the gates to the city and demolishing all the advanced military works that formed a 60m/200ft wide strip along the ramparts, in order to fully expose the complex in the manner of medieval fortifications.

As a result of Lord Dufferin's initiative, visitors can now stroll along the fortification walkways and enjoy panoramic views of the city and surrounding areas.

★★The Citadel

From Place d'Armes, follow Rue Saint-Louis to Côte de la Citadelle, turn left and follow the street to its end. Enter through the Durnford gate.

Though the Citadel was built at a time of peace and never used for defensive purposes, its conception dates back to the founding of the city. In 1615, Samuel de Champlain proposed that a citadel be erected on the Cap Diamant heights in order to control access to the hinterlands by way of the St. Lawrence River. Engineer Chaussegros de Léry submitted a similar project in 1716 and, in 1720, he drew the plans of a citadel much like the one that was built a century later, under the supervision of Lieutenant-Colonel Elias Walker Durnford.

The star-shaped plan of the present citadel (1820-1852) is typical of Vauban fortifications. Sébastien le Prestre, **marquis de Vauban** (1633-1707), military engineer and marshal of France under Louis XIV, perfected French military architecture by

The Citadel

developing advanced works (or outworks) that protected entrances and ramparts from enemy fire. So sophisticated was the Vauban system that the British used it until the beginning of the 19C.

Surrounding the citadel were sloping earthworks known as glacis, which forced the enemy to expose itself to cannon fire from the garrison. Enemy fire, on the other hand, could not reach the stone walls unless it was exceptionally precise. The enceinte is formed of bastions linked together by curtains (straight walls). The bastions were shaped so as to protect the ditches by means of cannon fire, while the tenailles (isolated bastions located in the ditches) protected the curtains and entrances to the citadel.

The Neoclassical **Porte Dalhousie** (Dalhousie Gate, 1830) is the main entrance to the citadel and the site of the changing of the guard ceremony *(Jun 24–Labour Day daily 10am; 35min)* and the retreat *(Jul–Aug Wed–Sat 6pm; 30min)*. Paired columns adorn the main facade, creating a monumental effect intended to evoke military might and rigour.

Visit – *Visit by guided tour (1hr) only. Apr–mid-May daily 10am–4pm. Mid-May–Jun 9am–5pm. July–Labour Day 9am–6pm. Sept 9am–4pm. Oct 10am–3pm. $5.50.* &. ☐ *www.lacitadelle.qc.ca/ ☎ 418-694-2815. Some areas of the Citadel are off-limits, as it is still a military base for the Royal 22nd Regiment.* Guided tours begin at the powder magazine (1831), which was renovated as a chapel in 1927. The tour then leads to one of the tenailles, which formerly housed a prison and today serves as an annex to the Museum of the Royal 22nd Regiment. On view here are many types of arms, military decorations, uniforms and World War I artifacts. From the King's Bastion, visitors can take in a superb **view★★** of the Château Frontenac and the Upper Town. The tour then leads past the Cap-Diamant redoubt (1693); the residence of the governor-general, partly destroyed by fire in 1976 and subsequently rebuilt; and the hospital (1849), which today functions as an administrative building. Occupying the old powder magazine (1750), the **Museum of the Royal 22nd Regiment** contains a collection of military objects from the 17C to the present, including uniformed mannequins posing as soldiers from the various regiments of New France, and several dioramas illustrating the major battles of the 18C. The tour also leads to the Prince of Whales bastion, the highest natural point in the city, from which a sweeping **view** extends over the St. Lawrence River and the Plains of Abraham.

Leave the citadel by the Durnford gate and take the path to the left, which ascends to the fortifications; continue towards the St. Lawrence River.

The path leading to the Governor's walk runs alongside the citadel's outer wall and the National Battlefields Park. One of the Martello towers is visible in the distance.

★★ **Promenade des Gouverneurs** (Governors' Walk) – *Closed in winter.* Rising over the park, a belvedere affording magnificent **views★★** of the St. Lawrence and the Quebec region marks the beginning of this spectacular walk. Precariously suspended between the heavens and the dark waters of the St. Lawrence along the steep cliff, the boardwalk leads from the belvedere to Dufferin Terrace. The **panorama★** extends northeast to the Île d'Orleans, Mt. Sainte-Anne and the Laurentians.

★★Walking Tour of Ramparts *2km/1.3mi. Map p 241.*

Begin the tour at Dufferin Terrace.

★★★**Terrasse Dufferin (Dufferin Terrace)** – Stretching 671m/2,200ft above the majestic river, this popular vantage point offers breathtaking **views**★★ of the Lower Town, St. Lawrence River and surrounding region. The terrace, a large wooden board-walk, is an extension of Lord Dufferin's beautification project. It was constructed to provide a view of the river at a time when the Lower Town was overrun by commercial buildings and warehouses.

The section of the terrace that faces Château Frontenac lies over the remains of the colonial governor's residence, the **Château Saint-Louis**, destroyed by fire in 1834. Governor Durham had a terrace built over the site. It bore his name until the present terrace was built.

Dufferin Terrace rapidly became a focal point of city life. It was electrified in 1885 and, shortly thereafter, ice slides were set up. The terrace's kiosks and public benches introduced Quebecers to urban fixtures akin to those found on Parisian boulevards and created a lively, bustling atmosphere.

Jardin des Gouverneurs (Governors' Garden) – This small park beside the Château Frontenac was created in the mid-17C for the enjoyment of the governor-general of New France. The **Wolfe-Montcalm Monument (4)** (1827) is a joint memorial to the two enemies who died in combat and, as was observed at the time, whose meeting resulted in the creation of the Canadian nation. The shape of the monument sym-bolizes death: note the cenotaph forming the base of the structure and, particularly, the dignified obelisk. The inscription reads in translation from Latin: "Valour gave them a common death, history a common fame, posterity a common monument."

To the right of the garden, follow Rue du Mont-Carmel to the Cavalier du Moulin park. Continue to the end of Dufferin Terrace.

Erected in 1898, the **Samuel de Champlain Monument (5)**, by Paul Chevré, honours the "father of New France." Nearby stands a monument made of bronze, granite and glass that commemorates the inscription of Quebec's historic district on UNESCO's World Heritage List, in December 1985. A **funicular** links Dufferin terrace to the Lower Town.

Take the Frontenac staircase and cross the Prescott gate to Montmorency Park.

Inaugurated on July 3, 1983 to commemorate the 375th anniversary of the founding of Quebec City, the **Porte Prescott** (Prescott Gate) is a reconstruction of a previous gate that was erected on the same spot in 1797, and demolished in 1871.

Parc Montmorency (Montmorency Park) – It is here, at the summit of Côte de la Montagne, that the intendant of New France, Jean Talon, had a house built in 1667. At the end of the 17C, Msgr. de Saint-Vallier, second bishop of Quebec, purchased the house and constructed a vast episcopal palace (1691-1696). The Legislative Assembly of Lower Canada occupied the building from 1792 onwards. Reconstructed in the early 19C, the structure housed the Parliament of the Union Government, which held sessions intermittently in Quebec City, Kingston, Montreal and Toronto. It was later destroyed by fire.

The park features a **monument (6)** to the memory of George-Étienne Cartier, and another **(7)** to Louis Hébert, Marie Rollet and Guillaume Couillard. Created by sculptor Alfred Laliberté (1918), the latter commemorates the tricentennial of the arrival of the first settlers in New France in 1617 (their names are inscribed on the back of the monument).

The park provides a good view of the Quebec Seminary, in particular the five-storey building currently housing Laval University's School of Architecture. From this vantage point, the visitor can appreciate the elegant **lantern** placed atop the central dome, which has become a familiar landmark in Old Quebec.

★**Rue des Remparts** – Until approximately 1875, this street was a mere path which ran alongside the ramparts, connecting bastions and batteries. Located across from the seminary buildings, the Sault-au-Matelot and Clergé batteries, erected in 1711, protected the Quebec harbour. Today, black cannons overlooking the Lower Town permit the visitor to recapture the atmosphere of the old fortified city.

Continue along Rue des Remparts to Rue Sainte-Famille.

Located at the foot of Rue Sainte-Famille until 1871, the Hope gate closed off access to the Upper Town. Branching off Rue des Remparts, the sinuous Côte de la Canoterie has linked the Upper and Lower Towns since 1634; it used to lead to a tiny cove, known as l'Anse à la Canoterie, that served as a merchandise landing and a shipyard for the construction of small crafts.

Maison Montcalm (Montcalm House) – *45-49 Rue des Remparts.* Situated in a slightly recessed spot, this majestic residence contains three separate structures. The middle part, built in 1725, was soon flanked by two similar buildings. The house is named for Louis-Joseph de Saint-Véran, **marquis de Montcalm**, who lived on the ground floor of the centre section from December 1758 to June 1759. In 1810, the middle structure was raised one storey; the two neighbouring houses followed suit in 1830.

Across the Montcalm House, the Montcalm Bastion, a small, tranquil square, offers lovely views of Rue des Remparts and the fortifications.

Bastion des Augustines (Augustine Bastion) – *Across from Augustine Monastery, 75 Rue des Remparts.* Facing the Saint-Charles River, the northern section of the fortifications was long neglected because the cliff provided an adequate natural defense. After the American invasion of 1775-1776, it was decided to complete this section of the walls surrounding the Upper Town. Completed in 1811, the masonry wall was so high that peering through the gun embrasures proved the only way to look out over the countryside.

The Palace Gate, demolished in 1871, once stood before the Augustine Monastery. In the monastery garden, adjacent to the entrance portal, note the former powder magazine, built in 1820 to supply the northern cannon batteries.

A few blocks past the Augustine Bastion, the **Gare du Palais** (Palais Station) and the **Old Post Office** are visible to the right. Constructed of local granite, stone and brick, both buildings reflect the architectural style imposed throughout Canada by the Canadian Pacific Railway on its buildings following the construction of the Château Frontenac in 1893. *A 20min detour to the train station is recommended for those wishing to visit the refurbished interior.* Restored to their former splendour, the original porcelain tiles and steel arches adorn a surprisingly modern and functional entrance hall.

Cross Côte du Palais and take Rue de l'Arsenal leading to the back entrance of the Artillery Park. If renovations are in progress and the back entrance is closed, proceed along Côte du Palais and turn right on Rue Saint-Jean, then right on Rue D'Auteuil.

★**Lieu historique national du Parc-de-l'Artillerie** (Artillery Park National Historic Site) – *The main entrance at 2 Rue d'Auteuil is located near the St. John Gate.* This vast site that includes barracks, a redoubt and an old foundry, commemorates three centuries of military, social and industrial life in Quebec City. Originally a residential district, the area now occupied by the Artillery Park was transformed by the construction of army barracks in 1749. After the Conquest, soldiers of the Royal Artillery Regiment took up residence here and erected several additional buildings over the years. The area's industrial vocation began in 1879, when the Canadian government acquired the site to convert it into a cartridge factory, later named the Dominion Arsenal. The industrial complex was abandoned in 1964 and in 1972, the Canadian Parks Service began a program of renovations. Today the site features several noteworthy buildings.

Ancienne Fonderie (Old Foundry) – *Open Apr–Oct daily 10am–5pm (Apr–early May by reservation). Rest of the year by reservation noon–4pm. Closed mid-Dec–mid-Jan. $3.25.* &. *www.parkscanada.gc.ca/artillerie* ☎ *418-648-4205.* The large windows and skylights of this 1903 foundry recall its original function. Today the building houses a reception and interpretation centre for the Artillery Park complex. Focal point of the exhibit, the **scale model**★★ of Quebec City presents a stunning picture of the city as it appeared at the beginning of the 19C. Created between 1806 and 1808 by military engineers, the model reproduces topographical features and public buildings with great precision. On the lower level, visitors can see the ruins of a powder magazine and its protective wall (1808), and objects recovered during archaeological digs at the site.

Economuseum of Dolls – *Open mid-Jun–mid-Aug daily Mon–Fri 9:30am–4:30pm, Sun noon–5pm. Mid-Aug–mid-Jun Mon–Sat 10am–5pm. Closed major holidays.* ☎ *418-692-1516.* This small museum and boutique occupies a shelter that formerly housed gun carriages. A charming collection of dolls greets visitors at the entrance, while in rooms to the left, artisans demonstrate the various steps in the creation of these timeless toys, from the forming of their features to the making of their clothes. Displays at the rear of the building reveal 19C artifacts discovered in the artillery park – including porcelain doll fragments – as well as a number of dolls from past years paired with contemporary examples to show how these popular playthings have evolved over the years.

Dauphine Redoubt – Construction of the impressive white edifice began in 1712 but was interrupted in 1713, following the signature of the Treaty of Utrecht. Remains of the bastioned stone wall along the structure can still be seen today. Completed in 1748 by Chaussegros de Léry, the redoubt was converted into barracks. After the Conquest, the British army built an additional storey over part of the structure and also added massive buttresses to contain the masonry and prevent the vaults from collapsing. The informative exhibits combine costumes, paintings and artifacts to offer insight into a soldier's life during the 18C and 19C.

Nouvelles Casernes (Barracks) – Chaussegros de Léry designed this 160m/525ft long stone structure in 1750 as a succession of row houses, an unusual concept at the time. The barracks contained armouries, stock rooms, a guard room and six prison cells. The building was partially reconstructed during the late 19C.

Exit at the St. John Gate.

Porte Saint-Jean (St. John Gate) – As of 1867, a larger gate replaced the one designed in the 18C. To facilitate traffic flow between the various parts of the city, this gate was demolished in 1897. The current structure was built in 1936.

Place d'Youville – Located on the site of the former Montcalm market, this lively square has been a cultural and entertainment centre for residents of Quebec City since 1900. Note the Montcalm Palace *(Palais Montcalm)*, erected in 1930; the sober architecture and lack of ornamentation testify to the magnitude of the economic crisis that marked that era. Adjacent stands the Capitole Theatre (Théâtre du Capitole); its rounded facade is typical of the Beaux Arts style popular during the early 20C.

> ### ● A Night at the Capitole ...
>
> *972 Rue Saint-Jean.*
> *Information & reservations*
> ☎ *418-694-4444.* Located just steps away from St. John Gate, this nearly century-old building houses one of Quebec's most prestigious live-performance theatres (cap. 1,300). The sumptuous interior decoration lends itself to large-scale productions as well as more intimate concerts. Before or after the show (or even for breakfast), stop in at **Il Teatro** (in the Capitole building; ☎ *418-694-9996)*, a charming eatery serving fine Italian cuisine in a modern, yet welcoming setting. In summer the terrace offers a wonderful view of Rue Saint-Jean.

Return through the St. John Gate and turn right on Rue d'Auteuil.

Porte Kent (Kent Gate) – Named in honour of the Duchess of Kent, this opening in the western rampart was created in 1879.

Chapelle des Jésuites (Jesuit Chapel) – *At the junction of Rue d'Auteuil and Rue Dauphine. Open year-round Mon–Fri 11:30am–1:30pm. Closed major holidays.* ☎ *418-694-9616.* This chapel has been dedicated to Canadian martyrs since 1925. The small structure (1820) stands on land formerly belonging to the Jesuit College. The building was enlarged in 1857 and a new facade added in 1930. The gilded wooden statues of the Virgin and St. Joseph were sculpted by Pierre-Noël Levasseur. Médard Bourgault, of Saint-Jean-Port-Joli, carved the Stations of the Cross.

© Malak, Ottawa

Porte Saint-Louis

Lieu historique national des Fortifications-de-Québec (Quebec Fortifications National Historic Site) – *100 Rue St-Louis. Open early-Apr–early-May by reservation only. Early-May–late-June daily 10am–5pm. Late-June–early-Sept daily 9am–5pm. Early-Sept–early-Oct daily 10am–5pm. $2.75.* & *www.parkscanada.gc.ca/fortifications* ☎ *418-648-7016.* Contained within the surrounding wall, the **Fortification interpretation centre** presents the history of Quebec via the evolution of its defense systems and organises guided tours of the imposing wall surrounding the city. Near the centre, to the right of the St. Louis Gate, lies the **poudrière**, built in 1810 or the Esplanade, a vast field used for military exercises between 1779 and 1783.

Porte Saint-Louis (St. Louis Gate) – The St. Louis gate – like its counterparts, the Kent, St. John and Prescott gates – no longer controls access to the city. Instead it provides a bridge for visitors using the fortifications walkway to tour the old city. Replete with towers, turrets, battlements and machicolations, the gate was designed in 1878 by Irish architect W.H. Lynn, a collaborator of Lord Dufferin. The St. Louis gate influenced the development of a Château-style architecture in Quebec City.

★ ④ GRANDE ALLÉE *5km/2.9mi. Maps pp 258-259.*

Begin the walking tour at the Parliament Building.

Departing from the St. Louis gate and extending southward of old Quebec, the Grande Allée is the city's Champs-Élysées. Lined with an abundance of restaurants, bars, outdoor cafés, boutiques and offices, Quebec City's premier thoroughfare provides an elegant setting for the city's nightlife.

Grande Allée developed along the east-west axis that separated the land plots allotted to a few major property holders on the Quebec plateau in the early 17C. Originally a country road, it acquired a sudden popularity in the late 18C when it was transformed into a resort district by the British. In just a few years, magnificent villas appeared along the south side of Grande Allée, and the Faubourg Saint-Louis began taking shape.

Adding to the shift of business activity to Montreal and the move of the Canadian Parliament to Ottawa, the departure of the British garrison in 1871 hastened the decline of Quebec City. Inspired by the new city of Edinburgh, which developed alongside the original medieval town, the municipal engineer Charles Baillairgé suggested that Grande Allée be transformed into one of Quebec City's main arteries.

A major fire destroyed the Faubourg Saint-Louis on July 1, 1876, clearing much of the area and prompting the decision to erect the Parliament Building on this site. Following construction of the imposing edifice in 1886, the boulevard was designed as a corridor for official processions, linking the Parliament Building to Bois-de-Coulonge Park, the official residence of the Lieutenant-Governor.

The first residents of the remodelled Grande Allée (1886-1890) were the political elite of the city, who built opulent villas in the Second Empire style. Between 1890 and 1900, the upper portion of the boulevard was further developed with the arrival of a new bourgeoisie reaping the benefits of the Lower Town's industrialization. The heyday of Grande Allée continued well after World War I, and came to an end with the opening of the Quebec City Bridge to car travel in 1929, which gradually transformed the elegant residential district into a busy thoroughfare.

Avenue Cartier

The comings and goings of neighbourhood denizens animate this attractive thoroughfare located well away from Quebec City's main tourist areas. Lining the street are a number of interesting restaurants, cafes and small shops well worth taking the time to explore. The menu at **Graffiti** *(1191 Ave. Cartier; ☎ 418-529-4949)* features high-quality Italian and French food accompanied by an excellent wine list. A glass-brick wall enhances the warm, welcoming interior. A bit farther down the street, **Café Krieghoff** *(1089 Ave. Cartier; ☎ 418-522-3711)* serves light meals and excellent breakfasts, attracting a varied clientele to its small, simply decorated dining rooms. Located just off Avenue Cartier, **Épicerie Méditerranéenne** *(64 Blvd. René-Lévesque EST; ☎ 418-529-9235)* excels in the fine art of presentation, with attractive displays of pastas, oils, breads and cheese to seduce the eye and awaken the appetite. Stop by at noon for a sandwich to go. At elegant **Quartier Général** *(1180 Ave. Cartier; ☎ 418-529-6083)*, every article appears to have been selected with the greatest of care, be it a frame, a candlestick or a decorative box.

★★Hôtel du Parlement (Parliament Building) – *Visit by guided tour (30min) only. Jun 24–Labour Day Mon–Fri 9am–4:30pm, weekends 10am–4:30pm. Rest of the year Mon–Fri 9am–4:30pm.* ☒ ☖ ☐ *www.assnat.qc.ca* ☎ *418-643-7239.* Overlooking the old city, this majestic edifice is the finest example of Second Empire architecture in Quebec City. In 1875, the deputy minister of the Department of Crown Lands, **Eugène-Étienne Taché** (1836-1912), was mandated by the provincial government to draw up the plans of a building to house the parliament and various government ministries. Originally designed to occupy the former site of the Jesuit college in Old Quebec (now City Hall), the project was transferred to the Cricket Field, in the Faubourg Saint-Louis, after the devastating fire of 1876.

The Parliament building forms a quadrangle surrounding an inner courtyard. The imposing **facade** presents a historic tableau featuring bronze figures that commemorate the great names of Quebec history. Some of these sculptures were created by Louis-Philippe Hébert. His *Nigog Fisherman* is encased in a niche before the main entrance; above the niche stands another one of his works, entitled *The Amerindian Family*, which was displayed during the 1889 Universal Exhibit in Paris. *In front of the facade is a diagram identifying the various bronze figures and their creators.*

The entrance hall bears the national emblems of various countries, a reminder that, at the time of construction, Quebec was chiefly comprised of immigrants from France, England, Ireland and Scotland. A staircase leads to Le Parlementaire, a sumptuous dining room *(open to the public)* decorated in the Beaux-Arts style (1917). Drawing attention to the restaurant entrance is a stained-glass passageway,

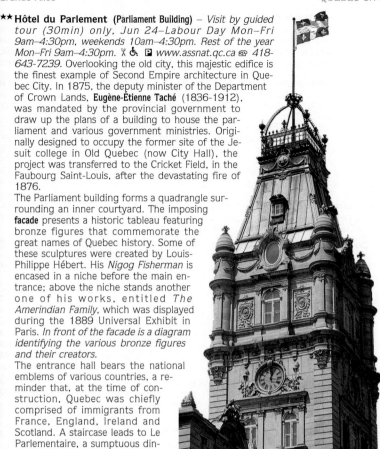

© Malak, Ottawa

Hôtel du Parlement

flooded with light, which evokes an Atlantic seascape.

Parliamentary Chambers – *On the first floor, an antechamber leads to both parliamentary chambers through finely chiselled doors.* Quebec's bicameral parliamentary system, as established by the Constitution Act of 1867, required two distinct halls: the Chamber of the National Assembly and the Chamber of the Legislative Council. Quebec's National Assembly (elected) now sits in the Chamber of the National Assembly. The Chamber of the Legislative Council, similar in size and decor, was used by the Legislative Council (appointed) until the council was abolished in 1968. Since then, it has hosted meetings of parliamentary committees and official receptions. Following the British parliamentary system, the majority party, which forms the government, sits face to face with the "loyal opposition" made up of one or several parties. Ministers and the principal members of the opposition are separated by a space, which in former times was said to equal "the length of two swords." The general plan of the chambers is modelled after the Banqueting Hall of London's Whitehall Palace. Above the throne of the National Assembly Speaker hangs a painting by Charles Huot (*The Debate on Languages*, 1910-1913) representing the January 21, 1793 sitting of the Legislative Assembly of Lower Canada, during which the historic linguistic debate that granted official status to the French language took place.

Gardens – Several commemorative monuments are strewn throughout the gardens of the Parliament Building. The monument to **Maurice Duplessis** (1890-1959), prime minister of Quebec (1936-1939, 1944-1959), is the work of the sculptor Émile Brunet. The monument commemorating the political career of **Honoré Mercier** (1840-1894), a champion of provincial autonomy and traditional rural values, who was prime minister of Quebec from 1887 to 1891, was sculpted by the French artist, Paul Chevré (1912). At the corner of Boulevard Dufferin and Grande Allée is a monument to **François-Xavier Garneau** (1809-1866), Quebec's first national historian.

Continue south on Grande Allée.

Manège militaire (Military Hall) – *Behind Place George-V.* Constructed between 1884 and 1887 by Eugène-Étienne Taché, the Château-style building formerly served as a provincial exhibit pavilion and a military exercise hall. At the turn of the century, an annex was added to the eastern wing of the original structure.

Turn right on Rue de la Chevrotière.

★**Chapelle historique Bon-Pasteur (Historic Good Shepherd Chapel)** – *1080 Rue de la Chevrotière. Open Jul–Aug Tue–Fri 1:30pm–4:30pm, Sun 9am–12:30pm. Rest of the year Mon–Fri 1:30pm–4:30pm, Sun 9am–12:30pm by appointment. Artists' Mass Sun 10:45am. Contribution requested ($2). Closed weeks of Jan 1 & Easter.* ☎ *418-648-9710.* Designed by Charles Baillairgé in 1866, the chapel is located on the second floor of the former convent of the Sisters of the Good Shepherd. The tall, narrow, Baroque-style nave is flanked by superimposed side galleries, enabling occupants on all levels to access the chapel.

Resting on the high altar (1730), the gilded retable from the Saint-Louis-de-Lotbinière church was sculpted in the Levasseur workshop in the 1730s. Above it hangs *The Assumption of the Virgin*, by Antoine Plamondon (1868). Several small paintings adorn the pilasters; they were created in the workshop of the Sisters, renowned for the many religious paintings executed for churches in the Quebec diocese in the late 19C.

Observatoire de la Capitale (Édifice Marie-Guyart) – *Entrance at 1037 Rue de la Chevrotière. Open late-June–mid-Oct daily 10am–5pm. Mid-Oct–late-June Tue–Sun 10am–5pm. $4 Closed Jan 1 & Dec 25.* ⴷ *www.observatoirecapitale.org* ☎ *418-644-9841.* The observatory occupying the 31st floor of this administrative building provides a splendid **view**★★ of Old Quebec, the citadel and fortifications as well as the surrounding areas.

Return to Grande Allée and turn right.

Église Saint-Cœur-de-Marie (Church of the Sacred Heart of Mary) – *At corner of Rue Scott and Grande Allée (no. 530).* Erected in 1920, the brick edifice was built for the Eudists, also known as the Congregation of Jesus and Mary, founded in the 17C. The quaint steeple distinctly contrasts with the otherwise modern structure.

La Laurentienne – *500 Grande Allée Est.* The headquarters of this insurance company occupy a structure (1962) that embodies the functionalist tendency of modern architecture in Quebec City. Towards the rear, a new facade of mirrored glass overlooks the Park of French America (Parc de l'Amérique française).

Take Ave. Taché on the left to view the Martello tower no. 2 (open May–Sept daily 10am-5:30pm; $2; ⴷ ☎ *418-648-4071). Return to Grande Allée.*

Maison Stewart (Stewart House) – *82 Grande Allée Ouest, at northeast corner of Ave. Cartier.* Surrounded by a small park, this 1849 cottage features large, French windows adorning the facade. Topped by a central chimney stack, the overhanging roof covers the lateral galleries.

At no. 95 stands the **Ladies' Protestant Home**, an elegant example of the Renaissance Revival style exemplified here by the massive cornice and lantern. To the right of the structure, facing the Avenue Cartier, the **Krieghoff House** *(not open to the public)* was named for the painter Cornelius Krieghoff (1815-1872) who lived here intermittently in 1859 and 1860. Built in 1850, this "rustic cottage" is in fact a country house for city dwellers; the style derives from Quebec vernacular architecture.

Turn left on Ave. Wolfe-Montcalm and follow signs to the Quebec Museum (Musée du Québec).

The avenue runs alongside a military parade ground used by the British army after they abandoned Place d'Armes in 1823. For years, major events such as the historic parades marking Quebec City's 300th anniversary took place on the site.

Facing the museum, the **Wolfe monument** marks the spot where the victor of the Battle of the Plains of Abraham, General James Wolfe, died on September 13, 1759.

★★**Musée du Québec (Quebec Museum)** – *The entrance to the museum is located between the two main buildings, on the ground level. Open Jun–Aug daily 10am–6pm (Wed 9pm). Rest of the year Tue–Sun 10am–5pm (Wed 9pm). Closed Dec 25. $7.* ⴲ ⴷ ⴷ *($2.50/hr) www.mdq.org* ☎ *418-643-2150.* Situated on the site of the National Battlefields Park, this remarkable museum complex provides a comprehensive overview of Quebec art from the 18C to the present. Temporary and permanent exhibits drawn from a collection of over 22,000 works of art are organised throughout three buildings.

Main Hall – Situated between the two other structures, the Main Hall serves as the main entrance to the museum. The modern structure, capped by skylights, houses the reception area, an auditorium and other amenities.

Gérard Morisset Pavilion – The monumental facade of this structure (named for a former museum director), reflects the Beaux-Arts style that was adopted for many of Quebec's government buildings. The granite-clad building features an imposing central staircase leading to an Ionic portico. The sculpted stone pediment evokes the

Province's economic history and the history of two groups: the Amerindians *(left side)* and the discoverers and missionaries *(right side)*. Aluminium-plated bas-reliefs representing various events in the history of Canada and traditional agricultural scenes adorn the structure's lateral wings. Pieces from the permanent collection are on view here, including ancient, modern and contemporary art; the works offer a sweeping view of the development of Quebec art.

Baillairgé Pavilion – Erected according to plans by Charles Baillairgé, this monumental Renaissance Revival-style structure (1871) housed, until 1967, the old "plains prison." An entire cell block has been preserved as an exhibit of prison life during the last century. One gallery here features one of the most important paintings in the history of Canada: the renowned *Assemblée des six comtés (Assembly of Six Counties)*. A masterpiece of Charles Alexander Smith, this impressive canvas illustrates one of the key moments of the insurrections of 1837-1838: in the foreground, Louis-Joseph Papineau, leader of the Patriots, addresses an attentive crowd.

In the tower of this structure *(4th floor)*, note the curious statue of a diver, entitled *aLomph aBram*, executed in the late 1960s by David Moore.

The Baillairgé Pavilion of the Musée du Québec houses the **Battlefields Park Interpretation Centre** (Centre d'interprétation du parc des Champs-de-Bataille), presenting the thrilling history of the battles of the Plains of Abraham *(open June–Labour Day daily 10am–5:30pm; rest of the year Tue–Sun 11am–5:30pm; $3.50;* ✗ ᵫ 🅿 *($1/hr) www.ccbn-nbc.gc.ca* ☎ *418-648-4071)*.

Upon exiting from the museum, turn left on Ave. Georges-VI and continue to Grey Terrace.

This observatory was named in honour of A.H. Grey, governor-general of Canada from 1904 to 1911, during which time the park was constructed.

Doubling back, take Ave. Ontario through National Battlefields Park.

★**Parc des Champs-de-Bataille** (Battlefields Park) – *Open Jun 24–Labour Day daily 8:30am–7:30pm. Early Sept–Jun 23 8:30am–5pm.* ✗ ᵫ 🅿 *($1/hr) www.ccbn-nbc.gc.ca* ☎ *418-648-4071. To the left of Ave. Ontario, Martello tower no. 1 is visible (open Jun–Sept daily 10am–5:30pm; $3.50). Continuing straight ahead, the Ave. du Cap-aux-Diamants leads to the Governors' Promenade (promenade des Gouverneurs) belvedere.* Created in 1908, on the tricentennial of the founding of the city, this national park stretches over 108ha/266 acres along a cliff on the south side of the Quebec City plateau. Overlooking the St. Lawrence River, the site commemorates the battles fought between the British and French armies during the Conquest. The park, completed in 1954, was landscaped by Frederick G. Todd, a student of Frederick Law Olmsted, renowned designer of New York City's Central Park and Montreal's Mt. Royal Park. Inspired by English country gardens, the rambling park introduces a green space into the cityscape, providing a natural-looking environment that contrasts with the structured, rational layout of classical gardens.

The Battle of the Plains of Abraham – A large section of the park occupies the former plains of Abraham, so named after Abraham Martin, a wealthy farmer living on the Quebec City heights in the 17C. On this site, the French and British armies fought the battle that eventually sealed the fate of the French colony.

On September 13, 1759, some 5,000 British troops under the command of General Wolfe scaled the steep cliff and launched an attack on the city. Without waiting for reinforcements, the French General Montcalm urged his ill-prepared army against the British lines, who in turn crushed the attempt in less than 15 minutes. Both generals were mortally wounded during the short, but decisive event. Five days later, Quebec had been completely occupied and the French troops, under the command of François-Gaston de Lévis (1719-1787), retreated to Montreal for the winter.

The following April, Lévis and the French army returned to battle the British at Sainte-Foy (a monument located in des-Braves Park north of Chemin Sainte-Foy commemorates the event). Though the French were victorious, their hopes were dashed the following month when a ship arrived bearing British reinforcements, sealing the fate of New France. The territory was officially turned over to the British by the Treaty of Paris in 1763.

Fearing that Americans would initiate another invasion following the failed attempt by Bostonians in 1775-1776, and still awaiting London's decision regarding the construction of a citadel, the British military erected four **Martello towers** between 1808 and 1812 as an advanced defensive line.

Café-Restaurant du Musée du Québec

In the National Battlefields Park. ☎ *418-644-6780.* Located within the Quebec Museum, this restaurant offers imaginative taste treats, carefully prepared and served with flair. Natural light floods the vast dining room, where immense windows offer a superb view of the Plains of Abraham. In summer, take a table on the terrace to admire the surrounding countryside.

Martello Tower

Mla et Klaus

Three towers remain, two located in the park and one on Rue Lavigueur (Faubourg Saint-Jean-Baptiste). Named after the Corsican point where they originated, Martello towers are circular defensive outposts, topped by a platform mounted with cannons. This platform is sometimes protected by a detachable roof which can be quickly dismantled in case of attack. The section of the wall built to resist the enemy is very thick, while the section facing the garrison is much thinner; thus, should the tower be overtaken by the enemy, it can be easily destroyed by the besieged troops.

EXCURSIONS *Map pp 258-259.*

Sillery and Sainte-Foy

Located on the banks of the St. Lawrence barely 1km/.6mi from Quebec, the community of Sillery was named after the French nobleman, Noël Brulart de Sillery. The settlement traces its origins to the Jesuit mission founded in 1637 to evangelize Amerindians. However, ravaging epidemic diseases and alcoholism led to the abandonment of the settlement in the 1680s. After the Conquest, Jesuits rented the territory to several wealthy merchants. The expanding lumber and shipbuilding industry prompted an economic surge during the mid-19C, as Sillery's coves and bays were used for unloading, squaring off, warehousing and exporting timber. Several of the sumptuous mansions erected during this prosperous era were later acquired by various religious organizations. After World War II, Sillery quickly developed as a residential suburb of Quebec City. Today, the town presents a subtle mix of old world charm and bustling city activities. Past National Battlefields Park, Grande Allée becomes Chemin Saint-Louis. A wooded median divides the boulevard, which is lined with prestigious office buildings.

★**Parc du Bois-de-Coulonge** (Bois-de-Coulonge Park) – *1215 Chemin Saint-Louis, in Sillery. Open daily year-round.* & 🅿 *www.capitale.gouv.qc.ca* ☎ *418-528-0773.* This pleasantly landscaped park constitutes a small part of the old Coulonge seigneury granted to Louis d'Ailleboust, Sieur de Coulonge, in 1649. During the Conquest, the British temporarily occupied the site. In 1780, the domain was subdivided, and one of the first country homes on this land was erected ten years later. Built in the Palladian style, the villa was renamed **Spencer Wood** in honour of British Prime Minister Lord Spencer, in 1811, and would become the residence of Lord Elgin, governor-general of the United Canadas, in 1852. It was rebuilt in 1860 after a fire. Following Confederation, it became the property of the provincial government and served as the residence of the Lieutenant-Governor.
Renamed Bois-de-Coulonge in 1947, the vice-regal residence was destroyed by fire in 1966. Since then, Bois-de-Coulonge Park has been open to the public. Visitors can admire the **guardian's house**★ – a small Château-style construction covered with decorative cedar shingles (1891), as well as various old buildings, gardens and a belvedere overlooking the river.

★**Villa Bagatelle** – *1563 Chemin Saint-Louis, in Sillery. Open year-round Tue–Sun 10am–5pm. $3. Closed Nov–Mar.* & *www.cataraqui.qc.ca* ☎ *418-688-8074.* Reconstructed in 1927 after a fire the previous year, the villa closely resembles a small Gothic Revival cottage erected in 1848 in the park. The house, surrounded by an English garden, houses an exhibit and documentation centre and mounts temporary thematic exhibitions.

Continue along Chemin Saint-Louis.

The road passes by the St. Michael Anglican church, with its squat steeple and large buttresses.

Turn left on Côte de l'Église.

Église Saint-Michel (St. Michael Church) – *1600 Rue Persico, in Sillery. Open year-round daily 8:30am–8pm.* ♿ ▣ ☎ *418-527-3390.* The Gothic Revival church dates from 1854. Five paintings from the Desjardins collection are preserved in the interior: *Emmaüs' Disciples, Death of St. Francis of Assisi, St. Francis of Assisi Receiving the Stigmata, the Annunciation,* and *the Adoration of the Magi.*

Outside, on a terrace below the church, the lookout at **Pointe-à-Puiseaux** affords a superb **view**★ of Quebec City, Sillery's coves, the Quebec City and Pierre-Laporte bridges and the south shore.

Return to Chemin Saint-Louis.

Domaine Cataraqui (Cataraqui Domain) – *2141 Chemin Saint-Louis, in Sillery. Open year-round Tue–Sun 10am–5pm. $5.* ♿ ▣ *www.cataraqui.qc.ca* ☎ *418-681-3010.* Erected during the 19C, the domain is one of the last survivors of Sillery's golden era. The vast park hugging the cliff encompasses a Gothic Revival villa as well as several greenhouses and outbuildings, including the studio of painter Henry Percyval Tudor-Hart, who lived here for several years. The house served as the Governor-General's temporary residence after the Bois-de-Coulonge fire, in 1860.

Maison Hamel-Bruneau (Hamel-Bruneau House) – *2608 Chemin Saint-Louis, in Sainte-Foy. Open year-round Tue–Sun 12:30pm–5pm (Wed 9pm).* ♿ ▣ ☎ *418-654-4325.* This little cottage, a synthesis between the ornate English cottage and the Quebec vernacular style, was built as a country home in 1858. It houses temporary exhibits and offers cultural activities.

Turn left on Ave. du Parc.

Aquarium du Québec (Quebec Aquarium) – *1675 Ave. des Hôtels, in Sainte-Foy. The aquarium will be closed for renovation indefinitely. For more information call* ☎ *418-622-0313.* Established in 1959, on a site overlooking the St. Lawrence River, the aquarium houses more than 1,700 specimens of indigenous and exotic fish, reptiles and sea mammals. Of special interest are the outdoor seal pools. Upon leaving the aquarium, stop at the little lookout in the parking lot to enjoy a magnificent **view**★ of the St. Lawrence River, Quebec City and Pierre-Laporte bridges.

Descend towards the St. Lawrence, take Blvd. Champlain and continue to Côte de Gignac. Turn left then right onto Chemin du Foulon.

★**Maison des Jésuites** (Jesuit House) – *2320 Chemin du Foulon, in Sillery. Open Jun–Aug Tue–Sun 11am–5pm.* ▣ ☎ *418-654-0259.* The current early-18C stone house was erected on the site of the St. Joseph mission (the first Jesuit mission in North America), established by Jesuits in 1637 in order to convert the Montagnais, Algonquins and Attikameks to a sedentary lifestyle. So as to protect themselves from attacks by Iroquois, the Jesuits and Amerindians lived in an enclosure surrounded by stakes, which was later replaced by a stone fort. Facing the house, vestiges of the fort and the Saint-Michel chapel have been unearthed. The British writer, Frances Moore Brookes, lived in this two-storey edifice in 1763. In 1769, she published *The History of Emily Montague,* which takes place in this house. By 1929, the Jesuit House was classified as one of the earliest historical monuments in Quebec. It now houses a small museum of exhibits focusing on the history of indige-

Maison des Jésuites, Sillery

nous peoples, as well as archaeology of the site and local history. In the gardens, note the recreated native camp, which highlights the site's importance as a meeting place between missionaries and indigenous peoples during the era of New France. Along Chemin du Foulon, note the old wooden houses, formerly inhabited by shipyard employees.

Université Laval (Laval University)

In Sainte-Foy, 7km/4mi from St. Louis Gate by Grande Allée, Chemin Saint-Louis and Blvd. Laurier (Rte. 175).

Founded in 1852 by the Quebec Seminary, Laval University began constructing a campus *(cité universitaire)* in the western suburb of Quebec City in 1949. The north-south axis opens onto a view of the Laurentian Mountains while the east-west draws attention to the Grand Seminary and the Faculty of Medicine. The university underwent considerable expansion in the 1960s; today its 13 departments, 9 specialty schools and several research centres accommodate a student body of more than 40,000 students.

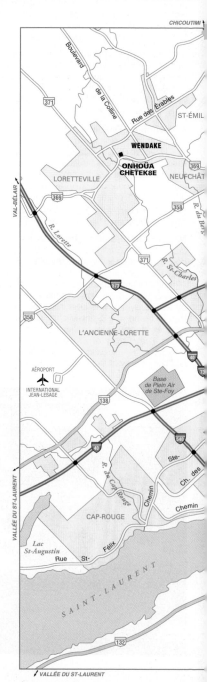

The Buildings – The **Louis-Jacques Casault Pavilion** (formerly the Grand Seminary) was built in 1958. Inside, the Gothic-style university chapel was redesigned to house the Quebec national archives. Facing the Casault Pavilion are two new buildings, erected in 1990: the **Laurentienne Pavilion** and the award-winning, Postmodern, **Alexandre-de-Sève Pavilion**.

With its classic composition, inner courtyard and facades articulated by sunshields of white concrete, the **Charles-de-Koninck Pavilion** (1964) is today considered the main building of the university complex. The **Comtois Pavilion** (1966) also reflects the desire to achieve a classical appearance through the use of prefabricated modules. With its inner courtyard and pillared structure, it is one of the most interesting buildings in the Quebec City region.

A squat building marked by horizontal lines, the sports complex known as **PEPS** (pavillon de l'éducation physique et des sports, 1971) stretches out over terraced grounds covering large underground parking areas. Facilities include an Olympic-size pool, an indoor stadium, skating rinks and several sporting areas.

★Cartier-Brébeuf National Historic Site

3km/2mi from St. John Gate, by Côte d'Abraham, Rue de la Couronne, Drouin Bridge and 1re Ave. Turn left on rue de l'Éspinay. *Open Apr–early May by appointment. Early May–early-Sept daily 10am–5pm. early-Sept–early-Oct daily 1pm–4pm. Rest of the year by appointment. $3.* & ▣ *www.parkscanada.gc.ca/brebeuf* ☎ *418-648-4038.* Located on the northern shore of the Lairet Basin, this park commemorates Jacques Cartier, who wintered on this spot in 1535-1536, and Jean de Brébeuf, a Jesuit missionary. The **interpretation centre** features insightful displays, which recall Cartier's second voyage to New France and his meetings with the Iroquois, as well as the Jesuit's first mission, established in 1626.

Charlesbourg

Take Rte. 73 Nord to Exit 150 (80e Rue Ouest).

★**Trait-Carré** – *Departure point for walking tour of the Trait-Carré: Moulin des Jesuites at 7960 Blvd. Henri-Bourassa (open Jun 24–mid-Aug daily 10am–9pm; ☎ 418-623-1877). Maps/brochures available.* The heart of old Charlesbourg, commonly referred to as the Trait-Carré historical district, comprises a square lot located in the midst of a star-shaped land division plan. Dating back to 1660, it

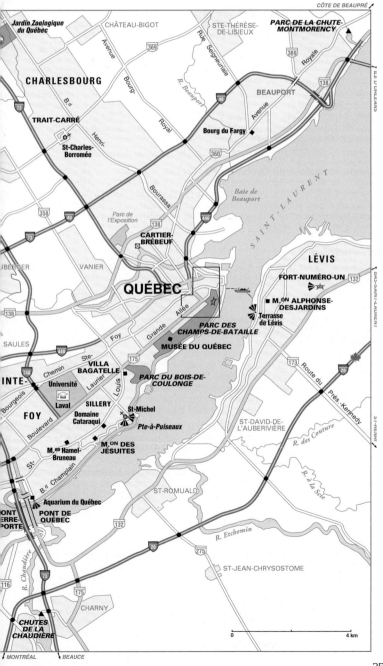

is the only such design in New France. Throughout Quebec, land concessions traditionally took the form of long, narrow strips of land known as *rangs*, which prevented large population concentrations.

The Trait-Carré design was devised in Charlesbourg by Jesuit priests and the intendant Jean Talon, who sought to ensure that all homes would be located near the main square, to improve defensibility in case of attack.

Today, the centre of Trait-Carré is bordered by four streets. In the middle is the institutional centre of old Charlesbourg, which includes a church, a municipal library housed in the old Saint Charles College (1903), and the Bon-Pasteur Convent, built in 1883.

Église Saint-Charles-Borromée (St. Charles Borromeo Church) – *Visit by guided tour only (by appointment).* ☎ *418-624-7720*. With its two steeples and high facade dominated by a large pediment, this edifice (1827-1830) exemplifies the influence of English Palladianism on the religious architecture of Quebec.

The focal point of the interior is the imposing triumphal arch adorning the flat apse. Salvaged from an earlier church erected on this site, two statues (1742) by Pierre-Noël Levasseur stand in lateral niches. Also worth noting are works by François Ranvoyzé, Louis Jobin, Charles Vézina and Paul Lambert.

At the southeast corner of the Trait-Carré stands the **Ephraïm Bédard House** *(7655 Chemin Samuel; open Jun 24–late Aug Wed–Sun 1pm–9pm; rest of the year Tue & Thu 1:30pm–4pm;* ♿ 🅿 ☎ *418-623-1877)*, a typical rural dwelling from early 19C. The **Pierre-Lefebvre House** *(7985 Trait-Carré Est; open Jun 24–late Aug Wed–Sun 1pm–7pm; rest of the year Thu–Fri 7pm–9pm, Sat 1pm–5pm, Sun 1pm–5pm;* ♿ 🅿 ☎ *418-623-1877)*, a typical 19C wood structure, has been converted into the Trait-Carré Gallery of Visual Arts. Other historic structures in the quarter have also been converted into cultural centers, among them the Magella-Paradis House (1833), which boasts a distinctive roofline.

Return to Rte. 73 and continue to Exit 154 (Rue de la Faune).

Jardin zoologique du Québec (Quebec City Zoo) – *The zoo will be closed for renovation indefinitely. For more information call* ☎ *418-622-0313*. A visit to the Quebec City Zoo ranks among the most popular family outings in the city. The zoo is home to over 600 animals representing some 125 species from around the globe. Local residents enjoy cross-country skiing and snowshoeing on the zoo grounds during the winter months.

Wendake

Take Rte. 73 Nord to Exit 154. Turn left on Rue de la Faune (which becomes Rue des Érables and Rue de la Rivière). Then turn right on Rue Max Gros-Louis.

Expelled from the Great Lakes region by the Iroquois, and by epidemics and famine, the Hurons sought the protection of the French in the mid-17C. Accompanied by Father Chaumonot, a Jesuit missionary, they settled in the Upper Town (near Fort Saint-Louis), and moved on to Ile d'Orleans in 1651. In 1668, they emigrated to Sainte-Foy, on the present site of Laval University, and then to Ancienne-Lorette, in 1673. From there they moved one last time to Jeune-Lorette, or Wendake, in 1697. Today, a stroll through the streets of the **Huron Village** (Village-des-Hurons) reveals the uniqueness of this place. The buildings on the reserve were erected on communal land in the Amerindian tradition, without individual land allotments or European cadastral boundaries. The community is located near the Saint Charles (or Kabir-Kouba) River, whose waterfalls have inspired numerous artists.

★ **Site traditionnel huron-wendat Onhoüa Chetek 8e (Huron-Wendat Onhoüa Chetek 8e Traditional Site)** – *575 Rue Stanislas-Kosca. Visit by guided tour (40min) only, early May–early Oct daily 9am–6pm. Rest of the year daily 9am–5pm. Closed Jan 1 & Dec 25. $8.* 🍴 ♿ 🅿 *www.huron-wendat.qc.ca* ☎ *418-842-4308*. "Koey Koey ataro…" (Welcome, friend…) Thus begins a visit to this recreated traditional Amerindian village, which offers a fascinating introduction to the history, heritage and customs of the First Nations, and of the Huron Nation in particular. Visitors will step inside a longhouse (multi-family dwelling), and view a smokehouse and a traditional sauna, a small structure in which steam is produced by pouring boiling water onto heated stones. From May to October experience the animation of Huron legends and traditional dance.

The **Notre-Dame-de-Lorette chapel** *(corner of Rues Chef-Maurice-Bastien and Chef-Nicholas-Vincent; open May–Oct Mon–Fri 9am–5pm, weekends 10am–5pm;* 🍴 ♿ 🅿 ☎ *418-845-1241)* occupies the site of the Jesuit Mission of 1697. The present structure (1865) was erected on the site of an earlier church (1730) that was destroyed by fire in 1862. The very simple decor includes a high altar tabernacle believed to have been executed in 1722 by Pierre-Noël Levasseur. Above the altar, a simple sculpture represents the Santa Casa of Loretto, in Italy, supported by two angels. The chapel treasure, which includes religious furnishings left behind by the Jesuit missionaries, is exhibited in the sacristy.

RAWDON★

Lanaudière

Population 3,855

Map p 133

Situated in the foothills of the Laurentian Mountains, this small community lies in the heart of a popular recreation area. The Rouge and Ouareau Rivers flanking the centre of town form spectacular waterfalls and cascades on their journey south to the St. Lawrence.

Originally part of lands granted to Loyalists in 1799, Rawdon was first settled in the late 1810s by Irish immigrants, who were followed by Scots and French Canadians (mainly Acadians). In the course of the 20C, the town has become home to a sizable Eastern European population. To this day, Rawdon remains a multicultural community, as evidenced by the presence of a diverse mix of religious edifices, including a Russian Orthodox church *(located at the junction of Rue Woodland and 15ᵉ Ave.)*. Also of particular interest is the small **Anglican Church** *(corner of Rue Metcalfe and 3ᵉ Ave.)*. The stone structure (1861), topped by a wooden belfry and bordered on one side by a small cemetery, is perhaps the town's most charming sight.

Access – *Rawdon is about 75km/46mi north of Montreal by Rtes. 25, 125 and 337.*

© Anne Gardon/REFLEXION

Parc des Chutes-Dorwin

SIGHTS

★**Parc des Chutes-Dorwin (Dorwin Falls Park)** – *Located in a park off Rte. 337, just before reaching the centre of Rawdon, coming from Montreal. Open May–Oct daily 9am–7pm. $2. ✗ ⅍ 🅿 ($2) www.ccdrawdon.qc.ca ☎ 450-834-2282.* In a wooded site, the Ouareau River cascades over rocks, then plunges 30m/98ft into a small pool and branches off into a narrow, rocky gorge.

According to an Amerindian legend, the falls sprang out when Nipissingue, a wicked sorcerer, pushed the beautiful maiden, Hiawitha, into a chasm. He was turned to stone by a clap of thunder, while she was transformed into a waterfall. Popular belief holds that the profile, carved into the rock at the edge of the falls, is that of the sorcerer *(best viewed from the observation deck midway down).*

The Rouge River also drops in a lovely waterfall, the Mason Falls *(on 3ᵉ Ave. and Rue Maple). Access to the bottom of the falls is difficult.*

★**Parc des Cascades (Cascades Park)** – *From Rue Queen, turn onto Rte. 341 towards Saint-Donat. Open mid-May–Thanksgiving Day daily 9am–6pm. $6/car. ⅍ 🅿 ☎ 514-834-2587.* The magnificent cascade, tumbling down a broad staircase of rocks, is located at the northern edge of Lake Pontbriand, on the Ouareau River. In summer, visitors can wade into the middle of the stream and enjoy the refreshing water. The paths, leading through the pine forest, and picnic areas make this site an enjoyable resting place.

★**Village Canadiana** – *4km/2.5mi. Leave Rawdon by Rue Queen and turn right onto 6ᵉ Ave. which becomes Chemin du Lac Morgan. The village is on the right. At press time, this site was closed for an undetermined period. Please call ahead for information before planning to visit. ☎ 450-834-4135.* This recreated village portrays the rural life of this region in the 19C. For many years, it was the private hobby of Earle Moore, who, in the 1960s, started moving houses and other structures slated for destruction to this enchanting site in the Laurentian foothills.

Built around the original site of an 1867 farmhouse, the village comprises more than 50 structures and is inhabited by costumed guides. Various farm animals roam the premises. Of particular interest are the graceful, white **church**; the settler's cabin of 1842, which was moved from Mille Îles (near Kingston, Ontario); and the inn *(auberge)* of 1843, which originally stood in Rawdon. The school house with its bell tower and upstairs living quarters for the teacher dates from 1835 and was relocated from Lakefield, Ontario. The presbytery (1835), where Brother André spent his vacations in Rawdon, and the General Store (1884) from Saint-Anicet can be visited. A covered bridge of 1888 from Coaticook spans the Rouge River, which is also tapped by an 1867 water mill from Rawdon.

Vallée du RICHELIEU★★

Montérégie

Map p 263

The majestic Richelieu River constitutes one of the links in the waterway flowing between Montreal and New York City. Approximately 130km/81mi long, the river flows from its source in New York State to join the St. Lawrence River at Sorel.

Samuel de Champlain discovered the waterway in 1609, and called it the Iroquois River. It was later named for Armand Jean du Plessis, Duke of Richelieu (1585-1642), better known as **Cardinal Richelieu**, chief minister of Louis XIII. Richelieu presided over the destiny of France from the 1620s until his death and actively supported the development of New France.

Settlers moved into the valley in the early 18C to cultivate the fertile land of this region, which remains one of the richest agricultural areas in Quebec. Today a popular weekend retreat for Montrealers, the Richelieu Valley attracts thousands of travellers and tourists every summer.

Historical Notes

Valley of Forts – Owing to its strategic location, the Richelieu Valley was fortified early in the French Regime. Forts were built at Chambly, Saint-Jean-sur-Richelieu, Lennox (on Île aux Noix) and Lacolle. These fortifications were initially built to protect Montreal against attacks by Iroquois, and later by British troops (1759–1760) and Americans (1775-1776).

In the mid-19C, the threat of invasion subsided, marking the beginning of a new era of trade. The objective was no longer to prevent access from the south but to facilitate transportation between Montreal and the United States. An extensive canal system was built to achieve this goal.

The Patriots' Rebellion (1837-1838) – The Richelieu Valley played an important role in the conflict that opposed the Patriots of Lower Canada to the British government. The grave constitutional struggles of the period, combined with a fierce sense of French Canadian nationalism, led Louis-Joseph Papineau, and his supporters, the Patriots, to denounce the British regime and to seek self-determination. As patriotic fervor increased, citizens loyal to the British government in power formed armed militias to support the army, and violent confrontations occured in the Richelieu Valley and around Montreal. British troops under Colonels Charles Gore and Charles Wetherall faced the rebels at Saint-Denis-sur-Richelieu, defeated them at Saint-Charles-sur-Richelieu, and finally crushed them at Saint-Eustache.

Route 133, on the east side of the river, is called the **Patriots' Road** (Chemin des Patriotes). The rifle, knitted hat, woven belt and sometimes the pipe are symbols of the Patriots and can be seen in numerous illustrations depicting the event. The green, white and red **Canadian tricolour** was their principal flag.

Access – *Chambly is located approximately 30km/19mi from Montreal by Rte. 10 (Exit 22). Itinerary 1 follows the Richelieu River on Rte. 133. Itinerary 2 follows Rte. 223, on the left bank (west side).*

① PATRIOTS' ROAD – Chambly to Sorel

78km/48mi by Rte. 133.

★**Chambly** – *See Entry Heading.*
Leave Chambly by Rte. 112, cross the Richelieu River in the village of Richelieu and take Rte. 133 Nord.

Saint-Mathias – *5km/3mi.* The first settlers came to Saint-Mathias in 1700, when it was still part of the seigneury of Chambly. Today, lovely homes and marinas border the Chambly Basin. The wayside cross on the right, where Route 133 straddles the Huron River, is one of several that still exist along the Richelieu River. The interior decor of the **church** (1784) dates from the 1820s and is the work of René Beauvais (known as Saint-James) and Paul Rollin, two companions of Louis-Amable Quévillon, who executed the pulpit and the main altar in 1797 *(visit by guided tour only; May–Oct Mon, Wed, Fri 9am–noon; contribution requested;* ☐ ⚙ *450-658-1671).*

Continue to Mont-St-Hilaire.

VALLÉE DU RICHELIEU
FORT LENNOX

0   10 km

Île aux Noix

St-Paul-de-l'Île-aux-Noix

Fort-Lennox ★

0   200 m

TROIS-RIVIÈRES

★ **Îles de Sorel**

Berthierville

St-Ignace-de-Loyola

★ **Ste-Anne-de-Sorel**

Sorel

NICOLET

St-Ours

St-Roch-de-Richelieu

St-Denis-sur-Richelieu ★

St-Antoine-sur-Richelieu

Repentigny

St-Marc-sur-Richelieu

St-Charles-sur-Richelieu

Varennes

DRUMMONDVILLE

St-Hyacinthe

Boucherville

Beloeil

McMasterville

Mt-St-Hilaire

MONTRÉAL

Mt Royal △ 233

Longueuil

Otterburn Park

Mt-St-Hilaire ★★ 411

Parc du Mt-St-Bruno

R. des Hurons

Mt Rougemont △ 381

St-Lambert

St-Mathias

Fort-Chambly ★★

GRANBY

La Prairie

★ **Chambly**

Richelieu

Mt St-Grégoire 267 △

SHERBROOKE

St-Jean-sur-Richelieu Iberville

Farnham

COWANSVILLE

Napierville

Sherrington

St-Paul-de-l'Île-aux-Noix

Fort-Lennox ★

Île aux Noix

Venise-en-Québec

STANBRIDGE EAST

Barrington

Lacolle

☆ **Blockhaus de la Rivière Lacolle ★**

R. Lacolle

Fort Montgomery

Baie Missisquoi (L. Champlain)

Hemmingford

Parc Safari ★★

U.S.A.   U.S.A.

Rouses Point

ALBANY, NY   PLATTSBURGH, NY   BURLINGTON, VT

The municipality of **Otterburn Park** *(9km/6mi)* boasts several splendid mansions. Across the river stands the McMasterville industrial complex, where explosives have been manufactured since 1878.

Mont-Saint-Hilaire – *12km/7mi*. Home of the renowned painter, **Ozias Leduc** (1864-1955) and birthplace of 20C artist, **Paul-Émile Borduas**. Mont-Saint-Hilaire is a well-known artistic centre.

Upon arriving in the community, notice the **Rouville-Campbell Manor** on the banks of the Richelieu River. This Tudor-style manor house with its tall brick chimneys was built in the 1850s for Major Thomas Edmund Campbell, who took over the Hertel de Rouville seigneury after the Rebellion of 1837. The mansion was modelled after the Campbell ancestral home in Inverane, Scotland. Artist Jordi Bonet (1932-1979) restored the manor in the 1970s; it now houses an inn and a fine restaurant.

The charming little stone **church** by the river was built in 1837 and decorated by Ozias Leduc in 1898 *(open Mon–Sat 9am–noon, 1:30pm–5pm; Sun 1pm–5pm; contribution requested;* & 🄿 ☎ *450-467-4434)*. On the opposite bank in the town of Belœil, the towers and turrets of the Église Saint-Mathieu-de-Belœil (St. Matthew of Belœil Church) are visible.

Make a detour (12km/7mi round-trip) to get to the Mt. Saint-Hilaire Nature Centre. Turn right on Rte. 116 (signed) and right again on Rue Fortier which becomes Chemin Ozias-Leduc. After 3km/2mi, turn left on Chemin de la Montagne, and left again on Chemin des Moulins.

★★ **Centre de la nature du mont Saint-Hilaire (Mt. Saint-Hilaire Nature Centre)** – *Open year-round daily 8am–1hr before dusk. $4.* ✗ & 🄿 ☎ *450-467-1755*. Rising abruptly above the Richelieu Valley, Mt. Saint-Hilaire (411m/1,348ft) is the most imposing of the Monteregian Hills. The lush forest covering about 11sq km/4sq mi of the mountain has remained practically intact since the arrival of Europeans in Canada. Apple orchards *(in bloom late May)* blanket the mountain's lower slopes, as the Richelieu Valley is one of Quebec's main apple-growing regions.

Mt. Saint-Hilaire is the former estate of Brigadier **Andrew Hamilton Gault** (1882-1958), founder of Princess Patricia's Canadian Light Infantry. He bequeathed his estate to McGill University in order to preserve its beauty and keep it from development. Today, a 6sq km/2.3sq mi section of the park is open to the public, while a 5sq km/1.9sq mi tract is reserved for scientific research. Some 22km/14mi of **trails** crisscross the mountain. From the main summit (known as Pain du Sucre, or "Sugarloaf"), visitors can enjoy sweeping **views**★★ of the Richelieu River, the St. Lawrence Valley and the Olympic Tower in Montreal. Some trails *(500m/1,640ft)* lead to Lake Hertel where Gault erected his residence; it has since been converted into a conference centre. A small rest area is available for hikers and cross-country skiers.

Return to Rte. 133.

Saint-Charles-sur-Richelieu – *15km/9mi*. It is here that the Patriots were defeated on November 25, 1837, by Colonel Wetherall, two days after the first victory at Saint-Denis *(below)*. In the waterfront park, note the small, bas-relief monument dedicated to the Patriots.

On the river, the boat *L'Escale* features theatrical productions during the summer.

★ **Saint-Denis-sur-Richelieu** – *12km/7mi*. This prosperous agricultural community was the site of the Patriot victory over Colonel Gore, on November 23, 1837. In a pleasant square located in the centre of the village, the Canadian tricolour flies above a wooden pedestal, beside a **monument** erected in honour of the Patriots. The inscription written by René Lévesque reads (in translation): "They fought for the recognition of our people, for political liberty and for a democratic system of government." It was placed here in 1987, to commemorate the 150th anniversary of the Rebellion.

Nearby, the **church**★ (1796) is surmounted by large, twin, copper towers, one of which contains the liberty bell used to call the Patriots to battle *(visit by 1hr guided tour only, Jun–Aug Tue–Sun 11am–6pm (closed noon–1pm); $4; reservations required 2 days in advance;* 🄿 *Maison Nationale des Patriotes* ☎ *450-787-3623)*. The first religious structure in Quebec to have been built on two storeys, it features a double row of windows on the exterior. A modern facade has hidden the original structure since 1922. The interior decor of carved wood dates, for the most part, from the 1810s and is attributed to Louis-Amable Quévillon.

★ **Maison Nationale des Patriotes** (Patriots' National House) – *610 Chemin des Patriotes (Rte. 133). Open Jun–Aug Tue–Sun 11am–6pm. May, Sept & Nov Tue–Sun 10am–5pm. Rest of the year by appointment. $4.* & 🄿 ☎ *450-787-3623*. Built in 1810 for Jean-Baptiste Mâsse, a blacksmith, innkeeper and merchant, this stone house serves as an interpretation centre on the Patriots' Rebellion of 1837-1838. Displays and an slide show explain the background of the uprising and highlight the events that led the Patriots in their long fight for freedom and democracy. The battles of Saint-Denis, Saint-Charles and Saint-Eustache are described. *Note: displays and slide show in French only.*

Saint-Ours – *12km/7mi.* In 1672, this seigneury was granted to Pierre de Saint-Ours. The river shoals impeded passing vessels until a dam and lock were completed in 1849. Erected in 1933, the present **Saint-Ours lock** *(open mid-Jun–early Aug daily 8:30am–8pm; mid-Aug–Labour Day Mon–Fri 8:30am–6pm, weekends 8:30am–7pm; mid-May–mid-Jun & early Sept–mid-Oct Mon–Fri 8:30am–10:30am & 2:30pm–4pm, weekends 8:30am–6pm;* 🚻 🅿 ☎ *450-785-2212)* is 103m/338ft long by 14m/46ft wide, and allows boats to be raised 1.5m/5ft in 5 minutes. At the turn of the century, ships carried timber, hay and cereals to the United States, and returned with coal, iron, copper and building materials. Today, a pleasant park equipped with picnic spots surrounds the lively lock area.

Beyond the lock (3km/2mi), a ferry links Saint-Ours to Saint-Roch.

Sorel – *18km/11mi.* Located at the confluence of the Richelieu and St. Lawrence Rivers, this community was named for Pierre de Saurel, who received the seigneury in 1672. In 1781, Sir Frederick Haldimand, Governor of Quebec, granted Sorel a municipal charter and renamed the town William-Henry (in honour of Prince William-Henry, the future King George IV). He also erected a garrison beside the Richelieu to counter the threat of an American invasion and ensure the security of the Loyalists established in the seigneury. Subsequently, the government acquired a large, wooden house to lodge the commander of the garrison, General von Riedesel. It was in this house, remodelled several times and today known as the **Governors' House** *(90 Chemin des Patriotes),* that the Riedesels, of German origin, introduced the Christmas tree to Canada.

★**Carré Royal** (Royal Square) – Created in 1791, to serve as the parade ground of the military town, this pleasant green space is today transformed into a park. Numerous footpaths crisscross it, so that from the air, it would resemble a British Flag *(bounded by Rue du Roi, Rue Charlotte, Rue du Prince and Rue George).*

Sorel is the site of the oldest Anglican mission in Canada (1784). The present **Christ Church** (1842), designed by John Wells in the Gothic Revival style, stands facing the Royal Square on Rue Prince. Between the square and the waterfront *(Rue du Roi),* a succession of bustling shops, restaurants and cafés leads to the old market, a yellow brick building constructed in the 1940s. To the east *(Rue Augusta),* a waterfront park with a raised gazebo offers panoramic **views** of the port, the confluence of the Richelieu and St. Lawrence Rivers, and the small, lively marina.

Sainte-Anne-de-Sorel – *4km/2mi east by chemin Sainte-Anne.* The vault and walls of the nave of **Église Sainte-Anne** (St. Anne's Church, 1876) are adorned with 13 superb frescoes executed by the painter, Suzor-Côté *(open year-round daily by appointment;* ☎ *450-743-7909).*

★**Cruise to the Islands of Sorel** – *Take Chemin du Chenal-du-Moine; follow signs to "Le Survenant." Depart from Sainte-Anne-de-Sorel 24 June–Labour Day daily 2pm & 4pm. Round-trip 1hr 30min. Commentary. Reservations required. $14.50.* 🚻 🅿 *Croisière des Îles de Sorel Inc.* ☎ *450-743-7227.* This boat trip allows visitors to discover the picturesque and enchanting Sorel Islands, and to see the majestic and powerful St. Lawrence in the distance. Starting at the Du Moine Canal, the boat passes a series of largely undeveloped islands, among them Île du Moine, Île de Grâce and Île d'Embarras. Several of the islands, laced with numerous intricate passageways, are accessible only by boat, and are popular with ornithologists, hunters and fishermen.

② FROM CHAMBLY TO HEMMINGFORD

80km/50mi by Rte. 223.

Leave Chambly by Rte. 223. The Chamby Canal is visible on the drive south.

Saint-Jean-sur-Richelieu – *16km/10mi. See Entry Heading*

Île aux Noix – *20km/12mi. Access by ferry from Saint-Paul-de-l'Île-aux-Noix. See Entry Heading.*

The Richelieu River widens as it approaches Lake Champlain and the US border. Numerous marinas dot its course.

★**Blockhaus de la rivière Lacolle** (Lacolle River Blockhouse) – *9km/6mi. Open Fête de Dollard–Labour Day daily 9am–5pm. Labour Day–Thanksgiving Day weekends 9am–5pm.* 🅿 ☎ *450-246-3227 or 450-359-4849.* This two-

Blockhaus de la rivière Lacolle (18C)

After photo by Tourisme Québec

level log structure was built in 1781 as part of the British defence system to repel American invasion. Standing on the Lacolle River, a tributary of the Richelieu, it is the only defence of its type remaining in Quebec. During the war of 1812, it withstood attack on three occasions, and bullet holes are still visible on the facade. Recently restored by the Quebec government, the interior houses displays on the military history of the blockhouse. Note the loopholes for muskets and the openings for cannons.

Continue south on Rte. 223 and turn right on Rte. 202.

★★ **Parc Safari (Safari Park)** – *26km/16mi, before entering Hemmingford. Open mid-May–mid-Jun Mon–Fri 10am–4pm, weekends 10am–5pm. Late Jun–mid-Sept daily 10am–5pm. $19.99.* ✗ ❷ 🅿 ☎ *450-247-2727.* Some 800 animals of 75 different species from Africa, Eurasia and the Americas roam freely in large enclosures in this zoological park. Required to remain in their vehicles, visitors can follow the **Car Safari** *(4km/2.5mi)* along which they can take photographs, touch and feed the animals. The **Enchanted Forest** combines an amusement park and water slides in a zoo-like setting. On the **jungle walk**, visitors can observe the monkeys on their island, walk through the deer compound and cross bridges to look down on lions, tigers and bears. Animal shows at the theatre (Théâtre sous les Arbres) and a circus in the stadium *(regular performances)* provide further entertainment; animal rides on elephants or ponies, and a petting zoo complete the visit.

RIGAUD
Montérégie
Population 6,057

This small residential town lies at the confluence of the Rigaud and Ottawa Rivers, on the border between Ontario and Quebec. Rigaud was originally part of the seigneury granted to Pierre and François Rigaud, sons of the Sieur de Vaudreuil, in 1732. In 1850, members of the Viatorian Clerics came to Rigaud to found a college at the request of Ignace Bourget, Bishop of Montreal. Today, Bourget College is the largest private boarding school in Canada, with more than 1,200 students. **Rigaud Mountain** (213m/699ft), renowned for its shrine and ski centre, dominates the town.

Access – *Rigaud is 70km/43mi west of Montreal by Rte. 40 (Exit 12).*

VISIT

★ **Sanctuaire Notre-Dame de Lourdes (Our Lady of Lourdes Shrine)** – *20 Rue Bourget. From Rue Saint-Jean-Baptiste, turn left on Rue Saint-Pierre, and follow signs. Open May–late Jun Mon–Fri 9:30am–5:15pm, Sat 9:30am–10pm, Sun 9:30am–6pm. Late Jun–Labour Day Mon–Fri 9:15am–6:30pm (Thu 9pm), Sat 9:15am–10pm, Sun 8:45am–6:30pm. Labour Day–Thanksgiving Day Mon–Fri 9:30am–5:15pm, Sat 9:30am–9pm, Sun 9am–5pm. Closed major holidays. Contribution requested.* ✗ ❷ 🅿 ☎ *450-451-4631.* Built into the rocky hillside, this open-air sanctuary was inspired by the shrine of Lourdes in France, site of a 1958 apparition of the Virgin Mary to Bernadette Soubirous, a 14-year-old peasant girl.

In 1874, Brother Ludger Pauzé, a teacher at the Bourget College, placed a statue of Our Lady of Lourdes in a niche on the mountainside. After his death, visitors, encouraged by the college's Superior, Father François-Xavier Chouinard, continued devotions to the Virgin Mary. In 1887, to accommodate the growing number of faithful, a larger statue was installed in a more accessible site, and a small chapel was built. A second, open-sided chapel was added in 1954.

Immediately upon arrival, the visitor discovers this latest chapel nestled in greenery *(masses are held in the summer months)*. A path leads up the hillside past the statue to the original chapel, shaped like an eight-sided belvedere. It offers a remarkable **view★** of the Ottawa and Rigaud Rivers and the surrounding area. The pink rock visible on the hillside is Potsdam sandstone.

RIMOUSKI★
Bas-Saint-Laurent
Population 31,773
Map p 81

Built along the banks of the St. Lawrence, this industrial city has developed in a semi-circular pattern around the mouth of the Rimouski River. Once a vast forest, the surrounding region long served as hunting grounds for the Micmac Indians. Granted as a seigneury in 1688, the territory was acquired in 1694 by the French merchant René Lepage, who settled here two years later. Rimouski is a Micmac term meaning "land of the moose."

The local economy, based on agriculture and seasonal fishing, experienced rapid growth during the early 20C, when the Price Brothers Company established sawmills and forestry operations. The city was rebuilt after the great fire of 1950 and is now considered the principal metropolis of eastern Quebec.

Access – *Rimouski is 312km/193mi from Quebec City by Rtes. 73 (Pierre-Laporte Bridge) and 20, and Rte. 132.*

SIGHTS

Musée régional de Rimouski (Rimouski Regional Museum) – *35 Rue Saint-Germain Ouest. Open mid-Jun–early-Sept daily 10am–6pm (Wed–Sat 9pm). Rest of the year Wed–Sun noon–5pm. $4.* ℀ *(summer only)* ᕕ ▯ ☎ *www.museerimouski.qc.ca* ☎ *418-724-2272.* The stone building that has housed the museum since the early 1970s was built in 1824 and served as the parish church until 1862. It was then used as a seminary, a convent and a primary school. Dedicated to contemporary art, the museum presents mainly temporary exhibits.

★**Maison Lamontagne** (Lamontagne House) – *3km/2mi east of the centre of town on Rte. 132, turn right onto Blvd. du Rivage at Rimouski-Est. Follow signs. Open mid-May–mid-Oct daily 9am–6pm. $3.* ᕕ ▯ ☎ *418-722-4038.* This large house was built in two phases. The longer section, of masonry half-timbering, dates from the second half of the 18C, while the full timbering section was completed around 1810. The structure is one of the few remaining examples of masonry half-timbering in North America; French settlers soon discovered that the stones between the timbering conducted cold and heat into the interior, making this type of construction unsuitable for the harsh Canadian climate. Occupied until 1959, the house was restored in 1981. Expositions mounted inside trace the development of Quebec domestic architecture and recreate rural life in the province during the late 18C.

★**Musée de la mer et lieu historique national du phare de Pointe-au-Père** (Maritime Museum and Pointe-au-Père Lighthouse National Historic Site) – *1034 Rue du Phare, Pointe-au-Père, 10km/6mi from Rimouski. Turn left off Rte. 132 onto Rue Père-Nouvel, then right to museum. Open late-Jun–late-Aug daily 9am–7pm. Early-Jun–late-Jun & late-Aug–mid-Oct 10am–5pm. $8.50.* ᕕ ▯ *www.musee-mer.qc.ca* ☎ *418-724-6214.* The first floor of the keeper's house is dedicated to the *Empress of Ireland,* nicknamed the "Titanic of the St. Lawrence," which sank close to shore on May 29, 1914, claiming 1,012 lives. Owing to the outbreak of World War I shortly thereafter, and the immigrant status of most of the passengers, the disaster lay forgotten for half a century. Since the mid-1960s, hundreds of diving expeditions have recovered numerous objects from the wreck. Many of these artifacts are on display in the museum. A multimedia exhibition re-creates the sinking of the *Empress of Ireland.* In the adjacent **lighthouse** (1909), the second tallest in Canada, exhibits trace the daily life of a lighthouse keeper at the beginning of the century. Climb the 128 steps to the top for a nice **view**★ of the coastline.

RIVIÈRE-DU-LOUP★

Bas-Saint-Laurent
Population 14,721
Map p 81

Situated in the heart of the Bas-Saint-Laurent region between Quebec City and the Gaspé Peninsula, Rivière-du-Loup commands a geographical position favourable to both commerce and tourism. A ferry links the industrial city to Saint-Siméon, on the north shore of the St. Lawrence in the Charlevoix region, and the Trans-Canada Highway leads south to New Brunswick.

Historical Notes

There are three theories on the origin of the name Rivière-du-Loup (literally "river of the wolf"). According to one, a French ship, named le *Loup*, may have wintered here around 1660. Local legend recounts that Champlain encountered an Amerindian tribe called the Mahigans, or wolves, in this area. The third possibility is that the name commemorates the seals, or *loups-marins*, that were commonly sighted at the mouth of the river.

The seigneury of Rivière-du-Loup was granted to Charles Aubert de la Chesnaye, ancestor of writer Philippe-Aubert de Gaspé, in 1673. Together with his companion, Sieur Charles Bazire, he became one of the wealthiest traders in New France, profiting from the furs and fish found in the region. The two partners had so little interest in settling the territory that from 1683 to 1765, the population grew from 4 to only 68. The colony began to expand significantly in 1802, when the seigneury was bought by Alexander Fraser, whose involvement in the lumber trade with England brought prosperity to Rivière-du-Loup. In 1860, the arrival of the railway linking the city with

Windsor (in the Eastern Townships) to the south provided another important boost to the economy. In 1887, the Témiscouata Railway in turn connected the city to New Brunswick.

The prosperity that flourished during the late 19C and early 20C is reflected in the opulent homes and public buildings erected during this period.

Access – *Rivière-du-Loup is located 193km/120mi northeast of Quebec City by Rte. 20 or Rte. 132.*

★TOWN CENTRE

Hôtel de ville (City Hall) – *At the corner of Rue Lafontaine and Blvd. Hôtel-de-Ville.* ☎ *418-862-9810.* Completed in 1917, the city hall occupies the former site of the public market building, destroyed by fire in 1910. An unusual architectural element of the structure is the main clock tower, typical of city halls found in the English-speaking provinces.

After leaving City Hall, turn right on Rue Lafontaine. Cross Rue Lafontaine to Rue de la Cour.

Located at the corner of Rue Lafontaine and Rue de la Cour, the limestone and brick **Courthouse** was designed by David Ouellet in 1881. It has undergone three major renovations. The **Old Post Office** (1889), a stately dark brick edifice on Rue Iberville *(turn right from Rue Lafontaine)*, exemplifies institutional architecture of Anglo-Saxon origin. It has been converted into a community centre.

Continue on Rue Iberville. Follow Rue du Domaine. Turn right on Rue du Domaine, continue to Rue du Rocher and turn right.

Bibliothèque municipale (Municipal Library) – The Second Empire stone structure was built in 1886 by David Ouellet. For nearly a century, it served as the convent of the Good Shepherd Sisters. After the religious community left in 1978, it was renovated and converted into a library (1983).

ADDITIONAL SIGHTS

Musée du Bas-Saint-Laurent (Bas-Saint-Laurent Museum) – *300 Rue Saint-Pierre. Open Jun–mid-Oct daily 10am–6pm. Rest of the year daily 1pm–5pm (Mon & Wed 7pm–9pm). Closed Jan 1 & Dec. 25. $5.* ⅙ ☐ *www.mbsl.qc.ca* ☎ *418-862-7547.* The themes of cultural heritage and contemporary art are incorporated into the museum's various temporary exhibits. Works by local artists are also shown regularly.

★**Chutes de la rivière du Loup (Rivière du Loup Falls)** – *Take Rue Lafontaine north to Rue Frontenac and turn right. The falls are two blocks away.* The level of the Loup River drops a total of 90m/295ft before joining the St. Lawrence, and a series of eight cascades interrupt the river flow over a distance of 1,500m/4,920ft. At this site, the falls are 38m/125ft high. Steps lead to a lookout providing an expansive view of the town and river. The **illuminated cross** on the cliff overlooking the river is also visible from this point.

EXCURSION

Cabano – *60km/37mi from Rivière-du-Loup by Rte. 185.* This lumbering centre on the Trans-Canada Highway occupies a pleasant **site**★ beside Lake Témiscouata. The lake was once part of an important portage route connecting the St. Lawrence and St. John Rivers. In 1839, during a dispute with the state of Maine over the location of the frontier, Fort Ingall was built to protect this route.

Fort Ingall – *2km/1.2mi by Rte. 232. Open early Jun–mid-Jun Mon–Fri*

Chutes de la rivière du Loup

10am–4pm. Late Jun–Aug daily 9:30am–6pm. Sept daily 10am–4pm. $6.50. 🔹 🅿 ☎ *418-854-2375.* Surrounded by a wooden stockade, this lakeside fort complex (1839-1842) once housed two hundred soldiers. Among its several reconstructed log buildings are the South Barracks, a blockhouse and the Officers' Quarters, where displays on regional history are presented.

> ### ■ Birders Beware
>
> La Société Duvetnor *(200 Rue Hayward* ☎ *418-867-1660)* offers you the chance to spot double-crested cormorants, great blue herons, and even black guillemots on a nature reserve composed of several islands - Les Pèlerins, Les Îles du Pot-de-l'Eau-de-vie, and l'Île-aux-Lièvres. Rich wildlife and a secluded environment guarantee a visit accompanied only by the sweet sounds of nature.

ROBERVAL

Saguenay–Lac-Saint-Jean
Population 11,640
Map p 280

Located on the southwestern shore of Lake Saint-Jean, this city is named after Jean-François de La Rocque, Sieur de Roberval, appointed First-Lieutenant of Canada by King François I. It was under Roberval's orders that Jacques Cartier led an ill-fated expedition to settle a colony in Charlesbourg, near Quebec City, in 1542. Founded in 1855, Roberval was the site of the prestigious Beemer Hotel at the end of the 19C, owned by the American lumber magnate Horace Jansen Beemer, who also operated two steamships on the lake. The magnificent mansion was destroyed by fire in 1908. Today, Roberval is an important service centre for the area and the finish point of the **international swim marathon** (Traversée internationale du lac Saint-Jean, *see Calendar of Events*).

Access – *Roberval is 259km/161mi north of Quebec City by Rtes. 175 and 169.*

SIGHTS

★**Église Notre-Dame-de-Roberval (Our Lady of Roberval Church)** – *On Blvd. Saint-Joseph at the corner of Ave. Lizotte, across from the hospital. Open year-round Sat 9:30am–8pm, Sun 8am–noon.* 🔹 🅿 ☎ *418-275-0272.* Built in 1967, this church resembles a large copper tent topped by a white steeple. The interior is shaped like a pyramid rising above the central altar. The brightly coloured stained-glass windows were fashioned by Guy Bruneau.

★**Centre historique et aquatique de Roberval (Roberval History and Aquatic Centre)** – *2.5km/1.6mi north of the town centre by Blvd. Saint-Joseph and Blvd. de la Traversée. Open Jun–Sept 10am–8pm. $5.50.* ⚠ 🔹 🅿 *www.ville.roberval.qc.ca* ☎ *418-275-0202.* Set beside the lake, this modern interpretation centre (1985) contains a series of insightful exhibits on the history, geology, flora and fauna of Lake Saint-Jean. An aquarium contains specimens of *ouananiche* (freshwater salmon), and there is a film on the international swim marathon. A special, submarine-shaped room illustrates the history of the lake.

EXCURSIONS

★★**Lac Saint-Jean** – *See Entry Heading.*

Mashteuiatsh – *9km/6mi north of Roberval by Blvd. Saint-Joseph.* This strip of land jutting into Lake Saint-Jean is the site of a reserve created in 1856 for the local indigenous population, mainly Montagnais Indians. Visitors can browse through the shops of the Pointe-Bleue village, featuring Amerindian handicrafts, and walk along the lake. An Amerindian celebration called **Jeux autochtones interbandes** is held in July.

Musée Amérindien de Mashteuiatsh (Mashteuiatsh Amerindian Museum) – *1787 Rue Amishk. Open mid-May–mid-Oct daily 9am–6:30pm. Rest of the year Mon–Fri 8am–4pm. $3.* 🔹 🅿 ☎ *418-275-4842.* Recent renovations have doubled the exposition space of this intriguing museum, which introduces visitors to the history and culture of the Pekuakamiulnuatsh (Montagnais Indians from the Lake Saint-Jean region) – their traditional lifestyle, customs, language and role in present-day society. A small shop offers handicrafts created in the village of Mashteuiatsh.

ROUYN-NORANDA

Abitibi-Témiscamingue
Population 28,819

Located in the heart of the Abitibi region, directly on the watershed line and astride the most mineral-rich portion of the Cadillac Fault, Rouyn-Noranda is both the regional capital of Abitibi and its main population centre. Abitibi, a relatively uncultivated region of forest, rock, lakes and rivers, takes its name from an Algonquian term meaning "watershed line." The region rests on a peneplain, or flat land surface created by erosion, gently sloping toward James Bay, carrying along the waters of Lake Abitibi and the Harricana River. Not just another mining town, the city is the region's cultural center boasting an international film festival and vibrant artistic community. In order to counteract the negative aesthetic effect of mining, residents are dedicated to the development of parks and their prize flower gardens. Rouyn-Noranda proudly claims Richard Dejardins, the popular singer and poet, as its native son.

Historical Notes

Natural Resources – Since commerce in the area depended entirely on water transportation, settlement only began in 1912, when the first railway line linking Abitibi to Ontario was inaugurated. However, the real catalyst for the sudden and rapid colonization of the Abitibi region was the discovery of the **Cadillac Fault**, a geological structure rich in copper, gold and silver, which traverses the Abitibi region west to east, through Rouyn-Noranda and Val-d'Or. The fault, which splays into innumerable secondary fractures, was the primary focus of mineral prospectors at the turn of the century, resulting in the region's phenomenal development. While the portion of the fault located in Quebec was being explored, mining of the Ontario portion was already underway, notably in Kirkland Lake. The region long remained within the commercial sphere of Ontario, where investors and capital were more abundant. In the 1950s, as the veins in the area were being depleted, mining operations moved further north, and mining remains one of this region's most important economic resources. Traditionally, miners were recruited in Eastern Europe, as most French-Canadians preferred to work the land. Following labour uprisings in the 1930s, immigrants were gradually replaced by French-Canadians. However, in 1942, the demands of the war industry attracted a large number of miners to the area, many of whom were foreigners.

Two mining towns – As its name indicates, Rouyn-Noranda is the result of a merger between the towns of Noranda and Rouyn. Although both are mining towns, their history is quite different. **Noranda** owed its creation to Ontarian interests and was primarily anglophone. The town's name is a contraction of the words *north* and *Canada*. In its early days, it was essentially a residential town, administered exclusively by the Noranda mine. The town of **Rouyn** was named after Sieur de Rouyn, a captain of the Royal Roussillon regiment, famed for his battle against the English at Sainte-Foy, near Quebec City. Rouyn was originally a meeting place for adventurers in search of a quick fortune; at that time, it was known as the "street of pleasures" *(rue des plaisirs)*. The town is truly a product of the gold rush (which in fact became a copper rush) of 1923. Primarily francophone, it was home to most of the miners and today is the business district of the city.

Access – *Rouyn-Noranda is located 638km/396mi from Montreal by Rte. 117. Air Alliance offers daily flights to the city from Montreal ☎ 514-393-3333.*

SIGHTS

★**Maison Dumulon (Dumulon House)** – *191 Ave. du Lac. Approaching from the direction of Val-d'Or, turn left off Rte. 117 onto Ave. du Lac and continue to Lake Osisko where a tourist information booth is located. Open Jun 24–Labour Day daily 9am–8pm. Rest of the year Mon–Fri 9am–noon & 1pm–5pm. $3.* ♿ 🅿 ☎ 819-797-7125. This reconstructed house recreates the atmosphere of the 1920s, when it served as Rouyn's first general store and post office. Photographs and various objects reminiscent of bygone days trace the history of the town. The local Tourism Office is located within the building.

Located in the **Parc des Pionniers (Pioneer Park)** next to the Dumulon House, the Tremoy promenade leads along Lake Osisko to the Rouyn-Noranda Nautical Centre (Centre nautique de Rouyn-Noranda).

> A walk in the park .... At the À Fleur d'Eau Botanical Park *(Aves. Montréal and Pinder. www.lino.com/~fleurdo ☎ 819-762-3178)* locals congregate after dinner to relax, chat and enjoy the scenery. Deciduous trees and beautiful landscaping surround Lac Edouard, the preferred swimming hole of the region's ducks. A Geological Garden familiarizes you with the region's geological composition.

Église orthodoxe russe Saint-Georges (St. George Russian Orthodox Church) – *201 Rue Taschereau Ouest; turn left off Rue Larivière. Open Jun 24–Labour Day daily 9am–5pm. $3. ☎ 819-797-7125*. Among the wave of immigrants arriving after World War II were about twenty Russian families and to serve them, Father Ustuchenko erected this small church according to the principles of Russian Orthodoxy. The two superimposed cupolas are intended to represent God embracing the earth. The church has been transformed into a small but extensively documented **museum**, full of picturesque details which lead the visitor to the very heart of another culture.

Théâtre du Cuivre (Copper Theatre) – *145 Rue Taschereau*. In 1987, this eminently contemporary building topped by a copper roof, won the prestigious Felix award for best theatre in the province. It hosts movies, plays and concerts as well as the Abitibi-Témiscamingue International Film Festival.

St. George Russian Orthodox Church

Noranda Metallurgie – *101 Rue Portelance*. The discovery of this mine led to the rush of 1923. In 1927, the mine started operations with the help of American and Canadian investors. A total of 51 million tonnes of high grade copper and gold ore were mined (on average, five tons of ore are required to produce one ounce of gold). A smelter now occupies the site of the former mine.

Fonderie Horne (Horne Smelter) – *Visit by guided tour (1hr 30min) only, Jun–early Sept daily 8:30am–6pm. Rest of the year by appointment. ☎ 819-762-7764*. The exhibit here focuses on the entire copper mining and refining process: from extraction to the production of an anode, a large 99 percent copper ingot weighing about 290kg/ 639lbs. After touring the home of Edmund Horne, discoverer of the Noranda Mine, visitors enter a railway compartment where a film on mining and the history of the region is presented. Finally, everyone is invited to don helmets and boots to visit the surface installations of the smelter.

EXCURSION

Angliers – *Just after reaching Arntfield, turn off Rte. 117 and head south on Rte. 101; 5km/3mi from of the village of Rollet, turn left on Rte. 391 to Angliers*. This peaceful village provides an ideal setting for nature lovers and fishing enthusiasts. It is also home of the old **T.E. Draper**, a tugboat used to haul lumber in the days when rivers were the only means of transporting materials and reaching remote areas (*open late Jun–early Sept daily 10am–6pm; $3.50; ♿ 🅿 ☎ 819-949-4431*). The vessel, in service from 1929 to 1979, supplemented the railway service that skirted the Long Sault Rapids on the Ottawa River, dropping off passengers at the southern end of Lake Témiscamingue. You can also tour the Gédéon logging site, a reconstructed logging camp.

Planning a trip to the United States?
*Don't forget to take along the **Michelin Road Map** (No. 930).*

Fjord du SAGUENAY★★★

Saguenay
Map below

Measuring 155km/96mi, the Saguenay River is the only river draining Lake Saint-Jean. Over its first 9km/6mi of the section between Alma and Jonquière, the once roaring torrent, which drops about 90m/295ft, has been harnessed and has spawned one of the most industrialized areas of the province. After 50km/31mi, at Saint-Fulgence, the river flows into the majestic Saguenay fjord that extends to Tadoussac, and empties into the St. Lawrence.

The deep channel through which the Saguenay flows beyond Saint-Fulgence was gouged in Precambrian rock by glaciers during the last ice age. As the ice receded, the sea swept into the valley, and to this day, tidewaters reach up as far as Chicoutimi. The channel is 1,500m/ 4,920ft wide in places and has an average depth of 240m/787ft. Rocky cliffs plunge into the dark waters from heights of up to 457m/ 1,500ft. The Saguenay is the southernmost fjord in the world.

Historical Notes

For over 4,000 years the Saguenay has been the *chemin qui cours*, or water route, for the First Nations who paddled upstream to go to their fur-trapping grounds. Upon landing here in 1534, Jacques Cartier first heard of the vast riches of the **Kingdom of the Saguenay**. Colonization began in 1838 when William Price created *Société des vingt et un*, twenty one hard-working men who left Charlevoix to start new lives in complete wilderness. The areas industrial riches proved illusive until the 19C, when the river was finally harnessed for hydroelectricity, giving the local economy an important boost. The Upper Saguenay (Haut-Saguenay) has since been extensively industrialized, and hydroelectric power plants, pulp mills and aluminium smelters dot its shores. In contrast, the undeveloped Lower Saguenay (Bas-Saguenay) is lined with long stretches of uninhabited land. The Saguenay's stark and untamed beauty has attracted visitors for years. Most choose to take a scenic river cruise, but the fjord can also be enjoyed by exploring the villages nestled along its shores. A spectacular natural park has been created to preserve part of the shoreline *(difficult access)*.

Access – *The fjord is accessible from Quebec City either by Rte. 175 to Chicoutimi (about 200km/124mi) or by Rte. 138 to Tadoussac (220km/136mi). Rte. 172 runs along the north shore of the fjord; Rte. 170 follows the south shore.*

FROM TADOUSSAC TO L'ANSE-SAINT-JEAN
250km/155mi.

There are several ways to visit this region-by boat, kayak, or car. As there are no bridges that cross the fjord for most of its length, begin on the north shore at Tadoussac, cross the fjord at Chicoutimi then visit the southern shore.

★★Tadoussac – *See Entry Heading.*

Take Rte. 138 north for 6km/4mi, then turn left on Rte. 172 and continue for 11km/7mi to Sacré-Cœur. Take another left and continue for 8km/5mi.

L'Anse de Roche (Rock Bay) – *25km/15mi. Turn left in Sacré-Cœur.* This tiny cove offers a splendid **view★** of the fjord and the massive power lines that span it, carrying electricity from the Manicouagan region to Montreal. *Return to Rte. 172.*

Sainte-Rose-du-Nord – *69km/43mi. Turn left at sign.* Founded in 1838, this charming village is nestled in a cove between two rocky escarpments. A stroll down to the wharf reveals an exceptional **site★★** while a walk to the scenic lookout will provide a great view of the village and fjord. The small **nature museum** contains a fascinating collection of nature's oddities, including wood twisted and polished into fantastic shapes, and wild mushrooms *(open year-round daily 8:30am–9pm; $4.50;* 🅿 ☎ *418-675-2348).*

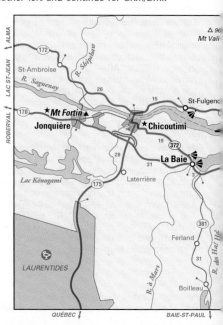

On its descent towards **Saint-Fulgence** *(28km/17mi)*, Route 172 affords a magnificent **panorama★** of the fjord's western end. **Mt. Valin** (968m/3,175ft) rises about 20km/12mi to the north of the town.

Follow Rtes. 172 and 175 south to Chicoutimi, crossing over the Saguenay.

★Chicoutimi – *16km/10mi from Saint-Fulgence. See Entry Heading.*

La Baie – *19km/12mi by Rte. 372. See Entry Heading.*
Follow Rte. 170 to Rivière-Éternité (43km/27mi). Turn left at sign.

Another stop along Rte. 172 that offers an impressive view of the fjord is Sacré-Coeur. Visit the wharf at **Anse-de-Roche**, engage in some aquatic activities, or for a real thrill rent a kayak for whale-watching. At Rivière Éternité enjoy the 175 nativity scenes from around the world at the Exposition Internationale de Crèches at the Église de Rivière-Éternité *(☎ 418-272-2807)*. In the winter, each home in the village is decorated with its own Nativity scene.

★★Parc du Saguenay (Saguenay Park) – *Open daily year-round. $7.75/car.* △ ☓ ☍ ☐ ☎ *418-272-2267 (in season) or 418-544-7388 (off-season). Cross-country skiing, ice fishing.* This park was created in 1983 to protect the banks of the fjord. It covers roughly 300sq km/116sq mi and extends a distance of about 100km/62mi from La Baie to Tadoussac. Popular areas within the park include Sainte-Marguerite Bay, Tadoussac Dunes and Éternité Bay. The latter is one of the prettiest coves on the fjord, dominated by the large twin cliffs, Cape Trinité and Cape Éternité.
The capes are best appreciated by taking a scenic **mini-cruise** *(depart from Éternité Bay late May–late Sept daily 11:30am & 2:30pm; additional departure Jul–Aug 1pm; round-trip 1hr; commentary; $15.50;* ☐ *Croisières du Cap Trinité Inc. ☎ 418-272-2591).* A footpath beside the bay also affords attractive **views**. A superb 25km/15.5mi hiking trail *(allow 2 days)* connects Rivière-Éternité to Anse-Saint-Jean *(cabins and campgrounds available).*
An **interpretation centre** located at the end of the Éternité River valley features exhibits tracing the origins of the fjord *(open late May–Jun 23 daily 10am–4pm; Jun 24–Labour Day daily 9am–5pm; early Sept–mid-Oct daily 8:30am–4:30pm;* ☓ ☍ ☎ *418-272-3027).*

★★Cap Trinité – *11km/7mi from Rivière-Éternité.* Named for its three ledges, this cape rises 518m/1,700ft over the fjord. It is renowned for the impressive statue of the Virgin Mary that stands on the first ledge about 180m/590ft above the black waters of the Saguenay. Known as **Our Lady of the Saguenay**, the statue was created in 1881 by Louis Jobin at the request of a businessman, Charles-Napoléon Robitaille, who had vowed to honour the Virgin after his life was spared on two occasions.

Over 8m/26ft tall, the statue was carved from three huge blocks of pine and then covered with a layer of lead. Hoisting the 3,175kg/7,000 lbs wood and metal creation into place proved to be a challenge. After numerous attempts, the statue was separated into pieces and later reassembled. A steep path leads from the interpretation centre to the statue *(about 7km/4mi round-trip, allow 4hrs)* and provides superb **panoramas★★**.

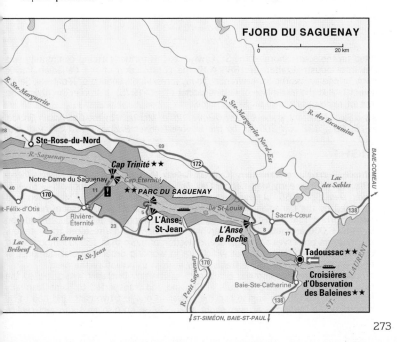

FJORD DU SAGUENAY

View of the fjord

Return to Rte. 170 (11km/7mi).

L'Anse-Saint-Jean – *23km/14mi. Turn left at sign.* This tiny community located at the mouth of the Saint-Jean River was founded in 1828. A magnificent **view**★ of the fjord can be enjoyed from the marina and the wharf. Note also the **Faubourg Bridge** (1929), a 37m/121ft-long covered bridge that spans the Saint-Jean River near the church.

Cross the bridge, continue for 5km/3mi and turn right.

Located on the only cape accessible by car, the lookout at Tabatière Bay (Anse de Tabatière) affords a superb **view** of the surrounding area.

EXCURSION

★★**Scenic Cruises** – *Departures from Chicoutimi and Tadoussac.*

SAINT-CONSTANT

Montérégie
Population 21,933
Map p 175

Located on the south shore of the St. Lawrence, this former farming community was thrust into industrialization in 1888 with the construction of the Canadian Pacific Railway bridge across the St. Lawrence. Today a residential suburb of Montreal, Saint-Constant is also the birthplace of **Gustave Lanctot** (1883-1975), historian, archivist, and author of numerous works on New France.

Access – *Saint-Constant is about 20km/12mi south of Montreal by the Champlain Bridge, Rte. 15, Rtes. 132 and 209; or by the Honoré-Mercier Bridge, Rtes. 132 and 209.*

SIGHT

★**Musée Ferroviaire Canadien (Canadian Railway Museum)** – *122A Rue Saint-Pierre (Rte. 209). Open early May–Labour Day daily 9am–5pm. Early Sept–mid-Oct weekends 9am–5pm. $6* ☐ *www.exporail.org* ☎ *450-632-2410.* Established and operated by the Canadian Railroad Historical Association, the museum highlights the important role played by railroads in the development of Canada. In addition to some 6,000 artifacts, 185,000 archival documents and a restored train station, the museum preserves an exceptional collection of more than 130 locomotives and other railway vehicles, many of which are in working order. Regular demonstrations on the operation of the trains allow visitors to recapture the past.

Among the steam locomotives is a replica of the tiny **Dorchester**, which pulled the first Canadian train in 1836. Built in England and transported to Saint-Jean-sur-Richelieu by barge, the engine had the power to pull just two cars, and had to be supplemented by horses at even slight inclines. Also on display is an exact replica of the **John Molson**, built in Scotland and shipped to Canada for use from 1850 to 1874 *(demonstrations in summer)*. The **CNR 5702**, a locomotive built for passenger service, reached speeds of over 160km/hour (99 mph) in 1930. One of the largest locomotives ever constructed, the **CP 5935** hauled trains over the Rockies and Selkirks in British Columbia in the 1950s. The **CP 7000**, Canadian Pacific's first electric locomotive with a diesel engine, was used from 1937 to 1964.

Among non-Canadian vehicles is a French locomotive, the **SNCF 030-C-841** "Chateaubriand," dating from 1883, which was retired after 83 years of service. A gift from British Rail, the **BR 60010** "Dominion of Canada," belonged to the class that established the world record for steam locomotives with a speed of 204km/hour (126.5mph) in 1938.

The museum also owns a large collection of streetcars, one of which is used to give tours of the site. Also visible are a bridge-style turntable and an enormous rotary snowplow used to clear the tracks during the long Canadian winters.

EXCURSION

Écluse de la Côte Sainte-Catherine (Côte Sainte-Catherine Lock) – *About 6km/4mi from the museum. Drive north to Rte. 132, turn left, then right on Rue Centrale. Open daily Apr–mid-Nov.* 🅿 ☏ *450-672-4110.* This is the second lock on the St. Lawrence Seaway system. At this point, vessels are raised 9m/30ft, from the level of the La Prairie Basin to that of Lake Saint-Louis, around the Lachine Rapids. The parking lot provides a good **view** of the vessels passing through the lock, and of the Montreal skyline in the distance.

SAINT-EUSTACHE
Laurentides
Population 39,848
Map p 174

This quiet residential and farming community is situated on the Mille Îles River as it leaves Lake Deux Montagnes and joins the Chêne River. Founded in 1768, it was named for the seigneur of Mille-Îles, Louis-Eustache Lambert-Dumont. In 1837, Saint-Eustache was the site of one of the most crushing defeats of the Patriots' Rebellion.

Historical Notes

On December 14, 1837, 150 French-speaking "rebels" led by **Jean-Olivier Chénier** faced 2,000 British soldiers under the command of General Sir John Colborne. The rebels took shelter in the church, which was bombarded and set on fire. Seventy patriots, including Chénier, had died before the rest surrendered. The survivors were imprisoned in Chénier's home, and Colborne burned the village during what was called "the bloody night" *(la nuit rouge)*. This event earned Colborne the nickname "Old Firebrand."

Access – *Saint-Eustache is about 35km/22mi west of Montreal by Rte. 15 and Rte. 640 (Blvd. Arthur-Sauvé Exit).*

SIGHTS

★**Église Saint-Eustache (St. Eustache Church)** – *123 Rue Saint-Louis. Visit by guided tour (30min) available, late-Jun–Labour Day Mon 1pm–4:30pm, Tue–Fri 9:30am–4:30pm, Sun noon–4:30pm. Contribution requested. Rest of the year call for reservation.* 🔸 🅿 *www.paroisse-steustache.qc.ca* ☏ *450-473-3200.* With its imposing facade and two elegant steeples, the St.-Eustache church was erected in 1783 and enlarged in 1831. Badly damaged in 1837 during the patriots battle against the British army, it was carefully rebuilt from the remains. Cannonball marks are still visible on the facade. The light and spacious interior contains an ornate barrel vault and is often used by the Montreal Symphony Orchestra for recording sessions because of its excellent acoustics.

To the right is the presbytery; to the left stands a former convent that now serves as the town hall. Behind the church, a pleasant park affords views of the Mille Îles River.

Manoir Globensky (Globensky Manor) – *235 Rue Saint-Eustache.* A huge porticoed entrance dominates the facade of this lovely Victorian manor (1903). The second manor erected on this site, this grandiose structure belonged to Charles-Auguste-Maximilien Globensky, last seigneur of the Chêne River seigneury. After his death, two local mayors used it as a residence. The manor became the city hall in 1962 and today still houses municipal offices.

Moulin Légaré (Légaré Mill) – *236 Rue Saint-Eustache, across from the manor. Open May–Oct Mon–Fri 8am–5pm, weekends & holidays 10am–5pm. Rest of the year Mon–Fri 8am–5pm.* 🔸 ☏ *450-472-9529.* The only building to survive "the bloody night" *(above)*, this seigneurial mill on the Chêne River was built in 1762 and has operated ever since. It is named for the Légaré family who ran it from 1908 to 1978. The original mechanism and equipment can be seen inside, and visitors can purchase wheat and buckwheat flour produced at the mill. From the bridge behind the structure, the turbine gate, the river and the towers of St. Eustache church are visible.

Rue Saint-Eustache – The city's main street is lined with several buildings of historical interest. The former Presbyterian Church (1910) at no. 271 now houses an art gallery presenting temporary exhibits. At no. 163, the gabled, red-brick Plessis-Bélair House has been converted into a restaurant. The building (1832) at no. 64, with its distinctive overhanging eaves, belonged to Hubert Globensky, and the store at no. 40 is the former Paquin House (1889).

EXCURSIONS

Parc d'Oka (Oka Park) – *14km/9mi by Rte. 148 and Rte. 640. Main entrance at the end of the Rte. 640. Open early May–mid-Sept daily 8am–8pm. Rest of the year daily 8am–6pm. $2. $5.25/car.* △ ✕ ⚹ 🅿 ☎ *450-479-8365.* Set beside Lake Deux Montagnes, this park covers 24sq km/9sq mi of a former seigneury belonging to the Sulpicians. Created in 1962, it was orginally named for Paul Sauvé, premier of Quebec (1959-1960) and a representative for the constituency. The park comprises a wide beach and several trails that wind through the magnificent deciduous forest *(an information booth is located near the main entrance)*.

Abbaye cistercienne (Cistercian Abbey) – *3km/2mi west of the intersection of Rte. 640 and Rte. 344. Parking lot after the main entrance, before the Calvary of Oka. Chapel open year-round daily 4am–8pm. Boutique open year-round daily.* ⚹ 🅿 ☎ *450-479-8361.* In 1881, the Sulpicians of Oka donated land to a group of Cistercian monks from the Bellefontaine abbey in France. The Cistercians erected a large monastery, la Trappe d'Oka, where, keeping a tradition of hospitality, the monks welcome visitors who wish to participate in their life of retreat.

★**Calvaire d'Oka (Calvary of Oka)** – *4km/2mi from the monastery on Rte. 344.* On the slopes of Oka Mountain (150m/492ft) stand a series of simple whitewashed stone sculptures representing the Stations of the Cross and Calvary. The four oratories and three chapels were built between 1740 and 1744 by Hamon Le Guen, a Sulpician from Brittany, in an effort to evangelize the indigenous population. The mountainside provides a good **view** of the park and of Lake Deux Montagnes. *Continue on Rte. 344 to Oka.*

Oka – *1km/.6mi from the Calvary; 21km/13mi from Saint-Eustache.* The name of this community on the shores of Lake Deux Montagnes comes from an Algonquian word for "pike," a fish once found in abundance in the lake. A mission was founded here in 1717 for Iroquois, Nipissing and Algonquin peoples; the reserve still exists. The community gained international notoriety in the summer of 1990 during the outbreak of the "Oka crisis," an Amerindian uprising centred on the issue of territorial and separatist claims of Canada's First Nations.

SAINT-FÉLICIEN

Saguenay–Lac-Saint-Jean
Population 10,972
Map p 280

Saint-Félicien is located on the western shore of Lake Saint-Jean, at the confluence of the Mistassini, Ticouapé and Ashuapmushuan rivers, which rush over falls and rapids for 266km/156mi before emptying into the lake. Founded in 1865, Saint-Félicien thrived on agriculture and lumber operations before becoming the gateway to the rich mining area of Chibougamau, to the northwest, in the 1950s. A major paper mill was established here in 1978, and a steam power plant in 1997.

On May 19, 1870, a conflagration known as the **Great Fire** started in Saint-Félicien and eventually ravaged the southern shores of the lake and the forests as far as La Baie. Entire communities were destroyed, and the long process of recovery was arduous. Today, the town is best known for its zoo, created in 1960 by local citizens. Soaring above Boulevard Sacré-Cœur in the centre of town are the twin steeples of Saint-Félicien's large pink granite church, erected in 1914. Across the street, Sacré-Cœur Park overlooks the Ashuapmushuan River.

Access – *Saint-Félicien is 285km/177mi north of Quebec City by Rtes. 175 and 169.*

SIGHTS

★★**Zoo "sauvage" de Saint-Félicien (Saint-Félicien Wild Zoo)** – *6km/4mi on Blvd. du Jardin (Rte. 167). Open mid-May–mid-Oct daily 9am–5pm. Rest of the year by appointment. $17.* ✕ ⚹ 🅿 *www.zoosauvage.qc.ca* ☎ *418-679-0543.* Occupying a pleasant site on a small island wedged in the Salmon River, the zoo offers a wonderful introduction to wild animals native to Canada. Some 950 specimens (caribou, wapiti, black bears, wolves and buffalo) roam freely in their natural habitat in the **Nature Trails Park**★★ (Parc des Sentiers de la nature) while visitors remain enclosed in a specially designed train. In addition, the pioneer era is recaptured in the authentic buildings on the site: a pioneer home from 1875, a trading post, a Montagnais camp, and a 1930s jobber (lumberjack) camp.

EXCURSIONS

★**Chute à l'Ours (Bear Falls)** – *After the Saint-Félicien bridge, turn left off Rte. 169 towards Dolbeau onto the road bordering Route Saint-Eusèbe Nord and continue on 15km/9mi. Follow signs for campground. Open late May–mid Sept daily 8am–11pm. $2.* ✕ ▯ ☏ *418-274-3411.* A foot-

White-Tailed Deer

path leads alongside these Ashuapmushuan River rapids, which extend over a distance of more than 1,500m/ 4,920ft. The falls were named by the early explorers, whose progress they hindered. Among these was a Jesuit father, Charles Albanel, the first Frenchman to reach the shores of James Bay, in 1672.

★**Moulin des Pionniers (Pioneers' Mill)** – *In La Doré, 20km/12mi from Saint-Félicien by Route 167. Open early Jun–Labour Day daily 9am–7pm. $8.* ✕ ▯ ☏ *418-256-3821.* Built in 1889 by Belarmain Audet, this wooden mill served to grind wheat, drive the blacksmith's forge, saw wood and cut shingles until 1977; the original mechanism is still in perfect working order. The site of the mill, on the Salmon River, is also the largest spawning ground for the landlocked salmon *(ouananiche)*, who return to their place of birth each year in from July to October to reproduce. The pioneer's house (1904), a two-storey log cabin, stands next to the mill. The oldest house in the town of La Doré, it was moved to this site in 1977 and is furnished with period pieces. Hiking trails provide fine **views** of the Salmon River; those interested in fishing can try for salmon in any of the fishing ponds located along the river's banks

Réserve faunique Ashuapmushuan (Ashuapmushuan Wildlife Reserve) – *South entrance is 33km/20mi (north entrance: 178km/110mi) northwest of Saint-Félicien on Route 167, towards Chibougamau (232km/144mi). Open mid-May–October daily 7am–9pm; open for hunting until mid-Oct.* ⛺ ♿ ▯ *www.sepaq.com ☏ 418-256-3806.* This 4,487sq km/ 1,732sq mi wildlife reserve is a hunting and fishing paradise, and one of the region's largest spawning grounds for the landlocked salmon *(ouananiche)*. Its name in Montaignais means "place where one stalks moose."

Dedicated to the preservation and promotion of wildlife, the reserve is governed by strict laws intended to protect both animals and visitors to the park. A stop at the welcome centre to obtain all necessary information and permits is highly recommended. Simply driving through the reserve requires no special permit.

The **Ashuapmushuan River** demarcates the territory of the reserve, which includes over 1,200 bodies of water. The river is 266km/165mi long and is one of the largest tributaries of Lake Saint-Jean. At one time, it served as a route for communication and trade between the Cree and the Montagnais. Also known as the doorway to Quebec's northern regions, it formed part of the route to James Bay. Fur trading became the principal activity with the arrival of the first Europeans. Several trading posts established along the shores and at the mouth of the river remained in use until the turn of the century.

Practical Information – Rte. 167 is equipped with security phones, as well as several observation posts and picnic areas. Pets are strictly forbidden in the reserve. Outfitters provide comfortable accommodation and the advice of well-trained guides for a variety of organised hunting and fishing trips. Reserve well in advance. Reservations are required for shelter rentals. Visitors can take part in any of several daily activities, such as fishing, hunting and canoe-camping (guide services available).

Chutes de la Chaudière (Chaudière Falls) – *68km/42mi, 1hr from Saint-Félicien; 17km/ 10mi are on a dirt road after obtaining a permit at the entrance. Open mid-June–Sept daily 8am–dusk.* ☎ *418-256-3806.* A magnificent lookout point on the Chaudière Falls allows visitors to appreciate the magnificent boreal forest comprised of birch, jack pine, black spruce and fir trees.

★★ **Lac Saint-Jean** – *See Entry Heading.*

SAINT-HYACINTHE

Montérégie
Population 38,981
Map p 263

Set on the western bank of the Yamaska River, Saint-Hyacinthe has become known as the "agro-industrial technopolis of Canada." Each year in July it hosts a large **Regional Agricultural Fair**. The city is also known for having one of the highest percentages of French-speaking people in the entire province (98.6 percent).

Historical Notes

In 1753, **Jacques-Hyacinthe-Simon Delorme**, a merchant and wood supplier, purchased the Maska seigneury from François-Pierre Rigaud, sieur de Vaudreuil, and the small community was quickly settled. During the late 18C, the Yamaska River was harnessed for power and in 1848 the railway line from Longueuil reached Saint-Hyacinthe. The town soon became a religious centre: the seminary was established in 1811 and the diocese in 1851.

■ **The Casavant Brothers**

In 1879, Joseph-Claver and Samuel-Marie Casavant, sons of the organ-maker Joseph Casavant, founded the company **Casavant Frères**, now world-renowned for the manufacture of fine organs. The company's most famous organ still graces the Notre Dame Basilica, in Montreal. The Casavant factory *(900 Rue Girouard Est)* produces about 16 organs per year.

Fire nearly destroyed the city on three occasions (1854, 1876 and 1903), and a flood carried away three bridges and devastated much of the downtown area in 1864. Nonetheless, by the end of the 19C Saint-Hyacinthe had become a major textile manufacturing centre.

Access – *Saint-Hyacinthe is about 65km/40mi east of Montreal by Rte. 20 (Exit 130 Sud) or Rte. 116.*

SIGHTS

Porte des anciens maires (Gate of the Former Mayors) – *Follow Rte. 137 (Rue Laframboise) into town; turn right on Rue Dessaulles (Rte. 116). Turn left on Ave. des Écoles, just before the Rte. 235 interchange. The gate is at the junction of Rue Girouard and Blvd. Laurier, near the banks of the Yamaska River.* Erected in 1927, this unusual brick gate with its two towers commemorates the first eleven mayors of Saint-Hyacinthe. It was inaugurated to celebrate the 100th birthday of the Honourable **Georges-Casimir Dessaulles**, who held the office of mayor from 1868 to 1879 and 1886 to 1897.

Cathédrale de Saint-Hyacinthe-le-Confesseur (Cathedral of St. Hyacinthe the Confessor) – *1900 Rue Girouard Ouest. Open year-round daily 6:30am–11:30am & 1:30pm–4:45pm.* ✗ ᕙ ◻ ☎ *450-773-8581.* This elegant, Romanesque-inspired cathedral (1878) is flanked by 50m/164ft stone towers topped by slender copper steeples. The Neoclassical interior, featuring an 1885 Casavant organ, was redecorated in 1942, 1964 and 1999. Ozias Leduc painted *The Eternal Father*, hanging in the choir.

★ **Riverfront Walk** – A pleasant walk along Rue Girouard winds along the banks of the Yamaska River, from the Gate of the Former Mayors to downtown. Several lovely Victorian homes line the wide artery, notably between Rue Després and Avenue Desaulniers. Closer to downtown, the street is bordered by imposing public buildings, including the cathedral and city hall dominating the Casimir-Dessaulles Park.

To the south lies Rue des Cascades, a lively street of shops and restaurants. The **Marché-Centre** (public market) *(no. 1555, at the intersection with Rue Saint-Denis),* dates back to 1877, and is considered the province's oldest public market. The Yamaska Rapids are visible from the Barsalou Bridge, at the eastern end of Rue des Cascades.

Lac SAINT-JEAN★★

Saguenay–Lac Saint-Jean

Map p 280

Located north of Quebec City, at the southern tip of the Saguenay region, Lake Saint-Jean fills a shallow glacial basin situated 98m/321ft above sea level. The current body of water, covering an area of 1,350sq km/521sq mi, is a small remnant of the original lake, created by melting glaciers over 10,000 years ago. Nowhere deeper than 63m/207ft, it has an average depth of 20m/66ft. The lake is fed by a number of rivers, including the Péribonka, Mistassini and Ashuapmushuan, but empties into only one: the Saguenay. The Lake Saint-Jean area resembles a crater with walls sloping downward toward the lake, creating spectacular rapids and falls.

Unlike its neighbouring industrial regions, the Saguenay and the Mauricie, the Lake Saint-Jean area supports agriculture; however, farming has only been practiced here since the Great Fire of 1870, which cleared much of the surrounding forest and opened broad tracts of land.

Historical Notes

First called Piékouagami ("flat lake") by the Montagnais, the lake was renamed for **Jean Dequen**, the first Frenchman to visit its shores in 1647. The fur trade between the Amerindians and the French, initially established at Tadoussac, soon moved into the region. In 1676, a trading post was built on the shores of the lake at the mouth of the Métabetchouane River, a site that later became the village of Desbiens.

The area remained unsettled until the mid-19C, when sawmills and pulp mills were built. The 20C was marked by the harnessing of the rivers for hydroelectricity and the building of an aluminium smelter at Alma. Despite industrialization, the shoreline communities still thrive on agriculture and tourism.

Today, Lake Saint-Jean is known for the **granite** found near its shores, notably at Saint-Gédéon, near Alma. Many of the large churches of the region are built of this stone, which has a pinkish hue once cut. The lake is famous for its abundance of landlocked salmon, known as **ouananiche**, a favourite catch for sports fishermen. *Gourgane* (a large bean) is among the region's predominant crops, and wild **blueberries**, or *bleuets*, grow so plentifully on the north shore of the lake that inhabitants are often referred to as "Bleuets."

Blueberry Picking

Assoc. touristique du Saguenay

Access – *Lake Saint-Jean is 180km/112mi north of Quebec City by Rte. 169 or Rte. 175 (via Chicoutimi), from Trois-Rivières by Rte. 155 and from Chicoutimi by Rte. 170.*

Activities – *The last week of July marks the beginning of the famous, nine-day international swim marathon (Traversée internationale du lac Saint-Jean), held every July since 1955. The one-way, straight-line swim from Péribonka to Roberval is 32km/19mi long and takes about 8hrs to complete. The round-trip, also part of the marathon, is completed by the more stalwart competitors in about 18hrs. In 1990, the marathon's route was lengthened to a 40km/25mi swim along the shore. For information:* ☎ *418-275-2851.*

TOUR AROUND THE LAKE *220km/132mi by Rte. 169.*

Alma – Just east of lake Saint-Jean at the mouth of the Saguenay River lies this regional capital of the island of Alma. Founded in 1864, the city was named in commemoration of that year's Anglo-French victory over the Russian army at the Alma River in the Crimea.

Experience the history of the region from the last ice age though industrialization at the **Musée d'Histoire du Lac-Saint-Jean** *(54 Rue Saint-Joseph; open Jun 24–Labour Day Mon–Fri 9am–6pm, weekends 1pm–5pm; rest of the year Mon–Fri 8:30am–noon & 1:30-4:30pm; $3 ⌸ ☎ 418-668-2606)*. On Rue Harvey, east of Avenue du Pont, lies the strikingly modern **Église Saint-Pierre.**

Dam-en-Terre – *8km/5mi. Exit the city center by Ave. du Pont, heading north, and turn left on Blvd. des Pins; turn right on Chemin de la Dam-en-Terre and right again on Chemin de la Marina.* The dam constructed between the islands of Alma and

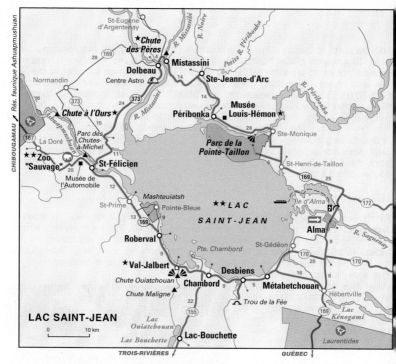

Maligne in the early 1950s was designed to harness the river and raise the level of the lake, thereby increasing its hydroelectric potential. Established on the bay in 1979, the **Dam-en-Terre Recreation Area** (*open mid-Jun–late Aug daily 8am–9pm; rest of the year daily 8am–4pm. $3.* △ ⚓ ♿ 🅿 ☎ *418-668-3016*) includes a campground, beach, picnic shelters, cottages for rent, restaurant and theatre, hiking trails and a marina. Visitors can also rent canoes, pedal-boats and bicycles. A **scenic cruise** is a nice way to visit the Alcan plant, the Isle-Maligne hydroelectric dam and the numerous villages of lake Saint-Jean (*depart Jun–early Sept Tue–Sun at 2pm & 6:30pm; round-trip 2hrs; commentary; reservations required; $22.95;* ♿ ☎ *418-668-3016*).

Take Rte. 169 for 25km/15mi to Saint-Henri-de-Taillon and continue 6km/4mi to Pointe-Taillon Park (follow signs).

Parc de la Pointe-Taillon (Pointe-Taillon Park) – *31km/19mi. Open Jun–early Sept daily 9am–7pm. May & Oct daily 10am–4pm. Opening times vary according to weather. $5/car.* △ ⚓ ♿ 🅿 *www.sepaq.com* ☎ *418-347-5371 or 418-695-7883 (off-season). Interpretation Centre open Jun–Sept daily 9am–2:30pm;* ♿ ☎ *418-347-5371.* Located at the mouth of the Péribonka River along the north bank of Lake Saint-Jean, the Pointe-Taillon peninsula was formed by post-glacial alluvial deposits. It stretches for nearly 20km/12mi and covers 92sq km/ 35sq mi. Mainly a land of marshes, swamps and peat bogs, it is also covered with a forest of black spruce and birch. On the shore of the lake, the forest gives way to a fine sandy beach that attracts migrating ducks and geese in the fall. The park offers several hiking trails and a 32km/20mi bike path, as well as canoeing, kayaking, pedal-boating and sailboarding.

Return to Rte. 169 and continue to Péribonka.

After Sainte-Monique, Route 169 crosses the Péribonka River and, 4km/2mi farther along, reaches a charming **viewpoint** and picnic area.

Péribonka – *34km/21mi from Pointe-Taillon Park.* This pretty community located on the banks of the Péribonka River, just above its outlet into Lake Saint-Jean, has subsisted on forestry and farming since its foundation in 1887. The mighty

Péribonka River, which means "river dug in the sand" in Montagnais, exceeds 460km/285mi in length, making it the largest tributary of Lake Saint-Jean. Today, its rushing waters are harnessed by two reservoirs and three power stations.

The French author, Louis Hémon (1880-1913), spent a few months in Péribonka in 1912 which inspired the creation of his posthumously published and best-known French Canadian novel, *Maria Chapdelaine, récit du Canada français*, a beautiful love story of bygone days. The community is also the departure point for the famous **Lake Saint-Jean International Swim Marathon** *(see Calendar of Events)*, which takes place during the last week of July.

Musée Louis-Hémon – *5km/3mi east of Péribonka on Rte. 169. Open Jun 24–Labour Day daily 9am–5pm. Rest of the year Mon–Fri 8am–4pm. $5.50.* ♿ ▯ *www.destination.ca/museelh* ☎ *418-374-2177.* Focusing on the life and work of Louis Hémon as well as literature in general, this vast museum complex possesses a collection of some 1,400 works of art, documents and ethnological artifacts from the world of letters. Also open to the public are the house of Samuel Bédard, where Louis Hémon stayed and worked as a farm hand in 1912, and a new, contemporary pavilion (1986) built of quartz. Exhibits here trace the author's life from his birth in Brittany to his tragic death in Chapleau (Ontario).

Continue on Rte. 169 to road junction (13km/8mi). Turn right and continue 1km/.6mi.

Sainte-Jeanne-d'Arc – *14km/9mi.* This village is located at the confluence of the Little Péribonka and the Noire Rivers. Erected beside a waterfall on the Little Péribonka in 1907, the **old mill** operated until 1974. Visitors can observe the original milling mechanisms and carding machine *(open mid-Jun–early Sept Mon–Thu 10am–5pm; Fri–Sun 10am–7pm;* ▯ ☎ *418-276-3166).* At one time, the river was harnessed to run a sawmill, shingle mill and flour mill, in addition to the carding mill.

Return to Rte. 169.

Dolbeau-Mistassini – *14km/9mi.* Now a shared municipality with Mistassini, Dolbeau was founded in 1927, with the establishment of the Domtar pulp and paper mill. Named after the Récollet missionary Jean Dolbeau, who arrived in Tadoussac in 1615, the town is famous for its **Festival des dix jours western de Dolbeau** *(see Calendar of Events)* held in July, and its **Astro Centre** which houses a huge sundial and a 45cm/18in telescope *(4km/2mi south of Dolbeau by Rte. 373; open Jun 24–early Sept daily 1pm–midnight; $7;* ♿ ▯ ☎ *418-276-0919).* Mistassini, meaning "large rock" in Cree, stands on the Mistassibi River beside a lovely waterfall, known as **Chute des Pères★** (Pères Falls), named after the Trappist Monks of Oka (*père* = priest) who came here in 1892. The twin towers of the original monastery are visible from a spot near the confluence of the Mistassini and Mistassibi Rivers. In 1980, the Trappists moved north to Saint-Eugène, but their chocolate and other products are still on sale at the factory near the old monastery. Mistassini is known as Quebec's blueberry capital. A **Blueberry Festival** *(see Calendar of Events)* is held here every August.

Saint-Félicien – *35km/22mi. See Entry Heading.*
Route 169 passes through Saint-Prime, a village renowned for its cheddar cheese and other dairy products.

Roberval – *25km/15mi. See Entry Heading.*
Route 169 hugs the lake for the entire distance between Roberval and Chambord, revealing a magnificent **panorama**.

■ Garden Paradise

Les Grands Jardins de Normandin *(1515 Avenue du Rocher, Normandin; www.cigp.com/jardin.html* ☎ *418-274-1993),* with over 55 hectares of beautifully manicured terrain, is sure to please even the most enthusiastic gardeners.

★Val-Jalbert – *9km/6mi. See Entry Heading.*
Beyond Val-Jalbert, a 2km/1.2mi drive along Route 169 leads to an excellent **viewpoint★** overlooking the lake.

Chambord – *9km/6mi.* Established in 1857, this community grew in importance after the arrival of the railway from Quebec City in 1888. It is named after Henry V, Count of Chambord, the last of the Bourbon royal line.

Desbiens – *9km/6mi.* Father Jean Dequen first saw Lake Saint-Jean from this spot, in 1647. He established a Jesuit mission five years later, followed by a fur-trading post in 1676. The community is named after Louis Desbiens, who founded the first pulp and paper mill in 1896.
A large wooden wharf just below the small Jean-Dequen Park is a wonderful spot to observe fishermen and admire the lake.

Centre d'histoire et d'archéologie de la Métabetchouane – *243 Rue Hébert, right after the bridge that spans the mouth of the Métabetchouane. Open Jun 20–Labour Day daily 10am–6pm. $4.* ♿ 🅿 ☎ *418-346-5341.* This interpretation centre traces the colonial history of Lake Saint-Jean and re-creates living conditions at a 19C fur-trading post. It also features displays on Amerindians and the prehistory of the region. The powder magazine at the entrance marks the exact spot of the original trading post, set on the banks of the Métabetchouane River. Note also the memorial honouring Jean de Quen.

Musée de la Motoneige (Snowmobile museum) – *1640 Chemin du Trou-de-la-Fée, access by 7ᵉ Ave. Open Jun 24–early Sept daily 9am–6pm. Rest of the year by appointment. $4.* ♿ 🅿 ☎ *418-346-5368.* This museum displays on a rotating basis its collection of more than 70 antique and classic snowmobiles. The informative displays document the incredible technological advances achieved over the last decades in the means of locomotion for traveling across snow-covered terrains.

Trou de la fée (Fairy Cavern) – *Located 6km/4mi south of Desbiens. Take 7ᵉ Ave. across from city hall (925 Rue Hébert) in Desbiens. Open mid-Jun–early-Oct daily 9am–5pm. $7.* 🅿 ☎ *418-346-5436.* Perched 68.5m/225ft above the Métabetchouane River, on the edge of an abrupt cliff where the Canadian Shield meets the Lake Saint-Jean basin, the cavern offers a spectacular **view** of the river. Deserters hiding in the cave during World War II claimed to have been saved by the fairy *(fée)* of the cavern. The 38m/125ft descent into the 10,000 year old grotto is impressive, but extremely steep *(sturdy shoes required; helmets provided).*

Return to Route 170.

Métabetchouan – *5km/3mi from Desbiens.* This village, founded in 1861, takes its name from the Métabetchouan River, (the name means "waters which unite before flowing in" in Cree). It is the site of a well-known summer music camp, Camp Musical du Lac-Saint-Jean *(Sunday evening concerts).* Perched on the hillside, the camp site provides a superb **view** of the lake.

SAINT-JEAN-PORT-JOLI★

Chaudière-Appalaches
Population 3,402
Map p 80

Known as the craft and wood-carving capital of Quebec, the small town of Saint-Jean-Port-Joli boasts the largest concentration of artisans in the province. Numerous craft shops, specializing primarily in wood carvings, line Route 132.

Philippe Aubert de Gaspé (1786-1871) moved to this community in 1824 from Quebec City, intending to write *Les Anciens Canadiens (The Canadians of Old)*, the novel that ultimately brought him great fame. Saint-Jean-Port-Joli is also the birthplace of a celebrated family of wood carvers, the **Bourgault brothers**: Médard (1897-1967), André (1898-1958) and Jean-Julien (born in 1910).

Access – *Saint-Jean-Port-Joli is 106km/66mi northeast of Quebec City by Rte. 73 (Pierre-Laporte Bridge) and Rte. 20 (Exit 414).*

SIGHTS

Site archéologique du Manoir du Sieur de Gaspé (Archaeological site of the Sieur de Gaspé Manor) – *5km/3mi west of town centre on Rte. 132.* On this site stood the manor house where Philippe Aubert de Gaspé wrote *Les Anciens Canadiens*, published in 1863. Fire destroyed the house in 1909, leaving only the bakery (1764), which today serves as a tourist information centre. Archaeological excavations take place here every summer.

Musée des Anciens Canadiens (Historial Museum) – *3km/2mi west of town centre on Rte. 132. Open May–Jun 23 daily 9am–5:30pm. Jun 24–Labour Day daily 8:30am–9pm. Labour Day–Oct daily 9am–5:30pm. $4.75.* ♿ 🅿 *www.quebecweb.com/ancienscanadiens* ☎ *418-598-3392.* The local history is illustrated by wood carvings crafted by Saint-Jean-Port-Joli's finest artists, including the Bourgault brothers. A video *(15min)* presents the art of sculpture in wood, stone and ice; sculpture demonstrations are held here during the summer.

★**Maison-musée Médard-Bourgault** (Médard-Bourgault House Museum) – *Two houses down from the Musée des Anciens Canadiens. Open Jun 24–Labour Day daily 10am–6pm. $2.50.* 🅿 ☎ *418-598-3880.* This 19C dwelling was purchased in 1920 by Médard Bourgault, the town's first wood carver, who restored it and embellished the walls and furnishings with his work. In the first room, the carvings by Médard and his son, Raymond, represent "the history of our ancestors."

© Yves Tessier/REFLEXION

Religious works by the master are exhibited in the second room, as is a magnificent armoire carved from linden wood. Also on display are Médard's first crucifix (1921) and his last sculpture, *Le Clochard* (The Hobo), begun in 1967 and never finished.

★**Église Saint-Jean-Baptiste (Church of St. John the Baptist)** – *In the town centre, 3km/2mi beyond the Musée des Anciens Canadiens. Open mid-Jun–mid-Oct Mon–Sat 9am–5pm, Sun noon–5pm.* ⚐ 🅿 ☎ *418-598-3023.* The slender spires and curved roof contribute to the charm of this edifice (1779). The ornate **interior** features works by Médard and Jean-Julien Bourgault. The main altar tabernacle (1740), attributed to Pierre-Noël Levasseur, stands in the sanctuary, decorated between 1794 and 1798 by Jean Baillairgé and his son, Florent. The barrel vault is composed of small coffers embellished with 4,300 carved flowers to simulate the heavens. The seigneurial pew has been preserved in honour of Philippe Aubert de Gaspé, last seigneur of Saint-Jean-Port-Joli, who is buried in the crypt of the church. In 1987, seventeen local wood carvers pooled their skills to create a magnificent **Nativity Scene**★ (Crèche de Noël). Although each linden figurine was carved by a different artist, the overall effect is remarkably harmonious.

SAINT-JEAN-SUR-RICHELIEU

Montérégie
Population 37,607
Map p 263

Birthplace of **Félix-Gabriel Marchand**, Premier of Quebec from 1897 to 1900, Saint-Jean is located on the west bank of the Upper Richelieu River, across from its twin city, Iberville. The history of the community can be traced back to 1666, when a small wooden fort was constructed here, forming one of the links in the chain of fortifications established by the French along the Richelieu River during the French-Iroquois wars. After the American Revolution, many Loyalists, faithful to the English Crown, settled in the town, which was then known as Dorchester. It was an important port for commerce with the states surrounding Lake Champlain, namely New York and Vermont.

Today, the city is well known for its fascinating balloon festival, the **Festival de montgolfières de Saint-Jean-sur-Richelieu**, which takes place every August.

Historical Notes

The 19C was a period of growth and prosperity for Saint-Jean-sur-Richelieu. In 1836, the Champlain and St. Lawrence Railroad Company built the first railway in Canada, connecting the town to La Prairie. The Chambly Canal was inaugurated seven years later. Benefiting from these two new transportation routes, Saint-Jean became a manufacturing centre for dishes, teapots, jugs and other pieces of white ceramic. In 1840, Moses Farrar opened the first stoneware factory, and one of his relatives began manufacturing glazed white earthenware for hotels and restaurants. With the financial support of several bankers, Moses created the **Saint-John's Stone Chinaware Company** in 1873. Pieces from both this company and the **Farrar** factories are now collectors' items.

The industry still exists, producing mainly structural porcelain and fixtures. Crane Canada is the only remaining industrial potter from that era.

Access – *Saint-Jean-sur-Richelieu is about 40km/25mi southeast of Montreal by Rtes. 10 and 35 (Exit at Blvd. du Séminaire).*

LE VIEUX-SAINT-JEAN (OLD SAINT-JEAN)

Musée du Haut-Richelieu (Upper Richelieu Museum) – *182 Rue Jacques-Cartier Nord, on the Market Square (Place du Marché). Open year-round Tue–Sun 9:30am–5pm. $2.* ☐ ☎ *450-347-0649.* Housed in the former market building (1859), this museum presents interesting displays on the Amerindian presence and the military history of the Upper Richelieu and the "Valley of Forts". It also features a unique collection of pottery and dishes signed "Saint-John's Stone Chinaware Company," notably several settings of the famous **Saint-John's Blue** dinner service, produced about 1890.

Continue along Place du Marché.

Adjoining the rear of the market building is the former **Fire Hall** (1877), topped by a small tower.

On the other side of Rue Longueuil, note the **St. John's United Church**, a dark brick structure dating from 1841. Several attractive Victorian-style homes line the neighbouring streets. The Neoclassical **Courthouse** (1850) stands at the corner of Rue Saint-Charles and Rue Longueuil.

Église anglicane St. James (St. James' Anglican Church) – *Corner of Rue Jacques-Cartier and Rue Saint-Georges.* With its white tower and Neoclassical entryway, the structure (1816) resembles a New England church. Today it serves the Roman Catholic parish of St. Thomas More, as well as the Anglican community.

Cathédrale de Saint-Jean-l'Évangéliste (Cathedral of St. John the Evangelist) – *Rue Longueuil. Open year-round daily 7:30am–5pm.* ☐ ☎ *450-347-2328.* Originally built between 1828 and 1853, this church features a central copper tower and an elaborate interior. It was enlarged in 1866 by Victor Bourgeau, and became a cathedral when the diocese was created in 1933.

Musée du Fort Saint-Jean (Fort Saint-Jean Museum) – *On grounds of the Fort Saint-Jean campus, Rue Jacques-Cartier Nord. Open late May–mid-Aug Tue–Sun 9:30am–4:30pm. $2.* ☐ ☎ *450-358-6500 (ext. 5769) or 450-358-6809 (off-season).* Housed in the former guardhouse (1850) of Fort Saint-Jean, this museum traces more than 300 years of military history. The collection of weapons, uniforms and other military artifacts is bolstered by an exhibit on the development of the fort. A first wooden structure, built by the French in 1666 as a defence against the Iroquois, was replaced by a second in 1748 to protect New France against British forces. In 1759, after the capture of Fort Lennox, Fort Saint-Jean was burned by the French defenders to avoid capture by the British. The structure was rebuilt by Guy Carleton in 1775 and captured by the Americans the same year, when the fort's small garrison finally surrendered after a long, 45-day siege. Having sustained severe fire damage, the fort was reconstructed after the Patriots' Rebellion of 1837.

After visiting the museum, visitors can tour the remains of the old ramparts on the grounds of the campus.

EXCURSIONS

Boat Trip – *Depart from Rue du Quai Jun 24–Labour Day daily 1:30pm & 3:30pm (round-trip 1hr 30min) Commentary. Reservations required. $15.50.* ☐ *Les Croisières Richelieu Inc.* ☎ *514-346-2446.* This 16km/10mi trip leads up the Richelieu River, past several marinas and lovely summer residences. The pleasant cruise begins near the locks and the entrance to the Chambly Canal, and provides lovely views of Iberville and the Royal Military Academy.

★★**Vallée du Richelieu** – *See Entry Heading.*

SAINT-JOACHIM
Région de Québec
Population 1,493
Map p 71

Located north of Quebec City, near the St. Lawrence, the present village of Saint-Joachim was founded soon after the Conquest. On their way to the capital, the British fleet burned the villages along the St. Lawrence shore. Wiser for the experience, the inhabitants of Saint-Joachim established their new community further inland. Today, the peaceful village is known for its lovely church *(below)*.

Access – *Saint-Joachim is 40km/25mi northeast of Quebec City. Take Rte. 360 to Beaupré and follow signs.*

SIGHTS

★★ **Église Saint-Joachim** (St. Joachim Church) – *Open mid-May–mid-Oct Mon–Fri daily 9am–5pm.* ☎ *418-827-4475.* Dedicated to the father of the Virgin Mary, this small church (1779) replaced an earlier sanctuary built in 1685 and destroyed by the British during the Conquest. The facade, designed by David Ouellet in 1895, blocks the view of the more traditional structure, which is best seen from the cemetery. The church is reputed for its **interior**★★ fashioned between 1815 and 1825 by **François Baillairgé** and his son **Thomas**, acting here as both architects and sculptors. François Baillairgé had already designed the sumptuous main altar and the chandeliers in 1785, when he was asked to add the finishing touches to the interior. The group of religious themes forms the most elaborate iconographic plan ever conceived for a church in Quebec. These representations, intended to affirm the legitimacy of the Church, depict men and sovereigns bowing to the Saviour, who empowered the Church to represent Him on earth. The parish priest, Father Corbin, left a considerable sum for this project in his will, which explains the extent of the undertaking and the opulence of the design.

© Malak, Ottawa

Église Saint-Joachim (Interior)

Choir – The panelling is enhanced by sculpted and gilded bas-reliefs. The two large sculpted panels on either side of the sanctuary represent Faith and Religion. The four medallions adorning the blind arcades depict scenes from the life of Christ: the Adoration of the Shepherds, the Adoration of the Magi, Jesus with the Doctors of the Church and the Presentation at the Temple.

The main altar is surrounded by majestic columns and four freestanding sculptures of the Evangelists. The bases of the statues are embellished with bas-reliefs depicting each Evangelist's symbol: the eagle for St. John, the ox for St. Luke, the lion for St. Mark and the angel for St. Matthew.

A sense of unity emanates from the graceful interior. The sculptures blend with the well-defined architectural scheme composed of a storey of pilasters of composite order, an imposing cornice and a finely decorated vault.

The painting above the main altar, *St. Joachim and the Virgin*, dates back to 1779. It is one of the few known works by Antoine Aide-Crequy, a parish priest from Baie-Saint-Paul, who developed his natural artistic talent to compensate for the lack of trained artists in the region during the mid-18C.

St. Joachim Church long served as the leading model for Neoclassical churches in Quebec. Thomas Baillairgé and his students went on to use the same aesthetic scheme repeatedly, thus helping establish a consistent and unified image of the Catholic Church.

Presbytère (Presbytery) – Across from the church stands the presbytery of Saint-Joachim. The large stone house incorporates a smaller old section (east) built in 1766 and covered with a high roof. The imposing west section and the sculpted Neoclassical wood portals were added in 1830.

Petit-Cap – *Just before the Cape Tourmente National Wildlife Reserve.* Petit-Cap is the site of the Seminary, a unique and monumental group of 18C buildings. The main edifice, Château Bellevue, overlooks the St. Lawrence. It dates back to 1779 and was enlarged in the original style in 1875. Adjacent to it are the late 18C chapel and the caretaker's house, a wooden structure covered with roughcast.

SAINT-LAMBERT

Montérégie
Population 20,971
Map p 175

This residential suburb of Montreal on the south shore of the St. Lawrence was originally part of the seigneury of Longueuil. Owing to the marshiness of the land, the district was commonly called *Mouille-pied* ("wet feet"). In 1857, the municipality adopted the name Saint-Lambert in honour of an associate of the Sieur de Maisonneuve, **Lambert Closse**, who settled in Montreal in 1642. Today, Saint-Lambert is the port of entry to the St. Lawrence Seaway.

The St. Lawrence Seaway – The opening of the seaway in 1959 marked the realization of a 400-year-old dream. In the early 16C, Jacques Cartier's quest for the Northwest Passage to the Orient was thwarted by the tumultuous Lachine Rapids, located west of present-day Montreal. The rapids were but the first of a daunting series of natural obstacles that rendered the river unnavigable between Montreal and the Great Lakes.

Conquering the river – Throughout the three hundred years that followed Cartier's discoveries, Amerindians, soldiers and settlers repeatedly attempted to conquer the shoals, rapids and falls of the St. Lawrence River upstream from Montreal by constructing canals and locks around such insurmountable obstacles as the mighty Niagara Falls.

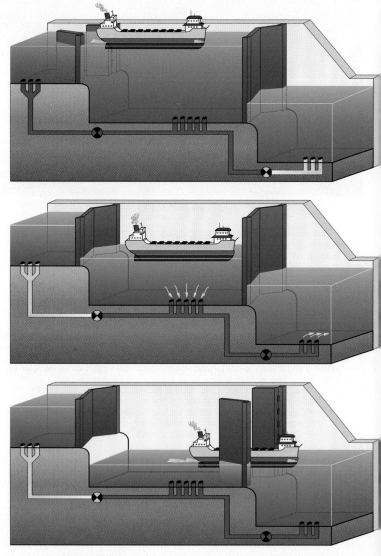

Schematic view of an Operating Lock on the St. Lawrence Seaway

The Industrial Revolution engendered an American interest in the creation of a seaway to facilitate the transport of goods between the United States and major ports in Canada and Europe. Years of negotiation between the Canadian and American governments led to a joint project to construct, maintain and operate the locks and canals. Finally, on April 25, 1959, the icebreaker *Iberville* began the first complete voyage through the St. Lawrence Seaway, which was officially inaugurated on June 26 of that same year, by Queen Elizabeth II, President Dwight Eisenhower and Canadian Prime Minister John Diefenbaker.

The seaway is 3,800km/2,356mi long and has a minimum depth of 8m/26ft. Sixteen locks raise and lower vessels a total of 177m/580ft, the difference in altitude between Montreal (6m/20ft) and Lake Superior (183m/600ft).

The massive seaway ships, known as **lakers**, measure up to 222m/728ft long and 23m/75ft wide. They transport ore (principally iron) from Quebec and Labrador to the steel mills of the Great Lakes region, and huge cargos of grain from the American heartland to ports on the St. Lawrence River.

Access – *Saint-Lambert is 10km/6mi east of Montreal by Rte. 112 (Victoria Bridge).*

SIGHTS

★**Écluse de Saint-Lambert (Saint-Lambert Lock)** – *From Victoria Bridge, follow signs for Rte. 20 Sud and turn right immediately, following signs. Open Apr–mid-Nov daily 8am–8pm.* & ▪ ☎ *450-672-4110.* This is the first lock in the St. Lawrence Seaway system. It raises and lowers vessels 4.6m/15ft, enabling them to bypass the treacherous rapids just upstream from the Montreal harbour.

The lock works in conjunction with the **Victoria Bridge**★, an impressive structure built between 1854 and 1859 to carry the Grand Trunk Railway across the river. At the time, the 2,742m/8,994ft bridge was deemed one of the world's great engineering feats. Rebuilt in the late 19C and again in the 1950s, it now carries cars in addition to trains. Drawbridges at each end of the lock allow a continuous flow of road traffic even when the locks are in operation.

From the lock's **observatory**, visitors can watch enormous lakers pass through the lock on their way upriver to the Great Lakes or down to Port-Cartier and Sept-Îles.

Musée Marsil (Marsil Museum) – *349 Riverside Drive. Open year-round Tue–Fri 10am–4pm, weekends 1pm–4pm. Closed major holidays. $2.* & ▪ *www.adaxces.com/museemarsil* ☎ *450-923-6601.* This lovely stone farmhouse, built by the Marsil family about 1749, remained in the family for nearly two centuries. With its steep roof, overhanging eaves, dormer windows and false chimney in the south gable, it is a good example of 18C vernacular architecture. The house was converted into a museum, and now mounts temporary exhibits demonstrating the ways in which textiles can reflect various cultures and historical periods.

Vallée du SAINT-LAURENT

Mauricie–Centre-du-Québec–Rég. Québec–Chaudière-Appalaches
Map pp 288-289

A vast agricultural plain in the region of Trois-Rivières, the St. Lawrence Valley narrows as the river flows toward Quebec City, where the foothills of the Laurentian Mountains rise to the north. Many small, older communities hug the shores of the St. Lawrence, and the roads lining the river are quiet and pleasant.

Access – *Trois-Rivières is situated halfway between Montreal (85km/53mi) and Quebec City (80km/50mi) on the north shore of the St. Lawrence and is accessible by Rte. 40 and Rte. 138. The itineraries described below cover the section of the St. Lawrence River Valley between Trois-Rivières and Quebec City, on both the north and south shores of the river.*

① NORTH SHORE – Trois-Rivières to Quebec City
130km/81mi by Rte. 138 and Rte. 40/440.

★★**Trois-Rivières** – *See Entry Heading.*
Leave the city by Rte. 138.

Cap-de-la-Madeleine – *6km. See Entry Heading.*
Along the drive to Batiscan, the Bécancour industrial park can be seen on the opposite shore.

★**Vieux presbytère de Batiscan (Old Presbytery of Batiscan)** – *24km/15mi. On right, before entering the village proper. Open Jun–Oct daily 10am–5pm. $3.* & ▪ ☎ *418-362-2051.* The first presbytery on this site was erected by Jesuit priests in 1696. In 1816, hoping to obtain the appointment of a resident parish priest, the parishioners replaced the dilapidated structure with the present edifice

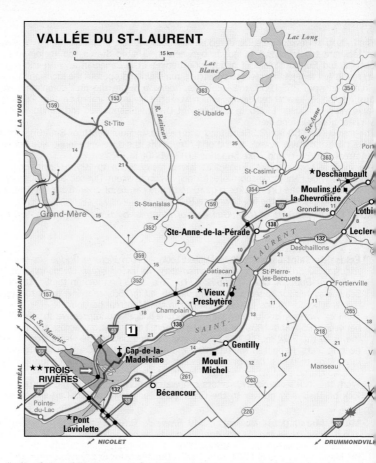

VALLÉE DU ST-LAURENT

(built of materials recovered from the original construction). The interior, typica of early 19C rural houses, is furnished with period pieces drawn from the collections of the Museum of Civilization in Quebec.

Continue into Batiscan (2km/1.2mi).

Batiscan's church (1866) stands overlooking the St. Lawrence River. The spires o the church in Saint-Pierre-les-Becquets are visible on the opposite shore. Soon after leaving the village, the road crosses the Batiscan River.

Sainte-Anne-de-la-Pérade – *10km/6mi from Batiscan.* This community on the Sainte-Anne River is known for its ice fishing. In January and February, tommy cod, commonly known as *petits poissons des chenaux*, leave the salt water to seek out fresh water. As the fish move through the river, a veritable village of colourfu shanties springs up on the frozen surface, inhabited by fishermen from all over the province. In the off-season, the huts are stacked on the riverbank. The Gothic Revival church (1859) was inspired by Montreal's Basilica.

After the town of **Grondines**, the road follows the St. Lawrence River, providing views of Lotbinière and of the ferry that crosses to the opposite bank. Quebec's first underwater transmission line passes through a tunnel beneath the St. Lawrence between Grondines and Lotbinière. The line is an important link in the 1,487km/922mi direct-current network between the Radisson substation (La Grande hydroelectric complex) in James Bay, and the Sandy Pond substation in Massachusetts.

Moulins de La Chevrotière (Chevrotière Mills) – *20km/12mi; after 15km/9mi, turn left on Rue de Chavigny. Open Jun 24–Labour Day daily 10am–4:30pm. $2.* ⬛ *www.multimania.com/deschambaultpat* ☎ *418-286-6862.* These two mills stand on a lovely site next to the La Chevrotière River. The smaller of the two dates to 1767; the larger, surmounted by a dormered roof, was built in 1802. Within, visitors will find temporary thematic exhibitions on such topics as sculpture, painting antique tools and others.

★**Deschambault** – *5km/3mi.* Overlooking the river, the **church** (1837, Thomas Baillairgé), distinguished by its wide, lateral galleries, was inspired by Quebec City's Anglican cathedral. Between its twin steeples is a statue of St. Joseph, attributed to Louis Jobin (1845-1928). Inside, the choir is adorned with statues of exceptional quality by François and Thomas Baillairgé *(open Jun 24–Labour Day Mon–Sat*

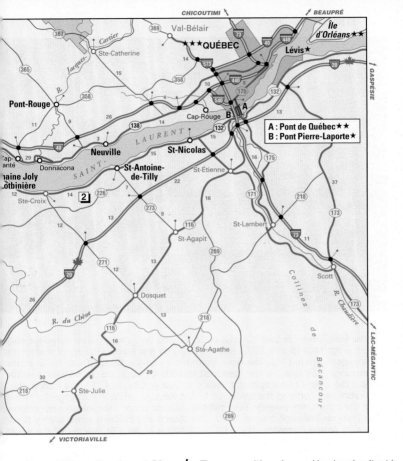

CHICOUTIMI ↗   ↗ BEAUPRÉ

A : Pont de Québec★★
B : Pont Pierre-Laporte★

10am–4:30pm, Sun 1pm–4:30pm; ♿ ☐ www.multimania.com/deschambaultpat/ ☎ 418-286-6891). In a pleasant park behind the church stands the former **presbytery,** built in 1815 *(open Jun 24–Labour Day daily 10am–5pm; ☎ 418-286-6891).* Recently restored, the structure houses exhibits, and offers cultural activities in summer. The former **assembly hall** (1840) now houses a café.

After Deschambault, a pleasant drive passes through Portneuf. At **Cap-Santé,** the village church features a lovely facade, modelled on that of Our Lady of Quebec Cathedral. Bordering the riverbank, the Vieux-Chemin extends from the parking lot behind the church. Originally part of the Chemin du Roy, this charming street is lined with 18C homes of French inspiration.

Route 138 then crosses the Jacques-Cartier River and enters **Donnacona,** known for its large pulp mill. From here, the **view** encompasses the river and the countryside around Neuville.

Continue for 28km/17mi to Rte. 365.

Detour to Pont-Rouge – *18km/11mi round-trip on Rte. 365.* This attractive community is located on the banks of the Jacques-Cartier River, which tumbles in a series of cascades on its descent to the St. Lawrence. Beside the bridge stands the four-store **Moulin Marcoux** (Marcoux Mill), erected in 1870. Restored in 1974, it houses an art gallery, a restaurant and a theatre.

Return to Rte. 138 and continue for 3km/2mi.

Neuville – *32km/20mi from Deschambault. Turn left on Rue des Érables.* Originally called Pointe-aux-Trembles, the parish of Neuville supplied freestone, a high-quality form of limestone, to construction sites in Quebec City beginning in the late 17C. Numerous families of stonecutters and masons settled here to work in the local quarries.

Rue des Érables – The availability of both materials and skilled labour explains the exceptional concentration of stone houses in the village. Although only a single main floor is apparent at street level, the houses on Rue des Érables were built to take advantage of the sloping ground, and actually comprise two or three storeys on the river, giving them a mill-like appearance. The Fiset house *(no. 679)* and the Pothier house *(no. 549),* both constructed around 1800, are good illustrations of such architecture. The seigneurial manor *(no. 500),* erected in 1835, reflects Quebec's vernacular architecture.

Pont de Québec and Pont Pierre-Laporte

Église Saint-François de Sales (Church of St. Francis de Sales) – *Open Jun–Sept daily 9am–5pm.* ☎ *418-876-2022.* Neuville's church was erected in several stages: the choir dates from 1761, the nave from 1854 and the facade from 1915. In the sanctuary is a baldachin commissioned in 1695 by Msgr. de Saint-Vallier to ornament the chapel of his episcopal palace in Quebec City. In 1717, the bishop, then in retirement, offered the baldachin to the Neuville parish in exchange for wheat for the community's needy. Four twisted columns encircle the tabernacle, sculpted by François Baillairgé around 1800. The church also contains some twenty paintings by **Antoine Plamondon** (1804-1895), a native of Neuville; several of the works were executed when the artist was 80 years old.

The road leaves the banks of the St. Lawrence and heads inland as it approaches the industrial suburbs of Quebec City. Highway 40 leads to **Cap-Rouge** *(Exit 302),* where a high trestle railway bridge (1906-1912) spans the river of the same name. It was here that Jacques Cartier and Sieur de Roberval attempted to establish a settlement in 1541.

★★★ **Quebec City** – *32km/20mi from Neuville. See Entry Heading.*

② SOUTH SHORE – Quebec City to Trois-Rivières
137km/85mi by Rte. 132.
Cross the St. Lawrence River on the Quebec City Bridge (Rte. 175).

★★ **Pont de Québec (Quebec City Bridge)** – This remarkable structure has a steel span extending 549m/1,801ft between its two main pylons; it was the world's longest cantilever-type bridge of its day. Construction proved to be a nightmare for the railroad company in charge: the bridge collapsed while under construction in 1907 and in 1916, the centre span fell into the river as it was being installed. Inaugurated in 1917 as a railway bridge, the Quebec City Bridge has been open to vehicular traffic since 1929. Just next to it is the **Pont Pierre-Laporte★**, opened in 1970. Measuring 668m/2,191ft, it is Canada's longest suspension bridge.
Take the first exit for Rte. 132.

Saint-Nicolas – *15km/9mi. Turn right on Rue de l'Entente, opposite the water tower.* Topped by a bell tower shaped like a sail, the intriguing church was erected in 1963 *(open year-round Mon–Fri 8:30am–noon & 1:30pm–4:30pm; closed July;* ♿ 🅿 ☎ *418-831-9622).* The centre altar is surrounded by pews and resembles, both visually and symbolically, a ship's helm. Natural light filters into the church at the edges of the dropped ceiling, reflecting on the marble and wood interior. The exterior balcony provides excellent **views** of the river and the two bridges leading to Quebec City.

Saint-Antoine-de-Tilly – *15km/9mi. Turn right on Chemin de Tilly.* A small road descends from the church (1788) to the St. Lawrence. From here, the view extends across the river to Neuville. The Manoir de Tilly, an old seigneurial manor built during the early 19C, has been converted into a country inn.

The road continues through Sainte-Croix with views of Donnacona and the church at Cap-Santé, on the opposite shore.

© Yves Tessier/REFLEXION

Domaine Joly de Lotbinière (Joly de Lotbinière Manor House) – *26km/16mi. After 23km/14mi turn right off Rte. 132 onto Rte. Pointe-Platon and follow signs for another 3km/2mi. Open mid-Jun–Labour Day daily 10am–6pm. Mid-May–mid-Jun & Labour Day–mid-Oct weekends 10am–5pm. $8.* ✗ ✦ 🅿 ☎ *418-926-2462.* This charming white clapboard structure surrounded by wide verandas adorned with a maple-leaf frieze was built in 1840 by Julie-Christine Chartier de Lotbinière and her husband, Pierre Gustave Joly, as a summer residence. It was also used by their son, **Henry-Gustave Joly de Lotbinière** (1829-1908), premier of Quebec (1878-1879), minister of Revenue in Wilfrid Laurier's cabinet (1896-1900) and Lieutenant-Governor of British Columbia (1900-1906).

The mansion has been converted into an **interpretation centre**, featuring displays on the history of the Lotbinière seigneury and the local natural environment. The grounds and gardens lend themselves to pleasant walks and picnics with views of the river.

Return to Rte. 132.

Lotbinière – *9km/6mi from Manor House.* Set amidst tranquil farming country, the village of Lotbinière offers views of Deschambault across the river.

Église Saint-Louis (St. Louis Church) – *Open mid-Jun–mid-Sept Tue–Sun 10am–4pm. Rest of the year weekends 10am–4pm.* ✗ ✦ 🅿 ☎ *418-796-2044.* The facade of this lovely white church (1818) overlooks a square bordered to the north by the former convent. The splendid interior was decorated by Thomas Baillairgé in 1845. The retable – shaped like a triumphant arch over the sanctuary – is surmounted by two neoclassical statues, *Faith* and *Hope*, both crafted by Baillairgé.

Maison Chavigny de la Chevrotière (Chavigny de la Chevrotière House) – *7640 Rue Marie-Victorin.* This monumental structure was erected in 1817 for Ambroise Chavigny, a notary from Chevrotière. The building's tall roof is evocative of the style of the French Regime.

Leclercville – *8km/5mi.* First settled by Acadians, this village overlooks the confluence of the Chêne and St. Lawrence Rivers. The brick church, dedicated to St. Emmélie, was built in 1863.

The road continues through Deschaillons and Saint-Pierre-les-Becquets, affording expansive views of the St. Lawrence. On the right *(7km/4mi from Leclercville)*, a plaque marks the huge 272kg/600lbs boulder allegedly placed here by Modeste Maillot (1763-1834), the legendary "Canadian Giant," who stood 7'4" tall. Maillot was born in Saint-Pierre-les-Becquets and died in Deschaillons.

West of Leclercville, the valley widens and gives way to plains. Further, the road passes through a region both agricultural and industrial, marked by the massive complex of Gentilly 2, Quebec's only nuclear power station.

Erected in 1774, the **Moulin Michel** (Michel Mill, *675 Blvd. Bécancour, 35km from Leclercville, on the left; open Jun 24–Aug Tue–Sun 10am–5pm; mid-May–Jun 23 & Sept–mid-Oct weekends noon–5pm;* ✗ ✦ 🅿 ☎ *819-298-2882*) offers a splendid look at the life and craft of a miller in New France. The mill was restored in 1992; during the summer, visitors can taste wheat bread milled from grains and baked on site. A short trail leads up the adjacent hillside to a lookout point offering a fine **view** encompassing the Bécancour industrial park and the plants at La Prade and Gentilly.

Bécancour – *14km/9mi.* Formerly part of the Pierre Le Gardeur de Repentigny seigneury, Bécancour was created in 1965 through the amalgamation of 11 villages and parishes. The name is now principally associated with the industrial park, the site of a huge aluminium smelter and other installations associated with the metallurgical industry.

Continue on Rte. 132 and Rte. 30.

From the road, views extend across the river to the Our Lady of the Cape Basilica in Cap-de-la-Madeleine and to the harbour and pulp mills of Trois-Rivières.

Take Rte. 55 across the Laviolette Bridge and then Rte. 40 to return to Trois-Rivières (17km/10.5mi).

★**Pont Laviolette (Laviolette Bridge)** – Completed in 1967, this elegantly curved bridge is over 3km/ 2mi long. It is the only bridge over the St. Lawrence River between Montreal and Quebec City.

SAINTE-AGATHE-DES-MONTS★
Laurentides
Population 5,669
Map p 135

Set on the shores of Sables Lake, amidst rolling mountains rising to 580m/1,902ft, this charming community is the capital of the Laurentides region. Settlers founded Sainte-Agathe in 1849, but construction of the Montreal and Occidental railway in 1892 hastened the development of the area, helping the town become the region's earliest tourist centre. A lively resort with numerous restaurants and inns, Sainte-Agathe is today home to Le Patriote, the best-known summer theatre in the Laurentians.

Access – *Sainte-Agathe is 86km/53mi north of Montreal by Rte. 15 and Rte. 117 (junction with Rte. 329).*

SIGHTS

★★**Lac des Sables (Sables Lake)** – Located at the foot of Rue Principale, Lagny Park provides excellent **views**★ of this lake, whose sparkling waters emanate from natural springs. The lake reaches a depth of 25m/83ft and is shaped like a wiggly H. It offers over 13km/8mi of public and private beaches.

A **scenic cruise** enables visitors to discover this magnificent lake and the homes lining its shores *(depart from dock at foot of Rue Principale mid-May–late Oct daily 10:30am, 11:30am, 1:30pm, 2:30pm & 3:30pm; additional departures Jun 24–late Aug 5pm & 7pm, Aug 24–Labour Day 5pm; round-trip 50min; commentary; $12;* ♿ ⃣ *Les Croisières Alouette ☎ 819-326-3656).* Among the many celebrities who have sojourned here are Jacqueline Kennedy, Queen Elizabeth II and Baron von Ribbentrop. The former residence of millionaire Lorne McGibbon was acquired by the Oblate Fathers after the stock market crash of 1929. The palatial mansion has been transformed into a hospital and rest home for their missionaries.

★**Lake Drive** – *About 11km/7mi. From Rue Principale, before dock, turn right on Rue Saint-Louis, then left on Chemin Tour du Lac.* The road crosses a tributary of the Nord River then reaches a small lookout *(7km/4mi)* from which there is a splendid view of the lake. It leads back to the village after passing lovely waterfront estates, a park and a long, sandy beach.

SAINTE-ANNE-DE-BEAUPRÉ★
Région de Québec
Population 3,023
Map p 71

Situated on the north shore of the St. Lawrence overlooking Île d'Orléans, Sainte-Anne-de-Beaupré is named for the patron saint of Quebec. Its shrine, administered by the Redemptorist Fathers, is a major Catholic pilgrimage centre, visited by over a million and a half people every year.

Historical Notes

According to legend, 17C French sailors caught in a storm on the river landed safely on the banks here after praying to St. Anne, the mother of the Virgin Mary. In thanks for their rescue, in 1658 they laid the foundations for a small wooden chapel in her honour. During construction, one of the workmen, Louis Guimont, was miraculously cured of lumbago. His was the first of many healings, and as a result, Sainte-Anne soon became a place of pilgrimage. Throngs of devotees, many seeking healing, came on foot, by canoe, and later by steamboat and by car.

The original wooden chapel was replaced by a sturdier structure in 1661, followed by a stone church in 1676. But so numerous were the pilgrims and parishioners that by the 19C, a larger building was required. Completed in 1876, the immense and imposing new structure was in turn destroyed by fire in 1922 and replaced by the present basilica, which was dedicated in 1934.

Access – *Sainte-Anne-de-Beaupré is 35km/22mi east of Quebec City by Rtes. 40 and 138.*

★★THE SHRINE

Basilica – *Open mid-Jun–mid-Sept daily 6:30am–9:30pm. Rest of the year daily 7am–4:30pm.* ♿ 🅿 ☎ *418-827-3781.* The enormous, twin-spired medieval-style basilica was designed by the architects Maxime Roisin and Louis-Napoléon Audet. Built in the shape of a Latin cross, with a steel frame and a veneer of white granite, it is 98m/ 321ft long, 60m/197ft wide at the transept, and 90m/ 295ft high. Between the two spires stands a large gilded statue of St. Anne, saved from the fire that destroyed the previous church.

Interior – Inside, the visitor is struck by the immense size of the basilica. The interior is divided into five naves separated by huge columns. Each column is topped by a carved capital, the work of Émile Brunet and Maurice Lord. The interior is lit by 240 **stained-glass windows**, fashioned by the French artist Auguste Labouret, assisted by the master glass maker Pierre Chaudière. Note especially the windows of the transepts and the rose window above the organ. The barrel vault above the main nave is decorated with glimmering **mosaics** portraying the life of St. Anne. Also the work of Auguste Labouret, aided by Jean Gaudin, they combine cream and brown colouring highlighted by red and gold. A particularly beautiful mosaic of the Holy Family is located above the main altar.

Basilica, Sainte-Anne-de-Beaupré

An ambulatory surrounds the sanctuary with ten radiating chapels. On a marble pedestal in the left wing of the transept stands a statue of St. Anne cradling the infant Mary in her arms. The chapel behind it contains a relic of St. Anne. Opposite, in the right wing of the transept, note the wooden sculpture (c.1920) of the Holy Family by Louis Jobin.

Chapelle Commémorative (Memorial Chapel) – *Open Apr–Nov daily 8am–7pm.* Built in 1878 on the site of the 1676 parish church, the structure incorporates elements of the original chapel, notably the steeple and its two cupolas. The tabernacle, dating from about 1700, is attributed to Jacques Leblond, also called Latour. The high altar was sculpted by Thomas Baillairgé in 1827.

Chapelle du Saint Escalier (Chapel of the Scala Santa) – Erected in 1891 next to the Memorial Chapel, this sanctuary contains a replica of the Scala Santa (Holy Stairs), which Christ climbed before being sentenced to death by Pontius Pilate. The original staircase was taken to Rome about AD 325 by St. Helena, mother of Emperor Constantine. Many pilgrims mount the steps on their knees.

Chemin de la Croix (The Stations of the Cross) – On the hillside behind the Chapel of the Scala Santa are life-size representations of the Stations of the Cross. They were cast in bronze by French craftsmen between 1913 and 1946.

ADDITIONAL SIGHTS

Musée de Sainte Anne (Sainte Anne Museum) – *9803 Blvd. Sainte-Anne, near the basilica. Open Apr–Oct daily 10am–5pm. Rest of the year weekends & holidays 10am–5pm. $5.* ♿ 🅿 ☎ *418-827-6873.* Opened in 1997, this museum of religious art presents the life of St. Anne and the development of the community, as well as the history of the shrine.

★ **Cyclorama de Jérusalem (Cyclorama of Jerusalem)** – *8 Rue Regina, beside the basilica. Open Jul–Aug daily 9am–8pm. May–Jun & Sept–Oct daily 9am–6pm. $6.* 🅿 *www.cyclorama.com* ☎ *418-827-3101.* The large edifice houses an enormous, impressively realistic painting measuring (1,540sq m/16,559 sq ft) showing Jerusalem on the day of the Crucifixion. Painted in Munich (1878-1882) by the French panoramist Paul Philippoteaux and five assistants, and installed at Sainte-Anne-de-Beaupré in 1895, it is 14m/46ft high by 110m/361ft in circumference.

EXCURSION

★★ **Côte de Beaupré** – *See Entry Heading.*

SCHEFFERVILLE
(Kawawachikamach)
Nord-du-Québec
Population 578

The mining town of Schefferville abuts the provincial boundary between Quebec and Labrador (province of Newfoundland). It lies on the northern fringe of the boreal forest, just south of the tundra, on the watershed of the Atlantic and Hudson Strait/Hudson Bay drainage basins.

Situated in the heart of the iron-rich **Labrador Trough**, Schefferville was built in 1854 by the Iron Ore Company of Canada, which operated here until 1982. During its heyday, close to 8,000 people lived in this frontier town; a gigantic statue, known as the *Iron Man*, located on the shore of Knob Lake, recalls the town's erstwhile prosperity. Today a ghost town when compared to its bustling past, Schefferville is mainly a service centre for the Amerindian population; mining continues, but at a much slower pace. It has also become a departure point for nature excursions to the Great North region of Quebec. Originally planned for a large population, Schefferville boasts a modern infrastructure. An extensive road system links the mining sites, their equipment still in place, and leads to a fascinating variety of lakes and mountain ridges. Permission is required to enter the company grounds *(inquire at municipal office)*.

For over 40 years, Montreal's McGill University has operated a **Subarctic Research Station** near the airport. The station accommodates students and researchers year-round but especially during the summer.

Access – **By air**: *Air Canada/Air Alliance (☎ 514-393-3333) via Sept-Îles, connecting with Aviation Québec Labrador (☎ 418-962-7901) to Wabush/Labrador City and Schefferville; or Inter Canadian (☎ 418-962-8321) via Sept-Îles, connecting with Air Schefferville to Schefferville.* **By train:** *The Quebec North Shore Labrador Railway (QNSL) once a week (Thu morning) from Sept-Îles. The train ride (12hrs) takes travellers from Sept-Îles across the Canadian Shield to the edge of the tundra.*

Activities – *This little-known region of northeastern Quebec is ideal for adventure tourism: caribou hunting, fishing, canoeing, wilderness treks. Outfitters offer a number of hunting and fishing excursions outside of Schefferville. Roads provide access to three Amerindian reserves: Kawawachikamach (Naskapis), Matimekosh and Lac-John (Montagnais).*

EXCURSIONS

Kawawachikamach – *15km/6mi northeast of Schefferville. Access by unpaved road.* Set amidst small lakes in the hilly region of the Canadian Shield, Kawawachikamach was built between 1981 and 1984, and is settled by Naskapi Indians.

The Naskapis – Related to the Cree and Montagnais Indians, the Naskapis belong to the Algonquian linguistic family. A nomadic people, they originated from the interior of the Ungava region, and followed the migratory route of the caribou to hunt. As their traditional hunting activities began to disappear, Naskapis settled at the Fort Chimo trading post, now called Kuujjuaq. In 1956, they left Fort Chimo for Schefferville, in the hope of improving their living standards.

When the **Northeastern Quebec Agreement** was signed in 1978, the Naskapis surrendered aboriginal title to their land and obtained financial compensation, land rights and new hunting, fishing and trapping rights. They decided to build their village on the shores of Matemace Lake, leaving behind the reserve of Matimekosh, which they had shared with the Montagnais. This new village was designed in collaboration with the Naskapis to be specifically adapted to their needs and to the local subarctic climate, one of the harshest in Canada.

Matimekosh – *Just north of Schefferville, on foot or by car by municipal road.* Around 1955, Montagnais Indians from Sept-Îles relocated to Schefferville to work in the mines. They settled in the village of Lac-John, created in 1960 on the shore of Lake John. The village later became an Amerindian reserve. The Montagnais, Algonquian-speaking Indians with French as their second language, operate an active crafts centre.

SEPT-ÎLES★

Duplessis
Population 25,224
Map p 88

This dynamic city occupies a superb site★★ in a large, almost circular bay on the north shore of the St. Lawrence. Protected by the islands at its mouth, the bay remains navigable during all seasons, allowing for industrial activity throughout the year. Today, Sept-Îles is the administrative centre of the Côte-Nord.

Historical Notes

The earliest known mention of the region of Sept-Îles, or "Seven Islands," dates back to 1535, when Jacques Cartier noted several round islands blocking the entrance to the large bay. In earlier times, Montagnais Indians hunted caribou here. In the 15C, Basques, French and Spanish fishermen came to the area in search of seals and whales from which they extracted oil much in demand in Europe.

In 1651, Father Jean Dequen arrived on these shores and founded the mission of Ange-Gardien. Several years later, the King of France agreed to the establishment of a series of trading posts, to be rented to French merchants. After the Conquest of New France, the King's posts were entrusted to a number of British merchants. The most influential of these, the Hudson's Bay Company, developed a monopoly on fishing, hunting and fur trading rights until 1859, after which the region was opened to settlement. In the early 20C, the paper industry became the principal economic activity, with the construction of a hydroelectric dam and pulp mill at Clarke City, today part of Sept-Îles. The paper mill shut down in 1967, but by the second half of the 20C, the transportation of coal and iron ore had boosted the community's economy. The city's natural deep water port enables ocean-bound ships to tranship coal here. Iron Ore Company of Canada (IOC) owns several wharves in the northeastern sector of the bay, and Wabush Mines Company operates ore-handling facilities in the Pointe Noire sector.

Access – *Sept-Îles is 640km/397mi northeast of Quebec City by Rte. 138. A ferry service links the community to Rimouski, on the south shore of the St. Lawrence, and to Port-Menier, on Anticosti Island. Service provided by Relais Nordik, Inc. Apr–Dec ☎ 418-723-8787. The major airport for the Côte-Nord is also located at Sept-Îles.*

SIGHTS

Parc du Vieux-Quai (Old Wharf Park) – A boardwalk lines the magnificent bay of Sept-Îles. Seafood enthusiasts can sample and buy shrimp and crab, while enjoying a leisurely stroll along the wharf. The shelters along the boardwalk display crafts by local artisans.

Musée régional de la Côte-Nord (North Shore Regional Museum) – *500 Blvd. Laure. Open mid-Jun–early Sept daily 9am–5pm. Rest of the year daily 9am–noon & 1pm–5pm, weekends & holidays 1pm–5pm. Closed Dec 25–Jan 1. $3.25.* ♿ 🅿 *www.bbsi.net/mrcn/* ☎ *418-968-2070.* The museum of art and history was created by the local artist, André Michel, as a reminder of the "eternal youth of this ancient land, its roots and the diverse origins of the great men and women who have lived here." The permanent exhibit, "A Never-Ending Shore," describes the 1,100km/682mi of shoreline and forests of black spruce, and the successive waves of population growth that resulted from the exploitation of the area's natural resources.

Le Vieux-Poste (Old Trading Post) – *Blvd. des Montagnais. Open early Jun–mid-Aug daily 9am–5pm. $3.25.* ♿ 🅿 *www.bbsi.net/mrcn/* ☎ *418-968-2070.* Reconstructed according to its 18C layout uncovered during archaeological excavations, this group of buildings surrounded by a palisade occupies a historically significant site. Montagnais Indians and European settlers first traded here three centuries ago, and the site was visited by Jacques Cartier, Louis Jolliet and merchants of the Hudson Bay Company. The site recreates the atmosphere of a trading post of years past; other exhibits offer an intriguing introduction to the Montagnais culture.

★PARC RÉGIONAL DE L'ARCHIPEL DES SEPT-ÎLES
(SEPT-ÎLES REGIONAL PARK)

Tour of the Islands – *Cruises depart from the Marina mid-Jun–mid-Sept. daily; several departures per day according to the cruise; round-trip 2hrs 30min; commentary; reservations suggested; $25–$30; tickets available at the Promenade ticket counter in front of the marina.* 🅿 *www.vitrine.net/ctsi* ☎ *418-968-1818; Corporation touristique de Sept-Îles* ☎ *418-962-1238.* Scenic **cruises** by ferry, riverboat and raft offer a good introduction to the region, its history and the natural

Lighthouse, Île du Corossol

beauty of the Sept-Îles archipelago. The lighthouse indicating the entrance to the bay is located on **Île du Corossol** (Corossol Island), a bird sanctuary with one of the greatest varieties of species in Canada, including gulls, terns, and puffins.

La Grande Basque – *Ferry to island departs from Old Wharf Park, mid-Jun–Aug. daily 9am–6pm. One-way 10–20min. Reservations suggested. $15, camping $7/day per tent. Tickets available at the Old Wharf ticket counter in front of the marina. & ▣ Corporation touristique de Sept-Îles www.vitrine.net/ctsi ☎ 418-968-9558.* Located closest to the city, La Grande Basque is the only island that has been developed for hiking, picnicking and camping. Numerous trails meander through grandiose and varied landscapes: huge rocky ridges, immense cliffs and a peat bog. Beautiful sandy beaches line the western shore.

SHERBROOKE★
Cantons-de-l'Est
Population 76,786
Map p 99

Located on the steep slopes of a valley, at the confluence of the Saint-François and Magog Rivers, Sherbrooke was originally called "the great fork" by Abenaki Indians. The first settlers arrived from Vermont about 1800. Soon thereafter, Gilbert Hyatt built a flour mill, and the community became known as Hyatt's Mills. In 1818, the name Sherbrooke was adopted in honour of the Governor-in-Chief of British North America, **Sir John Coape Sherbrooke** (1764-1830).

Owing to its industrial dominance during the 19C, Sherbrooke became the principal city of the Eastern Townships. Mills sprang up on the banks of the Magog River, soon followed by the textile mills. The advent of the railway accelerated Sherbrooke's economic growth, and a university opened in 1954, enhancing Sherbrooke's position as an important cultural centre. Originally anglophone, the population is now more than 94 percent francophone.

Today Sherbrooke serves the mining and agricultural concerns of the region. Mt. Bellevue, across the Magog River, is a popular ski centre.

Access – *Sherbrooke is 150km/93mi east of Montreal by Rte. 10 and Rte. 112.*

TOWN CENTRE

Monument aux morts (War Memorial) – *Rue King Ouest between Rue Gordon and Rue Brooks.* This imposing sculpture by George W. Hills stands in the centre of Rue King. It was erected in 1926 to commemorate the Sherbrooke residents who gave their lives in World War I. From this vantage point the **view** encompasses the city and the Saint-François River.

From the War Memorial, go east down the hill to Rue Wellington, turn left and continue for two blocks.

Hôtel de Ville (City Hall) – *145, Rue Wellington. Not open to the public.* Built between 1904 and 1906 as a courthouse, this imposing edifice exemplifies the Second Empire style. The architect, Elzéar Charest, reused the plans he had submitted to the 1890 city hall competition in Quebec City. Dominating lovely Strathcona Park, the structure has housed the city hall since 1988.

Musée des Beaux-Arts de Sherbrooke (Sherbrooke Museum of Fine Arts) – *241 Rue Dufferin. Open Jun 24–early Sept Tue–Sun 11am–5pm. Rest of the year Tue–Sun 1pm–5pm. Closed Dec 24–26 & Dec 31–Jan 2. $4.* ♿ ▯ *http://mba.ville.sherbrooke.qc.ca* ☎ *819-821-2115.* Housed in a historic structure in downtown Sherbrooke, this museum presents an interesting collection of Quebec art, focusing on the Eastern Townships. Note in particular works by Robert Whale (1805-1887), Suzor-Côté (1869-1937) and Wayne Seese (1918-1980). A collection of paintings in the naïve style includes pieces by Arthur Villeneuve, and by such international artists as Dragan Mihailovic and Jean-Marie Godefroy.

The museum also organises temporary exhibits of works by local artists and offers various educational activities.

★**Cathédrale Saint-Michel** (St. Michael's Cathedral) – *Rue de la Cathédrale, corner of Rue Marquette. Open year-round Mon–Fri 7:30am–noon & 1:30pm–4pm, Sat 9am–noon & 2pm–4pm, Sun 9am–noon & 2pm–6pm.* ♿ ▯ ☎ *819-563-9371.* This imposing Gothic Revival structure stands on a hill known as the Marquette Plateau, in the centre of Sherbrooke. Consecrated in 1958, the cathedral was built by Louis-Napoléon Audet, who also designed the basilica at Sainte-Anne-de-Beaupré. In the facade's principal stained-glass window hangs a 3m/10ft high aluminium crucifix, by the Montreal artist Cassini. Inside, ceilings over 20m/66ft high enclose a light and spacious interior. The large stained-glass windows, by Raphaël Lardeur and Gérard Brassard, portray Biblical scenes. To the left of the altar is a striking oak statue of the Virgin Mary by the 20C artist Sylvia Daoust.

Chapelle des Fondateurs (Founders' Chapel) – *Behind main altar to the left.* Added in 1980, this chapel features a mural of enamelled copper by Patricio Rivera, portraying the five founders of the Canadian Catholic Church: Marie de l'Incarnation, Marguerite d'Youville, Msgr. de Laval, Kateri Tekakwitha and Marguerite Bourgeoys.

Musée du Séminaire de Sherbrooke (Museum of the Sherbrooke Seminary) – *222 Rue Frontenac. Open Jun 24–early Sept daily 10am–5pm. Rest of the year Tue–Sun 12:30pm–4:30pm. $4.* ▯ *($1) www.mss.ville.sherbrooke.qc.ca* ☎ *819-564-3200.* This handsome museum boasting a fascinating collection of some 100,000 objects, is organised as two sections. Housed in an elegant brick tower of the Sherbrooke Seminary (1898), the **Musée de la Tour** (Tower Museum) incorporates religious items, weapons, furniture, and specimens of natural science, such as animals, shells and minerals. Note the series of wood carvings by Rodolphe Duguay, and the watercolours by William Henry Bartlett (1809-1854). Behind the seminary, the **Centre d'exposition Léon-Marcotte** (Léon Marcotte Exhibition Centre) features a variety of interactive exhibits on the sciences.

★THE OLD NORTH WARD (LE VIEUX-NORD)

The area north of the Magog River encompasses some of the oldest industries in Sherbrooke, as well as charming streets lined with large, lovely homes. Numerous Colonial and New England-style mansions lend the quarter a stately appearance, enlivened by fanciful examples of the Victorian styles, including Italian Villa, Châteauesque, Queen Anne and Gothic Revival. Their dormers, gables, towers and turrets are set off by splendid gardens dotted with tall trees.

Domaine Howard (Howard Estate) – *1300 Blvd. Portland. Buildings not open to the public.* Charles Benjamin Howard (1885-1964), businessman, politician and mayor of Sherbrooke, erected a stone house on this site in 1917, adding a second one a few years later for his mother. For several years, the buildings housed the offices of the Sherbrooke Historical Society *(now housed at 275 Rue Dufferin)*; today, both buildings belong to the city and house civic offices. The grounds form a pleasant park surrounding superb French formal gardens.

EXCURSIONS

Rocher Mena'Sen (Mena'Sen Rock) – *1.5km/1mi north of town. From Rue King Est, turn left on Rue Bowen, then bear left onto Blvd. Saint-François Nord.* An illuminated cross stands on this islet in the Saint-François River, replacing a lone pine tree (*mena'sen* in Abenaki) that was destroyed in a storm in 1913. According to Abenaki folklore, the tree commemorated the Abenaki victory over the Iroquois. Another legend tells of two young Amerindian lovers who, having escaped capture in Massachusetts, stopped here on their way to Odanak. The girl died at this spot and her lover planted the tree in her memory.

Sanctuaire de Beauvoir (Beauvoir Shrine) – *8km/4mi north of town by Blvd. Saint-François Nord and Chemin Beauvoir. Open May–Oct daily 9am–9pm. Rest of the year daily 9am–5pm.* ✗ *(summer)* ♿ ▯ *www.sanctuairedebeauvoir.qc.ca* ☎ *819-569-2535.* In 1915, Abbé Joseph-Arthur Laporte placed a statue of Christ at this spot, 360m/1,181ft above the Saint-François River. A simple stone chapel was constructed in 1920. Today, many pilgrims find their way here seeking peace and tranquillity, and to enjoy the panoramic **view**★ of the Sherbrooke area.

In the woods behind the chapel and the newer church (1945) is the Gospel Walk, consisting of eight **sculptures**★ representing scenes from the life of Christ. These stone sculptures were carved by Joseph Guardo. In summer, mass is celebrated in an outdoor chapel, which accommodates 1,600 pilgrims.

★★**Eastern Townships** – *See Cantons de l'Est.*

Coaticook – *See Entry Heading.*

TADOUSSAC★★
Manicouagan
Population 913
Map p 273

Situated at the mouth of the Saguenay River, Tadoussac occupies a beautiful **site**★★ on the cliffs and sand dunes lining the north shore of the St. Lawrence. Its name is derived from the Montagnais word *tatoushak*, meaning "knolls," a reference to the pair of small hills west of the community. A boardwalk extends alongside the St. Lawrence linking the old chapel and the Chauvin trading post, just beneath the **Hotel Tadoussac**, a long, red-roofed structure dating from 1941. Paths circle **Pointe de l'Islet**, which borders the bay, providing fine views of the landscape; others cross the knolls to a small cove (Anse-

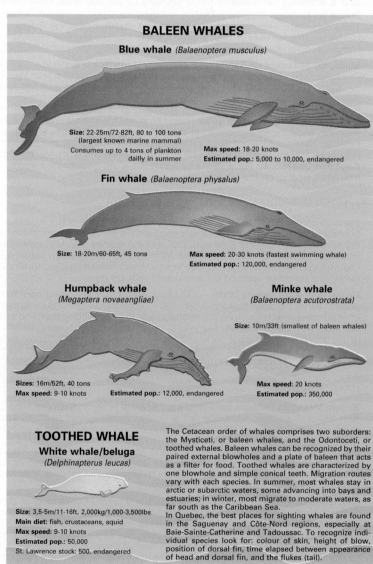

BALEEN WHALES

Blue whale *(Balaenoptera musculus)*

Size: 22-25m/72-82ft, 80 to 100 tons (largest known marine mammal)
Consumes up to 4 tons of plankton daily in summer
Max speed: 18-20 knots
Estimated pop.: 5,000 to 10,000, endangered

Fin whale *(Balaenoptera physalus)*

Size: 18-20m/60-65ft, 45 tons
Max speed: 20-30 knots (fastest swimming whale)
Estimated pop.: 120,000, endangered

Humpback whale
(Megaptera novaeangliae)

Sizes: 16m/52ft, 40 tons
Max speed: 9-10 knots
Estimated pop.: 12,000, endangered

Minke whale
(Balaenoptera acutorostrata)

Size: 10m/33ft (smallest of baleen whales)
Max speed: 20 knots
Estimated pop.: 350,000

TOOTHED WHALE

White whale/beluga
(Delphinapterus leucas)

Size: 3,5-5m/11-16ft, 2,000kg/1,000-3,500lbs
Main diet: fish, crustaceans, squid
Max speed: 9-10 knots
Estimated pop.: 50,000
St. Lawrence stock: 500, endangered

The Cetacean order of whales comprises two suborders: the Mysticeti, or baleen whales, and the Odontoceti, or toothed whales. Baleen whales can be recognized by their paired external blowholes and a plate of baleen that acts as a filter for food. Toothed whales are characterized by one blowhole and simple conical teeth. Migration routes vary with each species. In summer, most whales stay in arctic or subarctic waters, some advancing into bays and estuaries; in winter, most migrate to moderate waters, as far south as the Caribbean Sea.

In Quebec, the best places for sighting whales are found in the Saguenay and Côte-Nord regions, especially at Baie-Sainte-Catherine and Tadoussac. To recognize individual species look for: colour of skin, height of blow, position of dorsal fin, time elapsed between appearance of head and dorsal fin, and the flukes (tail).

à-l'eau), where the ferry from Baie-Sainte-Catherine docks. The lively town attracts a growing number of visitors, who come to observe the whales that visit the plankton-rich waters at the mouth of the Saguenay for a few months each year.

Historical Notes

Tadoussac was a meeting place for trade well before the arrival of Jacques Cartier on these shores, in 1535. In 1600, Pierre Chauvin built Canada's first fur trading post on this spot, and the Jesuits established a mission a few years later. On his first voyage to New France in 1603, Samuel de Champlain stopped here, and Tadoussac became a port of call for all vessels coming across the Atlantic. In 1628, the village was captured by the British adventurers, the Kirke Brothers, but it later returned to French hands and remained a trading centre until 1839. The first permanent residents arrived in the mid-19C and erected a sawmill. With the advent of the steamship in 1853, the community developed as a choice resort.

Mammals of the Deep

Every June, a flotilla of whales swims up the St. Lawrence River to the mouth of the Saguenay River. Here, the salty St. Lawrence and the fresh waters of the Saguenay combine to create a rich ecosystem for a multitude of flora and fauna. Krill and caplin drawn by the plankton flourishing in these waters attract the whales, which consume several tons of the small fish daily.

Many species of whale have been sighted here, the most common being the **fin** and **minke**. There is also a large population of white whales, better known as **belugas**. Occasionally, **humpback** whales are sighted, and lucky tourists may glimpse the huge **blue whale**, which is known to reach a length of 30m/98ft, making it the largest mammal on earth.

Access – *Tadoussac is about 220km/136mi northeast of Quebec City by Rtes. 40 and 138.*

SIGHTS

★★**Whale-Watching Cruises** – *Depart from the municipal wharf May–Oct daily 10am, 1pm, 2:30pm & 4:15pm. Round-trip 3hrs. Commentary. Choice of cruise in inflatable boat or passenger boat. Reservations required. Starting at $32.* ⟨ P

Croisières AML ☎ *418-237-4274.* At Tadoussac, the St. Lawrence is more than 10km/6mi wide. The boats head for the centre of the river where, miles from shore, the whales surface to breathe and dive to search for food. The spray that erupts from their blowholes just before they surface makes them very easy to spot. It is a magnificent experience to see these colossal creatures in the wild.

The entrance to the Saguenay Fjord is marked by a lighthouse that stands 15m/49ft high and is visible for nearly 50km/31mi. The fjord is known for its impressive tides which ebb and flow with remarkable speed.

© Yves Marcoux/PUBLIPHOTO

Whale-Watching

★★**Scenic Cruises** – *Depart from La Grève pier (near the marina) late May–late Oct daily 9am, 1pm & 4:15pm. Round-trip 3hrs. Commentary. Reservations suggested. $30.* ⟨ P *($3) Croisières à la Baleine* ☎ *418-235-4879.* To fully appreciate the deep and wide saguenay fjord, an ancient glacial valley flanked by precipitous cliffs, visitors are advised to take a boat trip. Cruises of varying lengths are offered to Anse-de-Roche, and as far as Baie-Trinité/Cape Éternité.

Centre d'interprétation des mammifères marins (Marine Mammal Interpretation Centre) – *108 Rue de la Cale Sèche, near the pier. Open mid-May–Jun 23 daily noon–5pm. Jun 24–mid-Sept daily 9am–8pm. Mid-Sept–mid-Oct daily noon–5pm.*

$5.50.   🔲 *www.gremm.org* ☎ *418-235-4701.* This interpretation centre presents interesting displays, videos and slide shows on the marine life of this area, in particular whales, seals and cormorants.

Chapelle des Indiens (Indian Chapel) – *On Rue du Bord-de-l'Eau. Open Jun–Sept daily 9am–9pm. May & Oct by appointment. $1.* & 🔲 ☎ *418-235-4324.* The small chapel, the oldest wooden church in Canada, was built in 1747 by the Jesuit missionary, Claude-Godefroy Cocquart. The chapel houses a fine collection of religious objects.

Poste de traite Chauvin (Chauvin Trading Post) – *157, Rue du Bord-de-l'Eau. Open Jul–Aug daily 9am–8:30pm. Jun & Sept daily 9am–noon & 3pm–6pm. $2.75.* & 🔲 ☎ *418-235-4657.* This log structure with its steeply pitched roof is a reconstruction of Pierre Chauvin's fur trading post of 1600. Inside, old photographs as well as archaeological and historical displays explain the fur trade between the Montagnais Indians and the French. The collection focuses on the Côte-Nord region.

For a legend of price listings for hotels and restaurants, see p 170.

Hotel Tadoussac – *165 Rue du Bord-de-l'Eau.* ✗ & 🔲 ☎ *418-235-4421.* **$$$** With its red roof made famous in the film *Hotel New Hampshire*, the Hotel Tadoussac invites you to step back in time. Its grand lawn stretching almost to the shore serves as an outdoor activity center with bowling and adirondack chairs perfect for relaxing and enjoying a nice summer day. Most of the simply decorated rooms have views of the Saint Lawrence.

Station piscicole de Tadoussac (Tadoussac Fish Hatchery) – *115 Rue du Bateau-Passeur. Open Jun 24–October daily 10am–6pm. $3.75.* 🔲 ☎ *418-235-4569 or* ☎ *418-236-4604 (off-season).* This centre is devoted to maintaining the levels of salmon populating the province's rivers. Workers in the centre fertilize and incubate salmon eggs and raise the fry. Visitors can learn about the biology and habitat of the salmon as well as the the various stages of the hatching process, and can observe the full-grown salmon in ponds and holding tanks.

Sand Dunes – *4km/2.5mi east by Rue des Pionniers.* Located in a stone house (1915), an **interpretation centre** *(open Jun–mid-Oct daily 10am–5pm;* & 🔲 ☎ *418-235-4238)* provides insight into the formation of the lovely marine terraces of fine sand lining the Saint Lawrence. Sparrows and birds of prey are visible here from August to October.

EXCURSIONS

★★★ **Fjord du Saguenay** – *See Entry Heading.*

★ **Côte-Nord** – *See Entry Heading.*

TERREBONNE★

Lanaudière
Population 42,214
Map p 133

This attractive city lies on the north shore of the Mille Îles River, north of Montreal. Terrebonne's refurbished old quarter, bounded by Rues Saint-Louis and Saint-Pierre, is a delightful place to stroll, with its quaint stone and wooden buildings, many of which house restaurants, cafés, boutiques and galleries.

Historical Notes

Terrebonne's story begins in 1673 when the seigneury was granted to Daulier des Landes, but settlement only began in the 18C. The community soon became known for its fertile soil, hence the name Terrebonne, meaning "good land." The first mills in the area were built by the abbot Louis Lepage, between 1718 and 1745, on one of the islands (Île des Moulins) in the Mille Îles River.

After the Conquest, Île des Moulins flourished under the Scottish merchants of the Northwest Company. Simon McTavish, one of the stockholders, acquired the Terrebonne seigneury in 1802. Within a few years, he had established an industrial and commercial centre on the island, whose fame extended well beyond the region's borders. In 1815, the mills of Terrebonne were reputedly the finest and best equipped in all of Canada. Activity subsided during the 1820s as electricity gradually replaced hydraulic power, and Île des Moulins was reduced to serving the needs of farmers in the area. In 1832, Joseph Masson, a banker from Montreal, acquired the seigneury and its mills. While he was unable to restore the village's past glory, his widow, Geneviève Sophie Raymond, tried to address the various needs of the community and created a road network, the Terrebonne Turnpike, extending from Saint-Vincent-de-Paul to Mascouche. However, business continued to decline and by the end of the 19C, all mills had shut down.

Access – *Terrebonne is 35km/22mi north of Montreal by Rte. 125 (Blvd.-Pie IX) and Rte. 25 (Exit 17).*

SIGHTS

Situated on high ground above the river, **Rue Saint-Louis** is lined with attractive stone buildings topped by steeply pitched roofs. At no. 901, note the former Masson Manor (1850), built in the neoclassical style with a symmetrical facade and pediments. The former residence of Geneviève Sophie Raymond, the building now serves as a school. The church (Église Saint-Louis-de-France), erected in 1878, with its tall central steeple and two side towers, stands nearby.

★**Île des Moulins (Mill Island)** – *From Blvd. des Seigneurs, turn right on Ave. Moody, left on Rue Saint-Louis and right Rue des Braves. Open late May–late Jun weekends 1pm–5pm. Late Jun–early Sept daily 1pm–9pm. Open-air theatre productions in summer.* ✕ ♿ *www.iledesmoulins.qc.ca* ☎ *450-471-0619.* The island presents an impressive collection of 19C buildings restored by the Quebec government. These structures can best be viewed from Rue des Braves, on the other side of Masson Pond, which was used as a reservoir.

Both types of mills that prevailed in Quebec in the 18C and 19C can be found here. The French Regime mills were often constructed on a causeway or bridge having supports high enough to permit the wheel to turn under them. By the late 18C, English technology had established mills on land, using diversion canals to augment the flow of water.

Crossing the causeway, the first building visible is the **flour mill** *(moulin à farine)*, built in 1846 on the site of the seigneurial mill of 1721. Both this restored mill and the adjacent **sawmill** (1804) have been converted into the municipal library, an acclaimed example of adaptive building re-use. The pleasant and innovative interior displays remnants of the mills. Visitors can gaze out the large rear windows and observe the pond water trickling down the original wheel mechanism to flow under the building.

The next building, on the island itself, is the **seigneurial office** *(bureau seigneurial)*, a stone structure built for the mill's foreman widow around 1850. It houses an **interpretation centre** with an exhibit on the history of the site *(same hours as Mill Island)*. Beside it is the old **bakery** *(boulangerie)*. Built for Simon McTavish in 1803, this massive building is reminiscent of traditional French architecture. The bakery used the flour produced on the island to bake biscuits, which were highly prized by travellers. The attic houses a gallery for contemporary art.

The last building, the so-called **new mill** *(moulin neuf)* of 1850, has two floors and an attic. It houses a cultural centre, an art gallery and a theatre The rest of the island is a pleasantly landscaped park dotted with modern sculptures, benches, picnic sites and an outdoor amphitheatre. Bike paths meander throughout the park.

Flour and Saw Mills, Île des Moulins

301

THETFORD MINES

Chaudière-Appalaches
Population 17,635
Map p 66

This community is located in the heart of the largest asbestos-producing region in the Western Hemisphere. Named for a small town in Norfolk, England, Thetford Mines sits in a naturally rolling area drained by the Bécancour River. The town is distinguished by its unique piles of **tailings**, artificial mountains composed of pulverized rock from the mines.

Historical Notes

In 1876, while ploughing his field, Joseph Fecteau found a strange piece of rock which frayed into silky white fibres: **asbestos**. The mineral had been recognized as "white gold" for over 2,000 years for its heat-resistance and insulating properties. Interest in Fecteau's discovery generated the area's development, particularly after the construction of a railway in 1879, which enabled rapid transport of raw and finished products. Asbestos yields a fibre used today in the construction and aerospace industries.

Despite restrictions governing the use of asbestos in recent years, Thetford Mines remains the largest producing centre, with both underground and open pit mines. A short drive south on Route 122 passes through **Black Lake**, and offers good views of the town's immense open-pit mine.

Access – *Thetford Mines is located 107km/66mi south of Quebec City by Rte. 73 and Rtes. 173 and 112.*

SIGHT

★ **Musée minéralogique et minier de Thetford Mines (Mineralogical and Mining Museum of Thetford Mines)** – *711 Blvd. Smith Sud (Rte. 112). Turn right on Blvd. Lemay and*

Musée Minéralogique et Minier

right again on Blvd. Smith. Open Jun 24–early Sept daily 9:30am–6pm. Early-Sept–Dec & Mar–Jun 24 daily 1pm–5pm. $5. ♿ ℗ *www.mmmtm.qc.ca* ☎ *418-335-2123.* This museum houses a superb collection of minerals from all over the world, with particular focus on the Appalachians, mountains renowned for the beauty and variety of their minerals. Displays help visitors identify the types of rock and describe their characteristics, such as hardness, translucence, colour and lustre. The exhibit highlights asbestos and other minerals found in Quebec.

EXCURSION

Kinnear's Mills – *24km/15mi by Rtes.112 and 269.* This tiny community in the Osgood River valley is known for the beauty of its site and for the four churches standing side by side *(not open to the public)* at its centre. Around 1842, several Scottish families settled in Kinnear's Mills and built the Presbyterian church. The more modest Methodist church (1876) and the Anglican church with its small steeple, were built by Loyalists after the American Revolution. The Catholic church was built by Irish Catholics who fled Ireland in the 1920s.

TROIS-RIVIÈRES★★

Mauricie
Population 49,419
Map opposite

Capital of the Mauricie–Bois-Francs region, this industrial centre is located on the north shore of the St. Lawrence River at the mouth of the Saint-Maurice River. Just before it enters the St. Lawrence, the Saint-Maurice River branches around two islands, thereby creating the three "rivers" for which the city is named. Major annual events in Trois-Rivières include an international poetry festival, an international festival of vocal arts and the **Grand Prix Player's Ltee** *(see Calendar of Events)*.

Historical Notes

First Settlers – In 1634, Samuel de Champlain sent Nicolas Goupil, Sieur de Laviolette (1604-c.1660) here to establish a fur trading post, and Trois-Rivières became the second oldest settlement in New France after Quebec City. For his fort, Laviolette chose a elevated spot (known as the Platon) high above the St. Lawrence. Furs were transported on the Saint-Maurice River until 1737, when the King's Road (Chemin du Roy) was inaugurated, connecting the settlement to the city of Quebec. During New France's heyday, Trois-Rivières was home to many great explorers, including Jean Nicolet and Nicolas Perrot. The joint explorations of **Pierre Radisson** and **Sieur des Groseilliers** led to the founding of the Hudson's Bay Company in 1670, and the renowned **Sieur de la Vérendrye** was the first European to reach the Rocky Mountains.

Pulp and Paper Capital – In the 1850s, major logging companies began exploiting the vast forests of the Saint-Maurice River valley. Large lumber mills sprang up in Trois-Rivières, along with a port, and later, hydroelectric installations. When a process for making paper from wood pulp was developed, a thriving pulp and paper industry took root in the area. In 1936, construction of grain silos and textile mills further stimulated the growth of the city. By the 1930s, Trois-Rivières was the world capital for the production of newsprint, a distinction the city holds to this day. Three large pulp mills currently operate in the city.

The **Pont Laviolette** across the St. Lawrence was inaugurated in December 1967, and is the only bridge linking the river's banks between Montreal and Quebec. Suspended 46m/150ft above the river, it is 3km/2mi long. The **University of Quebec at Trois-Rivières** (UQTR) opened outside the downtown district in 1969.

Access – *Trois-Rivières is situated about halfway between Montreal (85km/53mi) and Quebec City (80km/50mi) on the north shore of the St. Lawrence. It is connected to both by Rte. 40 (Centre-Ville exit) and Rte. 138.*

DOWNTOWN

2.9km/1.8mi. Map p 303.

A fire in 1908 destroyed or damaged hundreds of buildings, devastating the heart of the downtown area. The relatively few buildings that survived the disaster have been carefully restored.

Begin the walking tour at the Boucher de Niverville Manor.

★**Manoir Boucher-de-Niverville** (Boucher de Niverville Manor) – *168 Rue Bonaventure. Open Jun–Sept Mon & Tue 9am–5pm, Wed–Fri 9am–7pm, weekends 1pm–7pm. Rest of the year Mon–Fri 9am–5pm. Closed major holidays.* 🅿 ☎ 819-375-9628. This whitewashed stone manor house with red shutters was constructed about 1729 by François Châtelain. His son-in-law, Claude-Joseph Boucher, Sieur de Niverville, gave the manor its name when he inherited it in 1761. Restored in 1971,

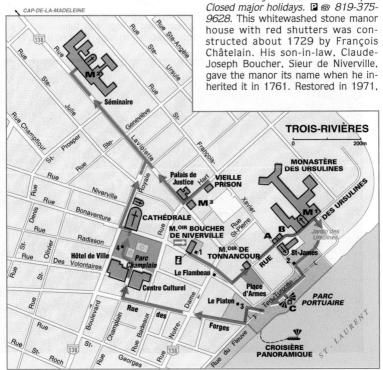

it houses the city's chamber of commerce and presents displays on the history of the area. The residence is decorated with typical 18C Quebec furniture. Climb the steep steps to the attic to admire the woodwork of the roof. Outside stands a **statue** (**1**) of Maurice Duplessis (1890-1959), a native of the city. Premier of Quebec from 1936 to 1939 and from 1944 to 1959, Duplessis lived down the street *(240 Rue Bonaventure)* and graduated from the Trois-Rivières Seminary.

Walk south on Rue Bonaventure.

Le Flambeau (The Flame) – *On Place Pierre Boucher. The monument is illuminated at night.* The striking obelisk in the centre of the Pierre Boucher Square was erected to celebrate Trois-Rivières' 325th anniversary. Pierre Boucher, Sieur de Grosbois (1622-1717), was the governor of Trois-Rivières in 1654, when the settlement was attacked by the Iroquois. He later founded Boucherville.

Walk south to Rue des Ursulines and turn left.

★ **Rue des Ursulines** – This charming street is lined with some of the oldest buildings in the city, most spared by the 1908 fire.

★ **Manoir de Tonnancour** (Tonnancour Manor) – *864 Rue des Ursulines. Open Jun 24–Aug Tue–Fri 9am–5pm, weekends 1pm–5pm. Feb–Jun 23 & Sept–Dec Tue–Fri 9am–noon & 1:30pm–5pm, weekends 1pm–5pm.* ☎ *819-374-2355.* This three-storey edifice was completed in 1725 by René Godefroy de Tonnancour, Seigneur of Pointe-du-Lac, and rebuilt by Judge Pierre-Louis Deschenaux after a fire in 1795. The structure served as an officers' barracks, a presbytery and a school. It has been restored and now houses an art gallery. Note the unusual style of the pitched roof, which reveals a Loyalist influence. The foundations and stone walls are original.

Opposite the manor house lies the **Place d'Armes**. Prior to 1800, the square served as a camping ground for Algonquin Indians who came to trade furs at the fort. Reserved for military use from 1751 to 1815, the square has been converted into a pleasant park. Note the bronze cannon made in Russia in 1828, a souvenir of the Crimean War (1853-1856).

St. James' Church – *787 Rue des Ursulines. Open Jun–Aug Tue–Sat 10am–5pm, Sun 2pm–5pm. Rest of the year by appointment.* ⚐ ▯ ☎ *819-374-6010.* The Récollets (reformed Franciscan monks) began construction here on a chapel and monastery in 1693, completing work in 1742. Added in 1754, the adjoining wing is now part of the structure. After the Conquest, the building was used as a court of law and a prison. The chapel was permanently converted to an Anglican church in 1823. Opposite the church, the **Maison de Gannes** (**A**) *(no. 834; private residence)*, built in 1756 by a French officer, is the only structure of French inspiration in the old quarter. At number 802, note also the historic **Maison Hertel de la Fresnière** (**B**), completed in 1829.

★ **Monastère des Ursulines** (Ursuline Monastery) – *784 Rue des Ursulines.* This religious complex, replete with a gracious dome and a large wall sundial, is the jewel of Trois-Rivières' old quarter. The Ursuline Sisters arrived in Quebec in 1639 from

Monastère des Ursulines

Tours, France, but were not summoned to Trois-Rivières until 1697. Their first monastery, completed in 1700, was enlarged with a chapel in 1714 and rebuilt after a fire in 1752. A second fire struck in 1806, but the French Regime style of the buildings was maintained during reconstruction. Six subsequent additions were made between 1835 and 1960. The Ursuline Sisters operate a private girls' school, which today has an enrollment of some 1,200 students. The inscription on the sundial (1860) reads, in Latin, *Dies Sicut Umbra* (Days flee like shadows).

★**Chapel** – *734 Rue des Ursulines. Open Mar–Apr Wed–Sun 1:30pm–5pm. May–Oct Tue–Fri 9am–5pm, weekends 1:30pm–5pm. Rest of the year by appointment* ☎ *819-375-7922.* The chapel is topped by a beautiful dome (1897) designed by Joseph and Georges Héroux and decorated with frescoes by Luigi Capello. The early 19C altar is the work of François Normand. Paintings executed in 1840 by the French Canadian artists, Antoine Plamondon *(left)* and Joseph Légaré *(right)*, hang above the altar.

Musée des Ursulines (Ursuline Museum) (**M'**) – *Same hours as the chapel. $2.50.* ☎ *819-375-7922.* The museum features fine collections of ceramics, silver, books, prints, furniture and decorative arts. Each year, exhibits are compiled on specific themes. A model shows the monastery as it appeared in the 19C. During summer vacations, temporary art exhibits are displayed in the refectory.

Cross the Ursuline Garden (in front of the monastery).

A **monument** (**2**) at the eastern end of the Waterfront Park commemorates Pierre Gaultier de Varennes, **Sieur de la Vérendrye**.

★**Parc Portuaire** (**Waterfront Park**) – Once part of the estate of Mayor Joseph-Édouard Turcotte, this attractive terrace affords superb **views** of the river. In 1857, Turcotte gave the land to the city for use as a public park.

Centre d'exposition sur l'industrie des pâtes et papiers (Pulp and Paper Industry Exhibition Centre) (**C**) – *800 Parc Portuaire. Enter from the upper terrace, or descend the steps to the main entrance on Parc Portuaire. Open Jun–Sept daily 9am–6pm. Apr–May & Oct by appointment. $3.* ✗ ♿ ⏸ *($1)* ☎ *819-372-4633.* The centre provides a fascinating glimpse of the industry that dominates Trois-Rivières' economy. The exhibit traces the history of paper from ancient China to the present. Audio-visual presentations and innovative displays explain the paper-making process and the different techniques for producing pulp. Large murals illustrate the future of the industry.

Walk along the waterfront to Le Platon.

Le Platon – In 1634, Sieur de Laviolette built his fort on this plateau 35m/115ft above the river. The area's name is derived from the word *peloton*, meaning "ball of wool." A **bust** (**3**) of Laviolette and a plaque were placed here in 1934 to celebrate the city's tricentennial.

★**Scenic Cruise** – *Landing at the foot of Rue des Forges. Depart from the harbour front May–Oct daily 1pm & 8pm. Round-trip 1hr 30min. Commentary. Reservations required. $11.* ✗ ⏸ *Navire M/V Le Draveur Inc.* ☎ *819-375-3000.* This cruise offers an unequalled **view** of the port of Trois-Rivières and its pulp and paper mills. Visitors can also get a good look at the Cap-de-la-Madeleine shrine and the impressive Laviolette Bridge. The nuclear power plant at Bécancour is visible on the south shore of the river.

Rue des Forges – Shops and restaurants line this busy street, which combines the flavour of the old port with the energy of a bustling university town.

From Rue des Forges between Rue Hart and Blvd. Royale, turn right between the city hall and the cultural centre and climb stairs to Parc Champlain.

Parc Champlain (**Champlain Park**) – The modern, concrete structures of Trois-Rivières' **City Hall** and **Cultural Centre** *(hôtel de ville* and *centre culturel)* border this pleasant square dotted with fountains and trees. The centre houses a theatre, library and art gallery. Built in 1967 to celebrate the centennial of Canada's confederation, this ensemble has been acclaimed for its architectural design.

In the square, a **monument** (**4**) to Benjamin Sulte (1841-1923) commemorates the well-known French-Canadian historian.

★**Cathédrale de Trois-Rivières** (**Cathedral**) – *362 Rue Bonaventure, at the edge of Parc Champlain. Open year-round daily 7am–11:30am & 2pm–5:30pm.* ♿ ⏸ ☎ *819-374-2400.* The Gothic Revival cathedral with its copper-clad steeple was designed by Victor Bourgeau. The building was consecrated in 1858, but financial difficulties delayed the erection of the steeple until 1905. The interior is dominated by Guido Nincheri's richly coloured **stained-glass windows**. Produced between 1935 and 1954, they depict the "Lorette Litanies" of the Virgin Mary.

Beside the cathedral stands a statue of Louis-François Laflèche, Bishop of Trois-Rivières from 1870 to 1898.

Walk along Blvd. Royale. Turn left on Rue Laviolette and continue 400m/1,312ft.

Séminaire de Trois-Rivières (Seminary) – *858 Rue Laviolette.* Founded in 1860, the St. Joseph Seminary was rebuilt after a fire in 1929. Embellished by columns and a statue of St. Joseph, the main entrance of the long, limestone structure is surmounted by a squat copper dome. Untouched by the fire, the Romanesque-style chapel *(behind the reception desk)* is open to visitors and displays the seminary's collection of religious objects, as well as artworks by Jordi Bonet (1932-1979). Galleries on each side of the entrance hall make up the **Pierre Boucher Museum (M²)**, which presents exhibits of the region's historic, ethnographic and artistic heritage *(open year-round Tue–Sun 1:30pm–4:30pm & 7pm–9pm;* ♿ 🅿 ☎ *819-376-4459).* On view here are works by Antoine Plamondon, Roy-Audy, Berczy, Ozias Leduc, Suzor-Côté, Rodolphe Duguay, Gaston Petit and Raymond Lasnier.

Double back on Rue Laviolette to Rue Hart.

The old **courthouse** (palais de justice) stands at the corner of Rue Laviolette and Rue Hart. Designed by François Baillairgé and built in 1823, it was enlarged and partially restored in 1913.

Continue on Rue Hart.

★**Musée des Arts et Traditions populaires du Québec (Museum of Quebec Folk Arts and Traditions) (M³)** – *200 Rue Laviollette, at the intersection with Rue Hart. The museum is currently closed with an expected reopening of summer 2001. Call for hours.* ☎ *819-372-0406.* Opened in 1996, this museum offers visitors an excellent opportunity to immerse themselves in Quebec culture. Permanent and temporary exhibitions display selections from a permanent ethnography collection of more than 80,000 objects (tools, furniture, textiles, toys, etc), illustrating provincial customs and mores; folk arts; traditional occupations; farming methods and domestic life. The museum also features a permanent archaeological collection of more than 20,000 artifacts of prehistoric Amerindians and European cultures.

★**Vieille Prison (Old Trois-Rivières Prison)** – *Same address as the Museum of Quebec Folk Arts and Traditions. Linked to the museum by covered walkway.* Designed by François Baillairgé and erected between 1816 and 1822, the imposing stone structure features some of the best surviving examples of Palladianism in Quebec. Note its massive size, three-storey framework, severe portal and wide pediment dominating the central facade, all characteristic of a style that marked the British presence throughout the Colonial Empire. The nine chimney stacks on the roof are evidence of a concern for the prisoners' comfort. The building ceased to function as a prison in 1986. Today it features an interpretation centre; twenty of its cells present different aspects of prison life, such as discipline, hygiene, visitation, etc.

EXCURSIONS

★**Pointe-du-Lac** – *About 20km/12mi from downtown by Rte. 138, on the shores of Lake Saint-Pierre.* In 1721, René Godefroy de Tonnancour established a **seigneurial mill**★ here, on the banks of the Saint-Charles River. By 1788, the two-storey stone structure was Quebec's sixth most productive wheat mill, and ground grain until 1965. The sawmill here operated until 1986. Restored in 1978 by the Quebec government, the mill has been converted into an art gallery and exhibit hall, presenting changing displays related to milling *(open late Jun–Labour Day daily 10am–5pm; $3;* 🅿 ☎ *819-377-1396).* Nearby, the Church of Our Lady of the Visitation (Église Notre-Dame-de-la-Visitation, 1882) is recognizable by its small steeple.

★**Mauricie** – *See Entry Heading.*

Vallée du Saint-Laurent – *See Entry Heading.*

VAL-D'OR★
Abitibi-Témiscamingue
Population 24,285

Situated in the heart of the Abitibi region, the area around Val-d'Or was the exclusive domain of Algonquin and Cree Amerindians prior to the arrival of Catholic missionaries and trappers in the 17C. The history of the city itself covers less than a century. The town was created in 1922 during the great gold rush that followed the discovery of major mineral deposits in Rouyn-Noranda. Located on the easternmost portion of the Cadillac Fault, Val-d'Or was the most important gold producer in the region during the 1929 economic crisis. Today, it remains one of the only active mining towns in the Abitibi region, with nine operating mines producing not only gold, but silver and copper as well. A thriving logging industry also supports the local economy. In summer, the many saloons, bars and restaurants light up the *Rue Principale* with the colorful neon signs reminiscent of 1950s and 1960s western towns.

Access – *Val-d'Or is accessible by Rte. 113 from Chibougamau (413km/256mi further north) or Rte. 117 from Montreal (531km/329mi). Air Alliance and Inter-Canadien offer daily flights from Montreal to Val-d'Or; Air Creebec flies to the James Bay region.*

SIGHTS

Village Minier de Bourlamaque (Mining Village of Bourlamaque) – *South of 3ᵉ Ave.* Upon entering Val-D'Or, take Rue Saint-Jacques, directly opposite the tourist information booth, up to Rue Perreault. Merged with Val-d'Or in 1965, this mining village was named after François-Charles de Bourlamaque, an aide of French General Montcalm. The village, which was declared a historic district in 1979, was administered exclusively by the Lamaque Mine, one of the main employers on the Cadillac Fault. The mine shaft, hospital and residence of the mine executives are intact, and the solid log cabins that housed the mine employees are still inhabited. The **Cité de l'Or** *(visit by guided tour only, mid-Jun–early Sept daily 8:30am–5:30pm; rest of the year by appointment; $18; tickets available at 90 Ave. Perreault;* ♿ 🅿 *www.citedelor.qc.ca* ☎ *819-825-7616)* provides guided tours of the village; in addition, visitors can see the surface buildings of the Lamaque Mine and descend some 91m/300ft into an authentic mine tunnel.

Tour d'observation (Observation Tower) – *Rue Sabourin, at the corner of Rue des Pins. Open Apr–Dec year-round daily until dusk.* Rising above an attractive forest setting, the Rotary tower (18m/59ft) overlooks the town and surrounding area, which has been nicknamed the "country of one hundred thousand lakes" *(le pays aux cent mille lacs).*

EXCURSION

Malartic – *25km/15mi west of Val-d'Or, on Rte. 117.* This mining and industrial town was created as a "mushroom city" in 1922, and flourished during the mid-20C, with seven active gold mines. Along the Avenue Royal, false-front buildings recall the city's gold rush days.

★**Musée régional des Mines de Malartic** (Malartic Regional Mining Museum) – *Arriving from Val-d'Or, turn right on Rue Centrale. The museum (no. 650) is located on the corner of Rue de la Paix. Visit by guided tour (1hr 30min) only, Jun–mid-Sept daily 9am–5pm. Rest of the year Mon–Fri 9am–noon & 1pm–5pm, weekends by appointment. $4.* ♿ 🅿 ☎ *819-757-4677.* This museum was established as a tribute to the mining heritage of the Abitibi-Témiscamingue. It features a fine collection of mineral samples from the region and from around the world, as well as an avant-garde exhibit that takes visitors on a simulated journey to the core of the ore.

VAL-JALBERT★

Saguenay–Lac Saint-Jean
Map p 280

Occupying a dramatic **site**★ near the falls of the Ouiatchouan River, this ghost town conjures up dreams of turn-of-the-century industrial life.

The community began as a company town around a pulp mill built by Damase Jalbert in 1902. After his death, the mill was taken over and expanded by Alfred Dubuc. At the height of production in 1910, it produced up to 50 tonnes of pulp a day, and in 1915, the town became a municipality. By 1926, the population had grown to a peak of 950 inhabitants.

Troubles began in 1926. Owing to a sudden lack of demand, the price of pulp dropped, and increased competition led the mill to close the following year. The population gradually drifted away, and the village fell into ruin. A program of renovations begun in 1970 saved Val-Jalbert from obscurity. Today a veritable open-air museum, this heritage site offers visitors a wide variety of activities.

Access – *The Val-Jalbert Historic Village is located 245km/162mi northwest of Quebec City by Rtes. 175 and 169.*

VAL-JALBERT HISTORIC VILLAGE

The village can be visited on foot or by tram. Open Jun 23–Aug 27 daily 9am–7pm. Early-May–Jun 22 & Aug 28–late-Oct daily 9am–5pm. $12. △ ✗ ♿ 🅿 ☎ *418-275-3132. The village belongs to the Quebec government. Some older homes have been renovated and are available to visitors as rental units year-round.*

Convent – The former convent-school of the Sisters of Our Lady of Good Counsel (1915) serves as an **interpretation centre** for the historic village. A slide show *(15min)* and a model of the site recount the history of Val-Jalbert. The nuns' quarters and chapel on the second floor can be visited. Across the street stand the remains of the St. George's Church and its presbytery, overrun with vegetation.

Rue Saint-Georges – Along the village's main artery lies the former **hotel** *(tourist accommodation is available on the second floor).* Destroyed by a fire in 1918, the structure was rebuilt soon after, to house the village's general store. Today, a small

Val-Jalbert Historic Village

boutique on the ground floor displays and sells a variety of objects from another era. Behind the general store in the old butcher's stall, an herbarium and a craft shop can be visited.

Residential Sector – The residential sector, now deserted, is situated on a plateau bounded by Rues Sainte-Anne, Saint-Joseph, Dubuc, Tremblay and Labrecque. At its peak, the village counted about 80 employee residences *(one is open to the public, on Rue Saint-Georges, near the post office).* When they were built between 1909 and 1920, these houses were considered state-of-the-art, equipped with central heating, electricity, running water, and even telephones. The houses belonged to the company, and were rented to employees for about $10 a month (employees' salaries averaged around $27 a month). Today, most of the sector is in decay, a ghostly reminder of its once-thriving past.

Vieux Moulin (Old Mill) – Standing at the base of the Ouiatchouan falls, this mill produced a large amount of pulp, which was subsequently transported south by train. The remains of the rail line are visible.

Once the vital centre of the village, the mill now houses an exhibit hall. A model explains the operation of the mill and a film *(20min)* describes the process of transforming wood pulp into paper. The old mill machinery is on display.

Chute Ouiatchouan (Ouiatchouan Falls) – These impressive 72m/236ft falls were once the sole source of power for the pulp mill and the community. A steep but sturdy stairway *(400 steps)* leads to the top of the falls; visitors can also make the ascent by cable car *($3.75)*. From this spot, the visitor will enjoy a magnificent **view★★** encompassing Lake Saint-Jean and the surrounding countryside. Downstream, the Ouiatchouan River is striking as it carves out a gorge in the rock.

Chute Maligne (Maligne Falls) – *4.4km/3mi, allow 11/2hrs round-trip. Trail begins in campground on west side of river. Note: steep descent to the falls.* A pleasant wooded trail climbs up above the Ouiatchouan River valley to a point where the river plunges over a second set of falls. A lock and sawmill were once located here, to prepare and cut the wood before it was floated down to the mill.

VALCOURT

Cantons de l'Est
Population 2,442
Map p 98

A tiny agricultural community until the 1930s, Valcourt has become famous for the **snowmobile**, the brainchild of one of its residents, and is now the site of a world-class industry.

Historical Notes

As a boy in Valcourt, **Joseph-Armand Bombardier** (1907-1964) envisioned creating an all-terrain vehicle that would travel over snow. He trained as a mechanic and worked in a garage next to his father's farm, inventing in his spare time. In 1937, he received his first patent, for a sprocket wheel/track system, which enabled him to develop vehicles guided by skis. Accommodating several passengers, the vehicle was primarily used for military applications. In 1959, he introduced the **Ski-Doo**, which went on to transform life in the north. A new vehicle and a new sport were born. Today, J.-A. Bombardier Industries develops and sells snowmobiles all over the world. It also makes locomotives, airplane engines, and other transportation-related items.

Access – *Valcourt is 130km/81mi from Montreal by Rte. 10 (Exit 90) and Rtes. 243 and 222.*

SIGHT

★ **Musée J.-Armand Bombardier (J.-Armand Bombardier Museum)** – *1001 Ave. J.-A.-Bombardier. From Rue Saint-Joseph, turn right on Blvd. du Parc, and then left on Ave. J.-A.-Bombardier. Follow signs. Open May–Labour Day daily 10am–5pm. Rest of the year Tue–Sun 10am–5pm. Closed Jan 1–2, Dec 24–26 & 31. $5.* ☈ ☐ *www.fjab.qc.ca* ☎ *450-532-5300.* Divided into three sections, this museum is a fascinating tribute to Valcourt's native son. The **J.-Armand Bombardier** Exhibit and the **Bombardier Garage** trace the inventor's life and re-create the atmosphere in which he worked during the early stages of his career. The **International Snowmobile Exhibit** illustrates the machine's assembly and its usage throughout the world from 1960 to the present. An additional room features temporary exhibits of science and technology.

VAUDREUIL-DORION

Montérégie
Population 18,466
Map p 174

Located just west of the island of Montreal, the seigneury of Vaudreuil was granted to Philippe Rigaud de Vaudreuil, Governor of Montreal, in 1702. Barely developed under the French Regime, the community was acquired in 1763 by Michel Chartier de Lotbinière, who furthered growth and established a parish. On October 25, 1783, he proposed a town plan in which a church and market place in the centre would be surrounded by a set of perpendicular streets. The 18C design was never carried out and the village kept its rural character. Engulfed by the Montreal suburbs during the 1970s, the twin communities of Vaudreuil and Dorion were eventually amalgamated, and today form the municipality of Vaudreuil-Dorion.

Access – *Vaudreuil-Dorion is about 50km/31mi west of Montreal. It is accessible either by Rte. 40 (Exit 35) or by Rte. 20 (Blvd. Saint-Henri exit).*

SIGHTS

★ **Maison Trestler (Trestler House)** – *85 Chemin de la Commune. From Rte. 20, turn right on Blvd. Saint-Henri, and right on Ave. Trestler. Open year-round Mon–Fri 9am–5pm, Sun 1pm–4pm. Closed Dec 23–Jan 3. $3.50.* ☐ *www.trestler.qc.ca* ☎ *450-455-6290.* This enormous stone house stands on a beautiful site overlooking Lake Deux Montagnes. It measures an impressive 44m/144ft long by 13m/42ft wide, and has a total of 14 dormer windows protruding from its wood shingle roof. The centre section dates from 1798 and was built by Jean-Joseph Trestler, a German who made his fortune in the fur trade. The wings were added in 1805 and 1806. Several rooms in the house are furnished with exemplary pieces of 18C and 19C furniture. The tour passes through the beautiful curved-ceiling vault, where furs were hung to dry and displayed for purchasers. During the summer, concerts are held in the house.

Maison Valois (Valois House) – *331 Ave. Saint-Charles, 1km/.6mi from the Trestler House. From Ave. Trestler, turn right onto Blvd. Saint-Henri, then bear right on Blvd. Saint-Charles. Open mid-Jun–late Aug daily 8:30am–7pm.* ☎ *450-455-7282.* Set in a pleasant park overlooking Lake Deux Montagnes, this edifice (1796) is typical of local residences, with its stone base and wooden walls. Note its steep roof, which measures about half the height of the structure and has no overhang. Restored by the municipality, it is used as an art gallery and hosts temporary exhibits.

Musée régional de Vaudreuil-Soulanges (Vaudreuil-Soulanges Regional Museum) – *431 Ave. St-Charles. Open year-round Tue–Fri 10am–5pm, weekends 1pm–5pm. Closed Dec 22–Jan 4. $3.* ♿ ☎ *450-455-2092.* This museum is located in a restored stone school building (1859), where **Lionel Groulx** (1878-1967), the great French-Canadian historian, studied. Typical of religious architecture of the period, it features a windowed mansard roof topped by a small lantern. The museum grew out of a local heritage preservation and development program. The main collection contains ethnographic objects used in various facets of domestic and artisanal life. In addition, the museum presents thematic and travelling exhibits.

Église Saint-Michel (St. Michael's Church) – *On Blvd. Roche, near the museum. Open year-round Mon–Fri 9am–10:30am, Sat 6pm–8pm, Sun 9am–noon.* ♿ 🅿 ☎ *450-455-4282.* Completed in 1789, this church – one of the oldest in the Montreal region – was declared a historic monument in 1957. The harmonious chevet, composed of an apse and a small sacristy, is best viewed from the cemetery. A new facade was added in 1856. Inside, note the liturgical pieces sculpted by Philippe Liébert in the late 18C: the main altar with its tabernacle, the side tabernacles and the pulpit. The choir panelling and stalls are by Louis-Amable Quévillon. The sculpted decor is complemented by an astonishingly realistic trompe-l'œil decor by F.-E. Meloche, a student of the 19C artist Napoléon Bourassa. The painting of St. Michael above the altar was executed by William Von Moll Berczy. Jean-Joseph Trestler *(above)* is buried in the crypt.

EXCURSIONS

Île Perrot – *About 16km/10mi by Rte. 20. See Entry Heading.*

Pointe-des-Cascades – *Take Rte. 338 from Vaudreuil-Dorion. The village is 7km/4mi from the intersection with Rte. 20.* Ancres Park lies near the point where the waters of the St. Lawrence and Ottawa Rivers meet, just upstream from Lake Saint-Louis. The park is set beside an old lock on the Soulanges Canal, one of the many canal systems that predated the St. Lawrence Seaway.

VICTORIAVILLE (Arthabaska)★
Centre-du-Québec
Population 38,174 (Victoriaville)

Now incorporated with the city of **Victoriaville**, the former town of Arthabaska lies on the shore of the Nicolet River, at the foot of Mt. Saint-Michel. It is the capital of the Bois-Francs (hardwood) region, so called because of the predominance of maple trees in the area. The town's name is derived from the Amerindian word *ayabaskaw*, meaning "place of bulrushes and reeds." The arrival of the first French-speaking settler, Charles Beauchesne, in 1834 heralded the influx of French Canadians into the southern part of the province, then primarily inhabited by English-speaking Loyalists. Maple products quickly became the backbone of the local economy and remain so today, although forestry and dairy cattle are equally important. After the opening of the railway in 1861, nearby Victoriaville replaced Arthabaska as a major industrial centre, although Arthabaska retained its plethora of cultural opportunities. The town was home to many notable Quebecers, including Prime Minister Wilfrid Laurier and the renowned painter-sculptor, **Marc-Aurèle de Foy Suzor-Côté**.

Sir Wilfrid Laurier – Lawyer, journalist and politician, Wilfrid Laurier (1841-1919) became the first French-Canadian prime minister of Canada (1896-1911) and a legend in his own time. Renowned for his liberalist views, he headed the Canadian Liberal Party from 1887 to 1919, and espoused Canadian unity and the country's emancipation from Great Britain. He also promoted the settlement of the Canadian West by supporting the construction of the Grand Trunk Railway and the creation of the provinces of Alberta and Saskatchewan.

Although he was born in the town of Saint-Lin (now known as Laurentides), 45km/28mi north of Montreal, Laurier spent most of his life in Arthabaska.

Access – *Victoriaville is located 164km/101mi from Montreal by Rtes. 20 and 122.*

SIGHTS

★**Musée Laurier (Laurier Museum)** – *16 Rue Laurier Ouest. The street intersects Blvd. Bois-Francs Sud just south of the town centre. Open Jul–Aug Mon–Fri 9am–5pm, weekends & holidays 1pm–5pm. Rest of the year Mon–Fri 9am–noon & 1pm–5pm, weekends 1pm–5pm. Closed Dec 23–early Jan. $3.50 (entrance to both buildings).*

🅿 ☎ *819-357-8655*. This museum commemorating Arthabaska's beloved native son occupies two separate buildings. The **Sir Wilfrid Laurier House** *(16 Rue Laurier Ouest)*, an attractive residence built for Laurier in 1876, features overhanging eaves, decorative brackets, quoins and bay windows. Laurier lived here until his death in 1919, although he spent most of his time in Ottawa after becoming prime minister in 1896.

The ground-floor rooms recreate the era during which Laurier lived here with his wife, Zoé Lafontaine. The bedroom,dining room (boasting a Tiffany lamp) and the living room, all appointed in the style of the day, are open to visitors. In the living room is an 1885 Kranick and Bach piano given to Lady Laurier by her husband. Laurier's political career and anecdotes about the couple's life in their home are presented in displays throughout the house. A striking portrait of Laurier, painted by his friend Suzor-Côté, hangs above the staircase. Laurier's study is located on the second floor.

Erected in 1910 in the Second Empire style, the Hôtel des Postes building *(949 Blvd. Bois-Francs Sud)* mounts temporary exhibitions of ethnology, history and art. Works by renowned Quebec artists such as Alfred Laliberté, Philippe Hébert, Suzor-Côté and others, drawn from the museum's permanent collection, are often on view. Outside the museum, note the **bust** of Sir Wilfrid Laurier by Alfred Laliberté.

Église Saint-Christophe d'Arthabaska (St. Christopher's Church) – *40 Rue Laurier Ouest. Open year-round daily 9am–5pm. Contribution requested.* ♿ 🅿 ☎ *819-357-2376*. Restored in 1997, this charming stone church (1873, J.-F. Peachy) in the Romanesque style has a remarkable **interior**. The ceiling is decorated with 76 frescoes and paintings, the work of an artist from Saint-Hyacinthe, J. T. Rousseau, aided by Suzor-Côté. The statue of St. Christopher, on top of the altar, was sculpted by students of Louis-Philippe Hébert. Also worth noting are Baroque-style scrolls, tromp-l'œil paintings and friezes, as well as 43 stained-glass windows by the **Hobbs Company**.

Mt. Saint-Michel – *From Rue Laurier, take Blvd. Bois-Francs Sud 1.5km/1mi. Turn left on Rue Mont-Saint-Michel.* A small park with benches and picnic tables affords a splendid **view**★ of Victoriaville and the Nicolet River valley. Among the prominent landmarks are the tower of Arthabaska College, operated by the Sacred Heart Brothers *(Frères du Sacré-Cœur)*, and the steeples of the churches of St. Christopher and St. Victoria. An iron cross, towering 24m/79ft high, was erected on the summit in 1928.

EXCURSIONS

★**Moulin La Pierre (La Pierre Mill)** – *6km/4mi by Rue Laurier Est, near Saint-Norbert-d'Arthabaska. Visit by guided group tour (1hr) only, year-round Tue–Fri 8am–5pm. $3.50.* ✗ ♿ 🅿 *Call ahead for reservations.* ☎ *819-369-9639*. Straddling the Gosselin River, this is one of the few remaining operating water mills in Quebec. It was built on this site by Jean Goulet in 1845.

Visitors can observe the milling process, purchase flour and enjoy home-made buckwheat biscuits in the café.

Église Sainte-Victoire (Church of St. Victoria) – *99 Rue Notre-Dame Ouest, in Victoriaville. About 5km/3mi by Rte. 161. Open year-round daily 8:30am–noon & 1:30pm–8pm.* ✗ ♿ 🅿 ☎ *819-752-2112*. This neoclassical-style church was completed in 1897; its main steeple measures 60m/197ft tall. The ornate **interior** features elaborate woodwork in the apse, a vault richly decorated with wood sculpture, and imposing lateral galleries. The stained-glass windows were produced in Montreal in 1928. Behind the church, to the left, is the presbytery topped by a mansard roof and a small tower.

Moulin La Pierre

VILLE-MARIE

Abitibi-Témiscamingue

Population 2,855

This small, yet vibrant community lies in the Témiscamingue region, southwest of Amos, on a vast and fertile plain that runs next to Lake Témiscamingue (an Algonquian word meaning "deep waters"). While farming continues as the city's economic mainstay, forestry and services also figure prominently in the local economy. Golf and tennis are popular pastimes here, and the city welcomes several international boating regattas during the month of July.

Historical Notes

Colonization of the region began in 1853 when lumbering laid bare large tracts of farmland. In 1863, the Oblate Fathers took up residence in the Old Fort Mission (Mission du Vieux Fort), located south of Fort Témiscamingue *(below)*. In 1887, they moved to Baie des Pères, Ville-Marie's former appellation. The Grey Nuns followed shortly thereafter. Since their arrival in the region, both orders have pursued their religious mission in the realms of education and culture. Nicknamed "the father of agriculture in Témiscamingue," Brother **Joseph Moffet** (1852-1932), from the Old Fort Mission, was a well-known organiser and negotiator as well as an intermediary between the settlers and lumber company officials. He also negotiated with produce buyers from Ontario, located on the other side of Lake Témiscamingue.

In 1897, the town established its own administrative body but did not become a municipality until 1962. To this day, the region has retained its agricultural vocation while diversifying its forest industry and services. The town boasts golf and tennis facilities and organises an international regatta on Pères Bay every July.

Access – *Ville-Marie is located 675km/420mi from Montreal. Take Rte. 138 through Hull, and continue on Rtes. 17, 533 and 101. The park suggests taking Rte. 63 from North Bay, Ontario, and then Rte.101. Air Alliance offers flights to Rouyn-Noranda, which is situated 133km/83mi to the north of Ville-Marie by Rtes. 117 and 101.*

SIGHTS

Grotte Notre-Dame-de-Lourdes (Our Lady of Lourdes Grotto) – *At the eastern edge of Rue Notre-Dame-de-Lourdes.* This mountain **site★** reveals a splendid view overlooking Lake Témiscamingue. The pleasant park is dotted with walking trails, picnic areas and Stations of the Cross.

On the corner of Rues Dollard and Notre-Dame-de-Lourdes stands the Medieval-style **town hall**. A school of agriculture from 1939 to 1965, it bears the name of the famed pioneer Brother Moffet. The Ville-Marie summer theatre is also located here *(programs are available at the tourist information booth at the corner of Rue Saint-André and Blvd. Industriel)* and the Augustin Chénier exhibition hall.

Maison du Colon (Settler House) – *7 Rue Notre-Dame-de-Lourdes, by the lake. Open Jun 24–Labour Day daily 10am–6pm (after 6pm by appointment only). $2.50.* ♿ 🅿 ☎ *819-629-3533.* The oldest house (1881) in the community now houses a small museum that presents various objects from the colonization period recounting the unique history of Ville-Marie and Témiscamingue. Facing the house is a small park affording superb **views** of the vast and very deep (up to 210m/688ft) Lake Témiscamingue. Stretching over 103km/64mi, the lake serves as a border between the provinces of Quebec and Ontario.

EXCURSIONS

★**Lieu historique national Fort-Témiscamingue (Fort Témiscamingue National Historic Site)** – *8km/6mi south of Ville-Marie, on 834 Chemin du Vieux-Fort. Turn right off Rte. 101 to Témiscaming. Open late-May–mid-Sept daily 1:30pm–4:30pm. Rest of the year by reservation.* ▲ ✗ ♿ 🅿 ☎ *819-629-3222.* In 1679, the French established a fur trading post on this site; the post was later abandoned. A second post was erected in 1720, and remained active for nearly two centuries. The post changed hands several times as a result of political and commercial fluctuations, passing from the Northwest Company to that company's rival, the Hudson's Bay Company. Today, several structures are all that testify to what may have been the region's earliest fur trading post.

The park's **interpretation centre** *(open Jul–early Sept 8:30am–6pm* ▲ ✗ ♿ 🅿 ☎ *819-629-3222)* offers a glimpse of life at a fur trading post during the 18C and 19C. Various types of furs and trade items are displayed; the centre also houses exhibits on the Voyageurs. Visitors can relax at the park's large **beach★**, picnic grounds and recreational areas.

★**Forêt enchantée** (Enchanted Forest) – This unusual natural site covers most of the park's 4ha/10 acres. Here the visitor can admire oddly shaped stands of silverberry, Eastern white cedar and red pine. It is said that strong northerly winds

Enchanted Forest

swept over the forest at the onset of winter, bending the trees under the forceful gales. Caught by the sudden frost, the small trees stayed bent under their cover of snow during the entire winter and retained an irregular shape even after the late thaw. A trail runs alongside the lake, leading to the ruins of old chimneys, remains of the original fort. Tombstones mark the graves of early European settlers.

Route 101 meanders near Lake Témiscamingue, which is in some places visible beyond a forest of oak, beech, maple, poplar and white or red pine. A few rest areas with picnic grounds and facilities are located along the road.

Témiscaming – *Rte. 101 to the Ontario border* ends in this small village located *90km/56mi south of Ville-Marie.* In 1917, the Riordon Company Ltd., a pulp and paper plant, was established in this charming town, which went on to become the site of a prosperous lumber industry.
The picturesque main road, known as the **Kipawa Route**, runs along the hillside to the southern end of Lake Témiscamingue, where it meets the Ottawa River.

Addresses, telephone numbers, opening hours and prices published in this guide are accurate at press time. We apologize for any inconvenience resulting from outdated information, and we welcome corrections and suggestions that may assist us in preparing the next edition. Please send us your comments:

Michelin Travel Publications
Editorial Department
P. O. Box 19001
Greenville, SC 29602-9001
TheGreenGuide-us@us.michelin.com

NUNAVIK ★★

Landscape with Inukshuk

Bounded on the west by Hudson Bay, on the north by the Hudson Strait, and on the east by Labrador, Nunavik ("the land to live" in Inuktitut) is the homeland of Quebec's Inuit population. Nunavik covers a total area of some 505,000sq km/ 194,980sq mi or approximately one-third of the provincial territory, and roughly corresponds to the region formerly known as Nouveau-Québec and still referred to as the Great or Far North.

The socio-cultural region of Nunavik was designated by referendum in the Inuit villages in 1986 and officially accepted by the provincial government two years later. Much of Nunavik's continental territory is situated within **Kativik**, the administrative region created by the James Bay and Northern Quebec Agreement in 1975 to represent the municipalities north of the 55th parallel.

Today, modern achievements have considerably transformed the Inuit lifestyle, but the traditional values and heritage of the people survive. In recent years, Nunavik has become a choice destination for adventurous travellers eager to explore one of the world's few remaining frontiers. The region's spectacular expanses of natural wonders offer a truly unique experience, but visitors must be equipped to cope with harsh conditions (nearly all visitors to Nunavik avail themselves of the services of an outfitter and/or guide).

Geographical Notes

The dominant feature of Nunavik's geography is the long, jagged coastline of the **Ungava Peninsula**, which juts north from the interior of the Quebec-Labrador peninsula, a subcontinental part of the Precambrian Canadian Shield. Most of Nunavik's 14 modern villages are located along this coast.

The northern half of the Ungava Peninsula is divided by the Povungnituk Mountains. This range stretches from east to west and includes the Nouveau-Québec Crater, thought to have been created by a meteorite some 1.4 million years ago. In the east, the **Torngat Mountains**, dominated by Quebec's highest peak, Mt. Iberville (1,662m/5,451ft), form the boundary between Quebec and Labrador.

Nunavik is a land of myriad lakes and rivers. These waterways, draining into Ungava Bay and Hudson Bay, have long been used by the Inuit to transport resources and raw materials such as wood, steatite and walrus ivory. In the 1950s, the Labrador Trough, a mineral-rich geological fault between Kangirsuk in the north and Schefferville/Labrador City/Gagnon in the south became a major centre for iron-ore mining.

Flora – Nunavik comprises three distinct zones of vegetation: to the north, the open **tundra** zone, which is a treeless area rich with lichens, mosses and shrubs; to the south, the northern woodlands or **taiga**, dotted with small stands of black spruce and jack pine; and in between, the **forest tundra**, characterized by spruce, larch and pine trees.

The tree line separating these environments extends between Umiujaq in the west to Tasiujaq, Kuujjuaq and Kangiqsualujjuaq in the northeast. Most of the Ungava Peninsula is under permafrost reaching 275m/902ft in depth at Salluit. Discontinuous permafrost (permafrost that appears in patches), occurs throughout Nunavik.

Climate – The climate of Nunavik is determined by the opposing influences of the cold continental landmass and the warmer Atlantic Ocean. The winters are long and cold; the summers are in general cool, but temperatures can reach up to 30°C/86°F. Spring usually provides long beautiful days, but similar to the fall can be marked by strong storms and unstable weather. The temperatures, which vary between the interior and the coast, range from -40°C/-40°F in January to 20°C/68°F in July. Snowfall is generally high (more than 200cm/78in) and snow cover can be expected between October and June. The coastal areas are locked in by sea ice between November and June depending on the location, allowing for only a very short boating and shipping season. Nunavik's northern location gives it long days in the summer (about 20 hours of light in June) and short ones in the winter (about 5 hours) in December.

Historical Notes

Early Inhabitants – The Inuit (*Inuit* means "the People:" *inu* = human being, *it* = many) are the aboriginal population of arctic Canada. Some 9,000 years ago, hunters from Asia crossed the land bridge that spanned the Bering Strait and settled in Alaska's coastal areas. About 2000 BC, these hunters began migrating eastward, leading to the creation of a second culture that developed along the Labrador Coast, towards Cape Dorset, south of Baffin Island. The so-called "Dorset People," are credited with introducing the igloo to the area. A third culture, known as Thule, developed in Alaska about AD 1000 and invaded the territory of the Dorset People, who eventually disappeared. The present-day Inuit are descendants from the Thule branch.

Like their ancestors, the early Inuit hunted marine mammals (seals, walrus and whales) along the coast and on the nearby islands. They also ventured inland along rivers and lakes to fish and hunt musk ox, caribou and waterfowl. Organised in small family groups, they travelled from camp to camp by dog sleds, kayaks, umiaks (large, open boat made from seal skins), or on foot, living in skin tents and sod houses in summer and in igloos in winter. Known for their keen navigational skills, the Inuit were able to travel great distances without the use of maps.

With the growth of the fur trade, the age-old rivalry between the Inuit and Amerindians living to the south escalated. Having been introduced to firearms before the Inuit, Algonquin Indians (Cree, Naskapi and Innu) forced the Inuit to abandon part of their territory.

Arrival of Europeans – About AD 1000, Vikings appeared on the east coast of Canada. Their visits were brief, however, and for several centuries Europe appeared to have forgotten the existence of the American continent, with the exception of Basque and English fishermen who frequented the fish-laden waters of North America. After the early 15C, European explorers probably found their way to the Arctic, but contact with the Inuit remained limited. In 1610, in his quest for the Northwest Passage, Henry Hudson, the British navigator and namesake of the immense bay off the western shores of Nunavik, met the Inuit in what later became known as the Hudson Strait. In 1670 Charles II of England granted a charter to the **Hudson's Bay Company** (HBC), allowing exclusive trading rights in the immense territory surrounding Hudson Bay. Named Rupert's Land in honour of Prince Rupert, cousin of Charles II, this remote expanse was virtually controlled by the HBC, which long dominated the lucrative North American fur trade. After 1750, the Inuit homeland became known to outsiders through subsequent explorations by the HBC. In 1870, Rupert's Land was legally transferred to the young Canadian Confederation in return for certain compensations.

Protestant Moravian missionaries arrived in the early 1810s, and Canadian scientific expeditions took place between the 1880s and 1900. In the early 20C, the French fur company **Révillon Frères**, established trading posts in the region, thereby competing with the well-established HBC. In 1936 the HBC reaffirmed its economic supremacy in the area by buying out its French competitor. The arrival of European traders and missionaries in the region dramatically transformed the local lifestyle: the economic organization of the indigenous populations shifted from a hunter-gatherer to a barter system, and the religious orders – Protestant and later Catholic – introduced European values and education. To a great degree the traders and missionaries brought about the abandonment of the semi-nomadic, self-sufficient existence of the indigenous peoples and the development of permanent, coastal settlements. American whale ships, which frequented the Hudson Strait after 1845, introduced the practice of remuneration, as well as rifles and wooden boats, which led the Inuit to abandon their traditional harpoons and sealskin kayaks. The new, more efficient hunting methods brought walruses and whales near to extinction, and the Inuit were forced to hunt on land to survive. The last whale ship was seen in 1915.

20C Transformations – In 1912, the Canadian government divided the former Rupert's Land among Manitoba, Ontario and Quebec. The Quebec border was moved up from the Eastmain River to the Hudson Strait, some 1,100km/682mi farther north. Federal laws confirming the new border included a clause requiring the province to buy the land belonging to the indigenous peoples. In the 1940s, the Canadian and Quebec governments and the American army began establishing facilities (Fort Chimo, or present-day Kuujjuaq, and Poste-de-la-Baleine, or Kuujjuarapik), and developing mineral and hydroelectric projects in the area. Modern villages with schools and wooden buildings were established by the Canadian federal government as part of its legal obligation toward the local population. Between 1950 and 1963, Inuit family groups became somewhat more sedentary, leaving their hunting and fishing camps for the new villages.

In the 1960s, Hydro-Québec launched a monumental hydroelectric project, which was made effective by the **James Bay and Northern Quebec Agreement**. This historic accord required the native population to surrender its land rights.

Since 1975, all 14 coastal villages have experienced major expansions in housing. In addition, airports, health care and schooling facilities have been upgraded. The HBC operated stores in many of the villages until the mid-1980s; currently these stores are operated by the Northwest Company, and are called Northern Stores. The Inuit have established commercial activities, creating employment opportunities in the villages. These enterprises range from commercial fishing and mining to construction and hotel management. The Inuit-owned Makivik Corporation manages the compensation packages established by the Agreement and has created a variety of subsidiaries, including Air Inuit and First Air airlines.

Nunavik Today – The 1986 grass-roots referendum that created the socio-cultural region of Nunavik sent out a clear signal throughout Quebec for wider acceptance of the distinct cultural identity of the Inuit. Two years later, Nunavik was officially recognized by the provincial government. Today, the vast majority of Inuit live in modern, prefabricated houses and can obtain schooling and professional training. Some Inuit study and have jobs in Montreal or other places outside their homeland. TV, video, telephone and fax machines are available in all villages. A wide variety of vehicles (motor boats and snowmobiles, for example) have made travel easier and faster.

Artist unknown. photo © Malak, Ottawa

Inuit Stone Sculpture
Mother and Child

NUNAVIK AIR ROUTES

- Air Inuit
- Air Creebec
- Canadian Airlines (and affiliates)
- First Air (Air Canada)

Despite their settlement in the new coastal villages, the Inuit have generally maintained their traditional economic activities, such as fishing and hunting. The Inuit hope to reap financial benefit from projects undertaken in Nunavik, such as the controversial James Bay project.

As in the past, the Inuit culture finds expression in art and family and community festivals. In addition, the Inuit have created projects and organizations to preserve their cultural heritage, such as the **Avataq Cultural Institute** in Inukjuak, which was established in 1980. An active **cooperative movement** has been another characteristic of the community since 1959. Today, the twelve co-ops, under the umbrella of the Fédération des Coopératives du Nouveau-Québec, hold an important position in regional commerce. Each one owns a general store on the local level and regulates the commercialisation of crafts, ensuring a livelihood for the many artists, painters, sculptors and engravers.

Current Population – Nunavik's current population today consists of three different groups: the Inuit (±8,300), occupying some 14 coastal villages; the **Naskapis** (at Kawawachikamach) and the **Cree** (at Whapmagoostui); and the **non-indigenous** or Caucasian, primarily francophones, most of whom reside in Kuujjuaq, the region's administrative centre. The Inuit of Nunavik today are geographically and culturally divided into those living in the northern and western Hudson Strait/Bay area and those in the eastern Ungava Bay area, who have ties with the Inuit on the Labrador coast. The Inuit of Canada have kept their language (±66 percent still speak Inuktitut), although English and French have become important languages in

Stone and Ivory Sculpture by George Kopak Tayarak

Practical Information

Getting There – Nunavik is accessible by airplane only *(for more details on air line routes, refer to the map on the preceding page)*. **First Air** *(☎ 613-738-0200)* offers daily service between Montreal and Kuujjuaq. **Air Inuit** *(☎ 613-738-0200)* based in Kuujjuaq and Kuujjuarapik, connects Montreal to Kuujjuarapik and Puvirnituq daily, and services all villages in Nunavik Monday through Friday. **Air Creebec** *(☎ 819-825-8355)* connects Montreal and Val-d'Or to Chisasibi and other villages along the coast of James Bay.

General Information – The villages in the arctic and subarctic regions of Quebec offer limited facilities to tourists, and travelling in these northern areas requires careful preparation. Four different types of travel for individuals or groups are offered: nature, culture, hunting and fishing, or adventure; the cost for one week is approximately $2,900 per person, all-inclusive. Before leaving, contact an official Nunavik tourism agency for exact information on the availability of accommodation and on different packages offered by adventure outfitters. Organisations that visitors may find helpful: Nunavik Tourism Assn., C.P. 218 Kuujjuaq, Quebec J0M 1C0 ☎ 819-964-2876 or 888-594-3424; Tourisme Québec Far North ☎ 418-643-6820.

Inform appropriate people about your movements in the area (location, routes, means of transportation and times). Never leave villages alone. When going on hikes and/or trips, take along sufficient provisions, proper clothing, shelter, and emergency equipment. Be aware of rapidly changing weather conditions depending on the season and area.

Accommodations – It is strongly recommended that all accommodations be arranged in advance. The *Nunavik Tourist Guide*, available from Nunavik Tourism Assn. *(above)* lists accommodations for Akulivik, Aupaluk, Inukjuak, Ivujivik Kangiqsualujjuaq, Kangiqsujuaq, Kangirsuk, Kuujjuaq, Kuujjuarapik, Puvirnituq Quaqtaq, Salluit and Umiujaq. Guest quarters in local homes are sometimes available. Double occupancy rates in hotels and inns range from $180 to $260; private baths are not always available.

Most restaurants serve American fast food. Tourists will generally buy and cook their own provisions, as most hotels are equipped with kitchenettes. The local diet consists of caribou, char and other fish, seal, and canned foods; fresh fruits and vegetables are scarce.

---

schools and public life in Nunavik. Since 1978, in accordance with the conditions of the James Bay and Northern Quebec Agreement, the Inuit have created their own school board, and Inuktitut is now taught in all schools.

The people maintain strong ties with other Inuit in Canada, Greenland, Alaska and Russia through cultural exchanges and political activities under the **Inuit Circumpolar Conference**, which was founded in 1977 and is recognized as a non-governmental agency by the United Nations. In late 1992, the Canadian government announced the creation of **Nunavut** ("our land" in Inuktitut), a 2,000,000sq km/770,000sq mi Inuit homeland carved out of the vast eastern expanses of the Northwest Territories stretching from the Saskatchewan-Manitoba provincial border to Greenland. In 1999 administration of this new nation passed to the Inuit.

EAST COAST

The villages described in this section are designated by their official names. Former names are given in parentheses.

★Kuujjuaq (Fort Chimo)   Pop. 2,055

Located on the western shore of the Koksoak River on flat, sandy land some 50km, 31mi upstream from Ungava Bay, this regional administrative centre is also Nunavik's largest village. Officially named Kuujjuaq, meaning "the great river" in Inuktitut, the settlement has retained its popular name, Fort Chimo. Upon first meeting Europeans the Inuit would say "Saïmuk! Saïmuk!," which meant "Shake hands!" However, the Europeans understood "Chimo" and so it remained the name of the first post they established. The original fort was founded on the opposite shore of the Koksoak as the first HBC trading post in northern Quebec. The settlement was transferred to its present site in 1945. The traditional red and white buildings of the post have been transported piece by piece to their new location on the western shore of the Koksoak River *(tours are available through local guides; check at hotel)*.

As the administrative centre of Kativik, Kuujjuaq is the seat of regional government offices, health services and a hospital, and a base for Air Inuit. A US Air Force base operated here between 1942 and 1949. Today its two major airfields are part of the current North Warning Systems, and the village serves as the transportation hub for northern Quebec, with several private air charter companies operating here. The present settlement was established around the base in the 1950s. The village has a hotel, restaurants, stores, banks and art shops. Between the 1960s and 1980s the provincial government maintained a musk-ox farm here; the animals were released in 1985 and now roam Nunavik.

Environs – A number of outfitters are available to arrange wilderness outings around Kuujjuaq for the arctic traveller (char and salmon fishing, as well as caribou hunting). A limited road system *(8km/5mi)* allows travel onto the tundra and to the tree line, in the vicinity of the settlement. These outings take travellers into isolated forested patches on a plateau of rolling hills between 80m/262ft and 250m/820ft in altitude. A highlight of the region is the **Koksoak River**, a tidal river whose character changes continuously with the ebb and flow of the tides. The tides reaching upstream into the river create a variety of fascinating and ever-changing landscapes.

Kangiqsualujjuaq   Pop. 648

This village is located on the eastern shore of **George River**, 25km/15.5mi south of Ungava Bay. It is situated in the shadow of an imposing granite outcrop in a narrow valley at the north end of a bay. Formerly known as George River and Port-Nouveau-Québec, Kangiqsualujjuaq, meaning "very large bay" in Inuktitut, is the northeasternmost permanent settlement in Nunavik. It was established on the initiative of local Inuit, who founded the first co-op in Nunavik, a char fishery, on this site in 1959. In the 1830s, an HBC post operated south of the contemporary village; it closed in the mid-20C.

The settlement hangs on the tree line, and a small lumber (spruce) mill operated here in the 1960s. The area appeals to canoeists, who ride the George River, and to fishermen attracted by the Atlantic salmon populating the river. The George River is also the feeding area of one of Northern Quebec's largest caribou herds. Outfitter camps are found upriver at the beautiful **Helen Falls** *(64km/40mi)*.

Tasiujaq (Leaf Bay, Baie-aux-Feuilles)   Pop. 191

This small settlement, whose name means "that which resembles a lake" in Inuktitut, is located on low-lying marshy flatland bordering the **Baie-aux-Feuilles**, the westernmost extension of Ungava Bay. The bay is noteworthy for its exceptional tidal movement (up to 17m/56ft) which is considered the highest in the world. Founded in the 1960s on the western shore of the Bérard River, the settlement was established in the vicinity of early 20C trading posts established by HBC and the Révillon Frères. Later, its economy was bolstered by mineral exploration that took place in the northern section of the Labrador Trough. The village lies just a few kilometres north of the tree line in the southern reaches of the barren tundra. The area is part of the large drainage basin of Feuilles River. Several outfitters' camps provide char, lake trout and brook trout fishing. Herds of caribou annually pass close to the village on their autumnal trek south.

Aupaluk   Pop. 159

This village is located on the southern shores of Hopes Advance Bay, an inlet on the western coast of Ungava Bay. Aupaluk owes its name, meaning "red place" in Inuktitut, to the reddish colour of the soil, which is the result of the high iron-ore content of the northern reaches of the Labrador Trough.

Originally a traditional hunting camp, Aupaluk was established in the late 1970s when Inuit from Kangirsuk and from some other villages relocated to this area, which is renowned for its abundance of caribou, fish and marine mammals. It was incorporated in 1981 and is today the smallest of the Inuit villages in Nunavik. As a new settlement, Aupaluk is the first arctic village in Canada whose town site was planned and conceived by the Inuit themselves. No outfitters operate here.

Kangirsuk (Payne Bay, Bellin)   Pop. 394

Situated on the northern shore of Arnaud River, 13km/8mi upstream from Ungava Bay, Kangirsuk ("the bay" in Inuktitut) began when trading and mission posts were established in the late 1880s. The HBC established a trading post in 1925. Government services were first introduced in the 1950s. Today, there are two stores (Northern Store and a co-op), and several outfitters operate fishing camps on the Ungava Peninsula.

Quaqtaq (Koartac)   Pop. 257

The village of Quaqtaq is located in a small valley on the eastern coast of Diana Bay at Cape Hopes Advance, which protrudes into the Hudson Strait. Frequented by the Inuit and their ancestors for 4,000 years, this region is rich in archaeological sites. Marine resources remain a mainstay of the Inuit to this day. Various

Flowering Tundra

trading posts existed here between the 1930s and 1960s, and a government weather station operated in the vicinity between 1927 and 1969. The local co-op store was founded in 1974. Quaqtaq lies on the arctic barrens with rugged mountains to the north and short and rocky hills to the south and east. The valleys and other protected places show a little vegetation in summer: moss, lichens, minuscule flowers in bright colours, berry bushes.

Diana Bay – The region around Diana Bay ("Tuvaaluk", in Inuktitut) is renowned for its rich hunting grounds, where abound land mammals (arctic fox, otter, rabbit, and sometimes the polar bear, which travels on ice for about 80km/50mi from the island of Akpatok) and sea mammals (various species of seals, walruses, beluga whales and some narwhals). Species of bird found here include the partridge; snow, Canada and barnacle geese (Quaqtaq is on their flyway); and the eider duck. Among the most common fish are the grey, red and speckled trout and the arctic char. Nature enthusiasts might even discover the musk-ox (approximately a million now flourish in the region), the legendary snowy owl or the loon.

Kangiqsujuaq (Wakeham, Maricourt)   Pop. 479

Occupying an exceptional **site★★** in a valley on the southeastern shore of Wakeham Bay, Kangiqsujuaq was established on the site of an early 20C trading post. In the 1930s the Oblate mission founded a station here. Government services were introduced in the 1960s, and today, the village has a Northern Store, a co-op, and two churches. Its present name, meaning "the great bay" in Inuktitut, replaced the earlier European appellations, Wakeham and Maricourt.

The village is located 88km/55mi northeast of the famous **Nouveau-Québec Crater★** measuring 3km/2mi in diameter and 267m/876ft deep. Outfitters arrange snowmobile excursions to the crater in winter.

Salluit (Saglouc, Sugluk)   Pop. 1,143

Located on the narrow Sugluk Fjord, about 10km/6mi from the Hudson Strait, this village is one of the largest settlements in northern Nunavik. The name, Salluit means "thin ones" in Inuktitut, because according to tradition, the Inuit had been told that the region abounded in animals to hunt, but when they arrived, they found almost none.

Salluit developed around trading and mission posts, which were established in the area after 1900. Government services were introduced in the 1950s. Today, there is an Anglican mission, a co-op and a Northern Store. Salluit is known for the beauty of its **site★★**, surrounded by high, rugged mountains and cliffs rising to 500m/1,640ft.

To the east of Salluit, asbestos mining at Purtuniq (Asbestos Hills) and Deception Bay introduced industrial activities and a modern infrastructure (jet airfield and harbour) in the early 1970s. Full-scale mining and shipping were abandoned in the 1980s.
Nature observation tours afford possibilities of viewing walrus herds, polar bears, and caribou.

Ivujivik   Pop. 274

Located in a cove south of Digges Sound, in a mountainous region near Cape Wolstenholme, Ivujivik ("place where ice accumulates during ice break" in Inuktitut) is the northernmost settlement in the entire province. After 1947, the Inuit of the neighbouring shores gradually settled in the small village established around the Catholic mission, which was founded in 1938 and closed in the 1960s. Shortly thereafter, government services were introduced and the co-op began operations in 1967. The Inuit of Ivujivik have not signed the James Bay and Northern Quebec Agreement of 1975. These dissenters have allied themselves with Inuit from Puvirnituq and Salluit to form the Inuit-Tungavingat-Nunamini movement. These groups administer their own schools, under the supervision of a locally elected committee.

Digges Island, north of Ivujivik in Hudson Strait, was the site of the first recorded encounter between Inuit from the Quebec-Labrador peninsula and Europeans. The historic event took place in 1610 during one of Henry Hudson's expeditions in search of a Northwest Passage to Asia.

WEST COAST

Akulivik (Cape Smith)   Pop. 411

Located on a peninsula bordered on the north by a deep water port, and on the south by the mouth of the Illukotat River, Akulivik is the westernmost village in Nunavik. Its name, meaning "middle part of a leister (fishing spear)," refers to the geographical aspect of the site.
Just off the coast lies the island of Cape Smith, on which the HBC operated a post between 1924 and 1951. Akulivik was founded by the Inuit in 1976 on the site that served as the summer camp of the Qikirtajuarmiut Inuit group before they moved to Puvirnituq in 1955. Qikirtajuarmiut means "the people of the island." The sandy texture of the soil is due to the crumbly, fossilized seashells that are vestiges of the last ice age. The co-op operates a store, a carving shop, and a recreation hall.

Puvirnituq (Puvirnituuq)   Pop. 1,169

The village is situated on the northern shore of the Puvirnituq River, 4km/2.5mi east of Povungnituk Bay. The name, Puvirnituq, meaning "place where there is a smell of putrefied meat," refers to a tragic episode in the short history of the

© Heiko Wittenborn

Igloo Building

village: an epidemic ravaged the settlement, and all the villagers died, leaving no one to bury the dead. When friends and family arrived from nearby camps in the spring, the stench of decaying bodies permeated the air.

As in other villages of the Far North, Puvirnituq developed after the establishment of a HBC fur trading post (1921). The Inuit who came to live in this post after 1951 had occupied, up to that time, summer camps near Akulivik and winter camps on the island of Cape Smith *(above)*.

In 1975, the citizens of Puvirnituq were joined by those of Ivujivik and 49 percent of those of Salluit in refusing to sign the James Bay and Northern Quebec Agreement. The position taken on this issue has instilled a strong sense of solidarity within the community.

The Hudson Bay Hospital Centre, a modern health facility serving the villages of the Hudson Bay coast, is located here.

Originating as the Carving Association, created in 1950 by Father André Steinman, a French Oblate missionary, the **Cooperative Association of Puvirnituq** is among the most dynamic co-ops of Nunavik. The Association operates a retail store, a hotel and manages the community's fuel supply. Several local artists have achieved international recognition.

Dogsled

Inukjuak (Port Harrison)   Pop. 1,184

Nunavik's second largest village, Inukjuak, is located on the mouth of the Innuksuac River near the Hopewell Islands. Non-natives arrived in the area in 1909 when the French fur company Révillon Frères installed a fur trading post on the site, which they called Port Harrison. The HBC, however, established a post here in 1920 and eventually bought out the French company in 1936. The HBC's monopoly on fur trade with the Inuit continued until 1958. The Anglican Mission arrived in 1927, and in 1935 postal service for the Far North was established.

Life in Inukjuak maintains a strong link with traditional activities. An important deposit of steatite, stone used for sculptures, was discovered here. The find has encouraged the growth of the arts.

Older buildings near the Co-op Hotel include the Anglican Mission, the Northern Store, the co-op store and the carving shop. The newer constructions of the village are concentrated along the route leading to the airport. On the eastern shore of the river, remnants of the old trading post, settlement and cemetery can be seen.

Avataq Cultural Institute – Inukjuak is the seat of the head officer of the Avataq Cultural Institute, a non-profit organization devoted to the preservation and development of the linguistic and cultural heritage of the Inuit in Nunavik. Activities linked to toponomy, history, the cultural centre, literature, games, traditional music, archaeology, etc., are offered. The Institute also collects various Inuit pieces from other museums and sponsors the annual Conference of the Inuit Elders, whose goal is to collect and preserve oral traditions and knowledge for the benefit of future generations.

Inuit Exhibit – In the lobby of the modern, brick schoolhouse, a series of bas-relief sculptures depicting everyday life in a traditional Inuit community demonstrate the skills of village carvers. The collection of hunting and fishing objects and practical cutting and scraping tools were assembled by a young Inuit archaeologist from Inukjuak, Daniel Weetaluktuk (1951-1982), who during his short career greatly contributed to arctic anthropology.

Environs – The gently rolling rock formations dominating the landscape around the village provide panoramic **views**★ of the village and port of Inukjuak, the river, the Hopewell Islands and Hudson Bay, and the mountains lying to the north.
A **walk** along the shore of the Innuksuac River toward the airport offers the possibility of discovering many varieties of the tiny wildflowers that miraculously survive in the Arctic climate. The clear waters of the meandering river form cascades and pools along the way.

Umiujaq   Pop. 315

This village was created for those Inuit of Kuujjuarapik who decided to relocate in light of phase 2 of the James Bay project, believing that implementation of the project would necessitate profound changes to their way of life. Archaeological, environmental and settlement-planning studies were conducted, and construction began during the summer of 1985. At this time, several hundred of the Inuit of Kuujjuarapik moved to the area and lived in temporary quarters until their homes were completed in early 1987.
Today, Umiujaq (meaning "which resembles a boat" in Inuktitut because of a hill that looks like an *umiak*, a large open boat made from seal skins) has a fresh and vibrant quality reflecting the pride of its citizens. This tranquil site near Lake Guillaume-Delisle (Richmond Bay) is remarkable for its escarpments along the seashore.
A municipal building houses the FM radio station, town hall, an Air Inuit bureau, and the post office. A **museum** in the town hall displays a collection of tools, household items, and other artifacts that were unearthed by archaeologists and village elders during the excavation of the site. Beside the municipal building stands the modern and well-equipped clinic, and the co-op, which also contains the carving shop.
Outfitters offer sightseeing trips to nearby islands and excursions on the Nastapoka River.

Kuujjuarapik   Pop. 579

Located on Hudson Bay,172km/106mi north of Radisson, Kuujjuarapik was established as a fur trading post by the HBC in 1813. The Anglican mission arrived in 1882, but the village did not become a permanent settlement until 1901. The first contacts with Catholic missionaries occurred in 1924. The French fur company, Révillon Frères, set up a post in 1908, at the mouth of the Little Whale River to trade with the Cree and Inuit living along the coast of the region. In the 1920s, the village was relocated to the mouth of the Great Whale River.
A weather station was established in 1895, but most government services did not reach the village until after 1949. From 1954 to 1959, Kuujjuarapik became a communication centre for northern Quebec through the construction of a series of radar stations known as the "mid-Canada line," between the Atlantic coast and Hudson Bay, north of the 55th parallel. The headquarters was established at Poste-de-la-Baleine. At this time the region around Kuujjuarapik experienced its greatest population growth. In 1965, the installation was evacuated and turned over to the province of Quebec.

© Julien Lama /PUBLIPHOTO

Kuujjuarapik

A Multi-ethnic community – Today the village of Kuujjuarapik is home to Inuit, Cree, and non-native populations. The post and village have gone through a number of name changes: first Great Whale River in English, then Poste-de-la-Baleine in French, Kuujjuarapik ("the little big river") in Inuktitut and Whapmagoostui ("Whale River") in Cree. The last three have gained official recognition, making the village one of the few places in Canada with three names.

The Inuit community is located near the mouth of Great Whale River, while the Cree community has settled further upstream. The Inuit and Cree have separate schools, infirmaries and municipal organizations. The Anglican Church holds services in Inuktitut and Cree. In the old church a collection of tools and typical costumes is on display. The Social Club provides recreational activities for all members of the community.

The village is bordered on the west by the airstrip which lies parallel to the Hudson Bay. Government offices and non-native housing are located near the airport in the former radar station complex. A research centre of the Laval University (Quebec) is also located here.

Environs – A wide, sandy beach stretches from the mouth of the Great Whale River to the opposite side of the village where high dunes provide good views of the Hudson Bay and the area around Kuujjuarapik.

Approximately 12km/7mi upstream from the village, a scenic **waterfall** is accessible by boat in summer or snowmobile in winter.

Inuk Girls with Puppy

J.P. Danvoye/PUBLIPHOTO

View of Montreal from Quai Victoria

Practical
Information

Calendar of Events

Following is a selection of Quebec's most popular annual events. Dates and duration of certain events may vary from year to year. For detailed information, contact the **Société des fêtes et festivals du Québec**, 4545 Pierre-De-Coubertin Ave., C.P. 1000, Succursale M, Montréal (PQ) H1V 3R2 www.festivals.qc.ca ☎ 514-252-3037, the regional tourist offices, or access **Tourisme Québec's** website at www.bonjourquebec.com. Regional tourist offices can also suggest other cultural or sporting events.

Spring

Mar	**Festival beauceron de l'érable** *Saint-Georges* (maple sugar festival) *(Chaudière-Appalaches)*
mid-Apr	**Exposition horticole "l'Effleure-Printemps !"** .... *Laval* (horticultural exhibit & contest) *www.lavaltechnopole.qc.ca*
early May	**Festival de l'érable** .... *Plessisville (Centre-du-Québec)* (maple tree festival)
mid-May	**Festival international de musique** .... *Victoriaville (Centre-du-Québec)* **actuelle de Victoriaville** (contemporary music)
late May	**La Féria du Vélo** .... *Montreal* (cycling race & festival)

Grand Prix Molson 2000

Summer

early Jun	**Festival de la chanson** .... *Tadoussac (Manicouagan)* (Quebec song festival)
mid-Jun	**Air Canada Grand Prix** .... *Île Notre-Dame (Montreal)* *www.grandprix.ca*
mid-Jun	**Maski-Courons International** .... *Saint-Gabriel-de-Brandon* (marathon) .... *(Lanaudière)* *www.maski-courons.com*
mid-Jun- late Jul	**International Benson & Hedges** .... *Île Sainte-Hélène (Montreal)* *www.parcjeandrapeau.com*
late Jun- early Jul	**Festival de la crevette** .... *Matane (Gaspésie)* (shrimp festival) .... *www.festivcrevette.com*
late Jun- early Jul	**Régates Molson Ex de Valleyfield** .... *Salaberry-de-Valleyfield* (international regatta) .... *(Montérégie)* *www.mmic.net/regates*
late Jun- early Jul	**Symposium de peinture** .... *Baie-Comeau (Manicouagan)* (painting symposium) *www.ville.baie-comeau.qc.ca/symposium*

late Jun Jul	**Festival international de Lanaudière** ....*Joliette (Lanaudière)* www.lanaudiere.org	
late Jun– mid-Aug	**La fabuleuse histoire d'un royaume** ....*La Baie (Saguenay–Lac-Saint-Jean)* www.d4m.com/grandsspectacles	
late Jun– late Aug	**Festival international du Domaine Forget** ....*Saint-Irénée (Charlevoix)* (classical music & jazz) www.domaineforget.com	
end Jun early Jul	**Festival International de Jazz de Montréal** ....**Montreal** www.montrealjazzfest.com	
end Jun– mid-Aug	**Festival Orford** ....*Magog (Eastern Townships)* www.arts-orford.org	
early Jul	**Festirame** ....*Alma (Saguenay–Lac-Saint-Jean)* www.sagamie.org/alma/festivalma	
early Jul	**Festival d'été de Québec du Maurier** ....*Quebec City* (international summer festival) www.infofestival.com	
early Jul	**Festival du pêcheur** ....*L'Étang-du-Nord (Magdalen Islands)* (fisherman's festival)	
early Jul	**Mondial des cultures de Drummondville** ....*Drummondville (Centre-du-Québec)*	
mid-Jul	**Traversée internationale du lac Memphrémagog** ....*Magog (Eastern* (international swim marathon)...*Townships)* www.traversee-memphremagog.com	
mid-Jul	**Festival juste pour rire** ....*Montreal* (comedy festival) .... www.hahaha.com	
mid-Jul	**Festival des dix jours** ....*Dolbeau (Saguenay–Lac-Saint-Jean)* **western de Dolbeau-Mistassini**	
mid-Jul	**Exposition agricole régionale** ....*Berthierville (Lanaudière)* **de Berthierville**	
mid-Jul	**Régates internationales de** ....*Ville-Marie (Abitibi-Témiscamingue)* **Ville-Marie** (international regatta)	
late Jul	**Exposition agricole** ....*Saint-Hyacinthe (Montérégie)* www.expo-agricole.com	
late Jul	**Grand Prix Player's de Trois-Rivières** ....*Trois-Rivières* (automobile racing) ....*(Mauricie–Bois-Francs)* www.gptr.qc.ca	
late Jul	**Traversée internationale** ....*Roberval (Saguenay–Lac-Saint-Jean)* **du lac Saint-Jean** www.traversee.qc.ca	
late Jul– early Aug	**Francofolies de Montréal**..*Montreal* (French music festival) www.francofolies.com	
early-Aug	**Festival de la baleine bleue**..........................*Bergeronnes (Manicouagan)* (blue whale festival)	
early Aug	**Festival du bleuet de Dolbeau-Mistassini** ....*Mistassini* www.festivaldubleuet.qc.ca ....*(Saguenay–Lac-Saint-Jean)*	
early Aug	**Fêtes de la Nouvelle-France** ....*Quebec City* (heritage festival) www.nouvellefrance.qc.ca	
early Aug	**Innu Nikamu** ....*Réserve de Maliotenam (Duplessis)* (Amerindian music festival)	
early Aug	**Symposium international de la** ....*Baie-Saint-Paul (Charlevoix)* **nouvelle peinture au Canada**	
early-mid-Aug	**Fêtes gourmandes internationales de Montréal** ....*Montreal* (festival of food & music) www.lesfetesgourmandes.com	
mid-Aug	**Concours de châteaux de sable** ....*Havre Aubert (Magdalen Islands)* (sandcastle-building contest) www.ilesdelamadeleine.com/chateaux	
mid-Aug	**Omnium du Maurier – Internationaux de tennis féminin** ....*Montreal* **du Canada** (women's tennis) www.tenniscanada.com	
mid-Aug	**Festival de montgolfières** ....*Saint-Jean-sur-Richelieu* **de Saint-Jean-sur-Richelieu** ....*(Montérégie)* www.montgolfieres.com	

International Jazz Festival, Montreal

late Aug– early Sept	**Festival des films du monde**.....................................*Montreal* (international film festival) *www.ffm-montreal.org*
late Aug– early Sept	**Classique internationale** ....*La Tuque (Mauricie–Bois-Francs)* **de canot de la Mauricie** (canoe competition)
late Aug– early Sept	**Festi Jazz international de Rimouski**.............*Rimouski (Bas-Saint-Laurent)* (jazz festival) *www.globetrotter.qc.ca/festijazz*
early Sept	**Festival de montgolfières de Gatineau** ....*Gatineau (Outaouais)* (hot air balloon festival) *www.ville.gatineau.qc.ca*
early Sept	**Brome Agricultural Fair**................................*Brome (Eastern Townships)*

Fall

mid-Sept	**Festival western de Saint-Tite**................*Saint-Tite (Mauricie–Bois-Francs)* (western festival) *www.festivalwestern.com*
early-mid-Oct	**Festival de l'oie blanche**.................*Montmagny (Chaudière-Appalaches)* (festival of the snow goose) *www.festivaldeloie.qc.ca*
late Oct	**Festival du cinéma international**.......................................*Rouyn-Noranda* (international film festival) ....*(Abitibi-Témiscamingue)*
early Nov	**Exposition d'antiquités** ....*Eastman (Eastern Townships)* (antique show)

Winter

late Nov– mid-Jan	**Exposition de crèches de Noël** ....*Rivière-Éternité* (nativity scenes exhibit) ....*(Saguenay–Lac-Saint-Jean)*
late Dec– mid-Feb	**Carnaval des petits poissons** ....*Sainte-Anne-de-la-Pérade* **des chenaux** (tommycod festival) ....*(Mauricie–Bois-Francs)*
late Jan– mid-Feb	**Fête des neiges** (winter festival)..*Montreal*
late Jan– mid-Feb	**Quebec Winter Carnival** ....*Quebec City* *www.carnaval.qc.ca*
Feb	**Bal de Neige** (winter festival) ....*Hull (Outaouais)*
mid-Feb	**Grand Prix de Valcourt** ....*Valcourt (Eastern Townships)* (snowmobile festival)
mid-Feb	**Carnaval-Souvenir** ....*Chicoutimi (Saguenay–Lac-Saint-Jean)*

Planning Your Trip

Tourism Offices – Contact the offices listed below for brochures giving details on points of interest, seasonal events and accommodation, as well as road and city maps. Regional offices, which distribute maps, brochures and other travel information free of charge, extend their operating hours from late June to September.

	In Quebec	☎
Tourisme Québec	CP 979 Montréal (PQ) H3C 2W3 www.bonjourquebec.com	514-873-2015 877-266-5687
Abitibi-Témiscamingue	170 Ave. Principale, bureau 103 Rouyn-Noranda (PQ) J9X 4P7 www.48nord.qc.ca	819-762-8181
Bas-Saint-Laurent	148 Rue Fraser Rivière-du-Loup (PQ) G5R 1C8 www.tourismebas-st-laurent.com	418-867-3015
Centre-du-Québec	20, Blvd. Carignan ouest Princeville (PQ) G6L 4M4 www.tourismecentreduqubec.com	819-364-7177
Charlevoix	630 Blvd. de Comporté, CP 275 La Malbaie (PQ) G5A 1T8 www.tourisme-charlevoix.com	418-665-4454
Chaudière-Appalaches	800 Autoroute Jean-Lesage Saint-Nicolas (PQ) G7A 1C9 www.chaudapp.qc.ca	418-831-4411
Duplessis	312 Ave. Brochu Sept-Îles (PQ) G4R 2W6 www.tourismecote-nord.com	418-962-0808
Eastern Townships	20 Rue Don-Bosco Sud Sherbrooke (PQ) J1L 1W4 www.tourisme-cantons.qc.ca	819-820-2020
Gaspésie	357 Route de la Mer Sainte-Flavie (PQ) G0J 2L0 www.tourisme-gaspesie.com	418-775-2223
Lanaudière	3647 Rue Queen, CP 1210 Rawdon (PQ) J0K 1S0 www.tourisme-lanaudiere.qc.ca	450-834-2535
Laurentides	14142 Rue de Lachapelle, RR 1 Mirabel (PQ) J7U 2C8 www.laurentides.com	450-436-8532
Laval	2900 Blvd. Saint-Martin Ouest Laval (PQ) H7T 2J2 www.tourismelaval.qc.ca	450-682-5522
Magdalen Islands	128 Rue Principale, CP 1028 Cap-aux-Meules (PQ) G0B 1B0 www.ilesdelamadeleine.com	418-986-2245
Manicouagan	337 Blvd. La Salle, Bureau 304 Baie-Comeau (PQ) G4Z 2Z1 www.tourismecote-nord.com	418-294-2876
Mauricie	5775 Blvd. Jean-XXIII Trois-Rivières (PQ) G8Z 4J2 www.tmbf.com	819-375-1222
Montérégie	11, Chemin Mariville Rougemont (PQ) J0L 1M0 www.tourisme-monteregie.qc.ca	450-469-0069
Montréal	1555 Rue Peel, bureau 600 Montréal (PQ) H3A 3LB www.tourisme-montreal.org	514-844-5400
Northern Quebec	**Nunavik Tourism Association** P.O. Box 218 Kuujjuaq (PQ) J0M 1C0 www.nunavik-tourism.com	819-964-2876
	Tourisme Baie-James 166 Blvd. Springer, P.O. Box 2270 Chapais (PQ) G0W 1H0	418-745-3969

Outaouais	103 Rue Laurier Hull (PQ) J8X 3V8 www.tourisme-outaouais.org	819-778-2222
Quebec City Region	835, Ave. Wilfrid Courier Québec (PQ) G1R 2L3	418-649-2608
Saguenay–Lac-Saint-Jean	198 Rue Racine Est, bureau 210 Chicoutimi (PQ) G7H 1R9 www.astraglac.d4m.com	418-543-9778
	Outside Quebec	☎
New York	1 Rockefeller Plaza, 26th floor New York NY 10020	212-397-0200
Toronto	20 Queen St. W., Suite 1504, Box 13 Toronto (ON) M5H 3S3	416-977-6060
United Kingdom	Bridge Marketing Ltd. P.O. Box 1939 Maidenhead, Berkshire SL6 1AJ	990 561 705

Consult the pages shown for detailed practical information on the following sights:
Anticosti Island (p 55), **Magdalen Islands** (p 144), **Montreal** (p 165), **Nunavik** (p 318) and **Quebec City** (p 226).

CYBER TOURISM

www.bonjourquebec.com

www.quebecregion.com

www.tourismej.qc.ca
(Youth Tourism Information)

www.tourism-montreal.org

www.montrealcam.com

www.planetarium.montreal.qc.ca

www.quebecadv.com

www.voir-quebec.qc.ca

www.skiquebec.qc.ca

Entry Requirements – Individuals visiting Canada must carry a valid passport; a visa is required for visitors from certain countries. It is advisable to check with the Canadian embassy or consulate in your country regarding entry regulations. No vaccinations are necessary. **US citizens** and legal residents of the US need proof of citizenship, such as a valid driver's license or valid passport. Permanent **US residents** who are not citizens must carry their Alien Registration Cards. Persons **under 18** who are not accompanied by an adult must have a letter from a parent or guardian stating the traveller's name and duration of trip. Students should carry a student ID; senior citizens (over 65) are required to present proof of age when requesting discounts at many attractions. For further information on all Canadian embassies and consulates abroad, contact the website of the Canadian Department of Foreign Affairs & International Trade: www.dfait-maeci.gc.ca.

Selected Canadian Consulates or Embassies ☎

Atlanta	1175 Peachtree St., NE 100 Colony Square, Suite 1700 Atlanta GA 30361	404-532-2000
Chicago	2 Prudential Plaza Chicago IL 60601	312-616-1860
Los Angeles	300 S. Grand Ave., 10th floor Los Angeles CA 90071	213-346-2700
New York	1251 Avenue of the Americas New York NY 10020-1175	212-596-1628
Washington DC	501 Pennsylvania Ave., NW Washington DC 20001	202-682-1740
Australia	Level 5, Quay West Building 111 Harrington St. Sydney, N.S.W. 2000	9364-3000
Germany	Friedrichstr. 95 10117 Berlin	030-2031-2470
United Kingdom	One Grosvenor Square Macdonald House London W1X 0AA	171-258-6600

Foreign Consulates in Quebec – Consulates of most foreign countries are located in Montreal. Embassies are located in Ottawa, the capital of Canada.

Selected Foreign Consulates in Quebec ☏

Germany	1250 Blvd. René-Lévesque Ouest Montreal (PQ) H5B 4W8	514-931-2277
Japan	600 Rue de la Gauchetière Ouest Montreal (PQ) H3B 4L8	514-866-3429
United Kingdom	1000 Rue de la Gauchetière Ouest Montreal (PQ) H3B 4W5	514-866-5863
United States	1155 Rue Saint-Alexandre Place Félix-Martin Montreal (PQ) H5B 1G1	514-398-9695

Insurance – Before leaving, it is advisable to check with your medical insurance provider to determine whether you are covered for doctor visits, medication, and hospital stays while visiting Quebec. A visitor insurance policy can be purchased either before leaving or within five days after arrival ($3.25–$8 per day according to age; $5,000–$60,000 limit). For details contact Blue Cross of Quebec, 550 Rue Sherbrooke Ouest, Montreal (PQ) H3A 1B9 ☏ 514-286-8400 or www.qc.bluecross.ca.

US visitors travelling by car must have proof of automobile insurance and should obtain a yellow card.

Customs and Immigration – Importation of **tobacco** is limited to 50 cigars or 200 cigarettes per adult. The limit for importing **alcoholic beverages** is 1.14 litres/1.2 quarts of liquor or wine, or 24 bottles of beer. Since Quebec has very strict laws concerning narcotics and other chemical substances, all prescription drugs should be identified; it is advisable to carry a copy of the prescription or a letter from your doctor.

Bringing **handguns** into Quebec is prohibited. Non-residents must declare all firearms. For further information on entry of firearms contact the Canadian Centre for Firearms ☏ 506-636-5064 or www.cfc-ccaf.gc.ca.

Pets must be accompanied by a certificate of vaccination against rabies (within last 3 years). For further information contact the Canadian Food Inspection Agency (Animal Health Division), 2001 Rue University, Suite 746, Montreal (PQ) H3A 3N2 ☏ 514-246-3889.

Disabled Travellers – Sights accessible to disabled travellers are indicated by the ♿ symbol in this guide. Most public buildings, churches, restaurants and hotels provide wheelchair access. Parking space is reserved for the disabled, and is strictly enforced. For more information or to obtain the guide *Accessible Québec Guide ($14 price includes shipping)*, contact KEROUL, 4545 Pierre-de-Coubertin Ave.; C.P. 1000, Station M, Montreal (PQ) H1V 3R2 ☏ 514-252-3104 or www.keroul.qc.ca. Another guide, *Handy Travel ($12.95 plus postage)*, is available from the Canadian Rehabilitation Council for the Disabled, 90 Eglinton Ave. East, Suite 511, Toronto (ON) M4P 2Y3; Easter Seals March of Dimes ☏ 416-932-8382.

The **Autocars Orléans Express Inc.** bus line offers transportation for persons with reduced mobility. For more information, contact the nearest Orléans Express office.

When to Visit – Quebec is a year-round vacation destination for sports enthusiasts, nature lovers, hunters and fishermen. Northern Quebec is subject to arctic temperatures, while the regions around the St. Lawrence are temperate in climate. Most cultural attractions are open from mid-May (Fête de Dollard) to the first weekend in September (Labour Day). *Sight descriptions contain more specific information.*

In early April the harvesting of maple syrup signals the coming of **spring** with sugaring-off parties. This season is brief with pleasant days and chilly evenings. In the southern part of Quebec, **summer**, extending from mid-June through mid-September, can be hot and humid. Light, loose-fitting clothes are best for hot weather but it is advisable to have a light jacket handy for cool evenings and excursions on lakes. Late May and June is black fly season and insect repellant is a must, especially for those planning to camp or hike. In **autumn**, beginning in early October, visitors can enjoy the many colours of "Indian Summer." **Winter** can begin as early as November, with an abundance of snow. Temperatures often fall below freezing and during January and February can drop below zero Fahrenheit (-17°C). Plenty of warm clothing and heavy jackets will protect the visitor from the frigid, but dry cold.

Seasonal Temperatures (°F/°C)

	April		July		October		January	
	min.	max.	min.	max.	min.	max.	min.	max.
Chicoutimi	25/-4	45/7	54/12	75/24	34/1	48/9	-9/-23	14/-10
Gaspé	27/-3	41/5	52/11	73/23	34/1	52/11	3/-16	21/-6
Kuujjuarapik	9/-13	28/-2	41/5	51/15	30/-1	41/5	18/-28	0/-18
Montreal	34/1	52/11	61/16	79/26	39/4	55/13	5/-15	21/-6
Quebec City	28/-2	19/7	55/13	77/25	36/2	52/11	1/-17	18/-8
Sherbrooke	28/-2	50/10	52/11	77/25	32/0	54/12	0/-18	21/-6

Getting There and Getting Around

By Air – International and domestic flights arrive at Montreal's **Dorval** airport ☎ 514-394-7377 as well as Quebec City's **Jean-Lesage** airport ☎ 418-640-2600. **Mirabel** airport ☎ 514-476-3010 is used for charter and cargo flights. Canada's national airlines, **Air Canada** and **Canadian Airlines**, service major European cities, Latin America and the Far East, and provide service along with their affiliates to most destinations within the country. Quebec is also serviced by a network of regional airlines. Service to remote areas, provided by charter companies, may be offered once or twice a week only. For telephone numbers of local air carriers, consult your travel agent or write to the appropriate provincial tourist office.

Airline	☎
Air Canada	514-393-3333
Air Alliance	418-692-0770
Air Nova	888-247-2262
Canadian Airlines	514-847-2211
Canadian Regional	418-692-1031
Air Inuit	613-738-0200
First Air	613-738-0200
Air Creebec	819-825-8355

By Train – Rail service within Quebec province is provided by **VIA Rail**. Fares are reasonable and trains are comfortable. The visitor should be aware of the great distances within Quebec (travel time between Montreal and the Gaspé Peninsula, for example, is 19 hours). First class, coach and sleeping accommodations are available for long trips. For information and schedules, contact VIA Rail, 895 Rue de la Gauchetière, Montreal (PQ) H3B 4G1 ☎ 514-989-2626 or www.viarail.com.

A **Canrailpass** *(Jun–mid-Oct $639; rest of the year $399)* can be purchased for unlimited train travel on the VIA Rail network for up to 30 days *(12 trips maximum; 3-day extension possible for $54/day)*. Special rates are offered for advance purchase, youth and senior citizens. Seat reservations should be made well in advance, especially during the summer months.

Amtrak provides daily service from Washington DC via New York City to Montreal. For schedules and information in the US and Canada ☎ 800-872-7245 or www.amtrak.com.

By Bus – **Autocars Orléans Express Inc.** ☎ 514-842-2281 serves the Montreal-Quebec City-Gaspésie corridor. The **Rout-Pass** *(May–Oct; $179)* is valid for 15 consecutive days; additional days may be added at the time of purchase for an additional charge. In some

regions local bus companies may provide additional service. For information and schedules contact Orléans Express, 420 Rue McGill, 2nd floor, Montreal (PQ) H2Y 2G1 or www.orleansexpress.com.

By Car – Foreign **driver's licenses** are valid in Quebec for six months. Drivers must carry the **vehicle registration** information and/or rental contract at all times. Visitors driving their own vehicles in Quebec should obtain a Canadian Non-Resident Inter-Province Motor Vehicle Insurance Liability Card **(Yellow Card)** which is available from insurance companies in the US.

The price of **gasoline**, sold in litres (3.78 litres to a US gallon), varies from province to province and is generally higher than in the US. **Service stations** are plentiful, except in isolated areas, and are usually full-service.

Extreme caution and low speed is recommended when driving on gravel roads. Extra precaution should be taken when driving in winter. **Winter tires** are recommended and an **emergency kit** should be carried. Except during winter storms, most highways are cleared and open for traffic, but it is always advisable to check traffic conditions before leaving. For up-to-date reports on road conditions, consult the blue pages in the local telephone book for the appropriate agencies, or call Environment Canada's road weather service and Transport Québec's roadworks ☎ 514-284-2363 (Montreal) or ☎ 418-684-2363 (Quebec City).

Road regulations – Quebec maintains a network of highways (called autoroutes) and secondary roads. All road signs are in French and distances are posted in metres or kilometres. The speed limit on inter-city highways is usually 100km/hr (60mph), 90km/hr (55mph) on secondary roads and 50km/hr (30mph) within city limits unless otherwise posted. Turning right on red is prohibited. The law requires that traffic in both directions halt for a stopped school bus. Seat belts are mandatory for all vehicle occupants. The possession or use of radar detection devices is illegal. Approach rail-road crossings with caution; most do not have barriers, but are signaled with flashing lights and sound. Blue road signs indicate services and points of interest for tourists, and brown signs indicate parks.

Canadian Automobile Association (CAA) – CAA Québec, 1180 Rue Drummond, Montreal (PQ) H3G 2R7 ☎ 514-861-7111 and 444 Rue Bouvier, Quebec City (PQ) G2J 1E3 ☎ 418-624-2424. All services of this national motorclub are offered to the US tourist upon presentation of the membership card of the American Automobile Association (AAA). The CAA is also affiliated with the Alliance Internationale de Tourisme (AIT), the Fédération Internationale de l'Automobile (FIA), the Federation of Interamerican Touring & Automobile Clubs (FITAC) and the Commonwealth Motoring Conference (CMC). CAA provides helpful travel information, insurance coverage and emergency road service: **24-hour emergency road service** ☎ 800-222-4357.

Car Rental – Major car rental companies operate offices in airports, train stations and larger cities. More favourable rates can usually be obtained with advance reservations. Minimum age for renting a car is 21, and payment is easiest by credit card. Some agencies offer special packages, but be aware of drop-off charges if you return the car to a location other than the one from which you rented it. The rental price does not include collision coverage. Liability coverage is mandatory. For any other information about car insurance or coverage while in Quebec, contact the Canadian Insurance Office, 500 Rue Sherbrooke West, Montreal (PQ) H3A 3C6 ☎ 514-288-1563 or www.saaq.gouv.qc.ca.

Below is a selection of rental car agencies operating in Quebec. The numbers listed are toll-free within Quebec:

	☎
Avis	800-321-3652
Budget	800-268-8900
Hertz	800-263-0678
Thrifty	800-367-2277
Tilden/National	800-227-7368

Camper Rental – Families or groups of four to six people may prefer to rent a camper with amenities (beds, kitchenette, shower, toilet, etc.) to travel around Quebec Province. Most campgrounds are operated by Parks Canada; some private camp-grounds offer more amenities (water and electrical hookups, sewage dump). Be aware that travelling with a camper is very popular; it is best to make your reservations at least six months in advance. Minimum age to rent or drive a camper is 21, with a valid driver's license or international driver's permit. Check with your local travel agent for information; in Quebec, camper rentals are listed in the telephone book Yellow Pages under "*Véhicules Récréatifs.*"

In case of accident – First-aid stations are well marked on the major roads. Non-residents sustaining vehicular damage and/or bodily injury should contact the local police and stay at the scene until an officer has completed an inspection. In certain cases, non-residents may be entitled to compensation under the Quebec Automobile Insurance Plan. For additional information contact the Quebec Automobile Insurance Corporation, 800 Victoria Place, C.P. 392, Montreal (PQ) H4Z 1L8 ☎ 514-873-7620.

By Boat – Quebec has an extensive ferry boat system. For schedules and other information contact the regional tourist office or Tourisme Québec, or the Société des Traversiers du Québec ☎ 418-643-2019.

Accommodations

Quebec offers a wide range of accommodation, from luxurious hotels to campgrounds. Reservations should be made well in advance, especially during the peak tourist season *(late June–Sept)*. It is advisable to guarantee reservations with a credit card. In remote areas, hotels may close during certain months of the year. Lower weekend rates may be available and some hotels offer packages that include meals.

Hotels – Thehotel chains listed below can be found in Quebec's larger cities. The accompanying telephone numbers are either toll-free within Quebec, Canada and the US, or are valid worldwide:

	☎ Quebec, Canada, US	☎ worldwide
Best Western International		800-528-1234
Canadian Pacifique	800-441-1414	514-861-3511
Hilton	800-221-2424	514-878-2332
Holiday Inn		800-465-4329
Hôtel des Gouverneurs	800-463-2820	514-842-4881
Radisson		800-333-3333
Ramada Inns		800-854-7854
Sheraton		800-325-3535

Small hotels, known for their ambience and excellent regional cuisine, are plentiful in urban areas and in the countryside. Quality accommodation at moderate prices is offered by **Comfort Inn, Quality Hotels & Suites** (reservations through Choice Hotels ☎ 800-221-2222) or **Days Inn** (☎ 800-325-2525). Family-owned motels and guest houses provide basic accommodation, often without a restaurant.

Youth Hostels – The Regroupement Tourisme Jeunesse, 4545 Pierre-de-Coubertin Ave., C.P. 1000, Succursale M, Montreal, H1V 3R2 ☎514-252-3117, operates hostels in conjunction with Hostelling International–Canada, providing inexpensive lodging *($9–$36/night)* for all ages. Hostels are centrally located in cities and villages, generally in close proximity to tourist attractions. Visitors must present their membership card to use the Hostelling International network. For additional information contact the Hostelling International office in your country or Hostelling International–Canada: 400-205 Catherine St., Ottawa (ON) Canada K2P 1C3 www.hostellingintl.ca ☎ 613-237-7884 or 800-461-8585 in the U.S. and Canada.

Bed & Breakfasts and Country Inns – An alternative to small hotels, bed & breakfasts *(gîtes du passant)* and country inns promise a welcoming atmosphere and range from elaborate to modest. Usually family-owned, they may consist of an extra room in a Victorian house, a cottage in backyard, a converted lighthouse, or a lovely townhouse on a quaint city street. Rates average $63/night (breakfast included); not all provide private bathrooms. Farm holidays for a day, a week or longer, are an especially appealing option for families with children who can participate in farm activities. The Fédération des Agricotours du Québec publishes a guide, *Gîtes du Passant au Québec ($21)*, which lists establishments and provides detailed information on facili-

Hotel Tadoussac

ties and locations. For further information contact the Fédération des Agricotours du Québec, 4545 Pierre-de-Coubertin Ave., CP 1000, Succursale M, Montréal (PQ) H1V 3R2 b514-252-3138, www.agricotours.qc.ca, or Hôtellerie Champêtre, 455 Rue Saint-Antoine Ouest, bureau 114, Montreal (PQ) H2Z 1J1 ☎ 514-861-4024, www.hotelleriechampetre.com.

Camping – Government-operated and private campgrounds accommodating tents, trailers and campers can be found throughout the province. Rates range from $10–25/night depending on services offered, higher when such amenities as washing machines, firewood, barbeque grills, children's playgrounds or a general store are included. Situated in scenic locations, government campgrounds are better maintained and fill up quickly. Some close during the winter depending on location. For detailed information contact the Fédération québécoise de camping et de caravaning ☎ 514-252-3003 (Montreal).
For information on camping, caravanning, canoeing and outdoor centers (Réseau Plein Air) and to order the annually published *Guide Camping Québec* (free), contact the Association des terrains de camping du Québec, 2001 Rue de la Métropole, Bureau 700, Longueuil (PQ) J4G 1S9 ☎ 450-651-7396, www.campingquebec.com.

Universities and Colleges – Some institutions rent dormitory space during the summer months *(May–Aug)* to individuals and families at moderate rates. Reservations are accepted. For a listing contact Tourisme Québec or the university's housing department. In Montreal: McGill University ☎ 514-398-6368; University of Montreal ☎ 514-343-6531; Concordia University ☎ 514-848-4757. In Trois-Rivières: Université du Québec ☎ 819-376-5016. In Rimouski: Université du Québec ☎ 418-723-4311.

Ski Resorts – Major ski resorts in Charlevoix, the Eastern Townships, Laurentians and Outaouais offer a complete range of accommodation, including slope-side lodgings, deluxe hotels and bed & breakfasts as well as condominium and chalet rentals. Some hotels offer their own ski schools and provide complete vacation packages. For information contact the Association des stations de ski ☎ 514-493-1810.

General Information

National Holidays – Most banks, government offices and schools are closed on the following legal holidays:

New Year's Day	*January 1*
Good Friday	*Friday before Easter Sunday*
Easter Monday	*Day following Easter Sunday*
Fête de Dollard	*3rd Monday in May*
Québec National Holiday	*June 24*
Canada Day	*July 1*
Labour Day	*1st Monday in September*
Thanksgiving Day	*2nd Monday in October*
Christmas	*December 25*
Boxing Day	*December 26*

Business Hours – Business hours are Monday to Friday 9am–5pm. Retail stores are usually open Monday to Friday 9am–6pm (until 9pm Thursday and Friday). Saturday hours are 10am–5pm. In the larger towns, stores may be open Sundays noon–5pm.

Money – The basic unit of currency is the Canadian dollar: one dollar = 100 cents. Bills are issued in denominations of $2, $5, $10, $20, $50 and $100. Coins are minted in denominations of 1 cent (**un sou** in French), 5 cents, 10 cents, 25 cents, 50 cents, $1 (**un dollar** in French) and $2. Major credit cards and traveller's cheques are widely accepted. Visitors may also use their credit cards or bank cards 24hrs/day to withdraw cash from automatic teller machines (ATMs). If necessary, it is also possible to receive cash sent to Canada through Western Union. The Canadian dollar fluctuates with the international money market. At press time: $1 Canadian = $0.68 US = $0.46 £ = $1.10 Australia = DEM 1.48 = 0.76 EUR. Exchange facilities tend to be limited in rural or remote areas. It is generally recommended to exchange money at banking institutions to receive the most favourable exchange rate.

Banks – Banks are generally open Monday to Friday 9am–5pm; hours may vary in certain locations. Banks at international airports have extended hours and foreign exchange counters. Banks with ATMs, affiliated with American or European banking institutions, will allow withdrawal of Canadian funds. Some banks charge a fee for cashing traveller's cheques.

Taxes and Tips – In Canada, as in the US, tax is not usually included in the purchase price, but is added at the time of payment. In addition to the national tax (GST) of 7% on all goods and services, there is an additional 7.5% provincial sales tax (TVQ) in Quebec. Foreign visitors can request a **tax refund** on short-term accommodations and most consumer goods purchased in Quebec by completing the application found in the back of the *Tax Refund for Visitors* brochure. This brochure, published by the government, is found in most major shopping centers, tourist information centers, hotel lobbies, and duty-free shops. For further information or a rebate application form, contact Revenue Canada, Visitor Rebate Program, Summerside Tax Centre, Summerside (PE) C1N 6C6 www.rc.gc.ca ☎ 902-432-5608.

Tips are not included in restaurant bills. It is customary to leave between 10–15% of the total as tip for good service. Taxi drivers, bellhops and hairdressers are usually tipped at the customer's discretion. There is no tipping in cinemas and theatres.

Electricity – 120 volts, 60 cycles. American small appliances can be used in Quebec while European appliances require adapters.

Metric System – In 1980, Quebec adopted the metric system. All distances and speed limits are posted in kilometres, (multiply by 5/8 or 0.625 to obtain the equivalent in miles). Gas is sold in litres.

1 kilometre (km) = 0.6 mile

1 metre (m) = 3.3 feet

1 kilogram (kg) = 1,000 grams (g) = 2.2 lbs

1 liter (l) = 33.8 fl.oz. = 1 quart = 0.26 gallons

Celsius to Fahrenheit:

multiply °C by 9, divide by 5, and add 32 = °F

Telephone – Quebec Province is divided into four area codes: **514** (Montreal), **450** (Laval, North & South Shores, Laurentians, Richelieu), **418** (Quebec City, Gaspé Peninsula and eastern Quebec), **819** (Eastern Townships, Hull and northern Quebec). It is not necessary to dial the area code for calls made within the same city unless the city is large enough to contain more than one area code. All numbers beginning with **800, 888** and **877** are **toll-free**. To call long distance within Canada and to the US, dial 1 + Area Code followed by the number. For overseas calls, dial 011 + country code, or dial 0 for operator assistance, available in both English and French. Directory assistance can be reached by dialing 411; for numbers outside the local area dial 1 + Area Code + 555-1212. A local call is 25 cents. Credit card calls and collect calls can be made from public pay phones. You can also purchase the "Allô!™" and "LaPuce™" cards which allow you to call from telephone booths without using coins or a credit card. These cards may be purchased in Bell Canada's Téléboutique™ stores, train stations and airports, tourist information centers and youth hostels.

Post Offices – Post offices are open Monday to Friday 9am–5:30pm. Some sample rates for first-class mail (letter or postcard): within Canada, 45 cents (up to 30 grams); to the US, 52 cents (up to 30 grams); international mail, 90 cents (up to 20 grams). Mail service for all but local deliveries is by air. Mail will be held at the "General Delivery" post office for 15 days and must be picked up by the addressee. Information regarding postal codes within Quebec is available by calling: ☎ 514-344-8822 or 800-267-1177.

When writing to Quebec, use the following format:

Company or Name
Street Address
City (PQ) Postal Code
CANADA

Saint-Jean-Baptiste Day, Montreal

Place d'Armes, Quebec City

Languages – The official language of Quebec is French, spoken by 82% of the population. The second language is English. Visitors can expect Quebecers in urban areas to be bilingual. In the rest of the province, however, French is spoken predominantly. All road signs are in French. Tourist information is generally available in both languages.

Time Zones – Quebec is located in the **Eastern Standard Time** (EST) zone, with the exception of the Magdalen Islands which are in the Atlantic Time zone (one hour ahead of the rest of Quebec). Daylight Savings Time (time advances one hour) is observed in Quebec from the first Sunday in April to the last Sunday in October.

The Press – In large cities, international newspapers are generally available at airports, major hotels and newsstands. The English paper *The Gazette*, published daily in Montreal, is available in other towns throughout Quebec, as is the *The Chronicle-Telegraph* published each Wednesday in Quebec City.

Liquor Laws – The minimum drinking age in Quebec is 18. The provincial government regulates the sale of wine and liquor sold in *"Société des Alcools du Québec"* or S.A.Q. stores. In Montreal and Quebec City, wine and liquor are also sold at *Maisons des Vins*. Stores are open during regular business hours. Beer and wine are also sold in grocery stores. The legal blood alcohol limit is 0.08%.

Tours and Nature

The options for touring and discovering nature in Quebec are plentiful. Tourisme Québec's regional tourist guides are helpful when planning an itinerary, and there is a variety of escorted tours by bus, private car or on foot. Additionally, CAA, in conjunction with Tourisme Québec and Kilomètre Voyages, publishes a brochure *($3.95)* containing vacation travel packages for the current year. To obtain a copy, contact Voyages CAA ☎ 514-861-7575, 800-686-9243 or www.caaquebec.com.

Organised Nature Tours – Organised nature tours are particularly popular. The Zoological Society of Montreal organises a variety of Field Trips which involve visiting different regions throughout the Montreal area. Trips are usually one or two days. For reservations and more information on available trips, contact the Zoological Society, 2055 Rue Peel, Montreal (PQ) H3A 1V4 ☎ 514-845-8317 or http://zoologicalsociet-ymtl.org. Visitors may also participate in organised observation tours of harp seals and their young (whitecoats) on the giant ice floes in the Gulf of St. Lawrence. All-inclusive five to thirteen-day excursions are led by expert guides. It is recommended to make reservations 6–9 months in advance due to limited group size *(late Feb–mid-Mar; US$1,795–$4,000 includes accommodations, meals & transportation during program; Natural Habitat Adventures, 2945 Center Green Court, Boulder, CO 80301, United States ☎ 303-449-3711 or www.nathab.com)*.

Adventure Travel – Experienced sportsmen can choose from a variety of excursions including ski-mountaineering, dogsledding expeditions, snowmobile trekking, or ice and rock climbing, canoeing and kayaking. These expeditions into the hinterland of

Quebec require careful planning; it is advisable to employ the services of experienced guides. For additional information on adventure travel contact CÉPAL, C.P. 963, 3350 Rue Saint-Dominique, Jonquière (PQ) G7X 7W8 ☎ 418-547-5728; Voyages Loisirs, 4545 Pierre-de-Coubertin Ave., C.P. 1000, Succursale M, Montreal (PQ) H1V 3R2 ☎ 514-252-3129 or www.loisirquebec.qc.ca; Rythmes du monde, 1221 Rue Saint-Hubert, Ste. 100, Montreal (PQ) H3L 3Y8 ☎ 514-288-4800; Passe Montagne (rock-climbing only), 1760 Montée 2ᵉ rang, Val-David (PQ) J0T 2N 0 ☎ 819-322-2123.

National Parks – **Parks Canada**, the Canadian park service, operates three national parks in Quebec. For detailed information, trail maps and brochures, contact Parks Canada, 25 Eddy Street, Hull (PQ) K1A 0M5 http://parkscanada.pch.gc.ca ☎ 418-648-4177 or 888-773-8888.

All parks offer interpretation programs, some of which include guided hikes, slide and video presentations, exhibits and seasonal lecture programs, to help visitors understand the natural environments. Visitors are asked to respect wildlife and park rules. Most parks have camping facilities operated on a first-come-first-served basis. Camping facilities fill quickly during the summer; for reservations call ☎ 902-426-3436 or ☎ 800-213-PARK (7275). The entrance fee varies from park to park, as do the fees charged for camping, fishing or other activities. Contact the appropriate park service for opening season dates.

Forillon National Park – Chemin du Portage, Forillon (PQ) G0E 1J0 ☎ 418-892-5553. Activities: hiking, backpacking, nature programs, biking trails, camping, swimming, sailing, scuba diving, boat tours, fishing, cross-country skiing.

Mauricie National Park – 794 5th St., C.P. 758, Shawinigan (PQ) G9N 6V9 ☎ 819-538-3232. Activities: hiking, backpacking, camping, canoeing, sailing, scuba diving, swimming, fishing, cross-country skiing.

Mingan Archipelago – 1303 Rue de la Digue, C.P. 1180, Havre-Saint-Pierre (PQ) G0G 1P0 ☎ 418-538-3285. Activities: hiking, backpacking, camping, sailing, boat tours.

Provincial Parks and Nature Reserves – In Quebec's 18 provincial parks *(below)*, the visitor can enjoy wildlife and forestry reserves year-round. Hiking, climbing, cycling, canoeing, fishing and hunting, cross-country or alpine skiing, and snowmobiling are just a few of the activities awaiting the outdoor enthusiast. A comprehensive guide, *Découvrez votre vraie nature* (free), covers the entire list of parks and their activities as well as detailed maps of park areas. Please note that some of these parks are closed off-season; for information, contact the Ministère de l'environnement et de la faune: 675 Blvd. René-Lévesque Est, 11th floor, Québec (PQ) G1R 5V7 www.menv.gouv.qc.ca ☎ 418-521-3830 or 800-561-1616 (Canada).

Aiguebelle *(Abitibi-Témiscamingue)* – Reception Centres Destor ☎ 819-763-3333; Mont-Brun ☎ 819-637-7322.

Bic *(Bas-Saint-Laurent)* – Interpretation Centre ☎ 418-869-3502.

Frontenac *(Estrie)* – Reception Centres Saint-Daniel ☎ 418-422-2136.

Gaspésie *(Gaspésie)* – Interpretation Centre ☎ 418-763-7811.

Grands-Jardins *(Charlevoix)* – Reception Centre Thomas-Fortin ☎ 418-457-3945; Interpretation Centre Château-Beaumont ☎ 418-846-2057.

Bonaventure-et-Rocher-Percé *(Gaspésie)* – Interpretation Centre ☎ 418-782-2240.

© Fred Klus /PUBLIPHOTO

Îles-de-Boucherville *(Montérégie)* – Reception Centre ☎ 450-670-2747.

Jacques-Cartier *(Quebec)* – Reception Centre ☎ 418-848-3169.

Miguasha *(Gaspésie)* – Reception Centre ☎ 418-794-2475.

Mont-Mégantic *(Eastern Townships)* – Reception Centre ☎ 819-888-2941.

Mont-Orford *(Eastern Townships)* – Reception Centre ☎ 819-843-4545.

Mont-Saint-Bruno *(Montérégie)* – Reception Centre ☎ 450-653-7544.

Mont-Tremblant *(Laurentides)* – Reception Centres Lake Monroe ☎ 819-688-2281; Saint-Donat ☎ 819-424-2954; Saint-Côme ☎ 450-883-1291.

Mont-Valin *(Saguenay–Lac-Saint-Jean)* – Information ☎ 418-674-1200.

Oka *(Laurentides)* – Reception Centre ☎ 450-479-8365.

Pointe-Taillon *(Saguenay–Lac-Saint-Jean)* – Interpretation Centre ☎ 418-347-5371.

Saguenay *(Saguenay–Lac-Saint-Jean)* – Interpretation and Observation Centres Pointe-Noire ☎ 418-544-7388 and Cap-de-Bon-Désir ☎ 418-232-6751.

Yamaska *(Eastern Townships)* – Reception Centre ☎ 450-777-5557.

Quebec also contains 14 **nature reserves** placed under the direction of **SÉPAQ** (Société des établissements de plein air du Québec), 801 Chemin Saint-Louis, bureau 180, Québec (PQ) G1S 1C1 www.sepaq.com ☎ 418-686-4875.

Sports and Recreation

For further information concerning the activities listed below, contact **Regroupement Loisir Québec (RLQ)**, 4545 Pierre-de-Coubertin Ave., Montreal (PQ) H1V 3R2 ☎ 514-252-3126, or www.loisirquebec.qc.ca, or contact the appropriate organisations directly.

Winter Activities – Owing to abundant snowfall, a variety of winter sports attracts both Quebecers and visitors from afar. The winter sports season begins mid-November and ends mid-April, although certain northern regions have good snow conditions through mid-May. Popular ski areas are easily accessible from most major cities. National and provincial parks allow all winter sports and many communities maintain skating rinks for ice hockey and recreational skating. Information on winter activities can be obtained by contacting regional tourist offices, ski resorts, or Tourisme Québec.

Alpine Skiing – Quebec boasts four major ski areas: Charlevoix, Eastern Townships, Laurentients and the Quebec region. One of the largest concentrations of ski resorts is in the Laurentians, less than an hour's drive from Montreal, with favourable snow conditions (average snowfall of almost 300cm/118in), renowned ski schools, night skiing and excellent slope-side accommodation. The imposing Appalachian Mountains stretch across the Eastern Townships region and have long been favoured by Americans and Quebecers for their cross-country trails and alpine ski slopes. Snowmaking equipment guarantees good skiing conditions all winter, although average snowfall is well above 350cm/136in. The World Cup Slalom and Giant Slalom Finals in 1993 were run on the slopes of Stoneham *(below)*. Four main resorts, located 60 minutes from Quebec City, provide slopes certified by the International Ski Federation. Snowfall averages 375cm/148in. For additional information, contact the Association des stations de ski du Québec, 7875 Blvd. Louis-H.-Lafontaine, bureau 104, Anjou (PQ) H1K 4E4 ☎ 514-493-1810 or www.assq.qc.ca.

Cross-country skiing – Quebec is renowned for cross-country skiing and offers a well-maintained network of trails totalling several thousand kilometres. Many national and international competitions, such as the Masters World Cup in 1989 and 1993, are held here. Trails for every level of difficulty are patrolled and dotted with heated cabins. Lessons, guided tours and ski rental are available in many areas. For additional information on cross-country ski trails, maps and services offered along trails, contact the Fédération québécoise de ski (Montreal) ☎ 514-252-3089.

Snowmobiling – Over 263 local clubs belong to the Fédération des Clubs de Motoneigistes du Québec, or FCMQ (Montreal) ☎ 514-252-3076, which maintains 32,000km/15,538mi of marked trails criss-crossing the province. Heated cabins, other accommodation and repair services can be found along the Trans-Quebec trail network. It is important to follow safety rules: exercise caution before crossing public roads, keep headlights on at all times and travel with at least one more vehicle.

A **registration card**, obtained by contacting the Federation, is required to operate a snowmobile. It is also advisable to acquire snowmobile liability insurance. The Federation publishes a yearly snowmobiler's guide to the Trans-Quebec Trails, listing locations of service areas, repair shops, snowmobile dealers offering equipment rental, and organized excursions. The Trans-Quebec Snowmobile Trail Network Map can be obtained by contacting Tourisme Québec or on the internet at www.fcmq.qc.ca.

Summer Activities – Blessed with innumerable lakes, rivers, parks and reserves, Quebec is a marvelous place to enjoy many forms of outdoor recreation during the summer months. A few are listed below.

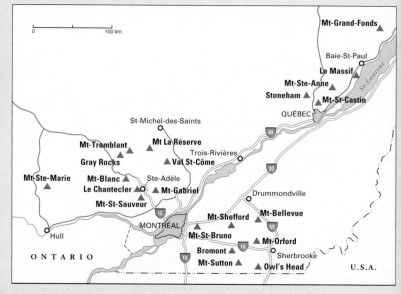

Canoeing – This summer activity is enjoyed on most of the river systems except those being used for logging. Canoe-camping trips are organised by several different organisations, including the Fédération québécoise de canot-camping (Montreal) ☎ 514-252-3001.

Cycling – Many parks include well-maintained cycling trails and offer bike rentals. For more information contact Vélo-Québec, 1251 Rue Rachel Est, Montreal (PQ) H2J 2J9 ☎ 514-521-8356 or www.velo.qc.ca.

Golf – Thegolfer can choose from nearly 300 golf courses in Quebec, most of them located in the Eastern Townships, Laurentians, Mauricie–Bois-Francs and Outaouais regions. Some are private clubs while others allow visitors. Amenities include equipment rental and use of club facilities. Advance reservation is recommended. For a listing contact the Association de golf du Québec, 1870 boul. des Sources, Pointe-Claire (PQ) ☎ 514-694-1990 or www.golfquebec.org. Publications by the regional tourist offices give detailed information on location of courses, travel directions, facilities offered, availability to non-members and rates.

Hiking – Nature lovers can escape the hustle and bustle of the city by hiking on well-marked trails over mountains, through dense forests or along windy seashores. The adventurous hiker may prefer off-the-beaten-path trails through undisturbed wilderness. For information, contact the Fédération québécoise de la marche (Montreal) ☎ 514-252-3157. To obtain topographic maps, contact the Canada Map Office, 130 Bentley Ave, Nepean (ON) K2E 6T9 ☎ 613-957-8861 or http://maps.nrcan.gc.ca.

Horseback riding – Many reputable stables can be found in the Eastern Townships, Gaspé Peninsula and Bas-Saint-Laurent regions. Farms specialising in ranch vacations often offer accommodation and riding lessons. Horseback riding is also available in most national and provincial parks. For more information contact Québec à cheval ☎ 514-252-3002 or www.cheval.qc.ca.

Kayaking – This sport is particularly popular in the northern regions of Abitibi-Témiscamingue, Saguenay and Nunavik, where camps have been set up. Kayaking is also practiced on the open sea in the Hudson or Ungava bays. Organisations offering excursions: CÉPAL, C.P. 963, Jonquière (PQ) G7X 7W8 ☎ 418-547-5728; Nouveau Monde Expéditions en Rivière, 100 Chemin Rivière-Rouge, Calumet (PQ) J0V 1B0 ☎ 819-242-7238 or www.newworld.ca; Trail Head, 1960 Scott Street, Ottawa, (ON) K1Z 8L8 ☎ 613-722-4229 or www.trailheadcnd.com.

Sailing – Enthusiasts can choose from a wealth of lakes in the Duplessis, Charlevoix, Laurentides, Manicouagan, and Montreal regions. A sail on the challenging St. Lawrence River is on top of every serious sailor's list. For more information contact the Fédération de voile du Québec (Montreal) ☎ 514-252-3097 or www.voile.qc.ca.

⛷	Information ☎	Vertical Drop		Total Runs	Runs			Total Lifts	Rooms
		M	ft		Beginner	Intermediate	Expert		
Bromont	450-534-2200	405	1329	25	8	5	12	4	305
Gray Rocks	819-425-2771	189	620	22	4	10	8	4	230
Le Chantecler	450-229-3555	183	600	22	7	10	5	8	260
Le Massif	418-632-5876	770	2525	20	5	4	11	2	
Mont-Bellevue	819-821-5872	81	266	6	3	3		3	
Mont-Blanc	819-688-2444	300	985	36	8	11	17	7	92
Mont-Gabriel	514-227-1100	200	655	12	2	4	6	10	140
Mont-Grand-Fonds	418-665-4405	335	1095	14	3	5	6	3	
Mont La Réserve	819-424-2377	305	1000	23	5	12	12	4	51
Mont-Orford	819-843-6548	540	1770	52	19	17	16	8	1100
Mont-St-Bruno	514-653-3441	134	440	15	2	7	6	8	
Mont-St-Sauveur	450-227-4671	213	700	29	5	9	15	9	85
Mont-Ste-Anne	418-827-4561	625	2050	56	13	26	17	12	1500
Mont-Ste-Marie	819-467-5200	381	1250	17	5	6	6	3	40
Mont-Shefford	514-372-1550	305	1000	12				3	
Mont-Sutton	450-538-2545	460	1500	53	17	15	21	9	75
Owl's Head	450-292-3342	540	1770	27	8	12	7	7	66
Stoneham	418-848-2411	420	1380	30	10	12	8	10	160
Tremblant	819-425-8711	650	2130	92	15	29	48	12	1200
Val St-Côme	514-883-0700	305	1000	24	6	8	10	4	66

Scuba diving – Popular diving spots include the coast of Forillon National Park, around Bonaventure and the Magdalen Islands, as well as the Côte-Nord. For more information contact the Fédération des activités subaquatiques du Québec (Montreal) ☎ 514-252-3009.

Rock climbing – Many regions of Quebec offer excellent climbing. Charlevoix, Côte-Nord, Eastern Townships, Gaspé Peninsula, Laurentians, as well as the Saguenay Fjord area have walls with drops from 30 to 300 metres (99 to 990 feet). Rock climbing season is between early May and late October. Ice climbing is also practiced in these areas during the winter. For further information contact the Fédération québécoise de la montagne (Montreal) ☎ 514-252-3004.

Windsurfing – This sport is popular on lakes, in parks and around the shores of the Gaspé Peninsula. The season runs from mid-June to the end of August. For more information contact the Fédération de voile de Québec (Montreal) ☎ 514-252-3097 or www.yachting.qc.ca.

Hunting and Fishing – Southern Quebec boasts plentiful reserves of fish and game. Renowned for their salmon fishing, the rivers of the Gaspé Peninsula also teem with speckled trout and small-mouth bass. A permit is required to fish in fresh water. Daily fees for fishing vary with the season, location and type of fish. The central Quebec region abounds in moose, black bear, grouse, and white-tailed deer among other types of game, and is also well-known for its variety of fish species. Anticosti Island is a favourite with sport fishers. In northern Quebec, above the 52nd parallel, non-residents are required to hire the services of an outfitter. Big game here includes caribou and moose. Regions known for their excellent hunting and fishing include Abitibi-Témiscamingue, Côte-Nord, Mauricie–Bois-Francs, Outaouais, Saguenay–Lac-Saint-Jean and Nunavik.

Outfitters – Outfitters' lodges are easy to reach by land or air and offer packages for the experienced sportsman as well as the novice. There are two types of outfitters, or *pourvoiries:* some have leased territories while others escort their expeditions to government-owned land. In addition to making all arrangements, including air transportation to remote locations, they provide accommodation and equipment needed to ensure a safe and carefree expedition. Furthermore, some outfitters offer fish and game storage, refrigeration and transport. **Registration Centres** are located along main roads and at airports in remote areas. A publication of **outfitters' lodges** is available at information kiosques or through the Fédération des pourvoyeurs du Québec, 5237 Blvd. Hamel, Quebec City (PQ) G2E 2H2 ☎ 418-877-5191 or www.fpq.com.

Hunting & Fishing Regulations – Hunting is prohibited in the parks; however, the reserves are open to hunters with permits except in areas where hunting is subject to quotas. Fishing is permitted in most parks and reserves. Hunting and fishing **permits** (required for freshwater fishing) can be obtained from most local sporting goods stores and outfitters. The price varies according to season, location and type of game or fish. You are required by law to **register** your game within 48 hours after leaving the hunting area. Registration centers are generally found along major roads and in the airports of more isolated regions. Strict **safety regulations** are enforced and every hunter is asked to help fight poaching. To report violators, the Ministère de l'environnement et de la faune du Québec operates A 24-hour telephone service ☎ 800-463-2191 (Canada only). For additional information contact the Ministère de l'environnement et de la faune du Québec, 675 Blvd. René-Lévesque Est, Quebec City (PQ) G1R 5V7 www.menv.gouv.qc.ca ☎ 418-521-3830.

Entertainment

Music – Two professional symphony orchestras are based in Quebec Province: the **Montreal Symphony Orchestra** (Orchestre Symphonique de Montréal ☎ 514-842-9951 or www.osm.ca) under the direction of Charles Dutoit; and Canada's oldest symphony orchestra, the **Quebec Symphony Orchestra** (Orchestre Symphonique du Québec ☎ 418-643-5598).

The prestigious Place des Arts performing arts complex comprises five multipurpose concert halls where the **Montreal Opera Company** (Opéra de Montréal ☎ 514-985-2258 or www.operademontreal.qc.ca) and McGill University's **McGill Chamber Orchestra** (☎ 514-487-5190) perform. On the McGill campus, Pollack Concert Hall (☎ 514-398-4547) hosts classical, jazz and chamber music. The **International Jazz Festival** (☎ 514-790-1245 or www.montrealjazzfest.com) held in June has become a major event in Montreal since its inception in 1977. The Molson Centre (1200 Ruede la Gauchetière ☎ 514-932-2582) offers a variety of performances throughout the year, including pop and rock concerts.

Dance – Montreal's **Les Grands Ballets Canadiens** (☎ 514-849-8681 or www.grandsballets.qc.ca), famous for its classical repertoire, performs nationally and abroad. Numerous cultural events and festivals feature ethnic folk dancers.

Theatres – Summer theatres are popular and can be enjoyed throughout the Province. Repertory theatres and dinner theatres perform in both French and English. For schedules see the arts and entertainment supplements in local newspapers (weekend editions) or free brochures distributed at hotels.

© Tourisme Québec/Marcel Gignac

Index

Islands and lakes are listed under their proper name (Île aux Coudres *see Coudres, Île aux*). The starred sights of Montreal and Quebec City, the principal sights of Nunavik and the Îles de la Madeleine (Magdalen Islands), and accommodations and hotels for Montreal, Quebec City, Gaspésie (Gaspé Peninsula), the Laurentides (Laurentians) and Hull are listed separately.

Notes

Notes